Spencer Ostrander

PAUL AUSTER is the bestselling author of *4 3 2 1*, *Sunset Park*, *Invisible*, *The Book of Illusions*, and *The New York Trilogy*, among many other works. In 2006, he was awarded the Prince of Asturias Prize for Literature. Among his other honors are the Prix Médicis étranger for *Leviathan*, the Independent Spirit Award for the screenplay of *Smoke*, and the Premio Napoli for *Sunset Park*. In 2012, he was the first recipient of the NYC Literary Honors in the category of fiction. He has also been a finalist for the International IMPAC Dublin Literary Award (*The Book of Illusions*), the PEN/Faulkner Award (*The Music of Chance*), the Edgar Award (*City of Glass*), and the Man Booker Prize (*4 3 2 1*). He is a member of the American Academy of Arts and Letters and a Commandeur de l'Ordre des Arts et des Lettres. His work has been translated into more than forty languages. He lives in Brooklyn, New York.

ALSO BY PAUL AUSTER

FICTION

The New York Trilogy (*City of Glass, Ghosts,* & *The Locked Room*)

In the Country of Last Things

Moon Palace

The Music of Chance

Leviathan

Mr. Vertigo

Timbuktu

The Book of Illusions

Oracle Night

The Brooklyn Follies

Day/Night (*Travels in the Scriptorium* & *Man in the Dark*)

Invisible

Sunset Park

4 3 2 1

NONFICTION

The Invention of Solitude

Hand to Mouth

The Red Notebook

Winter Journal

Here and Now (with J. M. Coetzee)

Report from the Interior

A Life in Words
(with I. B. Siegumfeldt)

Talking to Strangers

SCREENPLAYS

Three Films: Smoke, Blue in the Face, Lulu on the Bridge

The Inner Life of Martin Frost

POETRY

White Spaces

ILLUSTRATED BOOKS

The Story of My Typewriter
(with Sam Messer)

Auggie Wren's Christmas Story
(with Isol)

City of Glass (adapted by Paul Karasik and David Mazzucchelli)

EDITOR

The Random House Book of Twentieth-Century French Poetry

I Thought My Father Was God and Other True Tales from NPR's National Story Project

Samuel Beckett: The Grove Centenary Edition

GROUNDWORK

GROUNDWORK

Autobiographical Writings,
1979–2012

———

PAUL AUSTER

PICADOR
HENRY HOLT AND COMPANY
New York

picadorusa.com · instagram.com/picador
twitter.com/picadorusa · facebook.com/picadorusa

Picador® is a U.S. registered trademark and is used by Macmillan Publishing Group, LLC, under license from Pan Books Limited.

For book club information, please visit facebook.com/picadorbookclub or e-mail marketing@picadorusa.com.

The Library of Congress Cataloging-in-Publication Data is available upon request.

ISBN 978-1-250-24580-9 (trade paperback)
ISBN 978-1-250-24581-6 (e-book)

Designed by Gretchen Achilles

Our books may be purchased in bulk for promotional, educational, or business use. Please contact your local bookseller or the Macmillan Corporate and Premium Sales Department at 1–800-221-7945, extension 5442, or by e-mail at MacmillanSpecialMarkets@macmillan.com.

First Edition: May 2020

10   9   8   7   6   5   4   3   2   1

CONTENTS

PORTRAIT OF
AN INVISIBLE MAN

{1979}

The Invention of Solitude: I

In searching out the truth be ready
for the unexpected, for it is difficult to find
and puzzling when you find it.

HERACLITUS

One day there is life. A man, for example, in the best of health, not even old, with no history of illness. Everything is as it was, as it will always be. He goes from one day to the next, minding his own business, dreaming only of the life that lies before him. And then, suddenly, it happens there is death. A man lets out a little sigh, he slumps down in his chair, and it is death. The suddenness of it leaves no room for thought, gives the mind no chance to seek out a word that might comfort it. We are left with nothing but death, the irreducible fact of our own mortality. Death after a long illness we can accept with resignation. Even accidental death we can ascribe to fate. But for a man to die of no apparent cause, for a man to die simply because he is a man, brings us so close to the invisible boundary between life and death that we no longer know which side we are on. Life becomes death, and it is as if this death has owned this life all along. Death without warning. Which is to say: life stops. And it can stop at any moment.

The news of my father's death came to me three weeks ago. It was Sunday morning, and I was in the kitchen preparing breakfast for my small son, Daniel. Upstairs my wife was still in bed, warm under the quilts, luxuriating in a few extra hours of sleep. Winter in the country: a world of silence, wood smoke, whiteness. My mind was filled with thoughts about the piece I had been writing the night before, and I was looking ahead to the afternoon when I would be able to get back to work. Then the phone rang. I knew instantly that there was trouble. No one calls at eight o'clock on a Sunday morning unless it is to give news that cannot wait. And news that cannot wait is always bad news.

I could not muster a single ennobling thought.

Even before we packed our bags and set out on the three-hour drive to New Jersey, I knew that I would have to write about my father. I had no plan, had no precise idea of what this meant. I cannot even remember making a decision about it. It was simply there, a certainty, an obligation that began to impose itself on me the moment I was given the news. I thought: my father is gone. If I do not act quickly, his entire life will vanish along with him.

Looking back on it now, even from so short a distance as three weeks, I find this a rather curious reaction. I had always imagined that death would numb me, immobilize me with grief. But now that it had happened, I did not shed any tears, I did not feel as though the world had collapsed around me. In some strange way, I was remarkably prepared to accept this death, in spite of its suddenness. What disturbed me was something else, something unrelated to death or my response to it: the realization that my father had left no traces.

He had no wife, no family that depended on him, no one whose life would be altered by his absence. A brief moment of shock, perhaps, on the part of scattered friends, sobered as much by the thought of capricious death as by the loss of their friend, followed by a short period of mourning, and then nothing. Eventually, it would be as though he had never lived at all.

Even before his death he had been absent, and long ago the

people closest to him had learned to accept this absence, to treat it as the fundamental quality of his being. Now that he was gone, it would not be difficult for the world to absorb the fact that he was gone forever. The nature of his life had prepared the world for his death—had been a kind of death by anticipation—and if and when he was remembered, it would be dimly, no more than dimly.

Devoid of passion, either for a thing, a person, or an idea, incapable or unwilling to reveal himself under any circumstances, he had managed to keep himself at a distance from life, to avoid immersion in the quick of things. He ate, he went to work, he had friends, he played tennis, and yet for all that he was not there. In the deepest, most unalterable sense, he was an invisible man. Invisible to others, and most likely invisible to himself as well. If, while he was alive, I kept looking for him, kept trying to find the father who was not there, now that he is dead I still feel as though I must go on looking for him. Death has not changed anything. The only difference is that I have run out of time.

For fifteen years he had lived alone. Doggedly, opaquely, as if immune to the world. He did not seem to be a man occupying space, but rather a block of impenetrable space in the form of a man. The world bounced off him, shattered against him, at times adhered to him—but it never got through. For fifteen years he haunted an enormous house, all by himself, and it was in that house that he died.

For a short while we had lived there as a family—my father, my mother, my sister, and I. After my parents were divorced, everyone dispersed: my mother began a new life, I went off to college, and my sister stayed with my mother until she, too, went off to school. Only my father remained. Because of a clause in the divorce agreement which stipulated that my mother still owned a share of the house and would be given half the proceeds whenever it was sold (which made my father reluctant to sell), or from some secret refusal to change his life (so as not to show the world that the divorce had affected him in a way he could not control), or simply from inertia, an emotional lethargy that prevented him from taking any action, he stayed on, living alone in a house that could have accommodated six or seven people.

It was an impressive place: old, solidly built, in the Tudor style, with leaded windows, a slate roof, and rooms of royal proportions. Buying it had been a big step for my parents, a sign of growing wealth. This was the best neighborhood in town, and although it was not a pleasant place to live (especially for children), its prestige outweighed its deadliness. Given the fact that he wound up spending the rest of his life in that house, it is ironic that my father at first resisted moving there. He complained about the price (a constant theme), and when at last he relented, it was with grudging bad humor. Even so, he paid in cash. All in one go. No mortgage, no monthly payments. It was 1959, and business was going well for him.

Always a man of habit, he would leave for work early in the morning, work hard all day, and then, when he came home (on those days he did not work late), take a short nap before dinner. Sometime during our first week in the new house, before we had properly moved in, he made a curious kind of mistake. Instead of driving home to the new house after work, he went directly to the old one, as he had done for years, parked his car in the driveway, walked into the house through the back door, climbed the stairs, entered the bedroom, lay down on the bed, and went to sleep. He slept for about an hour. Needless to say, when the new mistress of the house returned to find a strange man sleeping in her bed, she was a little surprised. But unlike Goldilocks, my father did not jump up and run away. The confusion was eventually settled, and everyone had a good laugh. Even today, it still makes me laugh. And yet, for all that, I cannot help regarding it as a pathetic story.

It is one thing for a man to drive to his old house by mistake, but it is quite another, I think, for him not to notice that anything has changed inside it. Even the most tired or distracted mind has a corner of pure, animal response, and can give the body a sense of where it is. One would have to be nearly unconscious not to see, or at least not to feel, that the house was no longer the same. "Habit," as one of Beckett's characters says, "is a great deadener." And if the mind is unable to respond to the physical evidence, what will it do when confronted with the emotional evidence?

During those last fifteen years he changed almost nothing in the house. He did not add any furniture, he did not remove any furniture. The walls remained the same color, the pots and pans were not replaced, even my mother's dresses were not thrown out—but stored away in an attic closet. The very size of the house absolved him from having to make any decisions about the things it contained. It was not that he was clinging to the past, trying to preserve the house as a museum. On the contrary, he seemed to be unaware of what he was doing. It was negligence that governed him, not memory, and even though he went on living in that house all those years, he lived in it as a stranger might have. As the years went by, he spent less and less time there. He ate nearly all his meals in restaurants, arranged his social calendar so as to be busy every night, and used the house as little more than a place to sleep. Once, several years ago, I happened to mention to him how much money I had earned from my writing and translating during the previous year (a pittance by any standard, but more than I had ever made before), and his amused response was that he spent more than that just on eating out. The point is: his life was not centered around the place where he lived. His house was just one of many stopping places in a restless, unmoored existence, and this lack of center had the effect of turning him into a perpetual outsider, a tourist of his own life. You never had the feeling that he could be located.

Still, the house seems important to me, if only to the extent that it was neglected—symptomatic of a state of mind that, otherwise inaccessible, manifested itself in the concrete images of unconscious behavior. The house became the metaphor of my father's life, the exact and faithful representation of his inner world. For although he kept the house tidy and preserved it more or less as it had been, it underwent a gradual and ineluctable process of disintegration. He was neat, he always put things back in their proper place, but nothing was cared for, nothing was ever cleaned. The furniture, especially in the rooms he rarely visited, was covered with dust, cobwebs, the signs of total neglect; the kitchen stove was so encrusted with charred food that it had become unsalvageable; in the cupboard, sometimes languishing on the shelves for years: bug-infested packages of flour, stale crackers, bags of sugar that had turned into solid blocks, bottles of syrup that could no longer be opened. Whenever he prepared a meal for himself, he would immediately and assiduously do the dishes—but rinse them only, never using soap, so that every cup, every saucer, every plate was coated with a film of dingy grease. Throughout the house: the window shades, which were kept drawn at all times, had become so threadbare that the slightest tug would pull them apart. Leaks sprang and stained the furniture, the furnace never gave off enough heat, the shower did not work. The house became shabby, depressing to walk into. You felt as if you were entering the house of a blind man.

His friends and family, sensing the madness of the way he lived in that house, kept urging him to sell it and move somewhere else. But he always managed to ward them off with a non-committal "I'm happy here," or "The house suits me fine." In the end, however, he did decide to move. At the very end. In the last phone conversation we ever had, ten days before he died, he told me the house had been sold and that the closing was set for February first, about three weeks away. He wanted to know if there was anything in the house I could use, and I agreed to come down for a visit with my wife and Daniel on the first free day that opened up. He died before we had a chance to make it.

There is nothing more terrible, I learned, than having to face the objects of a dead man. Things are inert: they have meaning only in function of the life that makes use of them. When that life ends, the things change, even though they remain the same. They are there and yet not there: tangible ghosts, condemned to survive in a world they no longer belong to. What is one to think, for example, of a closetful of clothes waiting silently to be worn again by a man who will not be coming back to open the door? Or the stray packets of condoms strewn among brimming drawers of underwear and socks? Or an electric razor sitting in the bathroom, still clogged with the whisker dust of the last shave? Or a dozen empty tubes of hair coloring hidden away in a leather traveling case?—suddenly revealing things one has no desire to see, no desire to know. There is a poignancy to it, and also a kind of horror. In themselves, the things mean nothing, like the cooking utensils of some vanished civilization. And yet they say something to us, standing there not as objects but as remnants of thought, of consciousness, emblems of the solitude in which a man comes to make decisions about himself: whether to color his hair, whether to wear this or that shirt, whether to live, whether to die. And the futility of it all once there is death.

Each time I opened a drawer or poked my head into a closet, I felt like an intruder, a burglar ransacking the secret places of a man's mind. I kept expecting my father to walk in, to stare at me in disbelief, and ask me what the hell I thought I was doing. It didn't seem fair that he couldn't protest. I had no right to invade his privacy.

A hastily scrawled telephone number on the back of a business card that read: H. Limeburg—Garbage Cans of All Descriptions. Photographs of my parents' honeymoon in Niagara Falls, 1946: my mother sitting nervously on top of a bull for one of those funny shots that are never funny, and a sudden sense of how unreal the world has always been, even in its prehistory. A drawer full of hammers, nails, and more than twenty screwdrivers. A filing cabinet stuffed with canceled checks from 1953 and the cards I received for my sixth birthday. And then, buried at the bottom of a drawer in the bathroom: the monogrammed toothbrush that had once belonged to my mother and which had not been touched or looked at for more than fifteen years.

The list is inexhaustible.

It soon became apparent to me that my father had done almost nothing to prepare himself for his departure. The only signs of the impending move I could detect in the whole house were a few cartons of books—trivial books (out of date atlases, a fifty-year-old introduction to electronics, a high school Latin grammar, ancient law books) that he had been planning to give away to charity. Other than that, nothing. No empty boxes waiting to be filled. No pieces of furniture given away or sold. No arrangements made with a moving company. It was as though he had not been able to face it. Rather than empty the house, he had simply willed himself to die. Death was a way out, the only legitimate escape.

There was no escape for me, however. The thing had to be done, and there was no one else to do it. For ten days I went through his things, cleared out the house, got it ready for the new owners. It was a miserable time, but also an oddly humorous time, a time of reckless and absurd decisions: sell it, throw it out, give it away. My wife and I bought a big wooden slide for eighteen-month old Daniel and set it up in the living room. He thrived on the chaos: rummaging among the things, putting lampshades on his head, flinging plastic poker chips around the house, running through the vast spaces of the gradually emptying rooms. At night my wife and I would lie under monolithic quilts watching trashy movies on television. Until the television, too, was given away. There was trouble with the furnace, and if I forgot to fill it with water, it would shut off. One morning we woke up to find that the temperature in the house had dropped to forty degrees. Twenty times a day the phone rang, and twenty times a day I told someone that my father was dead. I had become a furniture salesman, a moving man, a messenger of bad tidings.

The house began to resemble the set for a trite comedy of manners. Relatives swooped in, asking for this piece of furniture or that piece of dinnerware, trying on my father's suits, overturning boxes, chattering away like geese. Auctioneers came to examine the merchandise ("Nothing upholstered, it's not worth a nickel"), turned up their noses, and walked out. Garbage men clumped in with heavy boots and hauled off mountains of trash. The water man read the water meter, the gas man read the gas meter, the oil men read the oil gauge. (One of them, I forget which, who had been given a lot of trouble by my father over the years, said to me with savage complicity, "I don't like to say this"—meaning he did—"but your father was an obnoxious bastard.") The real estate agent came to buy some furniture for the new owners and wound up taking a mirror for herself. A woman who ran a curio shop bought my mother's old hats. A junkman came with a team of assistants (four black men named Luther, Ulysses, Tommy Pride, and Joe Sapp) and carted away everything from a set of barbels to a broken toaster. By the time it was over, nothing was left. Not even a postcard. Not even a thought.

If there was a single worst moment for me during those days, it came when I walked across the front lawn in the pouring rain to dump an armful of my father's ties into the back of a Good Will Mission truck. There must have been more than a hundred ties, and many of them I remembered from my childhood: the patterns, the colors, the shapes that had been embedded in my earliest consciousness, as clearly as my father's face had been. To see myself throwing them away like so much junk was intolerable to me, and it was then, at the precise instant I tossed them into the truck, that I came closest to tears. More than seeing the coffin itself being lowered into the ground, the act of throwing away these ties seemed to embody for me the idea of burial. I finally understood that my father was dead.

Yesterday one of the neighborhood children came here to play with Daniel. A girl of about three and a half who has recently learned that big people were once children, too, and that even her own mother and father have parents. At one point she picked up the telephone and launched into a pretend conversation, then turned to me and said, "Paul, it's your father. He wants to talk to you." It was gruesome. I thought: there's a ghost at the other end of the line, and he really does want to talk to me. It was a few moments before I could speak. "No," I finally blurted out. "It can't be my father. He wouldn't be calling today. He's somewhere else."

I waited until she had hung up the phone and then walked out of the room.

In his bedroom closet I had found several hundred photographs— stashed away in faded manila envelopes, affixed to the black pages of warped albums, scattered loosely in drawers. From the way they had been stored I gathered he never looked at them, had even forgotten they were there. One very big album, bound in expensive leather with a gold-stamped title on the cover—This is Our

Life: The Austers—was totally blank inside. Someone, probably my mother, had once gone to the trouble of ordering this album, but no one had ever bothered to fill it.

Back home, I pored over these pictures with a fascination bordering on mania. I found them irresistible, precious, the equivalent of holy relics. It seemed that they could tell me things I had never known before, reveal some previously hidden truth, and I studied each one intensely, absorbing the least detail, the most insignificant shadow, until all the images had become a part of me. I wanted nothing to be lost.

Death takes a man's body away from him. In life, a man and his body are synonymous; in death, there is the man and there is his body. We say, "This is the body of X," as if this body, which had once been the man himself, not something that represented him or belonged to him, but the very man called X, were suddenly of no importance. When a man walks into a room and you shake hands with him, you do not feel that you are shaking hands with his hand, or shaking hands with his body, you are shaking hands with *him*. Death changes that. This is the body of X, not this is X. The syntax is entirely different. Now we are talking about two things instead of one, implying that the man continues to exist, but only as an idea, a cluster of images and memories in the minds of other people. As for the body, it is no more than flesh and bones, a heap of pure matter.

Discovering these photographs was important to me because they seemed to reaffirm my father's physical presence in the world, to give me the illusion that he was still there. The fact that many of these pictures were ones I had never seen before, especially the ones of his youth, gave me the odd sensation that I was meeting him for the first time, that a part of him was only just beginning to exist. I had lost my father. But at the same time, I had also found him. As long as I kept these pictures before my eyes, as long as I continued to study them with my complete attention, it was as though he were still alive, even in death. Or if not alive, at least not dead. Or rather, somehow suspended, locked in a universe that had nothing to do with death, in which death could never make an entrance.

Most of these pictures did not tell me anything new, but they helped to fill in gaps, confirm impressions, offer proof where none had existed before. A series of snapshots of him as a bachelor, for example, probably taken over a number of years, gives a precise account of certain aspects of his personality that had been submerged during the years of his marriage, a side of him I did not begin to see until after his divorce: my father as prankster, as man about town, as good time Charlie. In picture after picture he is standing with women, usually two or three, all of them affecting comical poses, their arms perhaps around each other, or two of them sitting on his lap, or else a theatrical kiss for the benefit of no one but the person taking the picture. In the background: a mountain, a tennis court, perhaps a swimming pool or a log cabin. These were the pictures brought back from weekend jaunts to various Catskill resorts in the company of his bachelor friends: play tennis, have a good time with the girls. He carried on in this way until he was thirty-four.

It was a life that suited him, and I can see why he went back to it after his marriage broke up. For a man who finds life tolerable only by staying on the surface of himself, it is natural to be satisfied with offering no more than this surface to others. There are few demands to be met, and no commitment is required. Marriage, on the other hand, closes the door. Your existence is confined to a narrow space in which you are constantly forced to reveal yourself—and therefore, constantly obliged to look into yourself, to examine your own depths. When the door is open there is never any problem: you can always escape. You can avoid unwanted confrontations, either with yourself or with another, simply by walking away.

My father's capacity for evasion was almost limitless. Because the domain of the other was unreal to him, his incursions into that domain were made with a part of himself he considered to be equally unreal, another self he had trained as an actor to represent him in the empty comedy of the world-at-large. This surrogate self was essentially a tease, a hyperactive child, a fabricator of tall tales. It could not take anything seriously.

Because nothing mattered, he gave himself the freedom to do anything he wanted (sneaking into tennis clubs, pretending to be a restaurant critic in order to get a free meal), and the charm he exercised to make his conquests was precisely what made these conquests meaningless. With the vanity of a woman he hid the truth about his age, made up stories about his business dealings, talked about himself only obliquely—in the third person, as if about an acquaintance of his ("There's a friend of mine who has this problem; what do you think he should do about it? . . ."). Whenever a situation became too tight for him, whenever he felt pushed to the verge of having to reveal himself, he would wriggle out of it by telling a lie. Eventually, the lie came automatically and was indulged in for its own sake. The principle was to say as little as possible. If people never learned the truth about him, then they couldn't turn around and use it against him later. The lie was a way of buying protection. What people saw when he appeared before them, then, was not really him, but a person he had invented, an artificial creature he could manipulate in order to manipulate others. He himself remained invisible, a puppeteer working the strings of his alter-ego from a dark, solitary place behind the curtain.

For the last ten or twelve years of his life he had one steady lady friend, and this was the woman who went out with him in public, who played the role of official companion. Every now and then there was some vague talk of marriage (at her insistence), and everyone assumed that this was the only woman he had anything to do with. After his death, however, other women began to step forward. This one had loved him, that one had worshipped him, another one was going to marry him. The principal girlfriend was shocked to learn about these other women: my father had never breathed a word about them to her. Each one had been fed a different line, and each one thought she had possessed him entirely. As it turned out, none of them knew the slightest thing about him. He had managed to elude them all.

Solitary. But not in the sense of being alone. Not solitary in the way Thoreau was, for example, exiling himself in order to find out where he was; not solitary in the way Jonah was, praying for deliverance in the belly of the whale. Solitary in the sense of retreat. In the sense of not having to see himself, of not having to see himself being seen by anyone else.

Talking to him was a trying experience. Either he would be absent, as he usually was, or he would assault you with a brittle jocularity, which was merely another form of absence. It was like trying to make yourself understood by a senile old man. You talked, and there would be no response, or a response that was inappropriate, showing that he hadn't been following the drift of your words. In recent years, whenever I spoke to him on the phone I would find myself saying more than I normally do, becoming aggressively talkative, chatting away in a futile attempt to hold his attention, to provoke a response. Afterwards, I would invariably feel foolish for having tried so hard.

He did not smoke, he did not drink. No hunger for sensual pleasures, no thirst for intellectual pleasures. Books bored him, and it was the rare movie or play that did not put him to sleep. Even at parties you would see him struggling to keep his eyes open, and more often than not he would succumb, falling asleep in a chair as the conversations swirled around him. A man without appetites. You felt that nothing could ever intrude on him, that he had no need of anything the world had to offer.

At thirty-four, marriage. At fifty-two, divorce. In one sense, it lasted years, but in fact it did not last more than a few days. He was never a married man, never a divorced man, but a life-long bachelor who happened to have had an interlude of marriage. Although he did not shirk his outward duties as a husband (he was faithful, he provided for his wife and children, he shouldered all his responsibilities), it was clear that he was not cut out to play this role. He simply had no talent for it.

My mother was just twenty-one when she married him. His conduct during the brief courtship had been chaste. No daring overtures, none of the aroused male's breathless assaults. Now and then they would hold hands, exchange a polite good-night kiss. Love, in so many words, was never declared by either one of them. By the time the wedding came, they were little more than strangers.

It was not long before my mother realized her mistake. Even before the honeymoon was over (that honeymoon, so fully documented in the photographs I found: the two of them sitting together, for instance, on a rock at the edge of a perfectly still lake, a broad path of sunlight behind them leading to the pine slope in shadow, my father with his arms around my mother, and the two of them looking at each other, smiling timidly, as if the photographer had made them hold the pose an instant too long), even before the honeymoon was over, my mother knew the marriage would not work. She went to her mother in tears and said she wanted to leave him. Somehow, her mother managed to persuade her to go back and give it a chance. And then, before the dust had settled, she found herself pregnant. And suddenly it was too late to do anything.

———

I think of it sometimes: how I was conceived in that Niagara Falls resort for honeymooners. Not that it matters where it happened. But the thought of what must have been a passionless embrace, a blind, dutiful groping between chilly hotel sheets, has never failed to humble me into an awareness of my own contingency. Niagara Falls. Or the hazard of two bodies joining. And then me, a random homunculus, like some dare-devil in a barrel, shooting over the falls.

A little more than eight months later, on the morning of her twenty-second birthday, my mother woke up and told my father that the baby was coming. Ridiculous, he said, that baby's not due for another three weeks—and promptly went off to work, leaving her without a car.

She waited. Thought maybe he was right. Waited a little more, then called a sister-in-law and asked to be driven to the hospital. My aunt stayed with my mother throughout the day, calling my father every few hours to ask him to come. Later, he would say, I'm busy now, I'll get there when I can.

At a little past midnight I poked my way into the world, ass first, no doubt screaming.

My mother waited for my father to show up, but he did not arrive until the next morning—accompanied by his mother, who wanted to inspect grandchild number seven. A short, nervous visit, and then off again to work.

She cried, of course. After all, she was young, and she had not expected it to mean so little to him. But he could never understand such things. Not in the beginning, and not in the end. It was never possible for him to be where he was. For as long as he lived, he was somewhere else, between here and there. But never really here. And never really there.

———

Thirty years later, this same little drama was repeated. This time I was there, and I saw it with my own eyes.

After my own son was born I had thought: surely this will please him. Isn't every man pleased to become a grandfather?

I had wanted to see him doting on the baby, for him to offer me proof that he was, after all, capable of demonstrating some feeling—that he did, after all, have feelings in the way other people did. And if he could show affection for his grandson, then wouldn't it be an indirect way of showing affection for me? You do not stop hungering for your father's love, even after you are grown up.

But then, people do not change. All told, my father saw his grandson only three or four times, and at no time was he able to distinguish him from the impersonal mass of babies born into the world every day. Daniel was just two weeks old when he first laid eyes on him. I can remember the day vividly: a blistering Sunday at the end of June, heatwave weather, the country air gray with moisture. My father pulled up in his car, saw my wife putting the baby into the carriage for a nap, and walked over to say hello. He poked his head into the carriage for a tenth of a second, straightened up and said to her, "A beautiful baby. Good luck with it," and then proceeded to walk on into the house. He might just as well have been talking about some stranger's baby encountered in line at the supermarket. For the rest of his visit that day he did not look at Daniel, and not once, ever, did he ask to hold him.

All this, merely as an example.

Impossible, I realize, to enter another's solitude. If it is true that we can ever come to know another human being, even to a small degree, it is only to the extent that he is willing to make himself known. A man will say: I am cold. Or else he will say nothing, and we will see him shivering. Either way, we will know that he is cold. But what of the man who says nothing and does not shiver? Where all is intractable, where all is hermetic and evasive, one can do no more than observe. But whether one can make sense of what he observes is another matter entirely.

I do not want to presume anything.

He never talked about himself, never seemed to know there was anything he *could* talk about. It was as though his inner life eluded even him.

He could not talk about it, and therefore he passed over it in silence.

If there is nothing, then, but silence, is it not presumptuous of me to speak? And yet: if there had been anything more than silence, would I have felt the need to speak in the first place?

My choices are limited. I can remain silent, or else I can speak of things that cannot be verified. At the very least, I want to put down the facts, to offer them as straightforwardly as possible, and let them say whatever they have to say. But even the facts do not always tell the truth.

He was so implacably neutral on the surface, his behavior was so flatly predictable, that everything he did came as a surprise. One could not believe there was such a man—who lacked feeling, who wanted so little of others. And if there was not such a man, that means there was another man, a man hidden inside the man who was not there, and the trick of it, then, is to find him. On the condition that he is there to be found.

To recognize, right from the start, that the essence of this project is failure.

Earliest memory: his absence. For the first years of my life he would leave for work early in the morning, before I was awake, and come home long after I had been put to bed. I was my mother's boy, and

I lived in her orbit. I was a little moon circling her gigantic earth, a mote in the sphere of her gravity, and I controlled the tides, the weather, the forces of feeling. His refrain to her was: Don't fuss so much, you'll spoil him. But my health was not good, and she used this to justify the attention she lavished on me. We spent a lot of time together, she in her loneliness and I in my cramps, waiting patiently in doctors' offices for someone to quell the insurrection that continually raged in my stomach. Even then, I would cling to these doctors in a desperate sort of way, wanting them to hold me. From the very beginning, it seems, I was looking for my father, looking frantically for anyone who resembled him.

Later memories: a craving. My mind always ready to deny the facts at the slightest excuse, I mulishly went on hoping for something that was never given to me—or given to me so rarely and arbitrarily that it seemed to happen outside the range of normal experience, in a place where I would never be able to live for more than a few moments at a time. It was not that I felt he disliked me. It was just that he seemed distracted, unable to look in my direction. And more than anything else, I wanted him to take notice of me.

Anything, even the least thing, was enough. How, for example, when the family once went to a crowded restaurant on a Sunday and we had to wait for our table, my father took me outside, produced a tennis ball (from where?), put a penny on the sidewalk, and proceeded to play a game with me: hit the penny with the tennis ball. I could not have been more than eight or nine years old.

In retrospect, nothing could have been more trivial. And yet the fact that I had been included, that my father had casually asked me to share his boredom with him, nearly crushed me with happiness.

More often, there were disappointments. For a moment he would seem to have changed, to have opened up a little, and then, suddenly, he would not be there anymore. The one time I managed to persuade him to take me to a football game (the Giants versus the Chicago Cardinals, at Yankee Stadium or the Polo Grounds, I forget which), he abruptly stood up from his seat in the middle of the fourth quarter and said, "It's time to go now." He wanted to "beat the crowd" and avoid getting stuck in traffic. Nothing I said could convince him to stay, and so we left, just like that, with the game going full tilt. Unearthly despair as I followed him down the concrete ramps, and then, even worse, in the parking lot, with the noise of the invisible crowd roaring behind me.

You could not trust him to know what you wanted, to anticipate what you might have been feeling. The fact that you had to tell him yourself vitiated the pleasure in advance, disrupted a dreamed-of harmony before a note could be played. And then, even if you did tell him, it was not at all sure that he would understand what you meant.

I remember a day very like today. A drizzling Sunday, lethargy and quiet in the house: the world at half-speed. My father was taking a nap, or had just awoken from one, and somehow I was on the bed with him, the two of us alone in the room. Tell me a story. It must have begun like that. And because he was not doing anything, because he was still drowsing in the languor of the afternoon, he did just what I asked, launching into a story without missing a beat. I remember it all so clearly. It seems as if I have just walked out of that room, with its gray light and tangle of quilts on the bed, as if, simply by closing my eyes, I could walk back into it any time I want.

He told me of his prospecting days in South America. It was a tale of high adventure, fraught with mortal dangers, hair-raising escapes, and improbable twists of fortune: hacking his way through the jungle with a machete, fighting off bandits with his bare hands, shooting his donkey when it broke its leg. His language was flowery and convoluted, probably an echo of the books he himself had read as a boy. But it was precisely this literary style that enchanted me. Not only was he telling me new things about himself, unveiling to me the world of his distant past, but he was telling it with new and strange words. This language was just as important as the story itself. It belonged to it, and in some sense was indistinguishable from it. Its very strangeness was proof of authenticity.

It did not occur to me to think this might have been a made-up story. For years afterward I went on believing it. Even when I had passed the point when I should have known better, I still felt there might have been some truth to it. It gave me something to hold on to about my father, and I was reluctant to let go. At last I had an explanation for his mysterious evasions, his indifference to me. He was a romantic figure, a man with a dark and exciting past, and his present life was only a kind of stopping place, a way of biding his time until he took off on his next adventure. He was working out his plan, figuring out how to retrieve the gold that lay buried deep in the heart of the Andes.

In the back of my mind: a desire to do something extraordinary, to impress him with an act of heroic proportions. The more aloof he was, the higher the stakes became for me. But if a boy's will is tenacious and idealistic, it is also absurdly practical. I was only ten years old, and there was no child for me to save from a burning building, no sailors to rescue at sea. On the other hand, I was a good baseball player, the star of my Little League team, and although my father had no interest in baseball, I thought that if he saw me play, just once, he would begin to see me in a new light.

Finally he did come. My mother's parents were visiting at the time, and my grandfather, a great baseball fan, showed up with him. It was a special Memorial Day game, and the seats were full. If I was ever going to do something remarkable, this was the moment to do it. I can remember catching sight of them in the wooden bleachers, my father in a white shirt with no tie and my grandfather wearing a white handkerchief on his bald head to protect him from the sun—the whole scene in my mind now drenched in this dazzling white light.

It probably goes without saying that I made a mess of it. I got no hits, lost my poise in the field, could not have been more nervous. Of all the hundreds of games I played during my childhood, this one was the worst.

Afterwards, walking to the car with my father, he told me I had played a nice game. No I hadn't, I said, it was terrible. Well, you did your best, he answered. You can't do well every time.

It was not that he was trying to encourage me. Nor was he trying to be unkind. Rather, he was saying what one says on such occasions, as if automatically. They were the right words to say, and yet they were delivered without feeling, an exercise in decorum, uttered in the same abstracted tone of voice he would use almost twenty years later when he said, "A beautiful baby. Good luck with it." I could see that his mind was somewhere else.

In itself, this is not important. The important thing is this: I realized that even if I had done all the things I had hoped to do, his reaction would have been exactly the same. Whether I succeeded or failed did not essentially matter to him. I was not defined for him by anything I did, but by what I was, and this meant that his perception of me would never change, that we were fixed in an unmoveable relationship, cut off from each other on opposite sides of a wall. Even more than that, I realized that none of this had anything to do with me. It had only to do with him. Like everything else in his life, he saw me only through the mists of his solitude, as if at several removes from himself. The world was a distant place for him, I think, a place he was never truly able to enter, and out there in the distance, among all the shadows that flitted past him, I was born, became his son, and grew up, as if I were just one more shadow, appearing and disappearing in a half-lit realm of his consciousness.

With his daughter, born when I was three and a half, it was somewhat easier for him. But in the end it was infinitely more difficult.

She was a beautiful child. Uncommonly fragile, with great brown eyes that would collapse into tears at the slightest prompting. She spent much of her time alone, a tiny figure wandering through an imaginary land of elves and fairies, dancing on tiptoe in lace-trimmed ballerina costumes, singing in a voice loud enough to be heard only by herself. She was a miniature Ophelia, already doomed, it would seem, to a life of constant inner struggle. She made few friends, had trouble keeping up in school, and was harassed by self-doubts, even at a very young age, that turned the simplest routines into nightmares of anguish and defeat. There were tantrums, fits of terrible crying, constant upheavals. Nothing ever seemed to go well for very long.

More sensitive to the nuances of the unhappy marriage around us than I was, her insecurity became monumental, crippling. At least once a day she would ask our mother if "she loved Daddy." The answer was always the same: Of course I do.

It could not have been a very convincing lie. If it had been, there would not have been any need to ask the question again the next day.

On the other hand, it is difficult to see how the truth would have made things any better.

It was almost as if she gave off a scent of helplessness. One's immediate impulse was to protect her, to buffer her against the assaults of the world. Like everyone else, my father pampered her. The more she seemed to cry out for coddling, the more willing he was to give it to her. Long after she was able to walk, for example, he insisted on carrying her down the stairs. There is no question that he did it out of love, did it gladly because she was his little angel. But underneath this coddling was the implicit message that she would never be able to do anything for herself. She was not a person to him, but an angel, and because she was never compelled to act as an autonomous being, she could never become one.

My mother, however, saw what was happening. When my sister was five years old, she took her to an exploratory consultation with a child psychiatrist, and the doctor recommended that some form of therapy be started. That night, when my mother told my father the results of the meeting, he exploded in a violent rage. No daughter of mine, etc. The idea that his daughter needed psychiatric help was no different from being told she was a leper. He would not accept it. He would not even discuss it.

This is the point I am trying to make. His refusal to look into himself was matched by an equally stubborn refusal to look at the world, to accept even the most incontrovertible evidence it thrust under his nose. Again and again throughout his life he would stare a thing in the face, nod his head, and then turn around and say it was not there. It made conversation with him almost impossible. By the time you had managed to establish a common ground with him, he would take out his shovel and dig it out from under your feet.

Years later, when my sister suffered through a series of debilitating mental breakdowns, my father continued to believe there was nothing wrong with her. It was as though he were biologically unable to recognize her condition.

In one of his books, R.D. Laing describes the father of a catatonic girl who on each visit to her in the hospital would grab her by the shoulders and shake her as hard as he could, telling her to "snap out of it." My father did not grab hold of my sister, but his attitude was essentially the same. What she needs, he would say, is to get a job, to clean herself up, to start living in the real world. Of course she did. But that was exactly what she could not do. She's just sensitive, he would say, she needs to overcome her shyness. By domesticating the problem to a quirk of personality, he could go on believing there was nothing wrong. It was not blindness so much as a failure of imagination. At what moment does a house stop being a house? When the roof is taken off? When the windows are removed? When the walls are knocked down? At what moment does it become a pile of rubble? She's just different, he would say, there's nothing wrong with her. And then one day the walls of your house finally collapse. If the door is still standing, however, all you have to do is walk through it, and you are back inside. It's pleasant sleeping out under the stars. Never mind the rain. It can't last very long.

Little by little, as the situation continued to get worse, he had to begin to accept it. But even then, at each stage along the way, his acceptance was unorthodox, taking on eccentric, almost self-nullifying forms. He became convinced, for example, that the one thing that could help her was a crash program in mega-vitamin therapy. This was the chemical approach to mental illness. Although it has never been proven to be an effective cure, this method of treatment has quite a large following. One can see why it would have attracted my father. Instead of having to wrestle with a devastating emotional fact, he could look upon the disease as a physical flaw, something that could be cured in the same way you cure the flu. The disease became an external force, a kind of bug that could be eradicated with an equal and opposite external force. In his eyes my sister was able to remain curiously untouched by all this. She was merely the *site* where the battle would take place, which meant that everything that was happening did not really affect *her*.

He spent several months trying to persuade her to begin this mega-vitamin program—even going so far as to take the pills himself, in order to prove that she would not be poisoned—and when at last she gave in, she did not take the pills for more than a week or two. The vitamins were expensive, but he did not balk at spending the money. On the other hand, he angrily resisted paying for other kinds of treatment. He did not believe that a stranger could possibly care about what happened to her. Psychiatrists were all charlatans, interested only in soaking their patients and driving fancy cars. He refused to pay the bills, which limited her to the shabbiest kind of public care. She was a pauper, with no income of her own, but he sent her almost nothing.

He was more than willing to take things into his own hands, however. Although it could not benefit either one of them, he wanted her to live in his house so that he could be the one responsible for looking after her. At least he could trust his own feelings, and he knew that he cared. But then, when she did come (for a few months, following one of her stays in the hospital), he did not disrupt his normal routine to accommodate her—but continued to spend most of his time out, leaving her to rattle around the enormous house like a ghost.

He was negligent and stubborn. But still, underneath it all, I know he suffered. Sometimes, on the phone, when he and I were discussing my sister, I could hear his voice break ever so slightly, as if he were trying to muffle a sob. Unlike everything else he ever came up against, my sister's illness finally *moved him*—but only to leave him with a feeling of utter helplessness. There is no greater sorrow for a parent than this helplessness. You have to accept it, even if you can't. And the more you accept it, the greater your despair becomes.

His despair became very great.

Wandering through the house today, without purpose, depressed, feeling that I have begun to lose touch with what I am writing, I chanced upon these words from a letter by Van Gogh: "Like everyone else, I feel the need of family and friendship, affection and friendly intercourse. I am not made of stone or iron, like a hydrant or a lamp-post."

Perhaps this is what really counts: to arrive at the core of human feeling, in spite of the evidence.

These tiniest of images: incorrigible, lodged in the mud of memory, neither buried nor wholly retrievable. And yet each one, in itself, a fleeting resurrection, a moment otherwise lost. The way he walked, for example, weirdly balanced, bouncing on the balls of his feet, as if he were about to pitch forward, blindly, into the unknown. Or the way he hunched over the table as he ate, his shoulders tensed, always merely consuming the food, never savoring it. Or else the smells that emanated from the cars he used for work: fumes, leaking oil, exhaust; the clutter of cold metal tools; the constant rattle as the car moved. A memory of the day I went driving with him through downtown Newark, no more than six years old, and he slammed down on the brakes, the jolt of it flinging my head against the dashboard: the sudden swarm of black people around the car to see if I was all right, especially the woman who thrust a vanilla ice cream cone at me through the open window, and my saying "no thank you," very politely, too stunned to know what I really wanted. Or else another day in another car, some years later, when my father spat out the window only to realize that the window had not been lowered, and my boundless, irrational delight at seeing the saliva slither down the glass. And still, as a little boy, how he would sometimes take me with him to Jewish restaurants in neighborhoods I had never seen before, dark places filled with old people, each table graced with a tinted blue seltzer bottle, and how I would grow queasy, leave my food untouched, and content myself with watching him wolf down borscht, pirogen, and boiled meats covered with horse radish. I, who was being brought up as an American boy, who knew less about my ancestors than I did about Hopalong Cassidy's hat. Or how, when I was twelve or thirteen, and wanted desperately to go somewhere with a couple of my friends, I called him at work to get his permission, and he said to me, at a loss, not knowing how to put it, "You're just a bunch of greenhorns," and how, for years afterward, my friends and I (one of them now dead, of a heroin overdose) would repeat those words as a piece of folklore, a nostalgic joke.

The size of his hands. Their calluses.

Eating the skin off the top of hot chocolate.

Tea with lemon.

The pairs of black, horn-rimmed glasses scattered through the house: on kitchen counters, on table tops, at the edge of the bathroom sink—always open, lying there like some strange, unclassified form of animal.

Watching him play tennis.

The way his knees sometimes buckled when he walked.

His face.

His resemblance to Abraham Lincoln, and how people always remarked on it.

His fearlessness with dogs.

His face. And again, his face.

Tropical fish.

———

Often, he seemed to lose his concentration, to forget where he was, as if he had lost the sense of his own continuity. It made him accident prone: smashed thumbnails from using a hammer, numerous little accidents in the car.

His absent-mindedness as a driver: to the point that it sometimes became frightening. I always thought it would be a car that did him in.

Otherwise, his health was so good that he seemed invulnerable, exempt from the physical ills that strike all the rest of us. As though nothing could ever touch him.

The way he spoke: as if making a great effort to rise up out of his solitude, as if his voice were rusty, had lost the habit of speaking. He always hemmed and hawed a lot, cleared his throat, seemed to sputter in midsentence. You felt, very definitely, that he was uncomfortable.

In the same way, it always amused me as a child to watch him sign his name. He could not simply put the pen against the paper and write. As if unconsciously delaying the moment of truth, he would always make a slight, preliminary flourish, a circular movement an inch or two off the page, like a fly buzzing in the air and zeroing in on its spot, before he could get down to business. It was a modified version of the way Art Carney's Norton used to sign his name on *The Honeymooners.*

He even pronounced his words a little oddly. "Upown," for example, instead of "upon," as if the flourish of his hand had its counterpart in his voice. There was a musical, airy quality to it. Whenever he answered the phone, it was a lilting "hellooo" that greeted you. The effect was not so much funny as endearing. It made him seem slightly daft, as if he were out of phase with the rest of the world—but not by much. Just a degree or two.

Indelible tics.

In those crazy, tensed-up moods he sometimes got into, he would always come out with bizarre opinions, not really taking them seriously, but happy to play devil's advocate in order to keep things lively. Teasing people put him in buoyant spirits, and after a particularly inane remark to someone he would often squeeze that person's leg—in a spot that always tickled. He literally liked to pull your leg.

Again the house.

No matter how negligent his care of it might have seemed from the outside, he believed in his system. Like a mad inventor protecting the secret of his perpetual motion machine, he would suffer no one to tamper with it. Once, when my wife and I were between apartments, we stayed in his house for three or four weeks. Finding the darkness of the house oppressive, we raised all the shades to let in the daylight. When my father returned home from work and saw what we had done, he flew into an uncontrollable rage, far out of proportion to any offense that might have been committed.

Anger of this sort rarely came out of him—only when he felt himself cornered, impinged upon, crushed by the presences of others. Money questions sometimes triggered it off. Or else some minor detail: the shades of his house, a broken plate, a little nothing at all.

Nevertheless, this anger was inside him—I believe constantly. Like the house that was well ordered and yet falling apart from within, the man himself was calm, almost supernatural in his imperturbability, and yet prey to a roiling, unstoppable force of fury within. All his life he strove to avoid a confrontation with this force, nurturing a kind of automatic behavior that would allow him to pass to the side of it. Reliance on fixed routines freed him from the necessity of looking into himself when decisions had to be made; the cliché was always quick to come to his lips ("A beautiful baby. Good luck with it.") instead of words he had gone out and looked for. All this tended to flatten him out as a personality. But at the same time, it was also what saved him, the thing that allowed him to live. To the extent that he was able to live.

From a bag of loose pictures: a trick photograph taken in an Atlantic City studio sometime during the Forties. There are several of him sitting around a table, each image shot from a different angle, so that at first you think it must be a group of several different men. Because of the gloom that surrounds them, because of the utter stillness of their poses, it looks as if they have gathered there to conduct a seance. And then, as you study the picture, you begin to realize that all these men are the same man. The seance becomes a real seance, and it is as if he has come there only to invoke himself, to bring himself back from the dead, as if, by multiplying himself, he had inadvertently made himself disappear. There are five of him there, and yet the nature of the trick photography denies the possibility of eye contact among the various selves. Each one is condemned to go on staring into space, as if under the gaze of the others, but seeing nothing, never able to see anything. It is a picture of death, a portrait of an invisible man.

Slowly, I am coming to understand the absurdity of the task I have set for myself. I have a sense of trying to go somewhere, as if I knew what I wanted to say, but the farther I go the more certain I am that the path toward my object does not exist. I have to invent the road with each step, and this means that I can never be sure of where I am. A feeling of moving around in circles, of perpetual back-tracking, of going off in many directions at once. And even if I do manage to make some progress, I am not at all convinced that it will take me to where I think I am going. Just because you wander in the desert, it does not mean there is a promised land.

When I first started, I thought it would come spontaneously, in a trance-like outpouring. So great was my need to write that I thought the story would be written by itself. But the words have come very slowly so far. Even on the best days I have not been able to write more than a page or two. I seem to be afflicted, cursed by some failure of mind to concentrate on what I am doing. Again and again I have watched my thoughts trail off from the thing in front of me. No sooner have I thought one thing than it evokes another thing, and then another thing, until there is an accumulation of detail so dense that I feel I am going to suffocate. Never before have I been so aware of the rift between thinking and writing. For the past few days, in fact, I have begun to feel that the story I am trying to tell is somehow incompatible with language, that the degree to which it resists language is an exact measure of how closely I have come to saying something important, and that when the moment arrives for me to say the one truly important thing (assuming it exists), I will not be able to say it.

There has been a wound, and I realize now that it is very deep. Instead of healing me as I thought it would, the act of writing has kept this wound open. At times I have even felt the pain of it concentrated in my right hand, as if each time I picked up the pen and pressed it against the page, my hand were being torn apart. Instead of burying my father for me, these words have kept him alive, perhaps more so than ever. I not only see him as he was, but as he is, as he will be, and each day he is there, invading my thoughts, stealing up on me without warning: lying in the coffin underground, his body still intact, his fingernails and hair continuing to grow. A feeling that if I am to understand anything, I

must penetrate this image of darkness, that I must enter the absolute darkness of earth.

Kenosha, Wisconsin. 1911 or 1912. Not even he was sure of the date. In the confusion of a large, immigrant family, birth records could not have been considered very important. What matters is that he was the last of five surviving children—a girl and four boys, all born within a span of eight years—and that his mother, a tiny, ferocious woman who could barely speak English, held the family together. She was the matriarch, the absolute dictator, the prime mover who stood at the center of the universe.

His father died in 1919, which meant that except for his earliest childhood he had no father. During my own childhood he told me three different stories about his father's death. In one version, he had been killed in a hunting accident. In another, he had fallen off a ladder. In the third, he had been shot down during the First World War. I knew these contradictions made no sense, but I assumed this meant that not even my father knew the facts. Because he had been so young when it happened—only seven—I figured that he had never been given the exact story. But then, this made no sense either. One of his brothers surely would have told him.

All my cousins, however, told me that they, too, had been given different explanations by their fathers.

No one ever talked about my grandfather. Until a few years ago, I had never seen a picture of him. It was as though the family had decided to pretend he had never existed.

Among the photographs I found in my father's house last month there was one family portrait from those early days in Kenosha. All the children are there. My father, no more than a year old, is sitting on his mother's lap, and the other four are standing around her in the tall, uncut grass. There are two trees behind them and

a large wooden house behind the trees. A whole world seems to emerge from this portrait: a distinct time, a distinct place, an indestructible sense of the past. The first time I looked at the picture, I noticed that it had been torn down the middle and then clumsily mended, leaving one of the trees in the background hanging eerily in mid-air. I assumed the picture had been torn by accident and thought no more about it. The second time I looked at it, however, I studied this tear more closely and discovered things I must have been blind to miss before. I saw a man's fingertips grasping the torso of one of my uncles; I saw, very distinctly, that another of my uncles was not resting his hand on his brother's back, as I had first thought, but against a chair that was not there. And then I realized what was strange about the picture: my grandfather had been cut out of it. The image was distorted because part of it had been eliminated. My grandfather had been sitting in a chair next to his wife with one of his sons standing between his knees—and he was not there. Only his fingertips remained: as if he were trying to crawl back into the picture from some hole deep in time, as if he had been exiled to another dimension.

The whole thing made me shake.

I learned the story of my grandfather's death some time ago. If not for an extraordinary coincidence, it never would have become known.

In 1970 one of my cousins went to Europe on a vacation with her husband. On the plane she found herself sitting next to an old man and, as people often do, they struck up a conversation to pass the time. It turned out that this man lived in Kenosha, Wisconsin. My cousin was amused by the coincidence and remarked that her father had lived there as a boy. Out of curiosity, the man asked her the name of her family. When she told him Auster, he turned pale. Auster? Your grandmother wasn't a crazy little woman with red hair, was she? Yes, that was my grandmother, my cousin answered. A crazy little woman with red hair.

And then he told her the story. It had happened more than fifty years before, and yet he still remembered the important details.

When this man returned home from his vacation, he tracked down the newspaper articles connected with the story, had them photocopied, and sent them to my cousin. This was his cover letter:

June 15, 70

Dear——and——.

   It was good to get your letter, and altho it did look like the task might be complicated, I had a stroke of luck.—Fran and I went out to dinner with a Fred Plons and his wife, and it was Fred's father who had bought the apartment bldg on Park Ave from your family.—Mr. Plons is about three years younger than myself, but he claimed that the case (at that time) fascinated him and he remembered quite a few details.—He stated that your grandfather was the first person to be buried in the Jewish Cemetery here in Kenosha.—(Previous to 1919 the Jewish people had no cemetery in Kenosha, but had their loved ones buried either in Chicago or Milwaukee.) With this information, I had no trouble locating the plot where your grandfather is buried.—And I was able to pin point the date. The rest is in the copy I am forwarding to you.—

   I only ask that your father should never learn of this knowledge that I am passing on to you—I would not want him to have any more grief than he already has suffered . . .

   I hope that this will shed some light on your Father's actions over the past years.

   Our fondest regards to you both—
   Ken & Fran

The newspaper articles are sitting on my desk. Now that the moment has come to write about them, I am surprised to find myself doing everything I can to put it off. All morning I have procrastinated. I have taken the trash to the dump. I have played with Daniel in the yard for almost an hour. I have read the entire newspaper—right down to the line scores of the spring training baseball games. Even now, as I write about my reluctance to write, I find myself impossibly restless: after every few words I pop up from my chair, pace the floor, listen to the wind outside as it bangs the loose gutters against the house. The least thing is able to distract me.

It is not that I am afraid of the truth. I am not even afraid to say it. My grandmother murdered my grandfather. On January 23, 1919, precisely sixty years before my father died, his mother shot and killed his father in the kitchen of their house on Fremont Avenue in Kenosha, Wisconsin. The facts themselves do not disturb me any more than might be expected. The difficult thing is to see them in print—unburied, so to speak, from the realm of secrets and turned into a public event. There are more than twenty articles, most of them long, all of them from the *Kenosha Evening News*. Even in this barely legible state, almost totally obscured by age and the hazards of photocopying, they still have the ability to shock. I assume they are typical of the journalism of the time, but that does not make them any less sensational. They are a mixture of scandalmongering and sentimentality, heightened by the fact that the people involved were Jews—and therefore strange, almost by definition—which gives the whole account a leering, condescending tone. And yet, granted the flaws in style, the facts seem to be there. I do not think they explain everything, but there is no question that they explain a great deal. A boy cannot live through this kind of thing without being affected by it as a man.

In the margins of these articles, I can just manage to decipher some of the smaller news stories of that time, events that were relegated to near insignificance in comparison to the murder. For example: the recovery of Rosa Luxemburg's body from the Landwehr Canal. For example: the Versailles peace conference. And on and on, day after day, through the following: the Eugene Debs case; a note on Caruso's first film ("The situations . . . are said to be highly dramatic and filled with stirring heart appeal"); battle reports from the Russian Civil War; the funerals of Karl Liebnecht and thirty-one other Spartacists ("More than fifty thousand persons marched in the procession which was five miles long. Fully twenty percent of these bore wreaths. There was no shouting or cheering"); the ratification of the national prohibition amendment ("William Jennings Bryan—the man who made grape juice famous—was there with a broad smile"); the textile strike in Lawrence, Massachusetts, led by the Wobblies; the death of Emiliano Zapata, "bandit leader in southern Mexico"; Winston Churchill; Bela Kun; Premier Lenine (sic); Woodrow Wilson; Dempsey versus Willard.

I have read through the articles about the murder a dozen times. Still, I find it hard to believe that I did not dream them. They loom up at me with all the force of a trick of the unconscious, distorting reality in the same way dreams do. Because the huge headlines announcing the murder dwarf everything else that happened in the world that day, they give the event the same egocentric importance we give to the things that happen in our private lives. It is almost like the drawing a child makes when he is troubled by some inexpressible fear: the most important thing is always the biggest thing. Perspective is lost in favor of proportion—which is dictated not by the eye but by the demands of the mind.

I read these articles as history. But also as a cave drawing discovered on the inner walls of my own skull.

———

The headlines on the first day, January 24, cover more than a third of the front page.

HARRY AUSTER KILLED
WIFE HELD BY POLICE

———

Former Prominent Real Estate Operator Is Shot
to Death in the Kitchen of the Home of His Wife on Thursday Night Following a Family Wrangle
Over Money—and a Woman.

WIFE SAYS HUSBAND WAS A SUICIDE

———

Dead Man Had Bullet Wound in His Neck
and in the Left Hip and Wife Admits That Revolver
With Which the Shooting Was Done Was Her Property—
Nine-Year-Old Son, Witness of the Tragedy,
May Hold Solution to the Mystery.

According to the newspaper, "Auster and his wife had separated some time ago and an action for divorce was pending in
the Circuit Court for Kenosha county. They had had trouble on
several occasions over money. They had also quarreled over the
fact that Auster [illegible] friendly with a young woman known
to the wife as 'Fanny.' It is believed that 'Fanny' figured in the
trouble between Auster and his wife immediately preceding the
shooting . . ."

Because my grandmother did not confess until the twenty-
eighth, there was some confusion about what really happened. My
grandfather (who was thirty-six years old) arrived at the house
at six o'clock in the evening with "suits of clothing" for his two

oldest sons "while it was stated by witnesses Mrs. Auster was in the bedroom putting Sam, the youngest boy, into bed. Sam [my father] declared that he did not see his mother take a revolver from under the mattress as he was tucked into bed for the night."

It seems that my grandfather had then gone into the kitchen to repair an electric switch and that one of my uncles (the second youngest son) had held a candle for him to see by. "The boy declared that he became panic stricken when he heard the shot and saw a flash of a revolver and fled the room." According to my grandmother, her husband had shot himself. She admitted they had been arguing about money, and "then he said, she continued, 'there is going to be an end for you or me,' and he threatened me. I did not know he had the revolver. I had kept it under the mattress of my bed and he knew it."

Since my grandmother spoke almost no English, I assume that this statement, and all others attributed to her, was invented by the reporter. Whatever it was she said, the police did not believe her. "Mrs. Auster repeated her story to the various police officers without making any decided change in it and she professed great surprise when she was told that she was to be held by the police. With a great deal of tenderness she kissed little Sam good night and then went off to the county jail.

"The two Auster boys were guests of the police department last night sleeping in the squad room and this morning the boys were apparently entirely recovered from any fright they had suffered as a result of the tragedy at their home."

Toward the end of the article, this information is given about my grandfather. "Harry Auster was a native of Austria. He came to this country a number of years ago and had resided in Chicago, in Canada, and in Kenosha. He and his wife, according to the story told the police, later returned to Austria but she rejoined her husband in this country about the time they came to Kenosha. Auster bought a number of homes in the second ward and for some time his operations were on a large scale. He built the big triple flat building on South Park avenue and another one known as the Auster flats on South Exchange street. Six or eight months ago he met with financial reverses ...

"Some time ago Mrs. Auster appealed to the police to aid her in watching Mr. Auster as she alleged that he had relations with a young woman which she believed should be investigated. It was in this way that the police first learned of the woman 'Fanny' ...

"Many people had seen and talked with Auster on Thursday afternoon and these people all declared that he appeared to be normal and that he showed no signs of desiring to take his own life ..."

The next day was the coroner's inquest. My uncle, as the only witness to the incident, was called on to testify. "A sad-eyed little boy, nervously twirling his stocking cap, wrote the second chapter in the Auster murder mystery Friday afternoon ... His attempts to save the family name were tragically pathetic. Again and again when asked if his parents were quarrelling he would answer 'They were just talking' until at last, apparently remembering his oath, he added 'and maybe quarrelling—well just a little bit.'" The article describes the jurors as "weirdly stirred by the boy's efforts to shield both his father and his mother."

The idea of suicide was clearly not going to wash. In the last paragraph the reporter writes that "developments of a startling nature have been hinted by officials."

Then came the funeral. It gave the anonymous reporter an opportunity to emulate some of the choicest diction of Victorian melodrama. By now the murder was no longer merely a scandal. It had been turned into a stirring entertainment.

WIDOW TEARLESS AT AUSTER GRAVE

Mrs. Anna Auster Under Guard Attends Funeral of
Husband, Harry Auster, Sunday.

"Dry-eyed and without the least sign of emotion or grief, Mrs. Harry Auster, who is held here in connection with the mysterious death of her husband, Harry Auster, attended Sunday morning, under guard, the funeral services of the man, in connection with whose death she is being held.

"Neither at the Crossin Chapel, where she looked for the first time since Thursday night upon the dead face of her husband nor at the burial ground did she show the least sign of weakening. The only intimation which she gave of breaking under the terrific strain of the ordeal was when over the grave, after the obsequies were finished, she asked for a conference this afternoon with the Rev. M. Hartman, pastor of the B'nai Zadek Congregation ...

"When the rites were completed Mrs. Auster calmly tightened the fox fur collar more closely about her throat and signified to the police that she was ready to leave ...

"After short ritualistic ceremonies the funeral procession was formed on Wisconsin street. Mrs. Auster asked that she also be allowed to go to the burial ground and the request was granted readily by the police. She seemed very petulant over the fact that no carriage had been provided for her, perhaps remembering that short season of apparent wealth when the Auster limousine was seen in Kenosha ...

"... The ordeal was made exceptionally long because some delay had occurred in the preparation of the grave and while she waited she called Sam, the youngest boy, to her, and tucked his coat collar more closely around his neck. She spoke quietly to him but with this exception she was silent until after the rites were finished ...

"A prominent figure at the funeral was Samuel Auster, of Detroit, the brother of Harry Auster. He took as his especial care the younger children and attempted to console them in their grief.

"In speeches and demonstrations Auster appeared very bitter about his brother's death. He showed clearly that he disbelieved the theory of suicide and uttered remarks which savoured of accusations of the widow . . .

"The Rev. M. Hartman . . . preached an eloquent sermon at the grave. He lamented the fact that the first person to be buried in the new cemetery should be one who had died by violence and who had been killed in his prime. He paid tribute to the enterprise of Harry Auster but deplored his early death.

"The widow appeared to be unmoved by the tributes paid to her dead husband. She indifferently opened her coat to allow the patriarch to cut a gash in her knitted sweater, a token of grief prescribed by the Hebrew faith.

"Officials in Kenosha fail to give up the suspicion that Auster was killed by his wife . . ."

The paper of the following day, January 26th, carried the news of the confession. After her meeting with the rabbi, she had requested a conference with the chief of police. "When she entered the room she trembled a little and was plainly agitated as the chief provided a chair. 'You know what your little boy told us,' the latter began when he realized that the psychological moment had come. 'You don't want us to think that he's lying to us, do you?' And the mother, whose face has been for days so masked as to reveal nothing of the horror hidden behind it, tore off the camouflage, became suddenly tender, and sobbed out her awful secret. 'He isn't lying to you at all; everything he has said is true. I shot him and I want to make a confession.'"

This was her formal statement: "My name is Anna Auster. I shot Harry Auster at the city of Kenosha, Wisconsin on the 23rd day of January A.D. 1919. I have heard people remark that three shots were fired, but I do not remember how many shots were fired that day. My reason for shooting the said Harry Auster is on account of the fact that he, the said Harry Auster, abused me. I was just like crazy when I shot the said Harry Auster. I never thought of shooting him, the said Harry Auster, until the moment I shot him. I think that this is the gun I shot the said Harry Auster with. I make this statement of my own free will and without being forced to do so."

The reporter continues, "On the table before Mrs. Auster lay the revolver with which her husband was shot to death. As she spoke of it she touched it falteringly and then drew her hand back with a noticeable tremor of horror. Without speaking the chief laid the gun aside and asked Mrs. Auster if there was more she cared to say.

"'That's all for now,' she replied composedly. 'You sign it for me and I'll make my mark.'

"Her orders—for a little moment she was almost regal again—were obeyed, she acknowledged the signature, and asked to be returned to her cell . . ."

At the arraignment the next day a plea of not guilty was entered by her attorney. "Muffled in a plush coat and a boa of fox fur, Mrs. Auster entered the court room . . . She smiled at a friend in the crowd as she took her seat before the desk."

By the reporter's own admission, the hearing was "uneventful." But still, he could not resist making this observation: "An incident occurred upon her return to her barred room which furnished a commentary on Mrs. Auster's state of mind.

"A woman, held on a charge of association with a married man, had been brought to the jail for incarceration in an adjoining cell. Upon seeing her, Mrs. Auster asked about the newcomer and learned the particulars in the case.

"'She ought to get ten years,' she said as the iron door clanged pitilessly. 'It was one of her kind that put me here.'"

After some intricate legal discussions concerning bail that were elaborately reported for the next few days, she was set free. "'Have you any notion that this woman will not appear for trial?' the court asked the attorneys. It was attorney Baker who answered: 'Where could a woman with five children like these go? She clings to them and the court can see that they cling to her.'"

For a week the press was quiet. Then, on February 8th, there was a story about "the active support that the cause is being given by some of the papers published in the Jewish language in Chicago. Some of these papers contained columns arguing the case of Mrs. Auster and it is declared that these articles have strongly urged her defense . . .

"Friday afternoon Mrs. Auster with one of her children sat in the office of her attorney while portions of these articles were read. She sobbed like a child as the interpreter read to the attorney the contents of these papers . . .

"Attorney Baker declared this morning that the defense of Mrs. Auster would be one of emotional insanity . . .

"It is expected that the trial of Mrs. Auster will be one of the most interesting murder trials ever tried in the Circuit Court for Kenosha county and the human interest story that has been featured in the defense of the woman up to this time is expected to be largely developed at the trial."

Then nothing for a month. On March 10th the headlines read:

ANNA AUSTER TRIED SUICIDE

The suicide attempt had taken place in Peterboro, Ontario in 1909—by taking carbolic acid and then turning on the gas. The attorney brought this information before the court in order to be granted a delay in the trial so that he would have enough time to secure affidavits. "Attorney Baker held that at the same time the woman had endangered the lives of two of her children and that the story of the attempted suicide was important in that it would show the mental condition of Mrs. Auster."

March 27th. The trial was set for April 7th. After that, another week of silence. And then, on April 4th, as if things had been getting just a bit too dull, a new development.

AUSTER SHOOTS BROTHER'S WIDOW

"Sam Auster, brother of Harry Auster . . . made an unsuccessful attempt to avenge the death of his brother just after ten o'clock this morning when he shot at Mrs. Auster . . . The shooting occurred just outside the Miller Grocery Store . . .

"Auster followed Mrs. Auster outside the door and fired once at her. Mrs. Auster, though she was not struck by the shot, fell to the sidewalk and Auster returned to the store declaring according to witnesses, 'Well, I'm glad I done that.' There he calmly awaited arrest . . .

"At the police station . . . Auster, entirely broken down nervously, gave his explanation of the shooting.

"'That woman,' he said, 'has killed my four brothers and my mother. I've tried to help but she won't let me.' Then as he was being led down to the cell, he sobbed out, 'God's going to take my part though, I know that.'

"At his cell Auster declared that he had tried everything within his power to help the children of his dead brother. The fact that the court had refused to appoint him administrator for the estate because they declared that the widow had some rights in the case had preyed on his mind recently . . . 'She's no widow,' he commented on that incident this morning. 'She is a murderer and should have no rights . . .'

"Auster will not be arraigned immediately in order to make a thorough investigation of the case. The police admit that the death of his brother and subsequent events may have so preyed on his mind that he was not entirely responsible for his deed. Auster expressed several times a hope that he should die too and every precaution is being taken to prevent him from taking his own life . . ."

The next day's paper had this to add: "Auster spent a rather troublesome night in the city lockup. Several times the officers found him sobbing in the cell and he appeared to be hysterical . . .

"It was admitted that Mrs. Auster had suffered from a 'bad case of nerves' as a result of the fright which had attended the attack on her life on Friday, but it was declared that she would be able to be in court when the case against her is called for trial on Monday evening."

After three days the state rested its case. Contending that the murder had been premeditated, the district attorney relied heavily on the testimony of a certain Mrs. Mathews, an employee at the Miller Grocery Store, who contended that "Mrs. Auster came to the store three times on the day of the shooting to use the telephone. On one of those occasions, the witness said, Mrs. Auster called up her husband and asked him to come to the house and fix a light. She said that Auster had promised to come at six o'clock."

But even if she invited him to the house, it does not mean that she intended to kill him once he was there.

It makes no difference anyway. Whatever the facts might have been, the defense attorney shrewdly turned everything to his own advantage. His strategy was to offer overwhelming evidence on two fronts: on the one hand, to prove infidelity on the part of my grandfather, and on the other, to demonstrate a history of mental instability on the part of my grandmother—the two of them combining to produce a case of justifiable homicide or homicide "by reason of insanity." Either one would do.

Attorney Baker's opening remarks were calculated to draw every possible ounce of sympathy from the jury. "He told how Mrs. Auster had toiled with her husband to build up the home and happiness which once was theirs in Kenosha after they had passed through years of hardships . . . 'Then after they had labored together to build up this home,' continued Attorney Baker, 'there came this siren from the city and Anna Auster was cast aside like a rag. Instead of supplying food for his family, her husband kept Fanny Koplan in a flat in Chicago. The money which she had helped to accumulate was being lavished on a more beautiful woman and after such abuse is there any wonder that her mind was shattered and that for the moment she lost control of her senses.'"

The first witness for the defense was Mrs. Elizabeth Grossman, my grandmother's only sister, who lived on a farm near Brunswick, New Jersey. "She made a splendid witness. She told in a simple manner the whole story of the life of Mrs. Auster; of her birth in Austria; of the death of her mother when Mrs. Auster was but six years of age; of the trip with her sister to this country eight years later; of long hours served as a maker of hats and bonnets in New York millinery shops; of how by this work the immigrant girl accumulated a few hundred dollars. She told of the marriage of the woman to Auster just after she reached her twenty-third birthday and of their business ventures; of their failure in a little candy store and their long trip to Lawrence, Kas., where they attempted to start over and where——, the first child was born; of the return to New York and the second failure in business which ended in bankruptcy and the flight of Auster into Canada. She told of Mrs. Auster following Auster to Canada; of the desertion by Auster of the wife and little children and how he had said that he was 'going to make way with himself' [sic] and how he had told the wife that he was taking fifty dollars so that when he was dead it might be found on him and used to give him a decent burial . . . She said that during their residence in Canada they were known as Mr. and Mrs. Harry Ball . . .

"A little break in the story which could not be furnished by Mrs. Grossman, was furnished by former Chief Constable Archie Moore and Abraham Low, both of Peterboro county, Canada. These men told of the departure of Auster from Peterboro and the grief of his wife. Auster, they said, left Peterboro July 14, 1909, and the following night Moore found Mrs. Auster in a room of their shabby home suffering from the effects of gas. She and the children lay on a mattress on the floor while the gas was flowing from four open jets. Moore told of the further fact that he had found a vial of carbolic acid in the room and that traces of the acid had been found on the lips of Mrs. Auster. She was taken to a hospital, the witness declared, and was ill for many days. Both of these men declared that in their opinion there was no doubt but that Mrs. Auster showed signs of insanity at the time she attempted her life in Canada."

Further witnesses included the two oldest children, each of whom chronicled the family's domestic troubles. Much was said about Fanny, and also the frequent squabbles at home. "He said that Auster had a habit of throwing dishes and glass ware and that at one time his mother's arm had been so badly cut that it was necessary to call a physician to attend her. He declared that his father used profane and indecent language toward his mother at these times . . ."

Another witness from Chicago testified that she had frequently seen my grandmother beat her head against the wall in fits of mental anguish. A police officer from Kenosha told how at "one time he had seen Mrs. Auster running wildly down a street. He stated that her hair was 'more or less' dishevelled and added that she acted much like a woman who had lost her mind." A doctor was also called in, and he contended that she had been suffering from "acute mania."

My grandmother's testimony lasted three hours. "Between stifled sobs and recourse to tears, she told the story of her life with Auster up to the time of the 'accident' . . . Mrs. Auster stood the ordeal of cross questioning very well, and her story was told over three times in almost the same way."

In his summation "Attorney Baker made a strong emotional plea for the release of Mrs. Auster. In a speech lasting nearly an hour and a half he retold in an eloquent manner the story of Mrs. Auster . . . Several times Mrs. Auster was moved to tears by the statements of her attorney and women in the audience were sobbing several times as the attorney painted the picture of the struggling immigrant woman seeking to maintain their home."

The judge gave the jury the option of only two verdicts: guilty or innocent of murder. It took them less than two hours to make their decision. As the bulletin of April 12th put it: "At four thirty o'clock this afternoon the jury in the trial of Mrs. Anna Auster returned a verdict finding the defendant not guilty."

April 14th. "'I am happier now than I have been for seventeen years,' said Mrs. Auster Saturday afternoon as she shook hands with each of the jurors following the return of the verdict. 'As long as Harry lived,' she said to one of them, 'I was worried. I never knew real happiness. Now I regret that he had to die by my hand. I am as happy now as I ever expect to be . . .'

"As Mrs. Auster left the court room she was attended by her daughter . . . and the two younger children, who had waited patiently in the courtroom for the return of the verdict which freed their mother . . .

"At the county jail Sam Auster . . . while he cannot understand it all, says he is willing to abide by the decision of the twelve jurors . . .

"'Last night when I heard of the verdict,' he said when interviewed on Sunday morning, 'I dropped on the floor. I could not believe that she could go clear free after killing my brother and her husband. It is all too big for me. I don't understand, but I shall let it go now. I tried once to settle it in my way and failed and I can't do anything now but accept what the court has said.'"

The next day he, too, was released. "'I am going back to my work in the factory,' Auster told the District Attorney. 'Just as soon as I get money enough I am going to raise a head stone over the grave of my brother and then I am going to give my energies to the support of the children of one of my brothers who lived in Austria and who fell fighting in the Austrian army.'

"The conference this morning brought out the fact that Sam Auster is the last of the five Auster brothers. Three of the boys fought with the Austrian army in the world war and all of them fell in battle."

In the last paragraph of the last article about the case, the newspaper reports that "Mrs. Auster is now planning to take the children and leave for the east within a few days . . . It was said that Mrs. Auster decided to take this action on the advice of her attorneys, who told her that she should go to some new home and start life without any one knowing the story of the trial."

It was, I suppose, a happy ending. At least for the newspaper readers of Kenosha, the clever Attorney Baker, and, no doubt, for my grandmother. Nothing further is said, of course, about the fortunes of the Auster family. The public record ends with this announcement of their departure for the east.

Because my father rarely spoke to me about the past, I learned very little about what followed. But from the few things he did mention, I was able to form a fairly good idea of the climate in which the family lived.

For example, they moved constantly. It was not uncommon for my father to attend two, or even three different schools in a single year. Because they had no money, life became a series of escapes from landlords and creditors. In a family that had already closed in on itself, this nomadism walled them off entirely. There were no enduring points of reference: no home, no town, no friends that could be counted on. Only the family itself. It was almost like living in quarantine.

My father was the baby, and for his whole life he continued to look up to his three older brothers. As a boy he was known as Sonny. He suffered from asthma and allergies, did well in school, played end on the football team, and ran the 440 for the track team at Central High in Newark. He graduated in the first year of the Depression, went to law school at night for a semester or two, and then dropped out, exactly as his brothers had done before him.

The four brothers stuck together. There was something almost medieval about their loyalty to one another. Although they had their differences, in many ways did not even like one another, I think of them not as four separate individuals but as a clan, a quadruplicate image of solidarity. Three of them—the youngest three—wound up as business partners and lived in the same town, and the fourth, who lived only two towns away, had been set up in business by the other three. There was scarcely a day that my father did not see his brothers. And that means for his entire life: every day for more than sixty years.

They picked up habits from one another, figures of speech,

little gestures, intermingling to such a degree that it was impossible to tell which one had been the source of any given attitude or idea. My father's feelings were unbending: he never said a word against any of his brothers. Again, it was the other defined not by what he did but by what he was. If one of the brothers happened to slight him or do something objectionable, my father would nevertheless refuse to pass judgment. He's my brother, he would say, as if that explained everything. Brotherhood was the first principle, the unassailable postulate, the one and only article of faith. Like belief in God, to question it was heresy.

As the youngest, my father was the most loyal of the four and also the one least respected by the others. He worked the hardest, was the most generous to his nephews and nieces, and yet these things were never fully recognized, much less appreciated. My mother recalls that on the day of her wedding, at the party following the ceremony, one of the brothers actually propositioned her. Whether he would have carried through with the escapade is another matter. But the mere fact of teasing her like that gives a rough idea of how he felt about my father. You do not do that sort of thing on a man's wedding day, even if he is your brother.

At the center of the clan was my grandmother, a Jewish Mammy Yokum, a mother to end all mothers. Fierce, refractory, the boss. It was common loyalty to her that kept the brothers so close. Even as grown men, with wives and children of their own, they would faithfully go to her house every Friday night for dinner—without their families. This was the relationship that mattered, and it took precedence over everything else. There must have been something slightly comical about it: four big men, each one over six feet, waiting on a little old woman, more than a foot shorter than they were.

One of the few times they came with their wives, a neighbor

happened to walk in and was surprised to find such a large gathering. Is this your family, Mrs. Auster? he asked. Yes, she answered, with great smiles of pride. This is—. This is—. This is—. And this is Sam. The neighbor was a little taken aback. And these lovely ladies, he asked. Who are they? Oh, she answered with a casual wave of the hand. That's—'s. That's—'s. That's—'s. And that's Sam's.

The picture painted of her in the Kenosha newspaper was by no means inaccurate. She lived for her children. (Attorney Baker: Where could a woman with five children like these go? She clings to them and the court can see that they cling to her.) At the same time, she was a tyrant, given to screaming and hysterical fits. When she was angry, she would beat her sons over the head with a broom. She demanded allegiance, and she got it.

Once, when my father had saved the huge sum of ten or twenty dollars from his newspaper route to buy himself a new bicycle, his mother walked into the room, cracked open his piggy bank, and took the money from him without so much as an apology. She needed the money to pay some bills, and my father had no recourse, no way to air his grievance. When he told me this story, his object was not to show how his mother had wronged him but to demonstrate how the good of the family was always more important than the good of any of its members. He might have been unhappy, but he did not complain.

This was rule by caprice. For a child, it meant that the sky could fall on top of him at any moment, that he could never be sure of anything. Therefore, he learned never to trust anyone. Not even himself. Someone would always come along to prove that what he thought was wrong, that it did not count for anything. He learned never to want anything too much.

My father lived with his mother until he was older than I am now. He was the last one to go off on his own, the one who had been left behind to take care of her. It would be wrong to say, however, that he was a mother's boy. He was too independent, had been too fully indoctrinated into the ways of manhood by his brothers. He was good to her, was dutiful and considerate, but not without a certain distance, even humor. After he was married, she called him often, haranguing him about this and that. My father would put the receiver down on the table, walk to the other end of the room and busy himself with some chore for a few minutes, then return to the phone, pick it up, say something innocuous to let her know he was there (uh-huh, uh-huh, mmmmmm, that's right), and then wander off again, back and forth, until she had talked herself out.

The comical side of his obtuseness. And sometimes it served him very well.

I remember a tiny, shriveled creature sitting in the front parlor of a two-family house in the Weequahic section of Newark reading the *Jewish Daily Forward*. Although I knew I would have to do it whenever I saw her, it made me cringe to kiss her. Her face was so wrinkled, her skin so inhumanly soft. Worse than that was her smell—a smell I was much later able to identify as that of camphor, which she must have put in her bureau drawers and which, over the years, had seeped into the fabric of her clothes. This odor was inseparable in my mind from the idea of "grandma."

As far as I can remember, she took virtually no interest in me. The one time she gave me a present, it was a second- or third-hand children's book, a biography of Benjamin Franklin. I remember reading it all the way through and can even recall some of the episodes. Franklin's future wife, for example, laughing at him the first time she saw him—walking through the streets of Philadelphia with an enormous loaf of bread under his arm. The book had a blue cover and was illustrated with silhouettes. I must have been seven or eight at the time.

After my father died, I discovered a trunk that had once belonged to his mother in the cellar of his house. It was locked, and I decided to force it open with a hammer and screwdriver, thinking it might contain some buried secret, some long lost treasure. As the hasp fell down and I raised the lid, there it was, all over again—that smell, wafting up toward me, immediate, palpable, as if it had been my grandmother herself. I felt as though I had just opened her coffin.

There was nothing of interest in it: a set of carving knives, a heap of imitation jewelry. Also a hard plastic dress-up pocketbook, a kind of octagonal box with a handle on it. I gave the thing to Daniel, and he immediately started using it as a portable garage for his fleet of little trucks and cars.

My father worked hard all his life. At nine he had his first job. At eighteen he had a radio repair business with one of his brothers. Except for a brief moment when he was hired as an assistant in Thomas Edison's laboratory (only to have the job taken away from him the next day because Edison learned he was a Jew), my father never worked for anyone but himself. He was a demanding boss, far more exacting than any stranger could have been.

The radio shop eventually led to a small appliance store, which in turn led to a large furniture store. From there he began to dabble in real estate (buying, for example, a house for his mother to live in), until this gradually displaced the store as the focus of his attention and became a business in its own right. The partnership with two of his brothers carried over from one thing to the next.

Up early every morning, home late at night, and in between, work, nothing but work. Work was the name of the country he lived in, and he was one of its greatest patriots. That is not to say, however, that work was pleasure for him. He worked hard because he wanted to earn as much money as possible. Work was a means to an end—a means to money. But the end was not something that could bring him pleasure either. As the young Marx wrote: "If *money* is the bond binding me to *human life*, binding society to me, binding me and nature and man, is not money the bond of all *bonds*? Can it not dissolve and bind all ties? Is it not, therefore, the universal *agent of separation?*"

He dreamed all his life of becoming a millionaire, of being the richest man in the world. It was not so much the money itself he wanted but what it represented: not merely success in the eyes of the world, but a way of making himself untouchable. Having money means more than being able to buy things: it means that the world need never affect you. Money in the sense of protection, then, not pleasure. Having been without money as a child, and therefore vulnerable to the whims of the world, the idea of wealth became synonymous for him with the idea of escape: from harm, from suffering, from being a victim. He was not trying to buy happiness, but simply an absence of unhappiness. Money was the panacea, the objectification of his deepest, most inexpressible desires as a human being. He did not want to spend it, he wanted to have it, to know that it was there. Money not as an elixir, then, but as an antidote: the small vial of medicine you carry in your pocket when you go out into the jungle—just in case you are bitten by a poisonous snake.

At times, his reluctance to spend money was so great it almost resembled a disease. It never came to such a point that he would deny himself what he needed (for his needs were minimal), but more subtly, each time he had to buy something, he would opt for the cheapest solution. This was bargain shopping as a way of life.

Implicit in this attitude was a kind of perceptual primitivism. All distinctions were eliminated, everything was reduced to its least common denominator. Meat was meat, shoes were shoes, a pen was a pen. It did not matter that you could choose between chuck and porterhouse, that there were throwaway ball points for thirty-nine cents and fifty-dollar fountain pens that would last for twenty years. The truly fine object was almost to be abhorred: it meant that you would have to pay an extravagant price, and that made it morally unsound. On a more general level, this translated itself into a permanent state of sensory deprivation: by closing his eyes to so much, he denied himself intimate contact with the shapes and textures of the world, cut himself off from the possibility of experiencing aesthetic pleasure. The world he looked out on was a practical place. Each thing in it had a value and a price, and the idea was to get the things you needed at a price that was as close to the value as possible. Each thing was understood only in terms of its function, judged only by how much it cost, never as an intrinsic object with its own special properties. In some way, I imagine it must have made the world seem a dull place to him. Uniform, colorless, without depth. If you see the world only in terms of money, you are finally not seeing the world at all.

As a child, there were times when I became positively embarrassed for him in public. Haggling with shopkeepers, furious over a high price, arguing as if his very manhood were at stake. A distinct memory of how everything would wither up inside me, of wanting to be anywhere in the world except where I was. A particular incident of going with him to buy a baseball glove stands out. Every day for two weeks I had visited the store after school to admire the one I wanted. Then, when my father took me to the store one evening to buy it, he so exploded at the salesman I was afraid he was going to tear him to pieces. Frightened, sick at heart, I told him not to bother, that I didn't want the glove after all. As we were leaving the store, he offered to buy me an ice cream cone. That glove was no good anyway, he said. I'll buy you a better one some other time.

Better, of course, meant worse.

Tirades about leaving too many lights on in the house. He always made a point of buying bulbs with low wattage.

His excuse for never taking us to the movies: "Why go out and spend a fortune when it will be on television in a year or two?"

The occasional family meal in a restaurant: we always had to order the least expensive things on the menu. It became a kind of ritual. Yes, he would say, nodding his head, that's a good choice.

Years later, when my wife and I were living in New York, he would sometimes take us out to dinner. The script was always precisely the same: the moment after we had put the last forkful of food into our mouths, he would ask, "Are you ready to go?" Impossible even to consider dessert.

His utter discomfort in his own skin. His inability to sit still, to make small talk, to "relax."

It made you nervous to be with him. You felt he was always on the verge of leaving.

He loved clever little tricks, prided himself on his ability to outsmart the world at its own game. A niggardliness in the most trivial aspects of life, as ridiculous as it was depressing. With his cars, he would always disconnect the odometers, falsifying the mileage in order to guarantee himself a better trade-in price. In his house, he would always do his own repair work instead of hiring a professional. Because he had a gift for machines and knew how things worked, he would take bizarre shortcuts, using whatever materials were at hand to rig up Rube Goldberg solutions to mechanical and electrical problems—rather than spending the money to do it right.

Permanent solutions never interested him. He went on patching and patching, a little piece here, a little piece there, never allowing his boat to sink, but never giving it a chance to float either.

The way he dressed: as if twenty years behind the times. Cheap synthetic suits from the racks of discount stores; unboxed pairs of shoes from the bins of bargain basements. Beyond giving proof of his miserliness, this disregard of fashion reinforced the image of him as a man not quite in the world. The clothes he wore seemed to be an expression of solitude, a concrete way of affirming his absence. Even though he was well off, able to afford anything he wanted, he looked like a poor man, a hayseed who had just stepped off the farm.

In the last years of his life, this changed a little bit. Becoming a bachelor again had probably given him a jolt: he realized that he would have to make himself presentable if he wanted to have any kind of social life. It was not that he went out and bought expensive clothes, but at least the tone of his wardrobe changed: the dull browns and grays were abandoned for brighter colors; the outmoded style gave way to a flashier, more dapper image. Checkered pants, white shoes, yellow turtlenecks, boots with big buckles. But in spite of these efforts, he never looked quite at home in these costumes. They were not an integral part of his personality. It made you think of a little boy who had been dressed up by his parents.

————

Given his curious relationship to money (his desire for wealth, his inability to spend), it was somehow appropriate that he made his living among the poor. Compared to them, he was a man of enormous riches. And yet, by spending his days among people who had next to nothing, he could keep before his eyes a vision of the thing he most feared in the world: to be without money. It put things in perspective for him. He did not consider himself stingy—but sensible, a man who knew the value of a dollar. He had to be vigilant. It was the only thing that stood between him and the nightmare of poverty.

When the business was at its peak, he and his brothers owned nearly a hundred buildings. Their terrain was the grim industrial region of northern New Jersey—Jersey City, Newark—and nearly all their tenants were black. One says "slumlord," but in this case it would not have been an accurate or fair description. Nor was he in any way an absentee landlord. He was *there*, and he put in hours that would have driven even the most conscientious employee to go out on strike.

The job was a permanent juggling act. There was the buying and selling of buildings, the buying and repairing of fixtures, the managing of several teams of repair men, the renting of apartments, the supervision of the superintendents, listening to tenant complaints, dealing with the visits of building inspectors, constant involvement with the water and electric companies, not to speak of frequent visits to court—both as plaintiff and defendant—to sue for back rent, to answer to violations. Everything was always happening at once, a perpetual assault from a dozen directions at the same time, and only a man who took things in his stride could have handled it. On any given day it was impossible to do everything that had to be done. You did not go home because you were finished, but simply because it was late and you had run out of time. The next day all the problems would be waiting for you—and several new ones as well. It never stopped. In fifteen years he took only two vacations.

He was soft-hearted with the tenants—granting them delays in paying their rent, giving clothes to their children, helping them to find work—and they trusted him. Old men, afraid of being robbed, would give him their most valuable possessions to store in his office safe. Of all the brothers, he was the one people went to with their troubles. No one called him Mr. Auster. He was always Mr. Sam.

While cleaning out the house after his death, I came across this letter at the bottom of a kitchen drawer. Of all the things I found, I am happiest to have retrieved this. It somehow balances the ledger, provides me with living proof whenever my mind begins to stray too far from the facts. The letter is addressed to "Mr. Sam," and the handwriting is nearly illegible.

April 19, 1976

Dear Sam,

I know you are so surprised to hear from me. first of all maybe I better introduce my self to you. I'm Mrs. Nash. I'm Albert Groover Sister in law—Mrs. Groover and Albert that lived at 285 pine Street in Jersey City so long and Mrs. Banks thats my Sister too. Any way. if you can remember.

You made arrangement to get the apartment for my children and I at 327 Johnston Ave right around the Corner from Mr. & Mrs. Groover my Sister.

Anyway I move away left of owing a $40. rent. this was the year of 1964 but I didn't for get I owed this earnest debt. So now here is your money. thanks for being so very nice to the children and I at that time. this is how much I appreciated what you done for us. I hope you can recall back to the time. So you was never forgotten by me.

About 3 weeks ago I called the office but weren't in at that time.
may the Good Lord ever to Bless you. I hardly comes to Jersey City
if so I would stop by see you.
No matter now I am happy to pay this debt. All for now.

Sincerely
Mrs. JB. Nash

As a boy, I would occasionally go the rounds with him as he collected rent. I was too young to understand what I was seeing, but I remember the impression it made on me, as if, precisely because I did not understand, the raw perceptions of these experiences went directly into me, where they remain today, as immediate as a splinter in the thumb.

The wooden buildings with their dark, inhospitable hallways. And behind each door, a horde of children playing in a bare apartment; a mother, always sullen, overworked, tired, bent over an ironing board. Most vivid is the smell, as if poverty were more than a lack of money but a physical sensation, a stench that invaded your head and made it impossible to think. Every time I walked into a building with my father, I would hold my breath, not daring to breathe, as if that smell was going to hurt me. Everyone was always happy to meet Mr. Sam's son. I was given innumerable smiles and pats on the head.

Once, when I was a bit older, I can remember driving with him down a street in Jersey City and seeing a boy wearing a T-shirt I had outgrown several months before. It was a very distinctive shirt, with a peculiar combination of yellow and blue stripes, and there was no question that this was the one that had been mine. Unaccountably, I was overcome with a feeling of shame.

Older still, at thirteen, fourteen, fifteen, I would sometimes go in with him to earn money working with the carpenters, painters, and repair men. Once, on an excruciatingly hot day in the middle of summer, I was given the job of helping one of the men tar a roof. The man's name was Joe Levine (a black man who had changed his name to Levine out of gratitude to an old Jewish grocer who had helped him in his youth), and he was my father's most trusted and reliable handyman. We hauled several fifty gallon barrels of tar up to the roof and got to work spreading the stuff over the surface with brooms. The sunlight beating down on that flat black roof was brutal, and after half an hour or so I became extremely dizzy, slipped on a patch of wet tar, fell, and somehow knocked over one of the open barrels, which then spilled tar all over me.

When I got back to the office a few minutes later, my father was greatly amused. I realized that the situation was amusing, but I was too embarrassed to want to joke about it. To my father's credit, he did not get angry at me or make fun of me. He laughed, but in a way that made me laugh too. Then he dropped what he had been doing, took me to the Woolworth's across the street, and bought me some new clothes. It had suddenly become possible for me to feel close to him.

As the years went by, the business started to decline. The business itself was not at fault, but rather the nature of the business: at that particular time, in that particular place, it was no longer possible to survive. The cities were falling apart, and no one seemed to care. What had once been a more or less fulfilling activity for my father now became simple drudgery. In the last years of his life he hated going to work.

Vandalism became such a severe problem that doing any kind of repairs became a demoralizing gesture. No sooner was plumbing installed in a building than the pipes would be ripped out by thieves. Windows were constantly being broken, doors smashed, hallways gutted, fires started. At the same time, it was impossible to sell out. No one wanted the buildings. The only way to get rid of them was to abandon them and let the cities take over. Tremendous amounts of money were lost in this way, an entire life's work. In the end, at the time of my father's death, there were only six or seven buildings left. The whole empire had disintegrated.

The last time I was in Jersey City (at least ten years ago) the place had the look of a disaster area, as if it had been pillaged by Huns. Gray, desolate streets; garbage piled everywhere; derelicts shuffling aimlessly up and down. My father's office had been robbed so many times that by now there was nothing left in it but some gray metal desks, a few chairs, and three or four telephones. Not even a typewriter, not one touch of color. It was not really a work place anymore, but a room in hell. I sat down and looked out at the bank across the street. No one came out, no one went in. The only living things were two stray dogs humping on the steps.

How he managed to pick himself up and go in there every day is beyond my understanding. Force of habit, or else sheer stubbornness. Not only was it depressing, it was dangerous. He was mugged several times, and once was kicked in the head so viciously by an attacker that his hearing was permanently damaged. For the last four or five years of his life there was a faint and constant ringing in his head, a humming that never went away, not even while he was asleep. The doctors said there was nothing that could be done about it.

In the end, he never went out into the street without carrying a monkey wrench in his right hand. He was over sixty-five years old, and he did not want to take any more chances.

Two sentences that suddenly come to mind this morning as I am showing Daniel how to make scrambled eggs.

"'And now I want to know,' the woman says, with terrible force, 'I want to know whether it is possible to find another father like him anywhere in the world.'" (Isaac Babel)

"Children have always a tendency either to depreciate or to exalt their parents, and to a good son his father is always the best of fathers, quite apart from any objective reason there may be for admiring him." (Proust)

I realize now that I must have been a bad son. Or, if not precisely bad, then at least a disappointment, a source of confusion and sadness. It made no sense to him that he had produced a poet for a son. Nor could he understand why a young man with two degrees from Columbia University should take a job after graduation as an ordinary seaman on an oil tanker in the Gulf of Mexico, and then, without rhyme or reason, take off for Paris and spend four years there leading a hand to mouth existence.

His most common description of me was that I had "my head in the clouds," or else that I "did not have my feet on the ground." Either way, I must not have seemed very substantial to him, as if I were somehow a vapor or a person not wholly of this world. In his eyes, you became part of the world by working. By definition, work was something that brought in money. If it did not bring in money, it was not work. Writing, therefore, was not work, especially the writing of poetry. At best it was a hobby, a pleasant way to pass the time in between the things that really mattered. My father thought that I was squandering my gifts, refusing to grow up.

Nevertheless, some kind of bond remained between us. We were not close, but stayed in touch. A phone call every month or so, perhaps three or four visits a year. Each time a book of my poetry was published I would dutifully send it to him, and he would always call to thank me. Whenever I wrote an article for a magazine, I would set aside a copy and make sure I gave it to him the next time I saw him. *The New York Review of Books* meant nothing to him, but the pieces in *Commentary* impressed him. I think he felt that if the Jews were publishing me, then perhaps there was something to it.

Once, while I was still living in Paris, he wrote to tell me he had gone to the public library to read some of my poems that had appeared in a recent issue of *Poetry*. I imagined him in a large, deserted room, early in the morning before going to work: sitting at one of those long tables with his overcoat still on, hunched over words that must have been incomprehensible to him.

I have tried to keep this image in mind, along with all the others that will not leave it.

The rampant, totally mystifying force of contradiction. I understand now that each fact is nullified by the next fact, that each thought engenders an equal and opposite thought. Impossible to say anything without reservation: he was good, or he was bad; he was this, or he was that. All of them are true. At times I have the feeling that I am writing about three or four different men, each one distinct, each one a contradiction of all the others. Fragments. Or the anecdote as a form of knowledge.

Yes.

The occasional flash of generosity. At those rare times when the world was not a threat to him, his motive for living seemed to be kindness. "May the good Lord ever to Bless you."

Friends called him whenever they were in trouble. A car stuck somewhere in the middle of the night, and my father would drag himself out of bed and come to the rescue. In certain ways it was easy for others to take advantage of him. He refused to complain about anything.

A patience that bordered on the superhuman. He was the only person I have ever known who could teach someone to drive without getting angry or crumpling in a fit of nerves. You could be careening straight toward a lamp post, and still he would not get excited.

Impenetrable. And because of that, at times almost serene.

Starting when he was still a young man, he always took a special interest in his oldest nephew—the only child of his only sister. My aunt had an unhappy life, punctuated by a series of difficult marriages, and her son bore the brunt of it: shipped off to military schools, never really given a home. Motivated, I think, by nothing more than kindness and a sense of duty, my father took the boy under his wing. He nursed him along with constant encouragement, taught him how to get along in the world. Later, he helped him in business, and whenever a problem came up, he was always ready to listen and give advice. Even after my cousin married and had his own family, my father continued to take an active interest, putting them up in his house at one point for more than a year, religiously giving presents to his four grand-nephews and grand-nieces on their birthdays, and often going to visit them for dinner.

This cousin was more shaken by my father's death than any of my other relatives. At the family gathering after the funeral he came up to me three or four times and said, "I ran into him by accident just the other day. We were supposed to have dinner together Friday night."

The words he used were exactly the same each time. As if he no longer knew what he was saying.

I felt that we had somehow reversed roles, that he was the grieving son and I was the sympathetic nephew. I wanted to put my arm around his shoulder and tell him what a good man his father had been. After all, he was the real son, he was the son I could never bring myself to be.

For the past two weeks, these lines from Maurice Blanchot echoing in my head: "One thing must be understood: I have said nothing extraordinary or even surprising. What is extraordinary begins at the moment I stop. But I am no longer able to speak of it."

To begin with death. To work my way back into life, and then, finally, to return to death.

Or else: the vanity of trying to say anything about anyone.

In 1972 he came to visit me in Paris. It was the one time he ever traveled to Europe.

I was living that year in a minuscule sixth-floor maid's room barely large enough for a bed, a table, a chair, and a sink. The windows and little balcony stared into the face of one of the stone angels that jutted from St. Germain l'Auxerrois: the Louvre to my left, Les Halles off to my right, and Montmartre in the far distance ahead. I had a great fondness for that room, and many of the poems that later appeared in my first book were written there.

My father was not planning to stay for any length of time, hardly even what you would call a vacation: four days in London, three days in Paris, and then home again. But I was pleased at the thought of seeing him and prepared myself to show him a good time.

Two things happened, however, that made this impossible. I became very ill with the flu; and I had to leave for Mexico the day after his arrival to work on a ghostwriting project.

I waited for him all morning in the lobby of the tourist hotel where he had booked reservations, sweating away with a high fever, almost delirious with weakness. When he did not show up at the appointed time, I stayed on for another hour or two, but finally gave in and went back to my room where I collapsed into bed.

Late in the afternoon he came and knocked on my door, waking me from a deep sleep. The encounter was straight out of Dostoyevsky: bourgeois father comes to visit son in a foreign city and finds the struggling poet alone in a garret, wasting away with fever. He was shocked by what he saw, outraged that anyone could live in such a room, and it galvanized him into action: he made me put on my coat, dragged me off to a neighborhood clinic, and then bought the pills that were prescribed for me. Afterwards, he refused to allow me to spend the night in my room. I was in no condition to argue, so I agreed to stay in his hotel.

The next day I was no better. But there were things to be done, and I picked myself up and did them. In the morning I took my father along with me to the vast Avenue Henri Martin apartment of the movie producer who was sending me to Mexico. For the past year I had been working on and off for this man, doing what amounted to odd jobs—translations, script synopses—things that were only marginally connected to the movies, which anyway did not interest me. Each project was more idiotic than the last, but the pay was good, and I needed the money. Now he wanted me to help his Mexican wife with a book she had been contracted to write for an English publisher: Quetzalcoatl and the mysteries of the plumed serpent. This seemed to be pushing it a bit, and I had already turned him down several times. But each time I said no, his offer had gone up, until now I was being paid so much money that I could no longer turn away. I would be gone for only a month, and I was being paid in cash—in advance.

This was the transaction my father witnessed. For once, I could see that he was impressed. Not only had I led him into this luxurious setting and introduced him to a man who did business in the millions, but now this man was calmly handing me a stack of hundred dollar bills across the table and telling me to have a pleasant trip. It was the money, of course, that made the difference, the fact that my father had seen it with his own eyes. I felt it as a triumph, as if I had somehow been vindicated. For the first time he had been forced to realize that I could take care of myself on my own terms.

He became very protective, indulgent of my weakened condition. Helped me deposit the money in the bank, all smiles and jokes. Then got us a cab and rode all the way to the airport with me. A big handshake at the end. Good luck, son. Knock 'em dead. You bet.

Nothing now for several days . . .

In spite of the excuses I have made for myself, I understand what is happening. The closer I come to the end of what I am able to say, the more reluctant I am to say anything. I want to postpone the moment of ending, and in this way delude myself into thinking that I have only just begun, that the better part of my story still lies ahead. No matter how useless these words might seem to be, they have nevertheless stood between me and a silence that continues to terrify me. When I step into this silence, it will mean that my father has vanished forever.

The dingy green carpet in the funeral home. And the director, unctuous, professional, suffering from eczema and swollen ankles, going down a checklist of expenses as if I were about to buy a suite of bedroom furniture on credit. He handed me an envelope that contained the ring my father had been wearing when he died. Idly fingering the ring as the conversation droned on, I noticed that the underside of the stone was smeared with the residue of some soapy lubricant. A few moments passed before I made the connection, and then it became absurdly obvious: the lotion had been used to remove the ring from his finger. I tried to imagine the person whose job it was to do such things. I did not feel horror so much as fascination. I remember thinking to myself: I have entered the world of facts, the realm of brute particulars. The ring was gold, with a black setting that bore the insignia of the Masonic brotherhood. My father had not been an active member for over twenty years.

The funeral director kept telling me how he had known my father "in the old days," implying an intimacy and friendship I was sure had never existed. As I gave him the information to be passed on to the newspapers for the obituary, he anticipated my remarks with incorrect facts, rushing ahead of me in order to prove how well acquainted he had been with my father. Each time this happened, I stopped and corrected him. The next day, when the obituary appeared in the paper, many of these incorrect facts were printed.

Three days before he died, my father had bought a new car. He had driven it once, maybe twice, and when I returned to his house after the funeral, I saw it sitting in the garage, already defunct, like some huge, stillborn creature. Later that same day I went off to the garage for a moment to be by myself. I sat down behind the wheel of this car, inhaling the strange factory newness of it. The odometer read sixty-seven miles. That also happened to have been my father's age: sixty-seven years. The brevity of it sickened me. As if that were the distance between life and death. A tiny trip, hardly longer than a drive to the next town.

Worst regret: that I was not given a chance to see him after he died. Ignorantly, I had assumed the coffin would be open during the funeral service, and then, when it wasn't, it was too late to do anything about it.

Never to have seen him dead deprives me of an anguish I would have welcomed. It is not that his death has been made any less real, but now, each time I want to see it, each time I want to touch its reality, I must engage in an act of imagination. There is nothing to remember. Nothing but a kind of emptiness.

When the grave was uncovered to receive the coffin, I noticed a thick orange root thrusting into the hole. It had a strangely calming effect on me. For a brief moment the bare fact of death could no longer be hidden behind the words and gestures of ceremony. Here it was: unmediated, unadorned, impossible to turn my eyes away from. My father was being lowered into the ground, and in time, as the coffin gradually disintegrated, his body would help to feed the same root I had seen. More than anything that had been said or done that day, this made sense to me.

The rabbi who conducted the funeral service was the same man who had presided over my Bar Mitzvah nineteen years earlier. The last time I had seen him he was a youngish, clean-shaven man. Now he was old, with a full gray beard. He had not known my father, in fact knew nothing about him, and half an hour before the service was to begin I sat down with him and told him what to say in the eulogy. He made notes on little scraps of paper. When it came time for him to deliver the speech, he spoke with great feeling. The subject was a man he had never known, and yet he made it sound as though he were speaking from the heart. Behind me, I could hear women sobbing. He was following what I had told him almost word for word.

It occurs to me that I began writing this story a long time ago, long before my father died.

Night after night, lying awake in bed, my eyes open in the darkness. The impossibility of sleep, the impossibility of not thinking about how he died. I find myself sweating between the sheets, trying to imagine what it feels like to suffer a heart attack. Adrenalin pumps through me, my head pounds, and my whole body seems to contract into a small area behind my chest. A need to experience the same panic, the same mortal pain.

And then, at night, there are the dreams, nearly every night. In one of them, which woke me up just hours ago, I learned from the teenage daughter of my father's lady friend that she, the daughter, had been made pregnant by my father. Because she was so young, it was agreed that my wife and I would raise the child after it was born. The baby was going to be a boy. Everyone knew this in advance.

It is equally true, perhaps, that once this story has ended, it will go on telling itself, even after the words have been used up.

The old gentleman at the funeral was my great uncle, Sam Auster, now almost ninety years old. Tall, hairless, a high-pitched, rasping voice. Not a word about the events of 1919, and I did not have the heart to ask him. I took care of Sam when he was a little boy, he said. But that was all.

When asked if he wanted anything to drink, he requested a glass of hot water. Lemon? No thank you, just hot water.

Again Blanchot: "But I am no longer able to speak of it."

From the house: a document from St. Clair County in the State of Alabama duly announcing my parents' divorce. The signature at the bottom: Ann W. Love.

From the house: a watch, a few sweaters, a jacket, an alarm clock, six tennis rackets, and an old rusted Buick that barely runs. A set of dishes, a coffee table, three or four lamps. A barroom statue of Johnnie Walker for Daniel. The blank photograph album, This Is Our Life: The Austers.

At first I thought it would be a comfort to hold on to these things, that they would remind me of my father and make me think of him as I went about my life. But objects, it seems, are no more than objects. I am used to them now, I have begun to think of them as my own. I read time by his watch, I wear his sweaters, I drive around in his car. But all this is no more than an illusion of intimacy. I have already appropriated these things. My father has vanished from them, has become invisible again. And sooner or later they will break down, fall apart, and have to be thrown away. I doubt that it will even seem to matter.

"... here it holds good that only he who works gets the bread, only he who was in anguish finds repose, only he who descends into the underworld rescues the beloved, only he who draws the knife gets Isaac ... He who will not work must take note of what is written about the maidens of Israel, for he gives birth to the wind, but he who is willing to work gives birth to his own father." (Kierkegaard)

Past two in the morning. An overflowing ashtray, an empty coffee cup, and the cold of early spring. An image of Daniel now, as he lies upstairs in his crib asleep. To end with this.

To wonder what he will make of these pages when he is old enough to read them.

And the image of his sweet and ferocious little body, as he lies upstairs in his crib asleep. To end with this.

THE BOOK OF MEMORY

{1980-1981}

The Invention of Solitude: II

"When the dead weep, they are beginning to recover,"
said the Crow solemnly.

"I am sorry to contradict my famous friend and colleague,"
said the Owl, "but as far as I'm concerned, I think that when
the dead weep, it means they do not want to die."

COLLODI, *The Adventures of Pinocchio*

He lays out a piece of blank paper on the table before him and writes these words with his pen. It was. It will never be again.

Later that same day he returns to his room. He finds a fresh sheet of paper and lays it out on the table before him. He writes until he has covered the entire page with words. Later, when he reads over what he has written, he has trouble deciphering the words. Those he does manage to understand do not seem to say what he thought he was saying. Then he goes out to eat his dinner.

That night he tells himself that tomorow is another day. New words begin to clamor in his head, but he does not write them down. He decides to refer to himself as A. He walks back and forth between the table and the window. He turns on the radio and then turns it off. He smokes a cigarette.

———

Then he writes. It was. It will never be again.

Christmas Eve, 1979. His life no longer seemed to dwell in the present. Whenever he turned on his radio and listened to the news of the world, he would find himself imagining the words to be describing things that had happened long ago. Even as he stood in the present, he felt himself to be looking at it from the future, and this present-as-past was so antiquated that even the horrors of the day, which ordinarily would have filled him with outrage, seemed remote to him, as if the voice in the radio were reading from a chronicle of some lost civilization. Later, in a time of greater clarity, he would refer to this sensation as "nostalgia for the present."

To follow with a detailed description of classical memory systems, complete with charts, diagrams, symbolic drawings. Raymond Lull, for example, or Robert Fludd, not to speak of Giordano Bruno, the great Nolan burned at the stake in 1600. Places and images as catalysts for remembering other places and images: things, events, the buried artifacts of one's own life. Mnemotechnics. To follow with Bruno's notion that the structure of human thought corresponds to the structure of nature. And therefore to conclude that everything, in some sense, is connected to everything else.

At the same time, as if running parallel to the above, a brief disquisition on the room. An image, for example, of a man sitting alone in a room. As in Pascal: "All the unhappiness of man stems from one thing only: that he is incapable of staying quietly in his room." As in the phrase: "he wrote The Book of Memory in this room."

———

The Book of Memory. Book One.

Christmas Eve, 1979. He is in New York, alone in his little room at 6 Varick Street. Like many of the buildings in the neighborhood, this one used to be nothing but a work place. Remnants of its former life are everywhere around him: networks of mysterious pipes, sooty tin ceilings, hissing steam radiators. Whenever his eyes fall on the frosted glass panel of his door, he can read these clumsily stencilled letters in reverse: R.M. Pooley, Licensed Electrician. People were never supposed to live here. It is a room meant for machines, cuspidors, and sweat.

He cannot call it home, but for the past nine months it is all he has had. A few dozen books, a mattress on the floor, a table, three chairs, a hot plate, and a corroded cold water sink. The toilet is down the hall, but he uses it only when he has to shit. Pissing he does in the sink. For the past three days the elevator has been out of service, and since this is the top floor, it has made him reluctant to go out. It is not so much that he dreads climbing the ten flights of stairs when he gets back but that he finds it disheartening to exhaust himself so thoroughly only to return to such bleakness. By staying in this room for long stretches at a time, he can usually manage to fill it with his thoughts, and this in turn seems to dispel the dreariness, or at least make him unaware of it. Each time he goes out, he takes his thoughts with him, and during his absence the room gradually empties of his efforts to inhabit it. When he returns, he has to begin the process all over again, and that takes work, real spiritual work. Considering his physical condition after the climb (chest heaving like a bellows, legs as tight and heavy as tree trunks), this inner struggle takes all that much longer to get started. In the interim, in the void between the moment he opens the door and the moment he begins to reconquer the emptiness, his mind flails in a wordless panic. It is as if he were being forced to watch his own disappearance, as if, by crossing the threshold of this room, he were entering another dimension, taking up residence inside a black hole.

Above him, dim clouds float past the tar-stained skylight, drifting off into the Manhattan evening. Below him, he hears the traffic rushing toward the Holland Tunnel: streams of cars heading home to New Jersey on the night before Christmas. Next door it is quiet. The Pomponio brothers, who arrive there each morning to smoke their cigars and grind out plastic display letters—a business they keep going by working twelve or fourteen hours a day—are probably at home, getting ready to eat a holiday meal. That is all to the good. Lately, one of them has been spending the night in his shop, and his snoring invariably keeps A. awake. The man sleeps directly opposite A., on the other side of the thin wall that divides their two rooms, and hour after hour A. lies in bed, staring into the darkness, trying to pace his thoughts to the ebb and flow of the man's troubled, adenoidal dreams. The snores swell gradually, and at the peak of each cycle they become long, piercing, almost hysterical, as if, when night comes, the snorer had to imitate the noise of the machine that holds him captive during the day. For once A. can count on a calm, unbroken sleep. Not even the arrival of Santa Claus will disturb him.

Winter solstice: the darkest time of the year. No sooner has he woken up in the morning than he feels the day beginning to slip away from him. There is no light to sink his teeth into, no sense of time unfolding. Rather, a feeling of doors being shut, of locks being turned. It is a hermetic season, a long moment of inwardness. The outer world, the tangible world of materials and bodies, has come to seem no more than an emanation of his mind. He feels himself sliding through events, hovering like a ghost around his own presence, as if he were living somewhere to the side of himself—not really here, but not anywhere else either. A feeling of having been locked up, and at the same time of being able to walk through walls. He notes somewhere in the margins of a thought: a darkness in the bones; make a note of this.

By day, heat gushes from the radiators at full blast. Even now, in coldest winter, he is forced to keep the window open. At night, however, there is no heat at all. He sleeps fully clothed, with two or three sweaters, curled up tightly in a sleeping bag. During the weekends, the heat is off altogether, both day and night, and there have been times lately when he has sat at his table, trying to write, and could not feel the pen in his hand anymore. In itself, this lack of comfort does not disturb him. But it has the effect of keeping him off balance, of prodding him into a state of constant inner watchfulness. In spite of what it might seem to be, this room is not a retreat from the world. There is nothing here to welcome him, no promise of a soma holiday to woo him into oblivion. These four walls hold only the signs of his own disquiet, and in order to find some measure of peace in these surroundings, he must dig more and more deeply into himself. But the more he digs, the less there will be to go on digging into. This seems undeniable to him. Sooner or later, he is bound to use himself up.

When night comes, the electricity dims to half-strength, then goes up again, then comes down, for no apparent reason. It is as though the lights were controlled by some prankster deity. Con Edison has no record of the place, and no one has ever had to pay for power. At the same time, the phone company has refused to acknowledge A.'s existence. The phone has been here for nine months, functioning without a flaw, but he has not yet received a bill for it. When he called the other day to straighten out the problem, they insisted they had never heard of him. Somehow, he has managed to escape the clutches of the computer, and none of his calls has ever been recorded. His name is off the books. If he felt like it, he could spend his idle moments making free calls to faraway places. But the fact is, there is no one he wants to talk to. Not in California, not in Paris, not in China. The world has shrunk to the size of this room for him, and for as long as it takes him to understand it, he must stay where he is. Only one thing is certain: he cannot be anywhere until he is here. And if he does not manage to find this place, it would be absurd for him to think of looking for another.

Life inside the whale. A gloss on Jonah, and what it means to refuse to speak. Parallel text: Gepetto in the belly of the shark (whale in the Disney version), and the story of how Pinocchio rescues him. Is it true that one must dive to the depths of the sea and save one's father to become a real boy?

Initial statement of these themes. Further installments to follow.

Then shipwreck. Crusoe on his island. "That boy might be happy if he would stay at home, but if he goes abroad he will be the most miserable wretch that was ever born." Solitary consciousness. Or, in George Oppen's phrase: "the shipwreck of the singular."

A vision of waves all around, water as endless as air, and the jungle heat behind. "I am divided from mankind, a solitaire, one banished from human society."

And Friday? No, not yet. There is no Friday, at least not here. Everything that happens is prior to that moment. Or else: the waves will have washed the footprints away.

First commentary on the nature of chance.

This is where it begins. A friend of his tells him a story. Several years go by, and then he finds himself thinking about the story again. It is not that it begins with the story. Rather, in the act of remembering it, he has become aware that something is happening to him. For the story would not have occurred to him unless whatever summoned its memory had not already been making itself felt. Unknown to himself, he had been burrowing down to a place of almost vanished memory, and now that something had surfaced, he could not even guess how long the excavation had taken.

During the war, M.'s father had hidden out from the Nazis for several months in a Paris *chambre de bonne*. Eventually, he managed to escape, made his way to America, and began a new life. Years passed, more than twenty years. M. had been born, had grown up, and was now going off to study in Paris. Once there, he spent several difficult weeks looking for a place to live. Just when he was about to give up in despair, he found a small *chambre de bonne*. Immediately upon moving in, he wrote a letter to his father to tell him the good news. A week or so later he received a reply: your address, wrote M.'s father, that is the same building I hid out in during the war. He then went on to describe the details of the room. It turned out to be the same room his son had rented.

It begins, therefore, with this room. And then it begins with that room. And beyond that there is the father, there is the son, and there is the war. To speak of fear, and to remember that the man who hid in that little room was a Jew. To note as well: that the city was Paris, a place A. had just returned from (December fifteenth), and that for a whole year he once lived in a Paris *chambre de bonne*—where he wrote his first book of poems, and where his own father, on his only trip to Europe, once came to see him. To remember his father's death. And beyond that, to understand— this most important of all—that M.'s story has no meaning.

Nevertheless, this is where it begins. The first word appears only at a moment when nothing can be explained anymore, at some instant of experience that defies all sense. To be reduced to saying nothing. Or else, to say to himself: this is what haunts me. And then to realize, almost in the same breath, that this is what he haunts.

He lays out a blank sheet of paper on the table before him and writes these words with his pen. Possible epigraph for The Book of Memory.

Then he opens a book by Wallace Stevens (*Opus Posthumous*) and copies out the following sentence.

"In the presence of extraordinary actuality, consciousness takes the place of imagination."

Later that same day he writes steadily for three or four hours. Afterwards, when he reads over what he has written, he finds only one paragraph of any interest. Although he is not sure what to make of it, he decides to keep it for future reference and copies it into a lined notebook:

When the father dies, he writes, the son becomes his own father and his own son. He looks at his son and sees himself in the face of the boy. He imagines what the boy sees when he looks at him and finds himself becoming his own father. Inexplicably, he is moved by this. It is not just the sight of the boy that moves him, nor even the thought of standing inside his father, but what he sees in the boy of his own vanished past. It is a nostalgia for his own life that he feels, perhaps, a memory of his own boyhood as a son to his father. Inexplicably, he finds himself shaking at that moment with both happiness and sorrow, if this is possible, as if he were going both forward and backward, into the future and into the past. And there are times, often there are times, when these feelings are so strong that his life no longer seems to dwell in the present.

———————

Memory as a place, as a building, as a sequence of columns, cornices, porticoes. The body inside the mind, as if we were moving around in there, going from one place to the next, and the sound of our footsteps as we walk, moving from one place to the next.

"One must consequently employ a large number of places," writes Cicero, "which must be well lighted, clearly set out in order, spaced out at moderate intervals; and images which are active, sharply defined, unusual, and which have the power of speedily encountering and penetrating the psyche . . . For the places are very much like wax tablets or papyrus, the images like the letters, the arrangement and disposition of the images like the script, and the speaking like the reading."

He returned from Paris ten days ago. He had gone there on a work visit, and it was the first time he had been abroad in more than five years. The business of traveling, of continual conversation, of too much drinking with old friends, of being away from his little son for so long, had finally worn him out. With a few days to spare at the end of his trip, he decided to go to Amsterdam, a city he had never been to before. He thought: the paintings. But once there, it was a thing he had not planned on doing that made the greatest impression on him. For no particular reason (idly looking through a guide book he found in his hotel room) he decided to go to Anne Frank's house, which has been preserved as a museum. It was a Sunday morning, gray with rain, and the streets along the canal were deserted. He climbed the steep and narrow staircase inside the house and entered the secret annex. As he stood in Anne Frank's room, the room in which the diary was written, now bare, with the faded pictures of Hollywood movie stars she had collected still pasted to the walls, he suddenly found himself crying.

Not sobbing, as might happen in response to a deep inner pain, but crying without sound, the tears streaming down his cheeks, as if purely in response to the world. It was at that moment, he later realized, that The Book of Memory began. As in the phrase: "she wrote her diary in this room."

From the window of that room, facing out on the backyard, you can see the rear windows of a house in which Descartes once lived. There are children's swings in the yard now, toys scattered in the grass, pretty little flowers. As he looked out the window that day, he wondered if the children those toys belonged to had any idea of what had happened thirty-five years earlier in the spot where he was standing. And if they did, what it would be like to grow up in the shadow of Anne Frank's room.

To repeat Pascal: "All the unhappiness of man stems from one thing only: that he is incapable of staying quietly in his room." At roughly the same time these words entered the *Pensées*, Descartes wrote to a friend in France from his room in that house in Amsterdam. "Is there any country," he asked with exuberance, "in which one can enjoy freedom as enormously as one does here?" Everything, in some sense, can be read as a gloss on everything else. To imagine Anne Frank, for example, had she lived on after the war, reading Descartes' *Meditations* as a university student in Amsterdam. To imagine a solitude so crushing, so unconsolable, that one stops breathing for hundreds of years.

He notes, with a certain fascination, that Anne Frank's birthday is the same as his son's. June twelfth. Under the sign of Gemini. An image of the twins. A world in which everything is double, in which the same thing always happens twice.

Memory: the space in which a thing happens for the second time.

The Book of Memory. Book Two.

Israel Lichtenstein's Last Testament. Warsaw; July 31, 1942.

"With zeal and zest I threw myself into the work to help assemble archive materials. I was entrusted to be the custodian. I hid the material. Besides me, no one knew. I confided only in my friend Hersh Wasser, my supervisor . . . It is well hidden. Please God that it be preserved. That will be the finest and best we achieved in the present gruesome time . . . I know that we will not endure. To survive and remain alive after such horrible murders and massacres is impossible. Therefore I write this testament of mine. Perhaps I am not worthy of being remembered, but just for my grit in working with the Society Oneg Shabbat and for being the most endangered because I hid the entire material. It would be a small thing to give my own head. I risk the head of my dear wife Gele Seckstein and my treasure, my little daughter, Margalit . . . I don't want any gratitude, any monument, any praise. I want only a remembrance, so that my family, brother and sister abroad, may know what has become of my remains . . . I want my wife to be remembered. Gele Seckstein, artist, dozens of works, talented, didn't manage to exhibit, did not show in public. During the three years of war worked among children as educator, teacher, made stage sets, costumes for the children's productions, received awards. Now together with me, we are preparing to receive death . . . I want my little daughter to be remembered. Margalit, 20 months old today. Has mastered Yiddish perfectly, speaks a pure Yiddish. At 9 months began to speak Yiddish clearly. In intelligence she is on a par with 3- or 4-year old children. I don't want to brag about her. Witnesses to this, who tell me about it, are the teaching staff of the school at Nowolipki 68 . . . I am not sorry about my life and that of my wife. But I am sorry for the gifted little girl. She deserves to be remembered also . . . May we be the redeemers for all the rest of the Jews in the whole world. I believe in the survival of our people. Jews will not be annihilated. We, the Jews of Poland, Czechoslovakia, Lithuania, Latvia, are the scapegoat for all Israel in all the other lands."

Standing and watching. Sitting down. Lying in bed. Walking through the streets. Eating his meals at the Square Diner, alone in a booth, a newspaper spread out on the table before him. Opening his mail. Writing letters. Standing and watching. Walking through the streets. Learning from an old English friend, T., that both their families had originally come from the same town (Stanislav) in Eastern Europe. Before World War I it had been part of the Austro-Hungarian Empire; between the wars it had been part of Poland; and now, since the end of World War II, part of the Soviet Union. In the first letter from T. there is some speculation that they might, after all, be cousins. A second letter, however, offers clarification. T. has learned from an ancient aunt that in Stanislav his family was quite wealthy; A.'s family, on the other hand (and this is consistent with everything he has ever known), was poor. The story is that one of A.'s relatives (an uncle or cousin of some sort) lived in a small cottage on the property of T.'s family. He fell in love with the young lady of the household, proposed marriage, and was turned down. At that point he left Stanislav forever.

What A. finds particularly fascinating about this story is that the man's name was precisely the same as his son's.

Some weeks later he reads the following entry in the Jewish Encyclopedia:

AUSTER, DANIEL (1893–1962). Israel lawyer and mayor of Jerusalem. Auster, who was born in Stanislav (then

Western Galicia), studied law in Vienna, graduated in 1914, and moved to Palestine. During World War I he served in the Austrian expeditionary force headquarters in Damascus, where he assisted Arthur Ruppin in sending financial help from Constantinople to the starving *yishuv*. After the war he established a law practice in Jerusalem that represented several Jewish-Arab interests, and served as secretary of the Legal Department of the Zionist Commission (1919, 20). In 1934 Auster was elected a Jerusalem councillor; in 1935 he was appointed deputy mayor of Jerusalem; and in 1936–38 and 1944–45 he was acting mayor. Auster represented the Jewish case against internationalization of Jerusalem brought before the United Nations in 1947–48. In 1948 Auster (who represented the Progressive Party) was elected mayor of Jerusalem, the first to hold that office in an independent Israel. Auster held that post until 1951. He also served as a member of the Provisional Council of Israel in 1948. He headed the Israel United Nations Association from its inception until his death.

All during the three days he spent in Amsterdam, he was lost. The plan of the city is circular (a series of concentric circles, bisected by canals, a cross-hatch of hundreds of tiny bridges, each one connecting to another, and then another, as though endlessly), and you cannot simply "follow" a street as you can in other cities. To get somewhere you have to know in advance where you are going. A. did not, since he was a stranger, and moreover found himself curiously reluctant to consult a map. For three days it rained, and for three days he walked around in circles. He realized that in comparison to New York (or New Amsterdam, as he was fond of saying to himself after he returned), Amsterdam was a small place, a city whose streets could probably be memorized in ten days. And yet, even if he was lost, would it not have been possible for him to ask directions of some passerby? Theoretically, yes, but in fact he was unable to bring himself to do so. It was not that he was afraid of strangers, nor that he was physically reluctant to speak. More subtly, he found himself hesitating to speak English to the Dutch. Nearly everyone speaks excellent English in Amsterdam. This ease of communication, however, was upsetting to him, as if it would somehow rob the place of its foreignness. Not in the sense that he was seeking the exotic, but in the sense that the place would no longer be itself—as if the Dutch, by speaking English, would be denied their Dutchness. If he could have been sure that no one would understand him, he would not have hesitated to rush up to a stranger and speak English, in a comical effort to make himself understood: with words, gestures, grimaces, etc. As it was, he felt himself unwilling to violate the Dutch people's Dutchness, even though they themselves had long ago allowed it to be violated. He therefore held his tongue. He wandered. He walked around in circles. He allowed himself to be lost. Sometimes, he later discovered, he would be only a few feet from his destination, but not knowing where to turn, would then go off in the wrong direction, thereby taking himself farther and farther from where he thought he was going. It occurred to him that perhaps he was wandering in the circles of hell, that the city had been designed as a model of the underworld, based on some classical representation of the place. Then he remembered that various diagrams of hell had been used as memory systems by some of the sixteenth century writers on the subject. (Cosmas Rossellius, for example, in his *Thesaurus Artificiosae Memoriae*, Venice, 1579.) And if Amsterdam was hell, and if hell was memory, then he realized that perhaps there was some purpose to his being lost. Cut off from everything that was familiar to him, unable to discover even a single point of reference, he saw that his steps, by taking him nowhere, were taking him nowhere but into himself. He was wandering inside himself, and he was lost. Far from troubling him, this state of being lost became a source of happiness, of exhilaration. He breathed it into his very bones. As if on the brink of some previously hidden knowledge, he breathed it into his very bones and said to himself, almost triumphantly: I am lost.

His life no longer seemed to dwell in the present. Each time he saw a child, he would try to imagine what it would look like as a grown-up. Each time he saw an old person, he would try to imagine what that person had looked like as a child.

It was worst with women, especially if the woman was young and beautiful. He could not help looking through the skin of her face and imagining the anonymous skull behind it. And the more lovely the face, the more ardent his attempt to seek in it the encroaching signs of the future: the incipient wrinkles, the later-to-be-sagging chin, the glaze of disappointment in the eyes. He would put one face on top of another: this woman at forty; this woman at sixty; this woman at eighty; as if, even as he stood in the present, he felt compelled to hunt out the future, to track down the death that lives in each one of us.

Some time later, he came across a similar thought in one of Flaubert's letters to Louise Colet (August 1846) and was struck by the parallel: ". . . I always sense the future, the antithesis of everything is always before my eyes. I have never seen a child without thinking that it would grow old, nor a cradle without thinking of a grave. The sight of a naked woman makes me imagine her skeleton."

Walking through the hospital corridor and hearing the man whose leg had been amputated calling out at the top of his voice: it hurts, it hurts. That summer (1979), every day for more than a month, traveling across town to the hospital, the unbearable heat. Helping his grandfather put in his false teeth. Shaving the old man's face with an electric razor. Reading him the baseball scores from the *New York Post*.

Initial statement of these themes. Further installments to follow.

Second commentary on the nature of chance.

He remembers cutting school one drizzly day in April 1962 with his friend D. and going to the Polo Grounds to see one of the first games ever played by the New York Mets. The stadium was nearly empty (attendance was eight or nine thousand), and the Mets lost soundly to the Pittsburgh Pirates. The two friends sat next to a boy from Harlem, and A. remembers the pleasant ease of the conversation among the three of them during the course of the game.

He returned to the Polo Grounds only once that season, and that was for a holiday doubleheader (Memorial Day: day of memory, day of the dead) against the Dodgers: more than fifty thousand people in the stands, resplendent sun, and an afternoon of crazy events on the field: a triple play, inside-the-park homeruns, double steals. He was with the same friend that day, and they sat in a remote corner of the stadium, unlike the good seats they had managed to sneak into for the earlier game. At one point they left their places to go to the hot dog stand, and there, just several rows down the concrete steps was the same boy they had met in April, this time sitting beside his mother. They all recognized one another and gave warm greetings, each amazed at the coincidence of meeting again. And make no mistake: the odds against this meeting were astronomical. Like the two friends, A. and D., the boy now sitting with his mother had not been to another game since that wet day in April.

Memory as a room, as a body, as a skull, as a skull that encloses the room in which a body sits. As in the image: "a man sat alone in his room."

"The power of memory is prodigious," observed Saint Augustine. "It is a vast, immeasurable sanctuary. Who can plumb its depths? And yet it is a faculty of my soul. Although it is part of my nature, I cannot understand all that I am. This means, then, that the mind is too narrow to contain itself entirely. But where is that part of it which it does not itself contain? Is it somewhere outside itself and not within it? How, then, can it be part of it, if it is not contained in it?"

The Book of Memory. Book Three.

It was in Paris, in 1965, that he first experienced the infinite possibilities of a limited space. Through a chance encounter with a stranger in a café, he was introduced to S. A. was just eighteen at the time, in the summer between high school and college, and he had never been to Paris before. These are his earliest memories of that city, where so much of his life would later be spent, and they are inescapably bound up with the idea of a room.

Place Pinel in the thirteenth arrondissement, where S. lived, was a working class neighborhood, and even then one of the last vestiges of the old Paris—the Paris one still talks about but which is no longer there. S. lived in a space so small that at first it seemed to defy you, to resist being entered. The presence of one person crowded the room, two people choked it. It was impossible to move inside it without contracting your body to its smallest dimensions, without contracting your mind to some infinitely small point within itself. Only then could you begin to breathe, to feel the room expand, and to watch your mind explore the excessive, unfathomable reaches of that space. For there was an entire universe in that room, a miniature cosmology that contained all that is most vast, most distant, most unknowable. It was a shrine, hardly bigger than a body, in praise of all that exists beyond the body: the representation of one man's inner world, even to the slightest detail. S. had literally managed to surround himself with the things that were inside him. The room he lived in was a dream space, and its walls were like the skin of some second body around him, as if his own body had been transformed into a mind, a breathing instrument of pure thought. This was the womb, the belly of the whale, the original site of the imagination. By placing himself in that darkness, S. had invented a way of dreaming with open eyes.

A former student of Vincent D'Indy's, S. had once been considered a highly promising young composer. For more than twenty years, however, none of his pieces had been performed in public. Naive in all things, but most especially in politics, he had made the mistake of allowing two of his larger orchestral works to be played in Paris during the war—*Symphonie de Feu* and *Hommage à Jules Verne*, each requiring more than one hundred-thirty musicians. That was in 1943, and the Nazi occupation was still at full strength. When the war ended, people concluded that S. had been a collaborator, and although nothing could have been farther from the truth, he was blackballed by the French music world—by innuendo and silent consent, never by direct confrontation. The only sign that any of his colleagues still remembered him was the annual Christmas card he received from Nadia Boulanger.

A stammerer, a child-man with a weakness for red wine, he was so lacking in guile, so ignorant of the world's malice, that he could not even begin to defend himself against his anonymous accusers. He simply withdrew, hiding behind a mask of eccentricity. He appointed himself an Orthodox priest (he was Russian), grew a long beard, dressed in a black cassock, and changed his name to the Abbaye de la Tour du Calame, all the while continuing—fitfully, between bouts of stupor—with the work of his life: a piece for three orchestras and four choruses that would take twelve days to perform. In his misery, in the totally abject conditions of his life, he would turn to A. and observe, stuttering helplessly, his gray eyes gleaming, "Everything is miraculous. There has never been an age more wonderful than this one."

The sun did not penetrate his room on the Place Pinel. He had covered his window with heavy black cloth, and what little light there was came from a few strategically placed and faintly glowing lamps. The room was hardly bigger than a second class train compartment, and it had more or less the same shape: narrow, high-ceilinged, with a single window at the far end. S. had cluttered this tiny place with a multitude of objects, the debris of an entire lifetime: books, photographs, manuscripts, private totems—everything that was of any significance to him. Shelves, densely packed with this accumulation, climbed up to the ceiling along each wall, each one sagging, tipping slightly inward, as if the slightest disturbance would loosen the structure and send the whole mass of things falling in on him. S. lived, worked, ate, and slept in his bed. Immediately to the left of him, fit snugly into the wall, was a set of small, cubbied shelves, which seemed to hold all he needed to get through the day: pens, pencils, ink, music paper, cigarette holder, radio, penknife, bottles of wine, bread, books, magnifying glass. To his right was a metal stand with a tray fastened to the top of it, which he could swing in and out, over the bed and away from it, and which he used as both his work table and his eating table. This was life as Crusoe would have lived it: shipwreck in the heart of the city. For there was nothing S. had not thought of. In his penury, he had managed to provide for himself more efficiently than many millionaires do. The evidence notwithstanding, he was a realist, even in his eccentricity. He had examined himself thoroughly enough to know what was necessary for his own survival, and he accepted these quirks as the conditions of his life. There was nothing in his attitude that was either faint-hearted or pious, nothing to suggest a hermit's renunciation. He embraced his condition with passion and joyful enthusiasm, and as A. looks back on it now, he realizes that he has never known anyone who laughed so hard and so often.

The giant composition, on which S. had spent the last fifteen years, was nowhere near completion. S. referred to it as his "work in progress," consciously echoing Joyce, whom he greatly admired, or else as the *Dodecalogue*, which he would describe as the-work-to-be-done-that-is-done-in-the-process-of-doing-it. It was unlikely that he ever imagined he would finish the piece. He seemed to accept the inevitability of his failure almost as a theological premise, and what for another man might have led to an impasse of despair was for him a source of boundless, quixotic hope. At some anterior moment, perhaps at his very darkest moment, he had made the equation between his life and his work, and now he was no longer able to distinguish between the two. Every idea fed into his work; the idea of his work gave purpose to his life. To have conceived of something within the realm of possibility—a work that could have been finished, and therefore detached from himself—would have vitiated the enterprise. The point was to fall short, but to do so only in attempting the most outlandish thing he could conjure for himself. The end result, paradoxically, was humility, a way of gauging his own insignificance in relation to God. For only in the mind of God were such dreams as S.'s possible. But by dreaming in the way he did, S. had found a way of participating in all that was beyond him, of drawing himself several inches closer to the heart of the infinite.

For more than a month during that summer of 1965, A. paid S. two or three visits a week. He knew no one else in the city, and S. therefore had become his anchor to the place. He could always count on S. to be in, to greet him with enthusiasm (Russian style; three kisses on the cheeks: left, right, left), and to be more than willing to talk. Many years later, at a time of great personal distress, he realized that what drew him continually to these meetings with S. was that they allowed him to experience, for the first time, what it felt to have a father.

His own father was a remote, almost absent figure with whom he had very little in common. S., for his part, had two grown sons, and both had turned away from his example and adopted an aggressive, hard-nosed attitude towards the world. Beyond the natural rapport that existed between them, S. and A. drew together out of a congruent want: the one for a son who would accept him as he was, the other for a father who would accept him as he was. This was further underscored by a parallel of births: S. had been born in the same year as A.'s father; A. had been born in the same year as S.'s younger son. For A., S. satisfied his paternal hunger through a curious combination of generosity and need. He listened to him seriously and took his ambition to be a writer as the most natural thing a young man could hope to do with himself. If A.'s father, in his strange, self-enclosed manner of being in the world, had made A. feel superfluous to his life, as if nothing he did could ever have an effect on him, S., in his vulnerability and destitution, allowed A. to become necessary to him. A. brought food to him, supplied him with wine and cigarettes, made sure he did not starve—which was a true danger. For that was the point about S.: he never asked anyone for anything. He would wait for the world to come to him, entrusting his deliverance to chance. Sooner or later, someone was bound to turn up: his ex-wife, one of his sons, a friend. Even then, he would not ask. But neither would he refuse.

Each time A. arrived with a meal (usually roast chicken, from a charcuterie on the Place d'Italie), it was turned into a mock feast, an excuse for celebration. "Ah, chicken," S. would exclaim, biting into a drumstick. And then again, chewing away at it, the juice dribbling into his beard: "Ah, chicken," with an impish, self-deprecatory burst of laughter, as if acknowledging the irony of his need and the undeniable pleasure the food gave him. Everything became absurd and luminous in that laughter. The world was turned inside out, swept away, and then immediately reborn as a kind of metaphysical jest. There was no room in that world for a man who did not have a sense of his own ridiculousness.

Further encounters with S. Letters between Paris and New York, a few photographs exchanged, all of this now lost. In 1967: another visit for several months. By then S. had given up his priest's robes and was back to using his own name. But the costumes he wore on his little excursions through the streets of his neighborhood were just as marvelous. Beret, silk shirt, scarf, heavy corduroy pants, leather riding boots, ebony walking stick with a silver handle: a vision of Paris via Hollywood, circa 1920. It was no accident, perhaps, that S.'s younger son became a film producer.

In February 1971, A. returned to Paris, where he would remain for the next three and a half years. Although he was no longer there as a visitor, which meant that more claims were made on his time, he still saw S. on a fairly regular basis, perhaps once every other month. The bond was still there, but as time went on A. began to wonder if it was not, in fact, a memory of that other bond, formed six years earlier, which sustained this bond in the present. For it turns out that after A. moved back to New York (July 1974), he no longer wrote any letters to S. It was not that he did not continue to think of him. But it was the memory of him, more than any need to carry on contact with S. into the future, that seemed to concern A. now. In this way he began to feel, as if palpably in his own skin, the passage of time. It sufficed him to remember. And this, in itself, was a startling discovery.

Even more startling to him, however, was that when he finally went back to Paris (November 1979), after an absence of more than five years, he failed to look up S. And this in spite of the fact that he had fully intended to do so. Every morning for the several weeks of his visit, he would wake up and say to himself, I must make time today to see S., and then, as the day wore on, invent an excuse for not going to see him. This reluctance, he began to realize, was a product of fear. But fear of what? Of walking back into his own past? Of discovering a present that would contradict the past, and thus alter it, which in turn would destroy the memory of the past he wanted to preserve? No, he realized, nothing so simple. Then what? Days went by, and gradually it began to come clear. He was afraid that S. was dead. Irrationally, he knew. But since A.'s father had died less than a year before, and since S. had become important to him precisely in relation to his thoughts about his father, he felt that somehow the death of one automatically entailed the death of the other. In spite of what he tried to tell himself, he actually believed this. Beyond that he thought: if I go to see S., then I will learn he is dead; but if I stay away, it will mean he is alive. By remaining absent, therefore, A. felt that he would be helping to keep S. in the world. Day after day, he walked around Paris with an image of S. in his mind. A hundred times a day, he imagined himself entering the little room on the Place Pinel. And still, he could not bring himself to go there. It was then that he realized he was living in a state of extreme duress.

Further commentary on the nature of chance.

From his last visit to S., at the end of those years in Paris (1974), a photograph has been preserved. A. and S. are standing outside, by the doorway of S.'s house. They each have an arm around the other's shoulder, and there is an unmistakeable glow of friendship and comraderie on their faces. This picture is one of the few personal tokens A. has brought with him to his room on Varick Street.

As he studies this picture now (Christmas Eve, 1979), he is reminded of another picture he used to see on the wall of S.'s room:

S. as a young man, perhaps eighteen or nineteen, standing with a boy of twelve or thirteen. Same evocation of friendship, same smiles, same arms-around-the-shoulders pose. The boy, S. had told him, was the son of Marina Tsvetayeva. Marina Tsvetayeva, who stands in A.'s mind along with Mandelstam as the greatest of Russian poets. To look at this 1974 photograph for him is to imagine her impossible life, which ended when she hanged herself in 1941. For many of the years between the Civil War and her death she had lived in the Russian emigré circles in France, the same community in which S. had been raised, and he had known her and had been a friend of her son, Mur. Marina Tsvetayeva, who had written: "It may be that a better way / To conquer time and the world / Is to pass, and not to leave a trace—/ To pass, and not to leave a shadow / on the walls . . ."; who had written: "I didn't want this, not / this (but listen, quietly, / to want is what bodies do / and now we are ghosts only) . . ."; who had written: "In this most Christian of worlds / All poets are Jews."

When A. and his wife returned to New York in 1974, they moved into an apartment on Riverside Drive. Among their neighbors in the building was an old Russian doctor, Gregory Altschuller, a man well into his eighties, who still did research work at one of the city hospitals and who, along with his wife, had a great interest in literature. Dr. Altschuller's father had been Tolstoy's personal physician, and propped up on a table in the Riverside Drive apartment was an enormous photograph of the bearded writer, duly inscribed, in an equally enormous hand, to his friend and doctor. In conversations with the younger Dr. Altschuller, A. learned something that struck him as nothing less than extraordinary. In a small village outside Prague, in the dead of winter in 1925, this man had delivered Marina Tsvetayeva's son: the same son who had grown up into the boy in the photograph on S.'s wall. More than that: this was the only baby he ever delivered in his career as a doctor.

"It was night," Dr. Altschuller wrote recently, "the last day of January, 1925 . . . The snow was falling, a terrible storm which snowed-in everything. A Czech boy came running to me from the village where Tsvetayeva now lived with her family, though her husband was not with her at the time. Her daughter was also away with her father. Marina was alone.

"The boy rushed into the room and said: 'Pani Tsvetayeva wants you to come to her immediately because she's already in labor! You have to hurry, it's already on the way.' What could I say? I quickly dressed and walked through the forest, snow up to my knees, in a raging storm. I opened the door and went in. In the pale light of a lonely electric bulb I saw piles of books in one corner of the room; they nearly reached the ceiling. Days of accumulated rubbish was shoveled into another corner of the room. And there was Marina, chain-smoking in bed, baby already on the way. Greeting me gaily: 'You're almost late!' I looked around the room for something clean, for a piece of soap. Nothing, not a clean handkerchief, not a piece of anything. She was lying in bed, smoking and smiling, saying: 'I told you that you'd deliver my baby. You came—and now it's your business, not mine' . . .

"Everything went smoothly enough. The baby, however, was born with the umbilical cord wrapped around his neck so tightly that he could hardly breathe. He was blue . . .

"I tried desperately to restore the baby's respiration and finally he started breathing; he turned from blue to pink. All this time Marina was smoking, silent, not uttering a sound, looking steadily at the baby, at me . . .

"I came back the next day and then saw the child every Sunday for a good many weeks. In a letter (May 10, 1925), Marina wrote: 'Altschuller directs everything concerning Mur with pride and love. Before eating, Mur gets one teaspoonful of lemon juice without sugar. He's fed according to the system of Professor Czerny, who saved thousands of newborn children in Germany during the war. Altschuller sees Mur every Sunday. Percussion, auscultation, some kind of arithmetic calculation. Then he writes down for me how to feed Mur next week, what to give him, how much butter, how much lemon, how much milk, how gradually to increase the amount. Every time he comes he remembers what was given last time, without carrying any notes . . . Sometimes I have a crazy desire just to take his hand and kiss it' . . .

"The boy grew quickly and became a healthy child adored by his mother and her friends. I saw him for the last time when he was not yet one year old. At that time Marina moved to France and there she lived for the next fourteen years. George (Mur's formal name) went to school and soon became an ardent student of literature, music, and art. In 1936 his sister Alia, then in her early twenties, left the family and France and returned to Soviet Russia, following her father. Marina stayed now with her very young son, alone in France . . . under extreme hardship, financial and moral. In 1939 she applied for a Soviet visa and returned to Moscow with her son. Two years later, in August 1941, her life came to a tragic end . . .

"The war was still on. Young George Efron was at the front. 'Good-bye literature, music, school,' he wrote to his sister. He signed his letter 'Mur.' As a soldier he proved to be a courageous and fearless fighter, took part in many battles, and died in July 1944, one of hundreds of victims of a battle near the village of Druika on the Western Front. He was only twenty years old."

The Book of Memory. Book Four.

Several blank pages. To be followed by profuse illustrations. Old family photographs, for each person his own family, going back as many generations as possible. To look at these with utmost care.

Afterwards, several sequences of reproductions, beginning with the portraits Rembrandt painted of his son, Titus. To include all of them: from the view of the little boy in 1650 (golden hair, red feathered hat) to the 1655 portrait of Titus "puzzling over his lessons" (pensive, at his desk, compass dangling from his left hand, right thumb pressed against his chin) to Titus in 1658 (seventeen years old, the extraordinary red hat, and, as one commentator has written, "The artist has painted his son with the same sense of penetration usually reserved for his own features") to the last surviving canvas of Titus, from the early 1660's: "The face seems that of a weak old man ravaged with disease. Of course, we look at it with hindsight—we know that Titus will predecease his father . . ."

To be followed by the 1602 portrait of Sir Walter Raleigh and his eight-year-old son Wat (artist unknown) that hangs in the National Portrait Gallery in London. To note: the uncanny similarity of their poses. Both father and son facing forward, left hands on hips, right feet pointing out at forty-five degree angles, the left feet pointing forward, and the somber determination on the boy's face to imitate the self-confident, imperious stare of the father. To remember: that when Raleigh was released after a thirteen-year incarceration in the Tower of London (1618) and launched out on the doomed voyage to Guiana to clear his name, Wat was with him. To remember that Wat, leading a reckless military charge against the Spanish, lost his life in the jungle. Raleigh to his wife: "I never knew what sorrow meant until now." And so he went back to England, and allowed the King to chop off his head.

To be followed by more photographs, perhaps several dozen: Mallarmé's son, Anatole; Anne Frank ("This is a photo that shows me as I should always like to look. Then I would surely have a chance to go to Hollywood. But now, unfortunately, I usually look different"); Mur; the children of Cambodia; the children of Atlanta. The dead children. The children who will vanish, the children who are dead. Himmler: "I have made the decision to annihilate every Jewish child from the face of the earth." Nothing but pictures. Because, at a certain point, the words lead one to conclude that it is no longer possible to speak. Because these pictures are the unspeakable.

He has spent the greater part of his adult life walking through cities, many of them foreign. He has spent the greater part of his adult life hunched over a small rectangle of wood, concentrating on an even smaller rectangle of white paper. He has spent the greater part of his adult life standing up and sitting down and pacing back and forth. These are the limits of the known world. He listens. When he hears something, he begins to listen again. Then he waits. He watches and waits. And when he begins to see something, he watches and waits again. These are the limits of the known world.

The room. Brief mention of the room and/or the dangers lurking inside it. As in the image: Hölderlin in his room.

To revive the memory of that mysterious, three-month journey on foot, crossing the mountains of the Massif Central alone, his fingers gripped tightly around the pistol in his pocket; that journey from Bordeaux to Stuttgart (hundreds of miles) that preceded his first mental breakdown in 1802.

"Dear friend . . . I have not written to you for a long time, and meanwhile have been in France and have seen the sad, lonely earth; the shepherds and shepherdesses of southern France and individual beauties, men and women, who grew up in fear of political uncertainty and of hunger . . . The mighty element, the fire of heaven and the silence of the people, their life in nature, their confinedness and their contentment, moved me continually, and as one says of heroes, I can well say of myself that Apollo has struck me."

Arriving in Stuttgart, "deathly pale, very thin, with hollow wild eyes, long hair and a beard, and dressed like a beggar," he stood before his friend Matthison and spoke one word only: "Hölderlin."

Six months later, his beloved Suzette was dead. By 1806, schizophrenia, and thereafter, for thirty-six years, fully half his life, he lived alone in the tower built for him by Zimmer, the carpenter from Tubingen—*zimmer,* which in German means *room.*

TO ZIMMER

> The lines of life are various as roads or as
> The limits of the mountains are, and what we are
> Down here, in harmonies, in recompense,
> In peace for ever, a god will finish there.

Toward the end of Hölderlin's life, a visitor to the tower mentioned Suzette's name. The poet replied: "Ah, my Diotima. Don't speak to me about my Diotima. Thirteen sons she bore me. One is Pope, another is the Sultan, the third is the Emperor of Russia . . ." And then: "Do you know what happened to her? She went mad, she did, mad, mad, mad."

During those years, it is said, Hölderlin rarely went out. When he did leave his room, it was only to take aimless walks through the countryside, filling his pockets with stones and picking flowers, which he would later tear to shreds. In town, the students laughed at him, and children ran away in fear whenever he approached to greet them. Towards the end, his mind became so muddled that he began to call himself by different names—Scardinelli, Killalusimeno—and once, when a visitor was slow to leave his room, he showed him the door and said, with a finger raised in warning, "I am the Lord God."

In recent years, there has been renewed speculation about Hölderlin's life in that room. One man contends that Hölderlin's madness was feigned, and that in response to the stultifying political reaction that overwhelmed Germany following the French revolution, the poet withdrew from the world. He lived, so to speak, underground in the tower. According to this theory, all of the writings of Hölderlin's madness (1806–1843) were in fact composed in a secret, revolutionary code. There is even a play that expands upon this idea. In the final scene of that work, the young Marx pays Hölderlin a visit in his tower. We are led to presume from this encounter that it was the old and dying poet who inspired Marx to write *The Economic and Philosophical Manuscripts of 1844*. If this were so, then Hölderlin would not only have been the greatest German poet of the nineteenth century but also a central figure in the history of political thought: the link between Hegel and Marx. For it is a documented fact that as young men Hölderlin and Hegel were friends. They were students together at the seminary in Tübingen.

Speculations of this sort, however, strike A. as tedious. He has no difficulty in accepting Hölderlin's presence in the room. He would even go so far as to say that Hölderlin could not have survived anywhere else. If not for Zimmer's generosity and kindness, it is possible that Hölderlin's life would have ended prematurely. To withdraw into a room does not mean that one has been blinded. To be mad does not mean that one has been struck dumb. More than likely, it is the room that restored Hölderlin to life, that gave him back whatever life it was left for him to live. As Jerome commented on the Book of Jonah, glossing the passage that tells of Jonah in the belly of the whale: "You will note that where you would think should be the end of Jonah, there was his safety."

"The image of man has eyes," wrote Hölderlin, during the first year of his life in that room, "whereas the moon has light. King Oedipus has an eye too many perhaps. The sufferings of this man, they seem indescribable, unspeakable, inexpressible. If the drama represents something like this, that is why. But what comes over me as I think of you now? Like brooks the end of something sweeps me away, which expands like Asia. Of course, this affliction, Oedipus has it too. Of course, that is why. Did Hercules suffer too? Indeed ... For to fight with God, like Hercules, that is an affliction. And immortality amidst the envy of this life, to share in that, is an affliction too. But this is also an affliction, when a man is covered with freckles, to be wholly covered with many a spot! The beautiful sun does that: for it rears up all things. It leads young men along their course with the allurements of its beams as though with roses. The afflictions that Oedipus bore seem like this, as when a poor man complains there is something he lacks. Son of Laios, poor stranger in Greece! Life is death, and death is a kind of life."

The room. Counter-argument to the above. Or: reasons for being in the room.

The Book of Memory. Book Five.

Two months after his father's death (January 1979), A.'s marriage collapsed. The problems had been brewing for some time, and at last the decision was made to separate. If it was one thing for him to accept this break-up, to be miserable about it and yet to understand that it was inevitable, it was quite another thing for him to swallow the consequences it entailed: to be separated from his son. The thought of it was intolerable to him.

He moved into his room on Varick Street in early spring. For the next few months he shuttled between that room and the house in Dutchess County where he and his wife had been living for the past three years. During the week: solitude in the city; on the weekends: visits to the country, one hundred miles away, where he slept in what was now his former work room and played with his son, not yet two years old, and read to him from the treasured books of the period: *Let's Go Trucks, Caps for Sale, Mother Goose.*

Shortly after he moved into the Varick Street room, the six-year old Etan Patz disappeared from the streets of that same neighborhood. Everywhere A. turned, there was a photograph of the boy (on lampposts, in shop windows, on blank brick walls), headlined by the words: LOST CHILD. Because the face of this child did not differ drastically from the face of his own child (and even if it had, it might not have mattered), every time he saw the photograph of this face he was made to think of his own son—and in precisely these terms: lost child. Etan Patz had been sent downstairs one morning by his mother to wait for the school bus (the first day following a long bus driver strike, and the boy had been eager to do this one little thing on his own, to make this small gesture of independence), and then was not seen again. Whatever it was that happened to him, it happened without a trace. He could have been kidnapped, he could have been murdered, or perhaps he simply wandered off and came to his death in a place where no one could see him. The only thing that can be said with any certainty is that he vanished—as if from the face of the earth. The newspapers made much of this story (interviews with the parents, interviews with the detectives assigned to the case, articles about the boy's personality: what games he liked to play, what foods he liked to eat), and A. began to realize that the presence of this disaster—superimposed on his own and admittedly much smaller disaster—was inescapable. Each thing that fell before his eyes seemed to be no more than an image of what was inside him. The days went by, and each day a little more of the pain inside him was dragged out into the open. A sense of loss took hold of him, and it would not let go. And there were times when this loss was so great, and so suffocating, that he thought it would never let go.

———

Some weeks later, at the beginning of summer. A radiant New York June: clarity of the light falling on the bricks; blue, transparent skies, zeroing to an azure that would have charmed even Mallarmé.

A.'s grandfather (on his mother's side) was slowly beginning to die. Only a year before he had performed magic tricks at A.'s son's first birthday party, but now, at eighty-five, he was so weak that he could no longer stand without support, could no longer move without an effort of will so intense that merely to think of moving was enough to exhaust him. There was a family conference at the doctor's office, and the decision was made to send him to Doctor's Hospital on East End Avenue and Eighty-eighth Street (the same hospital in which his wife had died of amniotropic lateral sclerosis—Lou Gehrig's disease—eleven years earlier). A. was at that conference, as were his mother and his mother's sister, his grandfather's two children. Because neither of the women could remain in New York, it was agreed that A. would be responsible for everything. A.'s mother had to return home to California to take care of her own gravely ill husband, while A.'s aunt was about to go to Paris to visit her first grandchild, the recently born daughter of her only son. Everything, it seemed, had quite literally become a matter of life and death. At which point, A. suddenly found himself thinking (perhaps because his grandfather had always reminded him of W.C. Fields) of a scene from the 1932 Fields film, *Million Dollar Legs*: Jack Oakey runs frantically to catch up with a departing stage coach and beseeches the driver to stop; "It's a matter of life and death!" he shouts. And the driver calmly and cynically replies: "What isn't?"

During this family conference A. could see the fear on his grandfather's face. At one point the old man caught his eye and gestured up to the wall beside the doctor's desk, which was covered with laminated plaques, framed certificates, awards, degrees, and testimonials, and gave a knowing nod, as if to say, "Pretty

impressive, eh? This guy will take good care of me." The old man
had always been taken in by pomp of this sort. "I've just received
a letter from the president of the Chase Manhattan Bank," he
would say, when in fact it was nothing more than a form letter.
That day in the doctor's office, however, it was painful for A. to
see it: the old man's refusal to recognize the thing that was looking him straight in the eyes. "I feel good about all this, doctor,"
his grandfather said. "I know you're going to get me better again."
And yet, almost against his will, A. found himself admiring this
capacity for blindness. Later that day, he helped his grandfather
pack a small satchel of things to take to the hospital. The old man
tossed three or four of his magic tricks into the bag. "Why are you
bothering with those?" A. asked. "So I can entertain the nurses,"
his grandfather replied, "in case things get dull."

A. decided to stay in his grandfather's apartment for as long as the
old man was in the hospital. The place could not remain empty
(someone had to pay the bills, collect the mail, water the plants),
and it was bound to be more comfortable than the room on Varick
Street. Above all, the illusion had to be maintained that the old
man was coming back. Until there was death, there was always
the possibility there would not be death, and this chance, slight
though it was, had to be credited.

A. remained in that apartment for the next six or seven weeks.
It was the same place he had been visiting since earliest childhood:
that tall, squat, oddly shaped building that stands on the corner
of Central Park South and Columbus Circle. He wondered how
many hours he had spent as a boy looking out at the traffic as it
wove around the statue of Christopher Columbus. Through those
same sixth floor windows he had watched the Thanksgiving Day
parades, seen the construction of the Coliseum, spent entire afternoons counting the people as they walked by on the streets below.

Now he was surrounded by this place again, with the Chinese telephone table, his grandmother's glass menagerie, and the old humidor. He had walked straight back into his childhood.

A. continued to hope for a reconciliation with his wife. When she agreed to come to the city with their son to stay at the apartment, he felt that perhaps a real change would be possible. Cut off from the objects and cares of their own life, they seemed to settle in nicely to these neutral surroundings. But neither one of them was ready at that point to admit that this was not an illusion, an act of memory coupled with an act of groundless hope.

Every afternoon A. would travel to the hospital by boarding two buses, spend an hour or two with his grandfather, and then return by the same route he had come. This arrangement worked for about ten days. Then the weather changed. An excruciating heat fell on New York, and the city became a nightmare of sweat, exhaustion, and noise. None of this did the little boy any good (cooped up in the apartment with a sputtering air conditioner, or else traipsing through the steamy streets with his mother), and when the weather refused to break (record humidity for several weeks running), A. and his wife decided that she and the boy should return to the country.

He stayed on in his grandfather's apartment alone. Each day became a repetition of the day before. Conversations with the doctor, the trip to the hospital, hiring and firing private nurses, listening to his grandfather's complaints, straightening the pillows under his head. There was a horror that went through him each time he glimpsed the old man's flesh. The emaciated limbs, the shriveled testicles, the body that had shrunk to less than a hundred pounds. This was a once corpulent man, whose proud, well-stuffed belly had preceded his every step through the world, and now he was hardly there. If A. had experienced one kind of death earlier in the year, a death so sudden that even as it gave him over to death it deprived him of the knowledge of that death, now he was experiencing death of another kind, and it was this slow, mortal exhaustion, this letting go of life in the heart of life, that finally taught him the thing he had known all along.

Nearly every day there was a phone call from his grandfather's former secretary, a woman who had worked in the office for more than twenty years. After his grandmother's death, she had become the steadiest of his grandfather's lady companions, the respectable woman he trotted out for public view on formal occasions: family gatherings, weddings, funerals. Each time she called, she would make copious inquiries about his grandfather's health, and then ask A. to arrange for her to visit the hospital. The problem was her own bad health. Although not old (late sixties at most), she suffered from Parkinson's disease and for some time had been living in a nursing home in the Bronx. After numerous conversations (her voice so faint over the telephone that it took all of A.'s powers of concentration to hear even half of what she said), he finally agreed to meet her in front of the Metropolitan Museum, where a special bus from the nursing home deposited ambulatory patients once a week for an afternoon in Manhattan. On that particular day, for the first time in nearly a month, it rained. A. arrived in advance of the appointed time, and then, for more than an hour, stood on the museum steps, keeping his head dry with a newspaper, on the lookout for the woman. At last, deciding to give up, he made one final tour of the area. It was then that he found her: a block or two up Fifth Avenue, standing under a pathetic sapling, as if to protect herself from the rain, a clear plastic bonnet on her head, leaning on her walking stick, body bent forward, all of her rigid, afraid to take a step, staring down at the wet sidewalk. Again that feeble voice, and A. almost pressing his ear against her mouth to hear her—only to glean some paltry and insipid remark: the bus driver had forgotten to shave, the newspaper had not been delivered. A. had always been bored by this woman, and even when she had been well he had cringed at having to spend more than five minutes in her company. Now he found himself almost angry at her, resenting the way in which she seemed to expect him to pity her. He lashed out at her in his mind for being such an abject creature of self-absorption.

More than twenty minutes went by before he could get a cab. And then the endless ordeal of walking her to the curb and putting her into the taxi. Her shoes scraping on the pavement: one inch and then pause; another inch and then pause; another inch and then another inch. He held her arm and did his best to encourage her along. When they reached the hospital and he finally managed to disentangle her from the back seat of the cab, they began the slow journey toward the entrance. Just in front of the door, at the very instant A. thought they were going to make it, she froze. She had suddenly been gripped by the fear that she could not move, and therefore she could not move. No matter what A. said to her, no matter how gently he tried to coax her forward, she would not budge. People were going in and out—doctors, nurses, visitors—and there they stood, A. and the helpless woman, locked in the middle of that human traffic. A. told her to wait where she was (as if she could have done anything else), and went into the lobby, where he found an empty wheelchair, which he snatched out from under the eyes of a suspicious woman administrator. Then he eased his helpless companion into the chair and bustled her through the lobby toward the elevator, fending off the shouts of the administrator: "Is she a patient? Is that woman a patient? Wheelchairs are for patients only."

When he wheeled her into his grandfather's room, the old man was drowsing, neither asleep nor awake, lolling in a torpor at the edge of consciousness. He revived enough at the sound of their entering to perceive their presence, and then, at last understanding what had happened, smiled for the first time in weeks. Tears suddenly filled his eyes. He took hold of the woman's hand and said to A., as if addressing the entire world (but feebly, ever so feebly): "Shirley is my sweetheart. Shirley is the one I love."

In late July, A. decided to spend a weekend out of the city. He wanted to see his son, and he needed a break from the heat and the hospital. His wife came into New York, leaving the boy with her parents. What they did in the city that day he cannot remember, but by late afternoon they had made it out to the beach in Connecticut where the boy had spent the day with his grandparents. A. found his son sitting on a swing, and the first words out of the boy's mouth (having been coached all afternoon by his grandmother) were surprising in their lucidity. "I'm very happy to see you, Daddy," he said.

At the same time, the voice sounded strange to A. The boy seemed to be short of breath, and he spoke each word in a staccato of separate syllables. A. had no doubt that something was wrong. He insisted that they all leave the beach at once and go back to the house. Although the boy was in good spirits, this curious, almost mechanical voice continued to speak through him, as though he were a ventriloquist's dummy. His breathing was extremely rapid: heaving torso, in and out, in and out, like the breathing of a little bird. Within an hour, A. and his wife were looking down a list of local pediatricians, trying to reach one who was in (it was dinner hour on Friday night). On the fifth or sixth try they got hold of a young woman doctor who had recently taken over a practice in town. By some fluke, she happened to be in her office at that hour, and she told them to come right over. Either because she was new at her work, or because she had an excitable nature, her examination of the little boy threw A. and his wife into a panic. She sat the boy up on the table, listened to his chest, counted his breaths per minute, observed his flared nostrils, the slightly bluish tint to the skin of his face. Then a mad rush about the office, trying to rig up a complicated breathing device: a vapor machine with a hood, reminiscent of a nineteenth century camera. But the boy would not keep his head under the hood, and the hissing of the cold steam frightened him. The doctor then tried a shot of adrenalin. "We'll try this one," she said, "and if it doesn't work we'll give him another." She waited a few minutes, went through the breath-rate calculations again, and then gave him the second shot. Still no effect. "That's it," she said. "We'll have to take him to the hospital." She made the necessary phone call, and with a furious energy that seemed to gather up everything into her small body, told A. and his wife how to follow her to the hospital, where to go, what to do, and then led them outside, where they left in separate cars. Her diagnosis was pneumonia with asthmatic complications—which, after X-rays and more sophisticated tests at the hospital, turned out to be the case.

The boy was put in a special room in the children's ward, pricked and poked by nurses, held down screaming as liquid medicine was poured into his throat, hooked up to an I.V. line, and placed in a crib that was then covered by a clear plastic tent—into which a mist of cold oxygen was pumped from a valve in the wall. The boy remained in this tent for three days and three nights. His parents were allowed to be with him continuously, and they took turns sitting beside the boy's crib, head and arms under the tent, reading him books, telling him stories, playing games, while the other sat in a small reading room reserved for adults, watching the faces of the other parents whose children were in the hospital: none of these strangers daring to talk to each other, since they were all thinking of only one thing, and to speak of it would only have made it worse.

It was exhausting for the boy's parents, since the medicine dripping into his veins was composed essentially of adrenaline. This charged him with extra doses of energy—above and beyond the normal energy of a two-year old—and much of their time was spent in trying to calm him down, restraining him from breaking out of the tent. For A. this was of little consequence. The fact of the boy's illness, the fact that had they not taken him to the doctor in time he might actually have died (and the horror that washed over him when he thought: what if he and his wife had decided to spend the night in the city, entrusting the boy to his grandparents—who, in their old age, had ceased to be observant of details, and who, in fact, had not noticed the boy's strange breathing at the beach and had scoffed at A. when he first mentioned it), the fact of all these things made the struggle to keep the boy calm as nothing to A. Merely to have contemplated the possibility of the boy's death, to have had the thought of his death thrown in his face at the doctor's office, was enough for him to treat the boy's recovery as a sort of resurrection, a miracle dealt to him by the cards of chance.

His wife, however, began to show the strain. At one point she walked out to A., who was in the adult sitting room, and said: "I give up, I can't handle him anymore"—and there was such resentment in her voice against the boy, such an anger of exasperation, that something inside A. fell to pieces. Stupidly, cruelly, he wanted to punish his wife for such selfishness, and in that one instant all the newly won harmony that had been growing between them for the past month vanished: for the first time in all their years together, he had turned against her. He stormed out of the room and went to his son's bedside.

The modern nothingness. Interlude on the force of parallel lives.

In Paris that fall he attended a small dinner party given by a friend of his, J., a well-known French writer. There was another American among the guests, a scholar who specialized in modern

French poetry, and she spoke to A. of a book she was in the process of editing: the selected writings of Mallarmé. Had A., she wondered, ever translated any Mallarmé?

The fact was that he had. More than five years earlier, shortly after moving into the apartment on Riverside Drive, he had translated a number of the fragments Mallarmé wrote at the bedside of his dying son, Anatole, in 1879. These were short works of the greatest obscurity: notes for a poem that never came to be written. They were not even discovered until the late 1950s. In 1974, A. had done rough translation drafts of thirty or forty of them and then had put the manuscript away. When he returned from Paris to his room on Varick Street (December 1979, exactly one hundred years after Mallarmé had scribbled those death notes to his son), he dug out the folder that contained the handwritten drafts and began to work up final versions of his translations. These were later published in the *Paris Review*, along with a photograph of Anatole in a sailor suit. From his prefatory note: "On October 6, 1879, Mallarmé's only son, Anatole, died at the age of eight after a long illness. The disease, diagnosed as child's rheumatism, had slowly spread from limb to limb and eventually overtaken the boy's entire body. For several months Mallarmé and his wife had sat helplessly at Anatole's bedside as doctors tried various remedies and administered unsuccessful treatments. The boy was shuttled from the city to the country and back to the city again. On August 22 Mallarmé wrote to his friend Henry Ronjon 'of the struggle between life and death our poor little darling is going through ... But the real pain is that this little being might vanish. I confess that it is too much for me; I cannot bring myself to face this idea.'"

It was precisely this idea, A. realized, that moved him to return to these texts. The act of translating them was not a literary exercise. It was a way for him to relive his own moment of panic in the doctor's office that summer: it is too much for me, I cannot face it.

For it was only at that moment, he later came to realize, that he had finally grasped the full scope of his own fatherhood: the boy's life meant more to him than his own; if dying were necessary to save his son, he would be willing to die. And it was therefore only in that moment of fear that he had become, once and for all, the father of his son. Translating those forty or so fragments by Mallarmé was perhaps an insignificant thing, but in his own mind it had become the equivalent of offering a prayer of thanks for the life of his son. A prayer to what? To nothing perhaps. To his sense of life. To *the modern nothingness*.

you can, with your little
hands, drag me
into the grave—you
have the right—
—I
who follow you, I
let myself go—
—but if you
wish, the two
of us, let us make . . .

an alliance
a hymen, superb
—and the life
remaining in me
I will use for——

*

no—nothing
to do with the great
deaths—etc.

—as long as we
go on living, he
lives—in us
it will only be after our
death that he will be dead
—and the bells
of the Dead will toll for
                              him

                *

sail—
navigates
river,
your life that
goes by, that flows

            *

    Setting sun
and wind
        now vanished, and
wind of *nothing*
that breathes
(here, the modern
? nothingness)

            *

death—whispers softly
—I am no one—
I do not even know who I am
(for the dead do not
know they are
dead—, nor even that they
                              die

—for children
at least
    —or

heroes—sudden
deaths

for otherwise
my beauty is
made *of last
moments*—
lucidity, beauty
face—of what would be

me, without myself

        *

Oh! you understand
that if I consent
to live—to seem
to forget you—
it is to
feed my pain
—and so that this apparent
forgetfulness
        can spring forth more
horribly in tears, at

some random
moment, in
the middle of this
life, when you
appear to me

*

true mourning in
     the apartment
—not cemetery—

     furniture
     *

to find *only*
absence—
—in presence
of little clothes
—etc—

          *

     no—I will not
give up
     nothingness

     father—I
feel nothingness
  invade me

Brief commentary on the word "radiance."

He first heard this word used in connection with his son when he had shown a photograph of the boy to his good friend, R., an American poet who had lived for eight years in Amsterdam. They were drinking in a bar that night, surrounded by a press of bodies and loud music. A. pulled the snapshot out of his wallet and handed it to R., who studied the picture for a long time. Then he turned to A., a little drunk, and said with great emotion in his voice: "He has the same radiance as Titus."

About one year later, shortly after the publication of "A Tomb for Anatole" in the *Paris Review*, A. happened to be visiting R. R. (who had grown extremely fond of A.'s son) explained to A.: "An extraordinary thing happened to me today. I was in a bookstore, leafing through various magazines, and I happened to open the *Paris Review* to a photograph of Mallarmé's son. For a second I thought it was your son. The resemblance was that striking."

A. replied: "But those were my translations. I was the one who made them put in that picture. Didn't you know that?"

And then R. said: "I never got that far. I was so struck by the picture that I had to close the magazine. I put it back on the shelf and then walked out of the store."

His grandfather lasted another two or three weeks. A. returned to the apartment overlooking Columbus Circle, his son now out of danger, his marriage now at a permanent standstill. These were probably the worst days of all for him. He could not work, he could not think. He began to neglect himself, ate only noxious foods (frozen dinners, pizza, take-out Chinese noodles), and left the apartment to its own devices: dirty clothes strewn in a bedroom corner, unwashed dishes piled in the kitchen sink. Lying on the couch, smoking cigarette after cigarette, he would watch old movies on television and read second-rate mystery novels. He did not try to reach any of his friends. The one person he did call— a girl he had met in Paris when he was eighteen—had moved to Colorado.

One night, for no particular reason, he went out to wander around the lifeless neighborhood of the West Fifties and walked into a topless bar. As he sat there at his table drinking a beer, he suddenly found himself sitting next to a voluptuously naked young woman. She sidled up to him and began to describe all the lewd things she would do to him if he paid her to go to "the back room." There was something so openly humorous and matter-of-fact about her approach that he finally agreed to her proposition. The best thing, they decided, would be for her to suck his penis, since she claimed an extraordinary talent for this activity. And indeed, she threw herself into it with an enthusiasm that fairly astonished him. As he came in her mouth a few moments later, with a long and throbbing flood of semen, he had this vision, at just that second, which has continued to radiate inside him: that each ejaculation contains several billion sperm cells—or roughly the same number as there are people in the world—which means that, in himself, each man holds the potential of an entire world. And what would happen, could it happen, is the full range of possibilities: a spawn of idiots and geniuses, of the beautiful and the deformed, of saints, catatonics, thieves, stock brokers, and high-wire artists. Each man, therefore, is the entire world, bearing within his genes a memory of all mankind. Or, as Leibniz put it: "Every living substance is a perpetual living mirror of the universe." For the fact is, we are of the same stuff that came into being with the first explosion of the first spark in the infinite emptiness of space. Or so he said to himself, at that moment, as his penis exploded into the mouth of that naked woman, whose name he has now forgotten. He thought: the irreducible monad. And then, as though taking hold of it at last, he thought of the furtive, microscopic cell that had fought its way up through his wife's body, some three years earlier, to become his son.

———

Otherwise nothing. He languished. He sweltered in the summer heat. Like some latter-day Oblomov curled on his couch, he did not move unless he had to.

There was a cable television in his grandfather's apartment, with more channels than A. had ever known existed. Whenever he turned it on, there seemed to be a baseball game in progress. Not only was he able to follow the Yankees and Mets of New York, but the Red Sox of Boston, the Phillies of Philadelphia, and the Braves of Atlanta. Not to speak of the little bonuses occasionally provided during the afternoon: the games from the Japanese major leagues, for example (and his fascination with the constant beating of drums during the course of the game), or, even more strangely, the Little League championships from Long Island. To immerse himself in these games was to feel his mind striving to enter a place of pure form. Despite the agitation on the field, baseball offered itself to him as an image of that which does not move, and therefore a place where his mind could be at rest, secure in its refuge against the mutabilities of the world.

He had spent his entire childhood playing it. From the first muddy days in early March to the last frozen afternoons of late October. He had played well, with an almost obsessive devotion. Not only had it given him a feeling for his own possibilities, convinced him that he was not entirely hopeless in the eyes of others, but it had been the thing that drew him out from the solitary enclosures of his early childhood. It had initiated him into the world of the other, but at the same time it was something he could also keep within himself. Baseball was a terrain rich in potential for reverie. He fantasized about it continually, projecting himself into a New York Giants uniform and trotting out to his position at third base in the Polo Grounds, with the crowd cheering wildly at the mention of his name over the loudspeakers. Day after day, he would come home from school and throw a tennis ball against the steps of his house, pretending that each gesture was a part of the World Series game unfolding in his head. It always came down to two outs in the bottom of the ninth, a man on base, the Giants trailing by one. He was always the batter, and he always hit the game-winning homerun.

As he sat through those long summer days in his grandfather's apartment, he began to see that the power of baseball was for him the power of memory. Memory in both senses of the word: as a catalyst for remembering his own life and as an artificial structure for ordering the historical past. 1960, for example, was the year Kennedy was elected president; it was also the year of A.'s Bar Mitzvah, the year he supposedly reached manhood. But the first image that springs to his mind when 1960 is mentioned is Bill Mazeroski's homerun that beat the Yankees in the World Series. He can still see the ball soaring over the Forbes Field fence—that high, dark barrier, so densely cluttered with white numbers—and by recalling the sensations of that moment, that abrupt and stunning instant of pleasure, he is able to re-enter his own past, to stand in a world that would otherwise be lost to him.

He reads in a book: since 1893 (the year before his grandfather was born), when the pitcher's mound was moved back ten feet, the shape of the field has not changed. The diamond is a part of our consciousness. Its pristine geometry of white lines, green grass, and brown dirt is an icon as familiar as the stars and stripes. As opposed to just about everything else in American life during this century, baseball has remained constant. Except for a few minor alterations (artificial turf, designated hitters), the game as it is played today is remarkably similar to the one played by Wee Willie Keeler and the old Baltimore Orioles: those long dead young men of the photographs, with their handlebar moustaches and heroic poses.

What happens today is merely a variation on what happened yesterday. Yesterday echoes today, and tomorrow will foreshadow what happens next year. Professional baseball's past is intact.

There is a record of every game played, a statistic for every hit, error, and base on balls. One can measure performances against each other, compare players and teams, speak of the dead as if they were still alive. To play the game as a child is simultaneously to imagine playing it as an adult, and the power of this fantasy is present in even the most casual pick-up game. How many hours of his boyhood, A. wonders, were spent trying to imitate Stan Musial's batting stance (feet together, knees bent, back hunched over in a taut French curve) or the basket catches of Willie Mays? Reciprocally, for those who grow up to be professionals, there is an awareness that they are living out their childhood dreams—in effect, being paid to remain children. Nor should the depth of those dreams be minimized. In his own Jewish childhood, A. can remember confusing the last words of the Passover Seder, "Next year in Jerusalem," with the ever-hopeful refrain of disappointed fandom, "Wait till next year," as if the one were a commentary on the other: to win the pennant was to enter the promised land. Baseball had somehow become entangled in his mind with the religious experience.

It was just then, as A. was beginning to sink into this baseball quicksand, that Thurman Munson was killed. A. noted that Munson was the first Yankee captain since Lou Gehrig, that his grandmother had died of Lou Gehrig's disease, and that his grandfather's death would come quickly in the wake of Munson's.

The newspapers were filled with articles about the catcher. A. had always admired Munson's play on the field: the quick bat flicking singles to right, the stumpy body chugging around the bases, the anger that seemed to consume him as he went about his business behind the plate. Now A. was moved to learn of Munson's work with children and the troubles he had had with his own hyperactive son. Everything seemed to be repeating itself. Reality was a Chinese box, an infinite series of containers within containers. For here again, in the most unlikely of places, the theme had reappeared: the curse of the absent father. It seemed that Munson himself was the only one who had the power to calm down the little boy. Whenever he was at home, the boy's outbursts stopped, his frenzies abated. Munson was learning how to fly a plane so that he could go home more often during the baseball season to be with his son, and it was the plane that killed him.

Inevitably, A.'s memories of baseball were connected with his memories of his grandfather. It was his grandfather who had taken him to his first game, had talked to him about the old players, had shown him that baseball was as much about talk as it was about watching. As a little boy, A. would be dropped off at the office on Fifty-seventh Street, play around with the typewriters and adding machines until his grandfather was ready to leave, and then walk out with him for a leisurely stroll down Broadway. The ritual always included a few rounds of Pokerino in one of the amusement arcades, a quick lunch, and then the subway—to one of the city ball parks. Now, with his grandfather disappearing into death, they continued to talk about baseball. It was the one subject they could still come to as equals. Each time he visited the hospital, A. would buy a copy of the *New York Post*, and then sit by the old man's bed, reading to him about the games of the day before. It was his last contact with the outside world, and it was painless, a series of coded messages he could understand with his eyes closed. Anything else would have been too much.

Toward the very end, with a voice that could barely produce a sound, his grandfather told him that he had begun to remember his life. He had been dredging up the days of his Toronto boyhood, reliving events that had taken place as far back as eighty years ago: defending his younger brother against a gang of bullies, delivering bread on Friday afternoon to the Jewish families in the neighbor-hood, all the trivial, long-forgotten things that now, coming back to him as he lay immobilized in bed, took on the importance of spiritual illuminations. "Lying here gives me a chance to remember," he told A., as if this were a new power he had discovered in himself. A. could sense the pleasure it gave him. Little by little, it had begun to dominate the fear that had been in his grandfather's face these past weeks. Memory was the only thing keeping him alive, and it was as though he wanted to hold off death for as long as possible in order to go on remembering.

He knew, and yet he would not say he knew. Until the final week, he continued to talk about returning to his apartment, and not once was the word "death" mentioned. Even on the last day, he waited until the last possible moment to say good-bye. A. was leaving, walking through the door after a visit, when his grandfather called him back. Again, A. stood beside the bed. The old man took hold of his hand and squeezed as hard as he could. Then: a long, long moment. At last, A. bent down and kissed his grandfather's face. Neither one of them said a word.

A. remembers a schemer, a maker of deals, a man of bizarre and grandiose optimisms. Who else, after all, could have named his daughter Queenie with a straight face? But at her birth he had declared, "she'll be a queen," and could not resist the temptation. He thrived on bluff, the symbolic gesture, on being the life of the party. Lots of jokes, lots of cronies, an impeccable sense of timing. He gambled on the sly, cheated on his wife (the older he got, the younger the girls), and never lost his taste for any of it. His locutions were particularly splendid. A towel was never just a towel, but a "Turkish towel." A taker of drugs was a "dope fiend." Nor would he ever say "I saw . . . ," but rather, "I've had an opportunity to observe . . ." In so doing, he managed to inflate the world, to turn it into a more compelling and exotic place for himself. He played the bigshot and reveled in the side-effects of the pose: the head-waiters calling him Mr. B., the delivery boys smiling at his excessive tips, the whole world tipping its hat to him. He had come down to New York from Canada just after the First World War, a poor Jewish boy on the make, and in the end he had done all right for himself. New York was his passion, and in his last years he refused to move away, resisting his daughter's offer of a life in sunny California with these words, which became a popular refrain: "I can't leave New York. This is where the action is."

A. remembers a day when he was four or five. His grandparents came for a visit, and his grandfather did a magic trick for him, some little thing he had found in a novelty shop. On the next visit, when he failed to show up with a new trick, A. raised a fuss of disappointment. From then on there was always a new piece of magic: disappearing coins, silk scarves produced from thin air, a machine that turned strips of blank paper into money, a big rubber ball that became five little rubber balls when you squeezed it in your hand, a cigarette extinguished in a handkerchief that made no burn, a pitcher of milk poured into a cone of newspaper that made no spill. What had started out as a curiosity to amuse his grandson became a genuine calling for him. He turned himself into an accomplished amateur magician, a deft sleight-of-hand artist, and he took special pride in his membership card from the Magician's Guild. He appeared at each of A.'s childhood birthday parties with his magic and went on performing until the last year of his life, touring the senior citizen clubs of New York with one of his lady friends (a blowsy woman with a pile of fake red hair) who would sing a song, accompanying herself on the accordion, that introduced him as the Great Zavello. It was only natural. His life was so steeped in the hocus-pocus of illusion, he had pulled off so many business deals by making people believe in him (convincing them that something not there was actually there, and vice versa) that it was a small matter for him to step up on stage and fool them in a more formal way. He had the ability to make people pay attention to him, and it was clear to everyone who saw him how delighted he was to be the center of their attention. No one is less cynical than a magician. He knows, and everyone else knows, that everything he does is a sham. The trick is not really to deceive them, but to delight them into wanting to be deceived: so that for the space of a few minutes the grip of cause-and-effect is loosened, the laws of nature countermanded. As Pascal put it in the *Pensées*: "It is not possible to have reasonable grounds for not believing in miracles."

A.'s grandfather, however, did not content himself merely with magic. He was equally fond of jokes, which he called "stories"—all of them written down in a little notebook that he carried around in his coat pocket. At some point during every family gathering, he would take out the notebook, skim through it quickly in some corner of the room, put it back in his pocket, sit down in a chair, and then launch into an hour's worth of verbal nonsense. Here, too, the memory is of laughter. Not, as with S., a laughter bursting from the belly, but a laughter that meandered outward from the lungs, a long sing-song loop of sound that began as a wheeze and dispersed, gradually, into a fainter and fainter chromatic whistle. That, too, is how A. would like to remember him: sitting in that chair and making everyone laugh.

His grandfather's greatest stunt, though, was neither a magic trick nor a joke, but a kind of extra-sensory voodoo that kept everyone in the family baffled for years. It was a game called the Wizard. A.'s grandfather would take out a deck of cards, ask someone to pick a card, any card, and hold it up for everyone to see. The five of hearts. Then he would go to the phone, dial a number, and ask to speak to the Wizard. That's right, he would say, I want to speak to the Wizard. A moment later he would pass around the telephone, and coming out of the receiver there would be a voice, a man's voice, saying over and over: five of hearts, five of hearts, five of hearts. Then he would thank the Wizard, hang up the phone, and stand there grinning at everyone.

Years later, when it was finally explained to A., it all seemed so simple. His grandfather and a friend had each agreed to be the Wizard for the other. The question, May I speak to the Wizard, was a signal, and the man on the other end of the line would start reeling off the suits: spade, heart, diamond, club. When he hit the right one, the caller would say something, anything, meaning go no further, and then the Wizard would go through the litany of numbers: ace, two, three, four, five, etc. When he came to the right one, the caller would again say something, and the Wizard would stop, put the two elements together, and repeat them into the phone: five of hearts, five of hearts, five of hearts.

The Book of Memory. Book Six.

He finds it extraordinary, even in the ordinary actuality of his experience, to feel his feet on the ground, to feel his lungs expanding and contracting with the air he breathes, to know that if he puts one foot in front of the other he will be able to walk from where he is to where he is going. He finds it extraordinary that on some mornings, just after he has woken up, as he bends down to tie his shoes, he is flooded with a happiness so intense, a happiness so naturally and harmoniously at one with the world, that he can feel himself alive in the present, a present that surrounds him and permeates him, that breaks through him with the sudden, overwhelming knowledge that he is alive. And the happiness he discovers in himself at that moment is extraordinary. And whether or not it is extraordinary, he finds this happiness extraordinary.

———————

Sometimes it feels as though we are wandering through a city without purpose. We walk down the street, turn at random down another street, stop to admire the cornice of a building, bend down to inspect a splotch of tar on the pavement that reminds us of certain paintings we have admired, look at the faces of the people who pass us on the street, trying to imagine the lives they carry around inside them, go into a cheap restaurant for lunch, walk back outside and continue on our way toward the river (if this city has a river), to watch the boats as they sail by, or the big ships docked in the harbor, perhaps singing to ourselves as we walk, or perhaps whistling, or perhaps trying to remember something we have forgotten. Sometimes it seems as though we are not going anywhere as we walk through the city, that we are only looking for a way to pass the time, and that it is only our fatigue that tells us where and when we should stop. But just as one step will inevitably lead to the next step, so it is that one thought inevitably follows from the previous thought, and in the event that a thought should engender more than a single thought (say two or three thoughts, equal to each other in all their consequences), it will be necessary not only to follow the first thought to its conclusion, but also to backtrack to the original position of that thought in order to follow the second thought to its conclusion, and then the third thought, and so on, and in this way, if we were to try to make an image of this process in our minds, a network of paths begins to be drawn, as in the image of the human bloodstream (heart, arteries, veins, capillaries), or as in the image of a map (of city streets, for example, preferably a large city, or even of roads, as in the gas station maps of roads that stretch, bisect, and meander across a continent), so that what we are really doing when we walk through the city is thinking, and thinking in such a way that our thoughts compose a journey, and this journey is no more or less than the steps we have taken, so that, in the end, we might safely say that we have been on a journey, and even if we do not leave our room, it has been a journey, and we might safely say that we have been somewhere, even if we don't know where it is.

He takes down from his bookshelf a brochure he bought ten years ago in Amherst, Massachusetts, a souvenir of his visit to Emily Dickinson's house, thinking now of the strange exhaustion that had afflicted him that day as he stood in the poet's room: a shortness of breath, as if he had just climbed to the top of a mountain. He had walked around that small, sun-drenched room, looking at the white bedspread, the polished furniture, thinking of the seventeen hundred poems that were written there, trying to see them as a part of those four walls, and yet failing to do so. For if words are a way of being in the world, he thought, then even if there were no world to enter, the world was already there, in that room, which meant it was the room that was present in the poems and not the reverse. He reads now, on the last page of the brochure, in the awkward prose of the anonymous writer:

"In this bedroom-workroom, Emily announced that the soul could be content with its own society. But she discovered that consciousness was captivity as well as liberty, so that even here she was prey to her own self-imprisonment in despair or fear . . . For the sensitive visitor, then, Emily's room acquires an atmosphere encompassing the poet's several moods of superiority, anxiety, anguish, resignation or ecstasy. Perhaps more than any other concrete place in American literature, it symbolizes a native tradition, epitomized by Emily, of an assiduous study of the inner life."

Song to accompany The Book of Memory. *Solitude,* as sung by Billie Holiday. In the recording of May 9, 1941 by Billie Holiday and Her Orchestra. Performance time: three minutes and fifteen seconds. As follows: In my solitude you haunt me / With reveries of days gone by. / In my solitude you taunt me / With memories that never die . . . Etc. With credits to D. Ellington, E. De Lange, and I. Mills.

First allusions to a woman's voice. To be followed by specific reference to several.

For it is his belief that if there is a voice of truth—assuming there is such a thing as truth, and assuming this truth can speak—it comes from the mouth of a woman.

It is also true that memory sometimes comes to him as a voice. It is a voice that speaks inside him, and it is not necessarily his own. It speaks to him in the way a voice might tell stories to a child, and yet at times this voice makes fun of him, or calls him to attention, or curses him in no uncertain terms. At times it willfully distorts the story it is telling him, changing facts to suit its whims, catering to the interests of drama rather than truth. Then he must speak to it in his own voice and tell it to stop, thus returning it to the silence it came from. At other times it sings to him. At still other times it whispers. And then there are the times it merely hums, or babbles, or cries out in pain. And even when it says nothing, he knows it is still there, and in the silence of this voice that says nothing, he waits for it to speak.

Jeremiah: "Then said I, Ah, Lord God! behold, I cannot speak: for I am a child. But the Lord said unto me, say not, I am a child: for thou shalt go to all that I shall send thee, and whatsoever I command thee thou shalt speak . . . Then the Lord put forth his hand, and touched my mouth. And the Lord said unto me, Behold, I have put my words in thy mouth."

The Book of Memory. Book Seven.

First commentary on the Book of Jonah.

One is immediately struck by its oddness in relation to the other prophetic books. This brief work, the only one to be written in the third person, is more dramatically a story of solitude than anything else in the Bible, and yet it is told as if from outside that solitude, as if, by plunging into the darkness of that solitude, the "I" has vanished from itself. It cannot speak about itself, therefore, except as another. As in Rimbaud's phrase: "Je est un autre."

Not only is Jonah reluctant to speak (as Jeremiah is, for example), but he actually refuses to speak. "Now the word of the Lord came unto Jonah . . . But Jonah rose up to flee from the presence of the Lord."

Jonah flees. He books passage aboard a ship. A terrible storm rises up, and the sailors fear they will drown. Everyone prays for deliverance. But Jonah has "gone down into the sides of the ship; and he lay, and was fast asleep." Sleep, then, as the ultimate withdrawal from the world. Sleep as an image of solitude. Oblomov curled on his couch, dreaming himself back into his mother's womb. Jonah in the belly of the ship; Jonah in the belly of the whale.

The captain of the ship finds Jonah and tells him to pray to his God. Meanwhile, the sailors have drawn lots, to see which among them has been responsible for the storm, ". . . and the lot fell upon Jonah.

"And then he said unto them, Take me up, and cast me forth into the sea; so shall the sea be calm unto you; for I know that for my sake this great tempest is upon you.

"Nevertheless the men rowed hard to bring it to the land; but they could not; for the sea wrought, and was tempestuous against them . . .

"So they took up Jonah, and cast him forth into the sea; and the sea ceased from her raging."

The popular mythology about the whale notwithstanding, the great fish that swallows Jonah is by no means an agent of destruction. The fish is what saves him from drowning in the sea. "The waters compassed me about, even to the soul: the depth closed me round about, the weeds were wrapped about my head." In the depth of that solitude, which is equally the depth of silence, as if in the refusal to speak there were an equal refusal to turn one's face to the other ("Jonah rose up to flee from the presence of the Lord")—which is to say: who seeks solitude seeks silence; who does not speak is alone; is alone, even unto death—Jonah encounters the darkness of death. We are told that "Jonah was in the belly of the fish three days and three nights," and elsewhere, in a chapter of the *Zohar*, we are told, "'Three days and three nights': which means the three days that a man is in his grave before his belly bursts apart." And when the fish then vomits Jonah onto dry land, Jonah is given back to life, as if the death he had found in the belly of the fish were a preparation for new life, a life that has passed through death, and therefore a life that can at last speak. For death has frightened him into opening his mouth. "I cried by reason of mine affliction unto the Lord, and he heard me; out of the belly of hell cried I, and thou heardest my voice." In the darkness of the solitude that is death, the tongue is finally loosened, and at the moment it begins to speak, there is an answer. And even if there is no answer, the man has begun to speak.

The prophet. As in false: speaking oneself into the future, not by knowledge but by intuition. The real prophet knows. The false prophet guesses.

This was Jonah's greatest problem. If he spoke God's message, telling the Ninevites they would be destroyed in forty days for their wickedness, he was certain they would repent, and thus be spared. For he knew that God was "merciful, slow to anger, and of great kindness."

"So the people of Ninevah believed God, and proclaimed a fast, and put on sackcloth, from the greatest of them even to the least of them."

And if the Ninevites were spared, would this not make Jonah's prophecy false? Would he not, then, be a false prophet? Hence the paradox at the heart of the book: the prophecy would remain true only if he did not speak it. But then, of course, there would be no prophecy, and Jonah would no longer be a prophet. But better to be no prophet at all than to be a false prophet. "Therefore now, O Lord, take, I beseech thee, my life from me; for it is better for me to die than to live."

Therefore, Jonah held his tongue. Therefore, Jonah ran away from the presence of the Lord and met the doom of shipwreck. That is to say, the shipwreck of the singular.

Remission of cause and effect.

A. remembers a moment from boyhood (twelve, thirteen years old). He was wandering aimlessly one November afternoon with his friend D. Nothing was happening. But in each of them, at that moment, a sense of infinite possibilities. Nothing was happening. Or else one could say that it was this consciousness of possibility, in fact, that was happening.

As they walked along through the cold, gray air of that afternoon, A. suddenly stopped and announced to his friend: One year from today something extraordinary will happen to us, something that will change our lives forever.

The year passed, and on the appointed day nothing extraordinary happened. A. explained to D.: No matter; the important thing will happen next year. When the second year rolled around, the same thing happened: nothing. But A. and D. were undaunted. All through the years of high school, they continued to commemorate that day. Not with ceremony, but simply with acknowledgement. For example, seeing each other in the school corridor and saying: Saturday is the day. It was not that they still expected a miracle to happen. But, more curiously, over the years they had both become attached to the memory of A.'s prediction.

The reckless future, the mystery of what has not yet happened: this, too, he learned, can be preserved in memory. And it sometimes strikes him that the blind, adolescent prophecy he made twenty years ago, that fore-seeing of the extraordinary, was in fact the extraordinary thing itself: his mind leaping happily into the unknown. For the fact of the matter is, many years have passed. And still, at the end of each November, he finds himself remembering that day.

Prophecy. As in true. As in Cassandra, speaking from the solitude of her cell. As in a woman's voice.

The future falls from her lips in the present, each thing exactly as it will happen, and it is her fate never to be believed. Madwoman, the daughter of Priam: "the shrieks of that ill-omened bird" from whom "... sounds of woe / Burst dreadful, as she chewed the laurel leaf, / And ever and anon, like the black Sphinx, / Poured the full tide of enigmatic song." (Lycophron's *Cassandra*, in Royston's translation, 1806). To speak of the future is to use a language that is forever ahead of itself, consigning things that have not yet happened to the past, to an "already" that is forever behind itself, and in this space between utterance and act, word after word, a chasm begins to open, and for one to contemplate such emptiness for any length of time is to grow dizzy, to feel oneself falling into the abyss.

A. remembers the excitement he felt in Paris in 1971, when he discovered the seventeen-hundred line poem by Lycophron (circa 300 B.C.), which is a monologue of Cassandra's ravings in prison before the fall of Troy. He came to the poem through a translation into French by Q., a writer just his own age (twenty-four). Three years later, when he got together with Q. in a cafe on the rue Condé, he asked him whether he knew of any translations of the poem into English. Q. himself did not read or speak English, but yes, he had heard of one, by a certain Lord Royston at the beginning of the nineteenth century. When A. returned to New York in the summer of 1974, he went to the Columbia University library to look for the book. Much to his surprise, he found it. *Cassandra, translated from the original Greek of Lycophron and illustrated with notes;* Cambridge, 1806.

This translation was the only work of any substance to come from the pen of Lord Royston. He had completed the translation while still an undergraduate at Cambridge and had published the poem himself in a luxurious private edition. Then he had gone on the traditional continental tour following his graduation. Because of the Napoleonic tumult in France, he did not head south—which would have been the natural route for a young man of his interests—but instead went north, to the Scandinavian countries, and in 1808, while traveling through the treacherous waters of the Baltic Sea, drowned in a shipwreck off the coast of Russia. He was just twenty-four years old.

Lycophron: "the obscure." In his dense, bewildering poem, nothing is ever named, everything becomes a reference to something else. One is quickly lost in the labyrinth of its associations, and yet one continues to run through it, propelled by the force of Cassandra's voice. The poem is a verbal outpouring, breathing fire, consumed by fire, which obliterates itself at the edge of sense. "Cassandra's word," as a friend of A.'s put it (B.: in a lecture, curiously enough, about Hölderlin's poetry—a poetry which he compares in manner to Cassandra's speech), "this irreducible sign—*deutungslos*—a word beyond grasping, Cassandra's word, a word from which no lesson is to be drawn, a word, each time, and every time, spoken to say nothing . . ."

After reading through Royston's translation, A. realized that a great talent had been lost in that shipwreck. Royston's English rolls along with such fury, such deft and acrobatic syntax, that to read the poem is to feel yourself trapped inside Cassandra's mouth.

line 240   An oath! an oath! they have an oath in heaven!
        Soon shall their sail be spread, and in their hands
        The strong oar quivering cleave the refluent wave;
        While songs, and hymns, and carols jubilant
        Shall charm the rosy God, to whom shall rise,
        Rife from Apollo's Delphic shrine, the smoke
        Of numerous holocausts: Well pleased shall hear
        Enorches, where the high-hung taper's light
        Gleams on his dread carousals, and when forth
        The Savage rushes on the corny field
        Mad to destroy, shall bid his vines entwist
        His sinewy strength, and hurl them to the ground.

*

line 426   . . . then Greece
        For this one crime, aye for this one, shall weep
        Myriads of sons: no funeral urn, but rocks
        Shall hearse their bones; no friends upon their dust
        Shall pour the dark libations of the dead;
        A name, a breath, an empty sound remains,
        A fruitless marble warm with bitter tears
        Of sires, and orphan babes, and widowed wives!

*

line 1686 Why pour the fruitless strain? to winds, and waves,
           Deaf winds, dull waves, and senseless shades of woods
           I chaunt, and sing mine unavailing song.
           Such woes has Lepsieus heaped upon my head,
           Steeping my words in incredulity;
           The jealous God! for from my virgin couch
           I drove him amorous, nor returned his love.
           But fate is in my voice, truth on my lips;
           What must come, will come; and when rising woes
           Burst on his head, when rushing from her seat
           His country falls, nor man nor God can save,
           Some wretch shall groan, "From her no falsehood
             flowed,
           True were the shrieks of that ill-omened bird."

    It intrigues A. to consider that both Royston and Q. had translated this work while still in their early twenties. In spite of the century and a half that separated them, each had given some special force to his own language through the medium of this poem. At one point, it occurred to him that perhaps Q. was a reincarnation of Royston. Every hundred years or so Royston would be reborn to translate the poem into another language, and just as Cassandra was destined never to be believed, the work of Lycophron would remain unread, generation after generation. A useless task therefore: to write a book that would stay forever closed. And still, the image rises up in his mind: shipwreck. Consciousness falling to the bottom of the sea, and the horrible noise of cracking wood, the tall masts tumbling into the waves. To imagine Royston's thoughts the moment his body smacked against the water. To imagine the havoc of that death.

The Book of Memory. Book Eight.

By the time of his third birthday, A.'s son's taste in literature had begun to expand from simple, heavily illustrated baby books to more sophisticated children's books. The illustration was still a source of great pleasure, but it was no longer crucial. The story itself had become enough to hold his attention, and when A. came to a page with no picture at all, he would be moved to see the little boy looking intently ahead, at nothing, at the emptiness of the air, at the blank wall, imagining what the words were telling him. "It's fun to imagine what we can't see," he told his father once, as they were walking down the street. Another time, the boy went into the bathroom, closed the door, and did not come out. A. asked through the closed door: "What are you doing in there?" "I'm thinking," the boy said. "I have to be alone to think."

Little by little, they both began to gravitate toward one book. The story of Pinocchio. First in the Disney version, and then, soon after, in the original version, with text by Collodi and illustrations by Mussino. The little boy never tired of hearing the chapter about the storm at sea, which tells of how Pinocchio finds Gepetto in the belly of the Terrible Shark.

"Oh, Father, dear Father! Have I found you at last? Now I shall never, never leave you again!"

Gepetto explains: "The sea was rough and the whitecaps overturned the boat. Then a Terrible Shark came up out of the sea and, as soon as he saw me in the water, swam quickly toward me, put out his tongue, and swallowed me as easily as if I had been a chocolate peppermint."

"And how long have you been shut away in here?"

"From that day to this, two long weary years—two years, my Pinocchio . . ."

"And how have you lived? Where did you find the candle? And the matches to light it with—where did you get them?"

"In the storm which swamped my boat, a large ship also suffered the same fate. The sailors were all saved, but the ship went right down to the bottom of the sea, and the same Terrible Shark that swallowed me, swallowed most of it . . . To my own good luck, that ship was loaded with meat, preserved foods, crackers, bread, bottles of wine, raisins, cheese, coffee, sugar, wax candles, and boxes of matches. With all these blessings, I have been able to live on for two whole years, but now I am at the very last crumbs. Today there is nothing left in the cupboard, and this candle you see here is the last one I have."

"And then?"

"And then, my dear, we'll find ourselves in darkness."

For A. and his son, so often separated from each other during the past year, there was something deeply satisfying in this passage of reunion. In effect, Pinocchio and Gepetto are separated throughout the entire book. Gepetto is given the mysterious piece of talking wood by the carpenter, Master Cherry, in the second chapter. In the third chapter the old man sculpts the Marionette. Even before Pinocchio is finished, his pranks and mischief begin. "I deserve it," says Gepetto to himself. "I should have thought of this before I made him. Now it's too late." At this point, like any newborn baby, Pinocchio is pure will, libidinous need without consciousness. Very rapidly, over the next few pages, Gepetto teaches his son to walk, the Marionette experiences hunger and accidentally burns his feet off—which his father rebuilds for him. The next day Gepetto sells his coat to buy Pinocchio an A-B-C book for school ("Pinocchio understood . . . and, unable to restrain his tears, he jumped on his father's neck and kissed him over and over"), and then, for more than two hundred pages, they do not see each other again. The rest of the book tells the story of Pinocchio's search for his father—and Gepetto's search for his son.

At some point, Pinocchio realizes that he wants to become a real boy. But it also becomes clear that this will not happen until he is reunited with his father. Adventures, misadventures, detours, new resolves, struggles, happenstance, progress, setbacks, and through it all, the gradual dawning of conscience. The superiority of the Collodi original to the Disney adaptation lies in its reluctance to make the inner motivations of the story explicit. They remain intact, in a pre-conscious, dream-like form, whereas in Disney these things are expressed—which sentimentalizes them, and therefore trivializes them. In Disney, Gepetto prays for a son; in Collodi, he simply makes him. The physical act of shaping the puppet (from a piece of wood that talks, that is *alive*, which mirrors Michaelangelo's notion of sculpture: the figure is already there in the material; the artist merely hews away at the excess matter until the true form is revealed, implying that Pinocchio's being precedes his body: his task throughout the book is to find it, in other words to find himself, which means that this is a story of becoming rather than of birth), this act of shaping the puppet is enough to convey the idea of the prayer, and surely it is more powerful for remaining silent. Likewise with Pinocchio's efforts to attain real boyhood. In Disney, he is commanded by the Blue Fairy to be "brave, truthful, and unselfish," as though there were an easy formula for taking hold of the self. In Collodi, there are no directives. Pinocchio simply blunders about, simply lives, and little by little comes to an awareness of what he can become. The only improvement Disney makes on the story, and this is perhaps arguable, comes at the end, in the episode of the escape from the Terrible Shark (Monstro the Whale). In Collodi, the Shark's mouth is open (he suffers from asthma and heart disease), and to organize the escape Pinocchio needs no more than courage. "Then, my dear Father, there is no time to lose. We must escape."

"Escape! How?"

"We can run out of the Shark's mouth and dive into the sea."

"You speak well, but I cannot swim, my dear Pinocchio."

"Why should that matter? You can climb on my shoulders and I, who am a fine swimmer, will carry you safely to shore."

"Dreams, my boy!" answered Gepetto, shaking his head and smiling sadly. "Do you think it possible for a Marionette, a yard high, to have the strength to carry me on his shoulders and swim?"

"Try it and see! And in any case, if it is written that we must die, we shall at least die together." Not adding another word, Pinocchio took the candle in his hand and going ahead to light the way, he said to his father: "Follow me and have no fear."

In Disney, however, Pinocchio needs resourcefulness as well. The whale's mouth is shut, and when it opens, it is only to let water in, not out. Pinocchio cleverly decides to build a fire inside the whale—which induces Monstro to sneeze, thereby launching the puppet and his father into the sea. But more is lost with this flourish than gained. For the crucial image of the story is eliminated: Pinocchio swimming through the desolate water, nearly sinking under the weight of Gepetto's body, making his way through the gray-blue night (page 296 of the American edition), with the moon shining above them, a benign smile on its face, and the huge open mouth of the shark behind them. The father on his son's back: the image evoked here is so clearly that of Aeneas bearing Anchises on his back from the ruins of Troy that each time A. reads the story aloud to his son, he cannot help seeing (for it is not thinking, really, so quickly do these things happen in his mind) certain clusters of other images, spinning outward from the core of his preoccupations: Cassandra, for example, predicting the ruin of Troy, and thereafter loss, as in the wanderings of Aeneas that precede the founding of Rome, and in that wandering the image of another wandering: the Jews in the desert, which, in its turn, yields further clusters of images: "Next year in Jerusalem," and with it the photograph in the Jewish Encyclopedia of his relative, who bore the name of his son.

A. has watched his son's face carefully during these readings of *Pinocchio*. He has concluded that it is the image of Pinocchio saving Gepetto (swimming away with the old man on his back) that gives the story meaning for him. A boy of three is indeed very little. A wisp of puniness against the bulk of his father, he dreams of acquiring inordinate powers to conquer the paltry reality of himself. He is still too young to understand that one day he will be as big as his father, and even when it is explained to him very carefully, the facts are still open to gross misinterpretations: "And some day I'll be the same tall as you, and you'll be the same little as me." The fascination with comic book super-heroes is perhaps understandable from this point of view. It is the dream of being big, of becoming an adult. "What does Superman do?" "He saves people." For this act of saving is in effect what a father does: he saves his little boy from harm. And for the little boy to see Pinocchio, that same foolish puppet who has stumbled his way from one misfortune to the next, who has wanted to be "good" and could not help being "bad," for this same incompetent little marionette, who is not even a real boy, to become a figure of redemption, the very being who saves his father from the grip of death, is a sublime moment of revelation. The son saves the father. This must be fully imagined from the perspective of the little boy. And this, in the mind of the father who was once a little boy, a son, that is, to his own father, must be fully imagined. *Puer aeternus*. The son saves the father.

Further commentary on the nature of chance.

He does not want to neglect to mention that two years after meeting S. in Paris, he happened to meet S.'s younger son on a subsequent visit—through channels and circumstances that had nothing to do with S. himself. This young man, P., who was precisely the same age as A., was working his way to a position of considerable power with an important French film producer. A. himself would later work for this same producer, doing a variety of odd jobs for him in 1971 and 1972 (translating, ghost writing), but none of that is essential. What matters is that by the mid to late seventies, P. had managed to achieve the status of co-producer, and along with the son of the French producer put together the movie *Superman*, which had cost so many millions of dollars, A. read, that it had been described as the most expensive work of art in the history of the Western world.

Early in the summer of 1980, shortly after his son turned three, A. and the boy spent a week together in the country, in a house owned by friends who were off on vacation. A. noticed in the newspaper that *Superman* was playing in a local theater and decided to take the boy, on the off-chance that he would be able to sit through it. For the first half of the film, the boy was calm, working his way through a bin of popcorn, whispering his questions as A. had instructed him to do, and taking the business of exploding planets, rocket ships, and outer space without much fuss. But then something happened. Superman began to fly, and all at once the boy lost his composure. His mouth dropped open, he stood up in his seat, spilled his popcorn, pointed at the screen, and began to shout: "Look! Look! He's flying!" For the rest of the film, he was beside himself, his face taut with fear and fascination, rattling off questions to his father, trying to absorb what he had seen, marveling, trying to absorb it again, marveling. Toward the end, it became a little too much for him. "Too much booming," he said. His father asked him if he wanted to leave, and he said yes. A. picked him up and carried him out of the theater—into a violent hail storm. As they ran toward the car, the boy said (bouncing up and down in A.'s arms), "We're having quite an adventure tonight, aren't we?"

For the rest of the summer, Superman was his passion, his obsession, the unifying purpose of his life. He refused to wear any shirt except the blue one with the S on the front. His mother sewed a cape together for him, and each time he went outside, he insisted on wearing it, charging down the streets with his arms in front of him, as if flying, stopping only to announce to each passerby under the age of ten: "I'm Superman!" A. was amused by all this, since he could remember these same things from his own childhood. It was not this obsession that struck him; nor even, finally, the coincidence of knowing the men who had made the film that led to this obsession. Rather, it was this. Each time he saw his son pretending to be Superman, he could not help thinking of his friend S., as if even the S on his son's T-shirt were not a reference to Superman but to his friend. And he wondered at this trick his mind continued to play on him, this constant turning of one thing into another thing, as if behind each real thing there were a shadow thing, as alive in his mind as the thing before his eyes, and in the end he was at a loss to say which of these things he was actually seeing. And therefore it happened, often it happened, that his life no longer seemed to dwell in the present.

The Book of Memory. Book Nine.

For most of his adult life, he has earned his living by translating the books of other writers. He sits at his desk reading the book in French and then picks up his pen and writes the same book in English. It is both the same book and not the same book, and the strangeness of this activity has never failed to impress him. Every book is an image of solitude. It is a tangible object that one can pick up, put down, open, and close, and its words represent many months, if not many years, of one man's solitude, so that with each word one reads in a book one might say to himself that he is confronting a particle of that solitude. A man sits alone in a room and writes. Whether the book speaks of loneliness or companionship, it is necessarily a product of solitude. A. sits down in his own room to translate another man's book, and it is as though he were entering that man's solitude and making it his own. But surely that is impossible. For once a solitude has been breached, once a solitude has been taken on by another, it is no longer solitude, but a kind of companionship. Even though there is only one man in the room, there are two. A. imagines himself as a kind of ghost of that other man, who is both there and not there, and whose book is both the same and not the same as the one he is translating. Therefore, he tells himself, it is possible to be alone and not alone at the same moment.

A word becomes another word, a thing becomes another thing. In this way, he tells himself, it works in the same way that memory does. He imagines an immense Babel inside him. There is a text, and it translates itself into an infinite number of languages. Sentences spill out of him at the speed of thought, and each word comes from a different language, a thousand tongues that clamor inside him at once, the din of it echoing through a maze of rooms, corridors, and stairways, hundreds of stories high. He repeats. In the space of memory, everything is both itself and something else. And then it dawns on him that everything he is trying to record in The Book of Memory, everything he has written so far, is no more than the translation of a moment or two of his life—those moments he lived through on Christmas Eve, 1979, in his room at 6 Varick Street.

The moment of illumination that burns across the sky of solitude.

Pascal in his room on the night of November 23, 1654, sewing the Memorial into the lining of his clothes, so that at any moment, for the rest of his life, he could find beneath his hand the record of that ecstasy.

In the Year of Grace 1654
On Monday, November 23rd, Feast of Saint Clement,
Pope and Martyr,
and of others in the Martyrology.
and eve of Saint Chrysogomus and other Martyrs.
From about half past ten at night until about half past twelve.
Fire
"God of Abraham, God of Isaac, God of Jacob,"
not of the philosophers and scientists.
Certainty. Certainty. Feeling. Joy. Peace.

. . .

Greatness of the human soul.

. . .

Joy, joy, joy, tears of joy.

. . .

I will not forget thy word. Amen.

. . .

Concerning the power of memory.

    In the spring of 1966, not long after meeting his future wife, A. was invited by her father (an English professor at Columbia) to the family apartment on Morningside Drive for dessert and coffee. The dinner guests were Francis Ponge and his wife, and A.'s future father-in-law thought that the young A. (just nineteen at the time), would enjoy meeting so famous a writer. Ponge, the master poet of the object, who had invented a poetry more firmly placed in the outer world perhaps than any other, was teaching a course at Columbia that semester. By then A. already spoke reasonably good French. Since Ponge and his wife spoke no English, and A.'s future in-laws spoke almost no French, A. joined in the discussion more fully than he might have, given his innate shyness and penchant for saying nothing whenever possible. He remembers Ponge as a gracious and lively man with sparkling blue eyes.

The second time A. met Ponge was in 1969 (although it could have been 1968 or 1970) at a party given in Ponge's honor by G., a Barnard professor who had been translating his work. When A. shook Ponge's hand, he introduced himself by saying that although he probably didn't remember it, they had once met in New York several years ago. On the contrary, Ponge replied, he remembered the evening quite well. And then he proceeded to talk about the apartment in which that dinner had taken place, describing it in all its details, from the view out the windows to the color of the couch and the arrangement of the furniture in each of the various rooms. For a man to remember so precisely things he had seen only once, things which could not have had any bearing on his life except for a fleeting instant, struck A. with all the force of a supernatural act. He realized that for Ponge there was no division between the work of writing and the work of seeing. For no word can be written without first having been seen, and before it finds its way to the page it must first have been part of the body, a physical presence that one has lived with in the same way one lives with one's heart, one's stomach, and one's brain. Memory, then, not so much as the past contained within us, but as proof of our life in the present. If a man is to be truly present among his surroundings, he must be thinking not of himself, but of what he sees. He must forget himself in order to be there. And from that forgetfulness arises the power of memory. It is a way of living one's life so that nothing is ever lost.

———

It is also true that "the man with a good memory does not remember anything because he does not forget anything," as Beckett has written about Proust. And it is true that one must make a distinction between voluntary and involuntary memory, as Proust does during the course of his long novel about the past.

What A. feels he is doing, however, as he writes the pages of his own book, is something that does not belong to either one of these two types of memory. A. has both a good memory and a bad memory. He has lost much, but he has also retained much. As he writes, he feels that he is moving inward (through himself) and at the same time moving outward (toward the world). What he experienced, perhaps, during those few moments on Christmas Eve, 1979, as he sat alone in his room on Varick Street, was this: the sudden knowledge that came over him that even alone, in the deepest solitude of his room, he was not alone, or, more precisely, that the moment he began to try to speak of that solitude, he had become more than just himself. Memory, therefore, not simply as the resurrection of one's private past, but an immersion in the past of others, which is to say: history—which one both participates in and is a witness to, is a part of and apart from. Everything, therefore, is present in his mind at once, as if each element were reflecting the light of all the others, and at the same time emitting its own unique and unquenchable radiance. If there is any reason for him to be in this room now, it is because there is something inside him hungering to see it all at once, to savor the chaos of it in all its raw and urgent simultaneity. And yet, the telling of it is necessarily slow, a delicate business of trying to remember what has already been remembered. The pen will never be able to move fast enough to write down every word discovered in the space of memory. Some things have been lost forever, other things will perhaps be remembered again, and still other things have been lost and found and lost again. There is no way to be sure of any of this.

Possible epigraph(s) for The Book of Memory.

"Thoughts come at random, and go at random. No device for holding on to them or for having them. A thought has escaped: I was trying to write it down: instead I write that it has escaped me." (Pascal)

"As I write down my thought, it sometimes escapes me; but this makes me remember my own weakness, which I am constantly forgetting. This teaches me as much as my forgotten thought, for I strive only to know my own nothingness." (Pascal)

The Book of Memory. Book Ten.

When he speaks of the room, he does not mean to neglect the windows that are sometimes present in the room. The room need not be an image of hermetic consciousness, and when a man or a woman stands or sits alone in a room there is more that happens there, he realizes, than the silence of thought, the silence of a body struggling to put its thoughts into words. Nor does he mean to imply that only suffering takes place within the four walls of consciousness, as in the allusions made to Hölderlin and Emily Dickinson previously. He thinks, for example, of Vermeer's women, alone in their rooms, with the bright light of the real world pouring through a window, either open or closed, and the utter stillness of those solitudes, an almost heartbreaking evocation of the everyday and its domestic variables. He thinks, in particular, of a painting he saw on his trip to Amsterdam, *Woman in Blue*, which nearly immobilized him with contemplation in the Rijksmuseum. As one commentator has written: "The letter, the map, the woman's pregnancy, the empty chair, the open box, the unseen window—all are reminders or natural emblems of absence, of the unseen, of other minds, wills, times, and places, of past and future, of birth and perhaps of death—in general, of a world that extends beyond the edges of the frame, and of larger, wider horizons that encompass and impinge upon the scene suspended before our eyes. And yet it is the fullness and self-sufficiency of the present moment that Vermeer insists upon—with such conviction that its capacity to orient and contain is invested with metaphysical value."

Even more than the objects mentioned in this list, it is the quality of the light coming through the unseen window to the viewer's left that so warmly beckons him to turn his attention to the outside, to the world beyond the painting. A. stares hard at the woman's face, and as time passes he almost begins to hear the voice inside the woman's head as she reads the letter in her hands. She, so very pregnant, so tranquil in the imminence of mother-hood, with the letter taken out of the box, no doubt being read for the hundredth time; and there, hanging on the wall to her right, a map of the world, which is the image of everything that exists out-side the room: that light, pouring gently over her face and shining on her blue smock, the belly bulging with life, and its blueness bathed in luminosity, a light so pale it verges on whiteness. To follow with more of the same: *Woman Pouring Milk, Woman Holding a Balance, Woman Putting on Pearls, Young Woman at a Window with a Pitcher, Girl Reading a Letter at an Open Window.*

"The fullness and self-sufficiency of the present moment."

If it was Rembrandt and Titus who in some sense lured A. to Am-sterdam, where he then entered rooms and found himself in the presence of women (Vermeer's women, Anne Frank), his trip to that city was at the same time conceived as a pilgrimage to his own past. Again, his inner movements were expressed in the form of paintings: an emotional state finding tangible representation in a work of art, as though another's solitude were in fact the echo of his own.

In this case it was Van Gogh, and the new museum that had been built to house his work. Like some early trauma buried in the unconscious, forever linking two unrelated objects (this shoe is my father; this rose is my mother), Van Gogh's paintings stand in his mind as an image of his adolescence, a translation of his deepest feelings of that period. He can even be quite precise about it, pinpointing events and his reactions to events by place and time (exact locations, exact moments: year, month, day, even hour and minute). What matters, however, is not so much the sequence of the chronicle as its consequences, its permanence in the space of memory. To remember, therefore, a day in April when he was sixteen, and cutting school with the girl he had fallen in love with: so passionately and hopelessly that the thought of it still smarts. To remember the train, and then the ferry to New York (that ferry, which has long since vanished: industrial iron, the warm fog, rust), and then going to a large exhibition of Van Gogh paintings. To remember how he had stood there, trembling with happiness, as if the shared seeing of these works had invested them with the girl's presence, had mysteriously varnished them with the love he felt for her.

Some days later, he began writing a sequence of poems (now lost) based on the canvases he had seen, each poem bearing the title of a different Van Gogh painting. These were the first real poems he ever wrote. More than a method for entering those paintings, the poems were an attempt to recapture the memory of that day. Many years went by, however, before he realized this. It was only in Amsterdam, studying the same paintings he had seen with the girl (seeing them for the first time since then—almost half his life ago), that he remembered having written those poems. At that moment the equation became clear to him: the act of writing as an act of memory. For the fact of the matter is, other than the poems themselves, he has not forgotten any of it.

————

Standing in the Van Gogh Museum in Amsterdam (December 1979) in front of the painting *The Bedroom*, completed in Arles, October 1888.

Van Gogh to his brother: "This time it is just simply my bedroom ... To look at the picture ought to rest the brain or rather the imagination ...

"The walls are pale violet. The floor is of red tiles.

"The wood of the bed and chairs is the yellow of fresh butter, the sheet and pillows very light lemon-green.

"The coverlet scarlet. The window green.

"The toilet table orange, the basin blue.

"The doors lilac.

"And that is all—there is nothing in this room with closed shutters ...

"This by way of revenge for the enforced rest I have been obliged to take ...

"I will make you sketches of the other rooms too some day."

As A. continued to study the painting, however, he could not help feeling that Van Gogh had done something quite different from what he thought he had set out to do. A.'s first impression was indeed a sense of calm, of "rest," as the artist describes it. But gradually, as he tried to inhabit the room presented on the canvas, he began to experience it as a prison, an impossible space, an image, not so much of a place to live, but of the mind that has been forced to live there. Observe carefully. The bed blocks one door, a chair blocks the other door, the shutters are closed: you can't get in, and once you are in, you can't get out. Stifled among the furniture and everyday objects of the room, you begin to hear a cry of suffering in this painting, and once you hear it, it does not stop. "I cried by reason of mine affliction ..." But there is no answer to this cry. The man in this painting (and this is a self-portrait, no different from a picture of a man's face, with eyes, nose, lips, and jaw) has been alone too much, has struggled too much in the depths of solitude. The world ends at that barricaded door. For the room is not a representation of solitude, it is the substance of solitude itself. And it is a thing so heavy, so unbreathable, that it cannot be shown in any terms other than what it is. "And that is all—there is nothing in this room with closed shutters . . ."

Further commentary on the nature of chance.

A. arrived in London and departed from London, spending a few days on either end of his trip visiting with English friends. The girl of the ferry and the Van Gogh paintings was English (she had grown up in London, had lived in America from the age of about twelve to eighteen, and had then returned to London to go to art school), and on the first leg of his trip, A. spent several hours with her. Over the years since their graduation from high school, they had kept in touch at best fitfully, had seen each other perhaps five or six times. A. was long cured of his passion, but he had not dismissed her altogether from his mind, clinging somehow to the feeling of that passion, although she herself had lost importance for him. It had been several years since their last meeting, and now he found it gloomy, almost oppressive to be with her. She was still beautiful, he thought, and yet solitude seemed to enclose her, in the same way an egg encloses an unborn bird. She lived alone, had almost no friends. For many years she had been working on sculptures in wood, but she refused to show them to anyone. Each time she finished a piece, she would destroy it, and then begin on the next one. Again, A. had come face to face with a woman's solitude. But here it had turned in on itself and dried up at its source.

A day or two later, he went to Paris, eventually to Amsterdam, and afterwards back to London. He thought to himself: there will be no time to see her again. On one of those days before returning to New York, he was to have dinner with a friend (T., the same friend who had thought they might be cousins) and decided to spend the afternoon at the Royal Academy of Art, where a large exhibition of "Post Impressionist" paintings was on view. The enormous crush of visitors at the museum, however, made him reluctant to stay for the afternoon, as he had planned, and he found himself with three or four extra hours before his dinner appointment. He went to a cheap fish and chips place in Soho for lunch, trying to decide what to do with himself during this free time. He paid up his bill, left the restaurant, turned the corner, and there, as she stood gazing into the display window of a large shoe store, he saw her.

It was not every day that he ran into someone on the London streets (in that city of millions, he knew no more than a few people), and yet this encounter seemed perfectly natural to him, as though it were a commonplace event. He had been thinking about her only a moment before, regretting his decision not to call her, and now that she was there, suddenly standing before his eyes, he could not help feeling that he had willed her to appear.

He walked toward her and spoke her name.

Paintings. Or the collapse of time in images.

In the Royal Academy exhibition he had seen in London, there were several paintings by Maurice Denis. While in Paris, A. had visited the widow of the poet Jean Follain (Follain, who had died in a traffic accident in 1971, just days before A. had moved to Paris) in connection with an anthology of French poetry that A. was preparing, which in fact was what had brought him back to Europe. Madame Follain, he soon learned, was the daughter of Maurice Denis, and many of her father's paintings hung on the walls of the apartment. She herself was now in her late seventies, perhaps eighty, and A. was impressed by her Parisian toughness, her gravel voice, her devotion to her dead husband's work.

One of the paintings in the apartment bore a title: Madelaine à 18 mois (Madelaine at 18 months), which Denis had written out across the top of the canvas. This was the same Madelaine who had grown up to become Follain's wife and who had just asked A. to enter her apartment. For a moment, without being aware of it, she stood in front of that picture, which had been painted nearly eighty years before, and A. saw, as though leaping incredibly across time, that the child's face in the painting and the old woman's face before him were exactly the same. For that one instant, he felt he had cut through the illusion of human time and had experienced it for what it was: as no more than a blink of the eyes. He had seen an entire life standing before him, and it had been collapsed into that one instant.

O. to A. in conversation, describing what it felt like to have become an old man. O., now in his seventies, his memory failing, his face as wrinkled as a half-closed palm. Looking at A. and shaking his head with deadpan wit: "What a strange thing to happen to a little boy."

Yes, it is possible that we do not grow up, that even as we grow old, we remain the children we always were. We remember ourselves as we were then, and we feel ourselves to be the same. We made ourselves into what we are now then, and we remain what we were, in spite of the years. We do not change for ourselves. Time makes us grow old, but we do not change.

The Book of Memory. Book Eleven.

He remembers returning home from his wedding party in 1974, his wife beside him in her white dress, and taking the front door key out of his pocket, inserting the key in the lock, and then, as he turned his wrist, feeling the blade of the key snap off inside the lock.

He remembers that in the spring of 1966, not long after he met his future wife, one of the keys of her piano broke: F above Middle C. That summer the two of them traveled to a remote part of Maine. One day, as they walked through a nearly abandoned town, they wandered into an old meeting hall, which had not been used for years. Remnants of some men's society were scattered about the place: Indian headdresses, lists of names, the detritus of drunken gatherings. The hall was dusty and deserted, except for an upright piano that stood in one corner. His wife began to play (she played well) and discovered that all the keys worked except one: F above Middle C.

It was at that moment, perhaps, that A. realized the world would go on eluding him forever.

If a novelist had used these little incidents of broken piano keys (or the wedding day accident of losing the key inside the door), the reader would be forced to take note, to assume the novelist was trying to make some point about his characters or the world. One could speak of symbolic meanings, of subtext, or simply of formal devices (for as soon as a thing happens more than once, even if it is arbitrary, a pattern takes shape, a form begins to emerge). In a work of fiction, one assumes there is a conscious mind behind the words on the page. In the presence of happenings in the so-called real world, one assumes nothing. The made-up story consists entirely of meanings, whereas the story of fact is devoid of any significance beyond itself. If a man says to you, "I'm going to Jerusalem," you think to yourself: how nice, he's going to Jerusalem. But if a character in a novel were to speak those same words, "I'm going to Jerusalem," your response is not at all the same. You think, to begin with, of Jerusalem itself: its history, its religious role, its function as a mythical place. You would think of the past, of the present (politics; which is also to think of the recent past), and of the future—as in the phrase: "Next year in Jerusalem." On top of that, you would integrate these thoughts into whatever it is you already know about the character who is going to Jerusalem and use this new synthesis to draw further conclusions, refine perceptions, think more cogently about the book as a whole. And then, once the work is finished, the last page read and the book closed, interpretations begin: psychological, historical, sociological, structural, philological, religious, sexual, philosophical, either singly or in various combinations, depending on your bent. Although it is possible to interpret a real life according to any of these systems (people do, after all, go to priests and psychiatrists; people do sometimes try to understand their lives in terms of historical conditions), it does not have the same effect. Something is missing: the grandeur, the grasp of the general, the illusion of metaphysical truth. One says: Don Quixote is consciousness gone haywire in a realm of the imaginary. One looks at a mad person in the world (A. at his schizophrenic sister, for example), and says nothing. This is the sadness of a wasted life, perhaps— but no more.

Now and then, A. finds himself looking at a work of art with the same eyes he uses to look at the world. To read the imaginary in this way is to destroy it. He thinks, for example, of Tolstoy's description of the opera in *War and Peace*. Nothing is taken for granted in this passage, and therefore everything is reduced to absurdity. Tolstoy makes fun of what he sees simply by describing it. "In the second act there were cardboard monuments on the stage, and a round hole in the backdrop representing a moon. Shades had been put over the footlights and deep notes were played on the horns and contrabass as a number of people appeared from both sides of the stage wearing black cloaks and flourishing what looked like daggers. Then some other men ran onto the stage and began dragging away the maiden who had been in white and was now in pale blue. They did not take her away at once, but spent a long time singing with her, until at last they dragged her off, and behind the scenes something metallic was struck three times, and everyone knelt down and sang a prayer. All these actions were repeatedly interrupted by the enthusiastic shouts of the audience."

There is also the equal and opposite temptation to look at the world as though it were an extension of the imaginary. This, too, has sometimes happened to A., but he is loath to accept it as a valid solution. Like everyone else, he craves a meaning. Like everyone else, his life is so fragmented that each time he sees a connection between two fragments he is tempted to look for a meaning in that connection. The connection exists. But to give it a meaning, to look beyond the bare fact of its existence, would be to build an imaginary world inside the real world, and he knows it would not stand. At his bravest moments, he embraces meaninglessness as the first principle, and then he understands that his obligation is to see what is in front of him (even though it is also inside him) and to say what he sees. He is in his room on Varick Street. His life has no meaning. The book he is writing has no meaning. There is the world, and the things one encounters in the world, and to speak of them is to be in the world. A key breaks off in a lock, and something has happened. That is to say, a key has broken off in a lock. The same piano seems to exist in two different places. A young man, twenty years later, winds up living in the same room where his father faced the horror of solitude. A man encounters his old love on a street in a foreign city. It means only what it is. Nothing more, nothing less. Then he writes: to enter this room is to vanish in a place where past and present meet. And then he writes: as in the phrase: "he wrote The Book of Memory in this room."

The invention of solitude.

He wants to say. That is to say, he means. As in the French, "vouloir dire," which means, literally, to want to say, but which means, in fact, to mean. He means to say what he wants. He wants to say what he means. He says what he wants to mean. He means what he says.

Vienna, 1919.

No meaning, yes. But it would be impossible to say that we are not haunted. Freud has described such experiences as "uncanny," or *unheimlich*—the opposite of *heimlich*, which means "familiar," "native," "belonging to the home." The implication, therefore, is that we are thrust out from the protective shell of our habitual perceptions, as though we were suddenly outside ourselves, adrift in a world we do not understand. By definition, we are lost in that world. We cannot even hope to find our way in it.

Freud argues that each stage of our development co-exists with all the others. Even as adults, we have buried within us a memory of the way we perceived the world as children. And not simply a memory of it: the structure itself is intact. Freud connects the experience of the uncanny with a revival of the egocentric, animistic world-view of childhood. "It would seem as though each one of us has been through a phase of individual development corresponding to that animistic stage in primitive men, that none of us has traversed it without certain traces of it which can be re-activated, and that everything which now strikes us as 'uncanny' fulfills the condition of stirring those vestiges of animistic mental activity within us and bringing them to expression." He concludes: "An uncanny experience occurs either when repressed infantile complexes have been revived by some impression, or when the primitive beliefs we have surmounted seem once more to be confirmed."

None of this, of course, is an explanation. At best it serves to describe the process, to point out the terrain on which it takes place. As such, A. is more than willing to accept it as true. Unhomeness, therefore, as a memory of another, much earlier home of the mind. In the same way a dream will sometimes resist interpretation until a friend suggests a simple, almost obvious meaning, A. cannot prove Freud's argument true or false, but it feels right to him, and he is more than willing to accept it. All the coincidences that seem to have been multiplying around him, then, are somehow connected with a memory of his childhood, as if by beginning to remember his childhood, the world were returning to a prior state of its being. This feels right to him. He is remembering his childhood, and it has appeared to him in the present in the form of these experiences. He is remembering his childhood, and it is writing itself out for him in the present. Perhaps that is what he means when he writes: "meaninglessness is the first principle." Perhaps that is what he means when he writes: "He means what he says." Perhaps that is what he means. And perhaps it is not. There is no way to be sure of any of this.

The invention of solitude. Or stories of life and death.

The story begins with the end. Speak or die. And for as long as you go on speaking, you will not die. The story begins with death. King Shehriyar has been cuckolded: "and they ceased not from kissing and clipping and clicketing and carousing." He retreats from the world, vowing never to succumb to feminine trickery again. Later, returning to his throne, he gratifies his physical desires by taking in women of the kingdom. Once satisfied, he orders their execution. "And he ceased not to do this for three years, till the land was stripped of marriageable girls, and all the women and mothers and fathers wept and cried out against the King, cursing him and complaining to the Creator of heaven and earth and calling for succor upon Him who heareth prayer and answereth those that cry to Him; and those that had daughters left fled with them, till at last there remained not a single girl in the city apt for marriage."

At this point, Shehrzad, the vizier's daughter, volunteers to go to the King. ("Her memory was stored with verses and stories and folklore and the sayings of Kings and sages, and she was wise, witty, prudent, and well-bred.") Her desperate father tries to dissuade her from going to this sure death, but she is unperturbed. "Marry me to this king, for either I will be the means of the deliverance of the daughters of the Muslims from slaughter, or I will die and perish as others have perished." She goes off to sleep with the king and puts her plan into action: "to tell ... delightful stories to pass away the watches of our night ...; it shall be the means of my deliverance and the ridding of the folk of this calamity, and by it I will turn the king from his custom."

The king agrees to listen to her. She begins her story, and what she tells is a story about story-telling, a story within which are several stories, each one, in itself, about story-telling—by means of which a man is saved from death.

Day begins to dawn, and mid-way through the first story-within-the-story, Shehrzad falls silent. "This is nothing to what I will tell tomorrow night," she says, "if the king let me live." And the king says to himself, "By Allah, I will not kill her, till I hear the rest of the story." So it goes for three nights, each night's story stopping before the end and spilling over into the beginning of the next night's story, by which time the first cycle of stories has ended and a new one begun. Truly, it is a matter of life and death. On the first night, Shehrzad begins with The Merchant and the Genie. A man stops to eat his lunch in a garden (an oasis in the desert), throws away a date stone, and behold "there started up before him a gigantic spirit, with a naked sword in his hand, who came up to him and said, 'Arise, that I may slay thee, even as thou hast slain my son.' 'How did I slay thy son?' asked the merchant, and the genie replied, 'When thou threwest away the date stone, it smote my son, who was passing at the time, on the breast, and he died forthright.'"

This is guilt out of innocence (echoing the fate of the marriageable girls in the kingdom), and at the same time the birth of enchantment—turning a thought into a thing, bringing the invisible to life. The merchant pleads his case, and the genie agrees to stay his execution. But in exactly one year the merchant must return to the same spot, where the genie will mete out the sentence. Already, a parallel is being drawn with Sherhzad's situation. She wishes to delay her execution, and by planting this idea in the king's mind she is pleading her case—but doing it in such a way that the king cannot recognize it. For this is the function of the story: to make a man see the thing before his eyes by holding up another thing to view.

The year passes, and the merchant, good to his word, returns to the garden. He sits down and begins to weep. An old man wanders by, leading a gazelle by a chain, and asks the merchant what is wrong. The old man is fascinated by what the merchant tells him (as if the merchant's life were a story, with a beginning, middle, and end, a fiction concocted by some other mind—which in fact it is), and decides to wait and see how it will turn out. Then another old man wanders by, leading two black dogs. The conversation is repeated, and then he, too, sits down and waits. Then a third old man wanders by, leading a dappled she-mule, and once again the same thing happens. Finally, the genie appears, in a "cloud of dust and a great whirling column from the heart of the desert." Just as he is about to drag off the merchant and slay him with his sword, "as thou slewest my son, the darling of my heart!," the first old man steps forward and says to the genie: "If I relate to thee my history with this gazelle and it seem to thee wonderful, wilt thou grant me a third of this merchant's blood?" Astonishingly, the genie agrees, just as the king has agreed to listen to Sherhzad's story: readily, without a struggle.

Note: the old man does not propose to defend the merchant as one would in a court of law, with arguments, counter-arguments, the presentation of evidence. This would be to make the genie look at the thing he already sees: and about this his mind has been made up. Rather, the old man wishes to turn him away from the facts, turn him away from thoughts of death, and in so doing delight him (literally, "to entice away," from the Latin *delectare*) into a new feeling for life, which in turn will make him renounce his obsession with killing the merchant. An obsession of this sort walls one up in solitude. One sees nothing but one's own thoughts. A story, however, in that it is not a logical argument, breaks down those walls. For it posits the existence of others and allows the listener to come into contact with them—if only in his thoughts.

The old man launches into a preposterous story. This gazelle you see before you, he says, is actually my wife. For thirty years she lived with me and in all that time she could not produce a son. (Again: an allusion to the absent child—the dead child, the child not yet born—referring the genie back to his own sorrow, but obliquely, as part of a world in which life stands equal to death.) "So I took me a concubine and had by her a son like the rising full moon with eyes and eyebrows of perfect beauty . . ." When the boy was fifteen, the old man went off to another city (he, too, is a merchant), and in his absence the jealous wife used magic to transform the boy and his mother into a calf and a cow. "Thy slave died and her son ran away," the wife told him on his return. After a year of mourning, the cow was slaughtered as a sacrifice—through the machinations of the jealous wife. When the man was about to slaughter the calf a moment later, his heart failed him. "And when the calf saw me, he broke his halter and came up to me and fawned on me and moaned and wept, till I took pity on him and said . . . 'Bring me a cow and let this calf go.'" The herdsman's daughter, also learned in the art of magic, later discovered the true identity of the calf. After the merchant granted her the two things she asked for (to marry the son and to bewitch the jealous wife, by imprisoning her in the shape of a beast—"else I shall not be safe from her craft"), she returned the son to his original form. Nor does the story quite end there. The son's bride, the old man goes on to explain, "dwelt with us days and nights and nights and days, till God took her to Himself; and after her death, my son set out on a journey to the land of Ind, which is this merchant's native country; and after a while I took the gazelle and travelled with her from place to place, seeking news of my son, till chance led me to this garden, where I found this merchant sitting weeping; and this is my story." The genie agrees that this is a marvelous story and remits to the old man a third part of the merchant's blood.

One after the other, the two remaining old men propose the same bargain to the genie and begin their stories in the same way. "These two dogs are my elder brothers," says the second old man. "This mule was my wife," says the third. These opening sentences contain the essence of the entire project. For what does it mean to look at something, a real object in the real world, an animal, for example, and say that it is something other than what it is? It is to say that each thing leads a double life, at once in the world and in our minds, and that to deny either one of these lives is to kill the thing in both its lives at once. In the stories of the three old men, two mirrors face each other, each one reflecting the light of the other. Both are enchantments, both the real and the imaginary, and each exists by virtue of the other. And it is, truly, a matter of life and death. The first old man has come to the garden in search of his son; the genie has come to the garden to slay his son's un-witting killer. What the old man is telling him is that our sons are always invisible. It is the simplest of truths: a life belongs only to the person who lives it; life itself will claim the living; to live is to let live. And in the end, by means of these three stories, the mer-chant's life is spared.

This is how *The Thousand and One Nights* begins. At the end of the entire chronicle, after story after story after story, there is a specific result, and it carries with it all the unalterable gravity of a miracle. Sherhzad has borne the king three sons. Again, the lesson is made clear. A voice that speaks, a woman's voice that speaks, a voice that speaks stories of life and death, has the power to give life.

"'May I then make bold to crave a boon of thy Majesty?'

"'Ask, O Sherhzad,' answered he, 'and it shall be given unto thee.'

"Whereupon she cried to the nurses and the eunuchs, saying, 'Bring me my children.'

"So they brought them to her in haste, and they were three male children, one walking, one crawling, and one sucking at the breast. She took them and, setting them before the king, kissed the ground and said, 'O King of the age, these are thy children and I crave that thou release me from the doom of death, for the sake of these infants.'"

When the king hears these words, he begins to weep. He gathers the little children up into his arms and declares his love for Sherhzad.

"So they decorated the city in splendid fashion, never before was seen the like thereof, and the drums beat and the pipes sounded, whilst all the mimes and mountebanks and players plied their various arts and the King lavished on them gifts and largesse. Moreover he gave alms to the poor and needy and extended his bounty to all his subjects and the people of his realm."

Mirror text.

If the voice of a woman telling stories has the power to bring children into the world, it is also true that a child has the power to bring stories to life. It is said that a man would go mad if he could not dream at night. In the same way, if a child is not allowed to enter the imaginary, he will never come to grips with the real. A child's need for stories is as fundamental as his need for food, and it manifests itself in the same way hunger does. Tell me a story, the child says. Tell me a story. Tell me a story, Daddy, please. The father then sits down and tells a story to his son. Or else he lies down in the dark beside him, the two of them in the child's bed, and begins to speak, as if there were nothing left in the world but his voice, telling a story in the dark to his son. Often it is a fairy tale, or a tale of adventure. Yet often it is no more than a simple leap into the imaginary. Once upon a time there was a little boy named Daniel, A. says to his son named Daniel, and these stories in which the boy himself is the hero are perhaps the most satisfying to him of all. In the same way, A. realizes, as he sits in his room writing The Book of Memory, he speaks of himself as another in order to tell the story of himself. He must make himself absent in order to find himself there. And so he says A., even as he means to say I. For the story of memory is the story of seeing. And even if the things to be seen are no longer there, it is a story of seeing. The voice, therefore, goes on. And even as the boy closes his eyes and goes to sleep, his father's voice goes on speaking in the dark.

The Book of Memory. Book Twelve.

He can go no farther than this. Children have suffered at the hands of adults, for no reason whatsoever. Children have been abandoned, have been left to starve, have been murdered, for no reason whatsoever. It is not possible, he realizes, to go any farther than this.

"But then there are the children," says Ivan Karamazov, "and what am I to do with them?" And again: "I want to forgive. I want to embrace. I don't want any more suffering. And if the sufferings of children go to make up the sum of sufferings which is necessary for the purchase of truth, then I say beforehand that the entire truth is not worth such a price."

Every day, without the least effort, he finds it staring him in the face. These are the days of Cambodia's collapse, and everyday it is there, looking out at him from the newspaper, with the inevitable photographs of death: the emaciated children, the grownups with nothing left in their eyes. Jim Harrison, for example, an Oxfam engineer, noting in his diary: "Visited small clinic at kilometer 7. Absolutely no drugs or medicines—serious cases of starvation— clearly just dying for lack of food . . . The hundreds of children were all marasmic—much skin disease, baldness, discolored hair and great fear in the whole population." Or later, describing what he saw on a visit to the 7th of January Hospital in Phnom Penh: ". . . terrible conditions—children in bed in filthy rags dying with starvation–no drugs—no food . . . The TB allied to starvation gives the people a Belsen-like appearance. In one ward a boy of thirteen tied down to the bed because he was going insane— many children now orphans—or can't find families—and a lot of nervous twitches and spasms to be seen among the people. The face of one small boy of eighteen months was in a state of destruction by what appeared to be infected skin and flesh which had bro-ken down under severe kwashiorkor—his eyes full of pus, held in the arms of his five-year-old sister . . . I find this sort of thing very tough to take—and this situation must be applicable to hundreds of thousands of Kampuchean people today."

Two weeks before reading these words, A. went out to din-ner with a friend of his, P., a writer and editor for a large weekly news magazine. It so happens that she was handling the "Cambo-dia story" for her publication. Nearly everything written in the American and foreign press about the conditions there had passed before her eyes, and she told A. about a story written for a North Carolina newspaper—by a volunteer American doctor in one of the refugee camps across the Thai border. It concerned the visit of the American President's wife, Rosalynn Carter, to those camps. A. could remember the photographs that had been published in the newspapers and magazines (the First Lady embracing a Cambodian child, the First Lady talking to doctors), and in spite of everything he knew about America's responsibility for creating the conditions Mrs. Carter had come to protest, he had been moved by those pictures. It turned out that Mrs. Carter visited the camp where the American doctor was working. The camp hospital was a make-shift affair: a thatched roof, a few support beams, the patients lying on mats on the ground. The President's wife arrived, followed by a swarm of officials, reporters, and cameramen. There were too many of them, and as they trooped through the hospital, patients' hands were stepped on by heavy Western shoes, I.V. lines were disconnected by passing legs, bodies were inadvertently kicked. Perhaps this confusion was avoidable, perhaps not. In any case, after the visitors had completed their inspection, the American doctor made an appeal. Please, he said, would some of you spare a bit of your time to donate blood to the hospital; even the blood of the healthiest Cambodian is too thin to be of use; our supply has run out. But the First Lady's tour was behind schedule. There were other places to go that day, other suffering people to see. There was just no time, they said. Sorry. So very sorry. And then, as abruptly as they had come, the visitors left.

In that the world is monstrous. In that the world can lead a man to nothing but despair, and a despair so complete, so resolute, that nothing can open the door of this prison, which is hopelessness, A. peers through the bars of his cell and finds only one thought that brings him any consolation: the image of his son. And not just his son, but any son, any daughter, any child of any man or woman.

In that the world is monstrous. In that it seems to offer no hope of a future, A. looks at his son and realizes that he must not allow himself to despair. There is this responsibility for a young life, and in that he has brought this life into being, he must not despair. Minute by minute, hour by hour, as he remains in the presence of his son, attending to his needs, giving himself up to this young life, which is a continual injunction to remain in the present, he feels his despair evaporate. And even though he continues to despair, he does not allow himself to despair.

The thought of a child's suffering, therefore, is monstrous to him. It is even more monstrous than the monstrosity of the world itself. For it robs the world of its one consolation, and in that a world can be imagined without consolation, it is monstrous.

He can go no farther than this.

This is where it begins. He stands alone in an empty room and begins to cry. "It is too much for me, I cannot face it" (Mallarmé). "A Belsen-like appearance," as the engineer in Cambodia noted. And yes, that is the place where Anne Frank died.

"It's really a wonder," she wrote, just three weeks before her arrest, "that I haven't dropped all my ideals, because they seem so absurd and impossible to carry out . . . I see the world gradually being turned into a wilderness, I hear the ever-approaching thunder, which will destroy us too, I can feel the sufferings of millions and yet, if I look up into the heavens, I think that it will all come right, that this cruelty too will end . . ."

No, he does not mean to say that this is the only thing. He does not even pretend to say that it can be understood, that by talking about it and talking about it a meaning can be discovered for it. No, it is not the only thing, and life nevertheless continues, for some, if not for most. And yet, in that it is a thing that will forever escape understanding, he wants it to stand for him as the thing that will always come before the beginning. As in the sentences: "This is where it begins. He stands alone in an empty room and begins to cry."

Return to the belly of the whale.

"The word of the Lord came unto Jonah . . . saying, Arise, go to Ninevah, that great city, and cry against it . . ."

In this command as well, Jonah's story differs from that of all the other prophets. For the Ninevites are not Jews. Unlike the other carriers of God's word, Jonah is not asked to address his own people, but foreigners. Even worse, they are the enemies of his people. Ninevah was the capital of Assyria, the most powerful empire in the world at that time. In the words of Nahum (whose prophecies have been preserved on the same scroll as the story of Jonah): "the bloody city . . . full of lies and rapine."

"Arise, go to Ninevah," God tells Jonah. Ninevah is to the east. Jonah promptly goes west, to Tarshish (Tartessus, on the farthest tip of Spain). Not only does he run away, he goes to the limit of the known world. This flight is not difficult to understand. Imagine an analogous case: a Jew being told to enter Germany during the Second World War and preach against the National Socialists. It is a thought that begs the impossible.

As early as the second century, one of the rabbinical commentators argued that Jonah boarded the ship to drown himself in the sea for the sake of Israel, not to flee from the presence of God. This is the political reading of the book, and Christian interpreters quickly turned it against the Jews. Theodore of Mopsuestia, for example, says that Jonah was sent to Ninevah because the Jews refused to listen to the prophets, and the book about Jonah was written to teach a lesson to the "stiff-necked people." Rupert of Deutz, however, another Christian interpreter (twelfth century), contends that the prophet refused God's command out of piety to his people, and for this reason God did not become very angry with Jonah. This echoes the opinion of Rabbi Akiba himself, who stated that "Jonah was jealous for the glory of the son (Israel) but not for the glory of the father (God)."

Nevertheless, Jonah finally agrees to go to Ninevah. But even after he delivers his message, even after the Ninevites repent and change their ways, even after God spares them, we learn that "it displeased Jonah exceedingly, and he was very angry." This is a patriotic anger. Why should the enemies of Israel be spared? It is at this point that God teaches Jonah the lesson of the book—in the parable of the gourd that follows.

"Doest thou well to be angry?" he asks. Jonah then removes himself to the outskirts of Ninevah, "till he might see what would become of the city"—implying that he still felt there was a chance Ninevah would be destroyed, or that he hoped the Ninevites would revert to their sinful ways and bring down punishment on themselves. God prepares a gourd (a castor plant) to protect Jonah from the sun, and "Jonah was exceedingly glad of the gourd." But by the next morning God has made the plant wither away. A vehement east wind blows, a fierce sun beats down on Jonah, and "he fainted, and wished himself to die, and said, it is better for me to die than to live"—the same words he had used earlier, indicating that the message of this parable is the same as in the first part of the book. "And God said to Jonah, Doest thou well to be angry for the gourd? And he said, I do well to be angry, even unto death. Then said the Lord, Thou hast had pity on the gourd, for which thou has not labored, neither madest it grow; which came up in a night and perished in a night; And should I not spare Ninevah, that great city, wherein are more than sixscore thousand persons that cannot discern between their right hand and their left hand; and also much cattle?"

These sinners, these heathen—and even the beasts that belong to them—are as much God's creatures as the Hebrews. This is a startling and original notion, especially considering the date of the story—eighth century B.C. (the time of Heraclitus). But this, finally, is the essence of what the rabbis have to teach. If there is to be any justice at all, it must be a justice for everyone. No one can be excluded, or else there is no such thing as justice. The conclusion is inescapable. This tiniest of books, which tells the curious and even comical story of Jonah, occupies a central place in the liturgy: it is read each year in the synagogue on Yom Kippur, the Day of Atonement, which is the most solemn day on the Jewish calendar. For everything, as has been noted before, is connected to everything else. And if there is everything, then it follows there is everyone. He does not forget Jonah's last words: "I do well to be angry, even unto death." And still, he finds himself writing these words on the page before him. If there is everything, then it follows there is everyone.

The words rhyme, and even if there is no real connection between them, he cannot help thinking of them together. Room and tomb, tomb and womb, womb and room. Breath and death. Or the fact that the letters of the word "live" can be rearranged to spell out the word "evil." He knows this is no more than a schoolboy's game. Surprisingly, however, as he writes the word "schoolboy," he can remember himself at eight or nine years old, and the sudden sense of power he felt in himself when he discovered he could play with words in this way—as if he had accidentally found a secret path to the truth: the absolute, universal, and unshakeable truth that lies hidden at the center of the world. In his schoolboy enthusiasm, of course, he had neglected to consider the existence of languages other than English, the great Babel of tongues buzzing and battling in the world outside his schoolboy life. And how can the absolute and unshakeable truth change from language to language?

Still, the power of rhyming words, of word transformations, cannot altogether be dismissed. The feeling of magic remains, even if it cannot be connected with a search for the truth, and this same magic, these same correspondences between words, are present in every language, even though the particular combinations are different. At the heart of each language there is a network of rhymes, assonances, and overlapping meanings, and each of these occurrences functions as a kind of bridge that joins opposite and contrasting aspects of the world with one another. Language, then, not simply as a list of separate things to be added up and whose sum total is equal to the world. Rather, language as it is laid out in the dictionary: an infinitely complex organism, all of whose elements—cells and sinews, corpuscles and bones, digits and fluids—are present in the world simultaneously, none of which can exist on its own. For each word is defined by other words, which means that to enter any part of language is to enter the whole of it. Language, then, as a monadology, to echo the term used by Leibniz. ("Since all is a plenum, all matter is connected and all movement in the plenum produces some effect on the distant bodies, in proportion to the distance. Hence every body is affected not only by those with which it is in contact, and thus feels in some way everything that happens to them; but through them it also feels those that touch the ones with which it is in immediate contact. Hence it follows that this communication extends over any distance whatever. Consequently, every body experiences everything that goes on in the universe, so much so that he who sees everything might read in any body what is happening anywhere, and even what has happened or will happen. He would be able to observe in the present what is remote in both time and space . . . A soul, however, can read in itself only what is directly represented in it; it is unable to unfold all at once all its folds; for these go on into infinity.")

Playing with words in the way A. did as a schoolboy, then, was not so much a search for the truth as a search for the world as it appears in language. Language is not truth. It is the way we exist in the world. Playing with words is merely to examine the way the mind functions, to mirror a particle of the world as the mind perceives it. In the same way, the world is not just the sum of the things that are in it. It is the infinitely complex network of connections among them. As in the meanings of words, things take on meaning only in relationship to each other. "Two faces are alike," writes Pascal. "Neither is funny by itself, but side by side their likeness makes us laugh." The faces rhyme for the eye, just as two words can rhyme for the ear. To carry the proposition one step further, A. would contend that it is possible for events in one's life to rhyme as well. A young man rents a room in Paris and then discovers that his father had hid out in this same room during the war. If these two events were to be considered separately, there would be little to say about either one of them. The rhyme they create when looked at together alters the reality of each. Just as two physical objects, when brought into proximity of each other, give off electromagnetic forces that not only effect the molecular structure of each but the space between them as well, altering, as it were, the very environment, so it is that two (or more) rhyming events set up a connection in the world, adding one more synapse to be routed through the vast plenum of experience.

These connections are commonplace in literary works (to return to that argument), but one tends not to see them in the world—for the world is too big and one's life is too small. It is only at those rare moments when one happens to glimpse a rhyme in the world that the mind can leap out of itself and serve as a bridge for things across time and space, across seeing and memory. But there is more to it than just rhyme. The grammar of existence includes all the figures of language itself: simile, metaphor, metonymy, synecdoche—so that each thing encountered in the world is actually many things, which in turn give way to many other things, depending on what these things are next to, contained by, or removed from. Often, too, the second term of a comparison is missing. It can be forgotten, or buried in the unconscious, or somehow made unavailable. "The past is hidden," Proust writes in an important passage of his novel, "beyond the reach of intellect, in some material object (in the sensation which that material object will give us) which we do not suspect. And as for that object, it depends on chance whether we come upon it or not before we ourselves must die." Everyone has experienced in one way or another the strange sensations of forgetfulness, the mystifying force of the missing term. I walked into that room, a man will say, and the oddest feeling came over me, as if I had been there before, although I cannot remember it at all. As in Pavlov's experiments with dogs (which, at the simplest possible level, demonstrate the way in which the mind can make a connection between two dissimilar things, eventually forget the first thing, and thereby turn one thing into another thing), something has happened, although we are at a loss to say what it is. What A. is struggling to express, perhaps, is that for some time now none of the terms has been missing for him. Wherever his eye or mind seems to stop, he discovers another connection, another bridge to carry him to yet another place, and even in the solitude of his room, the world has been rushing in on him at a dizzying speed, as if it were all suddenly converging in him and happening to him at once. Coincidence: to fall on with; to occupy the same place in time or space. The mind, therefore, as that which contains more than itself. As in the phrase from Augustine: "But where is the part of it which it does not itself contain?"

Second return to the belly of the whale.

"When he recovered his senses the Marionette could not remember where he was. Around him all was darkness, a darkness so deep and so black that for a moment he thought he had been dipped head first into an inkwell."

This is Collodi's description of Pinocchio's arrival in the belly of the shark. It would have been one thing to write it in the ordinary way: "a darkness as black as ink"—as a trite literary flourish to be forgotten the moment it is read. But something different is happening here, something that transcends the question of good or bad writing (and this is manifestly not bad writing). Take careful note: Collodi makes no comparisons in this passage; there is no "as if," no "like," nothing to equate or contrast one thing with another. The image of absolute darkness immediately gives way to an image of an inkwell. Pinocchio has just entered the belly of the shark. He does not know yet that Gepetto is also there. Everything, at least for this brief moment, has been lost. Pinocchio is surrounded by the darkness of solitude. And it is in this darkness, where the puppet will eventually find the courage to save his father and thereby bring about his transformation into a real boy, that the essential creative act of the book takes place.

By plunging his marionette into the darkness of the shark, Collodi is telling us, he is dipping his pen into the darkness of his inkwell. Pinocchio, after all, is only made of wood. Collodi is using him as the instrument (literally, the pen) to write the story of himself. This is not to indulge in primitive psychologizing. Collodi could not have achieved what he does in *Pinocchio* unless the book was for him a book of memory. He was over fifty years old when he sat down to write it, recently retired from an undistinguished career in government service, which had been marked, according to his nephew, "neither by zeal nor by punctuality nor by subordination." No less than Proust's novel in search of lost time, his story is a search for his lost childhood. Even the name he chose to write under was an evocation of the past. His real name was Carlo Lorenzini. Collodi was the name of the small town where his mother had been born and where he spent his holidays as a young child. About this childhood, a few facts are available. He was a teller of tall tales, admired by his friends for his ability to fascinate them with stories. According to his brother Ippolito, "He did it so well and with such mimickry that half the world took delight and the children listened to him with their mouths agape." In an autobiographical sketch written late in life, long after the completion of *Pinocchio*, Collodi leaves little doubt that he conceived of himself as the puppet's double. He portrays himself as a prankster and a clown—eating cherries in class and stuffing the pits into a schoolmate's pockets, catching flies and putting them into someone else's ears, painting figures on the clothes of the boy in front of him: in general, creating havoc for everyone. Whether or not this is true is beside the point. Pinocchio was Collodi's surrogate, and after the puppet had been created, Collodi saw himself as Pinocchio. The puppet had become the image of himself as a child. To dip the puppet into the inkwell, therefore, was to use his creation to write the story of himself. For it is only in the darkness of solitude that the work of memory begins.

Possible epigraph(s) for The Book of Memory.

"We ought surely to look in the child for the first traces of imaginative activity. The child's best loved and most absorbing occupation is play. Perhaps we may say that every child at play behaves like an imaginative writer, in that he creates a world of his own or, more truly, he rearranges the things of his world and orders it in a new way . . . It would be incorrect to think that he does not take this world seriously; on the contrary, he takes his play very seriously and expends a great deal of emotion on it." (Freud)

"You will not forget that the stress laid on the writer's memories of his childhood, which perhaps seems so strange, is ultimately derived from the hypothesis that imaginative creation, like day dreaming, is a continuation of and substitute for the play of child-hood." (Freud)

He watches his son. He watches the little boy move around the room and listens to what he says. He sees him playing with his toys and hears him talking to himself. Each time the boy picks up an object, or pushes a truck across the floor, or adds another block to the tower of blocks growing before him, he speaks of what he is doing, in the same way a narrator in a film would speak, or else he makes up a story to accompany the actions he has set in motion. Each movement engenders a word, or a series of words; each word triggers off another movement: a reversal, a continuation, a new set of movements and words. There is no fixed center to any of this ("a universe in which the center is everywhere, the circumference nowhere") except perhaps the child's consciousness, which is itself a constantly shifting field of perceptions, memories, and utterances. There is no law of nature that cannot be broken: trucks fly, a block becomes a person, the dead are resurrected at will. From one thing, the child's mind careens without hesitation to another thing. Look, he says, my broccoli is a tree. Look, my potatoes are a cloud. Look at the cloud, it's a man. Or else, feeling the food as it touches his tongue, and looking up, with a sly glint in his eyes: "Do you know how Pinocchio and his father escape from the shark?" Pause, letting the question sink in. Then, in a whisper: "They tiptoe quietly over his tongue."

It sometimes seems to A. that his son's mental perambulations while at play are an exact image of his own progress through the labyrinth of his book. He has even thought that if he could somehow make a diagram of his son at play (an exhaustive description, containing every shift, association, and gesture) and then make a similar diagram of his book (elaborating what takes place in the gaps between words, the interstices of the syntax, the blanks between sections—in other words, unraveling the spool of connections), the two diagrams would be the same: the one would fit perfectly over the other.

During the time he has worked on The Book of Memory, it has given him special pleasure to watch the boy remember. Like all preliterate beings, the boy's memory is astonishing. The capacity for detailed observation, for seeing an object in its singularity, is almost boundless. Written language absolves one of the need to remember much of the world, for the memories are stored in the words. The child, however, standing in a place before the advent of the written word, remembers in the same way Cicero would recommend, in the same way devised by any number of classical writers on the subject: image wed to place. One day, for example (and this is only one example, plucked from a myriad of possibilities), A. and his son were walking down the street. They ran into a nursery school playmate of the boy's standing outside a pizza parlor with his father. A.'s son was delighted to see his friend, but the other boy seemed to shy away from the encounter. Say hello, Kenny, his father urged him, and the boy managed to summon forth a feeble greeting. Then A. and his son continued on their walk. Three or four months later, they happened to be walking past the same spot together. A. suddenly heard his son muttering to himself, in a barely audible voice: Say hello, Kenny, say hello. It occurred to A. that if in some sense the world imprints itself on our minds, it is equally true that our experiences are imprinted on the world. For that brief moment, as they walked by the pizza parlor, the boy was literally seeing his own past. The past, to repeat the words of Proust, is hidden in some material object. To wander about in the world, then, is also to wander about in ourselves. That is to say, the moment we step into the space of memory, we walk into the world.

It is a lost world. And it strikes him to realize that it will be lost forever. The boy will forget everything that has happened to him so far. There will be nothing left but a kind of after-glow, and perhaps not even that. All the thousands of hours that A. has spent with him during the first three years of his life, all the millions of words he has spoken to him, the books he has read to him, the meals he has made for him, the tears he has wiped for him—all these things will vanish from the boy's memory forever.

The Book of Memory. Book Thirteen.

He remembers that he gave himself a new name, John, because all cowboys were named John, and that each time his mother addressed him by his real name he would refuse to answer her. He remembers running out of the house and lying in the middle of the road with his eyes shut, waiting for a car to run over him. He remembers that his grandfather gave him a large photograph of Gabby Hayes and that it sat in a place of honor on the top of his bureau. He remembers thinking the world was flat. He remembers learning how to tie his shoes. He remembers that his father's clothes were kept in the closet in his room and that it was the noise of hangers clicking together in the morning that would wake him up. He remembers the sight of his father knotting his tie and saying to him, Rise and shine, little boy. He remembers wanting to be a squirrel, because he wanted to be light like a squirrel and have a bushy tail and be able to jump from tree to tree as though he were flying. He remembers looking through the venetian blinds and seeing his newborn sister coming home from the hospital in his mother's arms. He remembers the nurse in a white dress who sat beside his baby sister and gave him little squares of Swiss chocolate. He remembers that she called them Swiss although he did not know what that meant. He remembers lying in his bed at dusk in midsummer and looking at the tree through his window and seeing different faces in the configuration of the branches. He remembers sitting in the bathtub and pretending that his knees were mountains and that the white soap was an ocean liner. He remembers the day his father gave him a plum and told him to go outside and ride his tricycle. He remembers that he did not like the taste of the plum and that he threw it into the gutter and was overcome by a feeling of guilt. He remembers the day his mother took him and his friend B. to the television studio in Newark to see a showing of Junior Frolics. He remembers that Uncle Fred had makeup on his face, just like his mother wore, and that he was surprised by this. He remembers that the cartoons were shown on a little television set, no bigger than the one at home, and the disappointment he felt was so crushing that he wanted to stand up and shout his protests to Uncle Fred. He remembers that he had been expecting to see Farmer Gray and Felix the Cat run around on a stage, as large as life, going at each other with real pitchforks and rakes. He remembers that B.'s favorite color was green and that he claimed his teddy bear had green blood running through its veins. He remembers that B. lived with both his grandmothers and that to get to B.'s room you had to go through an upstairs sitting room where the two white-haired women spent all their time watching television. He remembers that he and B. would go scavenging through the bushes and back-yards of the neighborhood looking for dead animals. He remembers burying them by the side of his house, deep in the darkness of the ivy, and that mostly they were birds, little birds like sparrows and robins and wrens. He remembers building crosses for them out of twigs and saying a prayer over their bodies as he and B. laid them in the hole they had dug in the ground, the dead eyes touching the loose damp earth. He remembers taking apart the family radio one afternoon with a hammer and screwdriver and explaining to his mother that he had done it as a scientific experiment. He remembers these were the words he used and that his mother spanked him. He remembers trying to chop down a small fruit tree in the back yard with a dull axe he had found in the garage and managing to make no more than a few dents in it. He remembers seeing the green on the underside of the bark and getting spanked for that too. He remembers sitting at his desk in the first grade away from the other children because he had been punished for talking in class. He remembers sitting at that desk and reading a book with a red cover and red illustrations with green-blue backgrounds. He remembers the teacher coming up to him from behind and very gently putting her hand on his shoulder and whispering a question into his ear. He remembers that she was wearing a white sleeveless blouse and that her arms were thick and covered with freckles. He remembers colliding with another boy during a softball game in the schoolyard and being thrown to the ground so violently that for the next five or ten minutes he saw everything as in a photographic negative. He remembers getting to his feet and walking toward the school building and thinking to himself, I'm going blind. He remembers how his panic gradually turned to acceptance and even fascination in the space of those few minutes and how, when his normal sight returned to him, he had the feeling that some extraordinary thing had taken place inside him. He remembers wetting his bed long after it was an acceptable thing to do and the icy sheets when he woke up in the morning. He remembers being invited for the first time to sleep over at a friend's house and how he stayed awake all night for fear of wetting the bed and humiliating himself, staring at the luminescent green hands of the watch he had been given for his sixth birthday. He remembers studying the illustrations in a children's Bible and accepting the fact that God had a long white beard. He remembers thinking that the voice he heard inside himself was the voice of God. He remembers going to the circus at Madison Square Garden with his grandfather and taking a ring off the finger of an eight and a half foot giant at the sideshow for fifty cents. He remembers keeping the ring on the top of his bureau beside the photograph of Gabby Hayes and that he could put four of his fingers through it. He remembers speculating that perhaps the entire world was enclosed in a glass jar and that it sat on a shelf next to dozens of other jar-worlds in the pantry of a giant's house. He remembers refusing to sing Christmas carols at school because he was Jewish and staying behind in the classroom while the other children went to rehearse in the auditorium. He remembers coming home from the first day of Hebrew school wearing a new suit and being pushed into a creek by older boys in leather jackets who called him a Jew shit. He remembers writing his first book, a detective story he composed with green ink. He remembers thinking that if Adam and Eve were the first people in the world, then everyone was related to everyone else. He remembers wanting to throw a penny out the window of his grandparents' apartment on Columbus Circle and his grandmother telling him that it would go straight through someone's head. He remembers looking down from the top of the Empire State Building and being surprised that the taxicabs were still yellow. He remembers visiting the Statue of Liberty with his mother and remembers that she got very nervous inside the torch and made him go back down the stairs sitting, one step at a time. He remembers the boy who was killed by lightning on a hike at summer camp. He remembers lying there in the rain next to him and seeing the boy's lips turn blue. He remembers his grandmother telling him how she remembered coming to America from Russia when she was five years old. He remembers that she told him she remembered waking up from a deep sleep and finding herself in the arms of a soldier who was carrying her onto a ship. He remembers that she told him this was the only thing she could remember.

The Book of Memory. Later that evening.

Not long after writing the words, "this was the only thing she could remember," A. stood up from his table and left his room.

Walking along the street, feeling drained by his efforts that day, he decided to go on walking for a while. Darkness came. He stopped for supper, spread out a newspaper on the table before him, and then, after paying his bill, decided to spend the rest of the evening at the movies. It took him nearly an hour to walk to the theater. As he was about to buy his ticket, he changed his mind, put the money back in his pocket, and walked away. He retraced his steps, following the same route that had taken him there in reverse. At some point along the way he stopped to drink a glass of beer. Then he continued on his walk. It was nearly twelve when he opened the door of his room.

That night, for the first time in his life, he dreamed that he was dead. Twice he woke up during the dream, trembling with panic. Each time, he tried to calm himself down, told himself that by changing position in bed the dream would end, and each time, upon falling back to sleep, the dream started up again at precisely the spot it had left off.

It was not exactly that he was dead, but that he was going to die. This was certain, an absolute and imminent fact. He was lying in a hospital bed, suffering from a fatal disease. His hair had fallen out in patches, and his head was half bald. Two nurses dressed in white walked into the room and told him: "Today you are going to die. It's too late to help you." They were almost mechanical in their indifference to him. He cried and pleaded with them, "I'm too young to die, I don't want to die now." "It's too late," the nurses answered. "We have to shave your head now." With tears pouring from his eyes, he allowed them to shave his head. Then they said: "The coffin is over there. Just go and lie down in it, close your eyes, and soon you'll be dead." He wanted to run away. But he knew that it was not permitted to disobey their orders. He went over to the coffin and climbed into it. The lid was closed over him, but once inside he kept his eyes open.

Then he woke up for the first time.

After he went back to sleep, he was climbing out of the coffin. He was dressed in a white patient's gown and had no shoes on. He left the room, wandered for a long time through many corridors, and then walked out of the hospital. Soon afterwards, he was knocking on the door of his ex-wife's house. "I have to die today," he told her, "there's nothing I can do about it." She took this news calmly, acting much as the nurses had. But he was not there for her sympathy. He wanted to give her instructions about what to do with his manuscripts. He went through a long list of his writings and told her how and where to have each of them published. Then he said: "The Book of Memory isn't finished yet. There's nothing I can do about it. There won't be time to finish. You finish it for me and then give it to Daniel. I trust you. You finish it for me." She agreed to do this, but without much enthusiasm. And then he began to cry, just as he had before: "I'm too young to die. I don't want to die now." But she patiently explained to him that if it had to be, then he should accept it. Then he left her house and returned to the hospital. When he reached the parking lot, he woke up for the second time.

After he went back to sleep, he was inside the hospital again, in a basement room next to the morgue. The room was large, bare, and white, a kind of old-fashioned kitchen. A group of his childhood friends, now grownups, were sitting around a table eating a large and sumptuous meal. They all turned and stared at him when he entered the room. He explained to them: "Look, they've shaved my head. I have to die today, and I don't want to die." His friends were moved by this. They invited him to sit down and eat with them. "No," he said, "I can't eat with you. I have to go into the next room and die." He pointed to a white swinging door with a circular window in it. His friends stood up from their chairs and joined him by the door. For a little while they all reminisced about their childhood together. It soothed him to talk to them, but at the same time he found it all the more difficult to summon the courage to walk through the door. Finally, he announced: "I have to go now. I have to die now." One by one, with tears pouring down his cheeks, he embraced his friends, squeezing them with all his strength, and said good-bye.

Then he woke up for the last time.

Concluding sentences for The Book of Memory.

From a letter by Nadezhda Mandelstam to Osip Mandelstam, dated 10/22/38, and never sent.

"I have no words, my darling, to write this letter ... I am writing it into empty space. Perhaps you will come back and not find me here. Then this will be all you have left to remember me by ... Life can last so long. How hard and long for each of us to die alone. Can this fate be for us who are inseparable? Puppies and children, did we deserve this? Did you deserve this, my angel? Everything goes on as before. I know nothing. Yet I know everything—each day and hour of your life are plain and clear to me as in a delirium—In my last dream I was buying food for you in a filthy hotel restaurant. The people with me were total strangers. When I had bought it, I realized I did not know where to take it, because I do not know where you are ... When I woke up, I said to Shura: 'Osia is dead.' I do not know whether you are still alive, but from the time of that dream, I have lost track of you. I do not know where you are. Will you hear me? Do you know how much I love you? I could never tell you how much I love you. I cannot tell you even now. I speak to you, only to you. You are with me always, and I who was such a wild and angry one and never learned to weep simple tears—now I weep and weep and weep ... It's me: Nadia. Where are you?"

————

He lays out a piece of blank paper on the table before him and writes these words with his pen.

The sky is blue and black and gray and yellow. The sky is not there, and it is red. All this was yesterday. All this was a hundred years ago. The sky is white. It smells of the earth, and it is not there. The sky is white like the earth, and it smells of yesterday. All this was tomorrow. All this was a hundred years from now. The sky is lemon and rose and lavender. The sky is the earth. The sky is white, and it is not there.

He wakes up. He walks back and forth between the table and the window. He sits down. He stands up. He walks back and forth between the bed and the chair. He lies down. He stares at the ceiling. He closes his eyes. He opens his eyes. He walks back and forth between the table and the window.

He finds a fresh sheet of paper. He lays it out on the table before him and writes these words with his pen.

It was. It will never be again. Remember.

REFERENCES

(Sources of quotations not mentioned in text)

91 "Israel Lichtenstein's Last Testament." *A Holocaust Reader*, edited by Lucy S. Dawidowicz. Behrman House. New York, 1976.

95 Flaubert. *The Letters of Gustave Flaubert*, selected, edited, and translated by Francis Steegmuller. Harvard University Press. Cambridge, 1979.

104 Marina Tsvetayeva. Quotations of translations by Elaine Feinstein. *Marina Tsvetayeva: Selected Poems*. Oxford University Press, 1971.

104 Gregory I. Altschuller, M.D. *Marina Tsvetayeva: A Physician's Memoir*. SUN. Volume IV, Number 3: Winter, 1980. New York.

107 Christopher Wright. *Rembrandt and His Art*. Galahad Books. New York, 1975.

108 Hölderlin. Prose quotations translated by Michael Hamburger. *Friedrich Hölderlin: Poems and Fragments*. University of Michigan Press. Ann Arbor, 1966.

109 Hölderlin. *To Zimmer*. Translated by John Riley and Tim Longville. *What I Own: Versions of Hölderlin*. Grosseteste Review Press, 1973.

143 B. = André du Bouchet. *Hölderlin Aujourd'hui*, a lecture delivered in Stuttgart, 1970.

146 Collodi. *The Adventures of Pinocchio*. Translated by Carol Della Chiesa. Macmillan. New York, 1925. All further quotations from this edition. Translations sometimes slightly adapted.

157 Edward A. Snow. *A Study of Vermeer*. University of California Press. Berkeley, 1979.

160 Van Gogh. *The Letters of Vincent Van Gogh*. Edited by Mark Roskill. Atheneum. New York, 1972.

165 Tolstoy. Ann Dunnigan's translation of *War and Peace*. New American Library. New York, 1968.

167 Freud. "The 'Uncanny.'" *On Creativity and the Unconscious*. Harper and Row. New York, 1958.

168 *The Thousand and One Nights*. All quotations from *The Portable Arabian Nights*. Translated by John Payne. Edited by Joseph Campbell. Viking. New York, 1952.

174 Dostoyevsky. *The Brothers Karamazov*. Translated by David Magarshack. Penguin. Baltimore, 1958.

175 Jim Harrison. Quoted in "The End of Cambodia?" by William Shawcross. *The New York Review of Books*. January 24, 1980.

177 Anne Frank. *The Diary of a Young Girl*. Doubleday. New York, 1952.

178 Quotations of commentaries on the Book of Jonah from "Jonah, or the Unfulfilled Prophecy" in *Four Strange Books of the Bible*, by Elias Bickerman. Schocken. New York, 1967.

181 Leibniz. *Monadology and Other Philosophical Essays*. Translated by Paul Schrecker and Anne Martin Schrecker. Bobbs-Merrill. Indianapolis, 1965.

183 Proust. *Swann's Way*. Translated by C.K. Scott Moncrieff. Random House. New York, 1928.

185 Freud. "The Relation of the Poet to Day-Dreaming." *On Creativity and the Unconscious*.

194 Nadezhda Mandelstam. *Hope Abandoned*. Translated by Max Hayward. Collins & Harvill. London, 1974.

THE RED NOTEBOOK

{1992}

———————

1

In 1972, a close friend of mine ran into trouble with the law. She was in Ireland that year, living in a small village not far from the town of Sligo. As it happened, I was visiting on the day a plain-clothes detective drove up to her cottage and presented her with a summons to appear in court. The charges were serious enough to require a lawyer. My friend asked around and was given a name, and the next morning we bicycled into town to meet with this person and discuss the case. To my astonishment, he worked for a firm called Argue and Phibbs.

This is a true story. If there are those who doubt me, I challenge them to visit Sligo and see for themselves if I have made it up or not. I have reveled in these names for the past twenty years, but even though I can prove that Argue and Phibbs were real men, the fact that the one name should have been coupled with the other (to form an even more delicious joke, an out-and-out sendup of the legal profession) is something I still find hard to believe.

According to my latest information (three or four years ago), the firm continues to do a thriving business.

2

The following year (1973), I was offered a job as caretaker of a farmhouse in the south of France. My friend's legal troubles were well behind her, and since our on-again off-again romance seemed to be on again, we decided to join forces and take the job together. We had both run out of money by then, and without this offer we would have been compelled to return to America—which neither one of us was prepared to do just yet.

It turned out to be a curious year. On the one hand, the place was beautiful: a large, eighteenth-century stone house bordered by vineyards on one side and a national forest on the other. The nearest village was two kilometers away, but it was inhabited by no more than forty people, none of whom was under sixty or seventy years old. It was an ideal spot for two young writers to spend a year, and L. and I both worked hard there, accomplishing more in that house than either one of us would have thought possible.

On the other hand, we lived on the brink of permanent catastrophe. Our employers, an American couple who lived in Paris, sent us a small monthly salary (fifty dollars), a gas allowance for the car, and money to feed the two Labrador retrievers who were part of the household. All in all, it was a generous arrangement. There was no rent to pay, and even if our salary fell short of what we needed to live on, it gave us a head start on each month's expenses. Our plan was to earn the rest by doing translations. Before leaving Paris and settling in the country, we had set up a number of jobs to see us through the year. What we had neglected to take into account was that publishers are often slow to pay their bills. We had also forgotten to consider that checks sent from one country to another can take weeks to clear, and that once they do, bank charges and exchange fees cut into the amounts of those checks. Since L. and I had left no margin for error or miscalculation, we often found ourselves in quite desperate straits.

I remember savage nicotine fits, my body numb with need as I scrounged among sofa cushions and crawled behind cupboards in search of loose coins. For eighteen centimes (about three and a half cents), you could buy a brand of cigarettes called Parisiennes, which were sold in packs of four. I remember feeding the dogs and thinking that they ate better than I did. I remember conversations with L. in which we seriously considered opening a can of dog food and eating it for dinner.

Our only other source of income that year came from a man

named James Sugar. (I don't mean to insist on metaphorical names, but facts are facts, and there's nothing I can do about it.) Sugar worked as a staff photographer for *National Geographic*, and he entered our lives because he was collaborating with one of our employers on an article about the region. He took pictures for several months, crisscrossing Provence in a rented car provided by his magazine, and whenever he was in our neck of the woods he would spend the night with us. Since the magazine also provided him with an expense account, he would very graciously slip us the money that had been allotted for his hotel costs. If I remember correctly, the sum came to fifty francs a night. In effect, L. and I became his private innkeepers, and since Sugar was an amiable man into the bargain, we were always glad to see him. The only problem was that we never knew when he was going to turn up. He never called in advance, and more often than not weeks would go by between his visits. We therefore learned not to count on Mr. Sugar. He would arrive out of nowhere, pulling up in front of the house in his shiny blue car, stay for a night or two, and then disappear again. Each time he left, we assumed that was the last time we would ever see him.

The worst moments came for us in the late winter and early spring. Checks failed to arrive, one of the dogs was stolen, and little by little we ate our way through the stockpile of food in the kitchen. In the end, we had nothing left but a bag of onions, a bottle of cooking oil, and a packaged pie crust that someone had bought before we ever moved into the house—a stale remnant from the previous summer. L. and I held out all morning and into the afternoon, but by two-thirty hunger had gotten the better of us, and so we went into the kitchen to prepare our last meal. Given the paucity of elements we had to work with, an onion pie was the only dish that made sense.

After our concoction had been in the oven for what seemed a sufficient length of time, we took it out, set it on the table, and dug in. Against all our expectations, we both found it delicious. I think we even went so far as to say that it was the best food we had ever tasted, but no doubt that was a ruse, a feeble attempt to keep our spirits up. Once we had chewed a little more, however, disappointment set in. Reluctantly—ever so reluctantly—we were forced to admit that the pie had not yet cooked through, that the center was still too cold to eat. There was nothing to be done but put it back in the oven for another ten or fifteen minutes. Considering how hungry we were, and considering that our salivary glands had just been activated, relinquishing the pie was not easy.

To stifle our impatience, we went outside for a brief stroll, thinking the time would pass more quickly if we removed ourselves from the good smells in the kitchen. As I remember it, we circled the house once, perhaps twice. Perhaps we drifted into a deep conversation about something (I can't remember), but however it happened, and however long we were gone, by the time we entered the house again the kitchen was filled with smoke. We rushed to the oven and pulled out the pie, but it was too late. Our meal was dead. It had been incinerated, burned to a charred and blackened mass, and not one morsel could be salvaged.

It sounds like a funny story now, but at the time it was anything but funny. We had fallen into a dark hole, and neither one of us could think of a way to get out. In all my years of struggling to be a man, I doubt there has ever been a moment when I felt less inclined to laugh or crack jokes. This was really the end, and it was a terrible and frightening place to be.

That was at four o'clock in the afternoon. Less than an hour later, the errant Mr. Sugar suddenly appeared, driving up to the house in a cloud of dust, gravel and dirt crunching all around him. If I think about it hard enough, I can still see the naive and goofy smile on his face as he bounced out of the car and said hello. It was a miracle. It was a genuine miracle, and I was there to witness it with my own eyes, to live it in my own flesh. Until that moment, I had thought those things happened only in books.

Sugar treated us to dinner that night in a two-star restaurant. We ate copiously and well, we emptied several bottles of wine, we laughed our heads off. And yet, delicious as that food must have been, I can't remember a thing about it. But I have never forgotten the taste of the onion pie.

3

Not long after I returned to New York (July 1974), a friend told me the following story. It is set in Yugoslavia, during what must have been the last months of the Second World War.

S.'s uncle was a member of a Serbian partisan group that fought against the Nazi occupation. One morning, he and his comrades woke to find themselves surrounded by German troops. They were holed up in a farmhouse somewhere in the country, a foot of snow lay on the ground, and there was no escape. Not knowing what else to do, the men decided to draw lots. Their plan was to burst out of the farmhouse one by one, dash through the snow, and see if they couldn't make it to safety. According to the results of the draw, S.'s uncle was supposed to go third.

He watched through the window as the first man ran out into the snow-covered field. There was a barrage of machine-gun fire from across the woods, and the man was cut down. A moment later, the second man ran out, and the same thing happened. The machine guns blasted, and he fell down dead in the snow.

Then it was my friend's uncle's turn. I don't know if he hesitated at the doorway, I don't know what thoughts were pounding through his head at that moment. The only thing I was told was that he started to run, charging through the snow for all he was worth. It seemed as if he ran forever. Then, suddenly, he felt pain in his leg. A second after that, an overpowering warmth spread through his body, and a second after that he lost consciousness.

When he woke up, he found himself lying on his back in a peasant's cart. He had no idea how much time had elapsed, no idea how he had been rescued. He had simply opened his eyes— and there he was, lying in a cart that some horse or mule was pulling down a country road, staring up at the back of a peasant's head. He studied the back of that head for several seconds, and then loud explosions began to erupt from the woods. Too weak to move, he kept looking at the back of the head, and suddenly it was gone. It just flew off the peasant's body, and where a moment before there had been a whole man, there was now a man without a head.

More noise, more confusion. Whether the horse went on pulling the cart or not I can't say, but within minutes, perhaps even seconds, a large contingent of Russian troops came rolling down the road. Jeeps, tanks, scores of soldiers. When the commanding officer took a look at S.'s uncle's leg, he quickly dispatched him to an infirmary that had been set up in the neighborhood. It was no more than a rickety wooden shack—a henhouse, maybe, or an outbuilding on some farm. There the Russian army doctor pronounced the leg past saving. It was too severely damaged, he said, and he was going to have to cut it off.

My friend's uncle began to scream. "Don't cut off my leg," he cried. "Please, I beg of you, don't cut off my leg!" But no one listened to him. The medics strapped him to the operating table, and the doctor picked up the saw. Just as he was about to pierce the skin of the leg, there was another explosion. The roof of the infirmary collapsed, the walls fell down, the entire place was obliterated. And once again, S.'s uncle lost consciousness.

When he woke up this time, he found himself lying in a bed. The sheets were clean and soft, there were pleasant smells in the room, and his leg was still attached to his body. A moment later, he was looking into the face of a beautiful young woman. She was smiling at him and feeding him broth with a spoon. With no knowledge of how it had happened, he had been rescued again and carried to another farmhouse. For several minutes after coming to, S.'s uncle wasn't sure if he was alive or dead. It seemed possible to him that he had woken up in heaven.

He stayed on in the house during his recovery and fell in love with the beautiful young woman, but nothing ever came of that romance. I wish I could say why, but S. never filled me in on the details. What I do know is that his uncle kept his leg—and that once the war was over, he moved to America to begin a new life. Somehow or other (the circumstances are obscure to me), he wound up as an insurance salesman in Chicago.

4

L. and I were married in 1974. Our son was born in 1977, but by the following year our marriage had ended. None of that is relevant now—except to set the scene for an incident that took place in the spring of 1980.

We were both living in Brooklyn then, about three or four blocks from each other, and our son divided his time between the two apartments. One morning, I had to stop by L.'s house to pick up Daniel and walk him to nursery school. I can't remember if I went inside the building or if Daniel came down the stairs himself, but I vividly recall that just as we were about to walk off together, L. opened the window of her third-floor apartment to throw me some money. Why she did that is also forgotten. Perhaps she wanted me to replenish a parking meter for her, perhaps I was supposed to do an errand, I don't know. All that remains is the open window and the image of a dime flying through the air. I see it with such clarity, it's almost as if I have studied photographs of that instant, as if it's part of a recurring dream I've had ever since.

But the dime hit the branch of a tree, and its downward arc into my hand was disrupted. It bounced off the tree, landed soundlessly somewhere nearby, and then it was gone. I remember bending down and searching the pavement, digging among the leaves and twigs at the base of the tree, but the dime was nowhere to be found.

I can place that event in early spring because I know that later the same day I attended a baseball game at Shea Stadium—the opening game of the season. A friend of mine had been offered tickets, and he had generously invited me to go along with him. I had never been to an opening game before, and I remember the occasion well.

We arrived early (something about collecting the tickets at a certain window), and as my friend went off to complete the transaction, I waited for him outside one of the entrances to the stadium. Not a single soul was around. I ducked into a little alcove to light a cigarette (a strong wind was blowing that day), and there, sitting on the ground not two inches from my feet, was a dime. I bent down, picked it up, and put it in my pocket. Ridiculous as it might sound, I felt certain that it was the same dime I had lost in Brooklyn that morning.

5

In my son's nursery school, there was a little girl whose parents were going through a divorce. I particularly liked her father, a struggling painter who earned his living by doing architectural renderings. His paintings were quite beautiful, I thought, but he never had much luck in convincing dealers to support his work. The one time he did have a show, the gallery promptly went out of business.

B. was not an intimate friend, but we enjoyed each other's company, and whenever I saw him I would return home with renewed admiration for his steadfastness and inner calm. He was not a man who grumbled or felt sorry for himself. However gloomy things had become for him in recent years (endless money problems, lack of artistic success, threats of eviction from his landlord, difficulties with his ex-wife), none of it seemed to throw him off course. He continued to paint with the same passion as ever, and unlike so many others, he never expressed any bitterness or envy toward less talented artists who were doing better than he was.

When he wasn't working on his own canvases, he would sometimes go to the Metropolitan Museum and make copies of the old masters. I remember a Caravaggio he once did that struck me as utterly remarkable. It wasn't a copy so much as a replica, an exact duplication of the original. On one of those visits to the museum, a Texas millionaire spotted B. at work and was so impressed that he commissioned him to do a copy of a Renoir painting—which he then presented to his fiancée as a gift.

B. was exceedingly tall (six-five or six-six), good-looking, and gentle in his manner—qualities that made him especially attractive to women. Once his divorce was behind him and he began to circulate again, he had no trouble finding female companions. I saw him only about two or three times a year, but each time I did, there was another woman in his life. All of them were obviously mad for him. You had only to watch them looking at B. to know how they felt, but for one reason or another, none of these affairs lasted very long.

After two or three years, B.'s landlord finally made good on his threats and evicted him from his loft. B. moved out of the city, and I lost touch with him.

Several more years went by, and then one night B. came back to town to attend a dinner party. My wife and I were also there, and since we knew that B. was about to get married, we asked him to tell us the story of how he had met his future wife.

About six months earlier, he said, he had been talking to a friend on the phone. This friend was worried about him, and after a while he began to scold B. for not having married again. You've been divorced for seven years now, he said, and in that time you could have settled down with any one of a dozen attractive and remarkable women. But no one is ever good enough for you, and you've turned them all away. What's wrong with you, B.? What in the world do you want?

There's nothing wrong with me, B. said. I just haven't found the right person, that's all.

At the rate you're going, you never will, the friend answered. I mean, have you ever met one woman who comes close to what you're looking for? Name one. I dare you to name just one.

Startled by his friend's vehemence, B. paused to consider the question carefully. Yes, he finally said, there was one. A woman by the name of E., whom he had known as a student at Harvard more than twenty years ago. But she had been involved with another man at the time, and he had been involved with another woman (his future ex-wife), and nothing had developed between them. He had no idea where E. was now, he said, but if he could meet someone like her, he knew he wouldn't hesitate to get married again.

That was the end of the conversation. Until mentioning her to his friend, B. hadn't thought about this woman in over ten years, but now that she had resurfaced in his mind, he had trouble thinking about anything else. For the next three or four days, he thought about her constantly, unable to shake the feeling that his one chance for happiness had been lost many years ago. Then, almost as if the intensity of these thoughts had sent a signal out into the world, the phone rang one night, and there was E. on the other end of the line.

B. kept her on the phone for more than three hours. He scarcely knew what he said to her, but he went on talking until past midnight, understanding that something momentous had happened and that he mustn't let her escape again.

After graduating from college, E. had joined a dance company, and for the past twenty years she had devoted herself exclusively to her career. She had never married, and now that she was about to retire as a performer, she was calling old friends from her past, trying to make contact with the world again. She had no family (her parents had been killed in a car crash when she was a small girl) and had been raised by two aunts, both of whom were now dead.

B. arranged to see her the next night. Once they were together, it didn't take long for him to discover that his feelings for her were just as strong as he had imagined. He fell in love with her all over again, and several weeks later they were engaged to be married.

To make the story even more perfect, it turned out that E. was independently wealthy. Her aunts had been rich, and after they died she had inherited all their money—which meant that not only had B. found true love, but the crushing money problems that had plagued him for so many years had suddenly vanished. All in one fell swoop.

A year or two after the wedding, they had a child. At last report, mother, father, and baby were doing just fine.

6

In much the same spirit, although spanning a shorter period of time (several months as opposed to twenty years), another friend, R., told me of a certain out-of-the-way book he had been trying to locate without success, scouring bookstores and catalogues for what was supposed to be a remarkable work that he very much wanted to read, and how, one afternoon as he made his way through the city, he took a shortcut through Grand Central Station, walked up the staircase that leads to Vanderbilt Avenue, and caught sight of a young woman standing by the marble railing with a book in front of her: the same book he had been trying so desperately to track down.

Although he is not someone who normally speaks to strangers, R. was too stunned by the coincidence to remain silent. "Believe it or not," he said to the young woman, "I've been looking everywhere for that book."

"It's wonderful," the young woman answered. "I just finished reading it."

"Do you know where I could find another copy?" R. asked. "I can't tell you how much it would mean to me."

"This one is for you," the woman answered.

"But it's yours," R. said.

"It *was* mine," the woman said, "but now I'm finished with it. I came here today to give it to you."

7

Twelve years ago, my wife's sister went off to live in Taiwan. Her intention was to study Chinese (which she now speaks with breathtaking fluency) and to support herself by giving English lessons to native Chinese speakers in Taipei. That was approximately one year before I met my wife, who was then a graduate student at Columbia University.

One day, my future sister-in-law was talking to an American friend, a young woman who had also gone to Taipei to study Chinese. The conversation came around to the subject of their families back home, which in turn led to the following exchange:

"I have a sister who lives in New York," my future sister-in-law said.

"So do I," her friend answered.

"My sister lives on the Upper West Side."

"So does mine."

"My sister lives on West 109th Street."

"Believe it or not, so does mine."

"My sister lives at 309 West 109th Street."

"So does mine!"

"My sister lives on the second floor of 309 West 109th Street."

The friend took a deep breath and said, "I know this sounds crazy, but so does mine."

It is scarcely possible for two cities to be farther apart than Taipei and New York. They are at opposite ends of the earth, separated by a distance of more than ten thousand miles, and when it is day in one it is night in the other. As the two young women in Taipei marveled over the astounding connection they had just uncovered, they realized that their two sisters were probably asleep at that moment. On the same floor of the same building in northern Manhattan, each one was sleeping in her own apartment, unaware of the conversation that was taking place about them on the other side of the world.

Although they were neighbors, it turned out that the two sisters in New York did not know each other. When they finally met (two years later), neither one of them was living in that building anymore.

Siri and I were married then. One evening, on our way to an appointment somewhere, we happened to stop in at a bookstore on Broadway to browse for a few minutes. We must have wandered into different aisles, and because Siri wanted to show me something, or because I wanted to show her something (I can't remember), one of us spoke the other's name out loud. A second later, a woman came rushing up to us. "You're Paul Auster and Siri Hustvedt, aren't you?" she said. "Yes," we said, "that's exactly who we are. How did you know that?" The woman then explained that her sister and Siri's sister had been students together in Taiwan.

The circle had been closed at last. Since that evening in the bookstore ten years ago, this woman has been one of our best and most loyal friends.

8

Three summers ago, a letter turned up in my mailbox. It came in a white oblong envelope and was addressed to someone whose name was unfamiliar to me: Robert M. Morgan of Seattle, Washington. Various post office markings were stamped across the front: *Not Deliverable, Unable to Forward, Return to Writer.* Mr. Morgan's name had been crossed out with a pen, and beside it someone had written *Not at this address.* Drawn in the same blue ink, an arrow pointed to the upper-left-hand corner of the envelope, accompanied by the words *Return to sender.* Assuming that the post office had made a mistake, I checked the upper-left-hand corner to see who the sender was. There, to my absolute bewilderment, I discovered my own name and my own address. Not only that, but this information was printed on a custom-made address label (one of those labels you can order in packs of two hundred from advertisements on matchbook covers). The spelling of my name was correct, the address was my address—and yet the fact was (and still is) that I have never owned or ordered a set of printed address labels in my life.

Inside, there was a single-spaced typewritten letter that began: "Dear Robert, In response to your letter dated July 15, 1989, I can only say that, like other authors, I often receive letters concerning my work." Then, in a bombastic, pretentious style, riddled with quotations from French philosophers and oozing with a tone of conceit and self-satisfaction, the letter-writer went on to praise "Robert" for the ideas he had developed about one of my books in a college course on the contemporary novel. It was a contemptible letter, the kind of letter I would never dream of writing to anyone, and yet it was signed with my name. The handwriting did not resemble mine, but that was small comfort. Someone was out there trying to impersonate me, and as far as I know he still is.

One friend suggested that this was an example of "mail art." Knowing that the letter could not be delivered to Robert Morgan (since there was no such person), the author of the letter was actually addressing his remarks to me. But that would imply an unwarranted faith in the U.S. Postal Service, and I doubt that someone who would go to the trouble of ordering address labels in my name and then sitting down to write such an arrogant, high-flown letter would leave anything to chance. Or would he? Perhaps the smart alecks of this world believe that everything will always go their way.

I have scant hope of ever getting to the bottom of this little mystery. The prankster did a good job of covering his tracks, and he has not been heard from since. What puzzles me about my own behavior is that I have not thrown away the letter, even though it continues to give me chills every time I look at it. A sensible man would have tossed the thing in the garbage. Instead, for reasons I do not understand, I have kept it on my work table for the past three years, allowing it to become a permanent fixture among my pens and notebooks and erasers. Perhaps I keep it there as a monument to my own folly. Perhaps it is a way to remind myself that I know nothing, that the world I live in will go on escaping me forever.

9

One of my closest friends is a French poet by the name of C. We have known each other for more than twenty years now, and while we don't see each other often (he lives in Paris and I live in New York), the bond between us remains strong. It is a fraternal bond, somehow, as if in some former life we had actually been brothers.

C. is a man of manifold contradictions. He is both open to the world and shut off from it, a charismatic figure with scores of friends everywhere (legendary for his kindness, his humor, his sparkling conversation) and yet someone who has been wounded by life, who struggles to perform the simple tasks that most other people take for granted. An exceptionally gifted poet and thinker about poetry, C. is nevertheless hampered by frequent writing blocks, streaks of morbid self-doubt, and surprisingly (for someone who is so generous, so profoundly lacking in mean-spiritedness), a capacity for long-standing grudges and quarrels, usually over some trifle or abstract principle. No one is more universally admired than C., no one has more talent, no one so readily commands the center of attention, and yet he has always done everything in his power to marginalize himself. Since his separation from his wife many years ago, he has lived alone in a number of small, one-room apartments, subsisting on almost no money and only fitful bouts of employment, publishing little, and refusing to write a single word of criticism, even though he reads everything and knows more about contemporary poetry than anyone in France. To those of us who love him (and we are many), C. is often a cause of concern. To the degree that we respect him and care about his well-being, we also worry about him.

He had a rough childhood. I can't say to what extent that explains anything, but the facts should not be overlooked. His father apparently ran off with another woman when C. was a little boy, and after that my friend grew up with his mother, an only child with no family life to speak of. I have never met C.'s mother, but by all accounts she is a bizarre character. She went through a series of love affairs during C.'s childhood and adolescence, each with a man younger than the man before him. By the time C. left home to enter the army at the age of twenty-one, his mother's boyfriend was scarcely older than he was. In more recent years, the central purpose of her life has been a campaign to promote the canonization of a certain Italian priest (whose name eludes me now). She has besieged the Catholic authorities with countless letters defending the holiness of this man, and at one point she even commissioned an artist to create a life-size statue of him—which now stands in her front yard as an enduring testament to her cause.

Although not a father himself, C. became a kind of pseudo-father seven or eight years ago. After a falling out with his girlfriend (during which they temporarily broke up), his girlfriend had a brief affair with another man and became pregnant. The affair ended almost at once, but she decided to have the baby on her own. A little girl was born, and even though C. is not her real father, he has devoted himself to her since the day of her birth and adores her as if she were his own flesh and blood.

One day about four years ago, C. happened to be visiting a friend. In the apartment there was a *Minitel,* a small computer given out for free by the French telephone company. Among other things, the *Minitel* contains the address and phone number of every person in France. As C. sat there playing with his friend's new machine, it suddenly occurred to him to look up his father's address. He found it in Lyon. When he returned home later that day, he stuffed one of his books into an envelope and sent it off to the address in Lyon—initiating the first contact with his father in over forty years. None of it made any sense to him. Until he found himself doing these things, it had never even crossed his mind that he wanted to do them.

That same night, he ran into another friend in a café—a woman psychoanalyst—and told her about these strange, unpremeditated acts. It was as if he had felt his father calling out to him, he said, as if some uncanny force had unleashed itself inside him. Considering that he had absolutely no memories of the man, he couldn't even begin to guess when they had last seen each other.

The woman thought for a moment and said, "How old is L.?," referring to C.'s girlfriend's daughter.

"Three and a half," C. answered.

"I can't be sure," the woman said, "but I'd be willing to bet that you were three and a half the last time you saw your father. I say that because you love L. so much. Your identification with her is very strong, and you're reliving your life through her."

Several days after that, there was a reply from Lyon—a warm and perfectly gracious letter from C.'s father. After thanking C. for the book, he went on to tell him how proud he was to learn that his son had grown up to become a writer. By pure coincidence, he added, the package had been mailed on his birthday, and he was moved by the symbolism of the gesture.

None of this tallied with the stories C. had heard throughout his childhood. According to his mother, his father was a monster of selfishness who had walked out on her for a "slut" and had never wanted anything to do with his son. C. had believed these stories, and therefore he had shied away from any contact with his father. Now, on the strength of this letter, he no longer knew what to believe.

He decided to write back. The tone of his response was guarded, but nevertheless it was a response. Within days he received another reply, and this second letter was just as warm and gracious as the first had been. C. and his father began a correspondence. It went on for a month or two, and eventually C. began to consider traveling down to Lyon to meet his father face to face.

Before he could make any definite plans, he received a letter from his father's wife informing him that his father was dead. He had been in ill health for the past several years, she wrote, but the recent exchange of letters with C. had given him great happiness, and his last days had been filled with optimism and joy.

It was at this moment that I first heard about the incredible reversals that had taken place in C.'s life. Sitting on the train from Paris to Lyon (on his way to visit his "stepmother" for the first time), he wrote me a letter that sketched out the story of the past month. His handwriting reflected each jolt of the tracks, as if the speed of the train were an exact image of the thoughts racing through his head. As he put it somewhere in that letter: "I feel as if I've become a character in one of your novels."

His father's wife could not have been friendlier to him during that visit. Among other things, C. learned that his father had suffered a heart attack on the morning of his last birthday (the same day that C. had looked up his address on the *Minitel*) and that, yes, C. had been precisely three and a half years old at the time of his parents' divorce. His stepmother then went on to tell him the story of his life from his father's point of view—which contradicted everything his mother had ever told him. In this version, it was his mother who had walked out on his father; it was his mother who had forbidden his father from seeing him; it was his mother who had broken his father's heart. She told C. how his father would come around to the schoolyard when he was a little boy to look at him through the fence. C. remembered that man, but not knowing who he was, he had been afraid.

C.'s life had now become two lives. There was Version A and Version B, and both of them were his story. He had lived them both in equal measure, two truths that canceled each other out, and all along, without even knowing it, he had been stranded in the middle.

His father had owned a small stationery store (the usual stock of paper and writing materials, along with a rental library of popular books). The business had earned him a living, but not much more than that, and the estate he left behind was quite modest. The numbers are unimportant, however. What counts is that C.'s stepmother (by then an old woman) insisted on splitting the money with him half and half. There was nothing in the will that required her to do that, and morally speaking she needn't have parted with a single penny of her husband's savings. She did it because she wanted to, because it made her happier to share the money than to keep it for herself.

10

In thinking about friendship, particularly about how some friendships endure and others don't, I am reminded of the fact that in all my years of driving I have had just four flat tires, and that on each of these occasions the same person was in the car with me (in three different countries, spread out over a period of eight or nine years). J. was a college friend, and though there was always an edge of unease and conflict in our relations, for a time we were close. One spring while we were still undergraduates, we borrowed my father's ancient station wagon and drove up into the wilderness of Quebec. The seasons change more slowly in that part of the world, and winter was not yet over. The first flat tire did not present a problem (we were equipped with a spare), but when a second tire blew out less than an hour later, we were stranded in the bleak and frigid countryside for most of the day. At the time, I shrugged off the incident as a piece of bad luck, but four or five years later, when J. came to France to visit the house where L.

and I were working as caretakers (in miserable condition, inert with depression and self-pity, unaware that he was overstaying his welcome with us), the same thing happened. We went to Aix-en-Provence for the day (a drive of about two hours), and coming back later that night on a dark, back-country road, we had another flat. Just a coincidence, I thought, and then pushed the event out of my mind. But then, four years after that, in the waning months of my marriage to L., J. came to visit us again—this time in New York State, where L. and I were living with the infant Daniel. At one point, J. and I climbed into the car to go to the store and shop for dinner. I pulled the car out of the garage, turned it around in the rutted dirt driveway, and advanced to the edge of the road to look left, right, and left before going on. Just then, as I waited for a car to pass by, I heard the unmistakable hiss of escaping air. Another tire had gone flat, and this time we hadn't even left the house. J. and I both laughed, of course, but the truth is that our friendship never really recovered from that fourth flat tire. I'm not saying that the flat tires were responsible for our drifting apart, but in some perverse way they were an emblem of how things had always stood between us, the sign of some impalpable curse. I don't want to exaggerate, but even now I can't quite bring myself to reject those flat tires as meaningless. For the fact is that J. and I have lost contact, and we have not spoken to each other in more than ten years.

11

In 1990, I found myself in Paris again for a few days. One afternoon, I stopped by the office of a friend to say hello and was introduced to a Czech woman in her late forties or early fifties—an art historian who happened to be a friend of my friend. She was an attractive and vivacious person, I remember, but since she was on the point of leaving when I walked in, I spent no more than five or ten minutes in her company. As usually happens in such situations, we talked about nothing of any importance: a town we both knew in America, the subject of a book she was reading, the weather. Then we shook hands, she walked out the door, and I have never seen her again.

After she was gone, the friend I had come to visit leaned back in her chair and said, "Do you want to hear a good story?"

"Of course," I said, "I'm always interested in good stories."

"I like my friend very much," she continued, "so don't get the wrong idea. I'm not trying to spread gossip about her. It's just that I feel you have a right to know this."

"Are you sure?"

"Yes, I'm sure. But you have to promise me one thing. If you ever write the story, you mustn't use anyone's name."

"I promise," I said.

And so my friend let me in on the secret. From start to finish, it couldn't have taken her more than three minutes to tell the story I am about to tell now.

The woman I had just met was born in Prague during the war. When she was still a baby, her father was captured, impressed into the German army, and shipped off to the Russian front. She and her mother never heard from him again. They received no letters, no news to tell them if he was alive or dead, nothing. The war just swallowed him up, and he vanished without a trace.

Years passed. The girl grew up. She completed her studies at the university and became a professor of art history. According to my friend, she ran into trouble with the government during the Soviet crackdown in the late sixties, but exactly what kind of trouble was never made clear to me. Given the stories I know about what happened to other people during that time, it is not very difficult to guess.

At some point, she was allowed to begin teaching again. In one of her classes, there was an exchange student from East Germany. She and this young man fell in love, and eventually they were married.

Not long after the wedding, a telegram arrived announcing the death of her husband's father. The next day, she and her husband traveled to East Germany to attend the funeral. Once there, in whatever town or city it was, she learned that her now dead father-in-law had been born in Czechoslovakia. During the war he had been captured by the Nazis, impressed into the German army, and shipped off to the Russian front. By some miracle, he had managed to survive. Instead of returning to Czechoslovakia after the war, however, he had settled in Germany under a new name, had married a German woman, and had lived there with his new family until the day of his death. The war had given him a chance to start all over again, and it seems that he had never looked back.

When my friend's friend asked what this man's name had been in Czechoslovakia, she understood that he was her father.

Which meant, of course, that insofar as her husband's father was the same man, the man she had married was also her brother.

12

One afternoon many years ago, my father's car stalled at a red light. A terrible storm was raging, and at the exact moment his engine went dead, lightning struck a large tree by the side of the road. The trunk of the tree split in two, and as my father struggled to get the car started again (unaware that the upper half of the tree was about to fall), the driver of the car behind him, seeing what was about to happen, put his foot on the accelerator and pushed my father's car through the intersection. An instant later, the tree came crashing to the ground, landing in the very spot where my father's car had just been. What was nearly the end of him proved to be no more than a close call, a brief episode in the ongoing story of his life.

A year or two after that, my father was working on the roof of a building in Jersey City. Somehow or other (I wasn't there to witness it), he slipped off the edge and started falling to the ground. Once again he was headed for certain disaster, and once again he was saved. A clothesline broke his fall, and he walked away from the accident with only a few bumps and bruises. Not even a concussion. Not a single broken bone.

That same year, our neighbors across the street hired two men to paint their house. One of the workers fell off the roof and was killed.

The little girl who lived in that house happened to be my sister's best friend. One winter night, the two of them went to a costume party (they were six or seven years old, and I was nine or ten). It had been arranged that my father would pick them up after the party, and when the time came I went along to keep him company in the car. It was bitter cold that night, and the roads were covered with treacherous sheets of ice. My father drove carefully, and we made the journey back and forth without incident. As we pulled up in front of the girl's house, however, a number of unlikely events occurred all at once.

My sister's friend was dressed as a fairy princess. To complete the outfit, she had borrowed a pair of her mother's high heels, and because her feet swam in those shoes, every step she took was turned into an adventure. My father stopped the car and climbed out to accompany her to the front door. I was in the back with the girls, and in order to let my sister's friend out, I had to get out first. I remember standing on the curb as she disentangled herself from the seat, and just as she stepped into the open air, I noticed that the car was rolling slowly in reverse—either because of the ice or because my father had forgotten to engage the emergency brake (I don't know)—but before I could tell my father what was happening, my sister's friend touched the curb with her mother's high heels and slipped. She went skidding under the car—which was still moving—and there she was, about to be crushed to death by the wheels of my father's Chevy. As I remember it, she didn't make a sound. Without pausing to think, I bent down from the curb, grabbed hold of her right hand, and in one quick gesture yanked her to the sidewalk. An instant later, my father finally noticed that the car was moving. He jumped back into the driver's seat, stepped on the brake, and brought the machine to a halt. From start to finish, the whole chain of misadventures couldn't have taken more than eight or ten seconds.

For years afterward, I walked around feeling that this had been my finest moment. I had actually saved someone's life, and in retrospect I was always astonished by how quickly I had acted, by how sure my movements had been at the critical juncture. I saw the rescue in my mind again and again; again and again I relived the sensation of pulling that little girl out from under the car.

About two years after that night, our family moved to another house. My sister fell out of touch with her friend, and I myself did not see her for another fifteen years.

It was June, and my sister and I had both come back to town for a short visit. Just by chance, her old friend dropped by to say hello. She was all grown up now, a young woman of twenty-two who had graduated from college earlier that month, and I must say that I felt some pride in seeing that she had made it to adulthood in one piece. In a casual sort of way, I mentioned the night I had pulled her out from under the car. I was curious to know how well she remembered her brush with death, but from the look on her face when I asked the question, it was clear that she remembered nothing. A blank stare. A slight frown. A shrug. She remembered nothing!

I realized then that she hadn't known the car was moving. She hadn't even known that she was in danger. The whole incident had taken place in a flash: ten seconds of her life, an interval of no account, and none of it had left the slightest mark on her. For me, on the other hand, those seconds had been a defining experience, a singular event in my internal history.

Most of all, it stuns me to acknowledge that I am talking about something that happened in 1956 or 1957—and that the little girl of that night is now over forty years old.

13

My first novel was inspired by a wrong number. I was alone in my apartment in Brooklyn one afternoon, sitting at my desk and trying to work when the telephone rang. If I am not mistaken, it was the spring of 1980, not many days after I found the dime outside Shea Stadium.

I picked up the receiver, and the man on the other end asked if he was talking to the Pinkerton Agency. I told him no, he had dialed the wrong number, and hung up. Then I went back to work and promptly forgot about the call.

The next afternoon, the telephone rang again. It turned out to be the same person asking the same question I had been asked the day before: "Is this the Pinkerton Agency?" Again I said no, and again I hung up. This time, however, I started thinking about what would have happened if I had said yes. What if I had pretended to be a detective from the Pinkerton Agency? I wondered. What if I had actually taken on the case?

To tell the truth, I felt that I had squandered a rare opportunity. If the man ever called again, I told myself, I would at least talk to him a little bit and try to find out what was going on. I waited for the telephone to ring again, but the third call never came.

After that, wheels started turning in my head, and little by little an entire world of possibilities opened up to me. When I sat down to write *City of Glass* a year later, the wrong number had been transformed into the crucial event of the book, the mistake that sets the whole story in motion. A man named Quinn receives a phone call from someone who wants to talk to Paul Auster, the private detective. Just as I did, Quinn tells the caller he has dialed the wrong number. It happens again on the next night, and again Quinn hangs up. Unlike me, however, Quinn is given another chance. When the phone rings again on the third night, he plays along with the caller and takes on the case. Yes, he says, I'm Paul Auster—and at that moment the madness begins.

Most of all, I wanted to remain faithful to my original impulse. Unless I stuck to the spirit of what had really happened, I felt there wouldn't have been any purpose to writing the book. That meant implicating myself in the action of the story (or at least someone who resembled me, who bore my name), and it also meant writing about detectives who were not detectives, about impersonation, about mysteries that cannot be solved. For better or worse, I felt I had no choice.

All well and good. I finished the book ten years ago, and since then I have gone on to occupy myself with other projects, other ideas, other books. Less than two months ago, however, I learned that books are never finished, that it is possible for stories to go on writing themselves without an author.

I was alone in my apartment in Brooklyn that afternoon, sitting at my desk and trying to work when the telephone rang. This was a different apartment from the one I had in 1980—a different apartment with a different telephone number. I picked up the receiver, and the man on the other end asked if he could speak to Mr. Quinn. He had a Spanish accent and I did not recognize the voice. For a moment I thought it might be one of my friends trying to pull my leg. "Mr. Quinn?" I said. "Is this some kind of joke or what?"

No, it wasn't a joke. The man was in dead earnest. He had to talk to Mr. Quinn, and would I please put him on the line. Just to make sure, I asked him to spell out the name. The caller's accent was quite thick, and I was hoping that he wanted to talk to Mr. Queen. But no such luck. "Q-U-I-N-N," the man answered. I suddenly grew scared, and for a moment or two I couldn't get any words out of my mouth. "I'm sorry," I said at last, "there's no Mr. Quinn here. You've dialed the wrong number." The man apologized for disturbing me, and then we both hung up.

This really happened. Like everything else I have set down in this red notebook, it is a true story.

WHY WRITE?

{1995}

1

A German friend tells of the circumstances that preceded the births of her two daughters.

Nineteen years ago, hugely pregnant and already several weeks past due, A. sat down on the sofa in her living room and turned on the television set. As luck would have it, the opening credits of a film were just coming on screen. It was *The Nun's Story*, a 1950s Hollywood drama starring Audrey Hepburn. Glad for the distraction, A. settled in to watch the movie and immediately got caught up in it. Halfway through, she went into labor. Her husband drove her to the hospital, and she never learned how the film turned out.

Three years later, pregnant with her second child, A. sat down on the sofa and turned on the television set once again. Once again a film was playing, and once again it was *The Nun's Story* with Audrey Hepburn. Even more remarkable (and A. was very emphatic about this point), she had tuned in to the film at the precise moment where she had left off three years earlier. This time she was able to see the film through to the end. Less than fifteen minutes later, her water broke, and she went off to the hospital to give birth for the second time.

These two daughters are A.'s only children. The first labor was extremely difficult (my friend nearly didn't make it and was ill for many months afterward), but the second delivery went smoothly, with no complications of any kind.

2

Five years ago, I spent the summer with my wife and children in Vermont, renting an old, isolated farmhouse on the top of a mountain. One day, a woman from the next town stopped by to visit with her two children, a girl of four and a boy of eighteen months. My daughter, Sophie, had just turned three, and she and the girl enjoyed playing with each other. My wife and I sat down in the kitchen with our guest, and the children ran off to amuse themselves.

Five minutes later, there was a loud crash. The little boy had wandered into the front hall at the other end of the house, and since my wife had put a vase of flowers in that hall just two hours earlier, it wasn't difficult to guess what had happened. I didn't even have to look to know that the floor was covered with broken glass and pools of water—along with the stems and petals of a dozen scattered flowers.

I was annoyed. Goddamn kids, I said to myself. Goddamn people with their goddamn clumsy kids. Who gave them the right to drop by without calling first?

I told my wife that I'd clean up the mess, and so while she and our visitor continued their conversation, I gathered up a broom, a dustpan, and some towels and marched off to the front of the house.

My wife had put the flowers on a wooden trunk that sat just below the staircase railing. This staircase was especially steep and narrow, and there was a large window not more than a yard from the bottom step. I mention this geography because it's important. Where things were has everything to do with what happened next.

I was about half finished with the clean-up job when my daughter rushed out from her room onto the second-floor landing. I was close enough to the foot of the stairs to catch a glimpse of her (a couple of steps back and she would have been blocked from view), and in that brief moment I saw that she had that high-spirited, utterly happy expression on her face that has filled my middle age with such overpowering gladness. Then, an instant later, before I could even say hello, she tripped. The toe of her sneaker had caught on the landing, and just like that, without any cry or warning, she was sailing through the air. I don't mean to suggest that she was falling or tumbling or bouncing down the steps. I mean to say that she was flying. The impact of the stumble had launched her into space, and from the trajectory of her flight I could see that she was heading straight for the window.

What did I do? I don't know what I did. I was on the wrong side of the banister when I saw her trip, but by the time she was midway between the landing and the window, I was standing on the bottom step of the staircase. How did I get there? It was no more than a question of several feet, but it hardly seems possible to cover that distance in that amount of time—which is next to no time at all. Nevertheless, I was there, and the moment I got there I looked up, opened my arms, and caught her.

3

I was fourteen. For the third year in a row, my parents had sent me to a summer camp in New York State. I spent the bulk of my time playing basketball and baseball, but as it was a co-ed camp, there were other activities as well: evening "socials," the first awkward grapplings with girls, panty raids, the usual adolescent shenanigans. I also remember smoking cheap cigars on the sly, "frenching" beds, and massive water-balloon fights.

None of this is important. I simply want to underscore what a vulnerable age fourteen can be. No longer a child, not yet an adult, you bounce back and forth between who you were and who you are about to become. In my own case, I was still young enough to think that I had a legitimate shot at playing in the Major Leagues, but old enough to be questioning the existence of God. I had read the Communist Manifesto, and yet I still enjoyed watching Saturday morning cartoons. Every time I saw my face in the mirror, I seemed to be looking at someone else.

There were sixteen or eighteen boys in my group. Most of us had been together for several years, but a couple of newcomers had also joined us that summer. One was named Ralph. He was a quiet kid without much enthusiasm for dribbling basketballs or hitting the cut-off man, and while no one gave him a particularly hard time, he had trouble blending in. He had flunked a couple of subjects that year, and most of his free periods were spent being tutored by one of the counselors. It was a little sad, and I felt sorry for him—but not too sorry, not sorry enough to lose any sleep over it.

Our counselors were all New York college students from Brooklyn and Queens. Wise-cracking basketball players, future dentists, accountants, and teachers, city kids to their very bones. Like most true New Yorkers, they persisted in calling the ground the "floor," even when all that was under their feet was grass, pebbles, and dirt. The trappings of traditional summer camp life were as alien to them as the I.R.T. is to an Iowa farmer. Canoes, lanyards, mountain climbing, pitching tents, singing around the campfire were nowhere to be found in the inventory of their concerns. They could drill us on the finer points of setting picks and boxing out for rebounds, but otherwise they mostly horsed around and told jokes.

Imagine our surprise, then, when one afternoon our counselor announced that we were going for a hike in the woods. He had been seized by an inspiration and wasn't going to let anyone talk him out of it. Enough basketball, he said. We're surrounded by nature, and it's time we took advantage of it and started acting like real campers—or words to that effect. And so, after the rest period that followed lunch, the whole gang of sixteen or eighteen boys along with two or three counselors set off into the woods.

It was late July, 1961. Everyone was in a fairly buoyant mood, I remember, and half an hour or so into the trek most people agreed that the outing had been a good idea. No one had a compass, of course, or the slightest clue as to where we were going, but we were all enjoying ourselves, and if we happened to get lost, what difference would that make? Sooner or later, we'd find our way back.

Then it began to rain. At first it was barely noticeable, a few light drops falling between the leaves and branches, nothing to worry about. We walked on, unwilling to let a little water spoil our fun, but a couple of minutes later it started coming down in earnest. Everyone got soaked, and the counselors decided we should turn around and head back. The only problem was that no one knew where the camp was. The woods were thick, dense with clusters of trees and thorn-studded bushes, and we had woven our way this way and that, abruptly shifting directions in order to move on. To add to the confusion, it was becoming hard to see. The woods were dark to begin with, but with the rain falling and the sky turning black, it felt more like night than three or four in the afternoon.

Then the thunder started. And after the thunder, the lightning started. The storm was directly on top of us, and it turned out to be the summer storm to end all summer storms. I have never seen weather like that before or since. The rain poured down on us so hard that it actually hurt; each time the thunder exploded, you could feel the noise vibrating inside your body. Immediately after that, the lightning would come, dancing around us like spears. It was as if weapons had materialized out of thin air: a sudden flash that turned everything a bright, ghostly white. Trees were struck, and the branches would begin to smolder. Then it would go dark again for a moment, there would be another crash in the sky, and the lightning would return in a different spot.

The lightning was what scared us, of course. It would have been stupid not to be scared, and in our panic we tried to run away from it. But the storm was too big, and everywhere we went we were met by more lightning. It was a helter-skelter stampede, a headlong rush in circles. Then, suddenly, someone spotted a clearing in the woods. A brief dispute broke out over whether it was safer to go into the open or continue to stand under the trees. The voice arguing for the open won, and we all ran in the direction of the clearing.

It was a small meadow, most likely a pasture that belonged to a local farm, and to get to it we had to crawl under a barbed-wire fence. One by one, we got down on our bellies and inched our way through. I was in the middle of the line, directly behind Ralph. Just as he went under the barbed wire, there was another flash of lightning. I was two or three feet away, but because of the rain pounding against my eyelids, I had trouble making out what happened. All I knew was that Ralph had stopped moving. I figured that he had been stunned, so I crawled past him under the fence. Once I was on the other side, I took hold of his arm and dragged him through.

I don't know how long we stayed in that field. An hour, I would guess, and the whole time we were there the rain and thunder and lightning continued to crash down upon us. It was a storm ripped from the pages of the Bible, and it went on and on and on, as if it would never end.

Two or three boys were hit by something—perhaps by lightning, perhaps by the shock of lightning as it struck the ground near them—and the meadow began to fill with their moans. Other boys wept and prayed. Still others, fear in their voices, tried to give sensible advice. Get rid of everything metal, they said, metal attracts the lightning. We all took off our belts and threw them away from us.

I don't remember saying anything. I don't remember crying. Another boy and I kept ourselves busy trying to take care of Ralph. He was still unconscious. We rubbed his hands and arms, we held down his tongue so he wouldn't swallow it, we told him to hang in there. After a while, his skin began to take on a bluish tinge. His body seemed colder to my touch, but in spite of the mounting evidence, it never once occurred to me that he wasn't going to come around. I was only fourteen years old, after all, and what did I know? I had never seen a dead person before.

It was the barbed wire that did it, I suppose. The other boys hit by the lightning went numb, felt pain in their limbs for an hour or so, and then recovered. But Ralph had been under the fence when the lightning struck, and he had been electrocuted on the spot.

Later on, when they told me he was dead, I learned that there was an eight-inch burn across his back. I remember trying to absorb this news and telling myself that life would never feel the same to me again. Strangely enough, I didn't think about how I had been right next to him when it happened. I didn't think, One or two seconds later, and it would have been me. What I thought about was holding his tongue and looking down at his teeth. His mouth had been set in a slight grimace, and with his lips partly open, I had spent an hour looking down at the tips of his teeth. Thirty-four years later, I still remember them. And his half-closed, half-open eyes. I remember those, too.

4

Not many years ago, I received a letter from a woman who lives in Brussels. In it, she told me the story of a friend of hers, a man she has known since childhood.

In 1940, this man joined the Belgian army. When the country fell to the Germans later that year, he was captured and put in a prisoner-of-war camp. He remained there until the war ended in 1945.

Prisoners were allowed to correspond with Red Cross workers back in Belgium. The man was arbitrarily assigned a pen pal— a Red Cross nurse from Brussels—and for the next five years he and this woman exchanged letters every month. Over the course of time they became fast friends. At a certain point (I'm not exactly sure how long this took), they understood that something more than friendship had developed between them. The correspondence went on, growing more intimate with each exchange, and at last they declared their love for each other. Was such a thing possible? They had never seen each other, had never spent a minute in each other's company.

After the war was over, the man was released from prison and returned to Brussels. He met the nurse, the nurse met him, and neither was disappointed. A short time later, they were married.

Years went by. They had children, they grew older, the world became a slightly different world. Their son completed his studies in Belgium and went off to do graduate work in Germany. At the university there, he fell in love with a young German woman. He wrote his parents and told them that he intended to marry her.

The parents on both sides couldn't have been happier for their children. The two families arranged to meet, and on the appointed day the German family showed up at the house of the Belgian family in Brussels. As the German father walked into the living room and the Belgian father rose to welcome him, the two men looked into each other's eyes and recognized each other. Many years had passed, but neither one was in any doubt as to who the other was. At one time in their lives, they had seen each other every day. The German father had been a guard in the prison camp where the Belgian father had spent the war.

As the woman who wrote me the letter hastened to add, there was no bad blood between them. However monstrous the German regime might have been, the German father had done nothing during those five years to turn the Belgian father against him.

Be that as it may, these two men are now the best of friends. The greatest joy in their lives is the grandchildren they have in common.

5

I was eight years old. At that moment in my life, nothing was more important to me than baseball. My team was the New York Giants, and I followed the doings of those men in the black-and-orange caps with all the devotion of a true believer. Even now, remembering that team which no longer exists, that played in a ballpark which no longer exists, I can reel off the names of nearly every player on the roster. Alvin Dark, Whitey Lockman, Don Mueller, Johnny Antonelli, Monte Irvin, Hoyt Wilhelm. But none was greater, none more perfect or more deserving of worship than Willie Mays, the incandescent Say-Hey Kid.

That spring, I was taken to my first big-league game. Friends of my parents had box seats at the Polo Grounds, and one April night a group of us went to watch the Giants play the Milwaukee Braves. I don't know who won, I can't recall a single detail of the game, but I do remember that after the game was over my parents and their friends sat talking in their seats until all the other spectators had left. It got so late that we had to walk across the diamond and leave by the center-field exit, which was the only one still open. As it happened, that exit was right below the players' locker rooms.

Just as we approached the wall, I caught sight of Willie Mays. There was no question about who it was. It was Willie Mays, already out of uniform and standing there in his street clothes not ten feet away from me. I managed to keep my legs moving in his direction and then, mustering every ounce of my courage, I forced some words out of my mouth. "Mr. Mays," I said, "could I please have your autograph?"

He had to have been all of twenty-four years old, but I couldn't bring myself to pronounce his first name.

His response to my question was brusque but amiable. "Sure, kid, sure," he said. "You got a pencil?" He was so full of life, I remember, so full of youthful energy, that he kept bouncing up and down as he spoke.

I didn't have a pencil, so I asked my father if I could borrow his. He didn't have one either. Nor did my mother. Nor, as it turned out, did any of the other grown-ups.

The great Willie Mays stood there watching in silence. When it became clear that no one in the group had anything to write with, he turned to me and shrugged. "Sorry, kid," he said. "Ain't got no pencil, can't give no autograph." And then he walked out of the ballpark into the night.

I didn't want to cry, but tears started falling down my cheeks, and there was nothing I could do to stop them. Even worse, I cried all the way home in the car. Yes, I was crushed with disappointment, but I was also revolted at myself for not being able to control those tears. I wasn't a baby. I was eight years old, and big kids weren't supposed to cry over things like that. Not only did I not have Willie Mays's autograph, I didn't have anything else either. Life had put me to the test, and in all respects I had found myself wanting.

After that night, I started carrying a pencil with me wherever I went. It became a habit of mine never to leave the house without making sure I had a pencil in my pocket. It's not that I had any particular plans for that pencil, but I didn't want to be unprepared. I had been caught empty-handed once, and I wasn't about to let it happen again.

If nothing else, the years have taught me this: If there's a pencil in your pocket, there's a good chance that one day you'll feel tempted to start using it.

As I like to tell my children, that's how I became a writer.

HAND TO MOUTH

{1996}

A Chronicle of Early Failure

In my late twenties and early thirties, I went through a period of several years when everything I touched turned to failure. My marriage ended in divorce, my work as a writer foundered, and I was overwhelmed by money problems. I'm not just talking about an occasional shortfall or some periodic belt tightenings—but a constant, grinding, almost suffocating lack of money that poisoned my soul and kept me in a state of never-ending panic.

There was no one to blame but myself. My relationship to money had always been flawed, enigmatic, full of contradictory impulses, and now I was paying the price for refusing to take a clear-cut stand on the matter. All along, my only ambition had been to write. I had known that as early as sixteen or seventeen years old, and I had never deluded myself into thinking I could make a living at it. Becoming a writer is not a "career decision" like becoming a doctor or a policeman. You don't choose it so much as get chosen, and once you accept the fact that you're not fit for anything else, you have to be prepared to walk a long, hard road for the rest of your days. Unless you turn out to be a favorite of the gods (and woe to the man who banks on that), your work will never bring in enough to support you, and if you mean to have a roof over your head and not starve to death, you must resign yourself to doing other work to pay the bills. I understood all that, I was prepared for it, I had no complaints. In that respect, I was immensely lucky. I didn't particularly want anything in the way of material goods, and the prospect of being poor didn't frighten me. All I wanted was a chance to do the work I felt I had it in me to do.

Most writers lead double lives. They earn good money at legitimate professions and carve out time for their writing as best they can: early in the morning, late at night, weekends, vacations. William Carlos Williams and Louis-Ferdinand Céline were doctors. Wallace Stevens worked for an insurance company. T. S. Eliot was a banker, then a publisher. Among my own acquaintances, the French poet Jacques Dupin is codirector of an art gallery in Paris. William Bronk, the American poet, managed his family's coal and lumber business in upstate New York for over forty years. Don DeLillo, Peter Carey, Salman Rushdie, and Elmore Leonard all worked for long stretches in advertising. Other writers teach. That is probably the most common solution today, and with every major university and Podunk college offering so-called creative writing courses, novelists and poets are continually scratching and scrambling to land themselves a spot. Who can blame them? The salaries might not be big, but the work is steady and the hours are good.

My problem was that I had no interest in leading a double life. It's not that I wasn't willing to work, but the idea of punching a clock at some nine-to-five job left me cold, utterly devoid of enthusiasm. I was in my early twenties, and I felt too young to settle down, too full of other plans to waste my time earning more money than I either wanted or needed. As far as finances went, I just wanted to get by. Life was cheap in those days, and with no responsibility for anyone but myself, I figured I could scrape along on an annual income of roughly three thousand dollars.

I tried graduate school for a year, but that was only because Columbia offered me a tuition-free fellowship with a two-thousand-dollar stipend—which meant that I was actually paid to study. Even under those ideal conditions, I quickly understood that I wanted no part of it. I had had enough of school, and the prospect of spending another five or six years as a student struck me as a fate worse than death. I didn't want to talk about books anymore, I wanted to write them. Just on principle, it felt wrong to me for a writer to hide out in a university, to surround himself with too many like-minded people, to get too comfortable. The risk was complacency, and once that happens to a writer, he's as good as lost.

I'm not going to defend the choices I made. If they weren't practical, the truth was that I didn't want to be practical. What I wanted were new experiences. I wanted to go out into the world and test myself, to move from this to that, to explore as much as I could. As long as I kept my eyes open, I figured that whatever happened to me would be useful, would teach me things I had never known before. If this sounds like a rather old-fashioned approach, perhaps it was. Young writer bids farewell to family and friends and sets out for points unknown to discover what he's made of. For better or worse, I doubt that any other approach would have suited me. I had energy, a head crammed full of ideas, and itchy feet. Given how big the world was, the last thing I wanted was to play it safe.

It's not difficult for me to describe these things and to remember how I felt about them. The trouble begins only when I question why I did them and why I felt what I felt. All the other young poets and writers in my class were making sensible decisions about their futures. We weren't rich kids who could depend on handouts from our parents, and once we left college, we would be out on our own for good. We were all facing the same situation, we all knew the score, and yet they acted in one way and I acted in another. That's what I'm still at a loss to explain. Why did my friends act so prudently, and why was I so reckless?

I came from a middle-class family. My childhood was comfortable, and I never suffered from any of the wants and deprivations that plague most of the human beings who live on this earth. I never went hungry, I never was cold, I never felt in danger of losing any of the things I had. Security was a given, and yet for all the ease and good fortune in the household, money was a subject of continual conversation and worry. Both of my parents had lived through the Depression, and neither one had fully recovered from those hard times. Each had been marked by the experience of not having enough, and each bore the wound in a different way.

My father was tight; my mother was extravagant. She spent; he didn't. The memory of poverty had not loosened its hold on his spirit, and even though his circumstances had changed, he could never quite bring himself to believe it. She, on the other hand, took great pleasure in those altered circumstances. She enjoyed the rituals of consumerism, and like so many Americans before her and since, she cultivated shopping as a means of self-expression, at times raising it to the level of an art form. To enter a store was to engage in an alchemical process that imbued the cash register with magical, transformative properties. Inexpressible desires, intangible needs, and unarticulated longings all passed through the money box and came out as real things, palpable objects you could hold in your hand. My mother never tired of reenacting this miracle, and the bills that resulted became a bone of contention between her and my father. She felt that we could afford them; he didn't. Two styles, two worldviews, two moral philosophies were in eternal conflict with each other, and in the end it broke their marriage apart. Money was the fault line, and it became the single, overpowering source of dispute between them. The tragedy was that they were both good people—attentive, honest, hardworking—and aside from that one ferocious battleground, they seemed to get along rather well. For the life of me I could never understand how such a relatively unimportant issue could cause so much trouble between them. But money, of course, is never just money. It's always something else, and it's always something more, and it always has the last word.

As a small boy, I was caught in the middle of this ideological war. My mother would take me shopping for clothes, sweeping me up in the whirlwind of her enthusiasm and generosity, and again and again I would allow myself to be talked into wanting the things she offered me—always more than I was expecting, always more than I thought I needed. It was impossible to resist, impossible not to enjoy how the clerks doted on her and hopped to her commands, impossible not to be carried away by the power of her performance. My happiness was always mixed with a large dose of anxiety, however, since I knew exactly what my father was going to say when he got the bill. And the fact was that he always said it. The inevitable outburst would come, and almost inevitably the matter would be resolved with my father declaring that the next time I needed something, he was the one who would take me shopping. So the moment would roll around to buy me a new winter jacket, say, or a new pair of shoes, and one night after dinner my father and I would drive off to a discount store located on a highway somewhere in the New Jersey darkness. I remember the glare of fluorescent lights in those places, the cinder-block walls, the endless racks of cheap men's clothing. As the jingle on the radio put it: "Robert Hall this season / Will tell you the reason—/ Low overhead / Bum, bum, bum / Low overhead!" When all is said and done, that song is as much a part of my childhood as the Pledge of Allegiance or the Lord's Prayer.

The truth was that I enjoyed this bargain hunting with my father as much as I enjoyed the buying sprees orchestrated by my mother. My loyalties were equally divided between my two parents, and there was never any question of pitching my tent in one camp or the other. My mother's approach was more appealing, perhaps, at least in terms of the fun and excitement it generated, but there was something about my father's stubbornness that gripped me as well, a sense of hard-won experience and knowledge at the core of his beliefs, an integrity of purpose that made him someone who never backed down, not even at the risk of looking bad in the eyes of the world. I found that admirable, and much as I adored my beautiful, endlessly charming mother for dazzling the world as she did, I also adored my father for resisting that same world. It could be maddening to watch him in action—a man who never seemed to care what others thought of him—but it was also instructive, and in the long run I think I paid more attention to those lessons than I ever realized.

As a young boy I fell into the mold of your classic go-getter. At the first sign of snow, I would run out with my shovel and start ringing doorbells, asking people if they would hire me to clear their driveways and front walks. When the leaves fell in October, I would be out there with my rake, ringing those same doorbells and asking about the lawns. At other times, when there was nothing to remove from the ground, I would inquire about "odd jobs." Straightening up the garage, cleaning out the cellar, pruning the hedges—whatever needed to be done, I was the man to do it. In the summer, I sold lemonade for ten cents a glass on the sidewalk in front of my house. I gathered up empty bottles from the kitchen pantry, loaded them in my little red wagon, and lugged them to the store to turn in for cash. Two cents for the small ones; five cents for the big. I mostly used my earnings to buy baseball cards, sports magazines, and comic books, and whatever was left over I would diligently put in my piggy bank, which was built in the shape of a cash register. I was truly the child of my parents, and I never questioned the principles that animated their world. Money talked, and to the degree that you listened to it and followed its arguments, you would learn to speak the language of life.

Once, I remember, I was in possession of a fifty-cent piece. I can't recall how I came to have that coin—which was just as rare then as it is now—but whether it had been given to me or whether I had earned it myself, I have a keen sense of how much it meant to me and what a large sum it represented. For fifty cents in those days you could buy ten packs of baseball cards, five comic books, ten candy bars, fifty jawbreakers—or, if you preferred, various combinations of all of them. I put the half-dollar in my back pocket and marched off to the store, feverishly calculating how I was going to spend my little fortune. Somewhere along the way, however, for reasons that still confound me, the coin disappeared. I reached into my back pocket to check on it—knowing it was there, just wanting to make sure—and the money was gone. Was there a hole in my pocket? Had I accidentally slid the coin out of my pants the last time I'd touched it? I have no idea. I was six or seven years old, and I still remember how wretched I felt. I had tried to be so careful, and yet for all my precautions, I had wound up losing the money. How could I have allowed such a thing to happen? For want of any logical explanation, I decided that God had punished me. I didn't know why, but I was certain that the All-Powerful One had reached into my pocket and plucked out the coin Himself.

Little by little, I started turning my back on my parents. It's not that I began to love them less, but the world they came from no longer struck me as such an inviting place to live. I was ten, eleven, twelve years old, and already I was becoming an internal émigré, an exile in my own house. Many of these changes can be attributed to adolescence, to the simple fact that I was growing up and beginning to think for myself—but not all of them. Other forces were at work on me at the same time, and each one had a hand in pushing me onto the road I later followed. It wasn't just the pain of having to witness my parents' crumbling marriage, and it wasn't just the frustration of being trapped in a small suburban town, and it wasn't just the American climate of the late 1950s—but put them all together, and suddenly you had a powerful case against materialism, an indictment of the orthodox view that money was a good to be valued above all others. My parents valued money, and where had it gotten them? They had struggled so hard for it, had invested so much belief in it, and yet for every problem it had solved, another one had taken its place. American capitalism had created one of the most prosperous moments in human history. It had produced untold numbers of cars, frozen vegetables, and miracle shampoos, and yet Eisenhower was President, and the entire country had been turned into a gigantic television commercial, an incessant harangue to buy more, make more, spend more, to dance around the dollar-tree until you dropped dead from the sheer frenzy of trying to keep up with everyone else.

It wasn't long before I discovered that I wasn't the only person who felt this way. At ten, I stumbled across an issue of *Mad* magazine in a candy store in Irvington, New Jersey, and I remember the intense, almost stupefying pleasure I felt at reading those pages. They taught me that I had kindred spirits in this world, that others had already unlocked the doors I was trying to open myself. Fire hoses were being turned on black people in the American South, the Russians had launched the first Sputnik, and I was starting to pay attention. No, you didn't have to swallow the dogma they were trying to sell you. You could resist them, poke fun at them, call their bluff. The wholesomeness and dreary rectitude of American life were no more than a sham, a halfhearted publicity stunt. The moment you began to study the facts, contradictions bubbled to the surface, rampant hypocrisies were exposed, a whole new way of looking at things suddenly became possible. We had been taught to believe in "liberty and justice for all," but the fact was that liberty and justice were often at odds with one another. The pursuit of money had nothing to do with fairness; its driving engine was the social principle of "every man for himself." As if to prove the essential inhumanity of the marketplace, nearly all of its metaphors had been taken from the animal kingdom: dog eat dog, bulls and bears, the rat race, survival of the fittest. Money divided the world into winners and losers, haves and have-nots. That was an excellent arrangement for the winners, but what about the people who lost? Based on the evidence available to me, I gathered that they were to be cast aside and forgotten. Too bad, of course, but those were the breaks. If you construct a world so primitive as to make Darwin your leading philosopher and Aesop your leading poet, what else can you expect? It's a jungle out there, isn't it? Just look at that Dreyfus lion strolling down the middle of Wall Street. Could the message be any clearer? Either eat or be eaten. That's the law of the jungle, my friend, and if you don't have the stomach for it, then get out while you still can.

I was out before I was ever in. By the time I entered my teens, I had already concluded that the world of business would have to get along without me. I was probably at my worst then, my most insufferable, my most confused. I burned with the ardor of a newfound idealism, and the stringencies of the perfection I sought for myself turned me into a pint-sized puritan-in-training. I was repulsed by the outward trappings of wealth, and every sign of ostentation my parents brought into the house I treated with scorn. Life was unfair. I had finally figured this out, and because it was my own discovery, it hit me with all the force of a revelation. As the months went by, I found it increasingly difficult to reconcile my good luck with the bad luck of so many others. What had I done to deserve the comforts and advantages that had been showered on me? My father could afford them—that was all—and whether or not he and my mother fought over money was a small point in comparison to the fact that they had money to fight over in the first place. I squirmed every time I had to get into the family car—so bright and new and expensive, so clearly an invitation to the world to admire how well off we were. All my sympathies were for the downtrodden, the dispossessed, the under-dogs of the social order, and a car like that filled me with shame—not just for myself, but for living in a world that allowed such things to be in it.

My first jobs don't count. My parents were still supporting me, and I was under no obligation to fend for myself or contribute to the family budget. The pressure was therefore off, and without any pressure, nothing important can ever be at stake. I was glad to have the money I earned, but I never had to use it on nuts-and-bolts necessities, I never had to worry about putting food on the table or not falling behind with the rent. Those problems would come later. For now I was just a high school kid looking for a pair of wings to carry me away from where I was.

At sixteen, I spent two months working as a waiter at a summer camp in upstate New York. The next summer, I worked at my uncle Moe's appliance store in Westfield, New Jersey. The jobs were similar in that most of the tasks were physical and didn't require much thought. If carrying trays and scraping dishes was somewhat less interesting than installing air conditioners and unloading refrigerators from forty-foot trailer trucks, I wouldn't want to make too big a point of it. This isn't a question of apples and oranges—but of two kinds of apples, both the same shade of green. Dull as the work might have been, however, I found both jobs immensely satisfying. There were too many colorful characters around, too many surprises, too many new thoughts to absorb for me to resent the drudgery, and I never felt that I was wasting my time just to earn a paycheck. The money was an important part of it, but the work wasn't just about money. It was about learning who I was and how I fit into the world.

Even at the camp, where my coworkers were all sixteen- and seventeen-year-old high school boys, the kitchen help came from a starkly different universe. Down-and-outs, Bowery bums, men with dubious histories, they had been rounded up from the New York streets by the owner of the camp and talked into accepting their low-paying jobs—which included two months of fresh air and free room and board. Most of them didn't last long. One day they would just disappear, wandering back to the city without bothering to say good-bye. A day or two later, the missing man would be replaced by a similar lost soul, who rarely lasted very long himself. One of the dishwashers, I remember, was named Frank, a grim, surly guy with a serious drinking problem. Somehow or other, we managed to become friends, and in the evening after work was done we would sometimes sit on the steps behind the kitchen and talk. Frank turned out to be a highly intelligent, well-read man. He had worked as an insurance agent in Springfield, Massachusetts, and until the bottle got the better of him, he had lived the life of a productive, tax-paying citizen. I distinctly remember not daring to ask him what had happened, but one evening he told me anyway, turning what must have been a complicated story into a short, dry account of the events that had done him in. In the space of sixteen months, he said, every person who had ever meant anything to him died. He sounded philosophical about it, almost as if he were talking about someone else, and yet there was an undertow of bitterness in his voice. First his parents, he said, then his wife, and then his two children. Diseases, accidents, and burials, and by the time they were all gone, it was as if his insides had shattered. "I just gave up," he said. "I didn't care what happened to me anymore, so I became a bum."

The following year, in Westfield, I made the acquaintance of several more indelible figures. Carmen, for example, the voluminously padded, wisecracking bookkeeper, who to this day is still the only woman I've known with a beard (she actually had to shave), and Joe Mansfield, the assistant repairman with two hernias and a ravaged Chrysler that had wiped out the odometer three times and was now up to 360,000 miles. Joe was sending two daughters through college, and in addition to his day job at the appliance store, he worked eight hours every night as a foreman in a commercial bakery, reading comic books beside the huge vats of dough so as not to fall asleep. He was the single most exhausted man I have ever met—and also one of the most energetic. He kept himself going by smoking menthol cigarettes and downing twelve to sixteen bottles of orange soda a day, but not once did I ever see him put a morsel of food in his mouth. If he ate lunch, he said, it would make him too tired and he would collapse. The hernias had come a few years earlier, when he and two other men were carrying a jumbo refrigerator up a narrow flight of stairs. The other men had lost their grip, leaving Joe to bear the entire weight of the thing himself, and it was exactly then, as he struggled not to be crushed by the several hundred pounds he was holding, that his testicles had shot up out of his scrotum. First one ball, he said, and then the other. Pop . . . pop. He wasn't supposed to lift heavy objects anymore, but every time there was an especially large appliance to deliver, he would come along and help us—just to make sure we didn't kill ourselves.

The *us* included a nineteen-year-old redhead named Mike, a tense, wiry shrimp with a missing index finger and one of the fastest tongues I had yet encountered. Mike and I were the air conditioner installation team, and we spent a lot of time together in the store van, driving to and from jobs. I never tired of listening to the onslaught of loopy, unexpected metaphors and outrageous opinions that came pouring out of him whenever he opened his mouth. If he found one of the customers too snotty, for example, he wouldn't say "that person's an asshole" (as most would) or "that person's stuck-up" (as some would), but "that person acts as if his shit doesn't smell." Young Mike had a special gift, and on several occasions that summer I was able to see how well it served him. Again and again we would enter a house to install an air conditioner, and again and again, just as we were in the middle of the job (screwing in the screws, measuring strips of caulking to seal up the window), a girl would walk into the room. It never seemed to fail. She was always seventeen, always pretty, always bored, always "just hanging around the house." The instant she appeared, Mike would turn on the charm. It was as if he knew she was going to come in, as if he had already rehearsed his lines and was fully prepared. I, on the other hand, was always caught with my guard down, and as Mike launched into his song and dance (a combination of bullshit, razzle-dazzle, and raw nerve), I would dumbly plod on with the work. Mike would talk, and the girl would smile. Mike would talk a little more, and the girl would laugh. Within two minutes they were old friends, and by the time I'd put the finishing touches on the job, they were swapping phone numbers and arranging where to meet on Saturday night. It was preposterous; it was sublime; it made my jaw drop. If it had happened only once or twice, I would have dismissed it as a fluke, but this scene was played out repeatedly, no less than five or six times over the course of the summer. In the end, I grudgingly had to admit that Mike was more than just lucky. He was someone who created his own luck.

In September, I started my senior year of high school. It was the last year I spent at home, and it was also the last year of my parents' marriage. Their breakup had been so long in coming that when the news was announced to me at the end of Christmas vacation, I wasn't upset so much as relieved.

It had been a mismatch from the start. If they hung in together as long as they did, it was more for "the children's sake" than for their own. I don't presume to have any answers, but I suspect that a decisive moment occurred two or three years before the end, when my father took over the grocery-shopping duties for the household. That was the last great money battle my parents fought, and it stands in my mind as the symbolic last straw, the thing that finally knocked the stuffing out of both of them. It was true that my mother enjoyed filling her cart at the local Shop-Rite until it was almost too heavy to push; it was true that she took pleasure in providing the treats my sister and I asked her for; it was true that we ate well at home and that the pantry was abundantly stocked. But it was also true that we could afford these things and that the family finances were in no way threatened by the sums my mother forked over at the checkout counter. In my father's eyes, however, her spending was out of control. When he finally put his foot down, it landed in the wrong place, and he wound up doing what no man should ever do to his wife. In effect, he relieved her of her job. From then on, he was the one who took responsibility for bringing food into the house. Once, twice, even three times a week, he would stop off somewhere on the way home from work (as if he didn't have enough to do already) and load up the back of his station wagon with groceries. The choice cuts of meat my mother had brought home were replaced by chuck and shoulder. Name-brand products became generic products. After-school snacks vanished. I don't remember hearing my mother complain, but it must have been a colossal defeat for her. She was no longer in charge of her own house, and the fact that she didn't protest, that she didn't fight back, must have meant that she had already given up on the marriage. When the end came, there were no dramas, no noisy showdowns, no last-minute regrets. The family quietly dispersed. My mother moved to an apartment in the Weequahic section of Newark (taking my sister and me along with her), and my father stayed on alone in the big house, living there until the day he died.

In some perverse way, these events made me extremely happy. I was glad that the truth was finally out in the open, and I welcomed the upheavals and changes that followed as a consequence of that truth. There was something liberating about it, an exhilaration in knowing that the slate had been wiped clean. An entire period of my life had ended, and even as my body continued to go through the motions of finishing up high school and helping my mother move to her new place, my mind had already decamped. Not only was I about to leave home, but home itself had disappeared. There was nothing to return to anymore, nowhere to go but out and away.

I didn't even bother to attend my high school graduation. I offer that as proof, evidence of how little it meant to me. By the time my classmates were donning their caps and gowns and receiving their diplomas, I was already on the other side of the Atlantic. The school had granted me a special dispensation to leave early, and I had booked passage on a student boat that sailed out of New York at the beginning of June. All my savings went into that trip. Birthday money, graduation money, bar mitzvah money, the little bits I'd hoarded from summer jobs—fifteen hundred dollars or so, I can't remember the exact amount. That was the era of Europe on Five Dollars a Day, and if you watched your funds carefully, it was actually possible to do it. I spent over a month in Paris, living in a hotel that cost seven francs a night ($1.40); I traveled to Italy, to Spain, to Ireland. In two and a half months, I lost more than twenty pounds. Everywhere I went, I worked on the novel I had started writing that spring. Mercifully, the manuscript has disappeared, but the story I carried around in my head that summer was no less real to me than the places I went to and the people I crossed paths with. I had some extraordinary encounters, especially in Paris, but more often than not I was alone, at times excessively alone, alone to the point of hearing voices in my head. God knows what to make of that eighteen-year-old boy now. I see myself as a conundrum, the site of inexplicable turmoils, a weightless, wild-eyed sort of creature, slightly touched, perhaps, prone to desperate inner surges, sudden about-faces, swoons, soaring thoughts. If someone approached me in the right way, I could be open, charming, positively gregarious. Otherwise, I was walled off and taciturn, barely present. I believed in myself and yet had no confidence in myself. I was bold and timid, light-footed and clumsy, single-minded and impulsive—a walking, breathing monument to the spirit of contradiction. My life had only just begun, and already I was moving in two directions at once. I didn't know it yet, but in order for me to get anywhere, I was going to have to work twice as hard as anyone else.

The last two weeks of the trip were the strangest. For reasons that had everything to do with James Joyce and *Ulysses*, I went to Dublin. I had no plans. My only purpose in going was to be there, and I figured the rest would take care of itself. The tourist office steered me to a bed-and-breakfast in Donnybrook, a fifteen-minute bus ride from the center of town. Besides the elderly couple who ran the place and two or three of the guests, I scarcely talked to anyone in all that time. I never even found the courage to set foot in a pub. Somewhere during the course of my travels, I had developed an ingrown toenail, and while it sounds like a comical condition, it wasn't the least bit funny to me. It felt as if the tip of a knife had been lodged in my big toe. Walking was turned into a trial, and yet from early in the morning to late in the afternoon, I did little else but walk, hobbling around Dublin in my too-tight, disintegrating shoes. I could live with the pain, I found, but the effort it called for seemed to drive me ever further into myself, to erase me as a social being. There was a crotchety American geezer in full-time residence at the boardinghouse—a seventy-year-old retiree from Illinois or Indiana—and once he got wind of my condition, he started filling my head with stories about how his mother had left an ingrown toenail untended for years, treating it with patchwork home remedies—dabs of disinfectant, little balls of cotton—but never *taking the bull by the horns*, and wouldn't you know it, she came down with *cancer of the toe*, which worked its way into her foot, and then into her leg, and then spread through her whole body and eventually did her in. He loved elaborating on the small, gruesome details of his mother's demise (for my own good, of course), and seeing how susceptible I was to what he told me, he never tired of telling the story again. I'm not going to deny that I was affected. A cumbersome annoyance had been turned into a life-threatening scourge, and the longer I delayed taking action, the more dismal my prospects would become. Every time I rode past the Hospital for Incurables on my way into town, I turned my eyes away. I couldn't get the old man's words out of my head. Doom was stalking me, and signs of impending death were everywhere.

Once or twice, I was accompanied on my rambles by a twenty-six-year-old nurse from Toronto. Her name was Pat Gray, and she had checked into the bed-and-breakfast the same evening I had. I fell desperately in love with her, but it was a hopeless infatuation, a lost cause from the start. Not only was I too young for her, and not only was I too shy to declare my feelings, but she was in love with someone else—an Irishman, of course, which explained why she'd come to Dublin in the first place. One night, I recall, she came home from a date with her beloved at around half-past twelve. I was still up at that hour, scribbling away at my novel, and when she saw light coming through the crack under my door, she knocked and asked to come in. I was already in bed, working with a notebook propped against my knees, and she burst in laughing, her cheeks flushed with drink, bubbling over with excitement. Before I could say anything, she threw her arms around my neck and kissed me, and I thought: Miracle of miracles, my dream has come true. But alas, it was only a false alarm. I didn't even have a chance to kiss her back before she was drawing away from me and explaining that her Irishman had proposed to her that night and that she was the happiest girl in the world. It was impossible not to feel glad for her. This straightforward, pretty young woman, with her short hair and innocent eyes and earnest Canadian voice, had chosen me as the person to share the news with. I did my best to congratulate her, to hide my disappointment after that brief, wholly implausible rush of expectation, but the kiss had undone me, had absolutely melted my bones, and it was all I could do not to commit a serious blunder. If I managed to control myself, it was only by turning myself into a block of wood. No doubt a block of wood has good manners, but it's hardly a fitting companion for a celebration.

Everything else was solitude, silence, walking. I read books in Phoenix Park, journeyed out to Joyce's Martello Tower along the strand, crossed and recrossed the Liffey more times than I could count. The Watts riots took place then, and I remember reading the headlines at a kiosk on O'Connell Street, but I also remember a small girl singing with a Salvation Army band early one evening as people shuffled home from work—some sad, plaintive song about human misery and the wonders of God—and that voice is still inside me, a voice so crystalline as to make the toughest person fall down and weep, and the remarkable thing about it was that no one paid the slightest attention to her. The rush-hour crowd rushed past her, and she just stood on the corner singing her song in the eerie, dusky, northern light, as oblivious of them as they were of her, a tiny bird in tattered clothes chanting her psalm to the broken heart.

Dublin is not a big city, and it didn't take me long to learn my way around. There was something compulsive about the walks I took, an insatiable urge to prowl, to drift like a ghost among strangers, and after two weeks the streets were transformed into something wholly personal for me, a map of my inner terrain. For years afterward, every time I closed my eyes before going to sleep, I was back in Dublin. As wakefulness dribbled out of me and I descended into semiconsciousness, I would find myself there again, walking through those same streets. I have no explanation for it. Something important had happened to me there, but I have never been able to pinpoint exactly what it was. Something terrible, I think, some mesmerizing encounter with my own depths, as if in the loneliness of those days I had looked into the darkness and seen myself for the first time.

I started Columbia College in September, and for the next four years the last thing on my mind was money. I worked intermittently at various jobs, but those years were not about making plans, not about preparing for my financial future. They were about books, the war in Vietnam, the struggle to figure out how to do the thing I was proposing to do. If I thought about earning a living at all, it was only in a fitful, haphazard sort of way. At most I imagined some kind of marginal existence for myself—scrounging for crumbs at the far edges of the workaday world, the life of a starving poet.

The jobs I had as an undergraduate were nevertheless instructive. If nothing else, they taught me that my preference for blue-collar work over white-collar work was well founded. At one point in my sophomore year, for example, I was hired by the subdivision of a publishing company to write material for educational film-strips. I had been subjected to a barrage of "audiovisual aids" during my childhood, and I remembered the intense boredom they invariably produced in me and my friends. It was always a pleasure to leave the classroom and sit in the dark for twenty or thirty minutes (just like going to the movies!), but the clunky images on screen, the monotone voice of the narrator, and the intermittent *ping* that told the teacher when to push the button and move on to the next picture soon took their toll on us. Before long, the room was abuzz with whispered conversations and frantic, half-suppressed giggles. A minute or two later, the spitballs would begin to fly.

I was reluctant to impose this tedium on another generation of kids, but I figured I'd do my best and see if I couldn't put some spark into it. My first day on the job, the supervisor told me to take a look at some of the company's past filmstrips and acquaint myself with the form. I picked out one at random. It was called "Government" or "Introduction to Government," something like that. He set up the spool on a machine and then left me alone to watch the film. About two or three frames into it, I came across a statement that alarmed me. The ancient Greeks had invented the idea of democracy, the text said, accompanied by a painting of bearded men standing around in togas. That was fine, but then it went on to say (*ping:* cut to a painting of the Capitol) that America was a democracy. I turned off the machine, walked down the hall, and knocked on the door of the supervisor's office. "There's a mistake in the filmstrip," I said. "America isn't a democracy. It's a republic. There's a big difference."

He looked at me as if I had just informed him that I was Stalin's grandson. "It's for little children," he said, "not college students. There's no room to go into detail."

"It's not a detail," I answered, "it's an important distinction. In a pure democracy, everyone votes on every issue. We elect representatives to do that for us. I'm not saying that's bad. Pure democracy can be dangerous. The rights of minorities need to be protected, and that's what a republic does for us. It's all spelled out in *The Federalist Papers.* The government has to guard against the tyranny of the majority. Kids should know that."

The conversation became quite heated. I was determined to make my point, to prove that the statement in the filmstrip was wrong, but he refused to swallow it. He pegged me as a troublemaker the instant I opened my mouth, and that was that. Twenty minutes after starting the job, I was given the boot.

Much better was the job I had in the summer after my freshman year—as groundskeeper at the Commodore Hotel in the Catskills. I was hired through the New York State Employment Agency in midtown Manhattan, a vast government office that found work for the unskilled and the unfortunate, the bottom dogs of society. Humble and badly paid as the position was, at least it offered a chance to get out of the city and escape the heat. My friend Bob Perelman and I signed on together, and the next morning we were dispatched to Monticello, New York, via the Short Line Bus

Company. It was the same setup I'd seen three years before, and our fellow passengers were the same bums and down-and-outs I'd rubbed shoulders with during my stint as a summer camp waiter. The only difference was that now I was one of them. The bus fare was deducted from the first paycheck, as was the employment agency's fee, and unless you hung in with the job for some little time, you weren't going to make any money. There were those who didn't like the work and quit after a couple of days. They wound up with nothing—dead broke and a hundred miles from home, feeling they'd been had.

The Commodore was a small, down-at-the-heels Borscht Belt establishment. It was no match for the local competition, the Concord and Grossinger's, and a certain wistfulness and nostalgia hung about the place, a memory of rosier days. Bob and I arrived several weeks in advance of the summer season, and we were responsible for getting the grounds into shape to welcome an influx of visitors in July and August. We mowed lawns, clipped bushes, collected trash, painted walls, repaired screen doors. They gave us a little hut to live in, a ramshackle box with less square footage than a beach cabana, and bit by bit we covered the walls of our room with poems—crazy doggerel, filthy limericks, flowery quatrains—laughing our heads off as we downed endless bottles of Budweiser chug-a-lug beer. We drank the beer because there was nothing better to do, but given the food we had to eat, the hops became a necessary component of our diet as well. There were only a dozen or so workers on the premises at the time, and they gave us the low-budget treatment where culinary matters were concerned. The menu for every lunch and dinner was the same: Chun King chicken chow mein, straight out of the can. Thirty years have gone by since then, and I would still rather go hungry than put another morsel of that stuff in my mouth.

None of this would be worth mentioning if not for Casey and Teddy, the two indoor maintenance men I worked with that summer. Casey and Teddy had been palling around together for more than ten years, and by now they were a pair, an indissoluble team, a dialectical unit. Everything they did, they did in tandem, traveling from place to place and job to job as if they were one. They were chums for life, two peas in a pod, buddies. Not gay, not the least bit interested in each other sexually—but buddies. Casey and Teddy were classic American drifters, latter-day hoboes who seemed to have stepped forth from the pages of a Steinbeck novel, and yet they were so funny together, so full of wisecracks and drunkenness and good cheer, that their company was irresistible. At times they made me think of some forgotten comedy duo, a couple of clowns from the days of vaudeville and silent films. The spirit of Laurel and Hardy had survived in them, but these two weren't bound by the constraints of show business. They were part of the real world, and they performed their act on the stage of life.

Casey was the straight man, Teddy was the card. Casey was thin, Teddy was round. Casey was white, Teddy was black. On their days off they would tramp into town together, drink themselves silly, and then return for their chow mein dinner sporting identical haircuts or dressed in identical shirts. The idea was always to spend all their money in one big binge—and to spend it in exactly the same way, even-steven, penny for penny. The shirts stand out in my mind as a particularly raucous event. They couldn't stop laughing when they showed up in those twin outfits, holding their sides and pointing at each other as if they'd just played an enormous joke on the world. They were the loudest, ugliest shirts imaginable, a double insult to good taste, and Casey and Teddy were positively seized with mirth as they modeled them for me and Bob. Teddy then shuffled off to the empty ballroom on the ground floor of the main building, sat down at the piano, and launched into what he called his Port Wine Concerto. For the next hour and a half, he clanged forth tuneless improvisations, filling the hall with a tempest of inebriation and noise. Teddy was a man of many gifts, but music was not one of them. Yet there he sat, happy as a clam in the fading light, a Dada maestro at peace with himself and the world.

Teddy had been born in Jamaica, he told me, and had joined the British Navy during World War II. Somewhere along the line, his ship was torpedoed. I don't know how much time elapsed before he was rescued (minutes? hours? days?), but whenever he was found, it was an American ship that found him. From then on he was in the American Navy, he said, and by the end of the war he was an American citizen. It sounded a little fishy to me, but that's the story he told, and who was I to doubt him? In the past twenty years, he seemed to have done everything a man can possibly do, to have run the entire gamut of occupations. Salesman, sidewalk artist in Greenwich Village, bartender, skid row drunk. None of it mattered to him. A great, rumbling basso laugh accompanied every story he told, and that laugh was like an unending bow to his own ridiculousness, a sign that his only purpose in talking was to poke fun at himself. He made scenes in public places, misbehaved like a willful child, was forever calling people's bluff. It could be exhausting to be with him, but there was also something admirable about the way he caused trouble. It had an almost scientific quality to it, as if he were conducting an experiment, shaking things up for the pure pleasure of seeing where they would land once the dust had settled. Teddy was an anarchist, and because he was also without ambition, because he didn't want the things that other people wanted, he never had to play by anybody's rules but his own.

I have no idea how or where he met Casey. His sidekick was a less flamboyant character than he was, and what I remember best about him was that he had no sense of taste or smell. Casey had been in a barroom fight some years back, had received a knock on the head, and had thenceforth lost all of his olfactory functions.

As a result, everything tasted like cardboard to him. Cover his eyes, and he couldn't tell you what he was eating. Chow mein or caviar, potatoes or pudding—there was no difference. Aside from this affliction, Casey was in excellent trim, a feisty welterweight with a New York Irish voice that made him sound like a Dead End Kid. His job was to laugh at Teddy's jokes and make sure his friend didn't take things too far and get himself hauled off to jail. Teddy got close to it one night that summer—standing up in a Monti-cello restaurant and waving around the menu as he shouted, "I ain't gonna eat this Japanese dog food!"—but Casey calmed him down, and we all managed to finish our meal. I don't suppose it's necessary to add that we weren't in a Japanese restaurant.

By any objective standard, Casey and Teddy were nobodies, a pair of eccentric fools, but they made an unforgettable impression on me, and I have never run across their likes since. That was the reason for going off to work at places like the Commodore Hotel, I think. It's not that I wanted to make a career of it, but those little excursions into the backwaters and shit holes of the world never failed to produce an interesting discovery, to further my educa-tion in ways I hadn't expected. Casey and Teddy are a perfect example. I was nineteen years old when I met them, and the things they did that summer are still feeding my imagination today.

In 1967, I signed up for Columbia's Junior Year Abroad Program in Paris. The weeks I'd spent there after finishing high school had whetted my appetite for the place, and I jumped at the chance to go back.

Paris was still Paris, but I was no longer the same person I'd been during my first visit. I had spent the past two years living in a delirium of books, and whole new worlds had been poured into my head, life-altering transfusions had reconstituted my blood. Nearly everything that is still important to me in the way of literature and philosophy I first encountered during those two years. Looking back on that time now, I find it almost impossible to absorb how many books I read. I drank them up in staggering numbers, consumed entire countries and continents of books, could never even begin to get enough of them. Elizabethan playwrights, pre-Socratic philosophers, Russian novelists, Surrealist poets. I read books as if my brain had caught fire, as if my very survival were at stake. One work led to another work, one thought led to another thought, and from one month to the next, I changed my ideas about everything.

The program turned out to be a bitter disappointment. I went to Paris with all sorts of grandiose plans, assuming I would be able to attend any lectures and courses I wanted to (Roland Barthes at the Collège de France, for example), but when I sat down to discuss these possibilities with the director of the program, he flat out told me to forget them. Out of the question, he said. You're required to study French language and grammar, to pass certain tests, to earn so many credits and half-credits, to put in so many class hours here and so many hours there. I found it absurd, a curriculum designed for babies. I'm past all that, I told him. I already know how to speak French. Why go backward? Because, he said, those are the rules, and that's the way it is.

He was so unbending, so contemptuous of me, so ready to interpret my enthusiasm as arrogance and to think I was out to insult him, that we immediately locked horns. I had nothing against the man personally, but he seemed bent on turning our disagreement into a personal conflict. He wanted to belittle me, to crush me with his power, and the longer the conversation went on, the more I felt myself resisting him. At last, a moment came when I'd had enough. All right, I said, if that's the way it is, then I quit. I quit the program, I quit the college, I quit the whole damn thing. And then I got up from my chair, shook his hand, and walked out of the office.

It was a crazy thing to do. The prospect of not getting a B.A. didn't worry me, but turning my back on college meant that I would automatically lose my student deferment. With the troop buildup in Vietnam growing at an alarming rate, I had suddenly put myself in a good position to be drafted into the army. That would have been fine if I supported the war, but I didn't. I was against it, and nothing was ever going to make me fight in it. If they tried to induct me into the army, I would refuse to serve. If they arrested me, I would go to jail. That was a categorical decision—an absolute, unbudgeable stance. I wasn't going to take part in the war, even if it meant ruining my life.

Still, I went ahead and quit college. I was utterly fearless about it, felt not the slightest tremor of hesitation or doubt, and took the plunge with my eyes wide open. I was expecting to fall hard, but I didn't. Instead, I found myself floating through the air like a feather, and for the next few months I felt as free and happy as I had ever been.

I lived in a small hotel on the rue Clément, directly across from the Marché Saint-Germain, an enclosed market that has long since been torn down. It was an inexpensive but tidy place, several notches up from the fleabag I'd stayed in two years before, and the young couple who ran it were exceedingly kind to me. The man's name was Gaston (stout, small mustache, white shirt, ever-present black apron), and he spent the bulk of his time serving customers in the café on the ground floor, a minuscule hole-in-the-wall that doubled as neighborhood hangout and hotel reception desk. That's where I drank my coffee in the morning, read the newspaper, and became addicted to pinball. I walked a lot during those months, just as I had in Dublin, but I also spent countless hours upstairs in my room, reading and writing. Most of the work I did then has been lost, but I remember writing poems and translating poems, as well as composing a long, exhaustingly complex screenplay for a silent film (part Buster Keaton movie, part philosophical tap dance). On top of all the reading I'd done in the past two years, I had also been going to the movies, primarily at the Thalia and New Yorker theaters, which were no more than a short walk down Broadway from Morningside Heights. The Thalia ran a different double feature every day, and with the price of admission just fifty cents for students, I wound up spending as much time there as I did in the Columbia classrooms. Paris turned out to be an even better town for movies than New York. I became a regular at the Cinémathèque and the Left Bank revival houses, and after a while I got so caught up in this passion that I started toying with the idea of becoming a director. I even went so far as to make some inquiries about attending IDHEC, the Paris film institute, but the application forms proved to be so massive and daunting that I never bothered to fill them out.

When I wasn't in my room or sitting in a movie theater, I was browsing in bookstores, eating in cheap restaurants, getting to know various people, catching a dose of the clap (very painful), and generally exulting in the choice I had made. It would be hard to exaggerate how good I felt during those months. I was at once stimulated and at peace with myself, and though I knew my little paradise would have to end, I did everything I could to prolong it, to put off the hour of reckoning until the last possible moment.

I managed to hold out until mid-November. By the time I returned to New York, the fall semester at Columbia was half over. I assumed there was no chance of being reinstated as a student, but I had promised my family to come back and discuss the matter with the university. They were worried about me, after all, and I figured I owed them that much. Once I had taken care of that chore, I intended to go back to Paris and start looking for a job. Let the draft be damned, I said to myself. If I wound up as a "fugitive from justice," so be it.

None of it worked out as I thought it would. I made an appointment to see one of the deans at Columbia, and this man turned out to be so sympathetic, so fully on my side, that he broke down my defenses within a matter of minutes. No, he said, he didn't think I was being foolish. He understood what I was doing, and he admired the spirit of the enterprise. On the other hand, there was the question of the war, he said. Columbia didn't want to see me go into the army if I didn't want to go, much less wind up in jail for refusing to serve in the army. If I wanted to come back to college, the door was open. I could start attending classes tomorrow, and officially it would be as if I had never missed a day.

How to argue with a man like that? He wasn't some functionary who was just doing his job. He spoke too calmly for that and listened too carefully to what I said, and before long I understood that the only thing in it for him was an honest desire to prevent a twenty-year-old kid from making a mistake, to talk someone out of fucking up his life when he didn't have to. There would be time for that later, n'est-ce pas? He wasn't very old himself—thirty, thirty-five, perhaps—and I still remember his name, even though I never saw him again. Dean Platt. When the university shut down that spring because of the student strike, he quit his job in protest over the administration's handling of the affair. The next thing I heard, he had gone to work for the UN.

The troubles at Columbia lasted from early 1968 until my class graduated the following June. Normal activity all but stopped during that time. The campus became a war zone of demonstrations, sit-ins, and moratoriums. There were riots, police raids, slugfests, and factional splits. Rhetorical excesses abounded, ideological lines were drawn, passions flowed from all sides. Whenever there was a lull, another issue would come up, and the outbursts would begin all over again. In the long run, nothing of any great importance was accomplished. The proposed site for a university gymnasium was changed, a number of academic requirements were dropped, the president resigned and was replaced by another president. That was all. In spite of the efforts of thousands, the ivory tower did not collapse. But still, it tottered for a time, and more than a few of its stones crumbled and fell to the ground.

I took part in some things and kept my distance from others. I helped occupy one of the campus buildings, was roughed up by the cops and spent a night in jail, but mostly I was a bystander, a sympathetic fellow traveler. Much as I would have liked to join in, I found myself temperamentally unfit for group activities. My loner instincts were far too ingrained, and I could never quite bring myself to climb aboard the great ship *Solidarity.* For better or worse, I went on paddling my little canoe—a bit more desperately, perhaps, a bit less sure of where I was going now, but much too stubborn to get out. There probably wouldn't have been time for that anyway. I was steering through rapids, and it took every ounce of my strength just to hold on to the paddle. If I had flinched, there's a good chance I would have drowned.

Some did. Some became casualties of their own righteousness and noble intentions, and the human loss was catastrophic. Ted Gold, one class ahead of me, blew himself to smithereens in a West Village brownstone when the bomb he was building accidentally went off. Mark Rudd, a childhood friend and Columbia dorm neighbor, joined the Weather Underground and lived in hiding for close to a decade. Dave Gilbert, an SDS spokesman whose speeches had impressed me as models of insight and intelligence, is now serving a seventy-five-year prison sentence for his involvement in the Brinks robbery. In the summer of 1969, I walked into a post office in western Massachusetts with a friend who had to mail a letter. As she waited in line, I studied the posters of the FBI's ten most wanted men pinned to the wall. It turned out that I knew seven of them.

That was the climate of my last two years of college. In spite of the distractions and constant turmoil, I managed to do a fair amount of writing, but none of my efforts ever added up to much. I started two novels and abandoned them, wrote several plays I didn't like, worked on poem after poem with largely disappointing results. My ambitions were much greater than my abilities at that point, and I often felt frustrated, dogged by a sense of failure. The only accomplishment I felt proud of was the French poetry I had translated, but that was a secondary pursuit and not even close to what I had in mind. Still, I must not have been totally discouraged. I kept on writing, after all, and when I began publishing articles on books and films in the *Columbia Daily Spectator*, I actually got to see my work in print fairly often. You have to start somewhere, I suppose. I might not have been moving as fast as I wanted to, but at least I was moving. I was up on my feet and walking forward, step by wobbly step, but I still didn't know how to run.

When I look back on those days now, I see myself in fragments. Numerous battles were being fought at the same time, and parts of myself were scattered over a broad field, each one wrestling with a different angel, a different impulse, a different idea of who I was. It sometimes led me to act in ways that were fundamentally out of character. I would turn myself into someone I was not, try wearing another skin for a while, imagine I had reinvented myself. The morose and contemplative stuffed shirt would dematerialize into a fast-talking cynic. The bookish, overly zealous intellectual would suddenly turn around and embrace Harpo Marx as his spiritual father. I can think of several examples of this antic bumbling, but the one that best captures the spirit of the time was a little piece of jabberwocky I contributed to the *Columbia Review*, the undergraduate literary magazine. For reasons that utterly escape me now, I took it upon myself to launch the First Annual Christopher Smart Award. I was a senior then, and the contest rules were published on the last page of the fall issue. I pluck these sentences from the text at random: "The purpose of the award is to give recognition to the great anti-men of our time... men of talent who have renounced all worldly ambition, who have turned their backs on the banquet tables of the rich ... We have taken Christopher Smart as our model ... the eighteenth-century Englishman who spurned the easy glory that awaited him as an inventor of rhymed couplets ... for a life of drunkenness, insanity, religious fanaticism, and prophetic writings. In excess he found his true path, in rejecting the early promise he showed to the academic poets of England, he realized his true greatness. Defamed and ridiculed over the past two centuries, his reputation run through the mud ... Christopher Smart has been relegated to the sphere of the unknowns. We attempt now, in an age without heroes, to resurrect his name."

The object of the competition was to reward failure. Not common, everyday setbacks and stumbles, but monumental falls, gargantuan acts of self-sabotage. In other words, I wanted to single out the person who had done the least with the most, who had begun with every advantage, every talent, every expectation of worldly success, and had come to nothing. Contestants were asked to write an essay of fifty words or more describing their failure or the failure of someone they knew. The winner would receive a two-volume boxed set of Christopher Smart's *Collected Works*. To no one's surprise but my own, not one entry was submitted.

It was a joke, of course, an exercise in literary leg pulling, but underneath my humorous intentions there was something disturbing, something that was not funny at all. Why the compulsion to sanctify failure? Why the mocking, arrogant tone, the know-it-all posturing? I could be wrong, but it strikes me now that they were an expression of fear—dread of the uncertain future I had prepared for myself—and that my true motive in setting up the contest was to declare myself the winner. The cockeyed, Bedlamite rules were a way of hedging my bets, of ducking the blows that life had in store for me. To lose was to win, to win was to lose, and therefore even if the worst came to pass, I would be able to claim a moral victory. Small comfort, perhaps, but no doubt I was already clutching at straws. Rather than bring my fear out into the open, I buried it under an avalanche of wisecracks and sarcasm. None of it was conscious. I was trying to come to terms with anticipated defeats, hardening myself for the struggles that lay ahead. For the next several years, my favorite sentence in the English language was from the Elizabethan poet Fulke Greville: "I write for those on whom the black ox hath trod."

As it happened, I wound up meeting Christopher Smart. Not the real Christopher Smart, perhaps, but one of his reincarnations, a living example of failed promise and blighted literary fortune. It was the spring of my senior year, just weeks before I was supposed to graduate. Out of nowhere, a man turned up on the Columbia campus and started causing a stir. At first I was only dimly aware of his presence, but little fragments of the stories circulating about him occasionally fell within my earshot. I'd heard that he called himself "Doc," for example, and that for obscure reasons that had something to do with the American economic system and the future of mankind, he was handing out money to strangers, no strings attached. With so many oddball doings in the air back then, I didn't pay much attention.

One night, a couple of my friends talked me into going down to Times Square with them to see the latest Sergio Leone spaghetti western. After the movie let out, we decided to cap off the evening with a little lark and repaired to the Metropole Café at Broadway and Forty-eighth Street. The Metropole had once been a quality jazz club, but now it was a topless go-go bar, complete with wall-to-wall mirrors, strobe lights, and half a dozen girls in glittering G-strings dancing on an elevated platform. We took a table in one of the back corners and started drinking our drinks. Once our eyes had adjusted to the darkness, one of my friends spotted "Doc" sitting alone in the opposite corner of the room. My friend went over and asked him to join us, and when the bearded, somewhat disheveled mystery man sat down beside me, mumbling something about Gene Krupa and what the hell had happened to this place, I turned my eyes away from the dancers for a moment and shook hands with the legendary, forgotten novelist, H. L. Humes.

He had been one of the founders of the *Paris Review* back in the fifties, had published two successful early books (*The Underground City* and *Men Die*), and then, just as he was beginning to make a name for himself, had vanished from sight. He just dropped off the literary map and was never heard from again.

I don't know the full story, but the bits and pieces I heard from him suggested that he'd had a rough time of it, had endured a long run of reversals and miseries. Shock treatments were mentioned, a ruined marriage, several stays in mental hospitals. By his own account, he'd been forced to stop writing for physical reasons—not by choice. The electroshock therapy had damaged his system, he said, and every time he picked up a pen, his legs would start to swell up, causing him unbearable pain. With the written word no longer available to him, he now had to rely on talk to get his "message" across to the world. That night, he gave a full-scale demonstration of how thoroughly he had mastered this new medium. First in the topless bar, and then on a nearly seventy-block walk up Broadway to Morningside Heights, the man talked a blue streak, rattling and rambling and chewing our ears off with a monologue that resembled nothing I had ever heard before. It was the rant of a hipster-visionary-neoprophet, a relentless, impassioned outflow of paranoia and brilliance, a careening mental journey that bounced from fact to metaphor to speculation with such speed and unpredictability that one was left dumbfounded, unable to say a word. He had come to New York on a mission, he told us. There were fifteen thousand dollars in his pocket, and if his theories about finance and the structures of capitalism were correct, he would be able to use that money to bring down the American government.

It was all quite simple, really. His father had just died, leaving Doc the aforementioned sum as an inheritance, and rather than squander the money on himself, our friend was proposing to give it away. Not in a lump, and not to any particular charity or person, but to everyone, to the whole world all at once. To that end he had gone to the bank, cashed the check, and converted it into a stack of fifty-dollar bills. With those three hundred portraits of Ulysses S. Grant as his calling cards, he was going to introduce himself to his coconspirators and unleash the greatest economic revolution in history. Money is a fiction, after all, worthless paper that acquires value only because large numbers of people choose to give it value. The system runs on faith. Not truth or reality, but collective belief. And what would happen if that faith were undermined, if large numbers of people suddenly began to doubt the system? Theoretically, the system would collapse. That, in a nutshell, was the object of Doc's experiment. The fifty-dollar bills he handed out to strangers weren't just gifts; they were weapons in the fight to make a better world. He wanted to set an example with his profligacy, to prove that one could disenchant oneself and break the spell that money held over our minds. Each time he disbursed another chunk of cash, he would instruct the recipient to spend it as fast as he could. Spend it, give it away, get it circulating, he would say, and tell the next person to do the same. Overnight, a chain reaction would be set in motion, and before you knew it, so many fifties would be flying through the air that the system would start to go haywire. Waves would be emitted, neutron charges from thousands, even millions of different sources would bounce around the room like little rubber balls. Once they built up enough speed and momentum, they would take on the strength of bullets, and the walls would begin to crack.

I can't say to what degree he actually believed this. Deranged as he might have been, a man of his intelligence surely would have known a stupid idea when he heard it. He never came out and said so, but deep down I think he understood what drivel it was. That didn't stop him from enjoying it, of course, and from spouting off about his plan at every opportunity, but it was more in the spirit of a wacko performance piece than a genuine political act. H. L. Humes wasn't some crackpot schizo taking orders from Martian command center. He was a ravaged, burnt-out writer who had run aground on the shoals of his own consciousness, and rather than give up and renounce life altogether, he had manufactured this little farce to boost his morale. The money gave him an audience again, and as long as people were watching, he was inspired, manic, the original one-man band. He pranced about like a buffoon, turning cartwheels and jumping through flames and shooting himself out of cannons, and from all I could gather, he loved every minute of it.

As he marched up Broadway that night with me and my friends, he put on a spectacular show. Between the cascading words and the barks of laughter and the jags of cosmological music, he would wheel around and start addressing strangers, breaking off in mid-sentence to slap another fifty-dollar bill in someone's hand and urge him to spend it like there was no tomorrow. Rambunctiousness took control of the street that night, and Doc was the prime attraction, the pied piper of mayhem. It was impossible not to get caught up in it, and I must admit that I found his performance highly entertaining. However, just as we neared the end of our journey and I was about to go home, I made a serious blunder. It must have been one or two in the morning by then. Somewhere off to my right, I heard Doc muttering to himself. "Any of you cats got a place to crash?" he said, and because he sounded so cool and nonchalant, so profoundly indifferent to the matters of this world, I didn't think twice about it. "Sure," I said, "you can sleep on my couch if you want to." Needless to say, he accepted my invitation. Needless to say, I had no idea what I had gotten myself into.

It's not that I didn't like him, and it's not that we didn't get along. For the first couple of days, in fact, things went rather smoothly. Doc planted himself on the couch and rarely stirred, rarely even brought the soles of his feet into contact with the floor. Aside from an occasional trip to the bathroom, he did nothing but sit, eat pizza, smoke marijuana, and talk. I bought the pizza for him (with his money), and after telling him five or six times that I wasn't interested in dope, he finally got the message and stopped offering it to me. The talk was incessant, however, the same repertoire of addled riffs he'd unfurled on the first night, but his arguments were more ample now, more fleshed out, more focused. Hours would go by, and his mouth never stopped moving. Even when I got up and left the room, he would go on talking, delivering his ideas to the wall, the ceiling, the light fixtures, and scarcely even notice that I was gone.

There wouldn't have been a problem if the place had been a little larger. The apartment had just two rooms and a kitchen, and since my bedroom was too small to hold anything but a bed, my work table was set up in the living room—which also happened to be where the couch was. With Doc permanently installed on the couch, it was all but impossible for me to get any work done. The spring semester was drawing to a close, and I had a number of term papers to write in order to complete my courses and graduate, but for the first two days I didn't even bother to try. I figured that I had a little margin and therefore didn't panic. Doc would be leaving soon, and once I had my desk back, I would be able to get down to work. By the morning of the third day, however, I realized that my houseguest had no intention of leaving. It wasn't that he was overstaying his welcome on purpose; the thought of leaving simply hadn't entered his head. What was I supposed to do? I didn't have the heart to kick him out. I already felt too sorry for him, and I couldn't find the courage to take such a drastic step.

The next few days were exceedingly difficult. I did what I could to cope, to see if some minor adjustments could improve the situation. In the end, things might have panned out—I don't know—but three or four days after I put Doc in the bedroom and took over the living room for myself, disaster struck. It happened on one of the most beautiful Sundays I can remember, and it was no one's fault but my own. A friend called to invite me to play in an outdoor basketball game, and rather than leave Doc alone in the apartment, I took him along with me. Everything went well. I played in the game and he sat by the side of the court, listening to the radio and yakking to himself or my friends, depending on whether anyone was within range. As we were returning home that evening, however, someone spotted us on the street. "Aha," this person said to me, "so that's where he's been hiding." I had never particularly liked this person, and when I told him to keep Doc's whereabouts under his hat, I realized that I might just as well have been talking to a lamppost. Sure enough, the buzzer of my apartment started ringing early the next morning. The campus celebrity had been found, and after his mysterious weeklong absence, H. L. Humes was more than happy to indulge his followers. All day long, groups of nineteen- and twenty-year-olds tramped into my apartment to sit on the floor and listen to Doc impart his skewed wisdom to them. He was the philosopher king, the metaphysical pasha, the bohemian holy man who saw through the lies their professors had taught them, and they couldn't get enough of it.

I was deeply pissed off. My apartment had been turned into a twenty-four-hour meeting hall, and much as I would have liked to hold Doc responsible for it, I knew that he wasn't to blame. His acolytes had come of their own accord, without invitations or appointments, and once the crowds began to gather, I could no more ask him to turn them away than I could ask the sun to stop shining. Talk was what he lived for. It was his final barrier against oblivion, and because those kids were there with him now, because they sat at his feet and hung on his every word, he could temporarily delude himself into thinking that all was not lost for him. I had no problem with that. For all I cared, he could go on talking until the next century. I just didn't want him doing it in my apartment.

Torn between compassion and disgust, I came up with a coward's compromise. It happened during one of the rare lulls of that period, at a moment when no unannounced visitors were in the apartment. I told Doc that he could stay—and that I would clear out instead. I had piles of work to do, I explained, and rather than dump him on the street before he'd found another place to live, I would go to my mother's apartment in Newark and write my school papers. In exactly one week I would return, and when I came back I expected him to be gone. Doc listened carefully as I outlined this plan to him. When I had finished, I asked him if he understood. "I dig, man," he said, speaking in his calmest, most gravelly jazzman's voice, "it's cool," and that was all there was to it. We went on to talk about other things, and somewhere in the course of our conversation that night he mentioned that many years back, as a young man in Paris, he had occasionally played chess with Tristan Tzara. This is one of the few concrete facts that has stayed with me. Over time, nearly everything else I heard from the mouth of H. L. Humes has disappeared. I can remember what his voice sounded like, but very little of what he said. All those great verbal marathons, those forced marches to the hinterlands of reason, those countless hours of listening to him unravel his plots and conspiracies and secret correspondences—all that has been reduced to a blur. The words are no more than a buzzing in my brain now, an unintelligible swarm of nothingness.

The next morning, as I was packing my bag and getting ready to leave, he tried to give me money. I turned him down, but he kept insisting, peeling off fifties from his wad like some racetrack gambler, telling me to take it, that I was a good kid, that we had to "share the wealth," and in the end I caved in to the pressure and accepted three hundred dollars from him. I felt terrible about it then and still feel terrible about it now. I had wanted to stay above that business, to resist taking part in the pathetic game he was playing, and yet when my principles were finally put on the line, I succumbed to temptation and allowed greed to get the better of me. Three hundred dollars was a large sum in 1969, and the lure of that money turned out to be stronger than I was. I put the bills in my pocket, shook Doc's hand good-bye, and hurried out of the apartment. When I returned a week later, the place was neat as a pin, and there was no sign of him anywhere. Doc had left, just as he had promised he would.

I saw him only once more after that. It was about a year later, and I was riding uptown on the number 4 bus. Just as we made the turn onto 110th Street, I spotted him through the window—standing on the corner of Fifth Avenue and the northern edge of Central Park. He appeared to be in bad shape. His clothes were rumpled, he looked dirty, and his eyes had a lost, vacant expression that had not been there before. He's slipped into hard drugs, I said to myself. Then the bus moved on, and I lost sight of him. Over the next days and weeks, I kept expecting to see him again, but I never did. Twenty-five years went by, and then, just five or six months ago, I opened *The New York Times* and stumbled across a small article on the obituary page announcing that he was dead.

Little by little, I learned how to improvise, trained myself to roll with the punches. During my last two years at Columbia, I took any number of odd freelance jobs, gradually developing a taste for the kind of literary hackwork that would keep me going until I was thirty—and which ultimately led to my downfall. There was a certain romance in it, I suppose, a need to affirm myself as an outsider and prove that I could make it on my own without kowtowing to anyone else's idea of what constituted the good life. My life would be good if and only if I stuck to my guns and refused to give in. Art was holy, and to follow its call meant making any sacrifice that was demanded of you, maintaining your purity of purpose to the bitter end.

Knowing French helped. It was hardly a rarefied skill, but I was good enough at it to have some translation jobs tossed my way. Art writings, for example, and an exceptionally tedious document from the French Embassy about the reorganization of its staff that droned on for more than a hundred pages. I also tutored a high school girl one spring, traveling across town every Saturday morning to talk to her about poetry, and another time I was collared by a friend (for no pay) to stand on an outdoor podium with Jean Genet and translate his speech in defense of the Black Panthers. Genet walked around with a red flower tucked behind his ear and rarely stopped smiling the whole time he was on the Columbia campus. New York seemed to make him happy, and he handled the attention he received that day with great poise. One night not long after that, I bumped into an acquaintance in the West End, the old student watering hole at Broadway and 114th Street. He told me that he had just started working for a pornography publisher, and if I wanted to try my hand at writing a dirty book, the price was fifteen hundred dollars per novel. I was more than willing to have a go at it, but my inspiration petered out after twenty or thirty pages. There were just so many ways to describe that one thing, I discovered, and my stock of synonyms soon dried up. I started writing book reviews instead—for a shoddily put together publication aimed at students. Sensing that the magazine wasn't going to add up to much, I signed my articles with a pseudonym, just to keep things interesting. Quinn was the name I chose for myself, Paul Quinn. The pay, I remember, was twenty-five dollars per review.

When the results of the draft lottery were announced at the end of 1969, I lucked out with number 297. A blind draw of the cards saved my skin, and the nightmare I had been girding myself against for several years suddenly evaporated. Who to thank for that unexpected mercy? I had been spared immense amounts of pain and trouble, had literally been given back control of my life, and the sense of relief was incalculable. Jail was no longer in the picture for me. The horizon was clear on all sides, and I was free to walk off in any direction I chose. As long as I traveled light, there was nothing to stop me from going as far as my legs would take me.

That I wound up working on an oil tanker for several months was largely a matter of chance. You can't work on a ship without a Merchant Seaman's card, and you can't obtain a Merchant Seaman's card without a job on a ship. Unless you know someone who can break through the circle for you, it's impossible to get in. The someone who did it for me was my mother's second husband, Norman Schiff. My mother had remarried about a year after her divorce from my father, and by 1970 my stepfather and I had been fast friends for nearly five years. An excellent man with a generous heart, he had consistently stood behind me and supported my vague, impractical ambitions. His early death in 1982 (at age fifty-four) remains one of the great sorrows of my life, but back then as I was finishing up my year of graduate work and preparing to leave school, his health was still reasonably good. He practiced law, mostly as a labor negotiator, and among his many clients at the time was the Esso Seaman's Union, for which he worked as legal counsel. That was how the idea got planted in my head. I asked him if he could swing me a job on one of the Esso tankers, and he said he would handle it. And without further ado, that was precisely what he did.

There was a lot of paperwork to take care of, trips to the union hall in Belleville, New Jersey, physical exams in Manhattan, and then an indefinite period of waiting until a slot opened up on one of the ships coming into the New York area. In the meantime, I took a temporary job with the United States Census Bureau, collecting data for the 1970 census in Harlem. The work consisted of climbing up and down staircases in dimly lit tenement buildings, knocking on apartment doors, and helping people fill out the government forms. Not everyone wanted to be helped, of course, and more than a few were suspicious of the white college boy prowling around their hallways, but enough people welcomed me in to make me feel that I wasn't completely wasting my time. I stayed with it for approximately a month, and then—sooner than I was expecting—the ship called.

I happened to be sitting in a dentist's chair at that moment, about to have a wisdom tooth pulled. Every morning since my name had gone on the list, I had checked in with my stepfather to let him know where I could be reached that day, and he was the one who tracked me down at the dentist's office. The timing couldn't have been more comical. The Novocain had already been injected into my gums, and the dentist had just picked up the pliers and was about to attack my rotten tooth when the receptionist walked in and announced that I was wanted on the phone. Extremely urgent. I climbed out of the chair with the bib still tied around my neck, and the next thing I knew, Norman was telling me that I had three hours to pack and get myself aboard the S.S. *Esso Florence* in Elizabeth, New Jersey. I stammered my apologies to the dentist and hightailed it out of there.

The tooth stayed in my mouth for another week. When it finally came out, I was in Baytown, Texas.

The *Esso Florence* was one of the oldest tankers in the fleet, a pipsqueak relic from a bygone age. Put a two-door Chevy next to a stretch limousine, and you'll have some idea of how it compared to the supertankers they build today. Already in service during World War II, my ship had logged untold thousands of watery miles by the time I set foot on it. There were enough beds on board to accommodate a hundred men, but only thirty-three of us were needed to take care of the work that had to be done. That meant that each person had his own room—an enormous benefit when you considered how much time we had to spend together. With other jobs you get to go home at night, but we were boxed in with one another twenty-four hours a day. Every time you looked up, the same faces were there. We worked together, lived together, and ate together, and without the chance for some genuine privacy, the routine would have been intolerable.

We shuttled between the Atlantic coast and the Gulf of Mexico, loading and unloading airplane fuel at various refineries along the way: Charleston, South Carolina; Tampa, Florida; Galveston, Texas. My initial responsibilities were mopping floors and making beds, first for the crew and then for the officers. The technical term for the position was "utilityman," but in plain language the job was a combination of janitor, garbage collector, and chambermaid. I can't say that I was thrilled to be scrubbing toilets and picking up dirty socks, but once I got the hang of it, the work turned out to be incredibly easy. In less than a week, I had polished my custodial skills to such a point that it took me only two or two and a half hours to finish my chores for the day. That left me with abundant quantities of free time, most of which I spent alone in my room. I read books, I wrote, I did everything I had done before—but more productively, somehow, with better powers of concentration now that there was so little to distract me. In many ways, it felt like an almost ideal existence, a perfect life.

Then, after a month or two of this blissful regimen, I was "bumped." The ship rarely traveled more than five days between ports, and nearly everywhere we docked some crew members would get off and others would get on. The jobs for the fresh arrivals were doled out according to seniority. It was a strict pecking order, and the longer you had worked for the company, the more say you had in what you were given. As low man on the totem pole, I had no say at all. If an old-timer wanted my job, he had only to ask for it, and it was his. After my long run of good luck, the boom finally fell on me somewhere in Texas. My replacement was a man named Elmer, a bovine Fundamentalist bachelor who happened to be the longest-serving, most famous utilityman of them all. What I had been able to do in two hours, Elmer now did in six. He was the slowest of the slow, a smug and untalkative mental lightweight who waddled about the ship in a world of his own, utterly ignored by the other crew members, and in all my experience I have never met a person who ate as much as he did. Elmer could pack away mountains of food—two, three, and four helpings at every meal—but what made it fascinating to watch him was not so much the scope of his appetite as the way he went about satisfying it: daintily, fastidiously, with a compulsive sense of decorum. The best part was the cleanup operation at the end. Once Elmer had eaten his fill, he would spread his napkin on the table before him and begin patting and smoothing the flimsy paper with his hands, slowly transforming it into a flat square. Then he would fold the napkin into precise longitudinal sections, methodically halving the area until it had been divided into eighths. In the end, the square would be turned into a long, rectilinear strip with all four edges exactly aligned. At that point, Elmer would carefully take hold of the edges, raise the napkin to his lips, and begin to rub. The action was all in the head: a slow back-and-forth swiveling that went on for twenty or thirty seconds. From start to finish, Elmer's hands never stirred. They would be fixed in the air as his large head turned left, right, and left again, and through it all his eyes never betrayed the slightest thought or emotion. The Cleaning of the Lips was a dogged, mechanical procedure, an act of ritual purification. Cleanliness is next to godliness, Elmer once told me. To see him with that napkin, you understood that he was doing God's work.

I was able to observe Elmer's eating habits at such close range because I had been bumped into the galley. The job of messman quadrupled my hours and made my life altogether more eventful. My responsibilities now included serving three meals a day to the crew (about twenty men), washing dishes by hand, cleaning the mess hall, and writing out the menus for the steward, who was generally too drunk to bother with them himself. My breaks were short—no more than an hour or two between meals—and yet in spite of having to work much harder than before, my income actually shrank. On the old job, there had been plenty of time for me to put in an extra hour or two in the evenings, scraping and painting in the boiler room, for example, or refurbishing rusty spots on deck, and those volunteer jobs had padded my paycheck quite nicely. Still, in spite of the disadvantages, I found working in the mess hall more of a challenge than mopping floors had been. It was a public job, so to speak, and in addition to all the hustling around that was now required of me, I had to stay on my toes as far as the men were concerned. That, finally, was my most important task: to learn how to handle the griping and rough-tempered complaints, to fend off insults, to give as good as I got.

Elmer aside, the crew was a fairly grimy, ill-mannered bunch. Most of the men lived in Texas and Louisiana, and apart from a handful of Chicanos, one or two blacks, and the odd foreigner who cropped up now and then, the dominant tone on board was white, redneck, and blue collar. A jocular atmosphere prevailed, replete with funny stories and dirty jokes and much talk about guns and cars, but there were deep, smoldering currents of racism in many of those men, and I made a point of choosing my friends carefully. To hear one of your coworkers defend South African apartheid as you sat with him over a cup of coffee ("they know how to treat niggers down there") doesn't bring much joy to the soul, and if I found myself hanging out mostly with the dark-skinned and Spanish-speaking men around me, there was a good reason for it. As a New York Jew with a college degree, I was an entirely alien specimen on that ship, a man from Mars. It would have been easy to make up stories about myself, but I had no interest in doing that. If someone asked me what my religion was or where I came from, I told him. If he didn't like it, I figured that was his problem. I wasn't going to hide who I was or pretend to be someone else just to avoid trouble. As it happened, I had only one awkward run-in the whole time I was there. One of the men started calling me Sammy whenever I walked by. He seemed to think it was funny, but as I failed to see any humor in the epithet, I told him to stop it. He did it again the next day, and once again I told him to stop it. When he did it again the day after that, I understood that polite words were not going to be enough. I grabbed hold of his shirt, slammed him against the wall, and very calmly told him that if he ever called me that again, I would kill him. It shocked me to hear myself talk like that. I was not someone who trafficked in violence, and I had never made that kind of threat to anyone, but for that one brief instant, a demon took possession of my soul. Luckily, my willingness to fight was enough to defuse the fight before it began. My tormentor threw up his hands in a gesture of peace. "It was just a joke," he said, "just a joke," and that was the end of it. As time went on, we actually became friends.

I loved being out on the water, surrounded by nothing but sky and light, the immensity of the vacant air. Seagulls accompanied us wherever we went, circling overhead as they waited for buckets of garbage to be dumped overboard. Hour after hour, they would hover patiently just above the ship, scarcely beating their wings until the scraps went flying, at which point they would plunge frantically into the foam, calling out to each other like drunks at a football game. Few pleasures can match the spectacle of that foam, of sitting at the stern of a large ship and staring into the white, churning tumult of the wake below. There is something hypnotic about it, and on still days the sense of well-being that washes through you can be overpowering. On the other hand, rough weather also holds its charms. As summer melted away and we headed into autumn, the inclemencies multiplied, bringing down some wild winds and pelting rains, and at those moments the ship felt no more safe or solid than a child's paper boat. Tankers have been known to crack in half, and all it takes is one wrong wave to do the job. The worst stretch, I remember, occurred when we were off Cape Hatteras in late September or early October, a twelve- or fifteen-hour period of flipping and flopping through a tropical storm. The captain stayed at the wheel all night, and even after the worst of it was over and the steward instructed me to carry the captain his breakfast the next morning, I was nearly blown overboard when I stepped onto the bridge with my tray. The rain might have stopped, but the wind speed was still at gale force.

For all that, working on the *Esso Florence* had little to do with high-seas adventure. The tanker was essentially a floating factory, and rather than introduce me to some exotic, swashbuckling life, it taught me to think of myself as an industrial laborer. I was one of millions now, an insect toiling beside countless other insects, and every task I performed was part of the great, grinding enterprise of American capitalism. Petroleum was the primary source of wealth, the raw material that fueled the profit machine and kept it running, and I was glad to be where I was, grateful to have landed in the belly of the beast. The refineries where we loaded and unloaded our cargo were enormous, hellish structures, labyrinthine networks of hissing pipes and towers of flame, and to walk through one of them at night was to feel that you were living in your own worst dream. Most of all, I will never forget the fish, the hundreds of dead, iridescent fish floating on the rank, oil-saturated water around the refinery docks. That was the standard welcoming committee, the sight that greeted us every time the tugboats pulled us into another port. The ugliness was so universal, so deeply connected to the business of making money and the power that money bestowed on the ones who made it—even to the point of disfiguring the landscape, of turning the natural world inside out—that I began to develop a grudging respect for it. Get to the bottom of things, I told myself, and this was how the world looked. Whatever you might think of it, this ugliness was the truth.

Whenever we docked somewhere, I made it my business to leave the ship and spend some time ashore. I had never been south of the Mason-Dixon line, and those brief jaunts onto solid ground took me to places that felt a lot less familiar or understandable than anything I'd met up with in Paris or Dublin. The South was a different country, a separate American universe from the one I'd known in the North. Most of the time, I tagged along with one or two of my shipmates, going the rounds with them as they visited their customary haunts. If Baytown, Texas, stands out with particular clarity, that is because we spent more time there than anywhere else. I found it a sad, crumbling little place. Along the main drag, a row of once elegant movie theaters had been turned into Baptist churches, and instead of announcing the titles of the latest Hollywood films, the marquees now sported fiery quotations from the Bible. More often than not, we wound up in sailors' bars on the back streets of broken-down neighborhoods. All of them were essentially the same: squalid, low-life joints; dim drinking holes; dank corners of oblivion. Everything was always bare inside. Not a single picture on the walls, not one touch of publican warmth. At most there was a quarter-a-rack pool table, a jukebox stuffed with country-and-western songs, and a drink menu that consisted of just one drink: beer.

Once, when the ship was in a Houston dry dock for some minor repairs, I spent the afternoon in a skid row bar with a Danish oiler named Freddy, a wild man who laughed at the slightest provocation and spoke English with an accent so thick that I scarcely understood a word he said. Walking down the street in the blinding Texas sun, we crossed paths with a drunken couple. It was still early in the day, but this man and woman were already so soused, so entrenched in their inebriation, they must have been going at the booze since dawn. They wobbled along the sidewalk with their arms around each other, listing this way and that, their heads lolling, their knees buckling, and yet both with enough energy left to be engaged in a nasty, foul-mouthed quarrel. From the sound of their voices, I gathered they'd been at it for years—a pair of bickering stumblebums in search of their next drink, forever repeating the same lines to each other, forever shuffling through the same old song and dance. As it turned out, they wound up in the same bar where Freddy and I chose to while away the afternoon, and because I was not more than ten feet away from them, I was in a perfect position to observe the following little drama:

The man leaned forward and barked out at the woman across the table. "Darlene," he said, in a drawling, besotted voice, "get me another beer."

Darlene had been nodding off just then, and it took her a good long moment to open her eyes and bring the man into focus. Another long moment ticked by, and then she finally said, "What?"

"Get me a beer," the man repeated. "On the double."

Darlene was waking up now, and a lovely, fuck-you sassiness suddenly brightened her face. She was clearly in no mood to be pushed around. "Get it yourself, Charlie," she snapped back at him. "I ain't your slave, you know."

"Damn it, woman," Charlie said. "You're my wife, ain't you? What the hell did I marry you for? Get me the goddamn beer!"

Darlene let out a loud, histrionic sigh. You could tell she was up to something, but her intentions were still obscure. "Okay, darling," she said, putting on the voice of a meek, simpering wife, "I'll get it for you," and then stood up from the table and staggered over to the bar.

Charlie sat there with a grin on his face, gloating over his small, manly victory. He was the boss, all right, and no one was going to tell him different. If you wanted to know who wore the pants in that family, just talk to him.

A minute later, Darlene returned to the table with a fresh bottle of Bud. "Here's your beer, Charlie," she said, and then, with one quick flick of the wrist, proceeded to dump the contents of the bottle onto her husband's head. Bubbles foamed up in his hair and eyebrows; rivulets of amber liquid streamed down his face. Charlie made a lunge for her, but he was too drunk to get very close. Darlene threw her head back and burst out laughing. "How do you like your beer, Charlie?" she said. "How do you like your fucking beer?"

Of all the scenes I witnessed in those bars, nothing quite matched the bleak comedy of Charlie's baptism, but for overall oddness, a plunge into the deepest heart of the grotesque, I would have to single out Big Mary's Place in Tampa, Florida. This was a large, brightly lit emporium that catered to the whims of dock-hands and sailors, and it had been in business for many years. Among its features were half a dozen pool tables, a long mahogany bar, inordinately high ceilings, and live entertainment in the form of quasi-naked go-go dancers. These girls were the cornerstone of the operation, the element that set Big Mary's Place apart from other establishments of its kind—and one look told you that they weren't hired for their beauty, nor for their ability to dance. The sole criterion was size. The bigger the better was how Big Mary put it, and the bigger you got, the more money you were paid. The effect was quite disturbing. It was a freak show of flesh, a cavalcade of bouncing white blubber, and with four girls dancing on the platform behind the bar at once, the act resembled a casting call for the lead role in *Moby-Dick*. Each girl was a continent unto herself, a mass of quivering lard decked out in a string bikini, and as one shift replaced another, the assault on the eyes was unrelenting. I have no memory of how I got there, but I distinctly recall that my companions that night were two of the gentler souls from the ship (Martinez, a family man from Texas, and Donnie, a seventeen-year-old boy from Baton Rouge) and that they were both just as flummoxed as I was. I can still see them sitting across from me with their mouths hanging open, doing everything they could not to laugh from embarrassment. At one point, Big Mary herself came over and sat down with us at our table. A splendid dirigible of a woman dressed in an orange pants suit and wearing a ring on every finger, she wanted to know if we were having a good time. When we assured her that we were, she waved to one of the girls at the bar. "Barbara," she yelled, belting out the word in a brassy, three-pack-a-day voice, "get your fat butt over here!" Barbara came, all smiles and good humor, laughing as Big Mary poked her in the stomach and pinched the ample rolls bulging from her hips. "She was a scrawny one at first," Mary explained, "but I've fattened her up pretty good. Ain't that so, Barbara?" she said, cackling like some mad scientist who's just pulled off a successful experiment, and Barbara couldn't have agreed with her more. As I listened to them talk, it suddenly occurred to me that I had it all wrong. I hadn't gone to sea. I'd run off and joined the circus.

Another friend was Jeffrey, the second cook (a.k.a. breakfast chef), from Bogalusa, Louisiana. We happened to have been born on the same day, and apart from the near-infant Donnie, we were the youngest members of the crew. It was the first time out for both of us, and since we worked together in the galley, we got to know each other reasonably well. Jeffrey was one of life's winners— a bright, handsome, fun-loving ladies' man with a taste for flashy clothes—and yet very practical and ambitious, a down-to-earth schemer who was quite consciously using his job on the ship to learn the ins and outs of cooking. He had no intention of making a career out of oil tankers, no desire to turn himself into an old salt. His dream was to become a chef in a high-class restaurant, maybe even to own that restaurant himself, and if nothing unexpected rose up to stop him, I don't doubt that that's exactly what he's doing today. We couldn't have been more unlike, Jeffrey and I, but we got along comfortably with each other. It was only natural that we should sometimes go ashore together when the ship was in port, but because Jeffrey was black, and because he had spent his whole life in the South, he knew that many of the places I went to with white crew members were off-limits to him. He made that perfectly clear to me the first time we planned an outing. "If you want me to go with you," he said, "you'll have to go where I can go." I tried to convince him that he could go anywhere he pleased, but Jeffrey wasn't buying the argument. "Maybe up North," he said. "Down here it's different." I didn't force the issue. When I went out for beers with Jeffrey, we drank them in black bars instead of white bars. Except for the skin color of the clientele, the atmosphere was the same.

One night in Houston, Jeffrey talked me into going to a dance club with him. I never danced and never went to clubs, but the thought of spending a few hours in a place that wasn't a low-rent dive tempted me, and I decided to take my chances. The club turned out to be a splashy disco hall thronged with hundreds of young people, the hottest black nightspot in town. There was a live band onstage, psychedelic strobe lights bouncing off the walls, hard liquor available at the bar. Everything pulsed with sex and chaos and loud music. It was Saturday night fever, Texas style.

Jeffrey was dressed to the teeth, and within four minutes he struck up a conversation with one of the many stunning girls floating around the bar, and four minutes after that they were out on the dance floor together, lost in an ocean of bodies. I sat down at a table and sipped my drink, the only white person in the building. No one gave me any trouble, but I got some odd, penetrating looks from a number of people, and by the time I finished my bourbon, I understood that I should be shoving off. I phoned for a cab and then went outside to wait in the parking lot. When the driver showed up a few minutes later, he started cursing. "Goddammit," he said. "Goddammit to hell. If I'd known you were calling from here, I wouldn't have come." "Why not?" I asked. "Because this is the worst fucking place in Houston," he said. "They've had six murders here in the past month. Every damn weekend, somebody else gets shot."

In the end, the months I spent on that ship felt like years. Time passes in a different way when you're out on the water, and given that the bulk of what I experienced was utterly new to me, and given that I was constantly on my guard because of that, I managed to crowd an astonishing number of impressions and memories into a relatively small sliver of my life. Even now, I don't fully understand what I was hoping to prove by shipping out like that. To keep myself off balance, I suppose. Or, very simply, just to see if I could do it, to see if I could hold my own in a world I didn't belong to. In that respect, I don't think I failed. I can't say what I accomplished during those months, but at the same time I'm certain I didn't fail.

I received my discharge papers in Charleston. The company provided airfare home, but you could pocket the money if you wanted to and make your own travel arrangements. I chose to keep the money. The trip by milk train took twenty-four hours, and I rode back with a fellow crew member from New York, Juan Castillo. Juan was in his late forties or early fifties, a squat, lumpy man with a big head and a face that looked like something pieced together with the skins and pulps of nineteen mashed potatoes. He had just walked off an oil tanker for the last time, and in appreciation of his twenty-five years of service to the company, Esso had given him a gold watch. I don't know how many times Juan pulled that watch out of his pocket and looked at it during the long ride home, but every time he did, he would shake his head for a few seconds and then burst out laughing. At one point, the ticket collector stopped to talk to us during one of his strolls down the aisle of the car. He looked very natty in his uniform, I remember, a black Southern gentleman of the old school. In a haughty, somewhat condescending manner, he opened the conversation by asking: "You boys going up North to work in the steel mills?"

We must have been a curious pair, Juan and I. I recall that I was wearing a beat-up leather jacket at the time, but other than that I can't see myself, have no sense of what I looked like or what other people saw when they looked at me. The ticket collector's question is the only clue I have. Juan had taken pictures of his shipmates to put in the family album at home, and I remember standing on the deck and looking into the camera for him as he clicked the shutter. He promised to send me a copy of the photo, but he never did.

I toyed with the idea of going out for another run on an Esso tanker, but in the end I decided against it. My salary was still being sent to me through the mail (for every two days I'd been on the ship, I received one day's pay on land), and my bank account was beginning to look fairly robust. For the past few months, I had been slowly coming to the conclusion that my next step should be to leave the country and live abroad for a while. I was willing to ship out again if necessary, but I wondered if I hadn't built up a large enough stake already. The three or four thousand dollars I'd earned from the tanker struck me as a sufficient sum to get started with, and so rather than continue in the merchant marine, I abruptly shifted course and began plotting a move to Paris.

France was a logical choice, but I don't think I went there for logical reasons. That I spoke French, that I had been translating French poetry, that I knew and cared about a number of people who lived in France—surely those things entered into my decision, but they were not determining factors. What made me want

to go, I think, was the memory of what had happened to me in
Paris three years earlier. I still hadn't gotten it out of my system,
and because that visit had been cut short, because I had left on the
assumption that I would soon be returning, I had walked around
with a feeling of unfinished business, of not having had my fill.
The only thing I wanted just then was to hunker down and write.
By recapturing the inwardness and freedom of that earlier time,
I felt that I would be putting myself in the best possible position
to do that. I had no intention of becoming an expatriate. Giving
up America was not part of the plan, and at no time did I think
I wouldn't return. I just needed a little breathing room, a chance
to figure out, once and for all, if I was truly the person I thought
I was.

What comes back to me most vividly from my last weeks in
New York is the farewell conversation I had with Joe Reilly, a
homeless man who used to hang around the lobby of my apartment building on West 107th Street. The building was a run-
down, nine-story affair, and like most places on the Upper West
Side, it housed a motley collection of people. With no effort at all,
I can summon forth a fair number of them, even after a quarter of
a century. The Puerto Rican mailman, for example, and the Chinese waiter, and the fat blonde opera singer with the Lhasa apso.
Not to mention the black homosexual fashion designer with his
black fur coat and the quarreling clarinetists whose vicious spats
would seep through the walls of my apartment and poison my
nights. On the ground floor of this gray brick building, one of the
apartments had been divided down the middle, and each half was
occupied by a man confined to a wheelchair. One of them worked
at the news kiosk on the corner of Broadway and 110th Street; the
other was a retired rabbi. The rabbi was a particularly charming
fellow, with a pointy artist's goatee and an ever-present black beret, which he wore at a rakish, debonair angle. On most days, he
would wheel himself out of his apartment and spend some time in

the lobby, chatting with Arthur, the superintendent, or with various tenants getting in and out of the elevator. Once, as I entered the building, I caught sight of him through the glass door in his usual spot, talking to a bum in a long, dark overcoat. It struck me as an odd conjunction, but from the way the bum stood there and from the tilt of the rabbi's head, it was clear that they knew each other well. The bum was an authentic down-and-outer, a scab-faced wino with filthy clothes and cuts dotting his half-bald scalp, a scrofulous wreck of a man who appeared to have just crawled out of a storm drain. Then, as I pushed open the door and stepped into the lobby, I heard him speak. Accompanied by wild, theatrical gestures—a sweep of the left arm, a finger darting from his right hand and pointing to the sky—a sentence came booming out of him, a string of words so unlikely and unexpected that at first I didn't believe my ears. "It was no mere fly-by-night acquaintance!" he said, rolling each syllable of that florid, literary phrase off his tongue with such relish, such blowhard bravura, such magnificent pomposity, that he sounded like some tragic ham delivering a line from a Victorian melodrama. It was pure W. C. Fields—but several octaves lower, with the voice more firmly in control of the effects it was striving to create. W. C. Fields mixed with Ralph Richardson, perhaps, with a touch of barroom bombast thrown in for good measure. However you wanted to define it, I had never heard a voice do what that voice did.

When I walked over to say hello to the rabbi, he introduced me to his friend, and that was how I learned the name of that singular gentleman, that mightiest of fallen characters, the one and only Joe Reilly.

According to the rabbi, who filled me in on the story later, Joe had started out in life as the privileged son of a wealthy New York family, and in his prime he had owned an art gallery on Madison Avenue. That was when the rabbi had met him—back in the old days, before Joe's disintegration and collapse. The rabbi had already left the pulpit by then and was running a music publishing company. Joe's male lover was a composer, and as the rabbi happened to publish that man's work, in the natural course of things he and Joe crossed paths. Then, very suddenly, the lover died. Joe had always had a drinking problem, the rabbi said, but now he hit the bottle in earnest, and his life began to fall apart. He lost his gallery; his family turned its back on him; his friends walked away. Little by little, he sank into the gutter, the last hole at the bottom of the world, and in the rabbi's opinion he would never climb out again. As far as he was concerned, Joe was a hopeless case.

Whenever Joe came around after that, I would dig into my pocket and hand him a few coins. What moved me about these encounters was that he never let his mask drop. Blustering forth his thanks in the highly embroidered, Dickensian language that came so effortlessly to him, he would assure me that I would be paid back promptly, just as soon as circumstances allowed. "I am most grateful to you for this bounty, young man," he would say, "most grateful indeed. It's just a loan, of course, so you needn't fret about being reimbursed. As you might or might not know, I've suffered some small setbacks lately, and this generosity of yours will go a long way towards helping me back to my feet." The sums in question were never more than a pittance—forty cents here, twenty-five cents there, whatever I happened to be carrying around with me—but Joe never flagged in his enthusiasm, never once let on that he realized what an abject figure he was. There he stood, dressed in a circus clown's rags, his unwashed body emitting the foulest of stinks, and still he persisted in keeping up his pose as a man of the world, a dandy temporarily down on his luck. The pride and self-deception that went into this act were both comical and heartbreaking, and every time I went through the ritual of giving him another handout, I had trouble keeping my balance. I never knew whether to laugh or cry, whether to admire him or shower him with pity. "Let me see, young man," he would continue, studying the coins I had just put in his palm. "I have, let's see, I have here in my hand, hmmm, fifty-five cents. Add that to the eighty cents you gave me the last time, and then add that, hmmm, add that to the forty cents you gave me the time before that, and it turns out that I owe you a grand total of, hmmm, let's see, a grand total of . . . one dollar and fifteen cents." Such was Joe's arithmetic. He just plucked figures out of thin air and hoped they sounded good. "No problem, Joe," I would say. "A dollar and fifteen cents. You'll give it to me the next time."

When I came back to New York from the Esso ship, he seemed to be floundering, to have lost some ground. He looked more bruised to me, and the old panache had given way to a new heaviness of spirit, a whining, tearful sort of despair. One afternoon, he broke down in front of me as he recounted how he had been beaten up in some alleyway the night before. "They stole my books," he said. "Can you imagine that? The animals stole my books!" Another time, in the middle of a snowstorm, as I left my ninth-floor apartment and walked to the elevator down the hall, I found him sitting alone on the staircase, his head buried in his hands.

"Joe," I said, "are you all right?"

He lifted his head. His eyes were infused with sorrow, misery, and defeat. "No, young man," he said. "I'm not all right, not the least bit all right."

"Is there anything I can do for you?" I asked. "You look terrible, just terrible."

"Yes," he said, "now that you mention it, there is one thing you can do for me," and at that point he suddenly reached out and took hold of my hand. Then, looking me straight in the eye, he gathered up his strength and said, in a voice trembling with emotion, "You can take me back into your apartment, lie down on the bed, and let me make love to you."

The bluntness of his request took me completely by surprise.

I had been thinking more along the lines of a cup of coffee or a bowl of soup. "I can't do that," I said. "I like women, Joe, not men. Sorry, but I don't do that kind of thing."

What he said next lingers in my mind as one of the best and most pungent statements I have ever heard. Without wasting a second, and without the slightest trace of disappointment or regret, he dismissed my answer with a shrug of the shoulders and said, in a buoyant, ringing tone of voice, "Well, you asked me— and I told you."

I left for Paris sometime in the middle of February 1971. After that encounter on the staircase, I didn't see Joe again for several weeks. Then, just days before my departure, I bumped into him on Broadway. He was looking much better, and the hangdog look had disappeared from his face. When I told him I was about to move to Paris, he was off and running again, as effusive and full of himself as ever. "It's odd that you should mention Paris," he said. "Indeed, it's a most timely coincidence. Not two or three days ago, I happened to be walking down Fifth Avenue, and who should I bump into but my old friend Antoine, director of the Cunard Lines. 'Joe,' he said to me, 'Joe, you're not looking too well,' and I said, 'No, Antoine, it's true, I haven't been at my best lately,' and Antoine said that he wanted to do something for me, lend a helping hand, so to speak, and put me back on track. What he proposed, right there on Fifth Avenue the other day, was to sail me over to Paris on one of his ships and put me up at the Hôtel George V. All expenses paid, of course, with a new wardrobe thrown into the bargain. He said I could stay there as long as I liked. Two weeks, two months, even two years if I wanted. If I decide to go, which I think I will, I'll be leaving before the end of the month. Which means, young man, that we'll be in Paris at the same time. A pleasant prospect, no? Expect to see me there. We'll have tea, dinner. Just leave a message for me at the hotel. On the Champs-Elysées. That's where we'll meet next, my friend. In Paris, on the Champs-Elysées." And then, bidding me farewell, he shook my hand and wished me a safe and happy voyage.

I never saw Joe Reilly again. Even before we said good-bye that day, I knew that I was talking to him for the last time, and when he finally disappeared into the crowd a few minutes later, it was as if he had already turned into a ghost. All during the years I lived in Paris, I thought of him every time I set foot on the Champs-Elysées. Even now, whenever I go back there, I still do.

My money didn't last as long as I thought it would. I found an apartment within a week of my arrival, and once I had shelled out for the agency commission, the security deposit, the gas and electric service, the first month's rent, the last month's rent, and the state-mandated insurance policy, I didn't have much left. Right from the start, therefore, I had to scramble to keep my head above water. In the three and a half years I lived in France, I had any number of jobs, bounced from one part-time gig to another, free-lanced until I was blue in the face. When I didn't have work, I was looking for work. When I had work, I was thinking about how to find more. Even at the best of times, I rarely earned enough to feel secure, and yet in spite of one or two close calls, I managed to avoid total ruin. It was, as they say, a hand-to-mouth existence. Through it all, I wrote steadily, and if much of what I wrote was discarded (mostly prose), a fair chunk of it (mostly poems and translations) was not. For better or worse, by the time I returned to New York in July 1974, the idea of not writing was inconceivable to me.

Most of the work I landed came through friends or the friends of friends or the friends of friends of friends. Living in a foreign country restricts your opportunities, and unless you know some people who are willing to help you, it is next to impossible to get started. Not only will doors not open when you knock on them, but you won't even know where to look for those doors in the first place. I was lucky enough to have some allies, and at one time or another they all moved small mountains on my behalf. Jacques Dupin, for example, a poet whose work I had been translating for several years, turned out to be director of publications at the Galerie Maeght, one of the leading art galleries in Europe. Among the painters and sculptors shown there were Miró, Giacometti, Chagall, and Calder, to mention just a few. Through Jacques's intervention, I was hired to translate several art books and catalogues, and by my second year in Paris, when my funds were perilously close to bottoming out, he saved the situation by giving me a room to live in—free of charge. These acts of kindness were essential, and I can't imagine how I would have survived without them.

At one point, I was steered to the Paris bureau of *The New York Times*. I can't remember who was responsible for the connection, but an editor named Josette Lazar began throwing translations my way whenever she could: articles for the Sunday *Book Review*, op-ed pieces by Sartre and Foucault, this and that. One summer, when my money was at low ebb again, she finagled a position for me as the nighttime switchboard operator at the *Times* office. The phone didn't ring very often, and mostly I just sat at a desk, working on poems or reading books. One night, however, there was a frantic call from a reporter stationed somewhere in Europe. "Sinyavsky's defected," she said. "What should I do?" I had no idea what she should do, but since none of the editors was around at that hour, I figured I had to tell her something. "Follow the story," I said. "Go where you have to go, do what you have to do, but stick with the story, come hell or high water." She thanked me profusely for the advice and then hung up.

Some jobs started out as one thing and ended up as another, like a botched stew you can't stop tinkering with. Just stir in some additional ingredients and see if it doesn't taste better. A good example would be my little adventure among the North Vietnamese in Paris, which began with an innocent phone call from Mary McCarthy to my friend André du Bouchet. She asked him if he knew of anyone who could translate poetry from French into English, and when he gave her my name, she called and invited me to her apartment to discuss the project. It was early 1973, and the war in Vietnam was still dragging on. Mary McCarthy had been writing about the war for several years, and I had read most of her articles, which I found to be among the best pieces of journalism published at the time. In the course of her work, she had come in contact with many Vietnamese from both the northern and southern halves of the country. One of them, a professor of literature, was putting together an anthology of Vietnamese poetry, and she had offered to help arrange for an English-language version to be published in America. The poems had already been translated into French, and the idea was to translate those translations into English. That was how my name had come up, and that was why she wanted to talk to me.

In her private life, Mary McCarthy was Mrs. West. Her husband was a well-to-do American businessman, and their Paris apartment was a large, richly appointed place filled with art objects, antiques, and fine furniture. Lunch was served to us by a maid in a black and white uniform. A china bell sat on the table next to my hostess's right hand, and every time she picked it up and gave it a little shake, the maid would return to the dining room to receive further instructions. There was an impressive, *grande dame* quality to the way Mary McCarthy handled these domestic protocols, but the truth was that she turned out to be everything I had hoped she would be: sharp-witted, friendly, unpretentious. We talked about many things that afternoon, and by the time I left her apartment several hours later, I was loaded down with six or seven books of Vietnamese poetry. The first step was for me to familiarize myself with their contents. After that, the professor and I would meet and get down to work on the anthology.

I read the books and enjoyed them, particularly *The Book of Kieu*, the national epic poem. The details escape me now, but I remember becoming interested in some of the formal problems presented by traditional Vietnamese verse structures, which have no equivalents in Western poetry. I was happy to have been offered the job. Not only was I going to be paid well, but it looked as if I might learn something into the bargain. A week or so after our lunch, however, Mary McCarthy called to tell me that there had been an emergency, and her professor friend had gone back to Hanoi. She wasn't sure when he would be returning to Paris, but for the time being at least, the project had been put on hold.

Such were the breaks. I pushed the books aside and hoped the job wasn't dead, even though I knew it was. Several days went by, and then, out of the blue, I received a telephone call from a Vietnamese woman living in Paris. "Professor So-and-so gave us your name," she said. "He told us you can translate into English. Is that true?" "Yes," I said, "it's true." "Good," she said. "We have a job for you."

The job turned out to be a translation of the new North Vietnamese constitution. I had no qualms about doing the work, but I found it strange that they should have come to me. You would think that a document of that sort would be translated by someone in the government—directly from Vietnamese into English, and not from French, and if from French, not by an enemy American living in Paris. I didn't ask any questions, however. I still had my fingers crossed about the anthology and didn't want to ruin my chances, so I accepted the job. The following evening, the woman came to my apartment to drop off the manuscript. She was a biologist in her mid-thirties—thin, unadorned, exceptionally reserved in her manner. She didn't say anything about a fee for the work, and from her silence I gathered that there wasn't going to be one. Given the tangled political nuances of the situation (the war between our two countries, my feelings about that war, and so on), I was hardly disposed to press her about money. Instead, I began asking her questions about the Vietnamese poems I had been reading. At one point, I got her to sit down at my desk with me and draw a diagram that explained the traditional verse forms that had piqued my curiosity. Her sketch proved to be very helpful, but when I asked her if I could keep it for future reference, she shook her head, crumpled up the paper, and put it in her pocket. I was so startled, I didn't say a word. In that one small gesture, an entire world had been revealed to me, an underground universe of fear and betrayal in which even a scrap of paper was suspect. Trust no one; cover your tracks; destroy the evidence. It wasn't that she was afraid of what I might do with the diagram. She was simply acting out of habit, and I couldn't help feeling sorry for her, sorry for both of us. It meant that the war was everywhere, that the war had tainted everything.

The constitution was eight or ten pages long, and apart from some standard Marxist-Leninist phrases ("running dogs of imperialism," "bourgeois lackeys"), it was pretty dry stuff. I did the translation the next day, and when I called my biologist friend to tell her that the work was finished, she sounded inordinately pleased and grateful. It was only then that she told me about my payment: an invitation to dinner. "By way of thanks," as she put it. The restaurant happened to be in the Fifth Arrondissement, not far from where I lived, and I had eaten there several times before. It was the simplest and cheapest Vietnamese restaurant in Paris, but also the best. The only ornament in the place was a black-and-white photograph of Ho Chi Minh hanging on the wall.

Other jobs were entirely straightforward, the essence of simplicity: tutoring a high school boy in English, serving as simultaneous translator at a small international conference of Jewish scholars (dinner included), translating material by and about Giacometti for the art critic David Sylvester. Few of these jobs paid well, but they all brought in something, and if I didn't always have great stocks of food in my refrigerator, I was rarely without a pack of cigarettes in my pocket. Still, I couldn't have sustained myself on odds and ends alone. They helped to keep me going, but add them all together, and they wouldn't have been enough to live on for more than a few weeks, a few months at most. I needed another source of income to pay the bills, and as luck would have it, I found one. To put it more accurately, it found me. For the first two years I spent in Paris, it was the difference between eating and not eating.

The story goes back to 1967. During my earlier stay as a student, an American friend had introduced me to a woman I will call Madame X. Her husband, Monsieur X, was a well-known film producer of the old style (epics, extravaganzas, a maker of deals), and it was through her that I started working for him. The first opportunity arose just a few months after I arrived. There was no telephone in the apartment I had rented, which was still the case with many Paris apartments in 1971, and there were only two ways of contacting me: by *pneumatique*, a rapid intracity telegram sent through the post office, or by coming to the apartment and knocking on the door. One morning, not long after I had woken up, Madame X knocked on the door. "How would you like to earn a hundred dollars today?" she said. The job seemed simple enough: read a movie script, then write out a six- or seven-page summary. The only constraint was time. A potential backer of the film was waiting on a yacht somewhere in the Mediterranean, and the outline had to be delivered to him within forty-eight hours.

Madame X was a flamboyant, stormy character, the first larger-than-life woman I had ever met. Mexican by birth, married since the age of eighteen or nineteen, the mother of a boy just a few years younger than I was, she lived her own independent life, drifting in and out of her husband's orbit in ways I was still too unsophisticated to understand. Artistic by temperament, she dabbled by turns at painting and writing, showing talent in both fields but with too little discipline or concentration to take those talents very far. Her true gift was encouraging others, and she surrounded herself with artists and would-be artists of all ages, hobnobbing with the known and the unknown as both a colleague and a patroness. Wherever she went, she was the center of attention, the gorgeous, soulful woman with the long black hair and the hooded cloaks and the clattering Mexican jewelry—moody, generous, loyal, her head full of dreams. Somehow or other, I had made it onto her list, and because I was young and just starting out, she counted me among those friends who needed looking after, the poor and struggling ones who required an occasional helping hand.

There were others too, of course, and a couple of them were invited along with me that morning to earn the same round figure I had been promised. A hundred dollars sounds like pocket change today, but back then it represented more than half a month's rent, and I was in no position to turn down a sum of that magnitude. The work was to be done at the Xs' apartment, an immense, palatial establishment in the Sixteenth Arrondissement with untold numbers of high-ceilinged rooms. The starting time was set for eleven o'clock, and I showed up with half an hour to spare.

I had met each of my coworkers before. One of them was an American in his mid-twenties, a fey unemployed pianist who walked around in women's high heels and had recently spent time in a hospital with a collapsed lung. The other was a Frenchman with decades of film experience, mostly as a second-unit director. Among his credits were the chariot scenes in *Ben-Hur* and the desert scenes in *Lawrence of Arabia*, but since those days of wealth and success, he had fallen on hard times: nervous breakdowns, periods of confinement in mental wards, no work. He and the pianist were major reclamation projects for Madame X, and throwing me together with them was just one example of how she operated. No matter how good her intentions were, they were invariably undermined by complex, impractical schemes, a desire to kill too many birds with a single stone. Rescuing one person is hard enough, but to think you can save the whole world at once is to ask for disappointment.

So there we were, the most mismatched trio ever assembled, gathered around the gigantic table in the dining room of the Xs' gigantic apartment. The script in question was also gigantic. A work of nearly three hundred pages (three times the length of the normal script), it looked like the telephone book of a large city. Because the Frenchman was the only one with any professional knowledge of the movies, the pianist and I deferred to him and allowed him to take charge of the discussion. The first thing he did was pull out a sheet of blank paper and begin jotting down the names of actors. Frank Sinatra, Dean Martin, Sammy Davis, Jr., followed by six or seven others. When he was finished, he slapped his hands on the table with great satisfaction. "You see this piece of paper?" he asked. The pianist and I nodded our heads. "Believe it or not, this little piece of paper is worth ten million dollars." He patted the list once or twice and then pushed it aside. "Ten, maybe twelve million dollars." He spoke with the utmost conviction, betraying not the slightest hint of humor or irony. After a brief pause, he opened the manuscript to the first page. "Well," he said, "are we ready to begin?"

Almost immediately, he became excited. On the second or third line of the first page, he noticed that the name of one of the characters began with the letter Z. "Aha!" he said. "Z. This is very important. Pay close attention, my friends. This is going to be a political film. Mark my words."

Z was the title of a film by Costa-Gavras, a popular hit two years earlier. That film had most assuredly been about politics, but the screenplay we had been asked to summarize was not. It was an action thriller about smuggling. Largely set in the Sahara Desert, it featured trucks, motorcycles, several gangs of warring bad guys, and a number of spectacular explosions. The only thing that set it apart from a thousand other movies was its length.

We had been at work for approximately a minute and a half, and already the pianist had lost interest. He stared down at the table and snickered to himself as the Frenchman rambled on, lurching from one bit of nonsense to another. Suddenly, without any transition or preamble, the poor man started talking about David Lean, recalling several philosophical discussions he'd had with the director fifteen years earlier. Then, just as abruptly, he broke off from his reminiscences, stood up from the table, and walked around the room, straightening the pictures on the walls. When he was finished with that task, he announced that he was going to the kitchen to look for a cup of coffee. The pianist shrugged. "I think I'll go play the piano," he said, and just like that, he was gone as well.

As I waited for them to return, I started reading the script. I couldn't think of anything else to do, and by the time it dawned on me that neither one of them would be coming back, I had worked my way through most of it. Eventually, one of Monsieur X's associates drifted into the room. He was a youngish, good-natured American who also happened to be Madame X's special friend (the complexities of the household were fathomless), and he instructed me to finish the job on my own, guaranteeing that if I managed to produce an acceptable piece of work by seven o'clock, all three of the hundred-dollar payments would be mine. I told him I would do my best. Before I hustled out of there and went home to my typewriter, he gave me an excellent bit of advice. "Just remember," he said. "This is the movies, not Shakespeare. Make it as vulgar as you can."

I wound up writing the synopsis in the extravagant, over-heated language of Hollywood coming attractions. If they wanted vulgar, I would give them vulgar. I had sat through enough movie trailers to know what they sounded like, and by dredging up every hackneyed phrase I could think of, by piling one excess on top of another, I boiled the story down to seven pages of frantic, non-stop action, a bloodbath wrought in pulsing, Technicolor prose. I finished typing at six-thirty. An hour later, a chauffeur-driven car arrived downstairs to take me and my girlfriend to the restaurant where Madame and Monsieur X had invited us for dinner. The moment we got there, I was supposed to deliver the pages to him in person.

Monsieur X was a small, enigmatic man in his mid to late fifties. Of Russian-Jewish origin, he spoke several languages with equal fluency, often shifting from French to English to Spanish in the course of a single conversation, but always with the same cumbersome accent, as if in the end he didn't feel at home in any of them. He had been producing movies for over thirty years, and in a career of countless ups and downs, he had backed good films and bad films, big films and small films, art films and trash films. Some had made piles of money for him, others had put him miserably in debt. I had crossed paths with him only a few times before that night, but he had always struck me as a lugubrious person, a man who played things close to the vest—shrewd, hidden, unknowable. Even as he talked to you, you sensed that he was thinking about something else, working out some mysterious calculations that might or might not have had anything to do with what he was saying. It's not that they didn't, but at the same time it would have been wrong to assume that they did.

That night in the restaurant, he was noticeably edgy when I arrived. A potentially lucrative deal hinged on the work of one of his wife's arty friends, and he was anything but optimistic. I had barely settled into my seat when he asked to see the pages I had written.

As the rest of us made small talk around the table, Monsieur X sat hunched in silence, reading through my florid, slam-bang paragraphs. Little by little, a smile began to form on his lips. He started nodding to himself as he turned the pages, and once or twice he was even heard to mutter the word "good" under his breath. He didn't look up, however. Not until he'd come to the last sentence did he finally raise his head and give me the verdict.

"Excellent," he said. "This is just what I wanted." The relief in his voice was almost palpable.

Madame X said something about how she'd told him so, and he confessed that he'd had his doubts. "I thought it would be too literary," he said. "But this is good. This is just right."

He became very effusive after that. We were in a large, gaudy restaurant in Montmartre, and he immediately started snapping his fingers for the flower girl. She came scurrying over to our table, and Monsieur X bought a dozen roses, which he handed to my girlfriend as an impromptu gift. Then he reached into his breast pocket, pulled out his checkbook, and wrote me a check for three hundred dollars. It was the first check I had ever seen from a Swiss bank.

I was glad to have delivered the goods under pressure, glad to have earned my three hundred bucks, glad to have been roped into the absurd events of that day, but once we left the restaurant and I returned to my apartment on the rue Jacques Mawas, I assumed that the story was over. It never once crossed my mind that Monsieur X might have further plans for me. One afternoon the following week, however, as I sat at my table working on a poem, I was interrupted by a loud knock on the door. It was one of Monsieur X's gofers, an elderly gentleman I'd seen lurking about the house on my visits there but had never had the pleasure of talking to. He wasted no time in getting to the point. Are you Paul Auster? he asked. When I told him I was, he informed me that Monsieur

X wanted to see me. When? I asked. Right now, he said. There's a taxi waiting downstairs.

It was a little like being arrested by the secret police. I suppose I could have refused the invitation, but the cloak-and-dagger atmosphere made me curious, and I decided to go along to see what was up. In the cab, I asked my chaperon why I had been summoned like this, but the old man merely shrugged. Monsieur X had told him to bring me back to the house, and that was what he was doing. His job was to follow orders, not ask questions. I therefore remained in the dark, and as I mulled over the question myself, the only answer I could think of was that Monsieur X was no longer satisfied with the work I had done for him. By the time I walked into his apartment, I was fully expecting him to ask me for the money back.

He was dressed in a paisley smoking jacket with satin lapels, and as he entered the room where I'd been told to wait for him, I noticed that he was rubbing his hands together. I had no idea what that gesture meant.

"Last week," he said, "you do good works for me. Now I want to make package deal."

That explained the hands. It was the gesture of a man ready to do business, and all of a sudden, on the strength of that dashed-off, tongue-in-cheek manuscript I'd concocted for him the other day, it looked as though I was about to be in business with Monsieur X. He had at least two jobs for me right away, and if all went well with those, the implication was that others would follow. I needed the money and accepted, but not without a certain wariness. I was stepping into a realm I didn't understand, and unless I kept my wits about me, I realized that strange things could be in store for me. I don't know how or why I knew that, but I did. When Monsieur X started talking about giving me a role in one of his upcoming movies, a swashbuckling adventure story for which I would need fencing and riding lessons, I held my ground. "We'll see," I said. "The fact is, I'm not much interested in acting."

Apparently, the man on the yacht had liked my synopsis just as much as Monsieur X had. Now he wanted to take things to the next level and was commissioning a translation of the screenplay from French into English. That was the first job. The second job was somewhat less cut-and-dried. Madame X was at work on a play, Monsieur X told me, and he had agreed to finance a production at the Round House Theatre in London next season. The piece was about Quetzalcoatl, the mythical plumed serpent, and since much of it was written in verse, and since much of that verse was written in Spanish, he wanted me to turn it into English and make sure that the drama was in playable shape. Fine, I said, and that was how we left it. I did both jobs, everyone was satisfied, and two or three months later, Madame X's play was performed in London. It was a vanity production, of course, but the reviews were good, and all in all the play was quite well received. A British publisher happened to attend one of the performances, and he was so impressed by what he'd seen that he proposed to Madame X that she turn the play into a prose narrative, which he would then publish as a book.

That was where things started getting sticky between me and Monsieur X. Madame X didn't have it in her to write the book on her own, and he believed that I was the one person on earth capable of helping her. I might have accepted the job under different circumstances, but since he also wanted me to go to Mexico to do the work, I told him I wasn't interested. Why the book had to be written in Mexico was never made clear to me. Research, local color, something along those lines, I'm not sure. I was fond of Madame X, but being thrown together with her for an unspecified length of time struck me as less than a good idea. I didn't even have to think about Monsieur X's offer. I turned him down on the spot, figuring that would close the matter once and for all.

Events proved me wrong. True indifference has power, I learned, and my refusal to take the job irritated Monsieur X and got under his skin. He wasn't in the habit of having people say no to him, and he became hell-bent on changing my mind. Over the next several months, he launched an all-out campaign to wear down my resistance, besieging me with letters, telegrams, and promises of ever greater sums of money. In the end, I reluctantly gave in. As with every other bad decision I've made in my life, I acted against my better judgment, allowing secondary considerations to interfere with the clarity of my instincts. In this case, what tipped the balance was money. I was having a hard time of it just then, desperately falling behind in my struggle to remain solvent, and Monsieur X's offer had grown so large, would eliminate so many of my problems at once, that I talked myself into accepting the wisdom of compromise. I thought I was being clever. Once I had climbed down from my high horse, I laid out my conditions in the toughest terms I could think of. I would go to Mexico for exactly one month, I told him—no more, no less—and I wanted full payment in cash before I left Paris. It was the first time I had ever negotiated for anything, but I was determined to protect myself, and I refused to yield on any of these points. Monsieur X was less than thrilled with my intractability, but he understood that I'd gone as far as I would go and gave in to my demands. The same day I left for Mexico, I deposited twenty-five one-hundred-dollar bills in my bank account. Whatever happened in the next month, at least I wouldn't be broke when I returned.

I was expecting things to go wrong, but not quite to the degree that they did. Without rehashing the whole complicated business (the man who threatened to kill me, the schizophrenic girl who thought I was a Hindu god, the drunken, suicidal misery that permeated every household I entered), the thirty days I spent in Mexico were among the grimmest, most unsettling days of my life. Madame X had already been there for a couple of weeks when I arrived, and I quickly learned that she was in no shape to work on the book. Her boyfriend had just left her, and this love drama had plunged her into the throes of an acute despair. It's not that I blamed her for her feelings, but she was so distraught, so distracted by her suffering, that the book was the last thing she wanted to think about. What was I supposed to do? I tried to get her started, tried to make her sit down with me and discuss the project, but she simply wasn't interested. Every time we took a stab at it, the conversation would quickly veer off onto other subjects. Again and again, she broke down and cried. Again and again, we got nowhere. After several of these attempts, I understood that the only reason she was bothering to make an effort was because of me. She knew that I was being paid to help her, and she didn't want to let me down, didn't want to admit that I had come all this way for nothing.

That was the essential flaw in the arrangement. To assume that a book can be written by a person who is not a writer is already a murky proposition, but granting that such a thing is possible, and granting that the person who wants to write the book has someone else to help with the writing of it, perhaps the two of them, with much hard work and dedication, can arrive at an acceptable result. On the other hand, if the person who is not a writer does not want to write a book, of what use is the someone else? Such was the quandary I found myself in. I was willing to help Madame X write her book, but I couldn't help her unless she wanted to write it, and if she didn't want to, there was nothing I could do but sit around and wait until she did.

So there I sat, biding my time in the little village of Tepotzolán, hoping that Madame X would wake up one morning and discover that she had a new outlook on life. I was staying with Madame X's brother (whose unhappy marriage to an American woman was on its last legs), and I filled my days with aimless walks around the dusty town, stepping over mangy dogs, batting flies out of my face, and accepting invitations to drink beers with the local drunks. My room was in a stucco outbuilding on the brother's property, and I slept under muslin netting to guard against the tarantulas and mosquitoes. The crazy girl kept showing up with one of her friends, a Central American Hare Krishna with a shaved head and orange robes, and boredom ate away at me like some tropical disease. I wrote one or two short poems, but otherwise I languished, unable to think, bogged down by a persistent, nameless anxiety. Even the news from the outside world was bad. An earthquake killed thousands of people in Nicaragua, and my favorite baseball player, Roberto Clemente, the most elegant and electrifying performer of his generation, went down in a small plane that was trying to deliver emergency relief to the victims. If anything pleasant stands out from the miasma and stupor of that month, it would be the hours I spent in Cuernavaca, the radiant little city that Malcolm Lowry wrote about in *Under the Volcano*. There, quite by chance, I was introduced to a man who was described to me as the last living descendant of Montezuma. A tall, stately gent of around sixty, he had impeccable manners and wore a silk ascot around his neck.

When I finally returned to Paris, Monsieur X arranged to meet me in the lobby of a hotel on the Champs-Elysées. Not the Hôtel George V, but another one directly across the street. I can't remember why he chose that place, but I think it had something to do with an appointment he'd scheduled there before mine, strictly a matter of convenience. In any case, we didn't talk in the hotel. The instant I showed up, he led me outside again and pointed to his car, which was waiting for us just in front of the entrance. It was a tan Jaguar with leather upholstery, and the man behind the wheel was dressed in a white shirt. "We'll talk in there," Monsieur X said. "It's more private." We climbed into the back seat, the driver started up the engine, and the car pulled away from the curb. "Just drive around," Monsieur X said to the chauffeur. I suddenly felt as if I had landed in a gangster movie.

Most of the story was known by then, but he wanted me to give him a full report, an autopsy of the failure. I did my best to describe what had happened, expressing more than once how sorry I was that things hadn't worked out, but with Madame X's heart no longer in the book, I said, there wasn't much I could do to motivate her. Monsieur X seemed to accept all this with great calm. As far as I could tell, he wasn't angry, not even especially disappointed. Just when I thought the interview was about to end, however, he brought up the subject of my payment. Since nothing had been accomplished, he said, it seemed only right that I should give him back the money, didn't it? No, I said, it didn't seem right at all. A deal is a deal, and I had gone to Mexico in good faith and had kept up my end of the bargain. No one had ever suggested that I write the book *for* Madame X. I was supposed to write it *with* her, and if she didn't want to do the work, it wasn't my job to force her to do it. That was precisely why I'd asked for the money in advance. I was afraid that something like this would happen, and I needed to know that I would be paid for my time—no matter how things turned out.

He saw the logic of my argument, but that didn't mean he was willing to back down. All right, he said, keep the money, but if you want to go on working for me, you'll have to do some more jobs to square the account. In other words, instead of asking me to return the money in cash, he wanted me to give it back in labor. I told him that was unacceptable. Our account was square, I said, I wasn't in debt to him, and if he wanted to hire me for other jobs, he would have to pay me what those jobs were worth. Needless to say, that was unacceptable to him. I thought you wanted a part in the movie, he said. I never said that, I answered. Because if you do, he continued, we'll have to clear up this business first. Once again,

I told him there was nothing to clear up. All right, he said, if that's how you feel about it, then we have nothing to say to each other anymore. And with that remark he turned away from me and told the driver to stop the car.

We had been riding around for about half an hour by then, slowly drifting toward the outer fringes of Paris, and the neighborhood where the car had stopped was unfamiliar to me. It was a cold January night, and I had no idea where I was, but the conversation was over, and there was nothing for me to do but say good-bye to him and get out of the car. If I remember correctly, we didn't even shake hands. I stepped out onto the sidewalk, shut the door, and the car drove off. And that was the end of my career in the movies.

I stayed on in France for another eighteen months—half of them in Paris and half of them in Provence, where my girlfriend and I worked as caretakers of a farmhouse in the northern Var. By the time I returned to New York, I had under ten dollars in my pocket and not a single concrete plan for the future. I was twenty-seven years old, and with nothing to show for myself but a book of poems and a handful of obscure literary essays, I was no closer to having solved the problem of money than I'd been before I left America. To further complicate the situation, my girlfriend and I decided to get married. It was an impulsive move, but with so many things about to change, we figured why not go ahead and change everything at once?

I immediately began casting about for work. I made telephone calls, followed up on leads, went in for interviews, explored as many possibilities as I could. I was trying to act sensibly, and after all the ups and downs I'd been through, all the tight corners and desperate squeezes that had trapped me over the years, I was determined not to repeat my old mistakes. I had learned my lesson, I told myself, and this time I was going to take care of business.

But I hadn't, and I didn't. For all my high-minded intentions, it turned out that I was incorrigible. It's not that I didn't find a job, but rather than accept the full-time position I had been offered (as junior editor in a large publishing house), I opted for a half-time job at half the pay. I had vowed to swallow my medicine, but just when the spoon was coming toward me, I shut my mouth. Until it happened, I had no idea that I was going to balk like that, no idea how stubbornly I was going to resist. Against all the odds, it seemed that I still hadn't given up the vain and stupid hope of surviving on my own terms. A part-time job looked like a good solution, but not even that was enough. I wanted total independence, and when some freelance translation work finally came my way, I quit the job and went off on my own again. From start to finish, the experiment lasted just seven months. Short as that time might have been, it was the only period of my adult life when I earned a regular paycheck.

By every standard, the job I had found was an excellent one. My boss was Arthur Cohen, a man of many interests, much money, and a first-rate mind. A writer of both novels and essays, a former publishing executive, and a passionate collector of art, he had recently set up a little business as an outlet for his excess energies. Part hobbyhorse, part serious commercial venture, Ex Libris was a rare-book concern that specialized in publications connected with twentieth-century art. Not books *about* art, but manifestations of the art itself. Magazines from the Dada movement, for example, or books designed by members of the Bauhaus, or photographs by Stieglitz, or an edition of Ovid's *Metamorphoses* illustrated by Picasso. As the back cover of each Ex Libris catalogue announced: "Books and Periodicals in Original Editions for the Documentation of the Art of the 20th Century: Futurism, Cubism, Dada, Bauhaus and Constructivism, De Stijl, Surrealism, Expressionism, Post War Art, as well as Architecture, Typography, Photography and Design."

Arthur was just getting the operation off the ground when he hired me as his sole employee. My chief task was to help him write the Ex Libris catalogues, which were issued twice a year and ran to a little over a hundred pages. Other duties included writing letters, preparing the catalogues for bulk mailings, fulfilling orders, and making tuna fish sandwiches for lunch. Mornings I spent at home, working for myself, and at twelve o'clock I would go downstairs to Riverside Drive and take the number 4 bus to the office. An apartment had been rented in a brownstone building on East Sixty-ninth Street to store Ex Libris's holdings, and the two rooms were crammed with thousands of books, magazines, and prints. Stacked on tables, wedged onto shelves, piled high in closets, these precious objects had overwhelmed the entire space. I spent four or five hours there every afternoon, and it was a bit like working in a museum, a small shrine to the avant-garde.

Arthur worked in one room and I worked in the other, each of us planted at a desk as we combed through the items for sale and prepared our meticulous catalogue entries on five-by-seven index cards. Anything having to do with French and English was given to me; Arthur handled the German and Russian materials. Typography, design, and architecture were his domain; I was in charge of all things literary. There was a certain fusty precision to the work (measuring the books, examining them for imperfections, detailing provenances when necessary), but many of the items were quite thrilling to hold, and Arthur gave me free rein to express my opinions about them, even to inject an occasional dose of humor if I felt like it. A few examples from the second catalogue will give some idea of what the job entailed:

233. **DUCHAMP, M. & HALBERSTADT**, V. L'Opposition et les cases conjuguées sont réconciliées par M. Duchamp et V. Halberstadt. Editions de L'Echiquier. St. Germain-en-Laye and Brussels, 1932. Parallel text in German

and English on left-hand pages. 112 double-numbered pp., with 2-color illustrations. 9 5/8 × 11". Printed paper covers.

The famous book on chess written and designed by Duchamp. (Schwarz, p. 589). Although it is a serious text, devoted to a real chess problem, it is nevertheless so obscure as to be virtually worthless. Schwarz quotes Duchamp as having said: "The endgames on which this fact turns are of no interest to any chess player; and that's the funniest thing about it. Only three or four people in the world are interested in it, and they're the ones who've tried the same lines of research as Halberstadt and myself, since we wrote the book together. Chess champions never read this book, because the problem it poses never really turns up more than once in a lifetime. These are possible endgame problems, but they're so rare that they're almost utopian." (p. 63). $1000.00

394. (STEIN, GERTRUDE). Testimony: Against Gertrude Stein. Texts by Georges Braque, Eugene Jolas, Maria Jolas, Henri Matisse, André Salmon, Tristan Tzara. Servire Press. The Hague, February, 1935. (Transition Pamphlet no. 1; supplement to Transition 1934–1935; no. 23). 16 pp. 511/16 × 87/8". Printed paper covers. Stapled.

In light of the great Stein revival of the Seventies, the continuing value of this pamphlet cannot be denied. It serves as an antidote to literary self-serving and, in its own right, is an important document of literary and artistic history. Occasioned by the inaccuracies and distortions of fact in The Autobiography of Alice B. Toklas, Transition produced this forum in order to allow some of the figures treated in Miss Stein's book to rebut her portrayal of them. The verdict seems to be unanimous. Matisse: "In short, it is more like a harlequin's costume the different pieces of which, having been more or less invented by herself, have been sewn together without taste and without relation to reality." Eugene Jolas: "The Autobiography of Alice B. Toklas, in its hollow, tinsel bohemianism and egocentric deformations, may very well become one day the symbol of the decadence that hovers over contemporary literature." Braque: "Miss Stein understood nothing of what went on around her." Tzara: "Underneath the 'baby' style, which is pleasant enough when it is a question of simpering at the interstices of envy, it is easy to discern such a really coarse spirit, accustomed to the artifices of the lowest literary prostitution, that I cannot believe it necessary for me to insist on the presence of a clinical case of megalomania." Salmon: "And what confusion! What incomprehension of an epoch! Fortunately there are others who have described it better." Finally, the piece by Maria Jolas is particularly noteworthy for its detailed description of the early days of Transition. This pamphlet was originally not for sale separately. $95.00

437. **GAUGUIN, PAUL.** Noa Noa. Voyage de Tahiti. Les Editions G. Crès & Cie. Paris, 1924. 154 pp., illustrated with 22 woodcuts after Paul Gauguin by Daniel de Monfreid. 5 3/4 × 7 15/16". Illustrated paper wrappers over paper.

This is the first definitive edition, including introductory material and poems by Charles Morice. The record of Gauguin's first two years in Tahiti, remarkable not only for its significant biographical revelations, but for its insightful anthropological approach to a strange culture. Gauguin follows Baudelaire's persuasive dictum: "Dites, qu'avez vous vu?" and the result is this miracle of vision: a Frenchman, at the height of European colonialism, traveling to an "underdeveloped country" neither to conquer nor convert, but to learn. This experience is the central event of Gauguin's life, both as an artist and as a man. Also: Noa Noa, translated into English by O.F. Theis. Nicholas L. Brown. New York, 1920. (Fifth printing; first printing in 1919). 148 pp. + 10 Gauguin reproductions. 5 5/16 × 7 13/16". Paper and cloth over boards. (Some minor foxing in French edition; slight fraying of spine in both French and English editions.) $65.00

509. **RAY, MAN**. Mr. and Mrs. Woodman. Edition Unida. No place, 1970. Pages unnumbered; with 27 original photographs and 1 signed and numbered engraving by Man Ray. 10 1/2 × 11 7/8". Leather bound, gilt-edged cardboard pages; leather and marbleized fitted box.

One of the very strangest of Man Ray's many strange works. Mr. and Mrs. Woodman are two puppet-like wood figures constructed by Man Ray in Hollywood in 1947, and the book, composed in 1970, is a series of mounted photographs of these witty, amazingly life-like characters in some of the most contorted erotic postures imaginable. In some sense, this book can best be described as a wood-people's guide to sex. Of an edition of only 50 copies, this is number 31, signed by Man Ray. All photographs are originals of the artist and carry his mark. Inserted is an original, numbered and signed engraving, specially made by Man Ray for this edition. $2100.00

Arthur and I got along well, with no strain or conflict, and we worked together in a friendly, unruffled atmosphere. Had I been a somewhat different person, I might have held on to that job for years, but seeing that I wasn't, I began to grow bored and restless after a few months. I enjoyed looking through the material I had to write about, but I didn't have the mind of a collector, and I could never bring myself to feel the proper awe or reverence for the things we sold. When you sit down to write about the catalogue that Marcel Duchamp designed for the 1947 Surrealist exhibition in Paris, for example—the one with the rubber breast on the cover, the celebrated bare falsie that came with the admonition "*Prière de Toucher*" ("Please Touch")—and you find that catalogue protected by several layers of bubble wrap, which in turn have been swathed in thick brown paper, which in turn has been slipped into a plastic bag, you can't help but pause for a moment and wonder if you aren't wasting your time. *Prière de toucher.* Duchamp's imperative is an obvious play on the signs you see posted all over France: *Prière de ne pas toucher* (Do Not Touch). He turns the warning on its head and asks us to fondle the thing he has made. And what better thing than this spongy, perfectly formed breast? Don't venerate it, he says, don't take it seriously, don't worship this frivolous activity we call art. Twenty-seven years later, the warning is turned upside down again. The naked breast has been covered. The thing to be touched has been made untouchable. The joke has been turned into a deadly serious transaction, and once again money has the last word.

This is not to criticize Arthur. No one loved these things more than he did, and if the catalogues we mailed out to potential customers were vehicles of commerce, they were also works of scholarship, rigorous documents in their own right. The difference between us was not that I understood the issues any better than he did (if anything, it was just the opposite), but that he was a businessman and I wasn't, which explained why he was the boss and I made just a few measly dollars per hour. Arthur took pleasure in turning a profit, enjoyed the push and pull of running the enterprise and making it succeed, and while he was also a man of great sophistication and refinement, a genuine intellectual who lived in and for the world of ideas, there was no getting around the fact that he was a crafty entrepreneur. Apparently, a life of the mind was not incompatible with the pursuit of money. I understood myself well enough to know that such a thing wasn't possible for me, but I saw now that it was possible for others. Some people didn't have to choose. They didn't have to divide the world into two separate camps. They could actually live in both places at the same time.

A few weeks after I started working for him, Arthur recommended me to a friend who was looking to hire someone for a short-term job. Arthur knew that I could use the extra money, and I mention this small favor as an example of how well he treated me. That the friend turned out to be Jerzy Kosinski, and that the job involved me in editing the manuscript of Kosinski's latest book, makes the episode worth talking about a little more. Intense controversy has surrounded Kosinksi in recent years, and since a large share of it emanated from the novel I worked on (*Cockpit*), I feel that I should add my testimony to the record. As Arthur explained it to me, the job was a simple matter of looking through the manuscript and making sure that the English was in good order. Since English wasn't Kosinski's first language, it seemed perfectly reasonable to me that he should want to have the prose checked before he handed the book to his publisher. What I didn't know was that other people had worked on the manuscript before me—three or four others, depending on which account you read. Kosinski never mentioned this earlier help to me, but whatever problems the book still had were not because the English didn't sound like English. The flaws were more fundamental than that, more about the book itself than how the story was told. I corrected a few sentences here, changed a few words there, but the novel was essentially finished by the time the manuscript was given to me. If left to my own devices, I could have completed the work in one or two days, but because Kosinski wouldn't let the manuscript out of his house, I had to go to his apartment on West Fifty-seventh Street to do the work, and because he hovered around me constantly, interrupting me every twenty minutes with stories, anecdotes, and nervous chatter, the job dragged on for seven days. I don't know why, but Kosinski seemed terribly eager to impress me, and the truth was that he did. He was so thoroughly high-strung, so odd and manic in his behavior, that I couldn't help but be impressed. What made these interruptions doubly odd and intriguing was that nearly every story he told me also appeared in the book he had written—the very novel spread out before me when he came into the room to talk. How he had masterminded his escape from Poland, for example. Or how he would prowl around Times Square at two in the morning disguised as a Puerto Rican under-cover cop. Or how, occasionally, he would turn up at expensive restaurants dressed in a sham military uniform (made for him by his tailor and representing no identifiable rank, country, or branch of service), but because that uniform looked good, and because it was covered with countless medals and stars, he would be given the best table in the house by the awestruck maître d'—without a reservation, without a tip, without so much as a glance. The book was supposedly a work of fiction, but when Kosinski told me these stories, he presented them as facts, real events from his life. Did he know the difference? I can't be sure, can't even begin to guess, but if I had to give an answer, I would say that he did. He struck me as too clever, too cunningly aware of himself and his effect on others not to enjoy the confusion he created. The common theme in the stories was deception, after all, playing people for fools, and from the way he laughed when he told them—as if gloating, as if reveling in his own cynicism—

I felt that perhaps he was only toying with me, buttering me up with compliments in order to test the limits of my credulity. Perhaps. And then again, perhaps not. The only thing I know for certain is that Kosinski was a man of labyrinthine complexity. When the rumors started circulating about him in the mid-eighties and magazine articles began to appear with accusations of plagiarism and the use of ghost writers and false claims concerning his past, I wasn't surprised. Years later, when he took his own life by suffocating himself with a plastic bag, I was. He died in the same apartment where I had worked for him in 1974, in the same bathroom where I had washed my hands and used the toilet. I have only to think about it for a moment, and I can see it all.

Otherwise, my months at Ex Libris passed quietly. Nothing much happened, and since most of the business was conducted through the mail, it was a rare day when anyone came to the apartment and disturbed us at our work. Late one afternoon, however, when Arthur was out on an errand, John Lennon knocked on the door, wanting to look at Man Ray photographs.

"Hi," he said, thrusting out his hand at me, "I'm John."

"Hi," I said, taking hold of the hand and giving it a good shake, "I'm Paul."

As I searched for the photographs in one of the closets, Lennon stopped in front of the Robert Motherwell canvas that hung on the wall beside Arthur's desk. There wasn't much to the painting— a pair of straight black lines against a broad orange background— and after studying it for a few moments, he turned to me and said, "Looks like that one took a lot of work, huh?" With all the pieties floating around the art world, I found it refreshing to hear him say that.

Arthur and I parted on good terms, with no hard feelings on either side. I made it my business to find a replacement for myself before I quit, and that made my departure relatively simple and painless. We stayed in touch for a little while, occasionally calling each other to catch up on the news, but eventually we lost contact, and when Arthur died of leukemia several years ago, I couldn't even remember the last time I had talked to him. Then came Kosinski's suicide. Add that to John Lennon's murder more than a decade earlier, and nearly everyone associated with the months I spent in that office has disappeared. Even Arthur's friend Robert Motherwell, the good artist responsible for the bad painting that provoked Lennon's comment, is no longer with us. Reach a certain moment in your life, and you discover that your days are spent as much with the dead as they are with the living.

The next two years were an intensely busy time. Between March 1975, when I stopped working for Ex Libris, and June 1977, when my son was born, I came out with two more books of poetry, wrote several one-act plays, published fifteen or twenty critical pieces, and translated half a dozen books with my wife, Lydia Davis. These translations were our primary source of income, and we worked together as a team, earning so many dollars per thousand words and taking whatever jobs we were offered. Except for one book by Sartre (*Life/Situations*, a collection of essays and interviews), the books the publishers gave us were dull, undistinguished works that ranged in quality from not very good to downright bad. The money was bad as well, and even though our rate kept increasing from book to book, if you broke down what we did on an hourly basis, we were scarcely a penny or two ahead of the minimum wage. The key was to work fast, to crank out the translations as quickly as we could and never stop for breath. There are surely more inspiring ways to make a living, but Lydia and I tackled these jobs with great discipline. A publisher would hand us a book, we would split the work in two (literally tearing the book in half if we had only one copy), and set a daily quota for ourselves. Nothing was allowed to interfere with that number.

So many pages had to be done every day, and every day, whether we felt in the mood or not, we sat down and did them. Flipping hamburgers would have been just as lucrative, but at least we were free, or at least we thought we were free, and I never felt any regrets about having left my job. For better or worse, this was how I had chosen to live. Between translating for money and writing for myself, there was rarely a moment during those years when I wasn't sitting at my desk, putting words on a piece of paper.

I didn't write criticism for money, but I was paid for most of the articles I published, and that helped pad my income to a certain degree. Still, getting by was a struggle, and from month to month we were no more than a short dry spell away from real poverty. Then, in the fall of 1975, just half a year into this tightrope walk *à deux*, my luck turned. I was given a five-thousand-dollar grant from the Ingram Merrill Foundation, and for the next little while the worst of the pressure was off. The money was so unexpected, so enormous in its ramifications, that I felt as if an angel had dropped down from the sky and kissed me on the forehead.

The man most responsible for this stroke of good fortune was John Bernard Myers. John didn't give me the money out of his own pocket, but he was the person who told me about the foundation and encouraged me to apply for the grant. The real benefactor, of course, was the poet James Merrill. In the quietest, most discreet manner possible, he had been sharing his family's wealth with other writers and artists for many years, hiding behind his middle name so as not to call attention to his astounding generosity. A committee met every six months to consider new applications and to dole out the awards. John was secretary of the committee, and although he didn't take part in choosing the recipients, he sat in on the meetings and knew how the members thought. Nothing was sure, he said, but he suspected that they would be inclined to support my work. So I put together a sampling of my poems and sent them in. At the next semiannual meeting, John's hunch proved to be correct.

I don't think I've ever known a funnier or more effusive person than John. When I first met him, in late 1974, he had been an integral part of the New York scene for the past thirty years, most famously as director of the Tibor de Nagy Gallery in the fifties, but also as cofounder of the Artists Theatre, editor of various short-lived literary magazines, and all-around champion and impresario of young talent. John was the first to give major shows to such artists as Red Grooms, Larry Rivers, Helen Frankenthaler, and Fairfield Porter, and he published the first books of Frank O'Hara, John Ashbery, and other poets of the New York School. The plays he produced were collaborations between many of these same poets and painters—O'Hara and Rivers, for example, or James Schuyler and Elaine de Kooning, the one writing the words and the other designing the sets. The Artists Theatre didn't bring in much at the box office, but John and his partner kept it running for years, and at a time when Off Broadway had yet to come into being, it was about the only experimental theater available in New York. What set John apart from all the other dealers, publishers, and producers I've known is that he wasn't in it for the money. Truth be told, he probably wasn't much of a businessman, but he had a genuine passion for art in all its forms, rigorous standards, openness of spirit, and an immense hunger for work that was different, challenging, new. A large man of six three or six four, he often made me think of John Wayne in his physical appearance. This John, however, in that he was proudly and flagrantly homosexual, in that he gleefully mocked himself with all manner of mincing gestures and extravagant poses, in that he took delight in silly jokes and ridiculous songs and a whole repertoire of childish humor, had nothing to do with that other John. No tough guy stuff for him. This John was all enthusiasm and goodwill, a man who had dedicated his life to beautiful things, and he wore his heart on his sleeve.*

When I met him, he was just starting up a new magazine—"of words and pictures"—called *Parenthèse*. I can't remember who suggested that I send him my work, but I did, and from then on John made a point of putting something of mine in nearly every issue. Later, when he discontinued the magazine and began publishing books instead, the first title on the list was a collection of my poems. John's belief in my work was absolute, and he backed me at a time when few people even knew that I was alive. In the endnotes to *Parenthèse 4*, for example, buried among the dry accounts of contributors' past achievements, he took it upon himself to declare that "Paul Auster has created a stir in the literary world by his brilliant analysis of the work of Laura Riding Jackson, by his essays on French paintings, and his poetry." It didn't matter that this statement wasn't true, that John was the only one paying attention. *Someone* was behind me, and in those early days of struggle and uncertainty, of not stirring up much of anything, that encouragement made all the difference. John was the first person who took a stand for me, and I have never stopped feeling grateful to him for that.

When the grant money came, Lydia and I hit the road again. We sublet our apartment and went to the Laurentian Mountains in Quebec, holing up in the house of a painter friend for a couple of months while he was away, then returned to New York for a week or two, and then promptly packed our bags again and took a cross-country train to San Francisco. We eventually settled in Berkeley, renting a small efficiency apartment not far from the university, and lived there for six months. We weren't flush enough to stop translating, but the pace was less frantic now, and

---

* For a vivid account of his adventures, see John's *Tracking the Marvelous: A Life in the New York Art World*, published by Random House in 1983.

that allowed me to spend more time with my own work. I went on writing poems, but new impulses and ideas started coming as well, and before long I found myself writing a play. That led to another play, which in turn led to another play, and when I returned to New York in the fall, I showed them to John. I didn't know what to make of what I had written. The pieces had surged up unexpectedly, and the results were quite different from anything I had done before. When John told me he liked them, I felt that perhaps I had taken a step in the right direction. The farthest thing from my mind was to do anything with them in a practical sense. I had given no thought to having them performed, no thought to publishing them. As far as I was concerned, they were hardly more than spare, minimalist exercises, an initial stab at something that might or might not turn out to be real. When John said that he wanted to take the longest of the plays and mount a production of it, I was caught totally by surprise.

No one was to blame for what happened. John jumped in with his customary excitement and energy, but things kept going wrong, and after a while it began to seem that we weren't putting on a play so much as trying to prove the indestructible power of Murphy's Law. A director and three actors were found, and shortly after that a reading was scheduled to drum up financial support for the production. That was the plan, in any case. It didn't help that the actors were young and inexperienced, not up to the task of delivering their lines with conviction or true feeling, but even worse was the audience who came to hear them deliver those lines. John had invited a dozen of his richest art collector friends, and not one of these potential backers was under sixty or had the slightest interest in the theater. He was counting on the play to seduce them, to overwhelm their hearts and minds with such stunning finality that they would feel no choice but to reach into their pockets and start pulling out their checkbooks. The event was held at a posh Upper East Side apartment, and my job was to charm these wealthy patrons, to smile and chat and reassure them that they were putting their money on the right horse. The problem was that I had no talent for smiling and chatting. I arrived in a state of extreme tension, nervous to the point of being ill, and quickly downed two bourbons to undo the knot in my stomach. The alcohol had precisely the opposite effect, and by the time the reading started, I had come down with a massive headache, a blistering, brain-bending assault that grew ever more unbearable as the evening wore on. The play thudded forward, and from start to finish the rich people sat in silence, utterly unmoved. Lines that I had imagined were funny did not produce the faintest titter. They were bored by the gags, indifferent to the pathos, perplexed by the whole thing. At the end, after some grim, perfunctory applause, I could only think about how to get out of there and hide. My head was cracking with pain. I felt stabbed and humiliated, unable to speak, but I couldn't abandon John, and so for the next half hour I listened to him talk about the play to his befuddled friends, doing everything I could not to pass out on the carpet. John put up a brave front, but every time he turned to me for help, I could do no more than stare down at my shoes and mumble a brief, unintelligible comment. Finally, apropos of nothing, I blurted out some lame excuse and left.

A lesser man would have given up after such a defeat, but John was undaunted. Not a penny of aid emerged from that gruesome evening, but he went ahead and started improvising a new plan, scuttling his dream of theatrical glory for a more modest, workable approach. If we couldn't afford a real theater, he said, we would make do with something else. The play was the only thing that mattered, and even if the run was limited to just a single, invitation-only performance, there was going to be a production of my play. If not for me, he said, and if not for him, then at least for his friend Herbert Machiz, who had died that summer. Herbert had directed the plays at the old Artists Theatre, and because he had been John's companion for twenty-five years, John was determined to revive the Theatre in Herbert's memory—if only for just one night.

A man who owned a restoration studio on East Sixty-ninth Street offered John the use of his space. It happened to be just down the block from the Ex Libris office—an interesting, if minor, coincidence—but more to the point was that in its previous incarnation the carriage house where John's friend now worked had been the studio of Mark Rothko. Rothko had killed himself there in 1970, and now, less than seven years later, my play was going to be presented in that same room. I don't want to sound overly superstitious about it, but given how things turned out, it feels that we were cursed, that no matter what any of us did or didn't do, the project was bound to fail.

Preparations began. The director and the three actors worked hard, and little by little the performances improved. I wouldn't go so far as to call them good, but at least they were no longer an embarrassment. One of the actors stood out from the others, and as the rehearsals went on, I began to pin my hopes on him, praying that his inventiveness and daring might pull the production up to a reasonably competent level. A date in early March was chosen for the performance, invitations were sent out, and arrangements were made for a hundred and fifty folding chairs to be delivered to the carriage house. I should have known better, but I actually began to feel optimistic. Then, just days before the big night, the good actor came down with pneumonia, and because there were no understudies (how could there have been?), it looked as if the performance would have to be canceled. The actor, however, who had put weeks of time and effort into the rehearsals, was not about to give up. In spite of a high temperature, in spite of the fact that he was coughing up blood just hours before the play was supposed to start, he crawled out of bed, pumped his system full of antibiotics, and staggered on at the appointed time. It was the noblest of noble gestures, the gutsy act of a born trouper, and I was impressed by his courage—no, more than impressed: filled with admiration—but the sad truth was that he was in no shape to do what he did. Everything that had sparkled in the rehearsals suddenly lost its shine. The performance was flat, the timing was off, scene after scene was blown. I stood at the back of the room and watched, powerless to do a thing. I saw my little play die in front of a hundred and fifty people, and I couldn't lift a finger to stop it.

Before putting the whole miserable experience behind me, I sat down and reworked the play. The performances had been only part of the problem, and I wasn't about to palm off responsibility for what had happened on the director or the actors. The play was too long, I realized, too rambling and diffuse, and radical surgery was needed to mend it. I began chopping and trimming, hacking away at everything that felt weak or superfluous, and by the time I was finished, half of the play was gone, one of the characters had been eliminated, and the title had been changed. I typed up this new version, now called *Laurel and Hardy Go to Heaven*, put it in a folder along with the other two plays I had written (*Blackouts* and *Hide and Seek*), and stuck the folder in a drawer of my desk. My plan was to keep it there and never look inside the drawer again.

Three months after the flop of the play, my son was born. Watching Daniel come into the world was a moment of supreme happiness for me, an event of such magnitude that even as I broke down and wept at the sight of his small body and held him in my arms for the first time, I understood that the world had changed, that I had passed from one state of being into another. Fatherhood was the dividing line, the great wall that stood between youth and adulthood, and I was on the other side now forever.

I was glad to be there. Emotionally, spiritually, and even

physically, there was nowhere else I wanted to be, and I was fully prepared to take on the demands of living in this new place. Financially, however, I wasn't the least bit prepared for anything. You pay a toll when you climb over that wall, and by the time I landed on the other side, my pockets were nearly empty. Lydia and I had left New York by then, moving to a house about two hours up the Hudson, and it was there that the hard times finally hit. The storm lasted for eighteen months, and when the wind died down enough for me to crawl out of my hole and inspect the damage, I saw that everything was gone. The entire landscape had been leveled.

Moving out of the city was the first step in a long series of miscalculations. We figured we could live on less money in the country, but the plain fact was that we couldn't. Car expenses, heating expenses, house repairs, and pediatrician's bills ate up whatever advantage we thought we had gained, and before long we were working so hard just to make ends meet that there was no time left for anything else. In the past, I had always managed to keep a few hours to myself every day, to push on with my poems and writing projects after spending the first part of the day working for money. Now, as our need for money rose, there was less time available to me for my own work. I started missing a day, then two days, then a week, and after a while I lost my rhythm as a writer. When I did manage to find some time for myself, I was too tense to write very well. Months went by, and every piece of paper I touched with my pen wound up in the garbage.

By the end of 1977, I was feeling trapped, desperate to find a solution. I had spent my whole life avoiding the subject of money, and now, suddenly, I could think of nothing else. I dreamed of miraculous reversals, lottery millions falling down from the sky, outrageous get-rich-quick schemes. Even the ads on matchbook covers began to hold a certain fascination. "Make Money Growing Worms in Your Basement." Now that I lived in a house with a basement, don't think I wasn't tempted. My old way of doing things had led to disaster, and I was ripe for new ideas, a new way of tackling the dilemma that had dogged me from the start: how to reconcile the needs of the body with the needs of the soul. The terms of the equation were still the same: time on the one hand, money on the other. I had gambled on being able to manage both, but after years of trying to feed first one mouth, then two mouths, and then three mouths, I had finally lost. It wasn't difficult to understand why. I had put too much of myself into working for time and not enough into working for money, and the result was that now I didn't have either one.

In early December, a friend came up from the city to visit for a few days. We had known each other since college, and he, too, had turned into a struggling writer—yet one more Columbia graduate without a pot to piss in. If anything, he was having an even rougher time of it than I was. Most of his work was unpublished, and he supported himself by bouncing from one pathetic temporary job to another, aimlessly traveling around the country in search of strange, down-and-out adventures. He had recently landed in New York again and was working in a toy store somewhere in Manhattan, part of the brigade of surplus help who stand behind the counters during the Christmas shopping season. I picked him up at the train station, and during the half-hour ride back to the house, we talked mostly about toys and games, the things he sold in the store. For reasons that still mystify me, this conversation dislodged a small pebble that had been stuck somewhere in my unconscious, an obstruction that had been sitting over a tiny pin-prick hole of memory, and now that I was able to look down that hole again, I found something that had been lost for nearly twenty years. Back when I was ten or twelve, I had invented a game. Using an ordinary deck of fifty-two playing cards, I had sat down on my bed one afternoon and figured out a way to play baseball with them. Now, as I went on talking to my friend in the car, the game came rushing back to me. I remembered everything about it: the basic principles, the rules, the whole setup down to the last detail.

Under normal circumstances, I probably would have forgotten all about it again. But I was a desperate man, a man with my back against the wall, and I knew that if I didn't think of something fast, the firing squad was about to fill my body with bullets. A windfall was the only way out of my predicament. If I could rustle up a nice large chunk of cash, the nightmare would suddenly stop. I could bribe off the soldiers, walk out of the prison yard, and go home to become a writer again. If translating books and writing magazine articles could no longer do the job, then I owed it to myself and my family to try something else. Well, people bought games, didn't they? What if I worked up my old baseball game into something good, something really good, and managed to sell it? Maybe I'd get lucky and find my bag of gold, after all.

It almost sounds like a joke now, but I was in dead earnest. I knew that my chances were next to nil, but once the idea grabbed hold of me, I couldn't shake free of it. Nuttier things had happened, I told myself, and if I wasn't willing to put a little time and effort into having a go at it, then what kind of spineless shit was I?

The game from my childhood had been organized around a few simple operations. The pitcher turned over cards: each red card from ace to 10 was a strike; each black card from ace to 10 was a ball. If a face card was turned over, that meant the batter swung. The batter then turned over a card. Anything from ace to 9 was an out, with each out corresponding to the position numbers of the defensive players: Pitcher = ace (1); Catcher = 2; First Baseman = 3; Second Baseman = 4; Third Baseman = 5; Shortstop = 6; Left Fielder = 7; Center Fielder = 8; Right Fielder = 9. If the batter turned over a 5, for example, that meant the out was made by the Third Baseman. A black 5 indicated a ground ball; a red 5 indicated a ball hit in the air (diamond = pop-up; heart = line drive). On balls hit to the outfield (7, 8, 9), black indicated a shallow fly ball, red a deep fly ball. Turn over a 10, and you had yourself a single. A jack was a double, a queen was a triple, and a king was a home run.

It was crude but reasonably effective, and while the distribution of hits was mathematically off (there should have been more singles than doubles, more doubles than home runs, and more home runs than triples), the games were often close and exciting. More important, the final scores looked like the scores of real baseball games—3 to 2, 7 to 4, 8 to 0—and not football or basketball games. The fundamental principles were sound. All I had to do was get rid of the standard deck and design a new set of cards. That would allow me to make the game statistically accurate, add new elements of strategy and decision making (bunts, stolen bases, sacrifice flies), and lift the whole thing to a higher level of subtlety and sophistication. The work was largely a matter of getting the numbers right and fiddling with the math, but I was well versed in the intricacies of baseball, and it didn't take me long to arrive at the correct formulas. I played out game after game after game, and at the end of a couple of weeks there were no more adjustments to be made. Then came the tedious part. Once I had designed the cards (two decks of ninety-six cards each), I had to sit down with four fine-tipped pens (one red, one green, one black, one blue) and draw the cards by hand. I can't remember how many days it took me to complete this task, but by the time I came to the end, I felt as if I had never done anything else. The design was nothing to brag about, but since I had no experience or talent as a designer, that was to be expected. I was striving for a clear, serviceable presentation, something that could be read at a glance and not confuse anyone, and given that so much information had to be crammed onto every card, I think I accomplished at least that. Beauty and elegance could come later. If anyone showed enough interest to want to manufacture the game, the problem could be turned over to a professional designer. For the time being, after much dithering back and forth, I dubbed my little brainchild Action Baseball.

Once again, my stepfather came to the rescue. He happened to have a friend who worked for one of the largest, most successful American toy companies, and when I showed the game to this man, he was impressed by it, thought it had a real chance of appealing to someone. I was still working on the cards at that point, but he encouraged me to get the game in order as quickly as I could and take it to the New York Toy Fair, which was just five or six weeks down the road. I had never heard of it, but by all accounts it was the most important annual event in the business. Every February, companies from around the world gathered at the Toy Center at Twenty-third Street and Fifth Avenue to display their products for the upcoming season, take note of what the competition was up to, and make plans for the future. What the Frankfurt Book Fair is for books and the Cannes Film Festival is for films, the New York Toy Fair is for toys. My stepfather's friend took charge of everything for me. He arranged to have my name put on the list of "inventors," which qualified me for a badge and an open pass to the fair, and then, as if that weren't enough, set up an appointment for me to meet with the president of his company—at nine o'clock in the morning on the first day of the fair.

I was grateful for the help, but at the same time I felt like someone who had just been booked on a flight to an unknown planet. I had no idea what to expect, no map of the terrain, no guidebook to help me understand the habits and customs of the creatures I would be talking to. The only solution I could think of was to wear a jacket and tie. The tie was the only one I owned, and it hung in my closet for emergency use at weddings and funerals. Now business meetings could be added to the list. I must have cut a ridiculous figure as I strode into the Toy Center that morning to collect my badge. I was carrying a briefcase, but the only thing inside it was the game, which was stowed inside a cigar box. That

FOUL OUT TO C — 2

STRIKE STRIKE STRIKE

E	DP	LDDP	SacB	SB(2)	SB(3)
2		(DP)			

SacF	SacF	EB	Inf in (3)	2 to 3

GROUND OUT TO 3B — 5

BALL BALL BALL

E	DP	LDDP	SacB	SB(2)	SB(3)
5					

SacF	SacF	EB	Inf in (3)	2 to 3

GROUND OUT TO 2B — 4

BALL BALL BALL

E	DP	LDDP	SacB	SB(2)	SB(3)
4					

SacF	SacF	EB	Inf in (3)	2 to 3

FOUL BALL — 6

SWING SWING SWING SWING

E	DP	LDDP	SacB	SB(2)	SB(3)
6					

SacF	SacF	EB	Inf in (3)	2 to 3

SINGLE
Runners advance 2 bases — 3

SWING SWING SWING

E	DP	LDDP	SacB	SB(2)	SB(3)
3					

SacF	SacF	EB	Inf in (3)	2 to 3

SINGLE
Runners advance 1 base — 4

SWING SWING SWING

E	DP	LDDP	SacB	SB(2)	SB(3)
4					

SacF	SacF	EB	Inf in (3)	2 to 3

GROUND OUT TO SS — 6

BALL BALL BALL BALL

E	DP	LDDP	SacB	SB(2)	SB(3)
6					

SacF	SacF	EB	Inf in (3)	2 to 3

GROUND OUT TO P — 1

BALL BALL BALL

E	DP	LDDP	SacB	SB(2)	SB(3)
1					

SacF	SacF	EB	Inf in (3)	2 to 3

was all I had: the game itself, along with several Xeroxed copies of the rules. I was about to go in and talk to the president of a multimillion-dollar business, and I didn't even have a business card.

Even at that early hour, the place was swarming with people. Everywhere you turned, there were endless rows of corporate stands, display booths decked out with dolls and puppets and fire engines and dinosaurs and extraterrestrials. Every kiddie amusement and gadget ever dreamed of was packed into that hall, and there wasn't one of them that didn't whistle or clang or toot or beep or roar. As I made my way through the din, it occurred to me that the briefcase under my arm was the only silent object in the building. Computer games were all the rage that year, the biggest thing to hit the toy world since the invention of the wind-up jack-in-the-box, and I was hoping to strike it rich with an old-fashioned deck of cards. Maybe I would, but until I walked into that noisy fun house, I hadn't realized how likely it was that I wouldn't.

My talk with the company president turned out to be one of the shortest meetings in the annals of American business. It didn't bother me that the man rejected my game (I was prepared for that, was fully expecting bad news), but he did it in such a chilling way, with so little regard for human decency, that it still causes me pain to think about it. He wasn't much older than I was, this corporate executive, and with his sleek, superbly tailored suit, his blue eyes and blond hair and hard, expressionless face, he looked and acted like the leader of a Nazi spy ring. He barely shook my hand, barely said hello, barely acknowledged that I was in the room. No small talk, no pleasantries, no questions. "Let's see what you have," he said curtly, and so I reached into my briefcase and pulled out the cigar box. Contempt flickered in his eyes. It was as if I had just handed him a dog turd and asked him to smell it. I opened the box and took out the cards. By then, I could see that all hope was gone, that he had already lost interest, but there was nothing to do but forge ahead and start playing the game. I shuffled the decks, said something about how to read the three levels of information on the cards, and then got down to it. One or two batters into the top half of the first inning, he stood up from his chair and extended his hand to me. Since he hadn't spoken a word, I had no idea why he wanted to shake my hand. I continued to turn over cards, describing the action as it unfolded: ball, strike, swing. "Thank you," the Nazi said, finally taking hold of my hand. I still couldn't figure out what was going on. "Are you saying you don't want to see any more?" I said. "I haven't even had a chance to show you how it works." "Thank you," he said again. "You can leave now." Without another word, he turned and left me with my cards, which were still spread out on the table. It took me a minute or two to put everything back in the cigar box, and it was precisely then, during those sixty or ninety seconds, that I hit bottom, that I reached what I still consider to be the low point of my life.

Somehow or other, I managed to regroup. I went out for breakfast, pulled myself together, and returned to the fair for the rest of the day. One by one, I visited every game company I could find, shook hands, smiled, knocked on doors, demonstrated the wonders of Action Baseball to anyone willing to spare me ten or fifteen minutes. The results were uniformly discouraging. Most of the big companies had stopped working with independent inventors (too many lawsuits), and the small ones either wanted pocket-sized computer games (beep-beep) or else refused to look at anything connected with sports (low sales). At least these people were polite. After the sadistic treatment I'd been given that morning, I found some consolation in that.

Sometime in the late afternoon, exhausted from hours of fruitless effort, I stumbled onto a company that specialized in card games. They had produced only one game so far, but that one had been wildly successful, and now they were in the market for a second. It was a small, low-budget operation run by two guys from

Joliet, Illinois, a back-porch business with none of the corporate trappings and slick promotional methods of the other companies at the fair. That was a promising sign, but best of all, both partners admitted to being avid baseball fans. They weren't doing much at that hour, just sitting around their little booth and chewing the fat, and when I told them about my game, they seemed more than happy to have a look at it. Not just a peek, but a thorough viewing—to sit down and play a full nine-inning contest to the end.

If I had rigged the cards, the results of the game I played with them could not have been more exciting, more true to life. It was nip and tuck the whole way, tension riding on every pitch, and after eight and a half innings of threats, rallies, and two-out strikeouts with the bases loaded, the score stood at two to one. The Joliet boys were the home team, and when they came up for their last turn at bat, they needed a run to tie and two to win. The first two batters did nothing, and quickly they were down to their last out, with no runners on base. The following batter singled, however, to keep them alive. Then, to everyone's astonishment, with the count at two balls and two strikes, the next batter hit a home run to win the game. I couldn't have asked for more than that. A two-out, two-run homer in the bottom of the ninth inning to steal a victory on the last pitch. It was a classic baseball thriller, and when the man from Joliet turned over that final card, his face lit up with an expression of pure, undisguisable joy.

They wanted to think about it, they said, to mull it over for a while before giving me an answer. They would need a deck to study on their own, of course, and I told them I would send a color Xerox copy to Joliet as soon as possible. That was how we left it: shaking hands and exchanging addresses, promising each other to be in touch. After all the dismal, demoralizing events of that day, there was suddenly cause for hope, and I walked out of the Toy Fair thinking that I might actually get somewhere with my crazy scheme.

Color Xeroxing was a new process then, and it cost me a small fortune to have the copies made. I can't remember the exact amount, but it was more than a hundred dollars, I think, perhaps even two hundred. I shipped the package off to them and prayed they would write back soon. Weeks passed, and as I struggled to concentrate on the other work I had to do, it gradually dawned on me that I was in for a disappointment. Enthusiasm meant speed, indecision meant delay, and the longer they delayed, the worse the odds would be. It took almost two months for them to answer, and by then I didn't even have to read the letter to know what was in it. What surprised me was its brevity, its utter lack of personal warmth. I had spent close to an hour with them, had felt I'd entertained them and aroused their interest, but their rejection consisted of just one dry, clumsily written paragraph. Half the words were misspelled, and nearly every sentence had a grammatical error in it. It was an embarrassing document, a letter written by dunces, and once my hurt began to wear off a little, I felt ashamed of myself for having misjudged them so thoroughly. Put your faith in fools, and you end up fooling only yourself.

Still, I wasn't quite ready to give up. I had gone too far to allow one setback to throw me off course, and so I put my head down and plunged ahead. Until I had exhausted all the possibilities, I felt duty bound to continue, to see the whole misbegotten business through to the end. My in-laws put me in touch with a man who worked for Ruder and Finn, a prominent New York public relations firm. He loved the game, seemed genuinely enthused when I showed it to him, and made an all-out effort to help. That was part of the problem. Everyone liked Action Baseball, enough people at any rate to keep me from abandoning it, and with a kind, friendly, well-connected man like this one pushing on my behalf, it wouldn't have made sense to give up. My new ally's name was George, and he happened to be in charge of the General Foods account, one of Ruder and Finn's most important clients. His plan, which struck me as ingenious, was to get General Foods to put Action Baseball on the Wheaties box as a special coupon offer. ("Hey, kids! Just mail in two Wheaties box tops and a check or money order for $3.98, and this incredible game can be yours!") George proposed it to them, and for a time it looked as if it might happen. Wheaties was considering ideas for a new promotional campaign, and he thought this one might just do the trick. It didn't. They went with the Olympic decathlon champion instead, and for the next umpteen years, every box of Wheaties was adorned with a picture of Bruce Jenner's smiling face. You can't really fault them. It was the Breakfast of Champions, after all, and they had a certain tradition to uphold. I never found out how close George came to getting his idea through, but I must confess (somewhat reluctantly) that I still find it hard to look at a box of Wheaties without feeling a little twinge.

George was almost as disappointed as I was, but now that he'd caught the bug, he wasn't about to quit trying. He knew someone in Indianapolis who was involved with the Babe Ruth League (in what capacity I forget) and thought something good might happen if he put me in contact with this man. The game was duly shipped to the Midwest again, and then followed another inordinately long silence. As the man hastened to explain to me when he finally wrote, he wasn't entirely responsible for the delay: "I am sorry to be so late in acknowledging receipt of your June 22 letter and your game, Action Baseball. They were late reaching me because of a tornado that wiped out our offices. I've been working at home since and did not get my mail until ten days or so ago." My bad luck was taking on an almost biblical dimension, and when the man wrote again several weeks later to tell me that he was passing on my game (sadly, with much regret, in the most courtly terms possible), I barely even flinched. "There is no question that your game is unique, innovative and interesting. There may well be a market for it since it is the only table-top baseball game without a lot of trappings, which makes it faster-moving, but the consensus here is that without big league players and their statistics, the established competition is insurmountable." I called George to give him the news and thank him for his help, but enough was enough, I said, and he shouldn't waste any more time on me.

Things stalled for a couple of months after that, but then another lead materialized, and I picked up my lance and sallied forth again. As long as there was a windmill somewhere in sight, I was prepared to do battle with it. I had not the least shred of hope anymore, but I couldn't quite let go of the stupid thing I had started. My stepfather's younger brother knew a man who had invented a game, and since that game had earned him a pile of money, it seemed reasonable for me to contact him and ask for advice. We met in the lobby of the Roosevelt Hotel, not far from Grand Central Station. He was a fast-talking wheeler-dealer of around forty, a wholly antipathetical man with every kind of bluff and angle up his sleeve, but I must admit that his patter had some verve to it.

"Mail order," he said, "that's the ticket. Approach a major-league star, get him to endorse the game for a share of the profits, and then take out ads in all the baseball magazines. If enough orders come in, use the money to produce the game. If not, send the money back and call it quits."

"How much would a thing like that cost?" I asked.

"Twenty, twenty-five thousand dollars. Minimum."

"I couldn't come up with that much," I said. "Not even if my life depended on it."

"Then you can't do it, can you?"

"No, I can't do it. I just want to sell the game to a company. That's all I've ever had in mind—to make some royalties from the copies they sold. I wouldn't be capable of going into business for myself."

"In other words," the man said, finally realizing what a numskull he was talking to, "you've taken a shit, and now you want someone to flush the toilet for you."

That wasn't quite how I would have expressed it myself, but I didn't argue with him. He clearly knew more than I did, and when he went on to recommend that I find a "game broker" to talk to the companies for me, I didn't doubt that he was pointing me in the right direction. Until then, I hadn't even known of the existence of such people. He gave me the name of someone who was supposed to be particularly good, and I called her the next day. That turned out to be my last move, the final chapter of the whole muddled saga. She talked a mile a minute to me, outlining terms, conditions, and percentages, what to do and what not to do, what to expect and what to avoid. It sounded like her standard spiel, a furious condensation of years of hard knocks and cutthroat maneuvers, and for the first several minutes I couldn't get a word in edgewise. Then, finally, she paused to catch her breath, and that was when she asked me about my game.

"It's called Action Baseball," I said.

"Did you say *baseball*?" she said.

"Yes, baseball. You turn over cards. It's very realistic, and you can get through a full nine-inning game in about fifteen minutes."

"Sorry," she said. "No sports games."

"What do you mean?"

"They're losers. They don't sell, and nobody wants them. I wouldn't touch your game with a ten-foot pole."

That did it for me. With the woman's blunt pronouncement still ringing in my ears, I hung up the phone, put the cards away, and stopped thinking about them forever.

Little by little, I was coming to the end of my rope. After the grim, garbled letter from Joliet, I understood that Action Baseball was no more than a long shot. To count on it as a source of money would have been an act of pure self-deception, a ludicrous error. I plugged away at it for several more months, but those final efforts took up only a small fraction of my time. Deep down, I had already accepted defeat—not just of the game, not just of my half-assed foray into the business world, but of all my principles, my lifelong stand toward work, money, and the pursuit of time. Time didn't count anymore. I had needed it in order to write, but now that I was an ex-writer, a writer who wrote only for the satisfaction of crumpling up paper and throwing it in the garbage, I was ready to abandon the struggle and live like everyone else. Nine years of freelance penury had burned me out. I had tried to rescue myself by inventing the game, but no one had wanted the game, and now I was right back where I had been—only worse, only more burned out than ever. At least the game had represented an idea, a temporary surge of hope, but now I had run out of ideas as well. The truth was that I had dug myself into a deep, dark hole, and the only way to crawl out of it was to find a job.

I made calls, wrote letters, traveled down to the city for interviews. Teaching jobs, journalism jobs, editorial jobs—it didn't matter what it was. As long as the job came with a weekly paycheck, I was interested. Two or three things almost panned out, but in the end they didn't. I won't go into the depressing details now, but several months went by without any tangible results. I sank further into confusion, my mind almost paralyzed with worry. I had made a total surrender, had capitulated on every point I had defended over the years, and still I was getting nowhere, was losing ground with every step I took. Then, out of the blue, a grant of thirty-five hundred dollars came in from the New York State Council on the Arts, and I was given an unexpected breather. It wouldn't last long, but it was something—enough to ward off the hour of doom for another minute or two.

One night not long after that, as I lay in bed battling against insomnia, a new idea occurred to me. Not an idea, perhaps, but a thought, a little notion. I had been reading a lot of detective novels that year, mostly of the hard-boiled American school, and beyond finding them to be good medicine, a balm against stress and chronic anxiety, I had developed an admiration for some of the practitioners of the genre. The best ones were humble, no-nonsense writers who not only had more to say about American life than most so-called serious writers, but often seemed to write smarter, crisper sentences as well. One of the conventional plot gimmicks of these stories was the apparent suicide that turns out to have been a murder. Again and again, a character would ostensibly die by his or her own hand, and by the end of the story, after all the tangled strands of the intrigue had finally been unraveled, it would be discovered that the villain was in fact responsible for the character's death. I thought: why not reverse the trick and stand it on its head? Why not have a story in which an apparent murder turns out to be a suicide? As far as I could tell, no one had ever done it.

It was no more than idle speculation, a two-in-the-morning brain wave, but I couldn't fall asleep, and with my heart beginning to race and flutter in my chest, I pursued the thought a little further, trying to calm myself by cooking up a story to go with my curveball premise. I had no stake in the results, was simply groping for a sedative to tranquilize my nerves, but one piece of the puzzle kept fitting beside another, and by the time I drifted off to sleep, I had worked out the bare-bones plot of a mystery novel.

The next morning, it occurred to me that it might not be such a bad idea to sit down and write the damn thing. It wasn't that I had anything better to do. I hadn't written a decent syllable in months, I couldn't find a job, and my bank account was down to almost nothing. If I could crank out a reasonably good detective novel, then surely there would be a few dollars in it. I wasn't dreaming of bags of gold anymore. Just an honest wage for an honest day's work, a chance to survive.

I started in early June, and by the end of August I had completed a manuscript of just over three hundred pages. The book was an exercise in pure imitation, a conscious attempt to write a book that sounded like other books, but just because I wrote it for money doesn't mean that I didn't enjoy myself. As an example of the genre, it seemed no worse than many others I had read, much better than some. It was good enough to be published, in any case, and that was all I was after. My sole ambition for the novel was to turn it into cash and pay off as many bills as I could.

Once again, I ran straight into problems. I was doing everything in my power to prostitute myself, offering up my wares for rock-bottom prices, and still no one would have me. In this case, the problem wasn't so much what I was trying to sell (as with the game), but my own astonishing ineptitude as a salesman. The only editors I knew were the ones who hired me to translate books, and they were ill qualified to pass judgment on popular fiction. They had no experience with it, had never read or published books like mine, and were scarcely even aware that such a thing as mystery novels existed, let alone the assorted subgenres within the field: private-eye novels, police procedurals, and so on. I sent off my manuscript to one of these editors, and when he finally got around to reading it, his response was surprisingly enthusiastic. "It's good," he said, "very good. Just get rid of the detective stuff, and you'll have yourself an excellent psychological thriller."

"But that's the whole point," I said. "It's a detective novel."

"Maybe so," he said, "but we don't publish detective novels. Rework it, though, and I guarantee that we'll be interested."

Altering the book might have interested him, but it didn't interest me. I had written it in a specific way for a specific purpose, and to begin dismantling it now would have been absurd. I realized that I needed an agent, someone to shop the novel around for me while I took care of more pressing matters. The rub was that I didn't have the first idea how to find one. Poets don't have agents, after all. Translators don't have agents. Book reviewers who make two or three hundred dollars per article don't have agents. I had lived my life in the remote provinces of the literary world, far removed from the commercial center where books and money have something to say to each other, and the only people I knew were young poets whose work appeared in little magazines, publishers of small, not-for-profit presses, and various other cranks, misfits, and exiles. There was no one to turn to for help, not one scrap of knowledge or information available to me. If there was, I was too dumb to know where to find it. Quite by chance, an old high school friend mentioned that his ex-wife happened to run a literary agency, and when I told him about my manuscript, he urged me to send it to her. I did, and after waiting nearly a month for an answer, I was turned down. There wasn't enough money in this kind of thing, she said, and it wasn't worth her trouble. No one read private-eye novels anymore. They were passé, old hat, a losing proposition all around. Word for word, it was identical to the speech the game broker had given me not ten days before.

Eventually, the book was published, but that didn't happen until four years later. In the meantime, all sorts of catastrophes occurred, one upheaval followed another, and the last thing on my mind was the fate of my pseudonymous potboiler. My marriage broke up in November 1978, and the typescript of the money novel was shoved into a plastic bag, all but lost and forgotten through several changes of address. My father died just two months after that—suddenly, unexpectedly, without ever having been sick a day in his life—and for many weeks the bulk of my time was spent taking care of estate business, settling his affairs, tying up loose ends. His death hit me hard, caused immense sorrow inside me, and whatever energy I had for writing I used to write about him. The terrible irony was that he had left me something in his will. It wasn't a great amount as far as inheritances go, but it was more money than I had ever had before, and it helped see me through the transition from one life into another. I moved back to New York and kept on writing. Eventually, I fell in love and married again. In the course of those four years, everything changed for me.

Sometime in the middle of that period, in late 1980 or early 1981, I received a call from a man I had met once before. He was the friend of a friend, and since the meeting had taken place a good eight or nine years earlier, I could scarcely remember who he was. He announced that he was planning to start a publishing company and wondered if I happened to have a manuscript he could look at. It wasn't going to be just another small press, he explained, but a real business, a *commercial operation*. Hmmm, I said, remembering the plastic bag at the bottom of my bedroom closet, if that's the case, then I just might have something for you. I told him about the detective novel, and when he said that he would be interested in reading it, I made a copy and sent it to him that week. Unexpectedly, he liked it. Even more unexpectedly, he said that he wanted to go ahead and publish it.

I was happy, of course—happy and amused, but also a trifle apprehensive. It seemed almost too good to be true. Publishing books wasn't supposed to be so easy, and I wondered if there wasn't a catch to it somewhere. He was running the company out of his Upper West Side apartment, I noticed, but the contract I received in the mail was a real contract, and after looking it over and deciding that the terms were acceptable, I couldn't think of a reason not to sign it. There was no advance, of course, no money up front, but royalties would begin with the first copy sold. I figured that was normal for a new publisher just getting off the ground, and since he had no investors or serious financial support, he couldn't very well cough up money he didn't have. Needless to say, his business didn't quite qualify as a *commercial operation*, but he was hoping it would become one, and who was I to throw a wet blanket on his hopes?

He managed to bring out one book nine months later (a

paperback reprint), but production of my novel dragged on for close to two years. By the time it was printed, he had lost his distributor, had no money left, and to all intents and purposes was dead as a publisher. A few copies made it into a couple of New York bookstores, hand-delivered by the publisher himself, but the rest of the edition remained in cardboard boxes, gathering dust on the floor of a warehouse somewhere in Brooklyn. For all I know, the books are still there.

Having gone that far with the business, I felt I should make one last effort and see if I couldn't conclude it once and for all. Since the novel had been "published," a hardcover edition was no longer possible, but there were still the paperback houses to consider, and I didn't want to walk away from the book until they'd had a chance to turn it down. I started looking for an agent again, and this time I found the right one. She sent the novel to an editor at Avon Books, and three days later it was accepted. Just like that, in no time at all. They offered an advance of two thousand dollars, and I agreed to it. No haggling, no counteroffer, no tricky negotiations. I felt vindicated, and I didn't care about the details anymore. After splitting the advance with the original publisher (as per contract), I was left with a thousand dollars. Deduct the ten percent agent's commission, and I wound up making a grand total of nine hundred dollars.

So much for writing books to make money. So much for selling out.

ACCIDENT REPORT

{1999}

1

When A. was a young woman in San Francisco and just starting out in life, she went through a desperate period in which she almost lost her mind. In the space of just a few weeks, she was fired from her job, one of her best friends was murdered when thieves broke into her apartment at night, and A.'s beloved cat became seriously ill. I don't know the exact nature of the illness, but it was apparently life-threatening, and when A. took the cat to the vet, he told her that the cat would die within a month unless a certain operation was performed. She asked him how much the operation would cost. He toted up the various charges for her, and the amount came to three hundred twenty-seven dollars. A. didn't have that kind of money. Her bank account was down to almost zero, and for the next several days she walked around in a state of extreme distress, alternately thinking about her dead friend and the impossible sum needed to prevent her cat from dying: three hundred twenty-seven dollars.

One day, she was driving through the Mission and came to a stop at a red light. Her body was there, but her thoughts were somewhere else, and in the gap between them, in that small space that no one has fully explored but where we all sometimes live, she heard the voice of her murdered friend. *Don't worry,* the voice said. *Don't worry. Things will get better soon.* The light turned green, but A. was still under the spell of this auditory hallucination, and she did not move. A moment later, a car rammed into her from behind, breaking one of the taillights and crumpling the fender. The man who was driving that car shut off his engine, climbed out of the car, and walked over to A. He apologized for doing such a stupid thing. No, A. said, it was my fault. The light turned green and I didn't go. But the man insisted that he was the one to blame. When he learned that A. didn't have collision insurance (she was too poor for luxuries like that), he offered to pay for any damages that had been done to her car. Get an estimate on what it will cost, he said, and send me the bill. My insurance company will take care of it. A. continued to protest, telling the man that he wasn't responsible for the accident, but he wouldn't take no for an answer, and finally she gave in. She took the car to a garage and asked the mechanic to assess the costs of repairing the fender and the taillight. When she returned several hours later, he handed her a written estimate. Give or take a penny or two, the amount came to exactly three hundred twenty-seven dollars.

2

W., the friend from San Francisco who told me that story, has been directing films for twenty years. His latest project is based on a novel that recounts the adventures of a mother and her teenage daughter. It is a work of fiction, but most of the events in the book are taken directly from the author's life. The author, now a grown woman, was once the teenage daughter, and the mother in the story—who is still alive—was her real mother.

W.'s film was shot in Los Angeles. A famous actress was hired to play the role of the mother, and according to what W. told me on a recent visit to New York, the filming went smoothly and the production was completed on schedule. Once he began to edit the movie, however, he decided that he wanted to add a few more scenes, which he felt would greatly enhance the story. One of them included a shot of the mother parking her car on a street in a residential neighborhood. The location manager went out scouting for an appropriate street, and eventually one was chosen—arbitrarily, it would seem, since one Los Angeles street looks more or less like any other. On the appointed morning, W., the actress, and the film crew gathered on the street to shoot the scene. The car that the actress was supposed to drive was parked in front of a house—no particular house, just one of the houses on that street—and as my friend and his leading lady stood on the sidewalk discussing the scene and the possible ways to approach it, the door of that house burst open and a woman came running out. She appeared to be laughing and screaming at the same time. Distracted by the commotion, W. and the actress stopped talking. A screaming and laughing woman was running across the front lawn, and she was headed straight for them. I don't know how big the lawn was. W. neglected to mention that detail when he told the story, but in my mind I see it as large, which would have given the woman a considerable distance to cover before she reached the sidewalk and announced who she was. A moment like that deserves to be prolonged, it seems to me—if only by a few seconds—for the thing that was about to happen was so improbable, so outlandish in its defiance of the odds, that one wants to savor it for a few extra seconds before letting go of it. The woman running across the lawn was the novelist's mother. A fictional character in her daughter's book, she was also her real mother, and now, by pure accident, she was about to meet the woman who was playing that fictional character in a film based on the book in which her character had in fact been herself. She was real, but she was also imaginary. And the actress who was playing her was both real and imaginary as well. There were two of them standing on the sidewalk that morning, but there was also just one. Or perhaps it was the same one twice. According to what my friend told me, when the women finally understood what had happened, they threw their arms around each other and embraced.

3

Last September, I had to go to Paris for a few days, and my publisher booked a room for me in a small hotel on the Left Bank. It's the same hotel they use for all their authors, and I had already stayed there several times in the past. Other than its convenient location—midway down a narrow street just off the Boulevard Saint-Germain—there is nothing even remotely interesting about this hotel. Its rates are modest, its rooms are cramped, and it is not mentioned in any guidebook. The people who run it are pleasant enough, but it is no more than a drab and inconspicuous hole-in-the-wall, and except for a couple of American writers who have the same French publisher I do, I have never met anyone who has stayed there. I mention this fact because the obscurity of the hotel plays a part in the story. Unless one stops for a moment to consider how many hotels there are in Paris (which attracts more visitors than any other city in the world) and then further considers how many rooms there are in those hotels (thousands, no doubt tens of thousands), the full import of what happened to me last year will not be understood.

I arrived at the hotel late—more than an hour behind schedule—and checked in at the front desk. I went upstairs immediately after that. Just as I was putting my key into the door of my room, the telephone started to ring. I went in, tossed my bag on the floor, and picked up the phone, which was set into a nook in the wall just beside the bed, more or less at pillow level. Because the phone was turned in toward the bed, and because the cord was short, and because the one chair in the room was out of reach, it was necessary to sit down on the bed in order to use the phone. That's what I did, and as I talked to the person on the other end of the line, I noticed a piece of paper lying under the desk on the opposite side of the room. If I had been anywhere else, I wouldn't have been in a position to see it. The dimensions of the room were so tight that the space between the desk and the foot of the bed was no more than four or five feet. From my vantage point at the head of the bed, I was in the only place that provided a low enough angle of the floor to see what was under the desk. After the conversation was over, I got off the bed, crouched down under the desk, and picked up the piece of paper. Curious, of course, always curious, but not at all expecting to find anything out of the ordinary. The paper turned out to be one of those little message forms they slip under your door in European hotels. To——and From——, the date and the time, and then a blank square below for the message. The form had been folded in three, and printed out in block letters on the outer fold was the name of one of my closest friends. We don't see each other often (O. lives in Canada), but we have been through a number of memorable experiences together, and there has never been anything but the greatest affection between us. Seeing his name on the message form made me very happy. We hadn't spoken in a while, and I had had no inkling that he would be in Paris when I was there. In those first moments of discovery and incomprehension, I assumed that O. had somehow gotten wind of the fact that I was coming and had called the hotel to leave a message for me. The message had been delivered to my room, but whoever had brought it up had placed it carelessly on the edge of the desk, and it had blown onto the floor. Or else that person had accidentally dropped it (the chambermaid?) while preparing the room for my arrival. One way or the other, neither explanation was very plausible. The angle was wrong, and unless someone had kicked the message after it had fallen to the floor, the paper couldn't have been lying so far under the desk. I was already beginning to reconsider my hypothesis when something more important occurred to me. O.'s name was on the outside of the message form. If the message had been meant for me, my name would have been there. The recipient was the one whose name belonged on the outside, not the sender, and if my name wasn't there, it surely wasn't going to be anywhere else. I opened the message and read it. The sender was someone I had never heard of—but the recipient was indeed O. I rushed downstairs and asked the clerk at the front desk if O. was still there. It was a stupid question, of course, but I asked it anyway. How could O. be there if he was no longer in his room? I was there now, and O.'s room was no longer his room but mine. I asked the clerk when he had checked out. An hour ago, the clerk said. An hour ago I had been sitting in a taxi at the edge of Paris, stuck in a traffic jam. If I had made it to the hotel at the expected time, I would have run into O. just as he was walking out the door.

IT DON'T MEAN
A THING

{2000}

———

1

We used to see him occasionally at the Carlyle Hotel. It would be an exaggeration to call him a friend, but F. was a good acquaintance, and my wife and I always looked forward to his arrival when he called to say that he was coming to town. A daring and prolific French poet, F. was also one of the world's leading authorities on Henri Matisse. So great was his reputation, in fact, that an important French museum asked him to organize a large exhibition of Matisse's work. F. wasn't a professional curator, but he threw himself into the job with enormous energy and skill. The idea was to gather together all of Matisse's paintings from a particular five-year period in the middle of his career. Dozens of canvases were involved, and since they were scattered around in private collections and museums all over the world, it took F. several years to prepare the show. In the end, there was only one work that could not be found—but it was a crucial one, the centerpiece of the entire exhibition. F. had not been able to track down the owner, had no idea where it was, and without that canvas years of travel and meticulous labor would go for naught. For the next six months, he devoted himself exclusively to the search for that one painting, and when he found it, he realized that it had been no more than a few feet away from him the whole time. The owner was a woman who lived in an apartment at the Carlyle Hotel. The Carlyle was F.'s hotel of choice, and he stayed there whenever he was in New York. More than that, the woman's apartment was located directly above the room that F. always reserved for himself—just one floor up. Which meant that every time F. had gone to sleep at the Carlyle Hotel, wondering where the missing painting could have been, it had been hanging on a wall directly above his head. Like an image from a dream.

2

I wrote that paragraph last October. A few days later, a friend from Boston called to tell me that a poet acquaintance of his was in bad shape. In his mid-sixties now, this man has spent his life in the far reaches of the literary solar system—the single inhabitant of an asteroid that orbits around a tertiary moon of Pluto, visible only through the strongest telescope. I have never met him, but I have read his work, and I have always imagined him living on his small planet like some latter-day Little Prince.

My friend told me that the poet's health was in decline. He was undergoing treatments for his illness, his money was at a low ebb, and he was being threatened with eviction from his apartment. As a way to raise some quick and necessary cash to rescue the poet from his troubles, my friend had come up with the idea of producing a book in his honor. He would solicit contributions from several dozen poets and writers, gather them into an attractive, limited-edition volume, and sell the copies by subscription only. He figured there were enough book collectors in the country to guarantee a handsome profit. Once the money came in, it would all be turned over to the sick and struggling poet.

He asked me if I had a page or two lying around somewhere that I might give him, and I mentioned the little story I had just written about my French friend and the missing painting. I faxed it to him that same morning, and a few hours later he called back to say that he liked the piece and wanted to include it in the book. I was glad to have done my little bit, and then, once the matter had been settled, I promptly forgot all about it.

Two nights ago (January 31, 2000), I was sitting with my twelve-year-old daughter at the dining room table in our house in Brooklyn, helping her with her math homework—a massive list of problems involving negative and positive numbers. My daughter is not terribly interested in math, and once we finished converting the subtractions into additions and the negatives into positives, we started talking about the music recital that had been held at her school several nights before. She had sung "The First Time Ever I Saw Your Face," the old Roberta Flack number, and now she was looking for another song to begin preparing for the spring recital. After tossing some ideas back and forth, we both decided that she should do something bouncy and up-tempo this time, in contrast to the slow and aching ballad she had just performed. Without any warning, she sprang from her chair and began belting out the lyrics of "It Don't Mean a Thing if it Ain't Got that Swing." I know that parents tend to exaggerate the talents of their children, but there was no question in my mind that her rendition of that song was remarkable. Dancing and shimmying as the music poured out of her, she took her voice to places it had rarely been before, and because she sensed that herself, could feel the power of her own performance, she immediately launched into it again after she had finished. Then she sang it again. And then again. For fifteen or twenty minutes, the house was filled with increasingly beautiful and ecstatic variations of a single unforgettable phrase: *It don't mean a thing if it ain't got that swing.*

The following afternoon (yesterday), I brought in the mail at around two o'clock. There was a considerable pile of it, the usual mixture of junk and important business. One letter had been sent by a small New York poetry publisher, and I opened that one first. Unexpectedly, it contained the proofs of my contribution to my friend's book. I read through the piece again, making one or two corrections, and then called the copy editor responsible for the production of the book. Her name and number had been provided in a cover letter sent by the publisher, and once we had had our brief chat, I hung up the phone and turned to the rest of my mail. Wedged inside the pages of my daughter's new issue of *Seventeen* magazine, there was a slim white package that had been sent from

France. When I turned it over to look at the return address, I saw that it was from F., the same poet whose experience with the missing painting had inspired me to write the short piece I had just read over for the first time since composing it in October. What a coincidence, I thought. My life has been filled with dozens of curious events like this one, and no matter how hard I try, I can't seem to shake free of them. What is it about the world that continues to involve me in such nonsense?

Then I opened the package. There was a thin book of poetry inside—what we would refer to as a chapbook; what the French call a *plaquette*. It was just thirty-two pages long, and it had been printed on fine, elegant paper. As I flipped through it, scanning a phrase here and a phrase there, immediately recognizing the exuberant and frenetic style that characterizes all of F.'s work, a tiny slip of paper fell out of the book and fluttered onto my desk. It was no more than two inches long and half an inch high. I had no idea what it was. I had never encountered a stray slip of paper in a new book before, and unless it was supposed to serve as some kind of rarefied, microscopic bookmark to match the refinement of the book itself, it seemed to have been put in there by mistake. I picked up the errant rectangle from my desk, turned it over, and saw that there was writing on the other side—eleven short words arranged in a single row of type. The poems had been written in French, the book had been printed in France, but the words on the slip of paper that had fallen out of the book were in English. They formed a sentence, and that sentence read: *It don't mean a thing if it ain't got that swing.*

3

Having come this far, I can't resist the temptation to add one more link to this chain of anecdotes. As I was writing the last words of the first paragraph in the second section printed above ("living on his small planet like some latter-day Little Prince"), I was reminded of the fact that *The Little Prince* was written in New York. Few people know this, but after Saint-Exupéry was demobilized following the French defeat in 1940, he came to America, and for a time he lived at 240 Central Park South in Manhattan. It was there that he wrote his celebrated book, the most French of all French children's books. *Le Petit Prince* is required reading for nearly every American high school student of French, and as was the case with so many others before me, it was the first book I happened to read in a language that wasn't English. I went on to read more books in French. Eventually, I translated French books as a way of earning my living as a young man, and at a certain point I lived in France for four years. That was where I first met F. and became familiar with his work. It might be an outlandish statement, but I believe it is safe to say that if I hadn't read *Le Petit Prince* as an adolescent in 1963, I never would have been in a position to receive F.'s book in the mail thirty-seven years later. In saying that, I am also saying that I never would have discovered the mysterious slip of paper bearing the words *It don't mean a thing if it ain't got that swing.*

240 Central Park South is an odd, misshapen building that stands on the corner overlooking Columbus Circle. Construction was completed in 1941, and the first tenants moved in just before Pearl Harbor and America's entrance into the war. I don't know the exact date when Saint-Exupéry took up residence there, but he had to have been among the first people to live in that building. By one of those curious anomalies that mean absolutely nothing, so was my mother. She moved there from Brooklyn with her parents and sister at the age of sixteen, and she did not move out until she married my father five years later. It was an extraordinary step for the family to take— from Crown Heights to one of the most elegant addresses in

Manhattan—and it moves me to think that my mother lived in the same building where Saint-Exupéry wrote *The Little Prince*. If nothing else, I am moved by the fact that she had no idea that the book was being written, no idea who the author was. Nor did she have any knowledge of his death some time later when his plane went down in the last year of the war. Around that same time, my mother fell in love with an aviator. As it happened, he, too, died in that same war.

My grandparents went on living at 240 Central Park South until their deaths (my grandmother in 1968; my grandfather in 1979), and many of my most important childhood memories are situated in their apartment. My mother moved to New Jersey after she married my father, and we changed houses several times during my early years, but the New York apartment was always there, a fixed point in an otherwise unstable universe. It was there that I stood at the window and watched the traffic swirling around the statue of Christopher Columbus. It was there that my grandfather performed his magic tricks for me. It was there that I came to understand that New York was my city.

Just as my mother had done, her sister moved out of the apartment when she married. Not long after that (in the early fifties), she and her husband moved to Europe, where they lived for the next twelve years. In thinking about the various decisions I have made in my own life, I have no doubt that their example inspired me to move to France when I was in my early twenties. When my aunt and uncle returned to New York, my young cousin was eleven years old. I had met him only once. His parents sent him to school at the French lycée, and because of the incongruities in our respective educations, we wound up reading *Le Petit Prince* at the same time, even though there was a six-year difference in our ages. Back then, neither one of us knew that the book had been written in the same building where our mothers had lived.

After their return from Europe, my cousin and his parents settled into an apartment on the Upper East Side. For the next several years, he had his hair cut every month at the barbershop in the Carlyle Hotel.

WINTER JOURNAL

{2011}

———

You think it will never happen to you, that it cannot happen to you, that you are the only person in the world to whom none of these things will ever happen, and then, one by one, they all begin to happen to you, in the same way they happen to everyone else.

Your bare feet on the cold floor as you climb out of bed and walk to the window. You are six years old. Outside, snow is falling, and the branches of the trees in the backyard are turning white.

Speak now before it is too late, and then hope to go on speaking until there is nothing more to be said. Time is running out, after all. Perhaps it is just as well to put aside your stories for now and try to examine what it has felt like to live inside this body from the first day you can remember being alive until this one. A catalogue of sensory data. What one might call a *phenomenology of breathing*.

You are ten years old, and the midsummer air is warm, oppressively warm, so humid and uncomfortable that even as you sit in the shade of the trees in the backyard, sweat is gathering on your forehead.

It is an incontestable fact that you are no longer young. One month from today, you will be turning sixty-four, and although that is not excessively old, not what anyone would consider to be an advanced old age, you cannot stop yourself from thinking about all the others who never managed to get as far as you have.

This is one example of the various things that could never happen, but which, in fact, have happened.

The wind in your face during last week's blizzard. The awful sting of the cold, and you out there in the empty streets wondering what possessed you to leave the house in such a pounding storm, and yet, even as you struggled to keep your balance, there was the exhilaration of that wind, the joy of seeing the familiar streets turned into a blur of white, whirling snow.

Physical pleasures and physical pains. Sexual pleasures first and foremost, but also the pleasures of food and drink, of lying naked in a hot bath, of scratching an itch, of sneezing and farting, of spending an extra hour in bed, of turning your face toward the sun on a mild afternoon in late spring or early summer and feeling the warmth settle upon your skin. Innumerable instances, not a day gone by without some moment or moments of physical pleasure, and yet pains are no doubt more persistent and intractable, and at one time or another nearly every part of your body has been subjected to assault. Eyes and ears, head and neck, shoulders and back, arms and legs, throat and stomach, ankles and feet, not to mention the enormous boil that once sprouted on the left cheek of your ass, referred to by the doctor as a *wen*, which to your ears sounded like some medieval affliction and prevented you from sitting in chairs for a week.

The proximity of your small body to the ground, the body that belonged to you when you were three and four years old, that is to say, the shortness of the distance between your feet and head, and how the things you no longer notice were once a constant presence and preoccupation for you: the little world of crawling ants and lost coins, of fallen twigs and dented bottle caps, of dandelions and clover. But especially the ants. They are what you remember best. Armies of ants traveling in and out of their powdery hills.

You are five years old, crouched over an anthill in the backyard, attentively studying the comings and goings of your tiny six-legged friends. Unseen and unheard, your three-year-old neighbor creeps up behind you and strikes you on the head with a toy rake. The prongs pierce your scalp, blood flows into your hair and down the back of your neck, and you run screaming into the house, where your grandmother tends to your wounds.

Your grandmother's words to your mother: "Your father would be such a wonderful man—if only he were different."

This morning, waking in the dimness of another January dawn, a scumbled, grayish light seeping into the bedroom, and there is your wife's face turned toward your face, her eyes closed, still fast asleep, the covers pulled all the way up to her neck, her head the only part of her that is visible, and you marvel at how beautiful she looks, how young she looks, even now, thirty years after you first slept with her, after thirty years of living together under the same roof and sharing the same bed.

More snow falling today, and as you climb out of bed and walk to the window, the branches of the trees in the back garden are turning white. You are sixty-three years old. It occurs to you that there has rarely been a moment during the long journey from boyhood to now when you have not been in love. Thirty years of marriage, yes, but in the thirty years before that, how many infatuations and crushes, how many ardors and pursuits, how many deliriums and mad surges of desire? From the very start of your conscious life, you have been a willing slave of Eros. The girls you loved as a boy, the women you loved as a man, each one different from the others, some round and some lean, some short and some tall, some bookish and some athletic, some moody and some outgoing, some white and some black and some Asian, nothing on the surface ever mattered to you, it was all about the inner light you would detect in her, the spark of singularity, the blaze of revealed selfhood, and that light would make her beautiful to you, even if others were blind to the beauty you saw, and then you would burn to be with her, to be near her, for feminine beauty is something you have never been able to resist. All the way back to your first days of school, the kindergarten class in which you fell for the girl with the long blond ponytail, and how often were you punished by Miss Sandquist for sneaking off with the little girl you had fallen for, the two of you together in a corner somewhere making mischief, but those punishments meant nothing to you, for you were in love, and you were a fool for love then, just as you are a fool for love now.

The inventory of your scars, in particular the ones on your face, which are visible to you each morning when you look into the bathroom mirror to shave or comb your hair. You seldom think about them, but whenever you do, you understand that they are marks of life, that the assorted jagged lines etched into the skin of your face are letters from the secret alphabet that tells the story of who you are, for each scar is the trace of a healed wound, and each wound was caused by an unexpected collision with the world—that is to say, an accident, or something that need not have happened, since by definition an accident is something that need not happen. Contingent facts as opposed to necessary facts, and the realization as you look into the mirror this morning that all life is contingent, except for the one necessary fact that sooner or later it will come to an end.

You are three and a half, and your twenty-five-year-old pregnant mother has taken you along with her on a shopping expedition to a department store in downtown Newark. She is accompanied by a friend of hers, the mother of a boy who is three and a half as well. At some point, you and your little comrade break away from your mothers and begin running through the store. It is an enormous open space, no doubt the largest room you have ever set foot in, and there is a palpable thrill in being able to run wild through this gargantuan indoor arena. Eventually, you and the boy begin belly-flopping onto the floor and sliding along the smooth surface, sledding without sleds, as it were, and this game proves to be so enjoyable, so ecstatic in the pleasure it produces, that you become more and more reckless, more and more daring in what you are willing to attempt. You reach a part of the store where construction work or repair work is under way, and without bothering to take notice of what obstacles might lie ahead, you belly-flop onto the floor again and sail along the glasslike surface until you find yourself speeding straight toward a wooden carpenter's bench. With a small twist of your small body, you think you can avoid crashing into the leg of the table that is looming before you, but what you do not realize in the split second you have to shift course is that a nail is jutting from the leg, a long nail low enough to be at the level of your face, and before you can stop yourself, your left cheek is pierced by the nail as you go flying past it. Half your face is torn apart. Sixty years later, you have no memories of the accident. You remember the running and the belly-flopping, but nothing about the pain, nothing about the blood, and nothing about being rushed to the hospital or the doctor who sewed up your cheek. He did a brilliant job, your mother always said, and since the trauma of seeing her firstborn with half his face ripped off never left her, she said it often: something to do with a subtle double-stitching method that kept the damage to a minimum and prevented you from being disfigured for life. You could have lost your eye, she would say to you—or, even more dramatically, You could have been killed. No doubt she was right. The scar has grown fainter and fainter as the years have passed, but it is still there whenever you look for it, and you will carry that emblem of good fortune (eye intact! not dead!) until you go to your grave.

Split eyebrow scars, one left and one right, almost perfectly symmetrical, the first caused by running full tilt into a brick wall during a dodgeball game in grade school gym class (the massively swollen black eye you sported for days afterward, which reminded you of a photograph of boxer Gene Fullmer, who had been defeated in a championship bout by Sugar Ray Robinson around the same time) and the second caused in your early twenties when you drove in for a layup during an outdoor basketball game, were fouled from behind, and flew into the metal pole supporting the basket. Another scar on your chin, origin unknown. Most likely from an early childhood spill, a hard fall onto a sidewalk or a stone that split open your flesh and left its mark, which is still visible whenever you shave in the morning. No story accompanies this scar, your mother never talked about it (at least not that you can recall), and you find it odd, if not downright perplexing, that this permanent line was engraved on your chin by what can only be called *an invisible hand*, that your body is the site of events that have been expunged from history.

It is June 1959. You are twelve years old, and in one week you and your sixth-grade classmates will be graduating from the grammar school you have attended since you were five. It is a splendid day, late spring in its most lustrous incarnation, sunlight pouring down from a cloudless blue sky, warm but not too warm, scant humidity, a soft breeze stirring the air and rippling over your face and neck and bare arms. Once school lets out for the day, you and a gang of your friends repair to Grove Park for a game of pickup baseball. Grove Park is not a park so much as a kind of village green, a large rectangle of well-tended grass flanked by houses on all four sides, a pleasant spot, one of the loveliest public spaces in your small New Jersey town, and you and your friends often go there to play baseball after school, since baseball is the thing you all love most, and you play for hours on end without ever growing weary of it. No adults are present. You establish your own ground rules and settle disagreements among yourselves—most often with words, occasionally with fists. More than fifty years later, you remember nothing about the game that was played that afternoon, but what you do remember is the following: The game is over, and you are standing alone in the middle of the infield, playing catch with yourself, that is, throwing a ball high into the air and following its ascent and descent until it lands in your glove, at which point you immediately throw the ball into the air again, and each time you throw the ball it travels higher than it did the time before, and after several throws you are reaching unprecedented heights, the ball is hovering in the air for many seconds now, the white ball going up against the clear blue sky, the white ball coming down into your glove, and your entire being is engaged in this witless activity, your concentration is total, nothing exists now except the ball and the sky and your glove, which means that your face is turned upward, that you are looking up as you follow the trajectory of the ball, and therefore you are no longer aware of what is happening on the ground, and what happens on the ground as you are looking up at the sky is that something or someone unexpectedly comes crashing into you, and the impact is so sudden, so violent, so overwhelming in its force that you instantly fall to the ground, feeling as though you have been hit by a tank. The brunt of the blow was aimed at your head, in particular your forehead, but your torso has been battered as well, and as you lie on the ground gasping for breath, stunned and nearly unconscious, you see that blood is flowing from your forehead, no, not flowing, gushing, and so you remove your white T-shirt and press it against the gushing spot, and within seconds the white T-shirt has turned entirely red. The other boys are alarmed. They come rushing toward you to do what they can to help, and it is only then that you find out what happened. It seems that one of your cohort, a gangly, good-hearted lunkhead called B.T. (you remember his name but will not divulge it here, since you do not want to embarrass him—assuming he is still alive), was so impressed by your towering, skyscraper throws that he got it into *his head* to take part in the action, and without bothering to tell you that he, too, was going to try to catch one of your throws started running in the direction of the descending ball, head turned upward, of course, and mouth hanging open in that oafish way of his (what person runs with his mouth hanging open?), and when he crashed into you a moment later, running at an all-out gallop, the teeth protruding from his open mouth went straight into *your head*. Hence the blood now gushing out of you, hence the depth of the gash in the skin above your left eye. Fortunately, the office of your family doctor is just across the way, in one of the houses that line the perimeter of Grove Park. The boys decide to lead you there at once, and so you cross the park holding your bloody T-shirt against your head in the company of your friends, perhaps four of them, perhaps six of them, you no longer remember, and burst en masse into Dr. Kohn's office. (You have not forgotten his name, just as you have not forgotten the name of your kindergarten teacher, Miss Sandquist, or the names of any of the other teachers you had as a boy.) The receptionist tells you and your friends that Dr. Kohn is seeing a patient just now, and before she can get up from her chair to inform the doctor that there is an emergency to attend to, you and your friends march into the consulting room without bothering to knock. You find Dr. Kohn talking to a plump, middle-aged woman who is sitting on the examination table dressed in a bra and slip only. The woman lets out a yelp of surprise, but once Dr. Kohn sees the blood gushing from your forehead, he tells the woman to get dressed and leave, tells your friends to make themselves scarce, and then hastens to the task of sewing up your wound. It is a painful procedure, since there is no time to administer an anesthetic, but you do your best not to howl as he threads the stitches through your skin. The job he does is perhaps not as brilliant as the one executed by the doctor who sewed up your cheek in 1950, but it is effective for all that, since you do not bleed to death and no longer have a hole in your head. Some days later, you and your sixth-grade classmates take part in your grammar school graduation ceremony. You have been selected to be a flag-bearer, which means that you must carry the American flag down an aisle of the auditorium and plant it in the flag stand on stage. Your head is wrapped in a white gauze bandage, and because blood still seeps occasionally from the spot where you were stitched up, the white gauze has a large red stain on it. After the ceremony, your mother says that when you were walking down the aisle with the flag, you reminded her of a painting of a wounded Revolutionary War hero. You know, she says, just like *The Spirit of '76*.

What presses in on you, what has always pressed in on you: the outside, meaning the air—or, more precisely, your body in the air around you. The soles of your feet anchored to the ground, but

all the rest of you exposed to the air, and that is where the story begins, in your body, and everything will end in the body as well. For
now, you are thinking about the wind. Later, if time allows for it, you
will think about the heat and the cold, the infinite varieties of rain,
the fogs you have stumbled through like a man without eyes, the
demented, machine-gun tattoo of hailstones clattering against the
tile roof of the house in the Var. But it is the wind that claims your
attention now, for the air is seldom still, and beyond the barely per-
ceptible breath of nothingness that sometimes surrounds you, there
are the breezes and wafting lilts, the sudden gusts and squalls, the
three-day-long mistrals you lived through in that house with the tile
roof, the soaking nor'easters that sweep along the Atlantic coast, the
gales and hurricanes, the whirlwinds. And there you are, twenty-one
years ago, walking through the streets of Amsterdam on your way to
an event that has been canceled without your knowledge, dutifully
trying to fulfill the commitment you have made, out in what will
later be called *the storm of the century*, a hurricane of such blistering
intensity that within an hour of your stubborn, ill-advised decision
to venture outdoors, large trees will be uprooted in every corner of
the city, chimneys will tumble to the ground, and parked cars will be
lifted up and go sailing through the air. You walk with your face to
the wind, trying to advance along the sidewalk, but in spite of your
efforts to get to where you are going, you cannot move. The wind is
blasting into you, and for the next minute and a half, you are stuck.

Your hands on the Ha'penny Bridge in Dublin thirteen Januarys
ago, the night following another hurricane with hundred-mile-
an-hour winds, the final night of the film you have been directing for the past two months, the last scene, the last shot, a simple
matter of fixing the camera on the gloved hand of your leading
actress as she turns her wrist and lets go of a small stone that will
fall into the waters of the Liffey. There is nothing to it, no shot has

demanded less effort or ingenuity in the entire film, but there you are in the dank and dark of the windswept night, as exhausted as you have ever been after nine weeks of grueling work on a production fraught with countless problems (budget problems, union problems, location problems, weather problems), fifteen pounds lighter than when you began, and after standing for hours on the bridge with your crew, the clammy, frigid Irish air has infiltrated your bones, and a moment comes just before the final shot when you realize that your hands are frozen, that you cannot move your fingers, that your hands have turned into two blocks of ice. Why aren't you wearing gloves? you ask yourself, but you are unable to answer the question, since the thought of gloves never even occurred to you when you left your hotel for the bridge. You film the last shot one more time, and then you and your producer, along with your actress, your actress's boyfriend, and several members of the crew, go to a nearby pub to thaw out and celebrate the completion of the film. The place is crowded, jammed full, an echo chamber packed with roaring, clamorous people bobbing back and forth in a state of apocalyptic merriment, but a table has been reserved for you and your friends, so you sit down at the table, and the moment your body makes contact with the chair you understand that you are depleted, drained of all physical energy, all emotional energy, utterly spent in a way you never could have imagined possible, so crushed that you feel you might burst into tears at any moment. You order a whiskey, and when you take hold of the glass and raise it to your lips, you are heartened to notice that your fingers can move again. You order a second whiskey, then a third whiskey, then a fourth whiskey, and suddenly you fall asleep. In spite of the frenzy all around you, you manage to go on sleeping until the good man who is your producer hoists you to your feet and half-drags you, half-carries you back to your hotel.

———

Yes, you drink too much and smoke too much, you have lost teeth without bothering to replace them, your diet does not conform to the precepts of contemporary nutritional wisdom, but if you shun most vegetables it is simply because you do not like them, and you find it difficult, if not impossible, to eat what you do not like. You know that your wife worries about you, especially about your smoking and drinking, but mercifully, until now, no X-ray has revealed any damage to your lungs, no blood test has revealed any devastation to your liver, and so you forge on with your vile habits, knowing full well that they will ultimately do you grave harm, but the older you become the less likely it seems that you will ever have the will or the courage to abandon your beloved little cigars and frequent glasses of wine, which have given you so much pleasure over the years, and you sometimes think that if you were to cut these things out of your life at this late date, your body would simply fall apart, your system would cease to function. No doubt you are a flawed and wounded person, a man who has carried a wound in him from the very beginning (why else would you have spent the whole of your adult life bleeding words onto a page?), and the benefits you derive from alcohol and tobacco serve as crutches to keep your crippled self upright and moving through the world. *Self-medication*, as your wife calls it. Unlike your mother's mother, she does not want you to be different. Your wife tolerates your weaknesses and does not rant or scold, and if she worries, it is only because she wants you to live forever. You count the reasons why you have held her close to you for so many years, and surely this is one of them, one of the bright stars in the vast constellation of enduring love.

Needless to say, you cough, especially at night, when your body is in a horizontal position, and on those nights when the breath tubes are excessively clogged, you climb out of bed, go into another room, and cough on madly until you have hacked up all the gunk. According to your friend Spiegelman (the most ardent smoker you know), whenever someone asks him why he smokes, he inevitably answers: "Because I like to cough."

1952. Five years old, naked in the bath, alone, big enough to wash yourself now, and as you lie on your back in the warm water, your penis suddenly springs to attention, popping out above the water line. Until this moment, you have seen your penis only from above, standing on your feet and looking down, but from this new vantage point, more or less at eye level, it occurs to you that the tip of your circumcised male organ bears a striking resemblance to a helmet. An old-fashioned sort of helmet, similar to those worn by firemen in the late nineteenth century. This revelation pleases you, since at that juncture of your life your greatest ambition is to grow up to become a fireman, which you consider to be the most heroic job on the face of the earth (no doubt it is), and how fitting that you should have a miniature fireman's helmet emblazoned on your very person, on the very part of your body, moreover, that looks like and functions as a hose.

The countless tight squeezes you have been in during the course of your life, the desperate moments when you have felt an urgent, overpowering need to empty your bladder and no toilet is at hand, the times when you have found yourself stuck in traffic, for example, or sitting on a subway stalled between stations, and the pure agony of forcing yourself *to hold it in*. This is the universal dilemma that no one ever talks about, but everyone has been there at one time or another, everyone has lived through it, and while there is no example of human suffering more comical that that of the bursting bladder, you tend not to laugh about these incidents until after you have managed to relieve yourself—for what person over the age of three would want to wet his pants in public? That is why you will never forget these words, which were the last words spoken to one of your friends by his dying father: "Just remember, Charlie," he said, "never pass up an opportunity to piss." And so the wisdom of the ages is handed down from one generation to the next.

Again, it is 1952, and you are in the backseat of the family car, the blue 1950 De Soto your father brought home the day your sister was born. Your mother is driving, and you have been on the road for some time now, going from where to where you can no longer remember, but you are on your way back, no more than ten or fifteen minutes from home, and for the past little while you have had to pee, the pressure in your bladder has been building steadily, and by now you are writhing on the backseat, legs crossed, your hand clamped over your crotch, uncertain whether you can hold out much longer. You tell your mother about your predicament, and she asks if you can hang in there for another ten minutes. No, you tell her, you don't think so. In that case, she says, since there's nowhere to stop between here and home, just go in your pants. This is such a radical idea to you, such a betrayal of what you consider to be your hard-won, manly independence, that you can scarcely believe what she has said. Go in my pants? you say to her. Yes, go in your pants, she says. What difference does it make? We'll throw your clothes in the wash the minute we get home. And so it happens, with your mother's full and explicit approval, that you pee in your pants for the last time.

Fifty years later, you are in another car, a rented car this time since you do not have one of your own, a spanking-new Toyota

Corolla that you have been driving for the past three hours on your way back from Connecticut to your house in Brooklyn. It is August 2002. You are fifty-five years old and have been driving since you were seventeen, always with skill and confidence, known to everyone who has ever driven with you as *a good driver*, with no accident on your record beyond a single scraped fender in close to forty years behind the wheel. Your wife is up front with you in the seat to your right, and in the back is your fifteen-year-old daughter (who has just finished a summer acting program at a school in Connecticut), sprawled out asleep on the quilts and pillows that have served as her bedding for the past month. Also sleeping in the back is your dog, the ragged stray mutt you and your daughter brought home off the streets eight years ago, whom you dubbed Jack (after Jack Wilton, the hero of Nashe's *The Unfortunate Travel- ler*) and who has been a much loved if lunatic member of the household ever since. Your wife, who worries about many things, has never worried about your driving, and in fact has often com- plimented you on how well you handle yourself in various kinds of traffic: passing other cars on multi-lane highways, for example, or negotiating the tangle of city streets, or easing your way around the twists and curves of backcountry roads. Today, however, she senses that something is wrong, that you are not concentrating properly, that your timing is slightly off, and more than once she has told you to watch what you are doing. You should know better by now than to doubt the wisdom of your wife's words, for she possesses an uncanny ability to read the minds of others, to see into the souls of others, to sniff out the hidden undercurrents of any human situation, and again and again you have marveled at how accurate her instincts have proven to be, but on this particu- lar day her anxiety is so acute that it has begun to get on your nerves. Are you not a famously *good driver*? you tell her. Have you ever had an accident? Would you ever do anything to put the lives of the people you love most in the world at risk? No, she says, of course not, she doesn't know what has gotten into her, and once you reach the tollbooths at the Triborough Bridge, you say to her, Look, here we are, New York City, nearly home now, and after that she promises not to say another word about your driving. But something is wrong, even if you are not willing to admit it, for this is 2002, and so many things have happened to you in this year of grim surprises, why shouldn't your mastery of cars suddenly and inexplicably abandon you? Worst of all, there was your mother's death in mid-May (heart attack), which stunned you not because you didn't know that people of seventy-seven can and do die without warning but because she was in apparent good health, and just the day before the last day of her life, you talked to her on the phone, and she was in buoyant spirits, cracking jokes and telling such funny stories that after you hung up you said to your wife: "She hasn't sounded this happy in years." Your mother's death worst of all, but there was also the blood clot that formed in your left leg during a nine-hour coach flight to Copenhagen in early February, which kept you flat on your back for several weeks and forced you to walk with a cane for months afterward, not to speak of the trouble you have been having with your eyes, the tear in the cornea of your left eye to begin with, then the tear in the right cornea some weeks later, followed by repeated, altogether random instances in one eye or the other over the past several months, and the damage is always done in your sleep, which means there is nothing you can do to prevent it (since the cream prescribed by the ophthalmologist has had no effect), and on those mornings when you wake up with yet another torn cornea, the pain is ferocious, an eye being without question the most sensitive and vulnerable part of the body, and after you put in the painkilling drops the doctor has prescribed for such emergencies, it generally takes from two to four hours before the pain begins to disappear, and during those hours there is nothing you can do but sit still with a cold washcloth over the afflicted eye, which you keep shut, since opening that eye will make you feel as if a pin were being jabbed into it. A six-month siege of *coach leg*, then, and a chronic case of *dry eye*, and also the first full-blown panic attack of your life, which occurred just two days after your mother's death, followed by several others in the days immediately after that, and for some time now you have felt that you are disintegrating, that you, who were once nature's strongman, able to resist all assaults from within and without, impervious to the somatic and psychological travails that dog the rest of humanity, are not the least bit strong anymore and are rapidly turning into a debilitated wreck. Your family doctor has prescribed pills to keep the panic attacks under control, and perhaps those pills have been affecting your ability to drive this afternoon, but that seems unlikely to you, since you have driven with these pills in your system before, and neither you nor your wife ever noticed any difference. Impaired or not, you have now passed through the tollbooth at the Triborough Bridge and have begun the final stage of your journey home, and as you drive through the city you are not thinking about your mother or your eyes or your leg or the pills you swallow to keep your panic attacks at bay. You are thinking only about the car and the forty or fifty minutes it will take to reach your house in Brooklyn, and now that your wife has calmed down and no longer seems concerned about your driving, you are calm as well, and nothing out of the ordinary happens as you cover the miles from the bridge to the outskirts of your neighborhood. It is true that you have to pee, that your bladder has been sending out signals to you for the past twenty minutes, ever more rapid and dire signals of distress, and therefore you drive a little faster than perhaps you should, since you are doubly eager to get home, home for the sake of home, of course, and with it the relief of being able to emerge from the stuffy confines of the car, but also because getting home will allow you to run upstairs to the bathroom and relieve *yourself*, and yet even if you are pressing a little more than you should, all is well, and by now you are just two and a half minutes from the street where you live. The car is traveling down Fourth Avenue, an ugly stretch of dilapidated apartment buildings and empty warehouses, and because pedestrian traffic is sparse along these blocks, drivers rarely have to worry about anyone crossing the street, and on top of that the lights stay green for longer intervals than on most avenues, which encourages drivers to go fast, too fast, often far above the speed limit. This poses no problem if you are going straight ahead (that is why you have chosen this route, after all: because it will get you home more quickly than any other), but the onrush of traffic can make left turns somewhat perilous, since you must turn while the light is green, and while the light is green for you, it is also green for the cars speeding toward you from the opposite direction. Now, as you come to the juncture of Fourth Avenue and Third Street, where you must make the left turn that will take you home, you stop the car and wait for an opening, and suddenly you forget the lesson you learned from your father when he taught you how to drive close to forty years ago. He himself was a wretched, incompetent driver, an inattentive, daydreaming motorist who courted disaster every time he put his key in the ignition, but for all his shortcomings behind the wheel, he was an excellent teacher of others, and the best piece of advice he ever gave you was this: drive defensively; work on the assumption that everyone else on the road is stupid and crazy; take nothing for granted. You have always held these words uppermost in your thoughts, and they have served you well for all these years, but now, because you are desperate to empty your bladder, or because a pill has affected your judgment, or because you are tired and not paying close attention, or because you have turned into a *debilitated wreck*, you impulsively decide to take a chance, which is to say, to go on the offensive. A brown van is coming toward you. Going fast, yes, but no more than forty-five miles an hour, you think, fifty at most, and after gauging the distance of the van from where you have stopped in relation to the speed of the van, you are certain you will be able to make the left turn and get through the intersection without any problem—but only if you act quickly and step on the accelerator *now*. Your calculations, however, are founded on the belief that the van is traveling at forty-five or fifty miles an hour, which is in fact not true. It is going faster than that, at least sixty, perhaps even sixty-five, and therefore, once you make the left turn and begin hustling through the intersection, the van is suddenly and unexpectedly upon you, and since you are looking forward and not to your right, you do not see the van as it comes crashing into your car—a ninety-degree-angle hit, straight into the front door on the passenger's side, the side on which your wife is sitting. The impact is thunderous, convulsive, cataclysmic— an explosion loud enough to end the world. You feel as if Zeus has hurled a lightning bolt at you and your family, and an instant later the car is spinning, out of control, madly rotating down the street until it collides with a metal lamppost and comes to an abrupt and jarring halt. Then everything goes silent, the entire universe is enveloped in silence, and when at last you are able to think again, the first thought that comes to you is that you are alive. You look at your wife and see that her eyes are open, that she is breathing and therefore alive as well, and then you turn around to look at your daughter in the back, and she too is alive, jolted from the depths of sleep by the double blow of van and lamppost, sitting up and looking at you with large, bewildered eyes, her lips whiter than any lips you have ever seen, lips as white as the paper you are writing on now, and you understand that she has been saved by the quilts and pillows she was sleeping on, saved by the fact that one's muscles are utterly relaxed in sleep, and therefore no bones are broken, her head has not been hurled into contact with any hard surface, and she will be all right, is all right, as is the dog, who was sleeping on the quilts and pillows as well. Then you turn back to have another look at your wife, who was closest to the impact of the collision, and from the way she is sitting there beside you, so still, so mute, so absent from her surroundings, you fear that her neck might be broken, her long and slender neck, the beautiful neck that is the very emblem of her extraordinary beauty. You ask her how she is, if she feels any pain and if so where, but if she manages to answer you, her response is muffled, spoken in such a low voice that you cannot hear what she says. By now, you have become aware of noise outside the car, things are happening around you, several things at once, most noticeably the shrieking voice of the woman who was driving the van, who is hopping around in the street, angrily insulting you for causing the accident. (You will later learn that she was driving without a license, that the van did not belong to her, and that she had been in trouble with the police on several occasions—which would account for the vehemence of her anger, since she was afraid of running afoul of the law—but as she stands there shouting at you now, you are appalled by her selfishness, stunned that she does not even bother to ask if you and your family are all right.) As if to blot out the vicious behavior of this woman (who, to use your father's words, is both stupid and crazy), a small miracle then occurs. A man is walking down Fourth Avenue, the only pedestrian on a thoroughfare that normally has no pedestrians, and against all reason, all logic, all presumptions about how the world supposedly works, this man is dressed in hospital whites, he is a young doctor, a native of India with smooth brown skin and an exceptionally handsome face, and seeing what has just happened, he approaches your car and calmly begins talking to your wife. There is no glass in the window anymore, which allows him to lean in and talk to her in a low voice, his soothing Indian voice, and as you listen to him ask all the standard questions a neurologist would pose to a patient— What is your name? What is the date? Who is the president?—you understand that he is doing everything he can to keep her conscious, to keep her from lapsing into a state of profound shock.

Given the impact of the crash, it does not surprise you that for the time being she can no longer see any colors, that the world in front of her eyes is visible only in black and white. The doctor, who is not an apparition, who is a real man (but how not to think of him as a divine spirit who has come to save your wife?), stays with her until the ambulance and emergency team arrive. You and your daughter and Jack have left the car by now, but your wife must not move, everyone is worried that her neck could be broken, and as you stand there watching the firemen cut open the right front door with an instrument known as *the jaws of life*, you study the demolished car and cannot comprehend why all of you are still breathing. The car looks like a squashed insect. All four tires are flat, splayed out, twisted, the passenger side is caved in, and the back, which you now realize is the part of the car that crashed into the lamppost, is crumpled up, with no glass left in the rear window. Slowly, the paramedics strap your wife onto a board to keep her immobilized, they slide her into an ambulance, you and your daughter are put in another ambulance, and then you all set out for the trauma unit at Lutheran Medical Center in Bay Ridge. After two CAT scans and a number of X-rays, the doctors announce that no bones are broken in your wife's back or neck. Happy, all of you happy, then, in spite of this brush with death, and as you leave the hospital together, your wife jokingly reports that the doctor in charge of conducting the CAT scans told her that she had the most perfect, most beautiful neck he had ever seen.

Eight and a half years have gone by since that day, and not once has your wife ever blamed you for the accident. She says the woman in the van was driving too fast and therefore was entirely responsible for what happened. But you know better than to exonerate yourself. Yes, the woman was driving too fast, but in the end that is of little consequence. You took a chance you shouldn't have taken, and that error of judgment continues to fill you with shame. That is why you vowed to quit driving after you left the hospital, why you have not sat behind the wheel of a car since the day you almost killed your family. Not because you don't trust yourself anymore, but because you are ashamed, because you understand that for one near-fatal moment you were just as stupid and crazy as the woman who crashed into you.

Two years after the crash, you are in the small French city of Arles, about to read from one of your books in public. Appearing with you will be the actor Jean-Louis Trintignant (a friend of your publisher's), who will take the passages you read in English and read them again in French translation. A double reading, as is customary in foreign countries where the audiences are not bilingual, with the two of you alternating from paragraph to paragraph as you march in tandem through the pages you have chosen for the event. You are glad to be in Trintignant's company tonight, since you hold his acting in great esteem, and when you think of the films you have seen him play in (Bertolucci's *The Conformist*, Rohmer's *Ma Nuit chez Maud*, Truffaut's *Confidentially Yours*, Kieslowski's *Red*—to cite just some of your favorites), you are hard-pressed to come up with the name of another European actor whose work you admire more. You also feel tremendous compassion for him, since you know about the brutal, highly publicized murder of his daughter some years back, and you are keenly aware of the terrible suffering he has lived through, continues to live through. Like many of the actors you have known and worked with, Trintignant is a shy and reticent person. Not that he doesn't exude an aura of goodwill and friendliness, but at the same time he is closed in on himself, a man who finds talking to others difficult. At the moment, the two of you are together on stage rehearsing the evening's performance, alone in the large church or former church where the reading will be held. You are impressed by the timbre of Trintignant's voice, the resonance of his voice, the qualities of voice that distinguish great actors from merely good ones, and it gives you enormous pleasure to hear the words you have written (no, not quite your words, but your words translated into another language) conveyed through the instrument of that exceptional voice. At one point, apropos of nothing, Trintignant turns to you and asks how old you are. Fifty-seven, you say, and then, after a brief pause, you ask him how old he is. Seventy-four, he replies, and then, after another brief pause, you both go back to work. Following the rehearsal, you and Trintignant are taken to a room somewhere in the church to wait until the audience has been seated and the performance can begin. Other people are in the room with you, various members of the company that publishes your work, the organizer of the event, anonymous friends of people you don't know, perhaps a dozen men and women in all. You are sitting in a chair and not talking to anyone, just sitting in silence and looking at the people in the room, and you see that Trintignant, who is about ten feet away from you, is sitting in silence as well, looking down at the floor with his chin cupped in his hand, apparently lost in thought. Eventually, he looks up, catches your eye, and says, with unexpected earnestness and gravity: "Paul, there's just one thing I want to tell you. At fifty-seven, I felt old. Now, at seventy-four, I feel much younger than I did then." You are confused by his remark. You have no idea what he is trying to tell you, but you sense it is important to him, that he is attempting to share something of vital importance with you, and for that reason you do not ask him to explain what he means. For close to seven years now, you have continued to ponder his words, and although you still don't know quite what to make of them, there have been glimmers, tiny moments when you feel you have almost penetrated the truth of what he was saying to you. Perhaps it is something as simple as this: that a man fears death more at fifty-seven than he does at seventy-four. Or perhaps he saw something in you that worried him: the lingering traces of what happened to you during the horrible months of 2002. For the fact is that you feel more robust now, at sixty-three, than you did at fifty-five. The problem with your leg is long gone. You have not had a panic attack in years, and your eyes, which still act up every now and then, do so far less frequently than before. Also to be noted: no more car crashes, and no more parents for you to mourn.

Thirty-two years ago today, meaning half your life ago almost to the minute, the news that your father had died the previous night, another night in January filled with snow, just as this one is, the cold wind, the wild weather, everything the same, time moving and yet not moving, everything different and yet everything the same, and no, he did not have the luck to reach seventy-four. Sixty-six, and because you always felt certain that he would live to a ripe old age, there was never any urgency about clearing the fog that had always hovered between you, and therefore, as the fact of his sudden, unexpected death finally sank in, you were left with a feeling of unfinished business, the hollow frustration of words not spoken, of opportunities missed forever. He died in bed making love to his girlfriend, a healthy man whose heart inexplicably gave out on him. In the years since that January day in 1979, numerous men have told you that this is the best way to die (the little death turned into real death), but no woman has ever said it, and you yourself find it a horrible way to go, and when you think of your father's girlfriend at the funeral and the shell-shocked look in her eyes (yes, she told you, it was truly horrible, the most horrible thing she had ever lived through), you pray that such a thing never happens to your wife. Thirty-two years ago today, and you have gone on regretting that too-abrupt departure ever since, for your father did not live long enough to see that his blundering, impractical son did not end up in the poorhouse, as he always feared you would, but several more years would have been necessary for him to understand this, and it saddens you that when your sixty-six-year-old father died in his girlfriend's arms, you were still struggling on all fronts, still eating the dirt of failure.

No, you do not want to die, and even as you approach the age of your father when his life came to an end, you have not called any cemetery to arrange for your burial plot, have not given away any of the books you are certain you will never read again, and have not begun to clear your throat to say your good-byes. Nevertheless, thirteen years ago, just one month past your fiftieth birthday, as you sat in your downstairs study eating a tuna fish sandwich for lunch, you had what you now call your false heart attack, a siege of ever-mounting pain that spread through your chest and down your left arm and up into your jaw, the classic symptoms of cardiac upheaval and destruction, the dreaded coronary infarction that can stop a man's life within minutes, and as the pain continued to grow, to reach higher and higher levels of incendiary force, burning up your insides and setting your chest on fire, you grew weak and dizzy from the onslaught, staggered to your feet, slowly climbed the stairs with both hands clutching the banister, and collapsed on the landing of the parlor floor as you called out to your wife in a feeble, barely audible voice. She came running down from the top floor, and when she saw you there lying on your back, she took you in her arms and held you, asking where it hurt, telling you she would call the doctor, and as you looked up at her face, you were convinced you were about to die, for pain of that magnitude could only mean death, and the odd thing about it, perhaps the oddest thing that has ever happened to you, is that you weren't afraid, you were in fact calm and altogether accepting of the idea that you were about to leave this world, saying to yourself, This is it, you're going to die now, and maybe death isn't as bad as you had thought it was, for here you are in the arms of the woman you love, and if you must die now, consider yourself blessed to have lived as long as fifty years. You were taken to the hospital, kept overnight in an emergency room bed, given blood tests every four hours, and by the next morning the heart attack had become an inflamed esophagus, no doubt aggravated by the heavy dose of lemon juice in your sandwich. Your life had been given back to you, your heart was sound and beating normally, and on top of all that good news, you had learned that death was not something to be feared anymore, that when the moment comes for a person to die, his being shifts into another zone of consciousness, and he is able to accept it. Or so you thought. Five years later, when you had the first of your panic attacks, the sudden, monstrous attack that ripped through your body and threw you to the floor, you were not the least bit calm or accepting. You thought you were going to die then, too, but this time you howled in terror, more afraid than you had ever been in your life. So much for other zones of consciousness and quiet exits from this valley of tears. You lay on the floor and howled, howled at the top of your lungs, howled because death was inside you and you didn't want to die.

Snow, so much snow these past days and weeks that fifty-six inches have fallen on New York in less than a month. Eight storms, nine storms, you have lost track by now, and all through January the song heard most often in Brooklyn has been the street music made by shovels scraping against sidewalks and thick patches of ice. Intemperate cold (three degrees one morning), drizzles and mizzles, mist and slush, ever-aggressive winds, but most of all the snow, which will not melt, and as one storm falls on top of another, the bushes and trees in your back garden are all wearing ever-longer and heavier beards of snow. Yes, it seems to have turned into one of *those* winters, but in spite of the cold and discomfort and your useless longing for spring, you can't help admiring the vigor of these meteorological dramas, and you continue to look at the falling snow with the same awe you felt when you were a boy.

Roughhousing. That is the word that comes to you now when you think about the pleasures of boyhood (as opposed to the pains). Wrestling with your father, a rare circumstance since he was seldom present during the hours when you were awake (off to work while you were still asleep and home after you had been put to bed), but all the more memorable because of that perhaps, and the outlandish size of his body and muscles, the sheer bulk of him as you grappled in his arms and strove to defeat the King of New Jersey in hand-to-hand combat, and also your older cousin by four years, on those Sunday afternoons when you and your family visited your aunt and uncle's house, the same excessive physicality as you rolled around on the floor with him, the joy of that physicality, the abandon. Running. Running and jumping and climbing. Running until you felt your lungs would burst, until your side ached. Day after day and on into the evening, the long, slowly fading dusks of summer, and you out there on the grass, running for all you were worth, your pulse pounding in your ears, the wind in your face. A bit later on, tackle football, Johnny on the Pony, Kick the Can, King of the Castle, Capture the Flag. You and your friends were so nimble, so flexible, so keen on waging these pretend wars that you went at one another with unrelenting savagery, small bodies crashing into other small bodies, knocking one another to the ground, yanking arms, grabbing necks, tripping and shoving, anything and everything to win the game—animals the lot of you, wild animals through and through. But how well you slept back then. Switch off the lamp, close your eyes . . . and see you tomorrow.

More subtly, more beautifully, more gratifying in the long run, there was your ever-evolving skill at playing baseball, the least violent of sports, and the passion you developed for it beginning at six or seven years old. Catching and throwing, fielding ground balls, learning where to position yourself at each moment throughout the course of a game, depending on how many outs there were, how many runners were on base, and knowing in advance what you must do should the ball be hit in your direction: throw home, throw to second, try for a double play, or else, because you played shortstop, run into left field after a base hit and then wheel around to make the long relay throw to the correct spot on the field. Never a dull moment, in spite of what critics of the game might think: poised in a state of constant anticipation, ever at the ready, your mind churning with possibilities, and then the sudden explosion, the ball speeding toward you and the urgent need to do what must be done, the quick reflexes required to perform your job, and the exquisite sensation of scooping up a ground ball hit to your left or right and making a hard, accurate throw to first. But no pleasure greater than that of hitting the ball, settling into your stance, watching the pitcher go into his windup, and to hit a ball squarely, to feel the ball making contact with the meat of the bat, the very sound of it as you followed through with your swing and saw the ball flying deep into the outfield—no, there was no feeling like it, nothing ever came close to the exaltation of that moment, and because you became better and better at this as time went on, there were many such moments, and you lived for them in a way you lived for nothing else, all wrapped up in this meaningless boy's game, but that was the apex of happiness for you back then, the very best thing your body was able to do.

The years before sex entered the equation, before you understood that the miniature fireman between your legs was good for anything but helping you empty your bladder. It must be 1952 again, but perhaps a little earlier or a little later than that, and you ask your mother the question all children ask their parents, the standard question about where babies come from, meaning where did you come from, and by what mysterious process did you enter the world as a human being? Your mother's answer is so abstract, so evasive, so metaphorical that it leaves you utterly confounded. She says: The father plants the seed in the mother, and little by little the baby begins to grow. At this point in your life, the only seeds you are familiar with are the ones that produce flowers and vegetables, the ones that farmers scatter over large fields at planting time to start a new round of crops for harvest in the fall. You instantly see an image in your head: your father dressed as a farmer, a cartoon version of a farmer in blue overalls with a straw hat on his head, and he is walking along with a large rake propped against his shoulder, walking with a jaunty, insouciant stride out in some rural nowhere, on his way to *plant the seed*. For some time afterward, this was the picture you saw whenever the subject of babies was mentioned: your old man as a farmer, dressed in blue overalls with a ragged straw hat on his head and a rake propped against his shoulder. You knew there was something wrong about this, however, for seeds were always planted in the earth, either in gardens or in large fields, and since your mother was neither a garden nor a field, you had no idea what to make of this horticultural presentation of the facts of life. Is it possible for anyone to be more stupid than you were? You were a stupid little boy who lacked the wit to ask the question again, but the truth was that you enjoyed imagining your father as a farmer, enjoyed seeing him in that ridiculous costume, and when it comes right down to it, you probably wouldn't have understood what your mother was talking about if she had given you a more precise answer to your question.

Some weeks or months before or after this conversation with your mother, the little neighbor boy who smashed you on the head with the toy rake inexplicably went missing. His frantic mother rushed into your backyard and told you and your friends to start looking for him, and off you all went, thrashing into the borderland of wild shrubbery and tangled undergrowth that served as your secret hiding place, calling out the name of the boy, which was Eric, although he was commonly referred to as Brat or Monster— a midget felon whose life thus far had been devoted exclusively to acts of terrorism and violence. You entered a dense patch of bushes, flicking leaves out of your face and parting branches as you moved forward, fully expecting to find the runaway hoodlum huddled at your feet, but what you found instead was a nest of wasps or hornets, which you inadvertently stepped on, and seconds later you were engulfed by those stinging creatures, who were attacking your face and arms, and even as you tried to swat them away, others had crawled inside your clothes and were stabbing you in your legs and chest and back. Horrific pain. You went running out of the bushes onto the grass in the backyard, no doubt screaming your head off, and there was your mother, who took one glance at you and immediately began stripping off your clothes, and when there was no longer a stitch on you, she swooped up your naked body into her arms and ran with you toward the house. Once inside, she carried you upstairs, turned on the water, and put you in a cold, cold bath.

The boy was found. If you remember correctly, he was discovered in his own house, asleep on the living room floor, either hidden behind the sofa or curled up under a table, but if you need further proof that he did not die or vanish that day, you have only to recall the afternoon four or five years later when you were in bed with a case of the flu, one of those dreary sick days spent in the airless confinement of pajamas, fever, and aspirin tablets every four hours, thinking about your friends, who had already been let out of school and were no doubt playing a game of pickup baseball in Grove Park, since the sun was shining and the weather was warm, which made it an ideal afternoon for baseball. You were nine or ten years old, and as you remember it now, more than half a century later, you were the only person in the house. Outside in the backyard, chained to the wire runner your father had built for him, the family dog was dozing on the grass. He had been a part of your life for a good two years or longer, and you were intensely fond of him—a frisky young beagle with an appetite for adventure and a mad penchant for chasing after cars. He had already been run over once, injuring his left hind leg so badly that he could no longer use it, which had turned him into a three-legged dog, a strange, peg-legged kind of dog, a swashbuckling pirate of a dog in your opinion, but he had adjusted to his infirmity well, and even with just three legs he could still outrun any four-legged dog in the neighborhood. So there you were lying in bed in your upstairs room, certain that your crippled dog was safely tethered to his runner in the backyard, when a sudden volley of loud noises burst in on the quiet: a screech of tires in front of your house, immediately followed by a high-pitched howl of pain, the howl of a dog in pain, and from the sound of that dog's voice, you instantly knew that it was your dog. You jumped out of bed and ran outside, and there was the Brat, the Monster, confessing to you that he had unhooked your dog from his leash because he "wanted to play with him," and there was the man who had been driving the car, a much rattled and deeply upset man, saying to the people who had gathered around him that he had no choice, that the boy and the dog ran straight into the middle of the street, and it was either hit the boy or hit the dog, so he swerved and hit the dog, and there was your dog, your mostly white dog lying dead in the middle of the black street, and as you picked him up and carried him into the house, you told yourself no, the man was wrong, he should have hit the boy and not the dog, he should have killed the boy, and so angry were you at the boy for what he had done to your dog, you did not stop to consider that this was the first time you had ever wished that another human being were dead.

There were fights, of course. No one can get through boyhood without some of them, or many of them, and when you consider the tussles and confrontations you took part in, the bloody noses you both gave and received, the punches to the stomach that knocked the wind out of you, the inane headlocks and hammer-locks that sent you and your opponent sprawling to the ground, you can't think of a single instance when you were the one who started it, for you hated the whole business of fighting, but because there was always a bully somewhere in the vicinity, some brainless tough who would taunt you with threats and dares and insults, there were times when you felt compelled to defend your-self, even if you were the smaller one and were almost certain to be thrashed. You loved the mock wars of tackle football and Cap-ture the Flag, the rough-and-tumble of barreling into a catcher at home plate, but real fighting made you sick. It was too fraught with emotional consequences, too wrenching in the angers it provoked, and even when you won your fights, you always felt like crying af-terward. The slug-or-be-slugged approach to settling differences lost all appeal to you after a boy at summer camp came at you by jumping down from the rafters of the cabin and you wound up breaking his arm when you retaliated by slamming him into a wooden table. You were ten years old, and from that point on you steered clear of fighting as best you could, but fights continued to come your way from time to time, at least until you were thirteen, when you finally figured out that you could win any fight against any boy by kneeing him in the balls, by driving your knee into his crotch with all the force you could muster, and just like that, within a matter of seconds, the fight would be over. You acquired a reputation for being a "dirty fighter," and perhaps there was some truth to it, but you fought like that only because you didn't want to fight, and after one or two of these bouts, word got around and no one ever attacked you again. You were thirteen years old and had permanently retired from the ring.

No more battles with boys, but an abiding passion for girls, for kissing girls and holding hands with girls, something that started for you long before the onset of puberty, at a time when boys are supposedly not interested in such matters. As far back as the kindergarten class in which you fell for the girl with the golden ponytail (whose name was Cathy), you were always mad for kissing, and even then, at age five or six, you and Cathy would sometimes exchange kisses—innocent pecks, to be sure, but deeply pleasurable for all that. In those years of so-called latency, your friends were unanimous in their public scorn for girls. They would mock them, tease them, pinch them, and pull up their dresses, but you never felt that antipathy, could never rouse yourself to participate in these assaults, and all during that early grammar school period of your life (that is, up to the age of twelve, when you carried the American flag with a blood-soaked bandage around your head during your class's graduation ceremony), you continued to succumb to various infatuations with girls such as Patty, Susie, Dale, Jan, and Ethel. No more than kissing and holding hands, of course (you were physically incapable of having sex, the mechanics of which were still rather vague to you, since you did not arrive at full-fledged puberty until you were turning fourteen), but the kissing had become altogether ferocious by the time you reached graduation day. There were dances and unchaperoned parties in that final year before you entered junior high school, nearly every weekend you and a gang of fifteen or twenty others were invited to someone's house, and in those suburban living rooms and finished basements, impotent boys and girls with newly sprouting breasts would dance to the latest rock-and-roll songs (the hits of 1958 and 1959), and eventually, as the evening wore on, the lights would be dimmed, the music would stop, and girls and boys would pair off in hidden corners of the room, where they'd all neck crazily until it was time to go home. You learned much about lips and tongues that year, were indoctrinated into the pleasures of feeling a girl's body in your arms, of feeling a girl's arms wrapped around you, but that was as far as it went. There were lines that could not be crossed, and for now you were happy not to cross them. Not because you were scared, but because it never even occurred to you.

Finally, the day came when you went hurtling across the threshold that separates boyhood from adolescence, and now that you had felt the feeling, now that you had discovered that your old friend the fireman was in fact an agent of divine bliss, the world you lived in became a different world, for the ecstasy of that feeling had given a new purpose to your life, a new reason for being alive. The years of phallic obsession began. Like every other male who has wandered this earth, you were in thrall to the miraculous change that had occurred in your body. On most days, you could think of little else—on some days, of nothing else.

Nevertheless, when you recall the years immediately following your transformation, you are struck by how cautious and backward you were. In spite of your ardor, in spite of your constant pursuit of girls in junior and senior high school, the romances and flirtations with Karen, Peggy, Linda, Brianne, Carol, Sally, Ruth, Pam, Starr, Jackie, Mary, and Ronnie, your erotic adventures were frightfully tame and insipid, barely one step beyond the make-out sessions you took part in when you were twelve. Perhaps you were unlucky, or perhaps you weren't bold enough, but you tend to think it had more to do with the place and the time, a middle-class suburban town in the early sixties, and the unwritten code that girls did not give themselves to boys, that good girls had reputations to uphold, and the line was drawn at kissing and petting, notably the least dangerous form of petting, that is, the boy's hand placed on a breast covered by two or three layers of clothing, a sweater (depending on the season), a blouse, and a bra, but woe to the boy who tried to put his hand inside a blouse, let alone reach for the forbidden territory inside a bra, for that hand would be swiftly pushed away by the girl who had a reputation to uphold, even if that girl secretly wanted the hand to be there as much as the boy did. How many times were you rebuffed in this way, you wonder, how many useless expeditions did your hands make into the skirts and blouses of your companions, how many partial journeys toward the realm of bare skin before being turned back at the gates? Such were the impoverished conditions of your early erotic life. No bare skin allowed, no shedding of clothes, and forget, once and for all, that genitals have any part in the game you are playing. And so you and Linda go on kissing, kissing and then kissing some more, kissing until your lips are chapped and drool is sliding down your cheeks, and all the while you pray that the erection bulging in your pants will not explode.

You live in a torment of frustration and never-ending sexual arousal, breaking the North American masturbation record every month throughout the years 1961 and 1962, an onanist not by choice but by circumstance, trapped inside your ever-growing, ever-mutating body, the five-feet-two-inch thirteen-year-old now transformed into a five-feet-ten-inch fifteen-year-old, still a boy, perhaps, but a boy in a man's body, who shaves a couple of times a week, who has hair on his forearms and legs, hair under his arms, pubic hair because he is no longer pubescent but almost fully formed, and even as you forge on with your schoolwork and your sporting activities and travel ever more deeply into the universe of books, your life is dominated by your thwarted sexual hunger, you feel that you are actually starving to death, and no ambition is more important to you, no cause is more central to the well-being of your aching, starving self than to lose your virginity as quickly as possible. Such is your desire, in any case, but nowhere is it written that desires must be fulfilled, and so the torture goes on, all the way through the delirious abnegations of 1962 and on into the fall of 1963, when finally, at long long last, an opportunity presents itself, and although it is less than ideal, not at all what you have been imagining, you don't hesitate to say yes. You are sixteen years old. In July and August, you worked as a waiter at a summer camp in upstate New York, and the fellow who served as your partner, a funny, fast-talking kid from Queens (a city boy who knows his way around the New York streets—as opposed to you, who know next to nothing), calls to tell you that he has the address and telephone number of a brothel on the Upper West Side. He will make the appointment for you if you wish, and because you indeed wish, you take a bus into the city the following Saturday and meet your friend in front of an apartment building in the mid-Eighties, just off the river. It is a damp, drizzly afternoon in late September, everything is gray and sodden, umbrella weather, or at least a day for wearing hats, but you have neither an umbrella nor a hat, which is nevertheless fine, perfectly fine, since the last thing you are thinking about now is the weather. The word *brothel* has conjured up a host of enticing mental images for you, and you are expecting to walk into a large, sumptuously decorated establishment with red plush-velvet walls and a staff of fifteen or twenty alluring young women (what wretched film put *that* idea in your head?), but as you and your friend step into the elevator, which is the slowest, dirtiest, most graffiti-scarred elevator in all of New York, you quickly readjust your expectations. The luxurious brothel turns out to be a shabby little one-bedroom apartment, and only two women are there, the proprietress, Kay, a round black woman pushing fifty, who greets your friend with a warm hug, as if they are old familiars, and a much younger woman, also black, who appears to be around twenty or twenty-two. They are both sitting on stools in the tiny kitchen, which is separated from the bedroom by a thin curtain that doesn't quite touch the floor, both are dressed in colorful silk robes, and, much to your relief, the young one is highly attractive, with a very pretty face, perhaps even a beautiful face. Kay announces the price (fifteen dollars? twenty dollars?) and then asks you and your friend which one wants to go first. No, no, your friend laughs, he's just come along for the ride (no doubt the girls in Queens are less reluctant to shed their clothes than the girls in New Jersey), and so Kay turns to you and says that you can choose, either her or her young co-worker, and when you do not choose Kay, she does not appear to be offended—merely shrugs, smiles, puts out her hand, and says, "A little money, honey," at which point you dig into your pocket and pull out the fifteen or twenty dollars you owe her. You and the young one (too shy or too nervous, you forget to ask what her name is, which means that she has been nameless to you for all these years) step into the other room as Kay pulls the curtain shut behind you. The girl leads you toward the bed in the corner, she slips out of her robe and tosses it onto a chair, and for the first time in your life you are in the presence of a naked woman. A beautiful naked woman, in fact, a young woman with a remarkably beautiful body, with glorious breasts, glorious arms and shoulders, glorious backside, glorious hips, glorious legs, and after three long years of frustration and failure, you are beginning to feel happy, as happy as you have felt at any time since your adolescence began. The girl instructs you to take off your clothes, and then the two of you are on the bed together, both naked, and all you really want, at least for now, is to touch her and kiss her and feel the smoothness of her skin, which is marvelously smooth skin, so smooth that it makes you tremble just to put your hand on her, but kissing on the mouth is not part of the program, since prostitutes do not kiss their customers on the mouth, and prostitutes have no interest in foreplay, no interest in touching or being touched for the simple pleasure of touching and being touched, for sex under these circumstances is not pleasure but work, and the sooner the client can finish the job he has paid for, the better. She knows it is your first time, that you are an absolute novice with no experience whatsoever, and she treats you kindly and patiently, she is a good person, you feel, and if she wants to get down to the fucking part right away, no problem, you are more than willing to play by her rules, for there is no question that you are ready, that you have been sporting an erection from the instant you saw her take off the robe, and therefore, as she eases herself onto her back, you happily climb on top of her and let her guide your penis to the place where it has longed to be for so many years. Good, everything is good, it feels as good as you always imagined it would, no, even better, much better, and all is good for the first little while, when it seems only a matter of seconds before you will finish the job, but then you become aware of Kay and your friend talking and laughing in the kitchen, which is no more than ten or twelve feet from the bed, and once you become aware of them, you start to feel distracted, and as soon as your mind begins to wander from the task at hand, you can feel how bored the girl is, how tiresome this whole business is for her, and even though you are lying on top of her, she is nowhere near you, she is in another city, another country, and then, losing patience, she asks you if you can finish, and you say yes, of course, and twenty seconds later she asks you again and you say yes, of course, but the next time she speaks to you, she says: "Come on out and let me jerk you off. You young kids. You jerk off all the time, but when it comes to the real thing, you don't have a clue." And so you let her jerk you off, which is precisely what you have been doing to yourself for the past three years—with one small difference: better her hand than yours.

You never went back. For the next year and a half, you continued to wrangle with sweaters, blouses, and bras, went on kissing and stroking and struggling against the embarrassment of unseemly ejaculations, and then, at eighteen, you connived to skip out on the last two months of high school, first by coming down with a case of mononucleosis that kept you weak and bedridden for most of May, and then by heading to Europe on a student ship three weeks before your class graduated. You were allowed to do this by the school authorities because your grades were good and you had already been admitted to college for the fall, so off you went, with the understanding that you would return at the beginning of September to take your final exams and officially earn your diploma. Airplanes were an expensive way to travel in 1965, but student ships were not, and since you were operating on a tight budget (money earned from summer jobs over the past two years), you opted for the S.S. *Aurelia* and a slow, nine-day crossing from New York to Le Havre. Approximately three hundred students were on board, most of whom had already finished one or two years of college, meaning that most were a bit older than you, and with little or nothing to do as you and your fellow passengers inched your way across the Atlantic, filling the time with sleep, food, books, and films, it was only natural, altogether inevitable it seems to you now, that the thoughts of three hundred young people between the ages of eighteen and twenty-one should have been largely preoccupied with sex. Boredom and proximity, the languors of a fair-weather ocean voyage, the knowledge that the ship was a world unto itself and nothing that happened there could have any enduring consequences—all these elements combined to create an atmosphere of unguarded sensual ease. The dalliances began before the sun set on the first day, and they continued until the ship touched land two hundred hours later. It was a floating palace of fornication out there on the high seas, with couples slinking in and out of darkened cabins, boys and girls changing partners from one day to the next, and twice during the crossing you found yourself in bed with someone, each time with a sympathetic and intelligent girl, not unlike the good girls you had grown up with in New Jersey, but these girls were from New York, and therefore more sophisticated, more experienced than the hand-swatting virgins from your hometown, and because there was a strong attraction on both sides, in the first instance between you and Renée, in the second instance between you and Janet, there was no compunction about shedding clothes, about crawling between the sheets and making love in a way that had not been possible in that sad flat on the Upper West Side, with kissing and touching and genuine feeling now part of the adventure, and this was the real breakthrough, your initiation into the pleasure of two partners participating equally in the pleasures of prolonged intimacy. There was still much to learn, of course. You were no more than a beginner at that point, but at least you were on your way, at least you had discovered how much there was to look forward to.

Later on, when you were living in Paris in the early seventies, there were long stretches when you were alone, sleeping night after night with no body next to yours in the narrow bed of your small maid's room, and there were times when you became half-mad in your womanless solitude, not just from lack of sexual release but from lack of any physical contact, and because there was no one to turn to, no woman you could count on for the companionship you craved, you would sometimes go out and find yourself a prostitute, perhaps five or six times in the several years you lived there, wandering down the side streets of the now demolished neighborhood of Les Halles, which was just around the corner from your room, or else, venturing a bit farther, walk to the rue Saint-Denis and its adjacent alleys, passageways, and cobbled lanes, the sidewalks crowded with women lined up against the walls of buildings and the *hôtels de passe*, an array of feminine possibilities that ran the gamut from good-looking girls in their early twenties to harshly made-up street veterans in their mid-fifties, hookers representing every imaginable body type, every race and color, from rotund Frenchwomen to willowy Africans to voluptuous Italians and Israelis, some provocatively dressed in miniskirts with breasts spilling out of low-cut bras and flimsy blouses, others in blue jeans and modest sweaters, not unlike the girls you had gone to school with in your hometown, but all of them in high heels or boots, black or white leather boots, and around the neck an occasional boa or silk scarf, or an occasional S&M girl decked out in flamboyant leather garb, or an occasional pretend schoolgirl in a plaid skirt and prim white blouse, something to accommodate every desire and predilection, and walking down the middle of the carless streets, the men, an endless procession of silent men, examining the possibilities on the sidewalks with furtive glances or bold stares, all kinds of women prepared to hire themselves out to all kinds of men, from lonely Arabs to middle-aged johns in suits, the throngs of womanless immigrants and frustrated students and bored husbands, and once you joined those processions, you suddenly felt that you were no longer part of the waking world, that you had slipped into an erotic dream that was at once thrilling and destabilizing, for the thought that you could go to bed with any one of those women merely by offering her a hundred francs (twenty dollars) made you dizzy, physically dizzy, and as you prowled the narrow streets looking for a companion to satisfy the need that had driven you out of your room into this labyrinth of flesh, you found yourself looking at faces rather than bodies, or faces first and bodies second, searching for a pretty face, the face of a human being whose eyes had not gone dead, someone whose spirit had not yet entirely drowned in the anonymity and artificiality of whoredom, and strangely enough, on your five or six excursions into the thoroughly legal, government-sanctioned red-light districts of Paris, you generally managed to find one. No bad experiences, then, no encounter that filled you with regret or remorse, and when you look back on it now, you suppose you were well treated because you were not an aging man with a protruding belly or a foul-smelling laborer with dirt under his fingernails but an unaggressive, not unpresentable young man of twenty-four or twenty-five who made no idiosyncratic or uncomfortable demands on the women he went upstairs with, who was simply grateful not to be alone in his own bed. On the other hand, it would be wrong to classify any of these experiences as memorable. Brisk and forthright, goodwilled but altogether businesslike in execution, a service competently rendered for an allotted fee, but since you were no longer the bumbling sixteen-year-old neophyte of yore, that was all you ever expected. Still, there was one time when something unusual occurred, when a spark of reciprocity was ignited between you and your provisional consort, which happened to be the last time you ever paid a woman to sleep with you, the summer of 1972, when you were earning some much needed cash with a job as switchboard operator at the local bureau of the *New York Times*, the graveyard shift, roughly six P.M. to one A.M., you no longer remember the exact hours, but you would arrive when the office was emptying out for the day and sit there alone at a desk, the only person on the darkened floor of a building on the Right Bank, waiting for the telephone to ring, which it seldom did, and using the unbroken silence of those hours to read books and work on your poems. One weekday night when your shift was done, you left the office and stepped outside into the summer air, the warm embrace of the summer air, and because the Métro was no longer running, you started walking home, strolling south in the soft summer air, not at all tired as you ambled through the empty streets on the way back to your small, empty room. Before long you were on the rue Saint-Denis, where a number of girls were still working in spite of the late hour, and then you turned down a nearby side street, the one where the prettiest girls tended to congregate, understanding that you had no desire to go home just yet, that you had been alone for too long and dreaded going back to your empty room, and midway down the block someone caught your attention, a tall brunette with a lovely face and an equally lovely figure, and when she smiled at you and asked if you wanted company (*Je t'accompagne?*), you didn't think twice about accepting her offer. She smiled again, pleased by the quickness of the transaction, and as you continued to look at her face, you understood that she would have been a heart-stopping beauty if her eyes had not been too close together, if she had not been ever so slightly cross-eyed, but that was of no importance to you, she was still the most appealing woman who had ever walked this street, and you were disarmed by her smile, which was a magnificent smile in your opinion, and it occurred to you that if everyone in the world could smile as she did, there would be no more wars or human conflicts, that peace and happiness would reign on earth forever. Her name was Sandra, a French girl in her mid-twenties, and as you followed her up the winding staircase to the third floor of the hotel, she announced that you were her last customer of the night, and consequently there would be no need to rush, you could take as much time as you liked. This was unprecedented, a violation of all professional standards and protocols, but it was already clear to you that Sandra was different from the other girls who worked that street, that she lacked the hardness and coldness that necessarily seemed to go with the job. Then you were in the room with her, and everything continued to be different from all your previous experiences in this part of the city. She was relaxed, in a warm and expansive mood, and even when you both took off your clothes, even when you discovered how uncommonly beautiful her body was (*majestic* was the word that came to you, in the same way that the bodies of certain dancers can be called majestic), she was talkative and playful, in no hurry to get down to business, not at all put out by your desire to touch her and kiss her, and as she lolled on the bed with you, she began demonstrating the various lovemaking positions she and her friends used with their clients, the Kama Sutra of the rue Saint-Denis, twisting around and over and in on top of herself as she helped you contort your body into matching configurations, laughing softly at the absurdity of it all as she told you the name of each position. Unfortunately, you can remember only one of them now, which was probably the dullest one, but also the funniest because it was so dull: *le paresseux*, the lazy man, which was simply a matter of stretching out on your side and copulating with your partner face to face. You had never met a woman who was so at home in her body, so serene in the way she carried her naked self, and eventually, even though you wanted these demonstrations to go on until morning, you became too aroused to hold back any longer. You assumed that would be the end of it, *jouissance* had always been the end of it in the past, but even after you were fin-

ished, Sandra did not press you to leave, she wanted to lie on the
bed with you and talk, and so you stayed with her for close to an
hour more, happily encircled in her arms as your head rested on
her shoulder, discussing things that have long since vanished from
your mind, and when she finally asked what you did with yourself
and you said that you wrote poems, you were expecting her to
shrug with indifference or make some noncommittal remark, but
no, no yet again, for once you started talking about poetry, Sandra
closed her eyes and began to recite Baudelaire, long passages delivered with intense feeling and perfectly accurate recall, and you
could only hope that Baudelaire had sat up in his grave and was
listening.

> *Mère des souvenirs, maîtresse des maîtresses,*
> *O toi, tous mes plaisirs! ô toi, tous mes devoirs!*
> *Tu te rappelleras la beauté des caresses,*
> *La douceur du foyer et le charme des soirs,*
> *Mère des souvenirs, maîtresse des maîtresses!*

It was one of the most extraordinary moments of your life,
one of the happiest moments of your life, and even after you were
back in New York and the next chapter of your story was being
written, you kept thinking about Sandra and the hours you had
spent with her that night, wondering if you shouldn't jump on a
plane, rush back to Paris, and ask her to marry you.

Always lost, always striking out in the wrong direction, always going around in circles. You have suffered from a lifelong inability to orient yourself in space, and even in New York, the easiest
of cities to negotiate, the city where you have spent the better
part of your adulthood, you often run into trouble. Whenever
you take the subway from Brooklyn to Manhattan (assuming you

have boarded the correct train and are not traveling deeper into Brooklyn), you make a special point to stop for a moment to get your bearings once you have climbed the stairs to the street, and still you will head north instead of south, go east instead of west, and even when you try to outsmart yourself, knowing that your handicap will set you going the wrong way and therefore, to rectify the error, you do the opposite of what you were intending to do, go left instead of right, go right instead of left, and still you find yourself moving in the wrong direction, no matter how many adjustments you have made. Forget tramping alone in the woods. You are hopelessly lost within minutes, and even indoors, whenever you find yourself in an unfamiliar building, you will walk down the wrong corridor or take the wrong elevator, not to speak of smaller enclosed spaces such as restaurants, for whenever you go to the men's room in a restaurant that has more than one dining area, you will inevitably make a wrong turn on your way back and wind up spending several minutes searching for your table. Most other people, your wife included, with her unerring inner compass, seem able to get around without difficulty. They know where they are, where they have been, and where they are going, but you know nothing, you are forever lost in the moment, in the void of each successive moment that engulfs you, with no idea where true north is, since the four cardinal points do not exist for you, have never existed for you. A minor infirmity until now, with no dramatic consequences to speak of, but that doesn't mean a day won't come when you accidentally walk off the edge of a cliff.

Your body in small rooms and large rooms, your body walking up and down stairs, your body swimming in ponds, lakes, rivers, and oceans, your body traipsing across muddy fields, your body lying in the tall grass of empty meadows, your body walking along city streets, your body laboring up hills and mountains, your body sitting down in chairs, lying down on beds, stretching out on beaches, cycling down country roads, walking through forests, pastures, and deserts, running on cinder tracks, jumping up and down on hardwood floors, standing in showers, stepping into warm baths, sitting on toilets, waiting in airports and train stations, riding up and down in elevators, squirming in the seats of cars and buses, walking through rainstorms without an umbrella, sitting in classrooms, browsing in bookstores and record shops (R.I.P.), sitting in auditoriums, movie theaters, and concert halls, dancing with girls in school gymnasiums, paddling canoes in rivers, rowing boats across lakes, eating at kitchen tables, eating at dining room tables, eating in restaurants, shopping in department stores, appliance stores, furniture stores, shoe stores, hardware stores, grocery stores, and clothing stores, standing in line for passports and driver's licenses, leaning back in chairs with your legs propped up on desks and tables as you write in notebooks, hunching over typewriters, walking through snowstorms without a hat, entering synagogues and churches, dressing and undressing in bedrooms, hotel rooms, and locker rooms, standing on escalators, lying in hospital beds, sitting on doctors' examination tables, sitting in barbers' chairs and dentists' chairs, doing somersaults on the grass, standing on your head on the grass, jumping into swimming pools, walking slowly through museums, dribbling basketballs in playgrounds, throwing baseballs and footballs in public parks, feeling the different sensations of walking on wooden floors, cement floors, tile floors, and stone floors, the different sensations of putting your feet on sand, dirt, and grass, but most of all the sensation of sidewalks, for that is how you see yourself whenever you stop to think about who you are: a man who walks, a man who has spent his life walking through the streets of cities.

———

Enclosures, habitations, the small rooms and large rooms that have sheltered your body from the open air. Beginning with your birth at Beth Israel Hospital in Newark, New Jersey (February 3, 1947) and traveling onward to the present (this cold January morning in 2011), these are the places where you have parked your body over the years—the places, for better or worse, that you have called home.

1. 75 South Harrison Street; East Orange, New Jersey. An apartment in a tallish brick building. Age 0 to 1½. No memories, but according to the stories you heard later in your childhood, your father managed to secure a lease by giving the landlady a television set—a bribe made necessary by the housing shortage that hit the country after the end of World War II. Since your father owned a small appliance store at the time, the apartment you lived in with your parents was equipped with a television as well, which made you one of the first Americans, one of the first people anywhere in the world, to grow up with a television set from birth.

2. 1500 Village Road; Union, New Jersey. A garden apartment in a complex of low brick buildings called Stuyvesant Village. Geometrically aligned sidewalks with large swaths of neatly tended grass. *Large* is surely a relative term, however, given how small you were at the time. Age 1½ to 5. No memories, then some memories, then memories in abundance. The dark green walls and venetian blinds in the living room. Digging for worms with a trowel. An illustrated book about a circus dog named Peewee, a toy dalmatian who miraculously grows to normal size. Arranging your fleet of miniature cars and trucks. Baths in the kitchen sink. A mechanical horse named Whitey. A scalding cup of hot cocoa that spilled on you and left a permanent scar in the crook of your elbow.

3. 253 Irving Avenue; South Orange, New Jersey. A two-story white clapboard house built in the 1920s, with a yellow front door, a gravel driveway, and a large backyard. Age 5 to 12. The site of

nearly all your childhood memories. You began living there so long ago, the milk was delivered by a horse-drawn wagon for the first year or two after you moved in.

4. 406 Harding Drive; South Orange, New Jersey. A larger house than the previous one, built in the Tudor style, awkwardly perched on a hilly corner with the tiniest of backyards and a gloomy interior. Age 13 to 17. The house in which you suffered through your adolescent torments, wrote your first poems and stories, and your parents' marriage dissolved. Your father went on living there (alone) until the day he died.

5. 25 Van Velsor Place; Newark, New Jersey. A two-bedroom apartment not far from Weequahic High School and the hospital where you were born, rented by your mother after she and your father separated and then divorced. Age 17 to 18. Bedrooms for your mother and little sister, but you slept on a fold-out couch in a minuscule den, not at all unhappy with the new arrangement, however, since you were glad your parents' painfully unsuccessful marriage was over, relieved that you were no longer living in the suburbs. You owned a car then, a secondhand Chevy Corvair bought for six hundred dollars (the same defective automobile that launched Ralph Nader's career—although you never had any serious trouble with yours), and every morning you would drive to your high school in not-too-distant Maplewood and go through the motions of being a high school student, but you were free now, unsupervised by adults, coming and going as you wished, getting ready to fly away.

6. Suite 814A, Carman Hall; Columbia University dormitory. Two rooms per suite, two occupants per room. Cinder-block walls, linoleum floors, two beds placed end to end under the window, two desks, a built-in cupboard for storing clothes, and a common bathroom shared with the occupants of 814B. Age 18 to 19. Carman Hall was the first new dorm built on the Columbia campus in more than half a century. An austere environment, ugly

and charmless, but nevertheless far better than the dungeonlike rooms to be found in the older dorms (Furnald, Hartley), where you sometimes visited your friends and were appalled by the stench of dirty socks, the cramped double-decker beds, the unending darkness. You were in Carman Hall during the New York City blackout of 1965 (candles everywhere, a mood of anarchic celebration), but what you remember best about your room are the hundreds of books you read there and the girls who occasionally wound up with you in your bed. The parietal rules of the all-male undergraduate college had been changed by the university administration just in time for the beginning of your freshman year, and females were now allowed into the rooms—with the door closed. For some time before that they had been allowed in if the door stayed open, followed by an interim period of a couple of years when the door could be left ajar by the width of a book, but then some brilliant boy with the mind of a Talmudic scholar challenged the authorities by using a matchbook, and that was the end of open doors. Your roommate was a childhood friend. He began dabbling in drugs midway through the first semester, became increasingly involved as the year wore on, and nothing you said to him ever made the smallest difference. You stood by helplessly and watched him disintegrate. By the next fall, he had dropped out of school—never to return. That was why you refused to dabble in drugs yourself, even as the Dionysian sixties roared around you. Alcohol yes, tobacco yes, but no drugs. By the time you graduated in 1969, two of your other boyhood friends were dead from overdoses.

7. 311 West 107th Street, Manhattan. A two-room apartment on the third floor of a four-story walkup between Broadway and Riverside Drive. Age 19 to 20. Your first apartment, which you shared with fellow sophomore Peter Schubert, your closest friend during your early days as an undergraduate. A derelict, ill-designed shit hole, with nothing in its favor but the low rent and

the fact that there were two entrance doors. The first opened onto the larger room, which served as your bedroom and workroom, as well as the kitchen, dining room, and living room. The second opened onto a narrow hallway that ran parallel to the first room and led to a small cell in the back, which served as Peter's bedroom. The two of you were lamentable housekeepers, the place was filthy, the kitchen sink clogged again and again, the appliances were older than you were and hardly functioned, dust mice grew fat on the threadbare carpet, and little by little the two of you turned the hovel you had rented into a malodorous slum. Because it was too depressing to eat there, and because neither one of you knew how to cook, you tended to go out to cheap restaurants together for your meals, either Tom's or the College Inn for breakfast, gradually preferring the latter because of its excellent jukebox (Billie Holiday, Edith Piaf), and night after night dinner at the Green Tree, a Hungarian restaurant on the corner of Amsterdam Avenue and West 111th Street, where you subsisted on goulash, overcooked green beans, and savory *palačinka* for dessert. For some reason, your memories of what happened in that apartment are dim, dimmer than those of the other places you inhabited before and after. It was a time of bad dreams—many bad dreams—that you remember well (the Montaigne seminar with Donald Frame and the Milton course with Edward Tayler are still vivid) but all in all what comes back to you now is a feeling of discontent, an urgent desire to be somewhere else. The war in Vietnam was growing, America had split in half, and the air around you was heavy, barely breathable, suffocating. You signed up with Schubert for the Junior Year Abroad Program in Paris, left New York in July, quarreled with the director in August and quit the program, stayed on until early November as a non-student, an ex-student, living in a small, bare-bones hotel (no telephone, no private bathroom), where you felt yourself beginning to breathe again, but then you were talked into going back to Columbia, a sensible move given the draft and your opposition to the war, but the time off had helped you, and when you reluctantly returned to New York, the bad dreams had stopped.

8. 601 West 115th Street; Manhattan. Another oddly shaped two-room apartment just off Broadway, but in a far more solid building than the last one, with the further advantage of having a true kitchen, which stood between the larger room and the smaller room and was big enough (barely) to squeeze in a runty, drop-leaf table. Age 20 to 22. Your first solo apartment, continuously dark because of its location on the second floor, but otherwise adequate, comfortable, sufficient to your needs of the moment. You spent your junior and senior years there, which were the wild years at Columbia, the years of demonstrations and sit-ins, of student strikes and police raids, of campus riots, expulsions, and paddy wagons carting off hundreds to jail. You diligently slogged through your course work, contributed film and book reviews to the student paper, wrote poems and translated poems, completed several chapters of a novel you eventually abandoned, but in 1968 you also participated in the weeklong sit-ins that led to your being thrown into a paddy wagon and driven downtown to a holding cell in the Tombs. As mentioned before, you had long since given up fighting, and you weren't about to tangle with the police when they smashed in the door of the room in Mathematics Hall where you and several other students were waiting to be arrested, but neither were you going to cooperate and walk out of there on your own two feet. You let your body grow limp—the classic strategy of passive resistance developed in the South during the civil rights movement—thinking the cops would carry you out of there without any fuss, but the members of the Tactical Patrol Force were angry that night, the campus they had invaded was turning into a bloody battleground, and they had no interest in your nonviolent, highly principled approach to the matter. They kicked you and pulled you by the hair, and when you still refused

to climb to your feet, one of them stomped on your hand with the heel of his boot—a direct hit, which left your knuckles swollen and throbbing for days afterward. In the next morning's edition of the *Daily News*, there was a photograph of you being dragged off to the paddy wagon. The caption read *Stubborn Boy*, and no doubt that was exactly what you were at that moment of your life: a stubborn, uncooperative boy.

9. 262 West 107th Street; Manhattan. Yet another two-room apartment with a sit-down kitchen, but not oddly shaped as the others had been, a large room and a somewhat smaller room, but the small room was nevertheless ample, nothing like the coffin-sized spaces of the previous two. The top floor of a nine-story building between Broadway and Amsterdam Avenue, which meant more light than in any of the other New York apartments, but a shoddier building than the last one, with sluggish, haphazard maintenance by the cheerful super, a stout, barrel-chested man named Arthur. Age 22 to a couple of weeks past your 24th birthday, a year and a half in all. You lived there with your girlfriend, the first time either one of you had attempted cohabitation with a member of the opposite sex. The first year, your girlfriend was finishing her B.A. at Barnard and you were a graduate student in the Columbia doctoral program in comparative literature, but you were only biding your time, you knew from the start that you would last no longer than one year, but the university had given you a fellowship and a stipend, so you worked on your M.A. thesis, which turned into a sixty-page essay called "The Art of Hunger" (which examined works by Hamsun, Kafka, Céline, and Beckett), consulted from time to time with your thesis advisor, Edward Said, attended a number of mandatory seminars, skipped your lecture classes, and went on writing your own fiction and poetry, some of which was beginning to be published in little magazines. When the year was over, you dropped out of the program as planned, quit student life forever, and went off to work on an Esso oil tanker

that shuttled among various refineries in the Gulf of Mexico and along the Atlantic coast—a job with decent pay, which you were hoping would finance a temporary move to Paris. Your girlfriend found someone to share the expense of the apartment with her during the months you were gone: a quick-tongued, sharp-witted young white woman who earned her living pretending to be a black D.J. for an all-black radio station—with great success, apparently, which you found deeply amusing, but how not to see it as one more symptom of the times, another example of the nuthouse logic that had taken over American reality? As for you and your girlfriend, the experiment in conjugal living had been something of a disappointment, and after you returned from your stint in the merchant marine and started preparing for the trip to Paris, you both decided that the romance had played itself out and that you would make the trip alone. One night about two weeks before your scheduled departure, your stomach rebelled against you, and the pains that shot into your gut were so severe, so agonizing in their assault, so unrelenting as you lay doubled up on the bed, you felt as if you had eaten a pot of barbed wire for dinner. The only plausible explanation was a ruptured appendix, which you figured would have to be operated on immediately. It was two o'clock in the morning. You staggered off to the emergency room at St. Luke's Hospital, waited in utmost misery for an hour or two, and then, when a doctor finally examined you, he confidently asserted that there was nothing wrong with your appendix. You were suffering from a bad attack of gastritis. Take these pills, he said, avoid hot and spicy foods, and little by little you'll begin to feel better. Both his diagnosis and his prediction were correct, and it was only later, many years later, that you understood what had happened to you. You were afraid—but afraid without knowing you were afraid. The prospect of uprooting yourself had thrown you into a state of extreme but utterly suppressed anxiety; the thought of breaking up with your girlfriend was no doubt far more upsetting than you had imagined it would be. You wanted to go to Paris alone, but a part of you was terrified by such a drastic change, and so your stomach went haywire and began to rip you in two. This has been the story of your life. Whenever you come to a fork in the road, your body breaks down, for your body has always known what your mind doesn't know, and however it chooses to break down, whether with mononucleosis or gastritis or panic attacks, your body has always borne the brunt of your fears and inner battles, taking the blows your mind cannot or will not stand up to.

10. 3, rue Jacques Mawas; 15th Arrondissement, Paris. Still another two-room apartment with a sit-down kitchen, on the third floor of a six-story building. Age 24. Not long after you arrived in Paris (February 24, 1971), you began having second thoughts about the breakup with your girlfriend. You wrote her a letter, asking if she had the courage to try to make another go of it, and when she said yes, your good-and-bad, off-and-on, up-and-down relations with her continued. She would be joining you in Paris in early April, and in the meantime you went out to look for a furnished apartment (the ship had paid well, but not well enough to allow you to buy furniture), and you soon found the place on the rue Jacques Mawas, which was clean, filled with light, not too expensive, and equipped with a piano. Since your girlfriend was an excellent and devoted pianist (Bach, Mozart, Schubert, Beethoven), you took the apartment on the spot, knowing how pleased she would be by this lucky turn. Not just Paris, but Paris with a piano. You moved in, and once you had taken care of the household fundamentals (bedding, pots and pans, dishes, towels, silverware), you arranged for someone to come and tune the out-of-tune piano, which had not been played in years. A blind man showed up the next day (you have rarely met a piano tuner who is not blind), a corpulent person of around fifty with a dough-white face and eyes rolling upward in their sockets. A strange presence, you found, but not just because of the eyes. It was the skin, the blanched, puffball

skin, which looked spongy and malleable, as if he lived underground somewhere and never let the light touch his face. With him was a young man of eighteen or twenty, who held on to his arm as he guided the tuner through the front door and on toward the instrument in the back room. The young man never said a word during the visit, so you failed to learn if he was a son, a nephew, a cousin, or a hired companion, but the tuner was a talkative fellow, and after he had completed his work, he paused for a while to chat with you. "This street," he said, "rue Jacques Mawas in the fifteenth arrondissement. It's a very small street, isn't it? Just a few buildings, if I'm not mistaken." You told him he wasn't mistaken, it was indeed a very small street. "It's funny," he continued, "but it turns out that I lived here during the war. It was a good place to find apartments back then." You asked him why. "Because," he said, "many Israelites used to live in this neighborhood, but then the war started and they went away." At first, you couldn't register what he was trying to tell you—or didn't want to believe what he was telling you. The word *Israelite* might have knocked you off balance a little, but your French was good enough for you to know that it was not an uncommon synonym for the word *juif* (Jew), at least for people of the war generation, although in your experience it had always carried a pejorative edge to it, not an outright declaration of anti-Semitism so much as a way of distancing the Jews from the French, of turning them into something foreign and exotic, that curious, ancient people from the desert with their funny customs and vengeful, primitive God. That was bad enough, but the next part of the sentence reeked of such ignorance, or such willful denial, that you weren't sure if you were talking to the world's biggest simpleton or a former Vichy collaborator. *They went away.* No doubt on a deluxe world cruise, an uninterrupted five-year holiday spent basking in the Mediterranean sun, playing tennis in the Florida Keys, and dancing on the beaches of Australia. You wanted the blind man gone, to remove

him from your sight as quickly as possible, but as you were handing him his money, you couldn't resist asking one last question.
"Oh," you said, "and where did they go when they went away?"
The piano tuner paused, as if searching for an answer, and when
no answer came, he grinned at you apologetically. "I have no idea,"
he said, "but most of them didn't come back." That was the first of
several lessons that were hammered home to you in that building
about the ways of the French—the next one being the War of the
Pipes, which began a couple of weeks later. The plumbing equipment in your apartment was not new, and the chain-pull toilet
with the overhead water tank was not in proper working order.
Each time you flushed, the water would run for a considerable
length of time and make a considerable amount of noise. You paid
no attention to it, the running toilet was no more than a minor
inconvenience to you, but it seemed that it created a great turbu-
lence in the apartment below yours, the thunderous sound of a
bath being drawn at full throttle. You were unaware of this until a
letter was slipped under your door one day. It was from your
downstairs neighbor, a certain Madame Rubinstein (how shocked
the piano tuner would have been to learn that his wartime address
still harbored some undead Israelites), an indignant letter complaining about the unbearable ruckus of midnight baths, informing you that she had written to the landlord in Arras about your
carryings-on, and if he didn't begin eviction procedures against
you at once, she would take the matter to the police. You were
astonished by the violence of her tone, dumbfounded that she had
not bothered to knock on your door and talk about the problem
with you face to face (which was the standard method of resolving
differences between tenants in New York apartment buildings)
but instead had gone behind your back and contacted *the authorities.* This was the French way, as opposed to the American way—
a boundless faith in the hierarchies of power, an unquestioning
belief in the channels of bureaucracy to right wrongs and rectify

the smallest injustices. You had never met this woman, had no idea what she looked like, and here she was attacking you with savage insults, declaring war over an issue that until then had escaped your notice. To avoid what you assumed would be immediate eviction, you wrote to the landlord, explained your side of the story, promised to have the malfunctioning toilet fixed, and received a jovial, thoroughly heartening letter in response: Youth must have its day, live and let live, no worries, but just go easy on the hydrotherapy, all right? (The nasty French as opposed to the good-natured French: in the three and a half years you lived among them, you met some of the coldest, meanest characters on the face of the earth, but also some of the warmest, most generous men and women you have ever known.) Peace reigned for a while. You still had not seen Madame Rubinstein, but the complaints from downstairs had stopped. Then your girlfriend arrived from New York and the silent apartment began to fill with the sounds of her piano playing, and because you loved music above all other things, it was inconceivable to you that anyone could object to the keyboard masterworks emanating from the third floor. One Sunday afternoon, however, an especially beautiful Sunday afternoon in late spring, as you sat on the couch listening to your girlfriend play Schubert's *Moments Musicaux*, a chorus of shrieking, irritated voices suddenly erupted downstairs. The Rubinsteins were entertaining guests, and what the angry voices were saying was: "Impossible! Enough! The last straw!" Then someone began whacking a broomstick on the ceiling directly below the piano, and a woman's voice cried out: "Stop! Stop that infernal racket now!" It was the last straw for you as well, and with the voice still screaming from the second floor, you burst out of your apartment, ran down the stairs, and knocked—knocked hard—on the Rubinsteins' door. It opened within three seconds (no doubt they heard you coming), and there you were, standing face to face with the formerly invisible Madame Rubinstein, who turned out to be an attractive woman in her mid-forties (why does one always want to suppose that unpleasant people are ugly?), and with no preamble of any kind, the two of you immediately launched into a full-bore shouting match. You were not someone who was easily agitated, you had little trouble keeping your temper under control, you would generally do anything possible to avoid an argument, but on that particular day you were beside yourself with anger, and because your anger seemed to lift your French to new levels of speed and precision, the two of you went at it as equals in the art of verbal combat. Your position: We have every right to play the piano on a Sunday afternoon, on any afternoon for that matter, at any time of any day of any week or month as long as the hour is not too early or too late. Her position: This is a respectable bourgeois house; if you want to play the piano, rent a studio; this is a good bourgeois house, and that means we follow the rules and behave in a civilized manner; loud noises are forbidden; when a police detective was living in your apartment last year, we had him thrown out of the building because he kept such irregular hours; this is a decent bourgeois house; we have a piano in our apartment, but do *we* ever play it? No, of course not. Her arguments struck you as lame, cliché-ridden tautologies, comic assertions worthy of Molière's Monsieur Jourdain, but she delivered them with such fury and venomous conviction that you were in no mood to laugh. The conversation was going nowhere, neither one of you would budge, you were building a wall of permanent animosity between you, and when you imagined how bitter the future would be if you kept on going at each other in this way, you decided the moment had come to pull out your trump card, to turn the dispute around and steer it in an entirely different direction. How sad it is, you said, how terribly sad and pathetic that two Jews should be fighting like this; think of all the suffering and death, Madame Rubinstein, all the horrors our people have been subjected to, and here we are shouting at each other over nothing;

we should be ashamed of ourselves. The ploy worked just as you had hoped it would. Something about the way you said what you had said got through to her, and the battle was suddenly over. From that day forward, Madame Rubinstein ceased to be an antagonist. Whenever you saw her in the street or in the entranceway of the building, she would smile and address you with the formal propriety such encounters called for: *Bonjour, monsieur*, to which you would respond, politely smiling back at her, *Bonjour, madame.* Such was life in France. People pushed by force of habit, pushed for the pure pleasure of pushing, and they would go on pushing until you showed them you were willing to push back, at which point you would earn their respect. Add in the contingent fact that you and Madame Rubinstein were fellow Jews, and there was no reason to fight anymore, no matter how often your girlfriend played the piano. It sickened you that you had allowed yourself to resort to such an underhanded tactic, but the trump card had done its job, and it bought you peace for the rest of the time you lived on the rue Jacques Mawas.

11. 2, rue du Louvre; 1st Arrondissement, Paris. A maid's room (*chambre de bonne*) on the top floor of a six-story building facing the Seine. Age 25. Your room was in the back, and what you saw when you looked out the window was a gargoyle thrusting from the bell tower of the church next door—Saint-Germain l'Auxerrois, the same church whose bells tolled without interruption on August 24, 1572, ringing out the news of the Saint Bartholomew's Day massacre. When you looked to your left, you saw the Louvre. When you looked to your right, you saw Les Halles, and far off, at the northern edge of Paris, the white dome of Montmartre. This was the smallest space you have ever inhabited, a room so small that only the barest essentials could fit in there: a narrow bed, a diminutive desk and straight-backed chair, a sink, and another straight-backed chair beside the bed, where you kept your one-burner electric hot plate and the single pot you owned, which

you used for heating water to make instant coffee and boiled eggs. Toilet down the hall; no shower or bath. You lived there because you were low on money and the room had been given to you for free. The agents of this extraordinary act of generosity were your friends Jacques and Christine Dupin (the very best and kindest of friends—may their names be hallowed forever), who lived downstairs in a large apartment on the second floor, and because this was a Haussmann-era building, their apartment came with an extra room for a maid on the top floor. You lived alone. Once again, you and your girlfriend had failed to make a go of it, and once again you had split up. She was living in the west of Ireland by then, sharing a turf-heated cottage with a high school friend a few miles outside of Sligo, and although you went to Ireland at one point to try to win her back, your gallant gesture went for naught, since her heart had become entangled with that of a young Irishman, and you had walked in at an early juncture of their affair (which eventually came to naught as well), meaning that you had mistimed your trip, and you left the green, windy hills of Sligo wondering if you would ever see her again. You returned to your room, to the loneliness of your room, that smallest of small rooms that sometimes drove you out in search of prostitutes, but it would be wrong to say you were unhappy there, for you had no trouble adjusting to your reduced circumstances, you found it invigorating to learn that you could get by on almost nothing, and as long as you were able to write, it made no difference where or how you lived. Day after day throughout the months you were there, construction crews worked directly across from your building, digging an underground parking garage four or five levels deep. At night, whenever you went to your window and looked down at the excavated earth, at the vast hole spreading in the ground below you, you would see rats, hundreds of wet, gleaming rats running through the mud.

12. 29, rue Descartes; 5th Arrondissement, Paris. Another

two-room apartment with a sit-down kitchen, on the fourth floor of a six-story building. Age 26. A number of well-paying free-lance jobs had lifted you out of penury, and your finances were now robust enough for you to sign a lease on another apartment. Your girlfriend had returned from Sligo, the Irishman was no longer in the picture, and once again the two of you decided to join forces and take another stab at living together. This time, things went fairly smoothly, not without some bumps along the way, perhaps, but less jolting ones than previously, and neither one of you threatened to walk out on the other. The apartment at 29, rue Descartes was surely the most pleasant space you occupied in Paris. Even the concierge was pleasant (a pretty young woman with short blonde hair who was married to a cop, always smiling, always with a friendly word, unlike the snooping, ill-tempered crones who traditionally managed Paris apartment buildings), and you were glad to be living in this part of town, the middle of the old Latin Quarter, just up the hill from the place de la Contres-carpe, with its cafés, restaurants, and vivid, boisterous, theatrical open-air market. But the good freelance jobs of the past year were drying up, and once again your resources were dwindling. You figured you would be able to hang on until the end of the summer, and then you would have to pack it in and return to New York. At the last minute, however, your stay in France was unexpectedly prolonged.

13. Saint Martin; Moissac-Bellevue, Var. A farmhouse in south-eastern Provence. Two stories, immensely thick stone walls, red-tile roof, dark green shutters and doors, several acres of surrounding fields flanked by a national forest on one side and a dirt road on the other: the middle of nowhere. One of the stones above the front door was engraved with the words *L'An VI*—year six—which you took to mean the sixth year of the Revolution, suggesting that the house was built in 1794 or 1795. Age 26 to 27. You and your girlfriend spent nine months as caretakers of that remote southern

property, living there from early September 1973 to the end of May 1974, and although you have already written about some of the things that happened to you in that house (*The Red Notebook*, Story No. 2), there was much that you did not talk about in those five pages. When you think about the time you spent in that part of the world now, what comes back to you first is the air, the scents of thyme and lavender that rose up around you whenever you walked through the fields that bordered the house, the redolent air, the muscular air when the wind was blowing, the languorous air when the sun lowered itself into the valley and lizards and salamanders crawled out from crevices in the stones to drowse in the heat, and then the dryness and roughness of the country, the gray, molten rocks, the chalky white soil, the red earth along certain paths and stretches of road, the scarab beetles in the forest pushing their mountainous spheres of dung, the magpies swooping over the fields and neighboring vineyards, the flocks of sheep that passed through the meadow just beyond the house, the sudden apparitions of sheep, hundreds of sheep bunched together and moving forward with the clattering sounds of their bells, the violence of the mistrals, the windstorms that would last for seventy-two unbroken hours, shaking every window, every shutter, every door and loosened tile of the house, the yellow broom that covered the hillsides in spring, the flowering almond tress, the rosemary bushes, the scrubby, stunted live oaks with gnarled trunks and shimmering leaves, the frigid winter that forced you to close off the second floor of the house and live in the three downstairs rooms, warmed by an electric heater in one and a wood fire in another, the ruins of the chapel on a nearby cliff where the Knights Templar used to stop on their way to fight in the Crusades, the static coming through your enfeebled transistor radio in the middle of the night for two weeks running as you strained to listen to the U.S. Armed Forces broadcasts from Frankfurt of the Mets versus Cincinnati in the National League play-offs, the Mets versus

Oakland in the World Series, and then the hailstorm you were thinking about the other day, the icy stones hammering against the terra-cotta roof and melting on the grass around the house, not as large as baseballs, perhaps, but golf balls for nine-foot men, followed by the one time it snowed and everything briefly turned white, and your nearest neighbor, a bachelor tenant farmer living alone with his truffle dog in a crumbling yellow house and dreaming of world revolution, the shepherds drinking in the hilltop bar of Moissac-Bellevue, their hands and faces black with dirt, the dirtiest men you have ever seen, and everyone speaking with the rolling *r*'s of the southern French accent, the added *g*'s that turned the words for wine and bread into *vaing* and *paing*, the *s*'s dropped elsewhere in France still surviving their Provençal origins, turning *étrangers* into *estrangers* (strangers, foreigners), and all through the region the rocks and walls painted with the slogan *Occitanie Libre!*, for this was the medieval land of *oc* and not of *oui*, and yes, you and your girlfriend were *estrangers* that year, but how much softer life was in this part of the country when compared to the brittle formalities and edginess of Paris, and how warmly you were treated during your time in the south, even by the stuffy, bourgeois couple with the impossible name of Assier de Pompignon, who would occasionally invite you to their house in the adjacent village of Régusse to watch films on TV, not to mention the people you came to know in Aups, seven kilometers from the house, where you went on your twice-weekly shopping expeditions, a town of three or four thousand people that came to feel like a vast metropole as the months of isolation rolled on, and because there were only two principal cafés in Aups, the right-wing café and the left-wing café, you frequented the left-wing café, where you were welcomed in by the regulars, the scruffy farmers and mechanics who were either Socialists or Communists, the rowdy, talkative locals who grew increasingly fond of the young American *estrangers*, and you remember sitting with them in that bar as you all watched the 1974 presidential election returns on TV, the campaign between Giscard and Mitterrand following Pompidou's death, the hilarity and ultimate disappointment of that evening, everyone soused and cheering, everyone soused and cursing, but also in Aups there was your friend the butcher's son, more or less your age, who worked in his father's shop and was being groomed to take over the business, but at the same time a passionate and highly skilled photographer, who spent that year documenting the evacuation and demolition of a small village that was scheduled to be inundated for the construction of a dam, the butcher's son with his heartbreaking photographs, the drunken men in the Socialist/ Communist bar, but also the dentist in Draguignan, the man your girlfriend had to visit again and again for the complicated root-canal work he performed on her, all the many hours she spent in his chair, and when the work was finally done and he presented her with the bill, it came to all of three hundred francs (sixty dollars), a sum so low, so incommensurate with the time and effort he had expended on her, that she asked him why he had charged her so little, to which he responded, with a wave of the hand and a diffident little shrug, "Forget it. I was young once myself."

14. 456 Riverside Drive; in the middle of the long block between West 116th Street and West 119th Street, Manhattan. Two rooms with a razor-thin galley kitchen between them, the northern penthouse or tenth floor of a nine-story building overlooking the Hudson. *Penthouse* was a deceptive term in this case, since your apartment and the southern penthouse next to it were not a structural part of the building you lived in. PHN and PHS were located inside a separate, freestanding, flat-roofed, diminutive one-story house built out of white stucco, which sat on the main roof like a peasant hut incongruously transported from the back street of a Mexican village. Age 27 to 29. The interior space was cramped, barely adequate for two people (you and your girlfriend were still together), but affordable New York apartments turned

out to be scarce, and after your return from three and a half years abroad, you spent more than a month looking for somewhere to live, anywhere to live, and you felt fortunate to have landed in this airy if too crowded perch. Brilliant light, gleaming hardwood floors, fierce winds blowing off the Hudson, and the singular gift of a large L-shaped roof terrace that equaled or surpassed the square footage of the apartment inside. In warm weather, the roof mitigated the effects of claustrophobia, and you never tired of going out there and looking at the view from the front of the building: the trees of Riverside Park, Grant's Tomb to the right, the traffic cruising along the Henry Hudson Parkway, and most of all the river, with its spectacle of unceasing activity, the countless numbers of boats and sailing vessels that traveled along its waters, the freighters and tugs, the barges and yachts and cabin cruisers, the daily regatta of industrial ships and pleasure craft that populated the river, which you soon discovered was another world, a parallel world that ran beside the patch of land you inhabited, a city of water just beyond the city of stones and earth. A stray hawk would settle onto the roof every now and then, but most often you were visited by gulls, crows, and starlings. One afternoon, a red pigeon landed outside your window (salmon-colored, speckled with white), a wounded fledgling with fearless curiosity and strange, red-rimmed eyes, and after you and your girlfriend fed him for a week and he was well enough to fly again, he kept coming back to the roof of your apartment, nearly every day for months, so often that your girlfriend eventually gave him a name, Joey, which meant that Joey the pigeon had acquired the status of pet, an outdoor companion who shared his address with you until the following summer, when he flapped his wings one last time and flew away for good. Early on: working from noon to five for a rare-book dealer on East Sixty-ninth Street, writing poems, reviewing books, and slowly reacclimating yourself to America, just as the country was living through the Watergate hearings and the fall of Richard Nixon, which made it a slightly different America from the one you had left. On October 6, 1974, about two months after you moved in, you and your girlfriend were married. A small ceremony held in your apartment, then a party thrown by a friend who lived in a nearby apartment that was much larger than yours. Given the frequent changes of heart that had afflicted the two of you from the beginning, the constant comings and goings, the affairs with other people, the breakups and makeups that followed one another as regularly as the changing of the seasons, the thought that either one of you should have considered marriage at this point now strikes you as an act of delusional folly. At the very least you were taking an enormous risk, gambling on the solidity of your friendship and your shared ambitions as writers to make marriage into something different from what you had already experienced together, but you lost the bet, you both lost because you were destined to lose, and therefore you managed to keep it going for only four years, marrying in October 1974 and calling it quits in November 1978. You were both twenty-seven when you took your vows, old enough to know better, perhaps, but at the same time neither one of you was anywhere close to full adulthood, you were both still adolescents at the core, and the hard truth was that you didn't have a chance.

15. 2230 Durant Avenue; Berkeley, California. A small efficiency apartment (two rooms and a kitchenette) across from the college football stadium, within walking distance of the university campus. Age 29. Restless, dissatisfied for no reason you could name, feeling ever more hemmed in by the too-tiny apartment in New York, you were rescued by a sudden infusion of cash (a grant from the Ingram Merrill Foundation), which opened the door to other possibilities, other solutions to the problem of how and where to live, and since you felt the moment had come to shake things up for yourself, you and your first wife boarded a train in New York, traveled to Chicago, where you disembarked and

switched to another train, and then headed for the West Coast, passing through the interminable flatlands of Nebraska, the Rockies, the deserts of Utah and Nevada, and pulled into San Francisco after a three-day journey. It was April 1976. The idea was to test out California for half a year and see if you might not want to move there permanently. You had several good friends in the area, you had visited the previous year and had come away with a favorable impression, and if you chose to conduct your experiment in Berkeley rather than in San Francisco, it was because the rents were lower there and you didn't have a car, and life without a car would be more manageable on that side of the Bay. The apartment wasn't much of anything, a low-ceilinged box with a faint odor of mildew and mold when the windows were shut, but not unlivable, not grim. You have no memory of making the decision to rent it, however, because not long after you arrived in town, sometime during the first week, when you were temporarily staying with friends, you were invited to play in a pickup softball game, in the second inning of which, with your back turned to the runner as you stood well out of the baseline waiting for a throw from the outfield, the runner intentionally went out of his way to crash into you from behind, leveling you with a murderous football block (wrong sport), and because he was a large man and you were not prepared for the blow, the collision snapped your head back before you fell to the ground, which caused a severe case of whiplash. (Your attacker, known for his bad sportsmanship and often referred to as "the Animal," was a highly sophisticated intellectual who went on to write books about seventeenth-century Dutch painting and translate a number of German poets. He turned out to be a former student of a former professor of yours, a man much admired by both of you, and when the Animal was informed of the connection, he was deeply contrite, saying he never would have run into you if he had known who you were. You have always been mystified by this apology. Was he trying to tell you that only former students of Angus Fletcher's were exempt from his dirty tactics but all others were fair game? You continue to scratch your head in wonder.) Your friends took you to the emergency room of the local hospital, where you were given a padded, Velcro-adjustable neck brace and a prescription for heavy doses of the muscle relaxant Valium, a drug you had never taken and which you hope you will never have to take again, for efficient as it was in alleviating the pain, it put you in a mindless stupor for the better part of a week, obliterating the memory of events an instant after those events occurred, meaning that several days of your life have been removed from the calendar. You cannot bring back a single thing that happened to you while you were walking around in your Frankenstein-monster neck brace and swallowing those amnesia-inducing pills, and therefore, when you and your first wife moved into the apartment on Durant Avenue, you praised her for having found such conveniently located digs, even though she had consulted with you at length before you both made the decision to live there. You stayed for the six months you had allotted yourselves, but no more. California had much to recommend it, and you fell in love with the landscape, the vegetation, the ever-present aroma of eucalyptus in the air, the fogs and all-encompassing showers of light, but after a while you found yourself missing New York, the vastness and confusion of New York, for the better you came to know San Francisco, the smaller and duller it seemed to you, and while you had no problem living in remotest seclusion (the nine months in the Var, for example, which had been an intensely fertile time for you), you decided that if you were going to live in a city, it had to be a big city, the biggest city, meaning that you could embrace the extremes of far-flung rural places and massive urban places, both of which seemed inexhaustible to you, but small cities and towns used themselves up too quickly, and in the end they left you cold. So you went back to New York in September, reclaimed the little apartment overlooking the Hudson (which had been rented out to a subtenant), and dug in again. But not for long. In October, the good news, the much-hoped-for news that a child was on the way—which meant that you would have to find another place to live. You wanted to stay in New York, you fully expected to stay in New York, but New York was too expensive, and after several months of searching for a larger apartment that you could afford, you accepted defeat and started looking elsewhere.

16. 252 Millis Road; Stanfordville, New York. A white, two-story house in northern Dutchess County. Construction date unknown, but neither new nor particularly old, which would suggest sometime between 1880 and 1910. Half an acre of land, with a vegetable garden in back, a dark, pine-shaded yard in front, and a small patch of woods between your property and the one to the south. A worn-out but not altogether decrepit place, something to be improved on over time if sufficient funds were available, with a living room, dining room, kitchen, and guest room/study on the ground floor and three bedrooms upstairs. Purchase price: $35,000. One of several houses on a rural side road with moderate traffic. Not the extreme isolation of Provence, but a life in the country for all that, and if you never ran into altruistic dentists or left-wing farmers, your neighbors on Millis Road were kind, solid citizens, many of them young couples with small children, all of whom you came to know to one degree or another, but what you remember best about your Dutchess County neighbors are the tragedies that took place in those houses, the twenty-eight-year-old woman who came down with M.S., for example, or the grieving middle-aged couple next door whose twenty-five-year-old daughter had died of cancer within the past year, the mother now reduced to skin and bone from a steady diet of gin and her tender husband doing his best to prop her up, so much suffering behind the locked doors and drawn shades of those houses, and among those houses your own house must be included as well. Age 30 to 31. A bleak time,

without question the bleakest time you have ever gone through, brightened only by the birth of your son in June 1977. But that was the place where your first marriage broke apart, where you were overwhelmed by constant money problems (as described in *Hand to Mouth*), and you came to a dead end as a poet. You don't believe in haunted houses, but when you look back on that time now, you feel that you were living under an evil spell, that the house itself was partly to blame for the troubles that descended on you. For many decades before you moved in, the owners had been a pair of unmarried sisters, German-Americans named Stemmerman, and by the time you bought the place from them, they were exceedingly old, in their late eighties or early nineties, one blind and the other deaf, and both had been in a nursing home for close to a year. A neighbor who lived a couple of doors down the road handled the negotiations for them—a vivacious woman who had been born in Cuba, was married to a quiet American auto mechanic, and collected glass figurines of elephants (!?)—and she told you a number of stories about the notorious Stemmerman sisters, who apparently hated each other and had been locked in mortal combat since childhood, the two of them bound together for life and yet bitter enemies to the last, who were known to engage in such loud, vicious quarrels that their voices could be heard up and down the length of Millis Road. When the neighbor started talking about how the deaf sister would punish the blind sister by locking her in the downstairs closet, you couldn't help conjuring up scenes from Gothic novels and remembering that tacky black-and-white movie with Bette Davis and Joan Crawford from the early sixties. How amusing, you thought, a couple of grotesque and crazy characters, but that's all in the past now, you and your pregnant wife would be bringing youth and vigor to the old house, and everything was about to change—all the while neglecting to consider that the Stemmermans had lived there for fifty or sixty years, perhaps seventy or eighty years, and that every inch of the house was impregnated with their malevolent spirits. You actually met the deaf sister one day at the Cuban woman's house (she nearly choked to death trying to drink a cup of tepid coffee), but she seemed benign enough to you, and you didn't give the matter another thought. Then you moved in, and in those early days of cleaning and rearranging furniture (some of which came with the house), you and your first wife pulled an armoire away from the wall in the upstairs hallway and found a dead crow on the floor behind it—a long-dead crow, utterly desiccated but intact. No, that wasn't amusing, not amusing at all, and even though you both tried to laugh it off, you went on thinking about that dead bird for months afterward, that dead black bird, the classic omen of bad tidings. The next morning, you discovered two or three boxes of books on the back porch, and because you were curious to see if anything was worth holding on to, you opened the boxes. One by one, you pulled out pamphlets from the John Birch Society, paperback books about the Communist plot to infiltrate the United States government, several volumes about the fluoride conspiracy to brainwash American children, pro-Nazi tracts published in English before the war, and then, most disturbing of all, a copy of *The Protocols of the Elders of Zion*, the book of books, the most repellent and influential defense of anti-Semitism ever written. You had never thrown away a book, had never been tempted to throw away a book, but these books you threw away, driving the boxes to the town dump and purposefully shoving them under a mound of rotting garbage. It wasn't possible to live in a house with such books in it. You hoped that would be the end of the story, but even after you got rid of the books, it still wasn't possible to live there. You tried, but it simply wasn't possible.

17. 6 Varick Street; Manhattan. One room on the top floor of a ten-story industrial building in what is now known as Tribeca. A sub-sublet, passed on to you by the sometime girlfriend of a childhood friend of yours. One hundred dollars a month for the

privilege of camping out in a former electrical supply office, a gutted shell not meant for human habitation, which until recently had served as a storage room for the artist's loft across the hall. A cold-water sink, but no bath, toilet, or kitchen facilities. Living conditions not unlike those in your maid's room on the rue du Louvre in Paris, but this room was three or four times larger than that one—as well as three or four times dirtier. Age 32. Before landing there in early 1979, a whirlwind of shocks, sudden changes, and inner upheavals that turned you around and set your life on a different course. With nowhere to go and no money to finance a move even if you had known where to go, you stayed on in the Dutchess County house after the breakup of your marriage, sleeping on the sofa-bed in the corner of your downstairs study, which you now realize had once been your bed as a child. A couple of weeks later, on a trip down to New York, you experienced the revelation, the scalding, epiphanic moment of clarity that pushed you through a crack in the universe and allowed you to start writing again. Three weeks after that, immersed in the prose text you had begun immediately after your resuscitation, your liberation, your new beginning, the unexpected hammer blow of your father's death. To your first wife's infinite credit, she stuck with you through the dismal days and weeks that followed, the ordeal of funeral arrangements and estate matters, disposing of your father's neckties, suits, and furniture, taking care of the sale of his house (which had already been in the works), standing by you through all the wrenching, practical business that follows death, and because you were no longer married, or married in name only, the pressures of marriage had been lifted, and once again you were friends, much as you had been in your early days together. You started writing the first part of *The Invention of Solitude*. By the time you moved to Varick Street in early spring, you were well into it.

18. 153 Carroll Street; Brooklyn. A railroad flat on the third

floor of a four-story building near Henry Street. Age 33 to 34. Three rooms, sit-down kitchen, and bathroom. The bedroom, overlooking the street in front, was large enough to fit in a double bed for yourself and a single bed for your son (the same sofa-bed you had used as a child and which you had now reclaimed after the sale of the house in Stanfordville). Two middle rooms, one without windows, which you converted into a makeshift study, the other the living room (one window overlooking the garden), followed by the kitchen (one window) and the bathroom in back— tawdry and run-down, yes, but a big step up from where you had been living before. You lost the place on Varick Street in January 1980 (the artist was giving up his loft), and when Manhattan rents proved to be too steep for an apartment that could accommodate both you and your two-and-a-half-year-old son (who spent three days a week with you), you crossed the East River and began searching in Brooklyn. Why hadn't you thought of this in 1976? you wondered. Surely this was a better solution than trekking one hundred miles to the north and buying a haunted house in Dutchess County, but the fact was that Brooklyn had never even crossed your mind back then, for New York was Manhattan and Manhattan only, and the outer boroughs were as alien to you as the distant countries of Oceania or the Arctic Circle. You wound up in Carroll Gardens, a self-enclosed Italian neighborhood where most people went out of their way to make you feel unwelcome, treating you with suspicion and silent stares, as if you were an intruder in their midst, an *estranger*, even if you could have passed for Italian yourself, but no doubt there was something wrong with you, the way you dressed, perhaps, or the way you moved, or simply the look in your eyes. Again and again for almost two years, walking down Carroll Street on the way to your apartment with the old women sitting on the stoops of their houses, cutting off their conversations when you were within earshot of them, watching you pass without a word, and the men standing around with nothing in their eyes, or else looking under the hoods of their cars, examining the engines of those cars with such persistence and dedication that they reminded you of philosophers in search of some ultimate truth about human existence, and the only time you ever received a nod from the women was when you were walking down that street with your son, your little blond-haired son, but otherwise you were a phantom, a man who was not there because he had no business being there. Fortunately, the owners of your building, John and Jackie Caramello, a couple in their early thirties who lived in the garden apartment on the bottom floor, were affable and friendly and never displayed the slightest resentment toward you, but they were your contemporaries, and they were no longer grinding the axes of their parents' generation. Joey Gallo's aunt lived on your block, there were the social clubs around the corner on Henry Street where the old-timers hung out during the day, and if Carroll Gardens was known as the safest neighborhood in the city, it was because it was ruled by an undercurrent of violence, the retaliatory violence and ethics of the mob. Black people steered clear of this well-guarded enclave, knowing they would be risking danger if they set foot within its borders, an unwritten law you might not have understood if you hadn't seen it executed with your own eyes, walking down Court Street one day in the brightness of an autumn afternoon, when a rangy black kid carrying a boom box on the other side of the street was jumped by three or four white teenagers, who pummeled him, bloodied him, and smashed his radio against the sidewalk, and before you could intervene the black kid was staggering away, stumbling forward, and then starting to run as the white kids shouted *nigger* at him and warned him never to come back. Another time, you did have a chance to intervene. A Sunday afternoon in late spring, walking down Carroll Street toward the subway station on Smith, when you stopped for a couple of minutes to watch a roller-skate hockey game being played on the asphalt surface of

Carroll Park and saw, hanging on the chain-link fence that surrounded the park, a large red, white, and black Nazi banner. You
went into the park, found the sixteen-year-old boy who had put it
up (the equipment manager of one of the teams), and told him to
take it down. Perplexed, not at all understanding why you would
ask him to do such a thing, he listened to you explain what the
banner represented, and when he heard you talk about the evils of
Hitler and the slaughter of innocent millions, he looked genuinely embarrassed. "I didn't know," he said. "I just thought it
looked cool." Rather than ask him where he had been all his life,
you waited until he had removed the banner and then continued
walking to the subway. Still, Carroll Gardens was not without its
advantages, the food in particular, the bakeries, the pork stores,
the watermelon man riding through the neighborhood with his
horse-drawn wagon in the summer, the coffee roasted on-site at
D'Amico's and the blast of sharp, beautiful smells that assaulted
you whenever you walked into that shop, but Carroll Gardens was
also the place where you asked the single most stupid question of
your adult life. You were upstairs in your apartment one afternoon, at work on the second half of *The Invention of Solitude* in your
windowless study, when a great clamor of voices rose up from the
street outside. You went downstairs to see what was going on, and
the whole block was out in force, clusters of men and women were
standing in front of their houses, twenty excited conversations
were going on at once, and there was your landlord, the burly
John Caramello, parked on the stoop of the building where you
both lived, calmly surveying the commotion. You asked him what
was wrong, and he told you that a man who had just been let out
of prison had been breaking into empty houses and apartments
along the block and stealing things—jewelry, silverware, anything
of value he could put his hands on—but he had been caught before he could get away. That was when you asked your question,
uttering the famous words that proved you were an out-and-out

dunce who still understood nothing about the little world in which you happened to be living. "Did you call the police?" John smiled. "Of course not," he said. "The boys beat the shit out of him, broke his legs with baseball bats, and threw him into a taxi. He won't be back in this neighborhood again—not if he wants to go on breathing." So much for your early days in Brooklyn, where you have been living for thirty-one years now, and in that transitional period of your life, beginning with the breakup of your marriage and your father's death, the nine months on Varick Street and the first eleven months in Carroll Gardens, a time marked by nightmares and inner struggle, alternating between fits of hope and no hope, tumbling into the beds of various women, women you tried to love and almost loved but couldn't, certain you would never marry again, working on your book, on your translations of Joubert and Mallarmé, on your mammoth anthology of twentieth-century French poetry, taking care of your confused and sometimes embattled three-year-old son, and with so many things happening to you at once, which included the near-fatal cardiac arrest of your mother's second husband just ten days after your father's funeral, the vigils in the hospital six months later as you watched over your grandfather's rapid decline and death, it was probably inevitable that your body should go haywire again, this time with a pounding heart, an irregular heart that would suddenly and inexplicably speed up inside your chest, the bouts of tachycardia that would take hold of you at night just as you were falling asleep, or wake you up just after you had fallen asleep, either alone in the room with your son or lying next to the sleeping bodies of Ann or Françoise or Ruby, the frantically beating heart that would echo inside your head with a percussiveness so loud and insistent you thought the noises were coming from somewhere in the room, a thyroid condition as you eventually found out, which had thrown your system entirely out of whack and for which you had to take pills for two or three years. Then, on February 23, 1981, twenty days after your thirty-fourth birthday, just four days after her twenty-sixth birthday, you met her, you found yourself being introduced to the One, the woman who has been with you ever since that night thirty years ago, your wife, the grand love that ambushed you when you were least expecting it, and in the first weeks you were together, when much of your time was spent in bed, you developed a ritual of reading fairy tales to each other, something you went on doing until your daughter was born six years later, and not long after you discovered the intimate pleasures of reading to each other in this way, your wife wrote a long prose poem entitled *Reading to You*, the fourteenth and last part of which evokes the erratic beating of your heart and is set in the bedroom of your third-floor apartment at 153 Carroll Street: *The cruel father sends the stupid boy into the woods to be killed, but the murderer cannot do it and lets him go, bringing back a deer's heart to the father instead, and this boy speaks to the dogs and the frogs and the birds and in the end the doves whisper into his ears, the words of the mass, the repetitions over and over into his ears, and somewhere else I whisper into your ears, messages, messages from me to you, about the back of your knees and the inside of your elbows and the impression above your upper lip, from me to you even if you are now away. I whisper like the birds in the story I read to you, repetitions in the room where you took me. The parts are the same, but changing, always in movement, altering imperceptibly like the expression on your face from a smile to seriousness leaning over me in the thin light. So I wish you a story in the reading of it, in the writing of it. We inherit stories, too, conditions, faces, hearts, bladders, weak and stricken. His heart has water around it, drowning, the sick heart, the heart sick, the stricken part, the beat measured in you that is sometimes too fast so you take pills to make it slower, to make it right and rhythmic, not random and slipping like other things. I wish you a story in bed where they hang the moon after the old men die so it shines forever on top of you, and will not stop even if it does not have its own light, but is borrowed and cyclic. I will take the moon, the*

borrowing and stealing and changing from large to small. The tiniest moon,
thin and weak behind a cloud in winter is the view I choose.

19. 18 Tompkins Place; Brooklyn. The top two floors of a four-
story brownstone on a one-block street of nearly identical row
houses in Cobble Hill, the neighborhood between Carroll Gardens and Brooklyn Heights. Age 34 to 39. Less than half a mile
from 153 Carroll Street, but an altogether different world, with
a population more mixed and various than the ethnic compound
you had lived in for the past twenty-one months. Not a duplex
shut off from the lower half of the house but two independent
floors, the low-ceilinged one on top with a nook-sized kitchen,
an ample dining area and unpartitioned living room beyond it,
as well as a small study for your wife; on the higher-ceilinged
floor below: a compact master bedroom, a larger bedroom/play-
room for your son, and a study for you, identical in size to your
wife's above. A bit ramshackle in overall design, but larger than
any apartment you had ever rented and located on a block of great
architectural beauty: every house constructed in the 1860s, gas
lamps burning at night in front of every door, and when the snow
covered the ground in winter, you felt that you had traveled back
to the nineteenth century, that if you shut your eyes and listened
closely enough, you would hear the sound of horses in the street.
You were married in that apartment on a sultry day in mid-June,
one of those hot, overcast days in early summer with storms building slowly at the far edge of the horizon, the sky darkening imperceptibly as the hours advanced, and an instant after you were
declared man and wife, at the very instant you took your wife in
your arms and kissed her, the storm finally broke, a tremendous
clap of thunder ripped through the air directly above you, rattling
the windows of the house, shaking the floor under your feet, and
as the people in the room gasped, it was as if the heavens were announcing your marriage to the world. An uncanny bit of dramatic

timing, which meant nothing and yet seemed to mean everything, and for the first time in your life, you felt that you were taking part in a cosmic event.

20. 458 Third Street, Apartment 3R; Brooklyn. A long, narrow apartment that took up one half of the third floor of a four-story building in Park Slope. Living room overlooking the street in front, dining room and galley kitchen in the middle, flanked by a book-lined hallway that led to three small bedrooms in the back. Age 40 to 45. When you moved to your previous apartment on Tompkins Place, your landlord, who also happened to be your downstairs neighbor, warned you that you could not live there forever, that eventually he and his family would be taking over the entire house. You must have understood this at the time, but after living there for five years and one month, your longest stint in any dwelling since your boyhood days on Irving Avenue, you had little by little pushed the thought of involuntary departure out of your mind, and because the years on Tompkins Place had been the happiest, most fulfilling period of your life so far, you simply refused to face the facts. Then, in November 1986—just one week after your wife discovered she was pregnant—the landlord politely informed you that time was up and he would not be renewing your lease. His announcement came as a jolt, and because you never wanted to be in such a position again, could not bear the idea of being thrown out of yet another place at some point in the future, you and your wife began searching for a place to buy, a co-op apartment that would belong to you and thereafter protect you from the whims of other people. The Wall Street crash of 1987 was still eleven months off, and the New York real estate frenzy was surging out of control, prices were going up every week, every day, every minute of every day, and because you had only so much money to spend on a down payment, you had to settle for something that did not quite measure up to your needs. The apartment

on Third Street was attractive, hands down the most attractive of
the many places you had visited on your search, but it was too
small for four people, especially when two of the people were writers, who not only had to live in that space but work there as well. All
three bedrooms were accounted for: one for you and your wife, one
for your son (who continued to live with you half the time), and
one for your infant daughter, and even the largest of the three, the
so-called master bedroom, was too tightly proportioned to accommodate a desk. Your wife volunteered to set up her work space in
a corner of the living room, and you went out and found yourself
a tiny studio in an apartment building on Eighth Avenue, a block
and a half from 458 Third Street (see entry 20A). Too cramped,
then, a less than ideal arrangement, but your circumstances were
far from tragic. You and your wife both preferred the anima-
tion of Park Slope to the quiet streets of Cobble Hill, and when
you started spending the summers in southern Vermont (three
months for five consecutive years—see entry 20B), there was little
or nothing to complain about, especially when you considered
some of the wretched places you had inhabited in the past. Living
in a co-op put you in more intimate contact with your neighbors
than at any time before or since, something you initially faced
with a certain amount of dread, but there were no Madame Rubinsteins in your building, no festering conflicts developed on any
front, and the co-op meetings you were obliged to attend were
relatively short, easygoing affairs. Six families were involved, four
of them with small children, and with an architect, a contractor,
and a lawyer among the members of the board, your neighbors
were conscientious about maintaining the physical and financial
health of the building. Your wife, who served as recording secretary for the five years you lived there, wrote up the minutes after
each board meeting—entertaining, tongue-in-cheek reports that
were warmly appreciated by everyone involved. Some excerpts:

10/19/87. BUGS: This highly unpleasant subject was addressed by the assembled company with utmost delicacy. The euphemism "problem" was used by at least one member. Marguerite went so far as to speak of "hundreds of babies." Dick recommended a product called COMBAT. Siri echoed the recommendation. It was also suggested that the exterminator be told to change his poison. Then, with a sigh of relief, the members turned to another subject.

3/7/88. THE FENCE: Theo was given a price of $500 for the fence by his students. Certain members felt this was exorbitant; others didn't. There was a faint agreement—that is, an agreement so vague, so slim, it might not be called an agreement at all—that if these students of Theo promised to do a good job, they could have their $500. But this is not certain . . .

10/18/88. OLD BUSINESS: There was a moment of hesitation. Would the members be able to reach into the past and recall just what our old business was? The president came to the rescue with a copy of the old minutes.

2/22/90. CEILING IN 3R: Paul announces to the group that the ceiling in #3R is about to collapse. Expressions of alarm can be seen on the faces of his fellow co-opers. His wife, otherwise known as the secretary, attempts to assuage the others by noting her husband's tendency to exaggerate. The man's bread and butter, after all, is in the making of fictions, and occasionally this submersion in the world of the imagination colors that other world, known for lack of a better expression as the Real World. Let it stand for the record that the ceiling in 3R is not about to collapse and that its occupants have taken appropriate action to make certain that this will not happen. The plasterers and painters shall take care of our slight sag . . .

3/28/90. CEILING IN 3R: It WAS falling in! The painters who restored that apartment to an acceptable condition confirmed Paul's gloomy prediction. It was just a matter of time before it fell on our heads.

6/17/92. FLOODING: The basement is flooding. Lloyd's acute remark that either we fix the flooding or stock the basement with trout hit home. The estimates for repair are running between $100 and $850, depending on what must be done. We agreed that lower was better than higher and that we should begin low with Roto-Rooter. The gentleman from Roto-Rooter, a friend, acquaintance, or at least a person KNOWN to Lloyd, is Raymond Clean, a name that inspires confidence, considering the nature of his work, and, who knows, may have inspired Mr. Clean's calling in life.

10/15/92. WINDOWS AND CRIME: Joe, the window man, was formally accused of absconding with the secretary's one hundred dollars and not answering his telephone. He may have left the country. Theo and Marguerite have also accused him of essentially NOT FIXING their balances, since they ceased to work again after one week. There was some speculation among the members as to how far one could get with $100. We may have to look for him in Hoboken.

12/3/92. Beyond the walls of 458 Third Street, the weather was cold and damp that night, and winter was upon us. We ended the meeting on a wistful note. Marguerite told stories about Cyprus, a definite longing in her voice. In that exotic place the weather is warm and the light brilliant and clothes dry on balconies in ten minutes.... And that is how it stands with us. There's always another place where the sun shines, where clothes dry fast, where there are no window men, no maintenances, no workmen's compensation, or flooded basements...

1/14/93. WORKMEN'S COMPENSATION: This issue of whether or not to cover officers of the co-op injured while performing their duties came to a head. We won't. Let come what may: fingers broken at the typewriter, necks strangled in a telephone cord while conducting co-op business, broken legs, arms, and heads from too much wine at a meeting. We'll have to live with it, the way people used to. We'll call it fate. We'll save about fifty bucks, and fifty bucks is fifty bucks is fifty bucks.

20A. 300 Eighth Avenue, Apartment 1-I; Brooklyn. A one-room studio on the ground floor of a six-story apartment building, located in the back, with a view of an air shaft and a brick wall. Larger than the maid's room on the rue du Louvre, less than half the size of the Varick Street hovel, but equipped with a toilet and bath as well as various kitchen appliances built into one of the walls: sink, stove, and minibar fridge, which you rarely bothered to use, since this was a space for work and not for living (or eating). A desk, a chair, a metal bookcase, and a couple of storage cabinets; a bare bulb hanging from the middle of the ceiling; an air conditioner in one of the windows, which you would turn on when you arrived in the morning to filter out noises from the building (COOL in summer; FAN in winter). Spartan surroundings, yes, but surroundings have never been of any importance as far as your work is concerned, since the only space you occupy when you write your books is the page in front of your nose, and the room in which you are sitting, the various rooms in which you have sat these forty-plus years, are all but invisible to you as you push your pen across the page of your notebook or transcribe what you have written onto a clean page with your typewriter, the same machine you have been using since your return from France in 1974, an Olympia portable you bought secondhand from a friend for forty dollars—a still functioning relic that was built in a West German factory more than half a century ago and will no doubt go on functioning long after you are dead. The number of your studio apartment pleased you for its symbolic aptness. 1-I, meaning the single self, the lone person sequestered in that bunker of a room for seven or eight hours a day, a silent man cut off from the rest of the world, day after day sitting at his desk for no other purpose than to explore the interior of his own head.

20B. Windham Road; West Townshend, Vermont. A two-story white clapboard house (circa 1800) on the crest of a steep dirt road three miles outside the village of West Townshend. June through August, 1989 through 1993. For the modest sum of one thousand dollars a month, you escaped the tropical heat of New York and the confines of your too-small apartment for this refuge in the hills of southern Vermont. A grassy, quarter-of-an-acre yard in front of the house; dense woods just beyond the yard that stretched on through several miles of wilderness; more woods on the other side of the dirt road; a small pond nearby; an outbuilding at the edge of the yard. Except for a sink and a cheap ancient stove in the kitchen, there were no amenities of any kind: no washing machine, no dishwasher, no television, no bathtub. Telephone communication via party line; radio reception touch and go at best. Freshly painted on the outside, the house was falling apart within: warped floors, buckling ceilings, squadrons of mice in the closets and bureaus, hideous, water-stained wallpaper in the bedrooms, and uncomfortable furniture throughout—lumpy, sagging beds; wobbly chairs; and a cushionless, understuffed couch in the living room. No one lived there anymore. The now-dead former owner, an aged spinster with no immediate heirs, had bequeathed the house to the children of various friends of hers, eight men and women who lived in different parts of the country, from California to Florida, but none in Vermont, none anywhere in New England. They were too scattered and uninvolved to do anything about the house, could not agree on whether to sell it, improve it, or tear it down, and left the oversight of the property to a local real estate agent. The last tenant, a young woman who had turned the place into a marijuana farm and had made a thriving business of it by employing a tough biker gang as her sales force, was now looking at a stiff prison term. After her arrest, the house had remained unoccupied for a couple of years, and when you and your wife rented it in the spring of 1989, on the strength of a single exterior shot of the house (so pretty), you had no idea what you were getting yourselves into. Yes, you had told the agent you were looking for something remote, that *rustic* was a word that did not frighten you or induce any qualms, but even though he'd warned you that the house was not in tip-top condition, neither one of you had imagined you would be walking into a tumbledown shanty. You remember the first night you spent there, wondering out loud if it would be possible to endure an entire summer in such a place, but your wife absorbed the shock more calmly than you did, telling you to be patient, to give it a week or so before you decided to jump ship, that it could turn out to be a lot better than you thought. The next morning, she launched into a furious campaign of scrubbing, bleaching, and disinfecting, opening windows to air out the stuffy rooms, discarding torn curtains and disintegrated blankets, cleaning the blackened stove and oven, removing trash and reorganizing the kitchen cupboards, sweeping, dusting, and polishing, her Scandinavian blood boiling with the righteousness and devotion of her frontier ancestors, while you went across the yard with your notebooks and typewriter to the outbuilding, a cabinlike structure of more recent vintage, which had been trashed by the marijuana girl and her biker friends and turned into a dump site of broken furniture, ripped screen windows, and graffiti-covered walls, a place beyond hope or salvation, and little by little you did what you could to clean up the mess, to get rid of the broken things, to wash the cracked linoleum floors, and within a couple of days you had installed yourself at a green wooden table in the front room and were back to work on your novel, and once you began to settle in, to occupy the house your wife had rescued from filth and disarray, you discovered that you liked being there, that what at first had seemed to be a ubiquitous, unalterable squalor was in fact no more than a state of weary dilapidation, and you could live with crooked floors and ceilings that were falling in, you could learn to ignore the house's defects because it wasn't your house, and little by little you came to appreciate the many advantages the place had to offer: the silence, the coolness of the Vermont air (sweaters in the morning, even on the warmest days), the afternoon strolls through the woods, the sight of your little daughter romping naked through the yard, the tranquil isolation that allowed you and your wife to pursue your work without interference. And so you kept going back, summer after summer, celebrating your daughter's second birthday there, her third birthday, her fourth birthday, her fifth birthday, her sixth birthday, and eventually you began to toy with the idea of buying the house, which wouldn't have cost much, far less than any other house for miles around, but when you considered the expense of restoring your summertime ruin, of rescuing it from imminent collapse and death, you realized that you couldn't afford such an undertaking and that if and when you had the money at your disposal, you should leave your too-small co-op apartment on Third Street and find a larger place to live in New York.

21. Somewhere in Park Slope; Brooklyn. A four-story brownstone with a small garden in back, built in 1892. Age 46 to the present. Your wife left Minnesota in the fall of 1978 to enter the Ph.D. program in English literature at Columbia. She chose Columbia because she wanted to be in New York, had turned down larger, more monumental fellowships from Cornell and Michigan in order to be in New York, and by the time you met her in February 1981, she was a veteran Manhattanite, a committed Manhattanite, a person who could no longer imagine living anywhere else. Then she threw her lot in with you and wound up settling in the urban hinterlands of Brooklyn. Not unhappily, perhaps, but Brooklyn had never been part of the plan, and now that the two of you had

decided to look for another place to live, you told her you were willing to go anywhere she wanted, that you were not so attached to Brooklyn that leaving it would cause you any regrets, and if she wanted to return to Manhattan, you would be happy to start looking with her there. No, she said, without pausing to think about it, without having to think about it, let's stay in Brooklyn. Not only did she not want to go back to Manhattan, she wanted to go on living in the same neighborhood where you were now. Fortunately, the real estate market had collapsed by then, and even though you had to sell your once overpriced apartment at a loss, the house you bought was just within your means—or just beyond them, but not by so much as to cause any lasting difficulties. It took you a year of dogged looking to find it, followed by another six months after the closing before you could move in, but then it was yours, a place finally big enough for all of you, all the bedrooms and studies you needed, all the wall space you needed to shelve the thousands of books you owned, a kitchen large enough to breathe in, bathrooms large enough to breathe in, a guest room for visiting friends and family, a deck off the kitchen for warm-weather drinks and meals, the little garden below, and bit by bit, over the eighteen years you have lived there, which is far longer than you have lived anywhere else, three times longer than your longest run in any other place, you have steadily repaired and improved every inch of every room on every floor, turning a somewhat shabby, down-at-the-heels old house into something sparkling and beautiful, a place that gives you pleasure every time you walk into it, and after eighteen years you are long past the point of thinking about houses in other neighborhoods, other cities, other countries. This is where you live, and this is where you want to go on living until you can no longer walk up and down the stairs. No, even more than that: until you can no longer *crawl* up and down the stairs, until they carry you out and put you in your grave.

Twenty-one permanent addresses from birth to the present, although *permanent* hardly seems to be the right word when you consider how often you have moved during the course of your life. Twenty stopping places, then, a score of addresses leading to the one address that may or may not prove to be permanent, and yet even though you have hung your hat in those twenty-one different houses and apartments, have paid your gas and electric bills there, have been registered to vote there, your body has rarely sat still for any length of time, and when you open a map of your country and begin to count, you discover that you have set foot in forty of the fifty states, sometimes just passing through (as with Nebraska on your train trip to the West Coast in 1976) but more often for visits of several days or weeks or even months, as with Vermont, for example, or California, where you not only lived for half a year but also visited from time to time after your mother and stepfather moved there in the early seventies, not to speak of the twenty-five or twenty-seven trips you have made to Nantucket, the annual summer visits to your friend who owns a house on the island, no less than a week each year, which would tally up to approximately six months total, or the many months you have spent in Minnesota with your wife, the two full summers you lived there when her parents were in Norway, the innumerable spring and winter visits throughout the eighties, nineties, and aughts, perhaps fifty times in all, meaning more than a year of your life, along with frequent trips to Boston starting when you were in your teens, the protracted rambles through the Southwest in 1985 and 1999, the various ports where your tanker docked along the gulf coasts of Texas and Florida when you worked as a merchant seaman in 1970, the visiting-writer jobs that have taken you to such places as Philadelphia, Cincinnati, Ann Arbor, Bowling Green, Durham, and Normal, Illinois, the Amtrak jaunts to Washington, D.C., when you were doing your National Story Project for NPR, the four months of summer camp in New Hampshire when you were eight and ten, the three long sojourns in Maine (1967, 1983, and 1999), and, not to be overlooked, your weekly returns to New Jersey from 1986 to 1990 when you were teaching at Princeton. How many days spent away from home, how many nights spent sleeping in beds that were not your bed? Not just here in America but abroad as well, for when you open your atlas to a map of the world, you see that you have been to all the continents except Africa and Antarctica, and even if you discount the three and a half years you lived in France (where, temporarily, you had several permanent addresses), your visits to foreign countries have been frequent and sometimes rather long: an additional year in France on numerous other trips both before and after the time you lived there, five months in Portugal (most of them in 2006, for the shooting of your last film), four months in the U.K. (England, Scotland, and Wales), three months in Canada, three months in Italy, two months in Spain, two months in Ireland, a month and a half in Germany, a month and a half in Mexico, a month and a half on the island of Bequia (in the Grenadines), a month in Norway, a month in Israel, three weeks in Japan, two and a half weeks in Holland, two weeks in Denmark, two weeks in Sweden, two weeks in Australia, nine days in Brazil, eight days in Argentina, one week on the island of Guadeloupe, one week in Belgium, six days in the Czech Republic, five days in Iceland, four days in Poland, and two days in Austria. You would like to tote up how many hours you have spent traveling to these places (that is, how many days, weeks, or months), but you wouldn't know how to begin, you have lost track of how many trips you have made in America, have no idea how often you have left America and gone abroad, and therefore you could never come up with an exact or even approximate number to tell you how many thousands of hours of your life have been spent in between places, going from here to there and back, the mountains of time you have given over to sitting in airplanes, buses, trains, and cars, the time squandered fighting to overcome the effects of jet lag, the boredom of waiting for your flight to be announced in airports, the deadly tedium of standing around the luggage carousel as you wait for your bag to tumble down the chute, but nothing is more disconcerting to you than the ride in the plane itself, the strange sense of being nowhere that engulfs you each time you step into the cabin, the unreality of being propelled through space at five hundred miles an hour, so far off the ground that you begin to lose a sense of your own reality, as if the fact of your own existence were slowly being drained out of you, but such is the price you pay for leaving home, and as long as you continue to travel, the nowhere that lies between the here of home and the there of somewhere else will continue to be one of the places where you live.

You would like to know who you are. With little or nothing to guide you, you take it for granted that you are the product of vast, prehistoric migrations, of conquests, rapes, and abductions, that the long and circuitous intersections of your ancestral horde have extended over many territories and kingdoms, for you are not the only person who has traveled, after all, tribes of human beings have been moving around the earth for tens of thousands of years, and who knows who begat whom begat whom begat whom begat whom begat whom to end up with your two parents begetting you in 1947? You can go back only as far as your grandparents, with some scant information about your great-grandparents on your mother's side, which means that the generations that came before them are no more than blank space, a void of conjecture and blind guesswork. All four of the grandparents were Eastern European Jews, the two on your father's side born in the late 1870s in the city of Stanislav in the backwater province of Galicia, then part of the Austro-Hungarian Empire, subsequently part of Poland after World War I, later part of the Soviet Union after World War II, and now part of Ukraine following the end of the Cold War, whereas the two on your mother's side were born in 1894 and 1895, your grandmother in Minsk and your grandfather in Toronto—a year after his family emigrated from Warsaw. Both of your grandmothers were redheads, and on both sides of your family there is a tumultuous mix of physical features in the many offspring who followed them, ranging from the dark-haired to the blond, from the brown-skinned to the pale and freckled, from curls and waves to no curls and no waves, from stout peasant bodies with thick legs and stubby fingers to the lithe and elongated contours of still other bodies. The Eastern European genetic pool, but who knows where those nameless ghosts had been wandering before they came to the cities of Russia, Poland, and the Austro-Hungarian Empire, for how else to account for the fact that your sister was born with a Mongolian blue spot on her back, something that occurs only in Asian babies, and how else to account for the fact that you, with your brownish skin and wavy hair and gray-green eyes, have eluded ethnic identification for your entire life and have been variously told by strangers that you must be and most certainly are an Italian, a Greek, a Spaniard, a Lebanese, an Egyptian, and even a Pakistani? Because you know nothing about where you come from, you long ago decided to presume that you are a composite of all the races of the Eastern Hemisphere, part African, part Arab, part Chinese, part Indian, part Caucasian, the melting pot of numerous warring civilizations in a single body. As much as anything else, it is a moral position, a way of eliminating the question of race, which is a bogus question in your opinion, a question that can only bring dishonor to the person who asks it, and therefore you have consciously decided to be everyone, to embrace everyone inside you in order to be most fully and freely yourself, since who you are is a mystery and you have no hope that it will ever be solved.

Your birthday has come and gone. Sixty-four years old now, inching ever closer to senior citizenship, to the days of Medicare and Social Security benefits, to a time when more and more of your friends will have left you. So many of them are gone already—but just wait for the deluge that is coming. Much to your relief, the event passed without incident or commotion, you calmly took it in your stride, a small dinner with friends in Brooklyn, and the impossible age you have now reached seldom entered your thoughts. February third, just one day after your mother's birthday, who went into labor with you on the morning she turned twenty-two, nineteen days before it was supposed to happen, and when the doctor pulled you out of her drugged body with a pair of forceps, it was twenty minutes past midnight, less than half an hour after her birthday had ended. You therefore always celebrated your birthdays together, and even now, almost nine years after her death, you inevitably think about her whenever the clock turns from the second of February to the third. What an unlikely present you must have been that night sixty-four years ago: a baby boy for her birthday, a birth to celebrate her birth.

May 2002. On Saturday, the long, highly spirited conversation with your mother on the telephone, at the end of which you turn to your wife and say: "She hasn't sounded this happy in years." On Sunday, your wife leaves for Minnesota. A large celebration for her father's eightieth birthday has been planned for next weekend, and she is going to Northfield in order to help her mother with the arrangements. You stay behind in New York with your daughter, who is fourteen and must attend school, but the two of you will of course be traveling to Minnesota for the party as well, and your tickets have been booked for Friday. In anticipation of the event, you have already written a humorous rhyming poem in your father-in-law's honor—which is the only kind of poem you write anymore: frivolous bagatelles for birthdays, weddings, and other family occasions. Monday comes and goes, and everything that happened that day has been obliterated from your memory. On Tuesday, you have a one o'clock meeting with a Frenchwoman in her mid-twenties who has been living in New York for the past several years. She has been engaged by a French publisher to write a guidebook of the city, and because you like this person and feel she is a promising writer, you have agreed to talk to her about New York, doubtful that anything you say will be of much use to her project, but nevertheless you are willing to give it a try. At noon, you are standing in front of the bathroom mirror with shaving cream on your face, about to pick up the razor and begin the job of making yourself presentable for the interview, but before you can attack a single whisker, the telephone rings. You go into the bedroom to answer it, awkwardly positioning the receiver in your hand so as not to cover it with shaving cream, and the voice on the other end is sobbing, the person who has called you is in a state of extreme distress, and little by little you understand that it is Debbie, the young woman who cleans your mother's apartment once a week and occasionally drives her on errands, and what Debbie is telling you now is that she just let herself into the apartment and found your mother on the bed, your mother's body on the bed, your dead mother's body on the bed. Your insides seem to empty out as you take in the news. You feel dazed and hollow, unable to think, and even if this is the last thing you were expecting to happen now (*She hasn't sounded this happy in years*), you are not surprised by what Debbie is telling you, not stunned, not shocked, not even upset. What is wrong with you? you ask yourself. Your mother has just died, and you've turned into a block of wood. You tell Debbie to wait where she is, you will get there as quickly as you can (Verona, New Jersey—next to Montclair), and an hour and a half later you are in your mother's apartment, looking at her corpse on the bed. You have seen several corpses in the past, and you are familiar with the inertness of the dead, the inhuman stillness that envelops the bodies of the no longer living, but none of those corpses belonged to your mother, no other dead body was the body in which your own life began, and you can look for no more than a few seconds before you turn your head away. The blue-tinged pallor of her skin, her half-closed eyes fixed on nothing, an extinguished self lying on top of the covers in her nightgown and bathrobe, the Sunday paper sprawled around her, one bare leg dangling over the edge of the bed, a spot of white drool hardened in a corner of her mouth. You cannot look at her, you will not look at her, you find it unbearable to look at her, and yet even after the paramedics have wheeled her out of the apartment in a black body bag, you continue to feel nothing. No tears, no howls of anguish, no grief—just a vague sense of horror growing inside you. Your cousin Regina is with you now, your mother's first cousin, who has driven over from her house in nearby Glen Ridge to lend you a hand, the daughter of your grandfather's only brother, five or six years younger than your mother, your first cousin once removed and one of the few people on either side of your family you feel any connection to, an artist, widow of another artist, the young bohemian woman who fled Brooklyn in the early fifties to live in the Village, and she stays with you throughout the day, she and her grown daughter, Anna, the two of them helping you sort through your mother's belongings and papers, conferring with you as you struggle to decide what to do about someone who left no will and never talked about her wishes after death (burial or cremation, funeral or no funeral), making lists with you of all the practical tasks that must be dealt with sooner rather than later, and that evening, after dinner in a restaurant, they take you back to their house and show you the guest room where you can spend the night. Your daughter is staying with friends in Park Slope, your wife is with her parents in Minnesota, and after a long talk with her on the phone after dinner, you are unable to sleep. You have bought a bottle of scotch to keep you company, and so you sit in a downstairs room until three or four in the morning, consuming half the bottle of Oban as you try to think about your mother, but your mind is still too numb to think about much of anything. Scattered thoughts, inconsequential thoughts, and still no impulse to cry, to break down and mourn your mother with an earnest display of sorrow and regret. Perhaps you are afraid of what will happen to you if you let yourself go, that once you allow yourself to cry you will not be able to stop yourself, that the pain will be too crushing and you will fall to pieces, and because you don't want to risk losing control of yourself, you hold on to the pain, swallow it, bury it in your heart. You miss your wife, miss her more than at any time since you have been married, for she is the only person who knows you well enough to ask the right questions, who has the assurance and understanding to prod you into revealing things about yourself that often elude your own understanding, and how much better it would be if you were lying in bed with her now instead of sitting alone in a darkened room at three in the morning with a bottle of whiskey. The next morning, your cousins continue to prop you up and help you with the tasks at hand, the visit to the mortuary and the selection of an urn (after consulting with your wife, your mother's sister, and your cousin, the unanimous decision was cremation and no funeral, with a memorial service to be held sometime after the summer), the calls to the real estate man, the car man, the furniture man, the cable television man, all the men you must contact in order to sell, disconnect, and discard, and then, after a long day submerged in the bleak miasma of *nothing*, they drive you back to your house in Brooklyn. You all share a takeout dinner with your daughter, you thank Regina for having *saved your life* (your exact words, since you truly don't know what you would have done without her), and once they have left, you stay up for a while talking to your daughter, but eventually she marches upstairs to go to bed, and now that you are alone again, you again find yourself resisting the lure of sleep. The second night is a repetition of the first: sitting alone in a darkened room with the same bottle of scotch, which you drain to the bottom this time, and still no tears, no cogent thoughts, and no inclination to call it a night and turn in. After many hours, exhaustion finally overwhelms you, and when you fall into bed at five-thirty, dawn is already breaking outside and the birds have begun to sing. You plan to sleep for as long as possible, ten or twelve hours if you can manage it, knowing that oblivion is the only cure for you now, but just after eight o'clock, when you have been sleeping for roughly two and a half hours, and sleeping in a way that only the drunk can sleep— *profondamente, stupidamente*—the telephone rings. If the phone were on the other side of the room, it is doubtful you would even hear it, but there it is on the nightstand next to your pillow, not twelve inches from your head, eleven inches from your right ear, and after how many rings (you will never know how many), your eyes involuntarily open. During those first seconds of semiconsciousness, you understand that you have never felt worse, that your body is no longer the body you are used to calling your own, that this new and alien physical self has been hammered by a hundred wooden mallets, dragged by horses for a hundred miles over a barren terrain of rocks and cacti, reduced to a heap of dust by a hundred-ton pile driver. Your bloodstream is so saturated with alcohol that you can smell it coming out of your pores, and the entire room stinks of bad breath and whiskey—fetid, noxious, disgusting. If you want anything now, if one wish could be granted to you, even at the cost of giving up ten years of your life in exchange, it is simply to shut your eyes again and go back to sleep. And yet, for reasons you will never understand (force of habit? a sense of duty? a conviction that the caller is your wife?), you roll over, extend your arm, and pick up the phone. It is one of your cousins, a female first cousin from your father's side of the family, ten years older than you are and a contentious, self-appointed moral judge, the last person on earth you want to talk to, but now that you have picked up the phone, you can't very well hang up on her, not when she is talking, talking, talking, scarcely pausing long enough to let you say a word, to give you a chance to break in and cut the conversation short. How is it possible, you wonder, for someone to rattle on as quickly as she does? It is as if she has trained herself not to breathe while she talks, to spew forth entire paragraphs in a single, uninterrupted exhale, long outrushes of verbiage with no punctuation and no need to stop for an occasional intake of air. Her lungs must be enormous, you think, the largest lungs in the world, and such stamina, such a burning compulsion to have the last word on every subject. You and this cousin have had numerous battles in the past, beginning with the publication of *The Invention of Solitude* in 1982, which in her eyes constituted a betrayal of Auster family secrets (your grandmother murdered your grandfather in 1919), and henceforth you were turned into an outcast, just as your mother was turned into an outcast after she and your father divorced (which is why you have decided against a funeral for her—in order to avoid having to invite certain members of that clan to the service), but at the same time this cousin is not a stupid woman, she is a summa cum laude college graduate, a psychologist with a large and successful practice, an expansive, energetic person who always makes a point of telling you how many of her friends read your novels, and it is true that she has made some efforts to patch things up between you over the years, to nullify the damage of her vicious outburst against your book two decades ago, but even if she professes to admire you now, there is nevertheless an abiding rancor in her as well, an animosity that continues to lurk inside her overtures of friendship, none of it is purely one thing or the other, and the whole situation between you is fraught with complications, for her health is not good, she has been undergoing cancer treatments for some time and you can't help feeling sorry for her, and because she has taken the trouble to call, you want to give her the benefit of the doubt, to allow her this short, perfunctory conversation and then roll over and go back to sleep. She begins by saying all the appropriate things. How sudden, how unexpected, how unprepared you must have been, and think of your sister, your poor schizophrenic sister, how will she cope now that your mother is gone? That is enough, you feel, more than enough to demonstrate her goodwill and sympathy, and you hope you will be able to hang up after another sentence or two, since your eyes are closing now, you are absolutely miserable with exhaustion, and if she would only stop talking within the next few seconds, you would have no trouble drifting off again into the deepest of slumbers. But your cousin is just getting started, rolling up her sleeves and spitting into her hands, as it were, and for the next five minutes she shares her earliest memories of your mother with you, meeting her as a girl of nine when your mother was still so young herself, just twenty or twenty-one, and how thrilling it was to have such a pretty new aunt in the family, so warm and full of life, and so you go on listening, you don't have the strength to interrupt her, and before long she is on another subject altogether, you don't know how she got there, but suddenly you hear her voice talking to you about your smoking, imploring you to stop, to give it up for good, or else you will become sick and die, die a horrendous early death, and as you die you will be filled with remorse for having *murdered yourself* in such a thoughtless way. She has been at it for nine or ten minutes at this point, and you are beginning to worry that you will not be able to go back to sleep, for the longer she goes on, the more you feel yourself being pulled toward consciousness, and once the line is crossed, there will be no turning back. You can't survive on two and a half hours' sleep, not in your present condition, not with so much alcohol still in your blood, you will be destroyed for the whole day, but even though you are feeling more and more tempted to hang up on her, you cannot find the will to do it. Then comes the onslaught, the barrage of verbal cannon fire you should have been expecting from the instant you picked up the phone. How could you have been so naïve as to think that kind words and quasi-hysterical warnings would be the end of it? There is still the question of your mother's character to be dealt with, and even if her body was discovered only two days ago, even if the crematorium in New Jersey has scheduled her body to be burned into ashes this very afternoon, that doesn't prevent your cousin from letting her have it. Thirty-eight years after she left your father, the family has codified its litany of complaints against your mother, it is the stuff of ancestral history by now, old gossip turned into solid facts, and why not go through the list of her misdeeds one last time—in order to give her a proper send-off to the place where she deserves to go? Never satisfied, your cousin says, always looking for something else, too flirtatious for her own good, a woman who lived and breathed to attract the attentions of men, oversexed, whorish, someone who slept around, an unfaithful wife—too bad that a person with so many other good qualities should have been such a mess. You always suspected your mother's ex-in-laws talked about her in that way, but until this morning you have never heard it with your own ears. You mumble something into the telephone and hang up, vowing never to talk to your cousin again, never to utter a single word to her for the rest of your life. Sleep is out of the question now. In spite of the supernatural exhaustion that has clobbered you into near senselessness, too much has been churned up inside you, your thoughts are sprinting off in myriad directions, adrenaline is surging through

your system again, and your eyes refuse to close. There is nothing
for it but to get out of bed and begin the day. You go downstairs
and prepare a pot of coffee, the strongest, blackest coffee you have
made in years, figuring that if you flood yourself with titanic doses
of caffeine, you will be lifted into something that resembles wakefulness, a partial wakefulness, which will allow you to sleepwalk
through the rest of the morning and on into the afternoon. You
drink the first cup slowly. It is exceedingly hot and must be swallowed in small sips, but then the coffee begins to cool down, and
you drink the second cup more rapidly than the first, the third
more rapidly than the second, and swallow by swallow the liquid
splashes into your empty stomach like acid. You can feel the caffeine accelerating your heart rate, agitating your nerves, and beginning to light you up. You are awake now, fully awake and yet
still weary, drained but ever more alert, and in your head there is
a buzzing that wasn't there before, a low-pitched mechanical
sound, a humming, a whining, as if from a distant, out-of-tune
radio, and the more you drink, the more you feel your body
changing, the less you feel that you are made of flesh and blood.
You are turning into something metallic now, a rusty contraption
that simulates human life, a thing put together with wires and
fuses, vast circuits of wires controlled by random electrical impulses, and now that you have finished the third cup of coffee, you
pour yourself another—which turns out to be the last one, the
lethal one. The attack begins simultaneously from the inside and
the outside, a sudden feeling of pressure from the air around you,
as if an invisible force were trying to push you through the chair
and knock you to the ground, but at the same time an unearthly
lightness in your head, a vertiginous jangle thrumming against the
walls of your skull, and all the while the outside continues to press
in on you, even as the inside grows empty, ever more dark and
empty, as if you are about to pass out. Then your pulse quickens,
you can feel your heart trying to burst through your chest, and a

moment after that there is no more air in your lungs, you can no longer breathe. That is when the panic overwhelms you, when your body shuts down and you fall to the floor. Lying on your back, you feel the blood stop flowing in your veins, and little by little your limbs turn to cement. That is when you start to howl. You are made of stone now, and as you lie there on the dining room floor, rigid, your mouth open, unable to move or think, you howl in terror as you wait for your body to drown in the deep black waters of death.

You couldn't cry. You couldn't grieve in the way people normally do, and so your body broke down and did the grieving for you. If not for the various incidental factors that preceded the onset of panic (your wife's absence, the alcohol, the lack of sleep, your cousin's phone call, the coffee), it is possible the attack never would have taken place. But in the end those elements are of only secondary importance. The question is why you couldn't let yourself go in the minutes and hours that followed your mother's death, why, for two full days, you were unable to shed any tears for her. Was it because a part of you was secretly glad she was dead? A dark thought, a thought so dark and disturbing that it scares you even to express it, but even if you are willing to entertain the possibility that it is true, you doubt that it would account for your failure to cry. You didn't cry after your father's death either. Nor after the deaths of your grandparents, nor after the death of your most beloved cousin, who died of breast cancer when she was thirty-eight, nor after the deaths of the many friends who have left you over the years. Not even at fourteen, when you were less than a foot away from a boy who was struck and killed by lightning, the boy whose dead body you sat next to and watched over for the next hour in a rain-drenched meadow, desperately trying to warm up his body and revive him because you didn't understand he was dead—not even that monstrous death could coax a single tear from you. Your eyes water up when you watch certain movies, you have dropped tears onto the pages of numerous books, you have cried at moments of immense personal sorrow, but death freezes you and shuts you down, robbing you of all emotion, all affect, all connection to your own heart. From the very beginning, you have gone dead in the face of death, and that is what happened to you with your mother's death as well. At least for the first little while, the first two days and nights, but then lightning struck again, and you were scorched.

Forget what your cousin said to you on the phone. You were angry at her, yes, appalled that she would stoop to slinging mud at such an inappropriate time, revolted by her nastiness, her sanctimonious contempt for a person who never did her an ounce of harm, but her accusations of infidelity against your mother were old business to you by then, and even if you had no proof, no evidence to support or deny the charges, you had long suspected that your mother *might* have strayed during her marriage to your father. You were fifty-five years old when you had that conversation with your cousin, and with so much time to have pondered the details of your parents' unfortunate marriage, you in fact hoped that your mother had found some comfort with another man (or men). But nothing was certain, and only once did you have any inkling that something might be amiss, a single moment when you were twelve or thirteen, which thoroughly perplexed you at the time: walking into the house one day after school, thinking no one else was there, picking up the telephone to make a call, and hearing a man's voice on the line, a voice that did not belong to your father, saying no more than *Good-bye*, an altogether neutral word perhaps, but spoken with great tenderness, and then your mother saying back to him, *Good-bye, darling*. That was the end of the conversation. You had no idea what the context was, could not identify the man, had heard almost nothing, and yet you worried about it for days, so much so that you finally found the courage to ask your mother about it, she who had always been honest and direct with you, you felt, who had never refused to answer your questions, but this time, this one time, she looked puzzled when you told her what you had heard, as if she had been caught off guard, and then a moment later she laughed, saying she couldn't remember, she didn't know what you were talking about. It was entirely possible that she didn't remember, that the conversation was of no importance and the endearment had not meant what you thought it had, but a tiny germ of doubt was planted in your head that day, doubt that quickly vanished in the weeks and months that followed, but four or five years later, when your mother announced that she was leaving your father, you couldn't help thinking back to the last sentences of that accidentally overheard conversation. Did any of it matter? No, not that you could think of. Your parents had been destined to split up from the day they were married, and whether your mother had slept with the man she called *darling*, whether there was another man or several men or no man at all, did not play a part in their divorce. Symptoms are not causes, and whatever ugly little thoughts your cousin might have harbored against your mother, she knew nothing about anything. It is undeniable that her call helped to unleash your panic attack—the timing of the call, the circumstances of the call—but what she said to you that morning was stale news.

On the other hand, even though you happened to be her son, you know next to nothing yourself. Too many gaps, too many silences and evasions, too many threads lost over the years for you to stitch together a coherent story. Useless to talk about her from the outside, then. Whatever can be told must be pulled from the inside, from your insides, the accumulation of memories and perceptions you continue to carry around in your body—and which left you, for reasons that will never be entirely known, gasping for breath on the dining room floor, certain you were about to die.

A hasty, ill-considered marriage, an impetuous marriage between two incompatible souls that ran out of steam before the honeymoon was over. A twenty-one-year-old girl from New York (born and bred in Brooklyn, translated to Manhattan at sixteen) and a thirty-four-year-old bachelor from Newark who had begun life in Wisconsin and had left there, fatherless, at the age of seven, when your grandmother shot and killed your grandfather in the kitchen of their house. The bride was the younger of two daughters, the product of yet another ill-considered, mismatched marriage (*Your father would be such a wonderful man—if only he were different*) who had dropped out of high school to work (clerical jobs in offices, later a photographer's assistant) and never told you much about her earlier loves and romances. A vague story about a boyfriend who had died in the war, an even vaguer story about a brief flirtation with actor Steve Cochran, but beyond that nothing at all. She finished up her diploma by going to school at night (Commercial High), but no college afterward, and no college for your father either, who was still a boy when he entered the Land of Work and began supporting himself as soon as he graduated from high school at eighteen. Those are the known facts, the few bits of verifiable information that have been passed down to you. Then come the invisible years, the first three or four years of your life, the blank time before any possibility of recall, and therefore you have nothing to go on but the various stories your mother told you later: your near death at sixteen months from tonsillitis (106° fever, and the doctor telling her: *It's in God's hands now*), the vagaries of your cranky, disobedient stomach, a condition that was diagnosed as an allergy or intolerance to something (wheat?

gluten?) and forced you to subsist for two and a half years on a
diet limited almost exclusively to bananas (so many bananas consumed in that time before memory that you still recoil from the
sight and smell of them and have not eaten one in sixty years), the
jutting nail that tore apart your cheek in the Newark department
store in 1950, your remarkable ability at age three to identify the
make and model of every car on the road (remarkable to your
mother, who read it as a sign of incipient genius), but most of
all the pleasure she communicated to you in the telling of these
stories, the way she seemed to exult in the mere fact of your existence, and because her marriage was such an unhappy one, you
realize now that she turned to you as a form of consolation, to
give her life a meaning and a purpose it was otherwise lacking.
You were the beneficiary of her unhappiness, and you were well
loved, especially well loved, without question deeply loved. That
first of all, that above and beyond everything else there might be
to say: she was an ardent and dedicated mother to you during your
infancy and early childhood, and whatever is good in you now,
whatever strengths you might possess, come from that time before
you can remember who you were.

Some early glimmers, a few small islands of recollection in an
otherwise endless sea of black. Waiting for your newborn sister to
come home from the hospital with your parents (age: three years
and nine months), looking through the slats of the venetian blinds
in the living room with your mother's mother and leaping up and
down when the car finally stopped in front of the house. According to your mother, you were an enthusiastic older brother, not
at all envious of the new baby who had entered your midst, but
she seems to have handled the matter with great intelligence, not
shutting you out but turning you into her *helper*, which gave you
the illusion that you were actively participating in your sister's

care. Some months later, you were asked if you wanted to give nursery school a try. You said yes, not quite sure what nursery school was, since preschools were far less common in 1951 than they are now, but after one day you had had enough. You remember having to line up with a group of other children and pretend you were in a grocery store, and when your turn finally came, after what seemed to have been hours, you handed a pile of pretend money to someone standing behind a pretend cash register, who gave you a bag of pretend food in return. You told your mother that nursery school was an idiotic waste of time, and she didn't try to talk you into going back. Then your family moved to the house on Irving Avenue, and when you started kindergarten the following September, you were ready for school, not the least bit fazed by the prospect of spending time away from your mother. You remember the chaotic prelude to the first morning, the children who ranted and screamed when their mothers said good-bye to them, the anguished cries of the abandoned echoing off the walls as you calmly waved good-bye to your own mother, and all that fuss was incomprehensible to you, since you were happy to be there and felt like a big person now. You were five years old, and already you were pulling away, no longer living exclusively in your mother's orbit. Better health, new friends, the freedom of the yard behind the house, and the beginnings of an autonomous life. You still wet the bed, of course, you still cried when you fell down and cut your knee, but the inner dialogue had begun, and you had crossed into the domain of conscious selfhood. Nevertheless, because of the hours he put in at work, and because of his penchant for taking long naps whenever he was at home, your father was largely absent from the household, and your mother continued to be the central force of authority and wisdom for all things that counted most. She was the one who put you to bed, the one who taught you how to ride a bicycle, the one who helped you with your piano lessons, the one you unburdened yourself to, the rock you clung to whenever the seas grew rough. But you were developing a mind of your own, and you were no longer in thrall to her every pronouncement and opinion. You hated practicing the piano, you wanted to be outside playing with your friends, and when you told her that you would prefer to quit, that baseball was vastly more important to you than music, she relented without putting up much of an argument. Then there was the issue of clothes. You mostly ran around in a T-shirt and a pair of jeans (called dungarees back then), but for special occasions—holidays, birthday parties, the visits to your grandparents in New York—she insisted on dressing you in finely tailored outfits, clothes that began to embarrass you by the time you reached six, especially the white-shirt-and-short-pants combo with the knee socks and sandals, and when you began to protest, claiming that you felt ridiculous in those things, that all you wanted was to look like every other American boy, she eventually gave ground and allowed you to have a say in what you wore. But she was pulling away by then, too, and not long after you turned six, she went off to the Land of Work, and you began seeing less and less of her. You don't remember feeling sad about it, but then again, what do you really know about what you felt? The important thing to keep in mind is that you know next to nothing—and nothing whatsoever about the state of her marriage, the depth of her unhappiness with your father. Years later, she told you that she tried to talk him into moving to California, that she felt there would be no hope for them unless he got away from his family, the suffocating presence of his mother and older brothers, and when he refused to consider it, she resigned herself to a marriage of no hope. The children were too small for her to contemplate divorce (not then, not there, not in middle-class America of the early fifties), and so she found another solution. She was only twenty-eight years old, and work opened the door, let her out of the house, and gave her a chance to build a life of her own.

You don't mean to suggest that she disappeared. She was simply less present than before, far less present, and if most of your memories from that period are confined to the little world of your boyhood pursuits (running around with your friends, riding your bicycle, going to school, playing sports, collecting stamps and baseball cards, reading comic books), your mother appears vividly in several instances, particularly when you were eight and for some reason joined the Cub Scouts with a dozen or so of your friends. You can't remember how often the meetings were held, but you suspect it was once a month, each time in the house of a different member, and these gatherings were run by a rotating squad of three or four women, the so-called den mothers, one of whom was your own mother, which proves that her work as a real estate broker was not so crushing that she couldn't afford to take an occasional afternoon off. You remember how much you enjoyed seeing her in her navy blue den mother's uniform (the absurdity of it, the novelty of it), and you also remember that she was the den mother the boys liked best, for she was the youngest and prettiest of all the mothers, the most entertaining, the most relaxed, the one who had no trouble commanding their complete attention. You can recall two of the meetings she ran with utmost clarity: working on the construction of wooden storage boxes (for what purpose you can no longer say, but everyone applied himself to the task with great diligence), and then, toward the end of the school year, when the weather was warm and the entire gang had grown bored with the rules and regulations of scouthood, there was a last or next-to-last meeting at your house on Irving Avenue, and because no one had the stomach for pretending to act like miniature soldiers anymore, your mother asked the boys how they would like to spend the afternoon, and when the unanimous response was *play baseball*, you all went out into the backyard and picked up sides for a game. Because there were only ten or twelve of you and the teams were shorthanded, your mother decided to play as well. You were immensely pleased, but since you had never seen her swing a bat, you weren't expecting her to do much of anything but strike out. When she came up in the second inning and smacked a ball far over the left fielder's head, you were more than pleased, you were flabbergasted. You can still see your mother running around the bases in her den mother's uniform and coming in to the plate with her home run—out of breath, smiling, soaking up the cheers from the boys. Of all the memories you have retained of her from your childhood, this is the one that comes back to you most often.

She probably wasn't beautiful, not beautiful in the classic sense of the term, but pretty enough, more than attractive enough to make men stare at her whenever she walked into a room. What she lacked in the way of pure good looks, the movie-star looks of certain women who may or may not be movie stars, she made up for by exuding an aura of glamour, especially when she was young, from her late twenties to her early forties, a mysterious combination of carriage, poise, and elegance, the clothes that pointed to but did not overstate the sensuality of the person inside them, the perfume, the makeup, the jewelry, the stylishly coiffed hair, and, above all, the playful look in the eyes, at once forthright and demure, *a look of confidence*, and even if she wasn't the most beautiful woman in the world, she acted as if she were, and a woman who can pull that off will inevitably make heads turn, which was no doubt what caused the dour matrons of your father's family to despise her after she left the fold. Those were difficult years, of course, the stretch of years before the long-deferred but inevitable breakup with your father, the years of *Good-bye, darling* and the car she wrecked one night when you were ten. You can still see her bloodied, banged-up face as she walked into the house early the next morning, and although she never told you much about the accident, only a bland, generic account that must have had little to do with the truth, you suspect that alcohol might have been involved, that there was a short period back then when she was drinking too much, for later on she dropped some hints about having been in A.A., and the fact was that she never drank any alcohol for the rest of her life—not one cocktail or glass of champagne, nothing, not even a sip of beer.

There were three of her, three separate women who seemed unconnected to one another, and as you grew older and began to look at her differently, to see her as someone who was not just your mother, you never knew which mask she would be wearing on any given day. At one end, there was the diva, the sumptuously decked-out charmer who dazzled the world in public, the young woman with the obtuse, distracted husband who craved having the eyes of others upon her and would not allow herself—not anymore—to be boxed into the role of traditional housewife. In the middle, which was far and away the largest space she occupied, there was a solid and responsible being, a person of intelligence and compassion, the woman who took care of you when you were young, the woman who went out to work, who ran several small businesses over the course of many years, the four-star joke teller and crossword-puzzle ace, a person with her feet firmly planted on the ground—competent, generous, observant of the world around her, a devoted liberal in her politics, a sage dispenser of advice. At the other end, the extreme end of who she was, there was the frightened and debilitated neurotic, the helpless creature prey to blistering assaults of anxiety, the phobic whose incapacities grew as the years advanced—from an early fear of heights to a metastatic flowering of multiple forms of paralysis: afraid of escalators, afraid of airplanes, afraid of elevators, afraid to drive a car, afraid of going near windows on the upper floors of buildings, afraid to be alone, afraid of open spaces, afraid to walk anywhere (she felt she would lose her balance or pass out), and an ever-present hypochondria that gradually reached the most exalted summits of dread. In other words: afraid to die, which in the end is probably no different from saying: afraid to live. When you were young, you were not aware of any of this. She seemed perfect to you, and even during her first attack of vertigo, which you happened to witness when you were six (the two of you climbing up the inner staircase of the Statue of Liberty), you were not alarmed, because she was a good and conscientious mother, and she managed to hide her fear from you by turning the descent into a game: sitting on the stairs together and going down one step at a time, asses on the rungs, laughing all the way to the bottom. When she was old, there was no more laughter. Only the void spinning around in her head, the knot in her belly, the cold sweats, a pair of invisible hands tightening around her throat.

Her second marriage was a grand success, the marriage everyone longs for—until it wasn't. You were glad to see her so happy, so clearly in love, and you took to her new husband without hesitation, not only because he was in love with your mother and knew how to love her in all the ways you felt she needed to be loved, but because he was an impressive man in his own right, a labor lawyer with an acute mind and a large personality, someone who seemed to take life by storm, who boomed out old standards at the dinner table and told hilarious stories about his past, who instantly embraced you not as a stepson but as a kind of younger brother, which turned you into close, steadfast friends, and all in all you thought this marriage was the best thing that had ever happened to your mother, the thing that would make everything right for her at last. She was still young, after all, still not forty years old, and because he was two years younger than she was, you had every reason to expect they would have a long life together and die in each other's arms. But your stepfather's health was not good. Strong and vigorous as he seemed, he had been cursed with a bad heart, and after a first coronary in his early thirties, he had his second big attack about a year into the marriage, and from then on there was an element of foreboding that hung over their life together, which only worsened when he suffered a third attack a couple of years later. Your mother lived in constant fear of losing him, and you saw with your own eyes how those fears gradually unhinged her, little by little exacerbating the weaknesses she had struggled for so long to keep hidden, the phobic self that roared into full bloom during their last years together, and when he died at fifty-four, she was no longer the person she had been when they were married. You remember her last heroic stand, the night in Palo Alto, California, when she told jokes nonstop to you and your wife as your stepfather lay in the intensive care unit of the Stanford Medical Center undergoing experimental cardiac treatments. The final, desperate move in a case that had been deemed all but hopeless, and the gruesome sight of your mortally ill stepfather lying in that bed hooked up to so many wires and machines that the room looked like the set from a science fiction film, and when you walked in and saw him there, you were so stunned and miserable that you found yourself fighting back tears. It was the summer of 1981, and you and your wife had known each other for about six months, you were living together but not yet married, and as the two of you stood at your stepfather's bedside, he reached out, took hold of both your hands, and said: "Don't waste any time. Get married now. Get married, take care of each other, and have twelve children." You and your wife were staying with your mother in a house somewhere in Palo Alto, an empty house that had been lent to her by some unknown friend, and that night, after eating dinner in a restaurant, where you nearly broke down again when the waitress came back to tell you that the kitchen had run out of the dish you had ordered (displaced anguish in its most pronounced form—to such a degree that the nonsensical tears you felt gathering in your eyes might be interpreted as the very embodiment of repressed emotions that can no longer be repressed), and once the three of you had returned to the house, the gloom of a house shadowed in death, all of you convinced that these were the last days of your stepfather's life, you sat down at the dining room table to have a drink, and just when you thought it would be impossible for anyone to say another word, when the heaviness in your hearts seemed to have crushed all the words out of you, your mother started telling jokes. One joke and then another joke, then another joke followed by the next joke, jokes so funny that you and your wife laughed until you could hardly breathe anymore, an hour of jokes, two hours of jokes, each one delivered with such crackerjack timing, such crisp, economical language that a moment came when you thought your stomach might burst through your skin. Jewish jokes mostly, an unending torrent of classic yenta routines with all the appropriate voices and accents, the old Jewish women sitting around a card table and sighing, each one sighing in turn, each one sighing more loudly that the last, until one of the women finally says, "I thought we agreed not to talk about the children." You all went a little crazy that night, but the circumstances were so grim and intolerable that you needed to go a little crazy, and somehow your mother managed to find the strength to let that happen. A moment of extraordinary courage, you felt, a sublime instance of who she was at her best—for great as your misery was that night, you knew that it was nothing, absolutely nothing compared to hers.

————

He survived the Stanford Medical Center and went home, but less than a year later he was dead. You believe that was when she died as well. Her heart went on beating for another twenty years, but the death of your stepfather was the end of her, and she never regained her footing after that. Little by little, her grief was transformed into a kind of resentment (*How dare he die on me and leave me alone?*), and while it pained you to hear her talk like that, you understood that she was frightened, searching for a way to hazard the next step and hobble on toward the future. She hated living on her own, was temperamentally not equipped to survive in a vacuum of solitude, and before long she was back in circulation, quite heavy now, many pounds overweight, but still attractive enough to turn the heads of several aging men. She had been living in southern California for over a decade at that point, and you saw each other infrequently, no more than once every six months or so, and what you knew about her was learned mostly through telephone conversations—useful in their way, but you seldom had a chance to observe her in action, and consequently you were both surprised and not surprised when she told you she was planning to get married again after just eighteen months of widowhood. It was a foolish marriage in your opinion, another hasty, ill-considered marriage, not unlike the marriage she made with your father in 1946, but she wasn't looking for a big love anymore so much as a refuge, someone to take care of her as she mended her fragile self. In his quiet, fumbling way, the third husband was devoted to her, which certainly counts for something, but for all his efforts and good intentions, he couldn't take care of her well enough. He was a dull man, an ex-marine and former NASA engineer, conservative in both his politics and his manner, either meek or weak (perhaps both), and therefore a one-hundred-and-eighty-degree turn from your effusive, charismatic, left-liberal stepfather—not a bad or cruel person, simply dull. He now worked as a self-employed inventor (of the struggling variety), but your mother had high hopes for his most recent invention—an intravenous medical device, both tubeless and portable, that would compete with and potentially supplant the traditional IV—and because it looked like a sure thing, she married him on the assumption that they would soon be rolling in money. There is no doubt that it was a clever invention, perhaps even a brilliant one, but the inventor had no head for business. Squeezed between fast-talking venture capitalists and double-talking medical supply firms, he eventually lost control of his own device, and while he walked off with some money in the end, it was hardly enough to roll in—so little, in fact, that within a year most of it was gone. Your mother, who was into her sixties by then, was forced to go back to work. She restarted the interior design business she had shut down some years earlier, and with her inventor husband serving as her office assistant and bookkeeper, she was the one who was supporting them now, or trying to support them, and whenever their bank account was in danger of dipping toward zero, she would call you to ask for help, always tearful, always apologetic, and because you were in a position to give that help, you sent them checks every so often, some large checks, some small checks, about a dozen checks and wire transfers over the next couple of years. You didn't mind sending them the money, but you found it strange, and more than a little disheartening, that her ex-marine had given up on himself so thoroughly that he was no longer able to pull his weight, that the man who was going to provide for her and lead them into the bower of a comfortable old age could not even summon the courage to thank you for your help. Your mother was the boss now, and bit by bit his role as husband was turned into that of faithful butler (breakfast in bed, shopping for groceries), but still they forged on, it wasn't so bad, surely it could have been worse, and even if she was disappointed by the way things had turned out, she also knew that something was better than nothing. Then, one morning in the spring of 1994, just after she had woken up, your mother walked into the bathroom and found her husband lying dead on the floor. Stroke, heart attack, cerebral hemorrhage—it is impossible to say, since no autopsy was ever performed, at least none that you are aware of. When she called your house in Brooklyn later that morning, her voice was filled with horror. Blood, she said to you, blood coming out of his mouth, blood everywhere, and for the first time in all the years you had known her, she sounded deranged.

She decided to move back east. Twenty years earlier, she had thought of California as a promised land, but now it was little more than a place of disease and death, the capital of bad luck and painful memories, and so she bolted across America to be near her family—you and your wife to begin with, but also her mentally ill daughter in Connecticut, her sister, and her two grandchildren. She was flat broke, of course, which meant that you would have to support her, but that was hardly a problem now, and you were more than willing to do it. You bought her a one-bedroom apartment in Verona, leased a car for her, and gave her what you both considered to be an adequate monthly allowance. You were hardly the first son in the world to find himself in this position, but that didn't make it any less strange or uncomfortable: to be taking care of the person who had once taken care of you, to have reached that point in life when your roles were reversed, with you now acting the part of parent while she was reduced to the part of helpless child. The financial arrangement occasionally caused some friction, since your mother found it difficult not to overspend her allowance, and even though you increased the amount several times, it was still difficult for her, which put you in the awkward spot of having to scold her every now and then, and once, when you were probably a bit too harsh with her, she broke down and cried on the telephone, telling you she was a useless old woman and maybe she should kill herself so she wouldn't be such a burden anymore. There was something comical about this gush of self-pity (you knew you were being manipulated), but at the same time it made you feel wretched, and in the end you always caved in and let her have whatever she wanted. More worrisome to you was her inability to do anything, to get out of her apartment and engage herself with the world. You suggested that she volunteer as a reading teacher for struggling children or illiterate adults, get involved with the Democratic Party or some other political organization, take courses, travel, join a social club, but she simply didn't have it in her to try. Until then, the lack of a formal education had never been an impediment to her—her native intelligence and quickness had seemed to make up for any deficiencies—but now that she was without a husband, without work, without anything to keep her occupied from day to day, you wished she could have developed an interest in music or art or books, in anything really, just so long as it was some kind of passionate, sustaining interest, but she had never formed the habit of nurturing inner pursuits of that kind, and therefore she continued to flail around without purpose, never quite sure what to do with herself when she woke up in the morning. The only novels she read were detective stories and thrillers, and even your books and your wife's books, which you both automatically gave her whenever they were published—and which she proudly displayed on a special shelf in her living room—were not the sorts of books she could read. She watched a lot of television. The TV was always on in her apartment, blasting forth from early in the morning until late at night, but it wasn't for watching programs so much as for the voices that came from the box. Those voices comforted her, were in fact necessary to her, and they helped her overcome her fear of living alone—which was probably her single greatest accomplishment of those years. No, they were not the best years, but you don't want to give the impression that it was a time of unbroken melancholy and disarray. She made regular visits to

Connecticut to see your sister, spent countless weekends with you at your house in Brooklyn, saw her granddaughter perform in school plays and sing her solos for the school chorus, followed her grandson's ever-deepening interest in photography, and after all those years in distant California, she was now a part of your life again, always present for birthdays, holidays, and special events—public appearances by you and your wife, the openings of your films (she was mad for the movies), and occasional dinners with your friends. She continued to charm people in public, even into her mid-seventies, for in some small corner of her mind she still saw herself as a star, as the most beautiful woman in the world, and whenever she emerged from her diminished, largely shut-in life, her vanity seemed to be intact. So much of what she had become saddened you now, but you found it impossible not to admire her for that vanity, for still being able to tell a good joke when people were listening.

You scattered her ashes in the woods of Prospect Park. There were five of you present that day—your wife, your daughter, your aunt, your cousin Regina, and yourself—and you chose Prospect Park in Brooklyn because your mother had played there often as a little girl. One by one, you all read poems out loud, and then, as you opened the rectangular metal urn and tossed the ashes onto the fallen leaves and underbrush, your aunt (normally undemonstrative, one of the most reserved people you have ever known) gave in to a fit of tears as she repeated the name of her baby sister over and over again. A week or two later, on a sparkling afternoon in late May, you and your wife took your dog for a walk in the park. You suggested returning to the spot where you had scattered your mother's ashes, but when you were still out on an open path, a good two hundred yards from the edge of the woods, you started feeling faint and dizzy, and even though you were taking pills to keep your new condition under control, you could feel another panic attack coming on. You took hold of your wife's arm, and the two of you turned around and went home. That was nearly nine years ago. You have not tried to go back to those woods since.

Summer 2010. Heat-wave weather, the Dog Star barking from sunup to sundown and on through the nights, a string of ninety-degree days and now, suddenly, all the way up to a hundred and six. It is a minute or two past midnight. Your wife has already gone to bed, but you are too restless for sleep, and so you have gone into the upstairs parlor, the room you both refer to as the library, an ample space with bookshelves lining three of the walls, and because those shelves are full now, crammed with the thousands of hardcovers and paperbacks you and your wife have accumulated over the years, there are piles of books and DVDs on the floor as well, the inevitable spillover that continues to grow as the months and years rush past you, giving the library a cluttered but sympathetic atmosphere of plenitude and well-being, the kind of room all visitors to the house describe as *cozy*, and yes, it is unquestionably your favorite room, with its soft leather couch and flat-screen TV, a perfect place for reading books and watching films, and because of the excruciating weather outside, the air-conditioning is on and the windows are closed, blocking out all sounds from the street, the nighttime medley of barking dogs and human voices, the weird, chubby man who wanders through the neighborhood singing show tunes in a piercing falsetto, the rumble of passing trucks, cars, and motorcycles. You turn on the television. The Mets game ended a couple of hours ago, and with no distraction available to you from the world of sport, you switch to the movie channel you like best, TCM, with its round-the-clock programming of old American films, and a few minutes into the story you have now begun to watch, something important occurs to you.

It begins when you see the man running through the streets of San Francisco, a crazed man charging down the stone steps of the medical center and dashing out into the streets, a man with nowhere to go, running along crowded sidewalks, darting into traffic, bumping into people as he sprints past them, a cannonball of frenzy and disbelief who has just been told he will be dead within days, if not hours, that his body has been contaminated by a *luminous toxin*, and because it is too late to flush the poison from his system, there is no hope for him, and even if he still appears to be alive, he is in fact already dead, he has in fact been murdered.

You have been that man, you tell yourself, and what you are watching on the television screen is a precise rendering of what happened to you two days after your mother's death in 2002: the hammer that descends without warning, and then the inability to breathe, the pounding heart, the dizziness, the sweats, the body that falls to the floor, the arms and legs that turn to stone, the howls that blast forth from maddened, airless lungs, and the certainty that the end is upon you, that one second from now the world will no longer exist, because you will no longer exist.

Directed by Rudolph Maté in 1950, the film is called *D.O.A.*, police shorthand for *dead on arrival*, and the hero-victim is one Frank Bigelow, a man of no particular distinction or interest, a no one, an anyone, roughly thirty-five years old, an accountant, auditor, and notary public who lives in Banning, California, a small desert town near Palm Springs. Bulky of build, with a fleshy, full-lipped face, he is a man with little else on his mind but women, and because he is feeling suffocated by his adoring, neurotic, obsessively clinging secretary, Paula, the woman he might or might not be planning to marry, he impulsively decides to take a week off from work and go to San Francisco on a solo vacation. When he checks in at the St. Francis Hotel, the lobby is swarming with boisterous guests. It happens to be "market week," the desk clerk tells him, an annual convention of traveling salesmen, and each time an attractive woman saunters past (all the women in the hotel are attractive), Bigelow turns to ogle her with the wide-eyed, slack-jawed lust of a man on the prowl. To push home the point, each of these glances is accompanied by a comic, slide-whistle rendition of the standard two-note wolf call, as if to suggest that Bigelow can't quite believe his good luck, that by landing in this particular hotel on this particular day he will in all likelihood chance upon some easy action. When he goes up to his room on the sixth floor, the hallway is hopping with semi-inebriated revelers (more slide-whistle wolf calls) and the door of the room directly opposite is open, giving Bigelow a clear view of a full-scale bash in progress. So the vacation begins.

Paula has telephoned from Banning, and before Bigelow un-packs and settles in, he returns the call. It seems there has been an urgent message from someone named Eugene Philips of Los An-geles, who said it was imperative that Bigelow contact him *at once*, that they must talk *before it's too late*. Bigelow has no idea who Phil-ips is. Have we done business with him? he asks Paula, but she has no memory of such a person either. All during this conversation, Bigelow is distracted by the goings-on across the hall. Women stop in his open doorway to wave hello and smile at him, and he waves and smiles back, even as he goes on talking to Paula. Forget about Philips, he tells her. He's on vacation now, he doesn't want to be bothered, and he'll deal with it when he returns to Banning.

After they hang up, Bigelow lights a cigarette, a waiter appears with a drink, and then a reveler from across the hall, who identi-fies himself as Haskell, enters the room and asks if he can use the phone. Three more bottles of bourbon and two more bottles of scotch are ordered for the party in 617. When Haskell learns that Bigelow is a stranger in town, he invites him to join in the merri-ment (*a few drinks, a few laughs*), and within two minutes Bigelow is dancing a rumba with Haskell's wife in the noisy room across the way. Sue is a brash, boozed-up piece of work, a frustrated woman looking for a good time, and because Bigelow turns out to be a skillful dancer, he becomes her number one target—not the most intelligent move, perhaps, given that her husband is right there to witness her antics, but Sue is both reckless and determined. Some minutes later, the gang from room 617 decides to leave the hotel and go out on the town. A reluctant Bigelow is dragged along with them, and suddenly they are in a crowded jazz club called the Fisherman, a frenetic place where an ensemble of black musicians is belting out an exultant, high-speed number with the word JIVE written on the wall behind them. One close-up after another shows the sax man, the piano man, the trumpet man, the bass man, and the drum man wailing on their instruments, intercut with wild reactions from the audience, and there is Bigelow sitting at the table with his new friends as the impetuous Sue clings tightly to him. Bigelow looks despondent, he is fed up, he wants no part of Sue or this cacophonous assault, and Haskell looks no less downhearted himself, studying his wife in silence as she throws herself at the stranger from across the hall. At some point in all this, the camera catches a man entering the club from behind, a tall man wearing a hat and an overcoat with an upturned collar, an odd and altogether curious collar, the reverse of which is marked by a black-and-white checkered pattern. The man approaches the bar, and a moment or two after that Bigelow finally manages to extricate himself from Sue and her companions. He goes to the bar as well and orders himself a bourbon, little knowing that the man with the curious collar is about to slip poison into his drink and that he, Bigelow, will be dead within twenty-four hours.

A stylish woman is sitting at the other end of the bar, and as Bigelow waits for his drink, he asks the bartender if the blonde is alone. The blonde turns out to be Jeanie, a *jive-crazy* rich girl who hangs out in clubs and uses words like *dig* and *easy* (i.e., copacetic, swell, no problem). Bigelow sidles over to her, and in those few seconds when he loses contact with his drink, which has now been poured and is waiting for him at his old spot at the other end of the bar, the man with the curious collar carries out his murderous mission, deftly pouring a measure of the toxic potion into the glass and then vanishing from sight. As Bigelow chats with the elegant Jeanie, who is at once cool and friendly, a self-possessed hipster queen, the bartender hands him his now doctored drink, his now deadly drink. Bigelow takes a sip, and instantly his face registers surprise, disgust. A second sip produces the same result. Pushing away the glass, he says to the bartender: "This isn't mine. I ordered bourbon. Give me another drink."

Meanwhile, Sue is on her feet, scanning the room for Bigelow, looking anxious, distraught, puzzled by his failure to return. Bigelow catches sight of her, then swings around and invites Jeanie to go somewhere else with him. There are people he wants to avoid, he says, and surely there must be other interesting places in San Francisco. Yes, Jeanie says, but she hasn't quite had her fill of the Fisherman. Why don't they meet up later when she hits her next spot of the evening, and then she writes down a telephone number on a piece of paper and tells him to call her there in an hour.

Bigelow returns to his hotel room, pulls out the scrap of paper with Jeanie's number on it, and picks up the phone, but before he can make the call, he glances up and sees that a bouquet of flowers has been delivered to the room. There is a card from Paula attached to the wrapping paper, and the message reads: *I'll keep a light burning in the window. Sweet dreams.* Bigelow is chastened. Instead of going out again to spend the night chasing skirts, he tears up Jeanie's number and tosses it in the trash, and a moment after that the story enters a different register, the real story begins.

The poison has already begun to do its work. Bigelow's head aches, but he assumes he has drunk too much and will feel better after he has slept it off. He climbs into bed, and as he does so the air fills with strange, disjointed sounds, the echoing voice of a distant female singer, mental debris from the jazz club, signs of mounting physical distress. When he wakes in the morning, Bigelow's condition has not improved. Still convinced that he drank too much and is suffering from a hangover, he calls room service and orders a pick-me-up, one of those tart, eye-opening nostrums spiced with horseradish and Worcestershire sauce that are supposed to jolt you into instant sobriety, but once the waiter shows up with the concoction, Bigelow can't face it, the mere sight of the drink fills him with nausea, and he asks the waiter to take it away. Something is seriously wrong. Bigelow clutches his stomach, appears dizzy and disoriented, and when the waiter asks if he is all right, the fatally ill victim-hero, still in the dark about what has befallen him, says he must have had too big a night of it and needs to get some fresh air.

Bigelow goes out, staggering ever so slightly, mopping his forehead with a handkerchief, and climbs onto a passing cable car. He jumps off at Nob Hill, and then he is walking, walking through deserted streets in broad daylight, walking with purpose, on his way somewhere—but what where and to what purpose?—until he finds the address he is looking for, a tall white structure with the words MEDICAL BUILDING chiseled into the stone façade. Bigelow is far more worried than he let on to the waiter at the hotel. He knows, indeed he knows, that something is seriously wrong with him.

At first, the results of the examination are encouraging. Looking at Bigelow's X-ray, a doctor says: "Lungs in good condition, blood pressure normal, heart fine. It's a good thing everybody isn't like you. It would put us doctors out of business." He instructs Bigelow to put on his clothes as they wait for the results of the blood tests administered by his colleague, Dr. Schaefer. As Bigelow knots his tie in the foreground, face to the camera, expressionless, a nurse walks into the room behind him, too addled to say a word, staring at him with a look that combines both horror and pity, and at that moment there can be no doubt that Bigelow is doomed. Dr. Schaefer enters, trying to mask his alarm. He and the first doctor confirm that Bigelow is unmarried, that he has no relatives in San Francisco, that he has come to the city alone. Why these questions? Bigelow asks. You're a very sick man, the doctor says. *You must steel yourself for a shock.* And then they tell him about the luminous toxic matter that has entered his system and will soon be attacking his vital organs. They wish there was something they could do, they say, but there is no antidote for this particular poison. He doesn't have long.

Bigelow is incredulous, filled with rage. This is impossible! he shouts. They must be wrong, there must be an error, but the doctors calmly defend their diagnosis, assuring him that there hasn't been an error—which only increases Bigelow's fury. "You're telling me I'm dead!" he roars. "I don't even know who you are! Why should I believe you?" Calling them both crazy, he pushes them aside and storms out of the office.

Cut to an even larger building—a hospital? another medical center?—and a shot of Bigelow bounding up the front steps. He barges into a room marked EMERGENCY, apoplectic, a man about to explode into a hundred fragments, and shoves his way past two bewildered and frightened nurses, insisting that he see a doctor at once, demanding that someone examine him for luminous poison.

The new doctor comes to the same conclusion as the first pair. *You've got it, all right. Your system has already absorbed it.* To prove the point, he switches off the overhead light and shows Bigelow the test tube containing the examination results. It is an eerie sight. The thing glows in the dark—as if the doctor were holding a vial of incandescent milk, a frosted bulb filled with radium, or worse, the liquefied fallout from a nuclear bomb. Bigelow's anger subsides. Faced with such overpowering evidence, he temporarily goes numb. "But I don't feel sick," he says quietly. "Just a little stomach ache, that's all."

The doctor warns him not to be fooled by his apparent lack of symptoms. Bigelow has no more than a day or two to live, a week at the most. *There's nothing that can be done now.* Then the doctor learns that Bigelow has no idea how, when, or where he swallowed the poison, which means that it was administered by another party, an unknown party, which further means that someone intentionally set out to kill him.

"This is a case for Homicide," the doctor says, reaching for the telephone.

"Homicide?"

"I don't think you understand, Bigelow. You've been murdered."

This is the moment when Bigelow snaps, when the monstrous thing that has happened to him turns into an all-out, unbridled panic, when the howl of agony begins. He bursts out of the doctor's office, bursts out of the building, and starts running through the streets, and as you follow this passage of the film, this long sequence of shots tracking Bigelow's mad fugue through the city, you understand that you are witnessing the outer manifestation of an inner state, that this senseless, headlong, unstoppable running is nothing less than the depiction of a mind filled with horror, that you are watching the choreography of dread. A panic attack has been translated into a breathless sprint through the streets of a city, for panic is nothing if not an expression of mental flight, the unbidden force that grows inside you when you are trapped, when the truth is too much to bear, when the injustice of this unavoidable truth can no longer be confronted, and therefore the only possible response is to flee, to shut down your mind by transforming yourself into a gasping, twitching, delirious body, and what truth could be more terrible than this one? Condemned to death within hours or days, cut down in the middle of your life for reasons that entirely escape your understanding, your life suddenly reduced to a thimbleful of minutes, seconds, heartbeats.

It doesn't matter what happens next. You watch the second half of the film attentively, but you know the story is over, that even as the story continues, there is nothing left to say. Bigelow will spend his last hours on earth trying to solve the mystery of his murder. He will learn that Philips, the man who called his office from Los Angeles, is dead. He will go to Los Angeles and investigate the activities of various thieves, psychopaths, and two-faced women. He will be shot at and punched. He will learn that his involvement in the story is purely accidental, that the villains want him dead because he happened to notarize a bill of sale pertaining to a stolen shipment of iridium and he is the only man alive who can identify the culprits. He will track down his murderer, the man with the curious collar, who is also the murderer of Philips, and kill him in a shoot-out on the landing of a darkened stairway. And then, shortly after that, Bigelow himself will die, just as the doctors said he would—in mid-sentence, telling his story to the police.

There is nothing wrong with playing it out like this, you suppose. It is the conventional thing to do, the manly, heroic option, the trope that befits all adventure stories, but why, you wonder, does Bigelow never divulge his imminent fate to anyone, not even to his doting, lovesick Paula? Perhaps because heroes must remain tough until the bitter end, and even when time is running out, they can't allow themselves to get bogged down in useless sentiment.

But you aren't tough anymore, are you? Ever since the panic attack of 2002, you have stopped being tough, and even though you work hard at trying to be a decent person, it has been a long time now since you last thought of yourself as heroic. If you ever found yourself in Bigelow's shoes, you are certain you would never do what Bigelow did. You would run through the streets, yes, you would run until you could no longer take another step, no longer breathe, no longer stand up, and then what? Call Paula, call Paula the instant you stopped running, but if her number happened to be busy when you called, then what? Prostrate yourself on the ground and weep, cursing the world for allowing you to have been born. Or else, quite simply, crawl off into a hole somewhere and wait to die.

You can't see yourself. You know what you look like because of mirrors and photographs, but out there in the world, as you move among your fellow human beings, whether friends or strangers or the most intimate beloveds, your own face is invisible to you. You can see other parts of yourself, arms and legs, hands and feet, shoulders and torso, but only from the front, nothing of the back except the backs of your legs if you twist them into the right position, but not your face, never your face, and in the end—at least as far as others are concerned—your face is who you are, the essential fact of your identity. Passports do not contain pictures of hands and feet. Even you, who have lived inside your body for sixty-four years now, would probably be unable to recognize your foot in an isolated photograph of that foot, not to speak of your ear, or your elbow, or one of your eyes in close-up. All so familiar to you in the context of the whole, but utterly anonymous when taken piece by piece. We are all aliens to ourselves, and if we have any sense of who we are, it is only because we live inside the eyes of others. Think of what happened to you when you were fourteen. For two weeks at the end of the summer, you worked for your father in Jersey City, joining one of the small crews that repaired and maintained the apartment buildings he and his brothers owned and managed: painting walls and ceilings, mending roofs, hammering nails into two-by-fours, pulling up sheets of cracked linoleum. The two men you worked with were black, every tenant in every apartment was black, every person in the neighborhood was black, and after two weeks of looking at nothing but black faces, you began to forget that your own face wasn't black. Since you couldn't see your own face, you saw yourself in the faces of the people around you, and bit by bit you stopped thinking of yourself as different. In effect, you stopped thinking about yourself at all.

Looking at your right hand as it grips the black fountain pen you are using to write this journal, you think of Keats looking at his own right hand under similar circumstances, in the act of writing one of his last poems and suddenly breaking off to scribble eight lines in the margin of the manuscript, the bitter outcry of a young man who knew he was headed for an early grave, darkly underscored by the word *now* in the first line, for every *now* necessarily implies a *later*, and what *later* could Keats look forward to but the prospect of his own death?

> *This living hand, now warm and capable*
> *Of earnest grasping, would, if it were cold*
> *And in the icy silence of the tomb,*
> *So haunt thy days and chill thy dreaming nights*
> *That thou would wish thine own heart dry of blood*
> *So in my veins red life might stream again,*
> *And thou be conscience-calm'd—see here it is—*
> *I hold it toward you.*

Keats to begin with, but no sooner do you think of *This living hand* than you are reminded of a story someone once told you about James Joyce, Joyce in Paris in the 1920s, standing around at a party eighty-five years ago when a woman walked up to him and asked if she could shake the hand that wrote *Ulysses*. Instead of offering her his right hand, Joyce lifted it in the air, studied it for a few moments, and said: "Let me remind you, madam, that this hand has done many other things as well." No details given, but what a delicious piece of smut and innuendo, all the more effective because he left everything to the woman's imagination. What did he want her to see? Wiping his ass, probably, picking his nose, masturbating in bed at night, sticking his fingers into Nora's cunt and diddling her bunghole, popping pimples, scraping food from his teeth, plucking out nostril hairs, disgorging wax from his ears—fill in the appropriate blanks, the central point being: whatever was most disgusting to her. Your hands have served you in similar ways, of course, everyone's hands have done those things, but mostly they are busy performing tasks that require little or no thought. Opening and closing doors, screwing light bulbs into sockets, dialing telephones, washing dishes, turning the pages of books, holding your pen, brushing your teeth, drying your hair, folding towels, taking money out of your wallet, carrying bags of groceries, swiping your MetroCard in subway turnstiles, pushing buttons on machines, picking up the newspaper from the front steps in the morning, turning down the covers of the bed, showing your ticket to the train conductor, flushing the toilet, lighting your little cigars, stubbing out your little cigars in ashtrays, putting on your pants, taking off your pants, tying your shoes, squirting shaving cream onto the tips of your fingers, clapping at plays and concerts, sliding keys into locks, scratching your face, scratching your arm, scratching your ass, wheeling suitcases through airports, unpacking suitcases, putting your shirts on hangers, zipping up your fly, buckling your belt, buttoning your jacket, knotting your tie, drumming your fingers on tables, loading paper into your fax machine, tearing checks out of your checkbook, opening up boxes of tea, switching on lights, switching off lights, plumping up your pillow before going to bed. Those same hands have sometimes punched people (as previously noted), and three or four times, in moments of intense frustration, they have also punched walls.

They have thrown plates onto the floor, dropped plates onto the floor, and picked up plates from the floor. Your right hand has shaken more hands than you could possibly count, has blown your nose, wiped your ass, and waved good-bye more often than the number of words in the largest dictionary. Your hands have held the bodies of your children, have wiped the asses and blown the noses of your children, have bathed your children, rubbed the backs of your children, dried the tears of your children, and stroked the faces of your children. They have patted the shoulders of friends, work comrades, and relatives. They have pushed and shoved, pulled people off the ground, gripped the arms of people who were about to fall, navigated the wheelchairs of those who could not walk. They have touched the bodies of clothed and naked women. They have moved down the length of your wife's naked skin and found their way onto every part of her. They are happiest there, you feel, have always been happiest there since the day you met her, for, to paraphrase a line from one of George Oppen's poems, some of the most beautiful places in the world are on your wife's body.

The day after the car crash in 2002, you went to the junkyard where the car had been towed to retrieve your daughter's belongings. It was a Sunday morning in August, warm as always, with a misty blur of rain dappling the streets as one of your friends drove you out to some godforsaken neighborhood in Brooklyn, a no-man's-land of crumbling warehouses, vacant lots, and boarded-up wooden buildings. The junkyard was run by a black man in his mid-sixties, a smallish fellow with long dreadlocks and clear, steady eyes, a gentle Rasta man who watched over his domain of wrecked automobiles like a shepherd tending a flock of dozing sheep. You told him why you were there, and when he led you over to the shiny new Toyota you had been driving the day before, you were stunned by how thoroughly destroyed it was, could not fathom how you and your family had managed to survive such a catastrophe. Immediately after the crash, you had noticed how badly damaged the car was, but you had been rattled by the collision, were not fully able to absorb what had happened to you, but now, a day later, you could see that the metal body of the car was so smashed in, it looked like a piece of crumpled paper. "Look at that," you said to the Rasta man. "We should all be dead now." He studied the car for a few seconds, looked you in the eye, and then turned his head upward as the fine rain fell onto his face and abundant hair. "An angel was watching over you," he said in a quiet voice. "You were supposed to die yesterday, but then an angel stretched out his hand and pulled you back into the world." He delivered those words with such serenity and conviction, you almost believed him.

When you sleep, you sleep soundly, seldom stirring until it is time to wake up in the morning. The problem you occasionally run into, however, is a reluctance to go to bed in the first place, a late-night surge of energy that prevents you from wanting to call it quits until you have polished off another chapter of the book you are reading, or watched a film on television, or, if it is baseball season and the Mets or the Yankees are playing on the West Coast, tuned in the broadcast from San Francisco, Oakland, or Los Angeles. Afterward, you crawl into bed beside your wife, and within ten minutes you are dead to the world until morning. Nevertheless, every now and then, something will interfere with your normally profound slumbers. If you accidentally wind up on your back, for example, you might begin to snore, in all likelihood you will begin to snore, and if the noise you produce is loud enough to wake your wife, she will softly urge you to roll over, and if that benign tactic should fail, she will give you a shove, or shake your shoulder, or

510 | PAUL AUSTER

pinch your ear. Nine times out of ten, you will unconsciously do
what she commands, and she will quickly fall back to sleep. The
other ten percent of the time, her shove will wake you up, and
because you don't want to trouble her sleep any further, you will
go down the hall to the library and stretch out on the sofa, which
is long enough to accommodate your fully extended body. More
often than not, you manage to fall back asleep on the sofa—but
sometimes you don't. Over the years, your sleep has also been
broken by flies and mosquitoes buzzing in the room (the perils
of summer), inadvertent punches in the face from your wife, who
tends to fling out her arms when she rolls over in bed, and once,
just once, you were rousted from your dreams when your wife
started singing in the middle of one of her own dreams—belting
out the lyrics of a song from a movie she had seen as a child, your
brilliant, erudite, supremely sophisticated wife returning to her
Midwestern childhood with a splendid, full-voiced rendition of
"Supercalifragilisticexpialidocious" as sung by Julie Andrews in
Mary Poppins. One of the rare instances when the eight-year difference in your ages has ever been apparent to you, since you were
too old for that film when it came out and therefore (mercifully)
have never seen it.

But what to do when it is the middle of the night, when you have
woken up sometime between two and four in the morning, have
stretched out on the sofa in the library, and are unable to go back
to sleep? It is too late to read, too late to turn on the television,
too late to watch a film, and so you lie in the dark and ruminate,
letting your thoughts go wherever they choose to go. Sometimes
you get lucky and are able to latch on to a word, or a character, or
a scene from the book you are working on, but more often you
will discover yourself thinking about the past, and in your experience, whenever your thoughts turn to the past at three o'clock in

the morning, those thoughts tend to be dark. One memory haunts you above all others, and on nights when you are unable to sleep, you find it difficult not to go back to it, to rehash the events of that day and relive the shame you felt afterward, have continued to feel ever since. It was thirty-two years ago, the morning of your father's funeral, and at some point you found yourself standing next to one of your uncles (the father of the cousin who called you on the morning of your panic attack), the two of you shaking hands with a line of mourners who shuffled past you as they offered their condolences, the ritual handshakes and empty words that punctuate every funeral service. Family members mostly, friends of your father's, men and women, faces you recognized and didn't recognize, and then you were shaking hands with Tom, one of the faces you didn't recognize, who told you he had been your father's chief electrician for many years and that your father had always treated him well, he was a good man, he said, this small Irishman with his Jersey City accent was telling you that your father was a good man, and you thanked him for that, you shook his hand again for that, and then he moved on to shake your uncle's hand, and when your uncle saw him, he immediately told Tom to leave, this was a private family funeral, he said, no outsiders were allowed, and when Tom mumbled that he only wanted to pay his respects, your uncle said sorry, he would have to leave, and so Tom turned around and left. Their conversation lasted no more than fifteen or twenty seconds, and you barely registered what was happening before Tom was on his way out. When you finally realized what your uncle had done, you were filled with disgust, appalled that he could have treated a person like that, any person, but especially this person, who was there only because he felt it was his duty to be there, and what still galls you today, what still floods you with shame, is that you said nothing to your uncle. Never mind that he was a man with a notorious temper, a hothead given to explosive rages and monumental shouting fits, and that if you had confronted him then, there was every chance he would have turned on you in the middle of your father's funeral. But so what? You should have confronted him, you should have had the courage to shout back at him if he had started shouting at you, and if not that, then why at least didn't you run after Tom and tell him he could stay? You have no idea why you didn't take a stand at that moment, and the shock of your father's sudden death is no excuse. You should have acted, and you didn't. All your life, you had been sticking up for people who had been pushed around, it was the one principle you believed in above all others, but on that particular day you held your tongue and did nothing. When you look back on it now, you understand that this failure to act is the reason why you have stopped thinking of yourself as heroic: because there was no excuse.

Nine years earlier (1970), while serving on the crew of the S.S. *Esso Florence*, you threatened to punch and even kill one of your shipmates for baiting you with anti-Semitic insults. You grabbed hold of his shirt, slammed him into a wall, and brought your right fist up against his face, telling him to stop calling you names or else. Martinez backed down immediately, apologized, and before long you became good friends. (Shades of Madame Rubinstein.) Nine years later, meaning nine years after your father's funeral (1988), you almost punched someone again, which was the last time you came close to engaging in a fight similar to the ones you fought as a boy. It was in Paris, and you remember the date well: September first, a special day on the French calendar, *la rentrée*, the official end of the summer holiday season, and therefore a day of crowds and inordinate confusion. For six weeks prior to that, you and your wife and children had been staying at your French publisher's house in the south, about fifteen kilometers east of Arles. It had been a restful time for all of you, a month and a half of quiet and work, of long walks and rambling excursions through the white hills of the Alpilles, of outdoor dinners under the plane tree in the yard, probably the most enjoyable summer of your life, with the added pleasure of seeing your one-year-old daughter take her first tottering steps without holding on to her parents' hands. You must not have been thinking clearly when you scheduled your return to Paris on September first, or perhaps you simply didn't understand what would be waiting for you when you got there. You had already put your eleven-year-old son on a plane back to New York (a direct flight from Nice), and so there were just three of you traveling north on the train that day, you and your wife and small daughter, along with a summer's worth of baggage and half a ton of baby supplies. You were looking forward to arriving in Paris, however, since your publisher had told you that an extensive article about your work would be appearing in that afternoon's *Le Monde*, and you wanted to buy a copy of the paper as soon as you climbed off the train. (You no longer read articles about yourself, no longer read reviews of your books, but this was then, and you still hadn't learned that ignoring what people say about you is beneficial to a writer's mental health.) The trip by T.G.V. from Avignon was a bit frazzling, largely because your daughter was too impressed by the high-speed train to sit still or sleep, which meant that you spent most of the three hours walking up and down the aisles of the cars with her, and by the time you pulled into the Gare de Lyon, you were ready for a nap. The station was mobbed with people, large masses of travelers surging forth in all directions, and you had to jostle and fight your way to the exit, your wife carrying the baby in her arms and you doing your best to push and pull the family's three large suitcases—not the easiest task, given that you had only two hands. In addition, there was a canvas bag slung over your shoulder, which held the first seventy-five pages of your novel in progress, and when you stopped to buy a copy of *Le Monde*, you slipped it into the bag as well. You wanted to read the article, of course, but after check-ing to see that it had indeed been printed in that afternoon's edi-tion, you put it away, assuming you could take a closer look at it while you were waiting in line for a taxi. Once the three of you made it through the exit door, however, you discovered that there was no line. There were taxis in front of the station, there were people waiting for those taxis, but there was no line. The crowd was immense, and unlike the English, who are in the habit of queuing up whenever more than three of them are present and who then stand there patiently until it is their turn, or even the Americans, who go about it more sloppily but always with an in-nate sense of justice and fair play, the French turn into fractious children whenever there are too many of them gathered in a con-fined space, and rather than collectively try to impose some order on the situation, it suddenly becomes every man for himself. The pandemonium in front of the Gare de Lyon that day reminded you of certain news clips you have seen of the New York Stock Exchange: Black Tuesday, Black Friday, the international markets are crashing, the world is in ruins, and there, on the floor of the exchange, a thousand frantic men are screaming their lungs out, each one about to drop dead of a heart attack. Such was the crowd you had joined that September first twenty-two and a half years ago: the rabble were on the loose and no one was in charge, and there you were, no more than a stone's throw from where the Bas-tille had once stood, stormed two centuries earlier by a mob no less unruly than this one, but revolution wasn't in the air just now, what the people wanted wasn't bread or freedom but *taxis*, and since the taxi supply was less than a fiftieth of what it should have been, the people were fuming, the people were shouting, the people were ready to tear one another apart. Your wife was calm, you remember, amused by the spectacle unfolding around her, and even your little daughter was calm, taking in everything with her big, curious eyes, but you were becoming aggravated, you have always been at your worst when traveling, edgy and irritable and never quite yourself, and more than anything you hate being trapped in the chaos of crowds, and therefore, as you sized up the predicament you had fallen into, you concluded that the three of you would have to wait there for a good hour or two before finding a cab, perhaps six hours, perhaps a hundred hours, and so you said to your wife that maybe it wouldn't be a bad idea to look for a taxi somewhere else. You pointed to another taxi stand down the hill, a few hundred yards away. "But what about the bags?" she said. "You'll never be able to carry three heavy bags all the way over there." "Don't worry," you said. "I can handle it." Of course you couldn't handle it, or could just barely handle it, and after lugging those monsters for just twenty or thirty yards, you understood that you had vastly overestimated your own strength, but at that point it would have been foolish to turn back, and so you kept on going, pausing every ten seconds to reorganize the load, switching the two bags and the one bag from your left arm to your right arm, from your right arm to your left arm, sometimes putting one of them on your back and carrying the other two with your hands, continually shifting the weight, which must have totaled about a hundred pounds, and naturally enough you were starting to sweat, your pores were gushing in the heat of the afternoon sun, and by the time you made it to the next taxi stand, you were thoroughly exhausted. "You see," you said to your wife, "I told you I could do it." She smiled at you in the way one smiles at an imbecilic ten-year-old, for the truth was, even though you had made it to the next taxi stand, there were no taxis waiting there, since every driver in the city was headed for the Gare de Lyon. Nothing to be done now except hang around and hope that one of them would eventually come your way. The minutes passed, your body started cooling down to more or less its normal temperature, and then, just as an approaching taxi came into view, you and your wife saw a woman walking in your direction, a young, extremely tall

African woman dressed in colorful African clothes and walking with perfectly erect posture, a small baby sleeping in a sling that was wrapped around her chest, a heavy bag of groceries hanging from her right hand, another heavy bag hanging from her left hand, and a third bag of groceries balanced on the top of her head. You were looking at a vision of human grace, you realized, the slow, fluid motion of her swaying hips, the slow, fluid motion of her walk, a woman bearing her burdens with what appeared to you as a kind of wisdom, the weight of each thing evenly distributed, her neck and head utterly still, her arms utterly still, the baby asleep on her chest, and after your embarrassing display of ineptitude as you hauled your own family's bags to this spot, you felt ridiculous in her presence, awed that a fellow human being could have mastered so well the very thing you yourself could not do. She was still walking toward you when the taxi pulled up and came to a stop. Relieved and happy now, you loaded the suitcases into the trunk and then slid into the backseat beside your wife and daughter. "Where to?" the driver asked, and when you told him where you were going, he shook his head and told you to get out of the cab. At first you didn't understand. "What are you talking about?" you said. "I'm talking about the trip," he replied. "It's too short, and I'm not going to waste my time on a measly fare like that." "Don't worry," you said. "I'll give you a good tip." "I don't care about your tip," he said. "I just want you out of the cab— now." "Are you blind?" you said. "We have a baby and a hundred pounds of luggage. What do you expect us to do—walk?" "That's your problem, not mine," he answered. "Out." There was nothing left to say to him. If the bastard in the front seat wouldn't take you to the address you had given him, what choice did you have but to get out of the taxi, unload your bags from the trunk, and wait for another cab? You were seething with anger by then, as angry and frustrated as you had been in years, no, more angry, more frustrated, more outraged than at any time you could remember, and when you had removed the bags from the trunk and the taxi man had started to drive away, you took the canvas bag that was slung over your shoulder, the bag that contained the only copy of the manuscript you were working on, not to mention the article in *Le Monde* that you were so anxious to read, and hurled it in the direction of the departing taxi. It landed with a great thud on the trunk of the car—a deeply satisfying thud that carried all the force of an exclamation mark set in fifty-point type. The driver slammed on the brakes, got out of the taxi, and began walking toward you with clenched fists, shouting at you for having attacked his precious vehicle, itching for a fight. You clenched your own fists and shouted back, warning him not to take another step toward you, or else you would dismantle him piece by piece and kick his sorry ass into the gutter. When you spoke those words, you had no doubt that you were prepared to tangle with him, that nothing was going to stop you from carrying out your promise to destroy this man, and when he looked into your eyes and saw that you meant what you were saying, he turned around, climbed into his cab, and drove off. You went out into the street to fetch your bag, and just then, as you bent down to pick it up, you saw the young African woman walking down the sidewalk with her baby and her three heavy bundles, well past you now, perhaps ten or twenty feet beyond where you were standing, and as you watched her move into the distance, you studied her slow and even gait, marveling at the stillness of her body, understanding that beyond the gentle swaying of her hips, not one part of her was moving except her legs.

One broken bone. Considering the thousands of games you took part in as a boy, you are surprised that there weren't others, at least several others. Twisted ankles, bruised thighs, sprained wrists, tender knees, sore elbows, shin splints, clunks on the head, but only one broken bone, your left shoulder, incurred during a football game when you were fourteen, which has prevented you from fully raising your arm for the past fifty years, but nothing of any great consequence, and you probably wouldn't bother to mention it now if not for the role your mother played in the story, which makes it her story in the end and not the story of how you, as the quarterback of your ninth-grade team, went diving for a fumbled ball in the backfield and wound up breaking your shoulder all by yourself, with no help from any of the players on the other team, leaping too far in your eagerness to recover the ball and landing in the wrong spot, on the wrong spot, and thereby breaking your bone when you crashed onto the hard ground. It was a frigid afternoon in late November, a game without referees or adult supervision, and after you hurt yourself you stood on the sideline and watched the rest of the game, disappointed that you couldn't play anymore, not yet understanding that your bone was broken but realizing that the injury was a bad one because you could no longer move your arm without feeling acute pain. Afterward, you hitchhiked back to your house with one of your friends, both of you still in your football uniforms, and you remember how difficult it was for you to remove your jersey and shoulder pads, so difficult in fact that you couldn't do it without your friend's help. It was a Saturday, and the house was empty. Your sister was off somewhere with friends, your father was at work, and your mother was at work as well, since Saturday was always a busy day for showing houses to prospective buyers. About two minutes after your friend helped you take off your shoulder pads, the telephone rang, and your friend went to answer it because you were finding it hard to move now without increasing the pain. It was your mother, and the first thing she said to your friend was: "Is Paul all right?" "Well," he answered, "not so good, actually. He seems to have hurt his arm." And then your mother said: "I knew it. That's why I called—because I've been worried." She told your friend that she was coming straight home and hung up. Later on, when she was driving you to the doctor for X-rays, she told you that a feeling had come over her that afternoon, a strange feeling that something had happened to you, and when you asked her when she had felt this feeling, it turned out that she had started worrying about you at the precise moment when you were diving onto the ground and breaking your shoulder.

You have no use for the *good old days.* Whenever you find yourself slipping into a nostalgic frame of mind, mourning the loss of the things that seemed to make life better then than it is now, you tell yourself to stop and think carefully, to look back at Then with the same scrutiny you apply to looking at Now, and before long you come to the conclusion that there is little difference between them, that the Now and the Then are essentially the same. Of course you have manifold grievances against the evils and stupidities of contemporary American life, not a day goes by when you are not wailing forth your harangues against the ascendency of the right, the injustices of the economy, the neglect of the environment, the collapsing infrastructure, the senseless wars, the barbarism of legalized torture and extraordinary rendition, the disintegration of impoverished cities like Buffalo and Detroit, the erosion of the labor movement, the debt we saddle our children with in order to attend our too-expensive colleges, the ever-growing crevasse that divides the rich from the poor, not to speak of the junk films we are making, the junk food we are eating, the junk thoughts we are thinking. It is enough to make one want to start a revolution—or live as a hermit in the Maine woods, feeding off berries and the roots of trees. And yet, go back to the year of your birth and try to remember what America looked like in its golden age of postwar prosperity: Jim Crow laws in full force throughout the South, anti-Semitic quota restrictions, back-alley abortions, Truman's executive order to establish a loyalty oath for all government

workers, the trials of the Hollywood Ten, the Cold War, the Red
Scare, the Bomb. Every moment in history is fraught with its own
problems, its own injustices, and every period manufactures its
own legends and pieties. You were sixteen when Kennedy was as-
sassinated, a junior in high school, and the legend now says that
the entire American population was bludgeoned into a state of
wordless grief by the trauma that occurred on November twenty-
second. You have another story to tell, however, for you and two
of your friends happened to travel down to Washington on the
day of the funeral. You wanted to be there because of your admiration for Kennedy, who had represented such a startling change
after eight long years of Eisenhower, but you also wanted to be
there because you were curious to know what it would feel like to
participate in a *historical event*. It was the Sunday after the Friday,
the day Ruby shot and killed Oswald, and you imagined that the
crowds of onlookers lining the avenues as the funeral procession
passed by would stand there in respectful silence, *in a state of wordless grief,* but what you encountered that afternoon was a throng of
rowdy, rubbernecking gawkers, people perched in trees with their
cameras, people shoving others out of the way to get a better look,
and more than anything else, what you were reminded of was the
atmosphere at a public hanging, the thrill that attends the spectacle of violent death. You were there, you witnessed those things
with your own eyes, and yet in all the years since then, not once
have you heard anyone talk about what really happened.

Nevertheless, there are things you miss from the old days, even if
you have no desire to see those days return. The ring of the old
telephones, the clacking of typewriters, milk in bottles, baseball
without designated hitters, vinyl records, galoshes, stockings and
garter belts, black-and-white movies, heavyweight champions, the
Brooklyn Dodgers and the New York Giants, paperback books for

thirty-five cents, the political left, Jewish dairy restaurants, double features, basketball before the three-point shot, palatial movie houses, nondigital cameras, toasters that lasted for thirty years, contempt for authority, Nash Ramblers, and wood-paneled station wagons. But there is nothing you miss more than the world as it was before smoking was banned in public places. From your first cigarette at age sixteen (in Washington with your friends at Kennedy's funeral) until the end of the previous millennium, you were free—with just a few exceptions—to smoke anywhere you liked. Restaurants and bars to begin with, but also college classrooms, movie theater balconies, bookstores and record stores, doctors' waiting rooms, taxicabs, ballparks and indoor arenas, elevators, hotel rooms, trains, long-distance buses, airports, airplanes, and the shuttle buses at airports that took you to the planes. The world is probably better off now with its militant anti-smoking laws, but something has also been lost, and whatever that thing is (a sense of ease? tolerance of human frailty? conviviality? an absence of puritanical anguish?), you miss it.

Some memories are so strange to you, so unlikely, so outside the realm of the plausible, that you find it difficult to reconcile them with the fact that you are the person who experienced the events you are remembering. At the age of seventeen, for example, on a flight from Milan to New York after your first trip abroad (to visit your mother's sister in Italy, where she had been living for the past eleven years), you sat next to an attractive, highly intelligent girl of eighteen or nineteen, and after an hour of conversation, you spent the rest of the journey kissing each other with lustful abandon, necking passionately in front of the other passengers without the slightest hint of shame or self-consciousness. It seems impossible that this could have happened, but it did. Even stranger, on the last morning of your European jaunt the following year, the one that began by crossing the Atlantic on the student ship, you boarded a plane at Shannon Airport in Ireland and found yourself sitting next to another pretty girl. After an hour of serious conversation about books, colleges, and your summer adventures, the two of you began necking as well, going at each other so fiercely that eventually you covered yourselves with a blanket, and under that blanket you moved your hands all over her body and up into her skirt, and it was only by sheer force of will that the two of you restrained yourselves from venturing into the forbidden territory of out-and-out fucking. How was it possible that such a thing could have happened? Are the sexual energies of youth so powerful that the mere presence of another body can serve as an inducement to sex? You would never do such a thing now, would not even dare to think of doing such a thing—but then again, you are no longer young.

No, you were never promiscuous, even if you sometimes wish you had allowed yourself to be wilder and more impulsive, but in spite of your temperate behavior, you had a couple of run-ins with the dreaded germs of intimacy. The clap. It happened to you once, when you were twenty years old, and once was more than enough. A viscous green slime oozing from the tip of your cock, a feeling that a metal pin had been jammed down your urethra, and the simple act of urination turned into an agony. You never knew how you contracted gonorrhea, the cast of possible candidates was limited, and none of them struck you as a likely carrier of that dismal scourge. Five years later, when you found yourself with a case of the crabs, you were equally in the dark. No pain this time, but an incessant itch in the pubic region, and when you finally looked down to see what was going on, you were astonished to discover that you had been infested with a battalion of midget crabs— identical in shape to the crabs that live in the ocean, but minute

in size, no bigger than ladybugs. You were so ignorant about ve-
nereal diseases that you had never heard of this affliction until
you caught it yourself, had no idea that such a thing as the crab
louse even existed. Penicillin had cured the gonorrhea, but nothing more than a powder was needed to rid you of the vermin who
were camping out in your pubes. A minor complaint, then, rather
comical when looked at from a distance, but at the same time another mystery, another conundrum you have never been able to
solve, for you had no idea who or what had caused those itchy
devils to invade your person, whether they were the product of a
sexual encounter, inadvertent contact with a tainted washcloth or
towel, or squatting on a swarm of microscopic eggs camped out
on a toilet seat in some Paris café or restaurant. Too small to be
detected by the human eye, but no less insidious than the armies
of invisible microbes that unleash the plagues and epidemics that
slaughter entire countries and civilization. Happily, the bugs were
on you and not in you, and when they finally hatched and come
to full-blown life, they were big enough for you to see them—and
to wipe them out .

Ladybugs were considered good luck. If one of them landed on
your arm, you were supposed to make a wish before it flew away.
Four-leaf clovers were also agents of good fortune, and you spent
countless hours in your early childhood on your hands and knees
in the grass, searching for those small prizes, which did indeed
exist but were found only rarely and therefore were a cause for
much celebration. Spring was heralded by the appearance of the
first robin, the brown, red-breasted bird who would suddenly and
unaccountably show up in your backyard one morning, hopping
around on the grass and digging for worms. You would count the
robins after that, taking note of the second one, the third one,
the fourth one, adding more robins to the tally each day, and by

the time you stopped counting them, the weather would be warm. The first summer after you moved into the house on Irving Avenue (1952), your mother planted a garden in the backyard, and among the clusters of annuals and perennials in the loamy earth of the flower bed, there was a single sunflower, which continued to grow as the weeks went by, first coming up to your shins, then up to your waist, then up to your shoulders, and then, after reaching the top of your head, shooting on past you to a height of about six feet. The sunflower's progress was the central event of the summer, a bracing plunge into the mysterious workings of time, and every morning you would run into the backyard to measure yourself against it and see how fast it was gaining on you. That same summer, you made your first close friend, the first true comrade of your childhood, a boy named Billy whose house was just a short distance from yours, and because you were the only person who could understand him when he talked (he garbled his words, which seemed to sink back into his saliva-clogged mouth before they could emerge as cleanly articulated sound), he relied on you as his interpreter to the rest of the world, and you relied on him as an intrepid Huck to your more cautious Tom. The next spring, you spent every afternoon combing through the bushes together, looking for dead birds—mostly fledglings, you now realize, who must have fallen out of their nests and could not make their way back home. You buried them in a patch of dirt that ran along the side of your house—intensely solemn rituals accompanied by made-up prayers and long moments of silence. You had both discovered death by then, and you knew that it was a serious business, something that did not allow for any jokes.

The first human death you remember with any clarity took place in 1957, when your eighty-year-old grandmother dropped down on the floor with a heart attack and died in a hospital later that day. You have no memory of going to the funeral, which would suggest you were not there, in all likelihood because you were ten years old and your parents thought you were too young. What you remember is the darkness that filled the house for days afterward, the people coming and going to sit shiva with your father in the living room, unknown men reciting incomprehensible Hebrew prayers in mumbled voices, the strangely quiet commotion of it all, your father's grief. You yourself were almost entirely untouched by this death. You had felt no connection to your grandmother, no love from her, no curiosity about who you were, not the slightest glimmer of affection, and the few times she'd wrapped her arms around you for a grandmotherly hug, you had felt frightened, eager for the embrace to end. The 1919 murder was still a family secret then, you would not learn about it until you were in your early twenties, but you had always sensed that your grandmother was mad, that this small immigrant woman with her broken English and violent screaming spells was someone to be kept at arm's length. Even as the mourners drifted in and out of the house, you went about your ten-year-old-boy's business, and when the rabbi put his hand on your shoulder and said it would be all right for you to go off and play in your Little League game that evening, you went up to your room, put on your baseball uniform, and ran out of the house.

Eleven years later, the death of your mother's mother was a different story. You were grown then, the bolt of lightning that had killed your friend when you were fourteen had taught you that the world was capricious and unstable, that the future can be stolen from us at any moment, that the sky is full of lightning bolts that can crash down and kill the young as well as the old, and always, always, the lightning strikes when we are least expecting it. This was the grandmother you cared about, the prim and slightly nervous woman you loved, the one who stayed with you often and was a consistent presence in your life, and now that you are thinking about her death, the nature of her death, which was slow and dreadful and anguishing to watch, you realize that all the other deaths in your family have been sudden, a series of lightning bolts similar to the one that killed your friend: your father's mother (heart attack, dead within hours), your father's father (shot and killed before you knew him), your father (heart attack, dead within seconds), your mother (heart attack, dead within minutes), and even your mother's father, whose death was not instantaneous, who made it to eighty-five in good health and then, after a swift decline of two or three weeks, died of pneumonia, which is to say, died of old age—a death to be envied, you feel, full-bore life into your ninth decade and then, rather than electrocution by lightning bolt, a chance to absorb the fact that you are on your way out, a chance to reflect for a while, and then you go to sleep and float off into the land of nothingness. Your grandmother didn't float anywhere. For two years she was dragged over a bed of nails, and when she died at seventy-three, there was little of anything left of her. Amyotrophic lateral sclerosis, commonly known as Lou Gehrig's disease. You have seen people's bodies consumed by the autocannibalism of virulent cancer, have watched the gradual strangulation of others by emphysema, but ALS is no less ravaging or cruel, and once you have been diagnosed with it, there is no hope, no remedy, nothing in front of you but a prolonged march toward disintegration and death. Your bones melt. The skeleton inside your skin turns to putty, and one by one your organs fail. What made your grandmother's case particularly hard to bear was that the first symptoms appeared in her throat, and her speech functions were attacked before anything else: larynx, tongue, esophagus. One day, out of nowhere, she found it difficult to pronounce her words clearly, the syllables came out slurred, slightly off. A month or two later, they were alarmingly off. Several months after

that, rattles of phlegm occluding her sentences, choked-off gur-
glings, the humiliations of impairment, and when no New York
doctor could figure out what was wrong with her, your mother
took her to the Mayo Clinic for a full workup. The men in Minnesota were the ones who pronounced her death sentence, and
before long her speech had become unintelligible. She was forced
to communicate in writing after that, carrying a little pencil and
a pad of paper wherever she went, though for the time being the
rest of her seemed well, she could still walk, still take part in the
life around her, but as the months passed and the musculature of
her throat continued to atrophy, swallowing became problematic,
eating and drinking became a permanent trial, and in the end the
rest of her body began to betray her as well. For the first week or
two in the hospital, she still had the use of her arms and hands,
could still use the pencil and pad to communicate, even though
her handwriting had deteriorated badly, and then she came under
the watch of a private nurse named Miss Moran (short and efficient, a rictus of perpetual false cheer glued onto her face), who
kept the pad and pencil from your grandmother, and the more
your grandmother howled in protest, the longer that pad was kept
from her. Once you and your mother got wind of what was going
on, Moran was fired, but the battle your grandmother had fought
with the sadistic nurse had depleted whatever strength she had
left. The gentle, self-effacing woman who had read you Maupas-
sant stories when you were ill, who had taken you to shows at
Radio City Music Hall, who had treated you to ice cream sundaes
and lunches at Schrafft's was dying in Doctors Hospital on the
Upper East Side of Manhattan, and not long after she became too
weak to hold the pencil anymore, she lost her mind. Whatever
force she still had in her was subsumed by rage, a demented anger that made her unrecognizable and expressed itself in constant
howls, the throttled, dammed-up howls of a helpless, immobilized
person struggling not to drown in a puddle of her own sputum.

Born in Minsk, 1895. Died in New York, 1968. *The end of life is bitter* (Joseph Joubert, 1814).

Things were the way they were, and you never stopped to question them. There were public schools and Catholic schools in your town, and because you were not Catholic, you attended the public schools, which were considered to be good schools, at least by the standards that were used to measure such things at the time, and according to what your mother later told you, it was for this reason that your family had moved to the house on Irving Avenue in the months before you were scheduled to begin kindergarten. You have nothing to compare your experience with, but in the thirteen years you spent in that system, the first seven at Marshall School (K–6), the next three at South Orange Junior High School (7–9), and the last three at Columbia High School in Maplewood (10–12), you had some good teachers and some mediocre teachers, a handful of exceptional and inspiring teachers and a handful of lousy and incompetent teachers, and your fellow students ranged from the brilliant to the average to the semimoronic. Such is the case with all public schools. Everyone who lives in the district can go for free, and because you grew up in a time before the advent of special education, before separate schools had been established to accommodate children with so-called problems, a number of your classmates were physically handicapped. No one in a wheelchair that you can remember, but you can still see the hunchbacked boy with the twisted body, the girl who was missing an arm (a fingerless stump jutting from her shoulder), the drooling boy who slobbered down the front of his shirt, and the girl who was scarcely taller than a midget. Looking back on it now, you feel that these people were an essential part of your education, that without their presence in your life your understanding of what it means to be human would have been impoverished, lacking all depth and compassion, all insight into the metaphysics of pain and adversity, for those children were the heroic ones, the ones who had to work ten times harder than any of the others to find a place for themselves. If you had lived only among the physically blessed, the children like yourself who took your well-formed bodies for granted, how would you have ever learned what heroism was? One of your friends from those early years was a plump, nonathletic boy with glasses and a homely, chinless sort of face, but he was much loved by the other boys for his sharp wit and humor, his prowess at math, and what struck you then as an uncommon generosity of spirit. He had a bedridden younger brother, a boy suffering from a disease that had stunted his growth and left him with brittle bones, bones that broke from the slightest contact with hard surfaces, bones that broke for no reason at all, and you can remember visiting your friend's house after school on several occasions and going in to see his brother, who was just a year or two younger than you were, lying in a hospital bed rigged with pulleys and wires, his legs in plaster casts, with his large head and impossibly pale skin, and you could hardly open your mouth in that room, you felt nervous, perhaps a bit scared, but the brother was a nice kid, friendly and affable and bright, and it always struck you as absurd, altogether outrageous that he should be lying in that bed, and every time you saw him you wondered what idiot god had decreed that he should be locked inside that body and not you. Your friend was devoted to him, they were as close to each other as any brothers you have ever known, and they shared a private, two-person world, a secret universe dominated by a mutual obsession with the fantasy baseball game they played, a board game with dice, cards, complex rules, and elaborate statistics, meticulously keeping records of every game they played, which evolved into entire seasons of games, every month or two another season, season after season of imaginary games as the years rolled on. How perfectly right, you realize now, that it should have been this friend of yours who called you one evening in the winter of 1957–58, not long after the Dodgers had announced their move from Brooklyn to Los Angeles, to tell you that Roy Campanella, the All-Star catcher, had been in a car accident, an accident so terrible that even if he pulled through, he would be paralyzed for the rest of his life. Your friend was weeping into the phone.

February twenty-third: the thirtieth anniversary of the day you met your wife, the thirtieth anniversary of the first night you spent together. The two of you leave your house in the late afternoon, cross the Brooklyn Bridge, and check into a hotel in lower Manhattan. A bit of an indulgence, perhaps, but you don't want these twenty-four hours to slip by without doing something to mark the occasion, and because the idea of throwing a party never came up (why would a couple want to celebrate its longevity in front of others?), you and your wife eat dinner alone in the hotel restaurant. Afterward, you take the elevator to the ninth floor and enter your room, where you polish off a bottle of champagne together, forgetting to turn on the radio, forgetting to turn on the television to investigate the four thousand movies that are available to you, and as you drink the champagne you talk to each other, for several hours you do nothing but talk, not about the past and the thirty years that are behind you but about the present, about your daughter and your wife's mother, about the work you are both engaged in now, about any number of things both pertinent and trivial, and in that respect this evening is no different from any other evening of your marriage, since the two of you have always talked, that is what defines you somehow, and for all these years you have been living inside the long, uninterrupted conversation that started the day you met. Outside, another cold winter night, another burst of freezing rain lashing against the windows, but you are in bed with your wife now, and the hotel bed is warm, the sheets are smooth and comfortable, and the pillows are positively gigantic.

Numerous crushes and flirtations, but only two big loves in your early life, the cataclysms of your mid-teens and late teens, both of which were disasters, followed by your first marriage, which ended in disaster as well. Starting in 1962, when you fell for the beautiful Belgian girl who lived in a neighboring town, you seemed to have a special talent for chasing after the wrong person, for wanting what you couldn't have, for giving your heart to girls who couldn't or wouldn't love you back. Occasional interest in your mind, flashes of interest in your body, but none whatsoever in your heart. Half-crazy girls, both of them ravishing and self-destructive and deeply exciting to you, but you understood almost nothing about them. You invented them. You used them as fictive embodiments of your own desires, ignoring their problems and personal histories, failing to grasp who they were outside of your own imagination, and yet the more they eluded you, the more passionately you longed for them. The one from your mid-teens was brilliant and pugnacious, at odds with everything American, which no doubt enhanced her allure in your eyes, but there were family difficulties, a mother who had hanged herself four years earlier in Brussels, and the girl's subsequent battles with her father's second wife, needless to say an American wife, which led to some frantic experiments with vodka, solo binges in her room that eventually landed her in the hospital. You remember trying to visit her there and being turned away, every afternoon turned away, out of your mind with love, with fear, and after they released her two months later, she called you to say good-bye, and then her father shipped her off to Belgium and you never saw her again. The second story began in the winter of your first year of college, when you fell for another unstable girl who both wanted you and didn't want you, and the more she didn't want you, the more ardently you pursued her. A sick troubadour and his inconstant lady, and even after she slashed her wrists in a halfhearted suicide attempt a few months later, you went on loving her, the one with the white bandages and the fetching, crooked smile, and then, after the bandages were removed, you made her pregnant, the condom you were using broke, and you spent every penny you had to pay for an abortion. A brutal memory, another one of the things that still keep you awake at night, and while you are certain the two of you made the correct decision not to have the baby (parents at nineteen and twenty, a grotesque thought), you are tormented by the memory of that unborn child. You always imagined it would be a girl, a girl with red hair, a wondrous firecracker of a girl, and it pains you to realize that she would be forty-three years old now, which means that in all probability you would have become a grandfather some time ago, perhaps a long time ago. If you had let her live.

In the light of your past failures, your misjudgments, your inability to understand yourself and others, your impulsive and erratic decisions, your blundering approach to matters of the heart, it seems curious that you should have wound up in a marriage that has lasted this long. You have tried to figure out the reasons for this unexpected reversal of fortune, but you have never been able to come up with an answer. You ran into a stranger one night and fell in love with her—and she fell in love with you. You didn't deserve it, but neither did you not deserve it. It just happened, and nothing can account for what happened to you except luck.

From the very start, everything was different with her. Not a figment this time, not some projection of your inner fancy, but a real person, and she imposed her reality on you the moment the two of you began to talk, which was one moment after the single acquaintance you had in common introduced you to each other in the lobby of the 92nd Street Y following a poetry reading, and because she was neither coy nor elusive, because she looked you in the eye and asserted herself as a wholly grounded presence, there was no way for you to turn her into something she was not—no way to invent her, as you had done with other women in the past, since she had already invented herself. Beautiful, yes, without question sublimely beautiful, a lean six-foot blonde with long, magnificent legs and the tiny wrists of a four-year-old, the biggest little person you had ever seen, or perhaps the littlest big person, and yet you were not looking at some remote object of female splendor, you were engaged in talking to a living, breathing human subject. Subject, not object, and therefore no delusions permitted. No deceptions possible. Intelligence is the one human quality that cannot be faked, and once your eyes had adjusted to the dazzle of her beauty, you understood that this was a brilliant woman, one of the best minds you had ever met.

Little by little, as you came to know her better in the weeks that followed, you discovered that you saw eye to eye on nearly everything of any importance. Your politics were the same, most of the books you cared about were the same books, and you had similar attitudes about what you wanted out of life: love, work, and children—with money and possessions far down on the list. Much to your relief, your personalities were nothing alike. She laughed more than you did, she was freer and more outgoing than you were, she was warmer than you were, and yet, all the way down at the bottom, at the nethermost point where you were joined together, you felt that you had met another version of yourself—but one that was more fully evolved than you were, better able to express what you kept bottled up inside you, a saner being. You adored her, and for the first time in your life, the person you adored adored you back. You came from entirely different worlds, a young Lutheran girl from Minnesota and a not so young Jew from New York, but just two and a half months after your chance encounter on February twenty-third thirty years ago, you decided to move in together. Until then, every decision you had made about women had been a wrong decision—but not this one.

She was a graduate student and a poet, and in the first five years you were together you watched her finish up her course work, study for and pass her oral exams, and then go through the arduous slog of writing her dissertation (on language and identity in Dickens). She published one book of poetry during that time, and because money was scarce in the early days of your marriage, she worked at several different jobs, editing a three-volume anthology published by Zone Books for one thing, secretly rewriting someone's doctoral dissertation on Jacques Lacan for another, and also teaching, most of all teaching. The first class was for low-level employees at an insurance company, ambitious young workers who wanted to improve their chances for promotion by taking an intensive course in English grammar and expository writing. Twice a week, your wife came home with stories about her students, some of them entertaining, some of them rather poignant, but the one you remember best concerns a howler that appeared on the final exam. Midway through the semester, your wife had given a lecture on various figures of speech, among them the concept of euphemism. By way of example, she had cited *pass away* as a euphemism for *die*. On the final exam, she asked the members of the class to give a definition of the word *euphemism*, and one vaguely attentive but challenged student answered: "Euphemism means *to die*." After the insurance company, she moved on to Queens College, where she worked as an adjunct for three years, a grinding, badly paid job, two courses per semester with classes in remedial English and English composition, twenty-five students per class, fifty papers a week to correct, three private conferences with each student every semester, a two-hour trip from Cobble Hill to Flushing that began at six in the morning and entailed two subways and a bus, then another two-hour trip in the opposite direction, all for a salary of eight thousand dollars a year with no benefits. The long days wore her out, not just because of the work and the travel but also because of the hours spent under the fluorescent lights at Queens, the rapidly flickering lights that can induce headaches in people who suffer from migraines, and because your wife had been saddled with that condition since childhood, it was the rare evening when she didn't walk through the door with dark circles under her eyes and a head bursting with pain. Her dissertation was advancing slowly, the weekly schedule was too fragmented for concentrated periods of research and writing, but suddenly your finances began to improve somewhat, enough for you to persuade her to quit the teaching job at any rate, and once she was free, she knocked off the rest of her Dickens thesis in six months. The bigger question was why she was still so determined to finish. Graduate school had made sense in the beginning: a single woman needs a job, especially if that woman comes from a family with no money, and even though her ambition was to write, she couldn't count on writing to sustain her, and therefore she would become a professor. But things were different now. She was married, her money situation was becoming less and less precarious, she was no longer planning to look for an academic job, and still she battled on until she had earned her doctorate. Again and again, you asked her why it was so important to her, and the various answers she gave you all go straight to the heart of who she was then, who she still is today. First: because she couldn't bring herself to quit something she had started. A question of stubbornness and pride. Second: because she was a woman. It was all very well that you had bailed out of graduate school after one year, you were a man, and men control the world, but a woman who wears the badge of an advanced degree will gain some respect in that man's world, will not be looked down upon as much as a woman who does not have that badge. Third: because she loved it. The hard work and discipline of intense study had improved her mind, had made her a better and more subtle thinker, and even if most of her time would be spent writing novels in the future (she had already started her first), she had no intention of abandoning her intellectual life once she had her Ph.D. These were discussions you had with her more than twenty-five years ago, but it was as if she had already begun to squint into the future and see the outlines of what lay in front of her. Since then: five published novels and a sixth in the works, but also four books of nonfiction, for the most part essays, dozens of essays on an enormous range of subjects: literature, art, culture, politics, films, daily life, fashion, neuroscience, psychoanalysis, the philosophy of perception, and the phenomenology of memory. In 1978, she was one of a hundred students who entered the graduate English program at Columbia. Seven years later, she was one of only three who had made it all the way to the end.

By marrying your wife, you married into her family as well, and because her parents still lived in the house where she had grown up, another country was gradually absorbed into your bloodstream: Minnesota, the northernmost province in the rural kingdom of the Upper Midwest. Not the flat world you'd imagined it would be, but an undulating land of small peaks and dipping curves, no mountains or hilly extrusions and yet clouds in the far distance that simulate mountains and hills, an illusory bulk, a mass of vaporous white to soften the monotony of mile after mile of undulating land, and on days when there are no clouds, the alfalfa fields that stretch all the way to the horizon, a low and distant horizon overarched by an enormous, never-ending sky, a sky so large that it comes all the way down to your toes. The coldest winters on earth, followed by broiling, humid summers, torrid heat bearing down on you with millions of mosquitoes, so many mosquitoes that T-shirts are sold bearing pictures of those homicidal dive-bombers with the legend MINNESOTA—THE STATE BIRD. The first time you went out there, for a two-month stay in the summer of 1981, you were writing the preface to your anthology of twentieth-century French poetry, a longish piece that ran to forty-something pages, and because your future wife's parents were out of town during your visit, you worked in your future father-in-law's office on the St. Olaf College campus, cranking out paragraphs about Apollinaire, Reverdy, and Breton in a room decorated with pictures of Viking helmets, driving each morning to the mostly deserted campus, which suddenly came to life one week when the college rented out some of its buildings to the annual Conference of Christian Coaches, and how you enjoyed seeing those coaches walk by when you parked your car in the morning, dozens of nearly identical-looking men with their crew cuts, potbellies, and Bermuda shorts, and then on to your room in the Norwegian Department, where you would write another couple of pages about French poets. You were in Northfield, which advertised itself as "The Home of Cows, Colleges, and Contentment," a town of about eight thousand people, best known as the place where Jesse James and his gang met their end during an attempted holdup (the bullet holes are still in the walls of the bank on Division Street), but your favorite spot quickly became the Malt-O-Meal factory on Highway 19, with its tall smokestacks pouring out white clouds of the nut-scented grain used in the recipe for that tawny, farina-textured breakfast cereal, located midway between your in-laws' house and the center of town, just a few hundred yards before the railroad tracks you stopped in front of with your wife one afternoon that summer as a slowly moving train passed by, the longest train you have ever seen, somewhere between one and two hundred freight cars, but you didn't have time to count them because you and your then future wife were talking, chiefly about the apartment you would be looking for when you returned to New York, and that was when the question of marriage first came up between you, not just living together under the same roof but bound by matrimony as well, that was what she wanted, that was what she insisted upon, and even though you had decided never to marry again, you said of course, you would gladly marry her if that was what she wanted, for you had loved her long enough by then to know that whatever she wanted was precisely what you wanted as well. That was why you paid such close attention to everything around you that summer, because this was the country where she had spent her girlhood and early womanhood, and by studying the details of that landscape you felt you would come to know her better, understand her better, and one by one, as you came to know her mother and father and three younger sisters, you began to acquire an understanding of her family as well, which also helped you understand her better, to feel the solidity of the ground she walked on, for this was a solid family, nothing like the fractured, provisional family you yourself had grown up in, and it wasn't long before you became one of them, for this, to your everlasting good fortune, was now your family, too.

Then came the winter visits, the turn-of-the-year homecomings, a week to ten days in a frozen world of silent air, of windborne daggers piercing your body, of looking at the thermometer through the kitchen window in the morning and seeing the red mercury stuck at twenty below zero Fahrenheit, thirty below zero, temperatures so inhospitable to human life you have often wondered

how anyone could live in such a place, your head filled with images of Sioux families wrapped from head to toe in buffalo pelts,
pioneer families freezing to death on the tundralike prairie. No
cold like this cold, an impossible cold that stuns the muscles in
your face the instant you step outdoors, that pummels your skin,
puckers your skin, that coagulates the blood in your veins, and yet
once, not many years ago, the entire family went out into the dark
to look at the northern lights, you saw them only that one time,
unforgettable, unimaginable—standing in the cold and gazing up
at an electric green sky, a sky flashing green against the black wall
of night, nothing you have witnessed has ever come close to the
hectic grandeur of that spectacle. On other nights, the clear nights
without clouds, a sky crammed with stars, packed full from horizon to horizon, more stars than you have seen anywhere else, so
many stars that they merge into dense liquid pools, a porridge of
whiteness overhead, and the white mornings that follow, the white
afternoons, the snow, the snow that falls endlessly all around you,
up to your knees, up to your waist, growing like the sunflower that
shot past your head in your mother's garden when you were a boy,
more snow than you have seen anywhere else, and suddenly you
are reliving a moment from the mid-nineties, when you and your
wife and daughter had made the annual Christmas pilgrimage to
Minnesota, and there you are behind the wheel on the night of
a blizzard, driving from the house of one of your wife's sisters in
Minneapolis to her parents' house in Northfield, just under forty
miles away. Sitting in the backseat are three generations of women
(your mother-in-law, wife, and daughter), and up front with you,
sitting in the passenger seat to your right, is your father-in-law, a
man who has treated you with kindness during the years of your
marriage to his oldest daughter, even if in many ways he is a remote and shut-down person, much as your own father was, both
men having endured rough and impoverished childhoods, and in
your father-in-law's case there was the added ordeal of having

served as a young foot soldier in World War II (the Battle of Lu-
zon, the Philippines, the jungles of New Guinea), but you are a
lifelong expert in the art of communicating with shut-down men,
and if your father-in-law sometimes resembles your father, you
feel that there is a larger reservoir of warmth and tenderness in
him, that he is more knowable than your father ever was, more
fully a member of the human race. You are forty-six or forty-
seven years old, in excellent physical condition, still youthful in
the middle of your middle age, and because you are still known
as a *good driver*, the female contingent in the backseat has absolute
faith in your ability to deliver them safely to the house in Northfield, and because they trust you, they are not alarmed by the potential dangers of the storm. All during the ride home, in fact, the
three of them engage in animated talk on any number of subjects,
acting as if it were a mild evening at the height of summer, but the
instant you start the car and pull away from your sister-in-law's
house, both you and your father-in-law know that you are in for
a hellish ride, that weather conditions are bad to the point of impossible. Once you reach the highway and begin traveling south
on I-35, the snow is lashing onto the windshield, and although
the wipers are working at full speed, you can see almost nothing,
since the snow starts gathering on the glass again the instant the
wipers complete their arc. There are no overhead lamps on the
highway, but the oncoming headlights of the cars traveling toward
you in the opposite lane illuminate the snow as it falls onto the
windshield, so that what you are seeing is no longer snow but a
shower of small, blinding lights. Worst of all, the road is slick, as
smooth and icy as a skating pond, and to go more than ten or fifteen miles an hour would rob the tires of their traction and render
the brakes useless. Every fifty or a hundred yards, both to your left
and to your right, you pass another car that has skidded off the
road, lying half-overturned in a mountainous snowbank or drift.
Your father-in-law, who has lived in Minnesota all his life, is all

too familiar with the hazards of driving in a storm like this one, and he is entirely with you as you inch the car along through the night, sitting in the navigator's seat and peering into the spangled clouds of snow that continue to pour down onto the windshield, warning you of upcoming curves, keeping you calm and focused, driving with you in his head, in the muscles of his body, and so it is that you finally make it to the house in Northfield, you and the old soldier in front, the women in back, a two-hour trek instead of the customary thirty or forty minutes, and when the five of you enter the house, the women are still talking and laughing, but your father-in-law, who knows what a trial this has been on your nerves, since it has been a trial on his nerves as well, pats you on the back and gives you a little wink. Fifty years after he hung up his uniform, the sergeant has saluted you.

Christmas dinner in Northfield, Minnesota, every year from 1981 until your father-in-law's death in 2004, after which the family house was sold, your mother-in-law moved to an apartment, and the tradition was altered to fit the new circumstances. But for close to a quarter century the meal was formalized down to the last detail, not one element different from the year before, and the table you first sat down to in 1981, which consisted of just seven people—your mother-in-law and father-in-law, your wife, her three sisters, and yourself—gradually expanded as one year melted into another and your wife's younger sisters married and began having children of their own, so by the end of that quarter-century run, nineteen people were sitting around the table, including the very old and the old, the young and the very young. It is important to note that Christmas was celebrated on the night of the twenty-fourth, not on the morning and afternoon of the twenty-fifth, for even though your wife's family lived in the American heartland, they were and are a Scandinavian family as well, a Norwegian family, and all Christmas protocols followed the conventions from that part of the world rather than this one. Your mother-in-law, born in the southernmost town of Norway in 1923, did not move across the Atlantic until she was thirty, and although her English is fluent, she continues to speak this second tongue with a pronounced Norwegian accent. She lived through the war and the German occupation as a young woman, was put in prison for nine days after participating in an early protest march against the Nazis when she was seventeen (if it had happened later in the war, she says, she would have been sent to a camp), and both of her older brothers were active members of the underground (one of them, after his cell was broken, skied to Sweden in order to escape the Gestapo). Your mother-in-law is an intelligent, well-read person, someone you greatly admire and feel much affection for, but her occasional struggles with the English language and American geography have produced some strange moments, none more hilarious, perhaps, than the night fifteen or sixteen years ago when the plane she and her husband were taking to Boston could not land because the airport was fogged in and consequently had to be rerouted to Albany, New York, and once they made it to Albany she called your wife and announced over the telephone: "We're in Albania! We're spending the night in Albania!" As for your father-in-law, he too was thoroughly Norwegian, even though he was a third-generation American, born in Cannon Falls, Minnesota, in 1922, the last of the nineteenth-century prairie children, a farm boy raised in a log house without electricity or indoor plumbing, and the rural community where he lived was so isolated, so unanimously populated by Norwegian immigrants and their descendents, that much of his early life was transacted in Norwegian rather than in English, so that he retained an accent throughout his adulthood and old age: not a heavy accent like your mother-in-law's but a soft musical brogue, an American English spoken in a way you have never heard from anyone else and which you always found highly pleasing to the ear. After the long interruption of the war, he finished college on the G.I. Bill, continued his studies through graduate school and a Fulbright year at the University of Oslo (where he and your mother-in-law met), and wound up as a professor of Norwegian language and literature. Your wife grew up in a Norwegian household, then, even if it happened to be located in Minnesota, and Christmas dinner was therefore strictly and resolutely Norwegian as well. In effect, it was a duplication of the Christmas dinners your mother-in-law ate with her own family as a child in southern Norway back in the 1920s and '30s, a time far removed from our current age of opulence and plenty, of supermarkets stocked with two hundred kinds of breakfast cereal and eighty-four flavors of ice cream. The meal never varied, and in twenty-three years not one dish was ever added to the menu or subtracted from it. Not turkey or goose or ham, as one might suppose for the main course, but pork ribs, covered lightly in salt and pepper, baked in the oven, and served without sauce or condiments. Accompanied by boiled potatoes, cauliflower, red cabbage, Brussels sprouts, carrots, lingonberries, and rice pudding for desert. No meal could be simpler than this one, more defiantly at odds with contemporary American notions about what constitutes acceptable holiday fare, and yet when you polled the youngest of your nieces and nephews a couple of years ago (the tradition still carries on in New York), asking them if they liked Christmas dinner as it was or if they would prefer to see some changes, they all cried out: "No changes!" This is food as ritual, as continuity, as family cohesion—a symbolic anchor to prevent you from drifting out to sea. Such is the tribe you have married into. When she was around fifteen, your witty daughter came up with a new term to describe her background: Jew-wegian. You doubt there are many people who can lay claim to that particular brand of hyphenated identity, but this is America, after all, and yes, you and your wife are the parents of a Jew-wegian.

The foods you loved as boy, from the time of your earliest memories to the threshold of puberty, and you wonder now how many thousands of forkfuls and spoonfuls went into you, how many bites and swallows, how many small sips and grand gulps, beginning with the myriad fruit juices you drank at various times during the day, orange juice in the morning, but also apple juice and grapefruit juice and tomato juice and pineapple juice, pineapple juice in a glass but also pineapple juice frozen in ice cube trays during the summer, which you and your sister referred to as "pineapple chunks," along with the soft drinks you downed whenever you were permitted to (Coca-Cola, root beer, ginger ale, 7 Up, Orange Crush), and the milkshakes you adored, especially chocolate, but sometimes vanilla for a change of pace, or a combination of the two known as a black-and-white, and then, in the summer, the delirium of the root beer float, traditionally made with vanilla ice cream, but for you even more delicious if the flavor of the ice cream was coffee. On any given morning, you would begin with a first course of cold cereal (Corn Flakes, Rice Krispies, Shredded Wheat, Puffed Wheat, Puffed Rice, Cheerios—whatever happened to be in the kitchen cupboard), which you would pour into a bowl, douse with milk, and then coat with a tablespoon (or two tablespoons) of white refined sugar. Followed by a serving of eggs (scrambled mostly, but occasionally fried or soft-boiled) and two pieces of buttered toast (white, whole wheat, or rye), often accompanied by bacon, ham, or sausage, or else a platter of French toast (with maple syrup), or, rarely, but always most coveted, a stack of pancakes (also with maple syrup). Several hours later, lunch meats piled between two slices of bread, ham or salami, corned beef or bologna, sometimes ham and American cheese together, sometimes American cheese alone, or else one of your mother's dependable tuna fish sandwiches. On cold days, cold winter days like this one, the sandwich was often preceded by a bowl of soup, which always came out of cans in the early fifties, your favorites being Campbell's chicken noodle and Campbell's tomato, which no doubt was the case with every other American child back then as well. Hamburgers and hot dogs, french fries and potato chips: once-a-week delicacies in the local malt shop known as the Cricklewood, where you and your school friends would eat lunch together every Thursday. (Your grammar school did not have a cafeteria. Everyone would go home for lunch, but starting when you were nine or ten, your mother and the mothers of your friends allowed you this treat: hamburgers and/or hot dogs at the Cricklewood every Thursday, which cost all of twenty-five or thirty cents.) The evening meal, interchangeably referred to as dinner or supper, was best if the main dish was lamb chops, but roast beef ran a close second, followed, in no particular order, by fried chicken, roast chicken, beef stew, pot roast, spaghetti and meatballs, sautéed liver, and fried fish fillets smothered in ketchup. Potatoes were a constant, and however they were served (primarily baked or mashed), they never failed to offer profound satisfaction. Corn on the cob surpassed all other vegetables, but that delight was confined to the last months of summer, and therefore you happily wolfed down the peas or peas and carrots or green beans or beets you found on your plate. Popcorn, pistachio nuts, peanuts, marshmallows, piles of saltines smeared with grape jelly, and the frozen foods that began appearing late in your childhood, in particular chicken pot pie and Sara Lee's pound cake. You have all but lost your taste for sweets at this point in your life, but when you look back on the distant days of your boyhood, you are staggered by how many sugary things you longed for and devoured. Ice cream most of all, for which you seemed to have an insatiable appetite, whether served up plain in a bowl or covered in chocolate sauce, whether presented in the form of a sundae or a float, ice cream on a stick (as in Good Humor bars and Creamsicles) as well as ice cream lurking inside spheres (Bon Bons), rectangles (Eskimo Pies), and domes (Baked Alaska). Ice cream was the tobacco of your youth, the addiction that slinked its way into your soul and endlessly seduced you with its charms, but you were also a pushover for cake (chocolate layer! angel food!) and every variety of cookie, from Vanilla Fingers to Burry's Double Dip Chocolate, from Fig Newtons to Mallomars, from Oreos to Social Tea Biscuits, not to mention the hundreds if not thousands of candy bars you consumed before the age of twelve: Milky Ways, Three Musketeers, Chunkys, Charleston Chews, York Mints, Junior Mints, Mars bars, Snickers bars, Baby Ruths, Milk Duds, Chuckles, Goobers, Dots, Jujubes, Sugar Daddys, and God knows what else. How is it possible that you managed to stay thin during the years when you were ingesting all this sugar, that your body somehow continued to grow upward rather than outward as you veered toward adolescence? Thankfully, all that is behind you now, but every now and then, perhaps once every two or three years, while you are killing time in an airport before a long-distance flight (for some reason, this happens only in airports), if you should wander into the magazine shop to look for a newspaper, an ancient longing will suddenly take hold of you, and then you will cast your eyes down at the sweets on display below the cash register, and if they happen to have Chuckles in stock, you will buy them. Within ten minutes, all five of the jellied candies will be gone. Red, yellow, green, orange, and black.

Joubert: *The end of life is bitter.* Less than a year after writing those words, at the age of sixty-one, which must have seemed considerably older in 1815 than it does today, he jotted down a different and far more challenging formulation about the end of life: *One must die lovable (if one can).* You are moved by this sentence, especially by the words in parentheses, which demonstrate a rare sensitivity of spirit, you feel, a hard-won understanding of how difficult it is to be lovable, especially for someone who is old, who is sinking into decrepitude and must be cared for by others. *If one can.* There is probably no greater human achievement than to be lovable at the end, whether that end is bitter or not. Fouling the deathbed with piss and shit and drool. We are all going there, you tell yourself, and the question is to what degree a person can remain human while hanging on in a state of helplessness and degradation. You cannot predict what will happen when the day comes for you to crawl into bed for the last time, but if you are not taken suddenly, as both of your parents were, you want to be lovable. *If you can.*

You mustn't neglect to mention that you nearly choked to death on a fish bone in 1971 or that you narrowly escaped killing yourself in a dark hallway one night in 2006 when you smashed your fore-head into a low door frame, stumbled backward, and then, trying to regain your balance, pitched forward, snagged your foot on the sill, and went flying face-first onto the floor of the apartment you had entered, the top of your head landing within inches of a thick table leg. Every day, in every country around the world, people die from falls like that one. Your friend's uncle, for example, the same man you wrote about nineteen years ago (*The Red Notebook*, Story No. 3), who survived gunshot wounds and multiple dangers as a partisan resistance fighter against the Nazis in World War II, a young man who managed to escape certain death and/or mu-tilation with dumbfounding regularity, and then, having moved to Chicago after the war, living in the tranquility of peacetime America, far from the battlefields and flying bullets and exploding land mines of his youth, awoke one night to go to the bathroom, tripped over a piece of furniture in the darkened living room, and died when his head smashed into a thick table leg. An absurd death, a nonsensical death, a death that could have been yours five years ago if your head had landed just a few inches to the left, and when you think about the ridiculous ways in which people can meet their end—tumbling down flights of stairs, slipping off ladders, accidentally drowning, being run over by cars, shot by stray bullets, electrocuted by radios that fall into bathtubs—you can only conclude that every life is marked by a number of close calls, that everyone who manages to reach the age you have come to now has already wriggled out of a number of potentially absurd, nonsensical deaths. All in the course of what you would call *ordinary life*. Needless to say, millions of others have confronted far worse, have not had the luxury of leading an ordinary life, soldiers in combat, for example, civilian casualties in wars, the murdered victims of totalitarian governments, and the countless many who have perished in natural disasters: floods, earthquakes, typhoons, epidemics. But even those who manage to survive catastrophe are no less prey to the whims of daily existence than those of us who have been spared such horrors—as with your friend's uncle, who eluded death in battle and died one night in a Chicago apartment on his way to the bathroom. In 1971, the fish bone lodged itself at the base of your throat. You were eating what you thought was a fillet of halibut, and for that reason you were not worried about encountering any bones, but suddenly you could no longer swallow without pain, something was *in there*, and none of the traditional remedies did the least bit of good: drinking water, eating bread, trying to pull the bone out with your fingers. The bone had traveled too far down your throat, and it was long enough and thick enough to have pierced the skin on both sides, and each time you made another attempt to cough it up, your saliva was mixed with blood. It was April or May, you had been living in Paris for two or two and a half months, and when it became clear that you would not be able to get rid of the bone yourself, you and your girlfriend left your apartment on the rue Jacques Mawas and walked to the nearest medical facility in the neighborhood, l'Hôpital Boucicaut. It was eight or nine o'clock in the evening, and the nurses had no idea what to do with you. They squirted a liquid numbing agent down your throat, they chatted with you, they laughed, but the stuck bone was inaccessible and therefore could not be extracted. Finally, at around eleven o'clock, the nighttime emergency doctor came on duty, a young man by the name of Meyer, yet one more Israelite in this neighborhood once inhabited by the blind piano tuner, and lo and behold, this young doctor, who couldn't have been more than four or five years older than you were, turned out to be an ear, nose, and throat specialist. After you spat up some blood for him during the preliminary examination, he told you to follow him through the courtyard to his private office in another one of the hospital's pavilions. You sat down in a chair, he sat down in a chair, and then he opened a large leather case filled with thirty or forty sets of tweezers, an impressive array of shining silver instruments, tweezers of every possible size and configuration, some with straight ends, some with curved ends, some with hooked ends, some with twisting ends, some with looping ends, some short and some long, some so intricate and bizarre-looking that you could not imagine how such things could travel down a person's throat. He told you to open your mouth, and one by one he gently guided various sets of tweezers into and down your gullet—so far down that you gagged and spat up more blood each time he pulled another one out. Patience, he said to you, patience, we're going to get it, and then, on the fifteenth try, using one of the largest pairs of tweezers, the grandfather pair with a grotesquely exaggerated scimitar of a hook at the end, he finally got a purchase on the bone, clamped down on it, wiggled it back and forth to free the points that were embedded in your flesh, and slowly lifted it up through the tunnel of your throat and out into the open air. He looked both pleased and astonished. Pleased by his success, but astonished by the size of the bone, which was a good three or four inches long. You were astonished as well. How could you have swallowed such a massive object? you asked yourself. It reminded you of an Eskimo sewing needle, a whalebone corset stay, a poison dart. "You're lucky," Dr. Meyer said, still looking at the bone as he held it up in front of your face. "This one easily could have killed you."

No snow of any significance since the night of February first, but a frigid month with little sun, much rain, much wind, hunkered down in your room every day writing this journal, this journey through winter, and now into March, still cold, still as cold as the winter cold of January and February, and yet every morning you go outside to peruse the garden now, looking for a sign of color, the smallest tip of a crocus leaf jutting from the ground, the first dab of yellow on the forsythia bush, but nothing to report so far, spring will be coming late this year, and you wonder how many more weeks will go by before you can begin searching for your first robin.

The dancers saved you. They are the ones who brought you back to life that evening in December 1978, who made it possible for you to experience *the scalding, epiphanic moment of clarity that pushed you through a crack in the universe* and allowed you to begin again. Bodies in motion, bodies in space, bodies leaping and twisting through empty, unimpeded air, eight dancers in a high school gym in Manhattan, four men and four women, all of them young, eight dancers in their early twenties, and you sitting in the bleachers with a dozen or so acquaintances of the choreographer's to watch an open rehearsal of her new piece. You had been invited by David Reed, a painter you met on the student ship that took you to Europe in 1965, now your oldest friend in New York, who had asked you to come because he was romantically involved with the choreographer, Nina W., a woman you did not know well and whose affair with David did not last long, but, if you are not distorting the facts, you believe she had started out as a dancer in Merce Cunningham's troupe, and now that she had turned her energies to choreography, her work bore some resemblance to Cunningham's: muscular, spontaneous, unpredictable. It was the darkest moment of your life. You were thirty-one years old, your first marriage had just cracked apart, you had an eighteen-month-old son and no regular job, no money to speak of, grinding out your meager, inadequate living as a freelance translator, author of three small books of poetry with at most one hundred readers in the world, padding your pittance of an income by writing critical pieces for *Harper's*, the *New York Review of Books*, and other magazines, and apart from a pseudonymous detective novel you had written the previous summer in an effort to generate some cash (which still had no publisher), your work had staggered to a halt, you were stuck and confused, you had not written a poem in more than a year, and you were slowly coming to the realization that you would never be able to write again. Such was the spot you were in that winter evening more than thirty-two years ago when you walked into the high school gym to watch the open rehearsal of Nina W.'s work in progress. You knew nothing about dance, still know nothing about dance, but you have always responded to it with a soaring inner happiness whenever you see it done well, and as you took your seat next to David, you had no idea what to expect, since at that point Nina W.'s work was unknown to you. She stood on the gym floor and explained to the tiny audience that the rehearsal would be divided into two alternating parts: demonstrations of the principal movements of the piece by the dancers and verbal commentary from her. Then she stepped aside, and the dancers began to move around the floor. The first thing that struck you was that there was no musical accompaniment. The possibility had never occurred to you—dancing to silence rather than to music—for music had always seemed essential to dance, inseparable from dance, not only because it sets the rhythm and speed of the performance but because it establishes an emotional tone for the spectator, giving a narrative coherence to what would otherwise be entirely abstract, but in this case the dancers' bodies were responsible for establishing the rhythm and tone of the piece, and once you began to settle into it, you found the absence of music wholly invigorating, since the dancers were hearing the music in their heads, the rhythms in their heads, hearing what could not be heard, and because these eight young people were good dancers, in fact excellent dancers, it wasn't long before you began to hear those rhythms in your head as well. No sounds, then, except the sounds of bare feet thumping against the wooden floor of the gym. You can't remember the details of their movements, but in your mind you see jumping and spinning, falling and sliding, arms waving and arms dropping to the floor, legs kicking out and running forward, bodies touching and then not touching, and you were impressed by the grace and athleticism of the dancers, the mere sight of their bodies in motion seemed to be carrying you to some unexplored place within yourself, and little by little you felt something lift inside you, felt joy rising through your body and up into your head, a physical joy that was also of the mind, a mounting joy that spread and continued to spread through every part of you. Then, after six or seven minutes, the dancers stopped. Nina W. stepped forward to explain to the audience what they had just witnessed, and the more she talked, the more earnestly and passionately she tried to articulate the movements and patterns of the dance, the less you understood what she was saying. It wasn't because she was using technical terms that were unfamiliar to you, it was the more fundamental fact that her words were utterly useless, inadequate to the task of describing the wordless performance you had just seen, for no words could convey the fullness and brute physicality of what the dancers had done. Then she stepped aside, and the dancers began to move again, immediately filling you with the same joy you had felt before they'd stopped. Five or six minutes later, they stopped again, and once more Nina W. came forward to speak, again failing to capture a hundredth part of the beauty you had just seen, and back and forth it went for the next hour, the dancers taking turns with the choreographer, bodies in motion followed by words, beauty followed by meaningless noise, joy followed by boredom, and at a certain point something began to open up inside you, you found yourself falling through the rift between world and word, the chasm that divides human life from our capacity to understand or express the truth of human life, and for reasons that still confound you, this sudden fall through the empty, unbounded air filled you with a sensation of freedom and happiness, and by the time the performance was over, you were no longer blocked, no longer burdened by the doubts that had been weighing down on you for the past year. You returned to your house in Dutchess County, to the downstairs workroom where you had been sleeping since the end of your marriage, and the next day you began to write, for three weeks you worked on a text of no definable genre, neither a poem nor a prose narrative, attempting to describe what you had seen and felt as you'd watched the dancers dance and the choreographer talk in that high school gym in Manhattan, writing many pages to begin with and then boiling them down to eight pages, the first work of your second incarnation as a writer, the bridge to everything you have written in the years since then, and you remember finishing during a snowstorm late one Saturday night, two o'clock in the morning, the only person awake in the silent house, and the terrible thing about that night, the thing that continues to haunt you, is that just as you were finishing your piece, which you eventually called *White Spaces*, your father was dying in the arms of his girlfriend. The ghoulish trigonometry of fate. Just as you were coming back to life, your father's life was coming to an end.

In order to do what you do, you need to walk. Walking is what brings the words to you, what allows you to hear the rhythms of the words as you write them in your head. One foot forward, and then the other foot forward, the double drumbeat of your heart. Two eyes, two ears, two arms, two legs, two feet. This, and then that. That, and then this. Writing begins in the body, it is the music of the body, and even if the words have meaning, can sometimes have meaning, the music of the words is where the meanings begin. You sit at your desk in order to write down the words, but in your head you are still walking, always walking, and what you hear is the rhythm of your heart, the beating of your heart. Mandelstam: "I wonder how many pairs of sandals Dante wore out while working on the *Commedia*." Writing as a lesser form of dance.

Cataloguing your travels ninety pages ago, you forgot to mention your journeys between Brooklyn and Manhattan, thirty-one years of traveling within your own city since your removal to Kings County in 1980, on average two or three times a week, which would add up to several thousand trips, many of them underground by subway, but many others back and forth across the Brooklyn Bridge in cars and taxis, a thousand crossings, two thousand crossings, five thousand crossings, it is impossible to know how many, but surely it is the trip you have taken more often than any other in your life, and not once have you failed to admire the architecture of the bridge, the curious but altogether satisfying blend of old and new that distinguishes this bridge from all others, the thick stone of the medieval Gothic arches at odds with and yet in harmony with the delicate spider webs of steel cables, once the tallest man-made structure in North America, and back in the days before the suicidal murderers visited New York, it was always the crossing from Brooklyn to Manhattan that you preferred, the anticipation of reaching the exact point where you could simultaneously see the Statue of Liberty in the harbor to your left and the downtown skyline looming in front of you, the immense buildings that would suddenly jump into sight, among them the Towers, of course, the unbeautiful Towers that gradually became a familiar part of the landscape, and even though you still marvel at the skyline whenever you approach Manhattan, now that the Towers are gone you can no longer make the crossing without thinking about the dead, about seeing the Towers burn from your daughter's bedroom window on the top floor of your house, about the smoke and ashes that fell onto the streets of your neighborhood for three days following the attack, and the bitter, unbreathable stench that forced you to shut all the windows of your house until the winds finally shifted away from Brooklyn on Friday, and even though you have continued to cross the bridge two or three times a week in the nine and a half years since then, the journey is no longer the same, the dead are still there, and the Towers are there as well—pulsating in memory, still present as an empty hole in the sky.

You heard the dead calling out to you—but only once, once in all the years you have been alive. You are not someone who sees things that are not there, and while you have often been confused by what you are seeing, you are not prone to hallucinations or fantastical alterations of reality. The same with your ears. Every now and then, while out on one of your walks through the city, you think you hear someone calling to you, think you hear the voice of your wife or daughter or son shouting your name from across the street, but when you turn around to look for them, it is always someone else saying *Paul* or *Dad* or *Daddy*. Twenty years ago, however, perhaps twenty-five years ago, under circumstances far removed from the flow of your daily life, you experienced an auditory hallucination that continues to bewilder you with its vividness and power, the sheer volume of the voices you heard, even though the chorus of the dead screamed out in you for no more than five or ten seconds. You were in Germany, spending the weekend in Hamburg, and on Sunday morning your friend Michael Naumann, who was also your German publisher, suggested that the two of you pay a visit to Bergen-Belsen—or, rather, to the site where Bergen-Belsen had once stood. You wanted to go, even if a part of you was reluctant to go, and you remember the drive there on the nearly empty autobahn that overcast Sunday morning, a white-gray sky hanging over mile after mile of flat land, seeing a car that had crashed into a tree by the side of the road and the corpse of the driver lying on the grass, a body so inert and twisted that you immediately knew the man was dead, and there you were, sitting in the car and thinking about Anne Frank and her sister, Margot, who had both died in Bergen-Belsen, along with tens of thousands of others, the many thousands of others who perished there from typhus and starvation, random beatings, murder. The dozens of films and newsreels you had seen of the death camps were spooling through your head as you sat in the passenger seat of the car, and as you and Michael approached your destination, you found yourself growing more and more anxious and withdrawn. Nothing was left of the camp itself. The buildings had been torn down, the barracks had been demolished and carted away, the barbed-wire fences had vanished, and what stood there now was a small museum, a one-story structure filled with poster-sized black-and-white photographs along with explanatory texts, a grim place, an awful place, but so denuded and antiseptic that you found it hard to imagine the reality of the place as it had been during the war. You couldn't feel the presence of the dead, the horror of so many thousands crammed into that nightmare village surrounded by barbed wire, and as you walked through the museum with Michael (in your memory, you were the only people there), you wished the camp had been left intact so the world could have seen what the architecture of barbarism had looked like. Then you went outside, onto the grounds where the death camp had stood, but it was a grassy field now, a domain of lovely, well-tended grass stretching for several hundred yards in all directions, and if not for the various markers planted in the ground that indicated where the barracks had once been, where certain buildings had once been, there would have been no way to guess what had gone on there several decades earlier. Then you came to a patch of grass that was slightly elevated, three or four inches higher than the rest of the field, a perfect rectangle that measured about twenty feet by thirty feet, the size of a large room, and in one corner there was a marker in the ground that read: *Here lie the bodies of 50,000 Russian soldiers.* You were standing on top of the grave of fifty thousand men. It didn't seem possible that so many dead bodies could fit into such a small space, and when you tried to imagine those bodies beneath you, the tangled corpses of fifty thousand young men packed into what must have been the deepest of deep holes, you began to grow dizzy at the thought of so much death, so much death concentrated in such a small patch of ground, and a moment later you heard the screams, a tremendous surge of voices rose up from the ground beneath you, and you heard the bones of the dead howl in anguish, howl in pain, howl in a roaring cascade of full-throated, earsplitting torment. *The earth was screaming.* For five or ten seconds you heard them, and then they went silent.

Talking to your father in your dreams. For many years now, he has been visiting you in a dark room on the other side of consciousness, sitting down at a table with you for long, unhurried conversations, calm and circumspect, always treating you with kindness and goodwill, always listening carefully to what you say to him, but once the dream is over and you wake up, you can't recall a single word either one of you said.

Sneezing and laughing, yawning and crying, burping and coughing, scratching your ears, rubbing your eyes, blowing your nose, clearing your throat, chewing your lips, rolling your tongue over the backs of your lower teeth, shuddering, farting, hiccuping, wiping sweat from your forehead, running your hands through your hair—how many times have you done those things? How many stubbed toes, smashed fingers, and knocks on the head? How many stumbles, slips, and falls? How many blinks of your eyes? How many steps taken? How many hours spent with a pen in your hand? How many kisses given and received?

Holding your infant children in your arms.

Holding your wife in your arms.

Your bare feet on the cold floor as you climb out of bed and walk to the window. You are sixty-four years old. Outside, the air is gray, almost white, with no sun visible. You ask yourself: How many mornings are left?

A door has closed. Another door has opened.

You have entered the winter of your life.

REPORT FROM THE INTERIOR

{2012}

In the beginning, everything was alive. The smallest objects were endowed with beating hearts, and even the clouds had names. Scissors could walk, telephones and teapots were first cousins, eyes and eyeglasses were brothers. The face of the clock was a human face, each pea in your bowl had a different personality, and the grille on the front of your parents' car was a grinning mouth with many teeth. Pens were airships. Coins were flying saucers. The branches of trees were arms. Stones could think, and God was everywhere.

There was no problem in believing that the man in the moon was an actual man. You could see his face looking down at you from the night sky, and without question it was the face of a man. Little matter that this man had no body—he was still a man as far as you were concerned, and the possibility that there might be a contradiction in all this never once entered your thoughts. At the same time, it seemed perfectly credible that a cow could jump over the moon. And that a dish could run away with a spoon.

Your earliest thoughts, remnants of how you lived inside yourself as a small boy. You can remember only some of it, isolated bits and pieces, brief flashes of recognition that surge up in you unexpectedly at random moments—brought on by the smell of something, or the touch of something, or the way the light falls on something in the here and now of adulthood. At least you think you can remember, you believe you remember, but perhaps you are not remembering at all, or remembering only a later remembrance of what you think you thought in that distant time which is all but lost to you now.

January 3, 2012, exactly one year to the day after you started composing your last book, your now-finished winter journal. It was one thing to write about your body, to catalogue the manifold knocks and pleasures experienced by your physical self, but exploring your mind as you remember it from childhood will no doubt be a more difficult task—perhaps an impossible one. Still, you feel compelled to give it a try. Not because you find yourself a rare or exceptional object of study, but precisely because you don't, because you think of yourself as anyone, as everyone.

The only proof you have that your memories are not entirely deceptive is the fact that you still occasionally fall into the old ways of thinking. Vestiges have lingered well into your sixties, the animism of early childhood has not been fully purged from your mind, and each summer, as you lie on your back in the grass, you look up at the drifting clouds and watch them turn into faces, into birds and animals, into states and countries and imaginary kingdoms. The grilles of cars still make you think of teeth, and the corkscrew is still a dancing ballerina. In spite of the outward evidence, you are still who you were, even if you are no longer the same person.

In thinking about where you want to go with this, you have decided not to cross the boundary of twelve, for after the age of twelve you were no longer a child, adolescence was looming, glimmers of adulthood had already begun to flicker in your brain, and you were transformed into a different kind of being from the small person whose life was a constant plunge into the new, who every day did something for the first time, even several things, or many things, and it is this slow progress from ignorance toward something less than ignorance that concerns you now. Who were you, little man? How did you become a person who could think, and if you could think, where did your thoughts take you? Dig up the old stories, scratch around for whatever you can find, then hold up the shards to the light and have a look at them. Do that. Try to do that.

The world was of course flat. When someone tried to explain to you that the earth was a sphere, a planet orbiting the sun with eight other planets in something called a solar system, you couldn't grasp what the older boy was saying. If the earth was round, then everyone below the equator would fall off, since it was inconceivable that a person could live his life upside down. The older boy tried to explain the concept of gravity to you, but that was beyond your grasp as well. You imagined millions of people plunging headlong through the darkness of an infinite, all-devouring night. If the earth was indeed round, you said to yourself, then the only safe place to be was the North Pole.

No doubt influenced by the cartoons you loved to watch, you thought there was a pole jutting out from the North Pole. Similar to one of those striped, revolving columns that stood in front of barbershops.

Stars, on the other hand, were inexplicable. Not holes in the sky, not candles, not electric lights, not anything that resembled what you knew. The immensity of the black air overhead, the vastness of the space that stood between you and those small luminosities, was something that resisted all understanding. Benign and beautiful presences hovering in the night, there because they were there and for no other reason. The work of God's hand, yes, but what in the world had he been thinking?

————

Your circumstances at the time were as follows: midcentury America; mother and father; tricycles, bicycles, and wagons; radios and black-and-white televisions; standard-shift cars; two small apartments and then a house in the suburbs; fragile health early on, then normal boyhood strength; public school; a family from the striving middle class; a town of fifteen thousand populated by Protestants, Catholics, and Jews, all white except for a smattering of black people, but no Buddhists, Hindus, or Muslims; a little sister and eight first cousins; comic books; Rootie Kazootie and Pinky Lee; "I Saw Mommy Kissing Santa Claus"; Campbell's soup, Wonder bread, and canned peas; souped-up cars (hot rods) and cigarettes for twenty-three cents a pack; a little world inside the big world, which was the entire world for you back then, since the big world was not yet visible.

Armed with a pitchfork, an angry Farmer Gray runs across a cornfield in pursuit of Felix the Cat. Neither one of them can talk, but their actions are accompanied by a steady clang of jaunty, highspeed music, and as you watch the two of them engage in yet another battle of their never-ending war, you are convinced they are real, that these raggedly drawn black-and-white figures are no less alive than you are. They appear every afternoon on a television program called *Junior Frolics*, hosted by a man named Fred Sayles, who is known to you simply as Uncle Fred, the silver-haired gatekeeper to this land of marvels, and because you understand nothing about the production of animated films, cannot even begin to fathom the process by which drawings are made to move, you figure there must be some sort of alternate universe in which characters like Farmer Gray and Felix the Cat can exist—not as pen scratches dancing across a television screen, but as fully embodied, three-dimensional creatures as large as adults. Logic demands that they be large, since the people who appear on television are always larger than their images on-screen, and logic also demands that they belong to an alternate universe, since the universe you live in is not populated by cartoon characters, much as you might wish it was. One day when you are five years old, your mother announces that she will be taking you and your friend Billy to the studio in Newark where *Junior Frolics* is broadcast. You will get to see Uncle Fred in person, she tells you, and be a part of the show. All this is exciting to you, inordinately exciting, but even more exciting is the thought that finally, after months of speculation, you will be able to set eyes on Farmer Gray and Felix the Cat. At long last you will discover what they really look like. In your mind, you see the action unfolding on an enormous stage, a stage the size of a football field, as the crotchety old farmer and the wily black cat chase each other back and forth in one of their epic skirmishes. On the appointed day, however, none of it happens as you thought it would. The studio is small, Uncle Fred has makeup on his face, and after you are given a bag of mints to keep you company during the show, you take your seat in the grandstand with Billy and the other children. You look down at what should be a stage, but which in fact is nothing more than the concrete floor of the studio, and what you see there is a television set. Not even a special television set, but one no bigger or smaller than the set you have at home. The farmer and the cat are nowhere in the vicinity. After Uncle Fred welcomes the audience to the show, he introduces the first cartoon. The television comes on, and there are Farmer Gray and Felix the Cat, bouncing around in the same way they always have, still trapped inside the box, still as small as they ever were. You are thoroughly confused. What error have you made? you ask yourself. Where has your thinking gone wrong? The real is so defiantly at odds with the imagined, you can't help feeling that a nasty trick has been played on you. Stunned with disappointment, you can barely bring yourself to look at the show.

Afterward, walking back to the car with Billy and your mother, you toss away the mints in disgust.

Grass and trees, insects and birds, small animals, and the sounds of those animals as their invisible bodies thrashed through the surrounding bushes. You were five and a half when your family left the cramped garden apartment in Union and installed itself in the old white house on Irving Avenue in South Orange. Not a big house, but the first house your parents had ever lived in, which made it your first house as well, and even though the interior was not spacious, the yard behind the house seemed vast to you, for in fact it was two yards, the first one a small grassy area directly behind the house, bordered by your mother's crescent-shaped flower garden, and then, because a white wooden garage stood just beyond the flowers, bisecting the property into independent terrains, there was a second yard behind it, the back backyard, which was wilder and bigger than the front backyard, a secluded realm in which you conducted your most intense investigations into the flora and fauna of your new kingdom. The only sign of man back there was your father's vegetable garden, which was essentially a tomato garden, planted not long after your family moved into the house in 1952, and every year for the twenty-six and a half years that remained of his life, your father spent his summers cultivating tomatoes, the reddest, plumpest New Jersey tomatoes anyone had ever seen, baskets overflowing with tomatoes every August, so many tomatoes that he would have to give them away before they went bad. Your father's garden, running along a side of the garage in the back backyard. His patch of ground, but your world—and there you lived until you were twelve.

Robins, finches, blue jays, orioles, scarlet tanagers, crows, sparrows, wrens, cardinals, blackbirds, and an occasional bluebird.

Birds were no less strange to you than stars, and because their true home was in the air, you felt that birds and stars belonged to the same family. The incomprehensible gift of being able to fly, not to mention the multitude of bright and dull colors, fit subjects for study and observation, but what intrigued you most about them were the sounds they made, a different language spoken by each kind of bird, whether tuneful songs or harsh, abrasive cries, and early on you were convinced that they were talking to one another, that these sounds were articulated words of a special bird language, and just as there were human beings of different colors who spoke an infinite number of languages, so too with the airborne creatures who sometimes hopped around on the grass in your back backyard, each robin talking to his fellow robins in a language with its own vocabulary and grammatical rules, as comprehensible to them as English was to you.

In the summer: splitting a blade of grass down the middle and whistling through it; capturing fireflies at night and walking around with your magic, glowing jar. In the fall: sticking the pods that fell from the maple trees onto your nose; picking up acorns from the ground and throwing them as far as you could—deep into the bushes and out of sight. Acorns were delicacies coveted by the squirrels, and since squirrels were the animals you admired most—their speed! their death-defying jumps through the branches of the oaks overhead!— you watched them carefully as they dug little holes and buried acorns in the ground. Your mother told you they were saving the acorns for the lean months of winter, but the truth was that not once did you ever see a squirrel dig up an acorn in winter. You concluded that they dug holes for the pure pleasure of digging, that they were mad for digging and simply couldn't stop themselves.

Until you were five or six, perhaps even seven, you thought the words *human being* were pronounced *human bean*. You found it mystifying that humanity should be represented by such a small, common vegetable, but somehow, twisting around your thoughts to accommodate this misunderstanding, you decided that the very smallness of the bean was what made it significant, that we all start out in our mother's womb no larger than a bean, and therefore the bean was the truest, most powerful symbol of life itself.

The God who was everywhere and reigned over everything was not a force of goodness or love but of fear. God was guilt. God was the commander of the celestial mind police, the unseen, all-powerful one who could invade your head and listen to your thoughts, who could hear you talking to yourself and translate the silence into words. God was always watching, always listening, and therefore you had to be on your best behavior at all times. If not, horrendous punishments would come blasting down upon you, unspeakable torments, incarceration in the darkest dungeon, condemned to live on bread and water for the rest of your days. By the time you were old enough to go to school, you learned that any act of rebellion would be crushed. You watched your friends undermine the rules with cunning and brilliance, invent new and ever more devious forms of mayhem behind the backs of the teachers and continually get away with it, whereas you, whenever you succumbed to temptation and participated in these antics, were always caught and punished. Without fail. No talent for mischief, alas, and as you imagined your angry God mocking you with a burst of contemptuous laughter, you realized that you had to be good—or else.

Six years old. Standing in your room one Saturday morning, having just dressed yourself and tied your shoes (such a big boy now, such a capable boy), all ready for action, about to go downstairs and begin the day, and as you stood there in the light of the early spring morning, you were engulfed by a feeling of happiness, an ecstatic, unbridled sense of well-being and joy, and an instant later you said to yourself: There is nothing better than being six years old, six is far and away the best age anyone can be. You remember thinking this as clearly as you remember what you did three seconds ago, it is still blazing inside you fifty-nine years after that morning, undiminished in its clarity, as bright as any one of the thousands or millions or tens of millions of memories you have managed to retain. What had happened to cause such an overpowering feeling? Impossible to know, but you suspect it had something to do with the birth of self-consciousness, that thing that happens to children at around the age of six, when the inner voice awakens and the ability to think a thought and tell yourself you are thinking that thought begins. Our lives enter a new dimension at that point, for that is the moment when we acquire the ability to tell our stories to ourselves, to begin the uninterrupted narrative that continues until the day we die. Until that morning, you just were. Now you knew that you were. You could think about being alive, and once you could do that, you could fully savor the fact of your own existence, which is to say, you could tell yourself how good it was to be alive.

1953. Still six years old, some days or weeks after that transcendent illumination, another turning point in your inner progress, which happened to take place in a movie theater somewhere in New Jersey. You had been to the movies just two or three times before that, in each case an animated film for children (*Pinocchio* and *Cinderella* spring to mind), but films with real people in them had been available to you only on television, principally low-budget Westerns from the thirties and forties, Hopalong Cassidy, Gabby Hayes, Buster Crabbe, and Al "Fuzzy" St. John, clunky old shoot-'em-ups in which the heroes wore white hats and the villains had black mustaches, all of which you thoroughly enjoyed and believed in with fervent conviction. Then, at some point during the year you turned six, you were taken by someone to a film that was shown at night—no doubt your parents, although you have no memory of them being there. It was your first movie experience that was not a Saturday matinee, not a Disney cartoon, not an antique black-and-white Western—but a new film in color that had been made for grown-ups. You remember the immensity of the crowded theater, the spookiness of sitting in the dark when the lights went out, a feeling of anticipation and unease, as if you were both there and not there at the same time, no longer inside your own body, in the way one disappears from oneself in the grip of a dream. The film was *The War of the Worlds*, based on the novel by H. G. Wells, lauded at the time as a breakthrough work in the realm of special effects—more elaborate, more convincing, more advanced than any film that had come before it. So you have read in recent years, but you knew nothing about that in 1953, you were merely a six-year-old boy watching a battalion of Martians invade the earth, and with the largest of large screens looming before you, the colors felt more vivid than any colors you had seen before, so lustrous, so clear, so intense that your eyes ached. Stone-round metal spaceships landed out of the night sky, one by one the lids of these flying machines would open, and slowly a Martian would emerge from within, a preternaturally tall insect-like figure with stick arms and eerily long fingers. The Martian would fix his gaze on an earthling, zero in on him with his grotesque, bulbous eyes, and an instant later there would be a flash of light. Seconds after that, the earthling would be gone. Obliterated, dematerialized, reduced to a shadow on the ground, and then the shadow would vanish as well, as if that person had never been there, had never even been alive. Oddly enough, you don't remember being scared. Transfixed is probably the word that best captures what

was happening to you, a sense of awe, as if the spectacle had hyp-
notized you into a state of numbed rapture. Then something terrible happened, something far more terrible than the deaths or
obliterations of the soldiers who had tried to kill the Martians
with their useless weapons. Perhaps these military men had been
wrong to assume the invaders had come with hostile intentions,
perhaps the Martians were simply defending themselves as any
other creatures would if they found themselves under attack. You
were willing to grant them the benefit of the doubt, in any case,
for it seemed wrong to you that the humans should have allowed
their fear of the unknown to turn so quickly into violence. Then
came the man of peace. He was the father of the leading lady, the
young and beautiful girlfriend or wife of the leading man, and this
father was a pastor or minister of some kind, a man of God, and
in a calm and soothing voice he counseled those around him to
approach the aliens with kindness and friendship, to come to them
with a love of God in their hearts. To prove his point, the brave
pastor-father started walking toward one of the ships, holding up
a Bible in one hand and a cross in the other, telling the Martians
they had nothing to fear, that we of the earth wanted to live in
harmony with everyone in the universe. His mouth was trembling
with emotion, his eyes were lit up with the power of his faith, and
then, as he came within a few feet of the ship, the lid opened, a
stick-like Martian appeared, and before the pastor-father could
take another step, there was a flash of light, and the bearer of the
holy word was turned into a shadow. Soon after that, not even a
shadow—turned into nothing at all. God, the all-powerful one,
had no power. In the face of evil, God was as helpless as the most
helpless man, and those who believed in him were doomed. Such
was the lesson you learned that night from *The War of the Worlds*. It
was a jolt you have never fully recovered from.

———

Forgive others, always forgive others—but never yourself. Say please and thank you. Don't put your elbows on the table. Don't brag. Never say unkind things about a person behind his back. Remember to put your dirty clothes in the hamper. Turn out the lights before you leave a room. Look people in the eye when you talk to them. Don't talk back to your parents. Wash your hands with soap and make sure to scrub under your nails. Never tell lies, never steal, never hit your little sister. Shake hands firmly. Be home by five o'clock. Brush your teeth before going to bed. And above all remember: don't walk under ladders, avoid black cats, and never let your feet touch the cracks in sidewalks.

You worried about the unfortunate ones, the downtrodden, the poor, and even though you were too young to understand anything about politics or the economy, to comprehend how crushing the forces of capitalism can be on the ones who have little or nothing, you had only to lift your head and look around you to realize that the world was unjust, that some people suffered more than others, that the word *equal* was in fact a relative term. It probably had something to do with your early exposure to the black slums of Newark and Jersey City, the Friday evenings when you would make the rounds with your father as he collected the rent from his tenants, the rare middle-class boy who had a chance to enter the apartments of the poor and desperately poor, to see and smell the conditions of poverty, the tired women and their children with only an occasional man in sight, and because your father's black tenants were always exceedingly kind to you, you wondered why these good people had to live with so little, so much less than you had, you so snug in your cozy suburban house, and they in their barren rooms with broken furniture or barely any furniture at all. It wasn't a question of race for you, at least not then it wasn't, since you felt comfortable among your father's black tenants and didn't care whether their skin was black or white, it all came down to a question of money, of not having enough money, of not having the kind of work to earn them enough money to live in a house like yours. Later on, when you were a bit older and started reading American history, at a moment in American history that happened to coincide with the flowering of the civil rights movement, you were able to understand a good deal more about what you had witnessed as a child of six and seven, but back then, in the obscure days of your dawning consciousness, you understood nothing. Life was kind to some and cruel to others, and your heart ached because of it.

Then, too, there were the *starving children of India*. This was more abstract to you, more difficult to grasp because more distant and alien, but nevertheless it exerted a powerful influence over your imagination. Half-naked children without enough to eat, emaciated limbs as thin as flutes, shoeless, dressed in rags, wandering through vast, crowded cities begging for crusts of bread. That was the vision you saw every time your mother talked about those children, which never happened anywhere except at the dinner table, for that was the standard ploy of all American mothers in the 1950s, who incessantly referred to the malnourished, destitute children of India in order to shame their own children into cleaning their plates, and how often you wished you could invite an Indian child to your house to share your dinner with you, for the truth was that you were a picky eater when you were small, no doubt the result of a faulty digestive system that afflicted you up to the age of three and a half or four, and there were certain foods that you couldn't abide, that made you ill just to look at them, and each time you failed to finish off what had been served to you, you would think about the boys and girls of India and feel riven with guilt.

You can't remember being read to, nor can you remember learning how to read. At most, you can recall talking to your mother about some of the characters you were fond of, characters from books, books she therefore must have read to you, but you have no memory of holding those books in your hands, no memory of sitting beside your mother or lying beside her as she pointed to the illustrations and read the words of the stories out loud to you. You cannot hear her voice, you cannot feel her body next to yours. If you strain hard enough, however, closing your eyes long enough to put yourself in a kind of semi-trance, you can just barely manage to summon up the impact certain fairy tales had on you, in particular "Hansel and Gretel," which was the one that frightened you most, but also "Rumpelstiltskin" and "Rapunzel," along with dim recollections of looking at pictures of Dumbo, Winnie the Pooh, and a little dalmatian named Peewee. But the story you cared about most, the one you still know more or less by heart, which means that it must have been read to you many dozens of times, was *Peter Rabbit*, the tale of poor naughty Peter, the wayward son of old Mrs. Rabbit, and his misadventures in Mr. McGregor's vegetable patch. As you flip through a copy of the book now, you are astonished by how familiar it is to you, every detail of every painting, nearly every word of the text, especially the chilling words from old Mrs. Rabbit on the second page: "You may go into the fields or down the lane, but don't go into Mr. McGregor's garden: your Father had an accident there; he was put in a pie by Mrs. McGregor." No wonder the story had such an effect on you. Charming and bucolic as the setting might be, Peter has not gone off on some lighthearted afternoon romp. By sneaking into Mr. McGregor's garden, he is boldly risking his own death, stupidly risking his own death, and as you study the contents of the book now, you can imagine how intensely you must have feared for

Peter's life—and how deeply you rejoiced at his escape. A memory that is not a memory, and yet it still lives on in you. When your daughter was born twenty-four years ago, one of the presents she received was a china cup decorated with two illustrations from Beatrix Potter books. The cup somehow managed to survive the perils of her infancy and childhood, and for the past fifteen years you have been using it to drink your tea in the morning. Just one month short of your sixty-fifth birthday, and every morning you drink from a cup designed for children, a Peter Rabbit cup. You tell yourself that you prefer this cup to all other cups in the house because of its perfect size. Smaller than a mug, larger than a traditional teacup, with a pleasing curve around the lip at the top, which feels comfortable against your own lips and allows the tea to go down your throat without spilling. A practical cup, then, an essential cup, but at the same time you would not be telling the truth if you claimed to be indifferent to the pictures that adorn it. You enjoy beginning the day with Peter Rabbit, your old friend from earliest childhood, from a time so distant that no conscious memories belong to it, and you live in dread of the morning when the cup will slip out of your hand and break.

At some point in your adolescence, your mother told you that you could identify the letters of the alphabet by the time you were three or four. You don't know if this assertion can be believed, since your mother tended to exaggerate whenever she talked about your youthful accomplishments, and the fact that you were put in the middle reading group when you started the first grade would seem to suggest that you were not as precocious as your mother thought you were. See Dick run. See Jane run. You were six years old, and your most vivid memory from that time places you at a desk that was set apart from the other children, a single desk at the back of the room, where you had been temporarily exiled for misbehaving in class (either talking to someone when you were supposed to be silent or as a result of one of the many punishments you received because of your ineptitude at making mischief), and as you sat at your solitary desk paging through a book that must have been printed in the 1920s (the boys in the illustrations were wearing knickers), your teacher came over to you, a kind young woman with thick, freckled arms named Miss Dorsey, or Dorsi, or perhaps Mrs. Dorsey or Dorsi, and put her hand on your shoulder, touching you gently, even tenderly, which surprised you at first but felt ever so good, and then she bent down and whispered in your ear, telling you that she was encouraged by the progress you had been making, that your work had improved dramatically, and therefore she had decided to shift you over to the top reading group. You must have been getting better, then. Whatever difficulties you had encountered in the early weeks of the school year were behind you now, and yet, when you retrieve the only other clear memory you have held on to from those days of learning how to read and write, you can do little more than shake your head in bafflement. You don't know if this incident took place before or after your promotion to the highest reading group, but you distinctly recall that you came to school a bit late that morning because of a doctor's appointment and that the first lesson of the day was already in progress. You slipped into your regular seat beside Malcolm Franklin, a large, hulking boy with exceptionally broad shoulders who was supposedly related to Benjamin Franklin, a fact or non-fact that always impressed you. Miss or Mrs. Dorsey-Dorsi was standing at the blackboard in front of the room, instructing the class on how to print the letter *w*. Each pupil, hunched over his or her desk with a pencil in hand, was carefully imitating her by writing out a row of *w*'s. When you looked to your left to see how Benjamin Franklin's relative was faring with the assignment, you were amused to discover that your classmate wasn't pausing to separate his *w*'s (*w w w w*) but was linking them all together (*wwww*). You were intrigued by how bold and interesting this elongated letter looked on the page, and even though you knew perfectly well that a real *w* had only four strokes, you rashly decided that you preferred Malcolm's version, and so, rather than do the assignment correctly, you copied your friend's example, willfully sabotaging the exercise and proving, once and for all, that in spite of the progress you had made, you were still a world-class dunderhead.

There was a time in your life, perhaps before six or after six—the chronology has blurred—when you believed the alphabet contained two extra letters, two secret letters that were known only to you. A backwards L: ⌐. And an upside-down A: ∀.

The best thing about the grammar school you attended, which lasted from kindergarten to the end of the sixth grade, was that no homework was ever assigned. The administrators who ran the local board of education were followers of John Dewey, the philosopher who had changed American teaching methods with his liberal, human approach to childhood development, and you were the beneficiary of Dewey's wisdom, a boy who was allowed to run free the moment the final bell sounded and school was done for the day, free to play with your friends, free to go home and read, free to do nothing. You are immensely grateful to those unknown gentlemen for keeping your boyhood intact, for not burdening you with unnecessary busywork, for having the intelligence to understand that children can take just so much, and then they must be left to their own devices. They proved that everything that needs to be learned can be learned within the confines of school, for you and your classmates received good primary educations under that system, not always with the most inventive teachers, perhaps, but competent for all that, and they drilled the three R's into you with indelible results, and when you think about your own two children, who grew up in an age of confusion and anxiety about pedagogical matters, you remember how they were subjected to grinding, unbearably tedious homework obligations night after night, often needing their parents' help in order to finish their assignments, and year after year, as you watched their bodies droop and their eyes begin to shut, you felt sorry for them, saddened that so many hours of their young lives were being thrown away in the service of a bankrupt idea.

There were few books in your house. The formal educations of both your parents had stopped at the end of high school, and neither one of them had any interest in reading. There was a decent public library in the town where you lived, however, and you went there often, checking out two or three or four books a week. By the time you were eight, you had acquired the habit of reading novels, for the most part mediocre ones, stories written and published for young people in the early fifties, countless volumes in the Hardy Boys series, for example, which you later learned had been created by someone who lived in Maplewood, the town next to yours, but the ones you liked best were novels about sports, in particular Clair Bee's Chip Hilton series, which followed the high school adventures of heroic Chip and his friend Biggie Cohen as they triumphed in one closely fought contest after another, games that always ended with a last-second touchdown pass, a half-court shot at the final buzzer, or a walk-off home run in the bottom of the eleventh inning. You also remember a gripping novel called *Flying Spikes*, about an aging, over-the-hill ex–major leaguer trying for one last shot at glory in the low minor leagues, as well as numerous nonfiction works about your favorite sport, such as *My Greatest Day in Baseball* and books about Babe Ruth, Lou Gehrig, Jackie Robinson, and the young Willie Mays. Biographies gave

you almost as much pleasure as novels did, and you read them
with passionate curiosity, especially the lives of people from the
distant past, Abraham Lincoln, Joan of Arc, Louis Pasteur, and
that man of multiple talents, the ancestor or not-ancestor of your
former classmate, Benjamin Franklin. Landmark Books—you remember those well, your grammar school library was filled with
them—but even more engaging were the hardcover books from
Bobbs-Merrill with the orange boards and spines, a vast collection of biographies with stark black silhouette illustrations inter-
spersed among the pages of text. You read dozens of them, if not
scores. And then there was the book your mother's mother gave
you as a present, which soon became one of your most cherished
possessions, a thick volume with the title *Of Courage and Valor*
(written by an author named Strong and published by the Hart
Book Company in 1955), a compendium of over fifty short biographies of the gallant, virtuous dead, including David (defeating
Goliath), Queen Esther, Horatius at the bridge, Androcles and the
lion, William Tell, John Smith and Pocahontas, Sir Walter Raleigh, Nathan Hale, Sacajawea, Simón Bolívar, Florence Nightin-
gale, Harriet Tubman, Susan B. Anthony, Booker T. Washington,
and Emma Lazarus. For your eighth birthday, that same beloved
grandmother gave you a multi-volume edition of the works of
Robert Louis Stevenson. The language of *Kidnapped* and *Treasure
Island* was too difficult for you at that age (you remember, for example, stumbling over the word *fatigue* the first time you encountered it in print and pronouncing it to yourself as *fat-a-gew*), but
you manfully struggled through the less bulky *Dr. Jekyll and Mr.
Hyde*, even if most of it went sailing clear over your head as well.
You adored the much simpler *A Child's Garden of Verses*, however,
and because you knew that Stevenson was a grown man when
those poems were written, you were impressed by how deftly and
persuasively he employed the first person throughout the book,
pretending to write from the point of view of a small child, and

you understand now, suddenly, that this was your first glimpse into the hidden wheelworks of literary creation, the mystifying process by which a person can leap into a mind that is not his own. The following year, you wrote your first poem, directly inspired by Stevenson, since he was the only poet you had read, a wretched piece of dried-out snot that began with the couplet: *Spring is here, / Give a cheer!* Thankfully, you have forgotten the rest, but what you do remember is the happiness that rushed through you as you composed what was, and undoubtedly still is, the worst poem ever written, for the time of year was indeed early spring, and as you walked alone across the newly resurgent grass in Grove Park and felt the warmth of the sun upon your face, you were in an exultant mood, and you felt the need to express that exaltation in words, in written, rhyming words. A pity that your rhymes were so impoverished, but no matter, what counted then was the impulse, the effort, the heightened sense of who you were and how deeply you felt you belonged to the world around you as your pencil inched across the page and you eked out your miserable verses. That same spring, for the first time in your life, you bought a book with your own money. You had had your eye on it for some weeks or months before that, but it took a while for you to save up the necessary cash ($3.95 is the figure that comes back to you now) in order to walk home with the gigantic Modern Library edition of Edgar Allan Poe's complete poems and stories. Poe was too difficult for you as well, too florid and complex a writer for your nine-year-old brain to grasp, but even if you understood only a small fraction of what you were reading, you loved the sound of the words in your head, the thickness of the language, the exotic gloom that permeated Poe's long, baroque sentences. Within a year, most of the difficulties had vanished, and by the time you were ten, you had made your next important discovery: Sherlock Holmes. Holmes and Watson, the dear companions of your solitary hours, that strange pair of Dr. Dull Common Sense and Mr. Eccentric Mastermind, and although you followed the ins and outs of their numerous cases with avid attention, what delighted you most were their conversations, the invigorating back-and-forth of opposing sensibilities, in particular one exchange that so startled you, so vehemently overturned everything you had been taught to think about the world, that the revelation went on troubling you and challenging you for years to come. Watson, the practical man of science, tells Holmes about the solar system—the same solar system you had struggled so hard to comprehend when you were younger—explaining that the earth and the other planets revolve around the sun in a precise and orderly fashion, and Holmes, the arrogant and unpredictable Mr. Know-It-All, promptly tells Watson that he has no interest in learning these things, that such knowledge is an utter waste of time and he will do everything in his power to forget what he has just been told. You were a ten-year-old fourth grader when you read that passage, perhaps an eleven-year-old fifth grader, and until then you had never heard anyone argue against the pursuit of learning, especially someone of Holmes's stature, a man who was recognized as one of the great thinkers of the century, and here he was telling his friend that *he didn't care.* In your world, you were supposed to care, you were supposed to show an interest in all realms of human knowledge, to study math as well as penmanship, music as well as science, and your much-admired Holmes was saying no, some things were more important than others, and the unimportant things should be tossed away and forgotten, since they served no purpose except to clutter one's mind with useless bits of *nothing.* Some years later, when you found yourself losing interest in science and math, you recalled Holmes's words—and used them to defend your indifference to those subjects. An idiotic position, no doubt, but you nevertheless embraced it. Further proof, perhaps, that fiction can indeed poison the mind.

———

The most celebrated figure from your part of the world was Thomas Edison, who had been dead for just sixteen years when you were born. Edison's laboratory was in West Orange, not far from your house in adjacent South Orange, and because it had been turned into a museum after the inventor's death, *a national landmark,* you visited it several times on school trips when you were a child, reverently paying homage to the Wizard of Menlo Park, who was responsible for more than a thousand inventions, including the incandescent lightbulb, the phonograph, and the movies, which to your mind made Edison one of the most important men who had ever lived, the number one scientist in human history. After a tour of the lab, visitors would be taken outside to a building called the Black Maria, a large tar-paper shack that had been the first film studio in the world, and there you and your classmates would watch a projection of *The Great Train Robbery,* the first feature film ever made. You felt that you had entered the innermost sanctum of genius, a holy shrine. Yes, Sherlock Holmes was your favorite thinker back then, a fearless exemplar of intellectual probity, the one who unveiled to you the miracle and the power of systematic, rational deduction, but Holmes was no more than a figment, an imaginary being who existed only in words, whereas Edison had been real, a flesh-and-blood man, and because his inventions had been created so close to where you lived, almost within shouting distance of your house, you felt a special connection to Edison, a singular intensity of admiration, if not whole-hog, out-and-out worship. You read at least two biographies of your hero before you were ten (a Landmark book first, then one of those orange books with the silhouette illustrations), saw television broadcasts of the two films that had been made about him—*Young Tom Edison* (with Mickey Rooney), *Edison the Man* (with Spencer Tracy)—and for some reason (it strikes you as preposterous now), you imagined there was something significant about the fact that both your birthday and Edison's birthday fell in early February and, even more significant, that you had been born exactly one hundred years after Edison (minus a week). But best of all, most important of all, the thing that solidified your bond with Edison to the point of profoundest kinship, was the discovery that the man who cut your hair had once been Edison's personal barber. His name was Rocco, a short, not-so-young man who wielded his comb and scissors in a shop just beyond the edge of the Seton Hall College campus, which was only a few blocks from your house. This was the mid-fifties, the late fifties, the era of the flattop and the crew cut, of white bucks and white socks and saddle shoes, of Keds sneakers and stiff, stiff jeans, and since you wore your hair short in the same way nearly every other boy did at the time, visits to the barbershop were frequent, on average twice a month, which meant that every other week throughout your childhood you sat in Rocco's chair looking at a large reproduction of a portrait of Edison that hung on the wall just to the left of the mirror, a picture with a handwritten note stuck into the lower right-hand corner of the frame that read: *To my friend Rocco: Genius is 1% inspiration, 99% perspiration—Thomas A. Edison.* Rocco was the link that tied you directly to Edison, for the hands that had once touched the inventor's head were now touching your head, and who was to say that the thoughts inside Edison's head had not traveled into Rocco's fingers, and because those fingers were now touching you, was it not reasonable to assume that some of those thoughts might now be sinking into your head? You didn't believe any of this, of course, but you liked to pretend you did, and each time you sat in Rocco's chair, you enjoyed playing this game of magical thought transference, as if you, who were destined to invent nothing, who would demonstrate not the smallest aptitude for things mechanical in years to come, were the legitimate heir of Edison's mind. Then, to your astonishment, your father quietly informed you one day that he had worked in Edison's lab after graduating from high school. Nineteen twenty-nine, his first full-time job, one of the many young men who had toiled under the master at Menlo Park. Nothing more than that. Perhaps he was trying to spare your feelings by not telling you the rest of the story, but the mere fact that Edison had been a part of your family's history, which meant that he was now a part of your history as well, quickly trumped Rocco's fingers as the most important link to the great man. You were immensely proud of your father. Surely this was the most vital piece of information he had ever shared about himself, and you never tired of passing that information on to your friends. *My father worked for Edison.* Meaning, you would now suppose, that your remote and uncommunicative father was no longer a complete cipher to you, that he was really someone, after all, a person who had made a contribution to the fundamental business of bettering the world. It wasn't until you were fourteen that your father told you the second half of the story. The job with Edison had lasted only a few days, you now learned—not because your father hadn't been doing well, but because Edison had found out he was Jewish, and since no Jews were allowed in the sacred precincts of Menlo Park, the old man summoned your father to his office and fired him on the spot. Your idol turned out to have been a rabid, hate-filled anti-Semite, a well-known fact that had not been included in any of the books you read about him.

Nevertheless, living heroes held far more sway over you than dead ones, even such exalted figures as Edison, Lincoln, and the young shepherd David, who slew the mighty Goliath with a single stone. Like all small boys, you wanted your father to be a hero, but your notion of heroism was too narrowly defined back then to grant your father a place in the pantheon. In your mind, heroism had to do with courage in battle, it was a question of how a person conducted himself in the midst of war, and your father was excluded from consideration because he hadn't fought in the war, the war being the Second World War, which had ended just eighteen months before you were born. The fathers of most of your friends had been soldiers, they had served the cause in one way or another, and when the little gang you belonged to gathered to stage mock battles in your suburban backyards, pretending to be fighting in Europe (against the Nazis) or on some island in the Pacific (against the Japanese), your friends often showed up with various pieces of military equipment that had been given to them by their fathers (helmets, canteens, metal cups, cartridge belts, binoculars) in order to make the games feel more authentic. You, however, always came empty-handed. Later on, you learned that your father had been exempted from military service because he was in the wire business, which the government had deemed essential to the war effort. That always felt a bit lame to you, but the truth was that your father was older than the other fathers, already thirty when America entered the war, which meant he might not have been drafted in any case. You were just five and six and seven when you played soldier with your friends, much too young to understand anything about your father's wartime situation, and so you began to question him about why he had no equipment to lend you for your games, perhaps even to pester him, and because your father could not bring himself to tell you that he hadn't served in the army (was he ashamed—or was it simply that he felt you would be disappointed?), he concocted a ruse to satisfy your wishes—and also, perhaps, to elevate himself in your eyes, to be seen as a hero—but the trick backfired on him and wound up disappointing you, just as your father had feared the truth would disappoint you. One night, he stole into your room after you had been put to bed. He thought you were asleep, but you weren't, your eyes were still open, and without saying a word you watched your father put two or three objects on your desk and then tiptoe out of the room. In the morning, you discovered that the objects were worn-out specimens of military gear—only one of which you can still see with any certainty: a tin canteen encased in thick green canvas. At breakfast, your father told you that he had dug up some of his old stuff from the war, but you weren't fooled, you knew in your heart that those things had never belonged to him, that he had bought them the previous afternoon in an army surplus store, and although you said nothing, pretending to be happy with your gifts, you hated your father for lying to you like that. Now, all these years later, you feel only pity.

By contrast, there was the counselor at the day camp you attended during the summer when you were five, a young man named Lenny, no more than twenty-three or twenty-four years old, much liked by all the boys in his charge, slight of build, funny, warm, strongly opposed to harsh discipline, who had recently come home to New Jersey after serving as a soldier in Korea. You knew that a war was being fought over there, but the details were entirely obscure to you, and as far as you can remember, Lenny never talked about his experiences in combat. It was your mother who told you about them, she only twenty-seven at the time and therefore a contemporary of Lenny's, and one afternoon when she came to fetch you, the two of them had a talk while you were gathering up your things, and when you and your mother were driving home in the car together, you could see how upset she was, more shaken than at any time you could remember (which surely accounts for why the incident has stayed with you all these years). She began telling you about frostbite, the intolerable cold of the Korean winters and the inadequate boots worn by the American soldiers, the badly designed boots that could do nothing to protect the feet of the infantrymen, causing frostbite, which blackened the toes and often led to amputation. Lenny, she said, poor Lenny had gone through all that, and now that your mother was explaining this to you, you realized that Lenny's hands had also suffered from the cold, for you had noticed there was something wrong with the top joints of his fingers, that they were harder and more wrinkled than normal adult fingers, and what you had assumed to be a genetic defect of some kind you now understood was the result of war. Much as you had always liked him, Lenny now rose in your estimation to the rank of exalted person.

If your father wasn't a hero to you, couldn't be a hero to you, that didn't mean you gave up searching for heroes elsewhere. Buster Crabbe and other movie cowboys served as early models, establishing a code of masculine honor to be studied and emulated, the man of few words who never looked for trouble but who would respond with daring and cunning whenever trouble found him, the man who upheld justice with quiet, self-effacing dignity and was willing to risk his life in the struggle between good and evil. Women could be heroic, too, at times even more courageous than men, but women were never your models for the simple reason that you were a boy, not a girl, and it was your destiny to grow up to become a man. By the time you were seven, the cowboys had given way to athletes, primarily baseball and football players, and while it puzzles you now that you should have thought that excelling at ball games could have taught you anything about how to live your life, there it was, for by now you had become a passionate young sportsman yourself, a boy who had turned these pastimes into the very center of his existence, and when you saw how the great ones performed under the pressure of do-or-die moments in stadiums thronged with fifty or sixty thousand people, you felt they were the incontestable heroes of your world. From courage under fire to skill under fire, the ability to thread a bullet pass through heavy coverage into the hands of a receiver or to lash a double to right-center field when the hit-and-run is on, physical prowess now instead of moral grandeur, or perhaps physical virtues translated into moral grandeur, but again, there it was, and you nurtured these admirations of yours all through the middle years of your childhood. Before you turned eight, you had already written your first fan letter, inviting Cleveland Browns quarterback Otto Graham, the top professional football player of the day, to attend your upcoming birthday party in New Jersey. To your everlasting surprise, Graham wrote back to you, sending a short, typewritten letter on official Cleveland Browns stationery. Needless to say, he declined the invitation, telling you that he had other obligations that morning, but the graciousness of his response mitigated the sting of disappointment—for even though you'd known it was a long shot, a part of you had thought he might actually come, and you had played out the scene of his arrival a hundred times in your head. Then, some months after that, you wrote to Bobby S., the captain and quarterback of the local high school football team, telling him what a magnificent player you thought he was, and because you were such a runt back then, which meant that your letter must have bordered on the ridiculous, filled with spelling errors and inane malapropisms, Bobby S. took the trouble to write back to you, no doubt touched to learn that he had such a young fan, and now that the football season had come to an end, he invited you to a basketball game as his guest (he played football in the autumn, basketball in the winter, and baseball in the spring—a three-sport superstar), instructing you to come down to the floor during warm-ups to identify yourself, which you did, and then Bobby S. found a spot for you on the bench, where you watched the game with the team. Bobby S. was all of seventeen or eighteen at the time, no more than an adolescent, but to you he was a full-grown man, a giant, as were all the other players on the squad. You watched the game in a blur of happiness, sitting in that old high school gym that had been built in the 1920s, both jangled and inspirited by the noise of the crowd around you, awed by the beauty of the cheerleaders who came prancing onto the floor during time-outs, rooting for your man Bobby S., who had made all this possible for you, but of the game itself you remember nothing, not a single shot, rebound, or stolen pass—only the fact that you were there, overjoyed to be sitting on the bench with the high school team, feeling as if you had stepped into the pages of a Chip Hilton novel.

A friend of your parents', Roy B., had played third base for the Newark Bears, the legendary minor league team that had once been part of the New York Yankees system. Nicknamed Whoops— for shouting out that word whenever he made an error in the field—he never made it to the major leagues, but he had played with and against any number of future all-stars, and since everyone liked the fast-talking, effervescent Whoops, a squat fireplug of a man who owned a men's discount clothing store out on Route 22, he was still in touch with many of his old ballplayer friends. He and his wife, Dolly, had three children, all girls, none of whom had any interest in baseball, and because he knew how much you cared about the game, both as a player and as a fan, he took you under his wing as a kind of surrogate son or nephew, a boy in any case, to share his baseball past with. One weekday night in the spring of 1956, just as you were about to go to bed, the telephone rang and, lo and behold, there was Phil Rizzuto on the other end of the line, the one and only Scooter, the Yankees' shortstop from 1941 until his retirement earlier that month, asking if you were Paul, Whoops's young friend. I've heard you're a terrific infielder, he said, speaking in that famously jovial voice of his, and I just wanted to say hello and tell you to keep up the good work. You had been caught off guard, you barely knew what to say, you were too flummoxed and tongue-tied to give more than one-syllable answers to Rizzuto's questions, but this was your first conversation with a legitimate hero, and even though it lasted no more than a couple of minutes, you nevertheless felt honored by that unexpected call, ennobled by your brush with the great man. Then, a week or two later, a postcard arrived in the mail. On the front, a color photograph of the interior of Whoops's clothing store: rack after rack of men's suits under the glare of fluorescent lights, ghost-like suits with no bodies in them, an army of the missing. On the back, a handwritten message: "Dear Paul, Hurry and grow up. The Cards can use a good third baseman. Yours, Stan Musial." Phil Rizzuto had been one thing, an excellent player whose career was now behind him, but Musial was one of the immortals, a .330 lifetime hitter who ranked as the National League equivalent of Ted Williams, a player still in his prime, Stan the Man, the left-handed slugger with the curved stance and lightning-quick bat, and you imagined him strolling into Whoops's store one afternoon to say hello to his old friend and the ever-vigilant Whoops asking Musial to write a few words to his little protégé, *a short message for the kid,* and now those words were sitting in your hands, which made you feel as if a god had reached out and touched you on the forehead. There was more, however, at least one more act of kindness from the good-hearted Whoops, a final display of generosity that surpassed all the other gifts he had bestowed on you. How would you like to meet Whitey Ford? he asked you one day. It was still 1956, but mid-October by then, not long after the end of the World Series. Of course you would like to meet Whitey Ford, you answered, you would love to meet Whitey Ford, who was the ace pitcher of the champion Yankees, the pitcher with the highest winning percentage in the history of the game, the short, brilliant lefty who had just completed his finest season. What person in his right mind would not want to meet Whitey Ford? And so it was arranged: Whoops and Whitey would stop by your house one afternoon next week, sometime between three-thirty and four, late enough to be certain you would be back from school. You had no idea what to expect, but you hoped the visit would be a long one, with Whoops and Whitey sitting around the living room with you for several hours talking baseball, during which Whitey would divulge the subtlest, most hidden secrets about the art of pitching, for in looking at you he would see straight into your soul and understand that, young as you might have been, you were someone worthy of being entrusted with that forbidden knowledge. On the appointed day, you rushed home from school, which was just a short distance from your house, and waited, waited for what must have been an hour and a half but felt as if it were a week, fretfully pacing around the rooms on the ground floor, all alone with your thoughts, your mother and father both off at work, your five-year-old sister God knows where, alone in the little clapboard house on Irving Avenue, growing more and more nervous about the supreme encounter, wondering if Whoops and Whitey would actually show up, fearing they had forgotten the rendezvous, or had been delayed by unforeseen circumstances, or had been killed in a car crash, and then, finally, when you were beginning to despair that Whitey Ford would ever set foot in your house, the doorbell rang. You opened the door, and there on the front steps was the five-foot-six-inch Whoops and the five-foot-ten-inch Yankee pitcher. A big smile from Whoops, followed by a terse but friendly handshake from the maestro. You invited them in, but Whoops or Whitey (impossible to remember which one) said they were running late and had only dropped by for a quick hello. You did your best to hide your disappointment, understanding that Whitey Ford would not in fact be setting foot in your house and that no secret knowledge would be imparted to you that day. The three of you stood there talking for what amounted to four minutes at most, which should have been enough to satisfy you, and surely would have been enough if you had not begun to suspect that the Whitey Ford standing on the front steps of your house was not the real Whitey Ford. He was the right size, his voice had the proper Queens accent, but something about his face looked different from the pictures you had seen of him, less handsome somehow, the round cheeks less round than they should have been, and even though his hair was blond, as Whitey's hair was, it was cut in a severe flattop, whereas in all the photos you had seen of Whitey his hair was longer, combed back in a kind of modified pompadour. You wondered if the real Whitey Ford had backed out of the visit and that Whoops, not wanting to let you down, had produced this more or less reasonable facsimile of Whitey as a substitute. To quiet your doubts, you began asking Whitey or not-Whitey questions about his record of the past season. Nineteen and six, he said, which was the correct answer. Two point four seven, which was also the correct answer, but still you couldn't shake the thought that a not–Whitey Ford might have done some homework before the visit so as not to be tripped up by a wiseass nine-year-old kid, and when he thrust out his right arm to shake your hand good-bye, you weren't sure if you were shaking Whitey Ford's hand or the hand of someone else. You still don't know. For the first time in your life, an experience had led you into a zone of absolute ambiguity. A question had been raised, and it could not be answered.

Boredom must not be overlooked as a source of contemplation and reverie, the hundreds of hours of your early childhood when you found yourself alone, uninspired, at loose ends, too listless or distracted to want to play with your little trucks and cars, to take the trouble to set up your miniature cowboys and Indians, the green and red plastic figures you would spread out on the floor of your room in order to send them into imaginary assaults and ambushes, or to start building something with your Lincoln Logs or your Erector set (which you never liked anyway, no doubt because of your ineptitude with mechanical things), feeling no impulse to draw (at which you were also painfully inept and derived little pleasure from) or search for your crayons to fill in another page of one of your stupid coloring books, and because it was raining outside or too cold to leave the house, you would languish in a mopey, ill-humored torpor, still too young to read, still too young to call up someone on the telephone, pining for a friend or a playmate to keep you company, most often sitting by the window and watching the rain slide down the glass, wishing you owned a horse, preferably a palomino with an ornate Western saddle, or if not a horse then a dog, a highly intelligent dog who could be trained to understand every nuance of human speech and would trot along beside you as you set out on your dangerous missions to save children in distress, and when you weren't dreaming about how you wished your life could be different, you tended to muse on eternal questions, questions you still ask yourself today and have never been able to answer, such as how did the world come into being and why do we exist, such as where do people go after they die, and even at that exceedingly young age you would speculate that perhaps the entire world was enclosed in a glass jar that sat on a shelf next to dozens of other jar-worlds in the pantry of a giant's house, or else, even more dizzying and yet logically irrefutable, you would tell yourself that if Adam and Eve were the first people in the world, then everyone was necessarily related to everyone else. Dreaded boredom, long and lonely hours of blankness and silence, entire mornings and afternoons when the world stopped spinning around you, and yet that barren ground proved to be more important than most of the gardens you played in, for that was where you taught yourself how to be alone, and only when a person is alone can his mind run free.

Every now and then, for no apparent reason, you would suddenly lose track of who you were. It was as if the being who inhabited your body had turned into an impostor, or, more precisely, into no one at all, and as you felt your selfhood dribble out of you, you would walk around in a state of stunned dissociation, not sure if it was yesterday or tomorrow, not sure if the world in front of you was real or a figment of someone else's imagination. This happened often enough during your childhood for you to give these mental fugues a name. *Daze,* you said to yourself, *I'm in a daze,* and even though these dream-like interludes were transitory, rarely lasting more than three or four minutes, the strangeness of feeling hollowed out like that would linger for hours afterward. It wasn't a good feeling, but neither did it scare you or disturb you, and as far as you could tell there was no identifiable cause, not fatigue, for example, or physical exhaustion, and no pattern to the comings and goings of these spells, since they occurred both when you were alone and when you were with other people. An uncanny sense of having fallen asleep with your eyes open, but at the same time knowing you were fully awake, conscious of where you were, and yet not there at all somehow, floating outside yourself, a phantom without weight or substance, an uninhabited shell of flesh and bone, a nonperson. The dazes continued throughout your childhood and well into your adolescence, coming over you once every month or two, sometimes a bit more often, sometimes a bit less, and even now, at your advanced age, the feeling still comes back once every four or five years, lasting for just fifteen or twenty seconds, which means that you have never completely outgrown this tendency to vanish from your own consciousness. Mysterious and unaccountable, but an essential part of who you were then and occasionally still are now. As if you were slipping into another dimension, a new configuration of time and space, looking at your own life with blank, indifferent eyes—or else rehearsing your death, learning what happens to you when you disappear.

Your family must be brought into this as well, your mother, father, and sister, with special attention paid to your parents' wretched marriage, for even though your purpose is to chart the workings of your young mind, to look at yourself in isolation and explore the internal geography of your boyhood, the fact is that you didn't live in isolation, you were part of a family, a strange family, and without question that strangeness had much to do with who you were as a child, perhaps everything to do with it. You have no horror stories to tell, no dramatic accounts of beatings or abuse, but instead a constant, underlying feeling of sadness, which you did your best to ignore, since by temperament you were not a sad or overtly miserable child, but once you were old enough to compare your situation to that of the other children you knew, you understood that your family was a broken family, that your parents had no idea what they were doing, that the fortress most couples try to build for their children was no more than a tumbledown shack, and therefore you felt exposed to the elements, unprotected, vulnerable—which meant that in order to survive it was essential that you toughen up and figure out a way to fend for yourself. They had no business being married, you realized, and once your mother began working when you were six, they rarely intersected, rarely seemed to have anything to talk about, coexisting in a chill of mutual indifference. No storms or fights, no shouting matches, no apparent hostility—simply a lack of passion on both sides, cellmates thrown together by chance and serving out their sentences in grim silence. You loved both of them, of course, you fervently wished that things could be better between them, but as the years went on you began to lose hope. They were both out most of the time, both working long into the evenings, and the house seemed permanently empty, with few family dinners, few chances for the four of you to be together, and after you were seven or eight you and your little sister were mostly fed by the housekeeper, a black woman named Catherine who entered the scene when you were five and remained a part of your life for many years, continuing to work for your mother after your parents divorced and your mother remarried, and you were still in touch with her well into her dotage, when the two of you exchanged letters after your father's death in 1979, but Catherine was hardly a maternal figure, she was an eccentric character from the backwoods of Maryland, several times married and several times divorced, a cackling jokester who drank on the sly and flicked the ashes of her Kool cigarettes into her open palm, more of a pal than a substitute mother, and therefore you and your sister were often alone together, your anxious, fragile sister, who would stand by the window waiting for your mother to return at some appointed hour, and if the car did not pull into the driveway at the precise minute it was expected, your sister would break down in tears, convinced that your mother was dead, and as the minutes rolled on, the tears would devolve into violent weeping and tantrums, and you, just eight and nine and ten years old, would do everything you could to reassure her and comfort her, but seldom to any avail, your poor sister, who finally cracked up in her early twenties and spent years spinning off into madness, held together today by doctors and psychopharmacological drugs, far more a victim of your strange family than you ever were. You know now how deeply unhappy your mother was, and you also know that in his own fumbling way your father loved her, that is, to the extent he was capable of loving anyone, but they made a botch of it, and to be a part of that disaster when you were a boy no doubt drove you inward, turning you into a man who has spent the better part of his life sitting alone in a room.

It took you a while to understand that not everyone thought the way you did, that there were angry, competitive boys who actively wished you ill, that even when you told the truth, there were those who would refuse to believe you, simply as a matter of principle. You were trusting and openhearted, you always began by assuming the best about others, and more often than not those attitudes were reciprocated by others, which led to many warm friendships when you were a child, and therefore it was especially hard on you when you crossed paths with the occasional mean-spirited boy, a person who rejected the rules of fair-mindedness that you and your friends lived by, who took pleasure in discord and conflict for their own sake. You are talking about ethical conduct here, not just good manners or the social benefits of polite behavior, but something more fundamental than that, the moral bedrock on which everything stands—and without which everything falls. To your mind, there was no greater injustice than to be doubted when you had told the truth, to be called a liar when you hadn't lied, for there was no recourse then, no way to defend your integrity in the face of your accuser, and the frustration caused by such a moral injury would burn deep into you, continue to burn into you, becoming a fire that could never be extinguished. Your first run-in with that sort of frustration occurred when you were five, during the summer of the heroic Lenny, the smallest of small disputes with another boy at the day camp you attended, so small as to qualify as ridiculously small, but you were a small boy then and the world you lived in was by definition small, and why else would you remember this incident if it hadn't felt large to you at the time, enormous in its impact, and by that you are referring not to the dispute itself, which was inconsequential, but to the outrage you felt afterward, the sense of betrayal that overwhelmed you when you told the truth and were not believed. The circumstances, such as you remember them—and you remember them well—were as follows: the boys in your group were making preparations for some kind of Indian pageant that was to be staged on the last day of the summer camp session, and among the things you were all supposed to do was construct a ceremonial rattle for the occasion, which consisted of ornamenting a can of Calumet baking powder with several colors of paint, filling the can with dried beans or pebbles, and pushing a stick through a hole in the bottom of the can to serve as a handle. The Calumet can was red, you recall, with a splendid portrait of an Indian chief in profile dominating the front, and you worked diligently on your project, you who had never excelled at art, but this time the results surpassed your expectations, your painted decorations were neat and precise and beautiful, and you felt proud of what you had accomplished. Of all the ceremonial rattles produced by the boys that day, yours was one of the best, if not the very best, but time ran out before anyone could put the finishing touches on the job, which meant that the work would have to be picked up again first thing the following morning. You missed the next day of camp because of a cold, however, and perhaps the day after that as well, and when you finally returned it was the last day, the morning of the pageant. You searched high and low for your masterpiece, but you couldn't find it, slowly understanding as you sifted through the pile that one of the boys had filched it in your absence. A counselor (not Lenny) pulled another rattle out of the box and told you to use that one instead, which needless to say disappointed you, for this substitute rattle had been done poorly and sloppily, it couldn't compare with the one you had made, but now you were stuck with this embarrassing piece of work, which everyone would assume you had decorated yourself, and as you marched off to take part in the pageant, you found yourself walking beside a boy named Michael, who was a year older than you were and had been subtly taunting you for the entire summer, treating you as a know-nothing dunce, a five-year-old incompetent, and when you held up the ugly rattle and showed it to Michael, explaining that it wasn't yours, that you had made a much better one, Michael laughed at you and said, Sure, a likely story, and when you defended yourself by saying no, this one really wasn't yours, Michael called you a liar and turned his back on you. A trivial matter, perhaps, but how you burned then, and how vast was your frustration to have been wronged in this way, not just because you had been wronged, but because you understood the wrong could never be made right.

Another episode from those early years concerns someone named Dennis, who moved to another town when you were seven or eight and subsequently disappeared from your life for good. With so many events from that time now erased from your memory, you find it interesting that this story, too, should revolve around a question of justice, of fairness, of trying to right a wrong. You believe you were six. Dennis was in your first-grade class, and before long the two of you became close friends. You remember your classmate as a quiet person, good-natured, quick to laugh, but somewhat withdrawn, pensive, as if he were carrying around some secret burden, and yet you admired him for his composure and what struck you as an uncommon air of dignity in someone still so young. Dennis came from a large Catholic family, one of several children, perhaps many children, and because there wasn't enough money to go around, his parents dressed him in shabby, hand-me-down clothes, ill-fitting shirts and pants inherited from his older brothers. Not a poor family exactly, but a struggling family, occupants of an enormous house that seemed to contain an infinite number of dank, sparsely furnished rooms, and each time you went there for lunch, the food was prepared by Dennis's father, a kind and amiable man, whose job or profession was unknown to you, but Dennis's mother was rarely to be seen. She spent her days alone in a downstairs room, and the few times she did make an appearance while you were visiting, she was always in her bathrobe and slippers, hair disheveled, chain-smoking, ornery, with dark circles under her eyes, a scary, witch-like character, you felt, and because you were so young, you had no idea what her problem was, whether she was an alcoholic, for example, or ill, or suffering from some mental or emotional trouble. You felt sorry for Dennis in any case, aggrieved that your friend had been sad- dled with such a woman for a mother, but of course Dennis never said a word about it, for small children never complain about their parents, not even the worst parents, they simply accept what they have been given and carry on from there. One Saturday, you and Dennis were invited to the birthday party of one of the boys in your class, which probably means that you were seven by then, or about to turn seven. Following the protocol for such occasions, your conscientious mother had supplied you with a present for the birthday boy, a prettily done-up package with bright wrap- ping paper and colorful ribbons. You and Dennis set out for the party together on foot, but all was not well, for your friend had no present of his own, his parents had neglected to buy him one, and when you saw Dennis studying the package under your arm, you understood how wretched he felt, how ashamed he was to be go- ing to the party empty-handed. The two of you must have talked about it, Dennis must have shared his feelings with you—the humiliation, the embarrassment—but you cannot recall a single word of that conversation. What you do remember is the pity and compassion you felt, the ache of misery that welled up in you when confronted by your friend's misery, for you loved and ad- mired this boy and couldn't bear to see him suffer, and so, as much for your sake as for Dennis's sake, you impulsively handed him your present, telling him that it was his now and that he should give it to the birthday boy when he walked into the house. But what about you? Dennis said. If I take this, then you'll be the one with nothing to give. Don't worry, you answered. I'll tell them I left my present at home, that I forgot to take it with me.

For the most part, you were obedient and well-behaved. Aside from that spontaneous burst of altruism with your friend, you were by no means a saintly child, and you did not make a habit of giving away your belongings in selfless acts of commiseration. You strove to tell the truth at all times, but occasionally you lied to cover up your misdeeds, and if you did not cheat at games or steal from your friends, it wasn't because you struggled to be good so much as that you never found yourself tempted to do those things. Every now and then, however, in fact only twice that you can recollect with any precision, a perverse impulse would take hold of you, an urge to destroy and mutilate, to sabotage, to smash things to bits, and you would turn around and do something fundamentally out of character, at odds with the self you had come to recognize as your own. In the first instance, which occurred when you were around five, you systematically dismantled the family radio, a large machine from the 1940s packed with glass tubes and six thousand wires, thinking at first that you would be able to put it back together, purposefully deceiving yourself by calling this exercise in vandalism a *scientific experiment,* but as you continued to extract the various parts from the innards of the machine, it soon became clear that rebuilding it was beyond your capacity as a scientist, and yet in spite of that you forged on, maniacally removing every bolt and wire housed within the box, doing it for the simple reason that you knew you weren't supposed to be doing it, that behavior of this kind was absolutely forbidden. What possessed you to attack that old Philco, to eviscerate it and render it useless, to annihilate it? Were you angry at your parents? Were you striking back at them for some wrong you felt they had done to you, or were you merely in one of those fractious, rebellious moods that sometimes get the better of small children? You have no idea, but you remember that you were soundly punished for what you did, even as you continued to protest your innocence, sticking to the story that your crime had been committed in the pursuit of scientific knowledge. Even more mystifying to you is the episode of the tree, which occurred about a year after the radio rampage, which means you were approximately six at the time, and there you were alone again, grumpily wishing there was someone you could play with, out of sorts, restless, wandering around in the yard behind your house, when it suddenly occurred to you what a good idea it would be to chop down the little fruit tree that stood near the flower bed, the new tree, a poor, scrawny sapling with a trunk so slender you could encircle it with your two hands. Such a small tree wouldn't pose much of a problem, you thought, and so you went into the garage to hunt for your father's axe, which turned out to be ancient, no doubt the oldest surviving axe in the Western Hemisphere, with a handle so long it was almost as tall as you were, and a blade so dull, so thick, and so rusted that it probably would have been hard-pressed to dent a stick of butter. On top of that, the axe was heavy, not too heavy to carry into the backyard, perhaps, but once you were in front of the tree, heavy enough to make it difficult to lift above your head, and far too heavy to swing with any force—not the baseball bat you had imagined it would be, but seven bats, twenty bats, and therefore you had trouble keeping it parallel to the ground, couldn't orient it in a straight line because your wrists and arms were wobbling as you drove the dull blade into the tree, and after six or seven whacks you were so exhausted that you had to give up. You had managed to pierce the bark in a few places, bits of the gray membrane were curled upward to show the fresh green underside and a hint of bare blond wood below, but nothing more than that, your plan to fell the tree had been a total failure, and even the wounds you had inflicted on it would heal in time. Again, the question was: why did you do it? You can't remember your motive—simply the desire to do it, the need to do it—but you suspect it might have been connected to the story about George Washington and the cherry tree, the essential American myth of your childhood, that inexplicable, confounding tale of young George chopping down the tree for no reason, doing it because he wanted to do it, because it struck him as a good idea, which was precisely what you had felt when you decided to cut down your tree, as if every boy at some point in his childhood were destined to cut down a tree for the pure pleasure of cutting down a tree, but then, of course, George Washington was the father of his country, of your country, and therefore he stood tall and confessed his misdeed to his own father—*I cannot tell a lie*—thus proving himself to be an honest boy, a boy of commendable virtue and moral strength, but you are the father of no country, and therefore you sometimes lied when you were a boy, lied because, unlike George Washington, you could tell a lie when the situation demanded you tell one, even if you knew that God would eventually punish you for it. But better God, you thought, than your parents.

Noble and august, unimpeachable in his honor, venerated by all Americans, Washington had fought a number of important battles on New Jersey ground during the Revolutionary War, and every year your class made a pilgrimage to the general's headquarters in Morristown, a shrine considered even more holy than the one dedicated to Edison in Menlo Park. The lightbulb and the phonograph were wondrous artifacts, but this white colonial mansion was the heart of America itself, the very seat of Columbia's glory, and in those early years of your childhood, you were taught to believe that everything about America was good. No country could compare to the paradise you lived in, your teachers told you, for this was the land of freedom, the land of opportunity, and every little boy could dream of growing up to become president. The courageous Pilgrims had crossed the ocean to found a nation out of raw wilderness, and the hordes of settlers who'd followed them had spread the American Eden across an entire continent, from the Atlantic to the Pacific, from Canada to Mexico, for Americans were industrious and clever, the most inventive people on earth, and every little boy could dream of growing up to become a rich and successful man. It was true that slavery had been a bad idea, but Lincoln had freed the slaves, and by now that unfortunate error was a thing of the past. America was perfect. America had won the war and was in charge of the world, and the only bad person it had ever produced was Benedict Arnold, the villainous traitor who had turned against his country and whose name was reviled by all patriots. Every other historical figure was wise and good and just. Every day brought further progress, and extraordinary as the American past had been, the future held even more promise. Never forget how lucky you are. To be an American is to take part in the greatest human enterprise since the creation of man.

Never a word about the poor black people in your father's buildings, of course, and never a word about the boots worn by the soldiers in Korea, but long after the summer had ended, you went on thinking about Lenny, and again and again you were haunted by the image of blackened, amputated toes, tens of thousands of discarded stumps, a mountain of digits severed from the feet of shivering, frostbitten soldiers: charred cigarette butts overflowing an ashtray as tall and wide as a house.

In the fall of that year, 1952, you experienced your first presidential campaign, Eisenhower versus Stevenson. Your parents were Democrats, which meant that you were pulling for the Democrat from Illinois as well, but being pro-Stevenson put you at odds with the squat, round-faced girl you had a crush on, Patty F., who wore her hair in braids, two identical and alluring braids that hung halfway down her back until, suddenly, the allure turned to disenchantment, for one morning, as you sat next to her on the front steps of your school, waiting for the doors to open so your kindergarten teacher could usher you inside to begin the day, you were appalled to hear her chanting a pro-Republican ditty, an aggressive bit of name-calling that shocked you with its vehemence: *Stevenson's a jerk, Stevenson's a jerk, Eisenhower has more power, Stevenson's a jerk!* How was it possible that you and your adored one did not see eye to eye on who should be the next president? Politics was a nasty sport, you now realized, a free-for-all of bitter, unending conflict, and it pained you that something as abstract and remote as a presidential election could cause a rift between you and plump little Patty, who turned out to be a ferocious partisan for the other side. What about the myth of a unified, harmonious America, you asked yourself, the idea that everyone should be pulling together for the common good? To call someone a jerk was a serious accusation. It destroyed the bonds of civility that supposedly prevailed in this most perfect of lands and proved not only that Americans were divided, but that those divisions were often inflamed by ugly passions and slanderous insults. The Cold War was in full bloom then, the Red Scare had entered its most poisonous phase, but you were too young to understand any of that, and as your childhood crept along through the early fifties, the only noise from the zeitgeist loud enough for you to hear was the bass drum sounding the alarm that the Communists were out to destroy America. No doubt all countries had enemies, you told yourself. That was why wars were fought, after all, but now that America had won the Second World War and had demonstrated its superiority over all other countries on earth, why would the Communists feel that America was bad, a country so bad that it was worthy of destruction? Were they stupid, you wondered, or did their animosity toward the United States suggest that people in other parts of the world had different ideas about how to live, *un-American ideas,* and if so, did that not further suggest that the greatness of America, which was self-evident to all Americans, was far from evident to those other people? And if they couldn't see what we saw, who was to say that what we saw was truly there?

Nothing about the boots—but scarcely a word about the Indians either. You knew they had been here first, that they had occupied the land now called America for two thousand years before white Europeans started coming to these shores, but when your teachers talked about America, the Indians were seldom part of the story. They were the natives, our aboriginal predecessors, the indigenous people who had once reigned over this part of the world, and two starkly opposing views about them prevailed in midcentury America, each one an absolute contradiction of the other, and yet they both stood as equals, each one pretending to have a valid claim on the truth. In the black-and-white Westerns you watched on television, the red men were invariably portrayed as ruthless killers, enemies of civilization, plundering demons who attacked white homesteaders out of pure, sadistic pleasure. On the other hand, there was the kingly portrait of the Indian chief on the can of Calumet baking powder, the same can you decorated for the ceremonial rattle when you were five, and the Indian pageant you took part in was not about the brutality of the Indians but their wisdom, their deeper understanding of nature than the white man's, their communion with the eternal forces of the universe, and the Great Spirit they believed in struck you as a warm and welcoming deity, unlike the vengeful God of your imagination, who ruled through terror and agonizing punishments. Later on, when you were cast in the role of Governor William Bradford for a play mounted by your second- or third-grade class, you presided over a reenactment of the first Thanksgiving with the munificent Squanto and Massasoit, knowing that the Indians were a good and kind people, and without their generosity and constant help, without their bountiful gifts of food and learned instruction about the ways of the land, the early Pilgrim settlers would not have survived their first winter in the New World. Such was the conflicting evidence: devils and angels both, violent primitives and noble savages, two irreconcilable visions of the same reality, and yet somewhere in this confusion there was a third term, a phrase that had fed the most secret part of your inner world for as long as you could remember: *wild Indian.* Those were the words your mother used whenever you misbehaved, when your normally subdued conduct turned to rambunctiousness and anarchy, for the truth was that there was a place in you that wanted to be wild, and that urge was expressed by imagining yourself to be an Indian, a boy who could run half-naked through gigantic pine forests with his bow and arrow, spend whole days galloping across the plains on his palomino stallion, and hunt buffalo with the warriors of his tribe. *Wild Indian* represented everything that was sensual, liberating, and unfettered, it was the id giving vent to its libidinous desires as opposed to the superego of cowboy heroes in white hats, the oppressive world of uncomfortable shoes and alarm clocks and airless, overheated classrooms. You had never met an Indian, of course, had never seen one except in films and photographs, but Kafka never set eyes on an Indian either, which did not stop him from composing a one-paragraph story entitled "The Wish to Be a Red Indian": "If only one were an Indian, instantly alert, and on a racing horse, leaning against the wind . . . ," a single run-on sentence that fully captures the desire to throw off restraints, to let go, to flee the stultifying conventions of Western culture. By the time you were in the third or fourth grade, this is what you had absorbed: the whites who came here in the 1620s were so few in number that they had no choice but to make peace with the surrounding tribes, but once their numbers swelled, once the invasion of English immigrants began to grow, and then continued to grow, the situation was reversed, and bit by bit the Indians were pushed out, dispossessed, slaughtered. The word *genocide* was unknown to you, but when you saw the Indians and whites going at each other in the old Westerns on TV, you knew there was more to the story than those stories ever told. The only Indian treated with any respect was Tonto, the faithful sidekick of the Lone Ranger, played by the actor Jay Silverheels, whom you admired for his courage, intelligence, and long, thoughtful silences. By the time you were in the fifth grade, that is, when you were ten and eleven years old, you had become an enthusiastic reader of *Mad* magazine, and in the now-famous parody of *The Lone Ranger* that appeared in one of its issues, the masked avenger of wrongs and his loyal comrade find themselves confronted by a band of hostile Indian warriors. The Lone Ranger turns to his friend and says: "Well, Tonto, it looks like we're surrounded." To which the Indian replies: "What do you mean *we?*" You got the joke, which was a superb and deeply funny joke, you felt, for the precise reason that in the end it wasn't a joke at all.

The Diary of Anne Frank. India becomes an independent country. Henry Ford dies. Thor Heyerdahl sails on a raft from Peru to Polynesia in 101 days. *All My Sons,* by Arthur Miller. *A Streetcar Named Desire,* by Tennessee Williams. The Dead Sea scrolls are discovered. Somewhere over a desert in the western United States, an American jet breaks the sound barrier. Truman appoints George C. Marshall secretary of state, and the Marshall Plan begins. Giacometti's sculpture *Man Pointing. The Plague,* by Albert Camus. The U.N. announces a plan for the partition of Palestine. The Actors Studio is founded in New York. André Gide wins the Nobel Prize. Pablo Casals vows not to perform in public as long as Franco is in power. Al Capone dies. Sugar rationing in the U.S. ends after five years. Jackie Robinson becomes the first black baseball player in the major leagues. Truman signs Executive Order 9835, requiring a loyalty oath from all government employees, and becomes the first president to address the American people on television. *I, the Jury,* by Mickey Spillane. *Doktor Faustus,* by Thomas Mann. HUAC opens its investigation into Communist influence in the movie industry. *Monsieur Verdoux,* by Charlie Chaplin. The Yankees beat the Dodgers in the World Series. Maria Callas makes her debut. More than twenty-eight inches of snow falls on New York, the largest blizzard in the city's history. *Out of the Past,* directed by Jacques Tourneur—as well as *Body and Soul, Brute Force, Crossfire, Born to Kill, Dead Reckoning, Desperate, Framed, Kiss of Death, Lady in the Lake, Nightmare Alley, Possessed, Railroaded, Dark Passage,* and *They Won't Believe Me.* Random, unrelated events, connected only by the fact that they all occurred in the year of your birth, 1947.

You remember the planes, the supersonic jets roaring across the blue skies of summer, cutting through the firmament at such exalted speeds that they were scarcely visible, a flash of silver glinting briefly in the light, and then, not long after they had vanished over the horizon, the thunderous boom that would follow, resounding for miles in all directions, the great detonation of blasting air that signified the sound barrier had been broken yet again. You and your friends were thunderstruck by the power of those planes, which always arrived without warning, announcing themselves as a furious clamor in the far distance, and within seconds they were directly overhead, and whatever game you and your friends might have been playing at that moment, you all stopped in mid-gesture to look up, to watch, to wait as those howling machines sped past you. It was the era of aviation miracles, of ever faster and faster, of ever higher and higher, of planes without torsos, planes that looked more like exotic fish than birds, and so prominent were those postwar flying machines in the imaginations of America's children that trading cards of the new planes were widely distributed, much like baseball cards or football cards, in packages of five or six with a slab of pink bubble gum inside, and on the front of each card there was a photograph of a plane instead of a ballplayer, with information about that plane printed on the back. You and your friends collected these cards, you were five and six years old and obsessed with the planes, dazzled by the planes, and you can remember now (suddenly, it is all so clear to you) sitting on the floor with your classmates in a school hallway during an air-raid drill, which in no way resembled the fire drills you were also subjected to, those impromptu exits into the warmth or the cold and imagining the school as it burned to the ground in front of your eyes, for an air-raid drill kept the children indoors, not in the classroom but the hallway, presumably to protect them against an attack from the air, missiles, rockets, bombs dropped from high-flying Communist planes, and it was during that drill that you saw the airplane cards for the first time, sitting on the floor with your back against the wall, silent, with no intention of breaking that silence, for talking was not allowed during these solemn exercises, these useless preparations against possible death and destruction, but one of the boys had a pack of those airplane cards with him that morning, and he was showing them to the other boys, surreptitiously passing them down the line of silent, seated bodies, and when your turn came to hold one of the cards in your hands, you were astonished by the design of the plane, its strangeness and unexpected beauty, all wing, all flight, a metal beast born in the empyrean, in a realm of pure, everlasting fire, and not once did you consider that the air-raid drill you were taking part in was supposed to teach you how to protect yourself from an attack by just such a plane, that is, a plane similar to the one on the card that had been built by your country's enemies. No fear. You never worried that bombs or rockets would fall on you, and if you welcomed the alarms that signaled the start of air-raid drills, it was only because they allowed you to leave the classroom for a few minutes and escape the drudgery of whatever lesson you were being taught.

In 1952, the year you turned five, which included the summer of Lenny, the beginning of your formal education, and the Eisenhower-Stevenson campaign, a polio epidemic broke out across America, striking 57,626 people, most of them children, killing 3,300 and permanently crippling untold numbers of others. That was fear. Not bombs or a nuclear attack, but polio. Roaming through the streets of your neighborhood that summer, you often came upon clusters of women talking to one another in doleful whispers, women pushing baby carriages or walking their dogs, women with dread in their eyes, dread in the hushed timbre of their voices, and the talk was always about polio, the invisible scourge that was spreading everywhere, that could invade the body of any man, woman, or child at any moment of the day or night. Worse still, there was the young man dying in the house across the street from where your closest friend lived, a Harvard student whose first name was Franklin, a brilliant person, according to your mother, someone destined to accomplish great things in life, and now he was wasting away with cancer, immobilized, doomed, and every time you visited your friend Billy, Billy's mother would instruct you to keep your voices down when you went outdoors so as not to disturb Franklin. You would look across the street at Franklin's white house, the shades drawn in every window, an eerily silent house where no one seemed to live anymore, and you would imagine the tall and handsome Franklin, whom you had seen several times in the past, stretched out on a white bed in his upstairs bedroom, waiting to die his slow and painful death. For all the fear caused by the polio epidemic, you never knew anyone who contracted the disease, but Franklin eventually died, just as your mother had told you he would. You saw the black cars lined up in front of the house on the day of the funeral. Sixty years later, you can still see the black cars and the white house. In your mind, they are still the quintessential emblems of grief.

You can't remember the precise moment when you understood that you were a Jew. It seems to you that it came sometime after you were old enough to identify yourself as an American, but you could be wrong, it could be that it was a part of you from the very beginning. Neither one of your parents came from a religious family. There were no rituals practiced in the household, no Sabbath meals on Friday night, no lighting of candles, no trips to the synagogue on the high holy days, let alone on any Friday night or Saturday morning of the year, and not a single word of Hebrew was uttered in your presence. A couple of desultory Passover seders in the company of relatives, Hanukkah gifts every December to offset the absence of Christmas, and just one serious rite that you took part in, which occurred when you were eight days old, far too early for you to remember anything about it, the standard circumcision ceremony, or *bris*, when the foreskin of your penis was lopped off by a fastidiously sharpened knife in order to seal the covenant between your newborn self and the God of your ancestors. For all their indifference to the particulars of their faith, your parents nevertheless considered themselves Jews, called themselves Jews, were comfortable with that fact and never sought to hide it, unlike countless other Jews over the centuries who did everything in their power to disappear into the Christian world that surrounded them, changing their names, converting to Catholicism or one of the Protestant sects, turning away from themselves and quietly obliterating their pasts. No, your parents stood firm and never questioned who they were, but in the early years of your childhood they had nothing to offer you on the subject of your religion or background. They were simply Americans who happened to be Jews, thoroughly assimilated after the struggles of their own immigrant parents, and therefore in your mind the notion of Judaism was above all associated with foreignness, as embodied in your grandmother, for example, your father's mother, an alien presence who still spoke and read mostly in Yiddish, whose English was nearly incomprehensible to you because of her heavy accent, and then there was the man who turned up occasionally at your mother's parents' apartment in New York, a relative of some kind by the name of Joseph Stavsky, an elegant figure who dressed in finely tailored three-piece suits and smoked with a long black cigarette holder, a sophisticated cosmopolitan whose Polish-accented English was perfectly understandable to you, and when you were old enough to understand such things (at seven? at eight? at nine?), your mother told you that cousin Joseph had come to America after the war with help from her parents, that back in Poland he had been married and the father of twin girls, but his wife and daughters had all been murdered in Auschwitz, and he alone had survived, once a prosperous lawyer in Warsaw, now scraping by as a button salesman in New York. The war had been over for some years by then, but the war was still present, still hovering around you and everyone you knew, manifested not only in the war games you played with your friends but in the words spoken in the households of your family, and if your first encounters with the Nazis took place as an imaginary GI in various backyards of your small New Jersey town, it wasn't long before you understood what the Nazis had done to the Jews, to Joseph Stavsky's wife and daughters, for instance, to members of your own family for the sole reason that they were Jews, and now that you had fully grasped the fact that you yourself were a Jew, the Nazis were no longer just the enemy of the American army, they were the incarnation of a monstrous evil, an anti-human force of global destruction, and even though the Nazis had been defeated, wiped off the face of the earth, they lived on in your imagination, lurking inside you as an all-powerful legion of death, demonic and insidious, forever on the attack, and from that moment on, that is, from the moment you understood that you were not only an American but a Jew, your dreams were populated by gangs of Nazi infantrymen, night after night you found yourself running from them, desperately running for your life, chased through open fields and dim, maze-like forests by packs of armed Nazis, faceless German soldiers who were bent on shooting you, on tearing off your arms and legs, on burning you at the stake and turning you into a pile of ashes.

By the time you were seven or eight, you were beginning to catch on. Jews were invisible, they had no part to play in American life, and they never appeared as heroes in books or films or television shows. *Gentleman's Agreement* notwithstanding, which won the Academy Award for best picture the year you were born, there were no cowboys called Bernstein or Schwartz, no private eyes called Greenberg or Cohen, and no presidential candidates whose parents had emigrated from the shtetls of eastern Poland and Russia. True, there were some boxers who had done well in the thirties and forties, there was the quarterback Sid Luckman and the three notables from the land of baseball (Hank Greenberg, Al Rosen, and Sandy Koufax, who broke in with the Dodgers in 1955), but they were such flagrant exceptions to the norm that they qualified as demographic flukes, mere statistical aberrations. Jews could play the violin and the piano, they could sometimes conduct symphony orchestras, but the popular singers and musicians were all Italian or black or hillbillies from the South. Vaudevillians, yes, funnymen, yes (the Marx Brothers, George Burns), but no movie stars, and even when the actors had been born Jewish, they invariably changed their names. George Burns had been

Nathan Birnbaum. Emanuel Goldenberg was transformed into Edward G. Robinson. Issur Danielovitch became Kirk Douglas, and Hedwig Kiesler was reborn as Hedy Lamarr. Tepid as *Gentleman's Agreement* might have been, with its contrived plot and sanctimonious positions (a non-Jewish journalist pretends to be Jewish in order to expose prejudices against the Jews), it is instructive to look at that film now as a snapshot of where Jews stood in American society in 1947. That was the world you entered as an infant, and while it was logical to assume that the German defeat in 1945 should have, or could have, snuffed out anti-Semitism for good, not much had changed on the home front. College admission quotas for Jews were still in force, clubs and other organizations were still restricted, kike jokes still got the boys laughing at the weekly poker game, and Shylock still reigned as the principal representative of his people. Even in the New Jersey town where you grew up, there were invisible barriers, impediments you were still too young to understand or notice, but when your best friend, Billy, moved away with his family in 1955, and your other good friend, Peter, vanished the following year—wrenching departures that both puzzled and saddened you—your mother explained that too many Jews were quitting Newark for the suburbs, that they too wanted their patch of grass, just like everyone else, and therefore the old guard was decamping, running away from this sudden influx of non-Christian home owners. Did she use the word *anti-Semitic?* You can't remember, but the implication was nevertheless clear: to be a Jew was to be different from everyone else, to stand apart, to be looked upon as an outsider. And you, who until then had seen yourself as thoroughly American, as American as any *Mayflower* blue blood, now understood that there were those who felt you didn't belong, that even in the place you called home, you were not fully at home.

To be a part of things and yet not a part of things. To be accepted by most and yet eyed with suspicion by others. After embracing the triumphal narrative of American exceptionalism as a little boy, you began to exclude yourself from the story, to understand that you belonged to another world besides the one you lived in, that your past was anchored in a somewhere else of remote settlements in Eastern Europe, and that if your grandparents on your father's side and your great-grandparents on your mother's side had not had the intelligence to leave that part of the world when they did, almost none of you would have survived, nearly every one of you would have been murdered during the war. Life was precarious. The ground under your feet could give way at any moment, and now that your family had landed in America, had been saved by America, that didn't mean you should expect America to make you feel welcome. Your sympathies turned toward the outcasts, the despised and mistreated ones, the Indians who had been chased off their lands and massacred, the Africans who had been shipped over here in chains, and even if you did not renounce your attachment to America, could not renounce it because in the end it was still your place, your country, you began to live in it with a new sense of wariness and unease. There were few opportunities in your little world to take a stand, but you did what you could do whenever an occasion presented itself, you fought back when the tough older boys in town called you Jewboy and Jew shit, and you refused to take part in Christmas celebrations at school, to sing Christmas carols at the annual holiday assembly, and therefore the teachers allowed you to stay alone in the room when the rest of the class tromped off to the auditorium to rehearse with the other classes in your grade. The sudden silence that surrounded you as you sat at your desk, the click of the minute hand on the old mechanical clock with the Roman numerals as you read your Poe and Stevenson and Conan Doyle, a self-declared outcast, stubbornly holding your ground, but proud, nevertheless proud in your stubbornness, in your refusal to pretend to be someone you were not.

In your mind, it had little or nothing to do with religion. You were aligning yourself with the forces of powerlessness, hoping to find some moral or intellectual strength by acknowledging your difference from others, but *Jew* signified a category of people rather than a theological system, a history of struggle and exclusion that had culminated in the disasters of World War II, and that history was all that concerned you. When you were nine, however, your parents joined one of the local synagogues. Needless to say, it was a Reform congregation, for that simplified, watered-down brand of Judaism best served the interests of people like them: the indifferent, unreligious, non-practicing American Jews who sought to reaffirm their bond with the traditions of their forebears. Bluntly put—but without question entirely true—Hitler was responsible. The resurgence of Jewish life in postwar America was a direct result of the death camps, and the engine that drove people like your parents to join up was guilt, a fear that unless their children were taught to become Jews, the very concept of Judaism in America would fade away to nothing. Your father had not studied Hebrew as a boy, had not gone through the rigors of preparing for his Bar Mitzvah, and your mother, who was the daughter of a socialist, had never once set foot in a synagogue, but together they conspired to force you into doing what they themselves had never done, and so, in the same September you entered the fourth grade, you also entered Hebrew school, which meant going to the synagogue to attend classes every Tuesday and Thursday afternoon from four o'clock to five-thirty as well as every Saturday morning from nine-thirty to noon. There were a thousand other things you would rather have been doing, but three times a week over the course of four long years you reluctantly dragged yourself into

that penitentiary of boredom, hating every moment of your im-
prisonment, slowly learning the rudiments of Hebrew, studying
the principal stories of the Old Testament, most of which horrified you to the core, in particular Cain's murder of Abel (why had
God rejected Cain's offering?), Noah and the Flood (why would
God want to destroy the world He had created?), Abraham's near
sacrifice of Isaac (what kind of God would ask a man to kill his
son?), and Jacob's theft of his father's birthright from Esau (why
would God bless a cheater, a man with no conscience?), all of
which confirmed your low opinion of God, who by turns came
across to you as an angry and demented psychopath, a petulant
child, and a wrathful, murdering criminal—a figure even more
frightening and dangerous than the God of your earliest imagin-
ings. To make matters worse, you were stuck in a class made up
entirely of boys, most of whom had even less interest in being
there than you did, who looked upon this forced extra schooling
as unjust punishment for the sin of merely being alive, fifteen or
twenty Jewish boys with ants in their pants and an insurrection-
ist contempt for every word spoken by the teacher, an assistant
rabbi with the unfortunate name of Fish, a short, bulky man with
a large face and a high forehead who spent most of his time in
class dodging spitballs, yelling at the boys to shut up, and pounding his fist on the table. Poor Rabbi Fish. He had been thrown into
a room with a pack of wild Indians, and three times a week he was
scalped.

You left your parents for the first time when you were eight. It was
your idea, you were the one who begged them to let you go, since you
wanted to be with Billy again, your closest friend since the age of
five, and now that he and his family had moved to another town,
far away from where the two of you had spent the past three years
together, your only chance to see him would be to go to the

summer camp he attended with his older brother in New Hampshire, a sleepaway camp that lasted for eight weeks, from the beginning of July until the end of August, a long stretch for a little boy who had never been away from home for more than a single night. Your mother was hesitant, fearing the long separation might be difficult for you to handle, but in the end, not wanting to disappoint you (or perhaps not knowing how else you should spend the summer), she and your father gave their consent. North-central New Hampshire, the area known as the White Mountains, was an exceedingly long car trip from New Jersey in 1955, since there were no interstate highways back then, at least not in that part of the country, and you remember the interminable drive with your parents, sitting in the backseat for ten, eleven, perhaps even twelve hours, and you wonder now if the journey wasn't stretched out over two days, with a pause for sleep in some inn or motel at the midpoint of your northward trek. Impossible to remember that detail, just as you cannot remember saying good-bye to your parents when they left you at the camp and drove away, which means that whatever you were thinking or feeling at that moment is inaccessible to you now—sorrow or joy, trepidation or excitement, second thoughts or proud resolve, you simply don't know. What you remember best about those eight weeks are the smells, the ever-present aroma of the surrounding pine forests, the dry scent of the afternoon sun cooking the dust on the heavily trodden footpath between your cabin and the mess hall, and the odor of the latrine, a primitive wooden structure with a long pissing trough and a row of toilet stalls with no doors on them, the stench of urine whenever you walked in there, like a whiff of ammonia burning up the insides of your nostrils, acrid and intense, never forgotten. Chilly nights under green woolen blankets, pseudo-Indian campfires extolling the wonders of nature and the beneficence of the Great Spirit, all the boys wearing headbands with gray feathers protruding from them, baseball, horseback riding, archery, firing .22 rifles at the shooting range, swimming in the lake, skinny-dipping. You felt far from everything there, farther away from what was familiar to you than at any time in your life, as if the long drive in the car had taken you to the edge of the world. Oddly, you don't remember much about Billy or the other boys, the continual newness that was thrust upon you every day seems to have blotted out almost all particulars, and only two events stand out for you with any clarity. The first was an unannounced, altogether unexpected visit from your grandfather, your mother's father, who stopped by on his way to Maine for his annual weeklong vacation with his male cronies, their principal daytime activity being "lobster fishing," which was something of a misnomer, since one doesn't "fish" for lobster, what one does is drop wooden cages into the water and hope the lobsters will crawl in, all the while sitting in a rowboat, which sounded like a tedious pastime to you, but "lobster fishing" also probably meant drinking and smoking and playing poker and telling dirty jokes, not to speak of some rustic hanky-panky, for your grandfather was a great one for jokes and cavorting with women he wasn't married to, the life of the party he was, and you loved him dearly. On the day of his visit, he arrived just as you were in the middle of the post-lunch rest period, a one-hour interregnum that came before the start of afternoon activities, and on that particular day, instead of reading or writing letters as you usually did, you fell asleep, and since as a child you were someone who slept as if you were in a coma, so profoundly unconscious that little or nothing could rouse you from your slumbers, neither hail nor thunder, neither swarming mosquitoes nor the loudest marching band, and therefore, on the day of your grandfather's visit, when one of your counselors finally managed to jostle you awake, you emerged from your nap with a groggy head, still half-asleep, barely understanding who you were, or even if you were, and stumbled outdoors to find your grandfather, who was waiting for you at the office near the main entrance to the camp. You were of course happy to see him, but because you were not quite yourself yet, still struggling to shake free of the blur and confusion inside you, you found it difficult to speak, to answer his questions with sentences longer than one or two words, and all through your brief conversation with him you wondered if you were still asleep and only imagining he was there, for this was the first time you had seen him without his suit and tie and white shirt, how curious your bald and portly grandfather looked in that bright short-sleeved shirt with the open collar, and before you could settle into one of your free-flowing talks about baseball, a sport he followed as closely as you did, your grandfather was slapping his knees, standing up, and saying that he had to be moving along. There for an instant—and then gone, like an unholy apparition. You were disgusted with yourself for not having done better, for having behaved like a moronic lump of flesh, but some days or weeks later you were even more disgusted with yourself when you woke up one morning to discover that you had wet your bed. This problem had plagued you throughout your childhood, it was the curse you carried around with you far longer than was seemly for a boy of your age, past five, past six, and year after year the humiliation of the rubber sheet stretched out below you to protect the mattress, not the result of some psychological trouble or frailty of the bladder, your mother said (who knows if she was right or wrong?), but quite simply because you slept too soundly, because the arms of Morpheus not only enfolded you in his embrace but crushed you, smothered you, and how often during those early years did your mother tiptoe into your room in the dead of night to wake you up and lead you to the toilet, how often did she struggle to pull you from the land of dreams and fail? By the time you were six or seven, you had largely overcome this disability, the shame of your nocturnal incontinence was no longer a constant torture to you, but every now and then you would fall back into your old ways, once every month or two it would happen again, and to wake to the sickening feeling of cold, wet sheets at that point in your life was so demoralizing, so outrageously juvenile and idiotic, that you sometimes wondered if you would ever grow up. Now, at the advanced age of eight, you had done it again. Not in the sanctuary of your family's house, where everyone was aware of your condition and never said a word about it, but in the public space of a summer-camp cabin inhabited by seven other boys and a counselor in his early twenties. Fortunately, it happened to be a Sunday, the one day of the week when reveille sounded later than usual, when breakfast was extended over an hour and a half rather than thirty or forty-five minutes, and so you waited until the other boys had left the cabin for the mess hall before you climbed out of bed, took off your clammy pajamas, and shoved them into your laundry bag. When you joined the others at the breakfast table, you sat there in an ever-mounting panic, wondering what to do next. Peeing in your bed had been bad enough, an insult to your pride and boyish dignity, but much worse was the fear of being found out, of being ridiculed by the other boys and forever branded as a baby, a fool, a person beneath contempt. Time was growing short, in another fifteen or twenty minutes everyone would be returning to the cabin, and because you didn't know who else to turn to, you decided you would have to risk talking to your counselor, a young man named George, a quiet, serious person who until then had always treated you with kindness, but how could you know he wouldn't laugh at you when you made your confession? And yet who else but George had the authority to release you from the mess hall and let you rush back to the cabin? There was no choice, you would have to talk to him and hope for the best, and so you stood up and walked over to George, who was sitting at the head of the table, and whispered into his ear that you had had an accident and would he please let you go now so you could wash out your sheet and hang it up to dry on the clothesline behind the cabin? George nodded and told you to go ahead. Just like that—an unanticipated miracle of compassion and understanding, but not so strange in the end, for later that morning he confided to you that he had suffered from similar lapses himself when he was your age. A fellow member of the secret fraternity of anguished, guilty bed wetters! Off you ran, then, sprinting back to the cabin, stripping the bottom sheet from your bed, the white sheet with its incriminating yellow stain, which looked something like a map of France, and then rushed over to the latrine, the foul-smelling piss house with its corrosive, all-engulfing reek of urine, and scrubbed out the stain in one of the sinks. You were never caught. George's mercy had protected you from the ultimate embarrassment, the mortifying shame of discovery, but it was a close call, a matter of minutes or even seconds, and your pounding heart was proof of just how scared you had been.

Why hark back to this story now, this ancient scrape with fear that turned out rather well for you in the end, so well, in fact, that you walked away from it without suffering any of the consequences you had anticipated with such dread? Because, finally, there were consequences, even if they were not the ones that made your heart beat so fast when you were afraid. You had a secret. There was a flaw in you that had to be kept hidden from the world, and because merely to think about being discovered filled you with a wretchedness beyond all imagining, you were forced to dissemble, to present a face to the world that was not your true face. Later that morning, when George made his confession to you, revealing that he too had once lived with that same secret himself, it occurred to you that most people had secrets of their own, perhaps all people, an entire universe of people treading the earth with thorns of guilt and shame stabbing their hearts, all of them forced to dissemble, to present a face to the world that was not their true

624 | PAUL AUSTER

face. What did this mean about the world? That everyone in it was more or less hidden, and because we were all other than what we appeared to be, it was next to impossible to know who anyone was. You wonder now if that sense of not knowing wasn't responsible for making you so passionate about books—because the secrets of the characters who lived inside novels were always, in the end, made known.

It would be an exaggeration to say you were homesick that summer. You didn't long for your parents, you didn't write letters complaining about your situation or feel any desire to be rescued, no, you were reasonably content throughout that long sojourn in the pine woods of New Hampshire, but at the same time not quite up to par, a bit depleted and lonely, and when the next year rolled around and your mother asked you if you wanted to return to the camp, you said no, you would prefer to stay at home and spend the summer playing baseball with your friends. Not the wisest decision, as it turned out, for even though you played ball for three or four hours a day, there were the other hours to be filled when you weren't playing, not to speak of the rain-drenched mornings when there was no playing at all, which meant you had too much time on your hands, you were idle for long stretches without knowing what to do with yourself, and even if those solitary periods were in fact nourishing to you in the end, back in the summer of 1956 you felt rather lost. You still had your first bicycle, the old orange two-wheeler with the foot brakes and the fat tires that your parents had bought for you when you were six (the following year, you would graduate to a larger one to accommodate your growing body—sleek and black, with hand brakes and thin tires), and every morning you would mount that too-small bike and peddle over to your friend Peter J.'s house, about a quarter of a mile away. The baseball field was in Peter's backyard, not a regulation field, of course, but an open area of worn-out grass and dirt that felt abundant to you at the time, or at least sufficient for games played by nine-year-olds, with stones for bases and a triangle etched into the bare ground for home plate, and on a typical morning there would be eight or ten of you in that yard with your gloves and bats and balls, dividing up into two teams, with the members of each team taking turns fielding various positions because everyone wanted a chance to pitch at least one inning per game, and there were many games, a double-header every day, sometimes even triple-headers, and you all took the games seriously, playing hard, with everyone keeping track of the number of home runs he hit (a fly ball into the bushes beyond left field), and so passed the most engaging hours of that summer, playing on a makeshift field in your friend's backyard, swatting fifty home runs, a hundred home runs, five hundred home runs into the bushes.

You liked Peter more than any other boy in your class, he had replaced the now-absent Billy as your closest friend, but within a year he too would be gone, departing to another town and disappearing from your life forever. You don't know why his family left, so you will not attribute it to the fact that too many Jews were settling in the neighborhood, which was how your mother tended to read all such departures, but there was no question that your friend's family looked upon you as someone from a different world, especially his Swedish grandfather, an old man with white hair and heavily accented English who, in an outburst of anger against you one afternoon, banished you from the house and forbade you ever to set foot in there again. It must have been sometime after the summer of backyard baseball, early September perhaps, about a month before you met the real or not-real Whitey Ford, and one day after school had been let out you and Peter went back to his house, and because it was raining that afternoon, the two of you stayed inside, eventually going downstairs to explore the cellar. Among the packing crates and spiderwebs and discarded pieces of furniture, you found an old set of golf clubs, which struck you both as an important discovery, since neither one of you had ever held a golf club in your hands, and so for the next little while you took turns swinging a seven-iron in the dampness of that subterranean room, taking turns because the cellar was crowded and there wasn't enough space for both of you to swing at the same time. At one point, without your knowledge, just as you were about to launch into another practice swing, Peter crept up behind you to have a better look, crept up too close to you, entering the area that encompassed the arc of your backswing, and because you hadn't heard him and couldn't see him, you flung your fully extended arms backward with the club in your two hands, not expecting to meet any resistance, confident that your backswing would fly unencumbered through the empty air, but because Peter had crossed the invisible threshold of what should have been all air and nothing else, the backswing of your club was interrupted in midflight when it struck something solid, and an instant after your backswing was stopped, you heard a scream, a sudden, all-out scream blasting against the walls of the cellar. The tip of the iron had gone straight into Peter's forehead, it had pierced the skin, blood was flowing from the wound, and your friend was shrieking in pain. You felt horrified, sick with fear, guiltless and yet filled with guilt, but before you could do anything to help, Peter's grandfather was charging down the stairs to the cellar, shoving you aside, and commanding you to leave the house. Even then, you understood why he should have been so angry, it seemed altogether natural for him to lose his temper at that moment, for there was his grandson, weeping and bleeding after a golf club had cracked him in the head, and whether it was your fault or not, you were responsible for injuring his beloved boy, so he let you have it. Understandable as that anger was to you, however, it must be said that you had rarely witnessed anger on that scale—perhaps never. It was a monumental anger, an outburst of rage worthy of the God of the Old Testament, the vengeful, homicidal Yahweh of your darkest dreams, and as you listened to the old man shout at you, it soon became apparent that not only was he sending you home, he was barring you from his house forever, telling you that you were no good, a wicked boy, and that *we have no use for your kind.* You staggered out of there feeling pummeled and shaken, miserable about what you had done to Peter, but worst of all were the old man's words ringing in your head. What had he meant by *your kind?* you wondered. The kind of boy who hits his friends with golf clubs and makes them bleed—or something even more sinister, some stain on your soul that could never be rubbed out? Was *your kind* simply another way of calling you a dirty Jew? Perhaps. And then again, perhaps not. That evening, when you told your mother about the seven-iron, the blood, and your friend's grandfather, the word *perhaps* did not once cross her lips.

The following summer, you went back to the sleepaway camp in New Hampshire. The experiment in unstructured time had been no more than a partial success, that is, largely a failure, so once again you asked to go up north for July and August, and your parents, who were neither rich nor poor but well enough off to spring for the several hundred dollars it would cost to send you there, gave their consent. Bed-wetting was a thing of the past now, but beyond that dubious if necessary accomplishment, nearly everything about you was different as well. The gap between eight and ten was more than just a distance of two years, it was a chasm of decades, an enormous leap from one period of your life into another, equal to the distance you would eventually cover, say, from twenty to forty, and now that it was 1957, you were a bigger, stronger, smarter person than you had been in 1955, vastly more competent in negotiating all aspects of your life, an ever more independent boy who could march away from his parents without the slightest twinge of anxiety or regret. For the next two months you lived in the country of baseball, it was the moment of your greatest, most fanatical attachment to the sport, and you played it every day, not just during the regular activity periods in the morning and afternoon but during free time in the after-dinner hours as well, working conscientiously to become a better short-stop, a more disciplined hitter, but such was your enthusiasm for the game that you often volunteered to stand in as catcher, savoring the challenge of that unfamiliar position, and little by little the counselors who were in charge of coaching baseball began to notice how quickly you were improving, the strides you had made in just a few short weeks, and by the middle of the summer you were promoted to the big boys' team, the twelve-, thirteen-, and fourteen-year-olds who traveled around the state playing teams from other camps, and though you struggled in the beginning to adjust to the new size of the infield (ninety feet between bases instead of sixty, sixty feet, six inches from the mound to home plate instead of forty-five feet, the standard measurements of all professional diamonds), the coaches stuck with you, you were the shortstop and leadoff hitter, the smallest player on the team, but you managed to hold your own, and so intent were you on doing well that you pushed all thoughts of failure from your mind, punishing yourself for every throwing error and strikeout you made, and even if you didn't stand out among the older boys, you didn't disgrace yourself either. Then came the final banquet, the big ceremonial meal that signaled the end of summer, the awards dinner at which various trophies were handed out to the boys who had been selected as the best swimmer, the best horseman, the best citizen, the best all-around camper, and so on, and suddenly you heard your name being called out by the head counselor, announcing that you had won the trophy for baseball. You weren't sure you had heard him correctly, for it wasn't possible that you could have won, you were too young, and you knew full well that you weren't the best baseball player in the camp—the best for your age, perhaps, but that was a far cry from being the best of all. Nevertheless, the head counselor was summoning you to the podium, they were giving you the trophy, and since it was the first award you had ever won, you felt proud to be up there shaking the head counselor's hand, if also a trifle embarrassed. A few minutes later, you ducked out of the mess hall to go to the latrine, that rank, stinking place that will never be expunged from your memory, and there, standing around and talking among themselves, were four or five of your older teammates, all of them eyeing you with animosity and revulsion, and as you emptied your bladder into the trough, they told you that you didn't deserve to win the trophy, that it should have gone to one of them, and because you were nothing more than a ten-year-old punk, maybe they should beat you up to put you in your place, or else smash your trophy, or, even better, smash the trophy and then smash you. You were beginning to feel a little intimidated by these threats, but the only response you could come up with was the truth: you hadn't asked for the award, you said, you hadn't expected to win, and even if you agreed with them that you shouldn't have won, what could you do about it now? Then you walked out of the latrine and returned to the dinner. Between that night and your departure from the camp two days later, no one beat you up and no one smashed your trophy.

You were inching toward the end of your childhood. The years between ten and twelve sent you on a journey no less gargantuan than the one between eight and ten, but day by day you never had the sense that you were moving quickly, hurtling forward to the brink of your adolescence, for the years passed slowly then, unlike now, when you have only to blink your eyes to discover that to-morrow is your birthday again. By eleven, you were mutating into a creature of the herd, struggling through that grotesque period of prepubescent dislocation when everyone is thrust into the micro-cosm of a closed society, when gangs and cliques begin to form, when some people are in and some people are out, when the word *popular* becomes a synonym for *desire*, when the childhood wars between girls and boys come to an end and fascination with the opposite sex begins, a period of extreme self-consciousness, when you are constantly looking at yourself from the outside, wonder-ing and often fretting about how others perceive you, which nec-essarily makes it a time of much tumult and silliness, when the rift between one's inner self and the self one presents to the world is never wider, when soul and body are most drastically at odds. In your own case, you found yourself becoming preoccupied with how you looked, worrying about whether you had the right hair-cut, the right shoes, the right pants, the right shirts and sweaters, never in your life have you been so concerned with clothes as you were at eleven and twelve, participating in the game of who was in and who was out with a desperate longing to be in, and at the Friday- and Saturday-night girl-boy parties that began some-time in the fifth grade, you always wanted to look your best for the girls, the young girls who were living through their own up-heavals and torments, with their training bras stretched over flat chests or barely swollen nipples, decked out in their party dresses with the stiff crinolines and whooshing silk slips, wearing garter belts and stockings for the first time, and now, so many years later, you remember the pathos of seeing those stockings sag and droop on their scrawny legs as the evening wore on, even if you can also remember breathing in the scents of their perfume as you held them in your arms and danced with them. Rock and roll had suddenly become interesting and exciting to you. Chuck Berry, Buddy Holly, and the Everly Brothers were the musicians you liked best, and you started collecting their records so you could listen to them alone in your upstairs bedroom, stacking the little 45s on their fat spindle and blasting up the volume when no one was around, and on days when you had nothing to do after school, you would rush home and turn on the television to watch *American Bandstand,* that spectacle of the new rock-and-roll universe injected daily into the country's living rooms, but it was more than music that attracted you to the show, it was the sight of a roomful of teenagers dancing to the music that kept you watching, for that was what you aspired to most now, to become a teenager, and you studied those kids on the screen as a way to learn something about the next, impending step of your life. Last year it had been the Three Stooges; now it was Dick Clark and his gang of youthful rockers. The era of pimples and braces had begun. Mercifully, those days come only once.

Still, you went on reading your books and writing your little stories and poems, not at all suspecting that you would end up doing those things for the rest of your life, doing them at that early age simply because you enjoyed doing them. At eleven, you made your second major purchase of a Modern Library book, the selected stories of O. Henry, and for a time you reveled in those brittle, ingenious tales with their surprise endings and narrative jolts (in much the same way that you fell for the early episodes of *The Twilight Zone* the following year, since Rod Serling's imagination was nothing if not a midcentury version of O. Henry's), but at bottom you knew there was something cheap about those stories, something far below what you considered to be literature of the first rank. In 1958, when Boris Pasternak won the Nobel Prize, his situation was prominently reported in the news, article after article told of how the Soviet police state had blocked the genius writer from going to Stockholm to accept his award, and now that

Doctor Zhivago had been translated into English, you went out and bought a copy for yourself (your next major purchase), eager to read the great man's work, confident that this was most assuredly literature of the first rank, but how could an eleven-year-old absorb the complexities of a Russian symbolist novel, how could a boy with no true literary foundation read such a long and nuanced work? You couldn't. You tried with the best will in the world, you doggedly read passages three and four and five times, but the book was beyond your capacity to understand a tenth part of what was in it, and after untold hours of struggle and mounting frustration, you reluctantly accepted defeat and put the book aside. It wasn't until you were fourteen that you were ready to tackle the masters, but back when you were eleven and twelve the books you could handle were considerably less challenging. A. J. Cronin's *The Citadel,* for example, which temporarily made you want to become a doctor, as well as *Green Mansions,* by W. H. Hudson, which teased your gonads with its exotic, jungle sensuality—those were two of your favorites at the time, the ones you remember best. As for your own juvenile efforts at scribbling, you were still under the sway of Stevenson, and most of your stories began with immortal sentences like this one: "In the year of our Lord, 1751, I found myself staggering around blindly in a raging snowstorm, trying to make my way back to my ancestral home." How you loved that lofty claptrap when you were eleven, but at twelve you happened to read a couple of detective novels (you forget which ones) and you understood that you would be better served by using a simpler, less bombastic kind of prose, and in your first attempt to turn out something in this new style, you sat down and wrote your own detective novel. It couldn't have come to more than twenty or thirty handwritten pages, but it felt so long to you, so much longer than anything you had written in the past, that you called it a novel. You can't remember the title or much about the story (something to do with two pairs of identical twins, you think, and a stolen pearl necklace stashed away in the cylinder of a type-writer), but you remember showing it to your sixth-grade teacher, the first male teacher you had ever had, and when he professed to like it, you felt heartened by his encouragement. That would have been enough, but then he went on to suggest that you read your little book to the class in installments, five or ten minutes at the end of each day, until the final bell rang at three o'clock, and so there you were, suddenly thrust into the role of *writer*, standing up in front of your classmates and reading your words out loud to them. The critics were kind. Everyone seemed to enjoy what you had written—if only as an escape from the monotony of the standard routine—but that was as far as it went, and several years would go by before you attempted to write anything that long again. Still, even if that youthful effort didn't seem important at the time, when you look back on it now, how not to think of it as a beginning, a first step?

In June 1959, four months after your twelfth birthday, you and your sixth-grade classmates graduated from the small grammar school you had been attending since kindergarten. After the summer, you started junior high, a three-year school with thirteen hundred students, the assembled population of children who had gone to the various neighborhood grammar schools scattered across your town. Everything was different there: no longer did you sit in a single classroom all day, there was not one teacher now but several, one for each of the subjects you took, and when the bell rang after each forty-six-minute period, you would leave the room and walk through the hallways to another room for your next class. Homework became a fact of life, daily assignments in all your academic subjects (English, math, science, history, and French), but there was also gym class, with its boisterous locker room, regulation jock straps, and communal showers, as well as shop class, taught by a half-bald, dandruff-ridden old-timer named Mr. Biddlecombe, a Dickensian throwback not only in name but in manner, who referred to his young charges as twerps and rapscallions and punished the unruly by locking them up in the storage closet. The best thing about the school was also the worst thing about it. A rigid tracking system was in force, meaning that each student was a member of a particular group, designated by a random letter of the alphabet—to disguise the fact that there was a hierarchy embedded in these groupings—but only the blind and deaf were unaware of what those letters stood for: fast track, medium track, and slow track. Pedagogically, there were definite advantages to this system—the progress of the bright students wasn't thwarted by the presence of dull students in the class, the plodders weren't cowed by the sprinters, each student could advance at his or her own speed—but socially it was something of a disaster, creating a community of preordained winners and losers, the ones who were destined to succeed and the ones who were destined to fail, and because everyone understood what the groupings meant, there was an element of snobbery or disdain among the fast toward the slow, and an element of resentment or animosity among the slow toward the fast, a subtle form of class warfare that occasionally erupted into actual fighting, and if not for the neutral territories of gym, shop, and home economics, where members of all groups were thrown together, the school would have resembled chopped-up Berlin after the war: Slow Zone, Medium Zone, Fast Zone. Such was the institution you entered in the waning months of the 1950s, a newly built pink-brick building with the latest in educational facilities and equipment, the pride of your hometown, and so excited were you to be going there, to be moving up in the world, that you set your alarm clock for exactly seven A.M. the night before the first day of school, and when you opened your eyes in the morning—before the alarm had sounded—you saw that it was exactly seven A.M., that the second hand was sweeping

past the nine on its way to the twelve, meaning that you had woken up ten seconds before you had to, and you, who had always
slept so soundly, who could never wake up without the blasting
bell of an alarm, had woken to silence for the first time in memory,
as if you had been counting down the seconds in your dreams.

There were many new faces, hundreds of new faces, but the one
that intrigued you the most belonged to a girl named Karen, a
fellow member of your fast-track brigade. It was unquestionably a
pretty face, perhaps even a beautiful face, but Karen had a sharp
mind as well, she was filled with confidence and humor, all lit up
and alive to the world, and within days of meeting her you were
smitten. A week or two into the school year, a dance was held for
the seventh graders, a Friday-night dance in the gym, and you
went, as did nearly everyone else, about three or four hundred of
you in all, and you made it your business to dance with Karen as
often as you could. Toward the end of the evening, the principal
announced that there was going to be a competition, a dance contest, and couples who wished to participate should go to the center of the floor. Karen wanted to give it a try, and since you were
happy to do whatever she wanted to do, you became her partner.
It was the first dance contest of your life, the only dance contest
of your life, and even if you weren't much of a dancer, you weren't
entirely hopeless, and because Karen was good, in fact very good,
with quick toes and an innate feel for the music, you understood
that you had to put yourself out for her, give it everything you
had. Early rock-and-roll dancing was still touch-dancing. The
Twist was a year or two off in the future, the revolution of isolate
partners had not yet caught on, and the dancers of 1959 were not
unlike the jitterbuggers of the forties, although by then the name
of the dance had changed to the Lindy. Couples held on to each
other, there was much spinning and twirling, and feet were more

important than hips: fast footwork was all. When you and Karen went to the center of the floor, you both decided to dance as fast as you could, to go two or three times faster than normal, hoping to keep it up long enough to impress the judges. Yes, Karen was a spirited girl, a person ready for any challenge, and so the two of you launched into your crazy routine, flying around the floor like a pair of monkeys in a speeded-up silent film, both of you secretly laughing at the excessiveness of your performance, the hilarity of your performance, tireless in your twelve-year-old bodies, and what you remember best was how tightly she held on to your hand, never losing her grip as you flung her out from you and then pulled her back in one wild turn after another, and because no other couple could keep up with you—or would even want to keep up with you—and because you were both half out of your minds, you won the contest. An absurd but memorable flash from your early life. The principal gave each of you a trophy, and when the dance was over you held hands with Karen as you walked to the ice cream shop in the middle of town, gloria, gloria, the rapture of holding hands with Karen on the night of the dance when you were twelve, and then, a block or two from the ice cream shop, Karen's trophy slipped out of her free hand and shattered on the sidewalk. You could see how upset she was— a small devastation because of its suddenness, because of the sudden sound, the unexpected crash of the trophy as it hit the pavement and splintered to pieces, and because it could never be mended, and because winning a dance trophy was of no importance to you (baseball was another matter), you handed her your trophy and told her to keep it. By the following year, you didn't see much of Karen anymore. You traveled in different circles, you were no longer in the same classes together, she was nearly a woman now and you were still a boy, and from then until you both graduated from high school in 1965, you barely spoke to each other. When you attended your twentieth high school reunion, however, a full twenty-six years after the night of the shattered trophy, Karen was there, a young widow of thirty-eight, and you danced with her again, a slow dance this time, and she told you that she remembered everything about that night when you were twelve, remembered it, she said, as if it were yesterday.

Your seventh-grade English teacher, Mr. S., wanted to encourage the students to read as many books as possible. A noble aim, but the system he devised to achieve that goal was not without its flaws, since he was more interested in quantity than quality, and a mediocre book of one hundred pages was worth just as much to him as a good book of three hundred. Even more troubling, he framed this project in the form of a competition, setting up a large pegboard on the back wall of the classroom and assigning each student a column, a vertical pathway in that grid of circular holes. The students were given pegs, which they were instructed to fashion into something that resembled rocket ships (these were the early years of the space race between America and the Soviet Union), and then Mr. S. told the children to stick the pegs into the bottom holes of their columns. Every time you read a book, you were supposed to move your peg up one notch. He wanted to keep the game going for two months, and then he would examine the results and see where everyone stood. You knew it was a bad idea, but this was the beginning of the first semester in your new school, and you wanted to do well, to stand out in some way, so you played along, diligently reading as many books as you could, which wasn't a problem, since you were already a committed reader of books, nor were you averse to the principle of competition, for the years you had spent playing baseball, football, and various other sports had turned you into a competitive boy, and not only were you going to do well, you decided, you were going to win. The two months passed, and every second or third day you would advance your peg another notch. Before long, you were ahead of the others, and as more time passed you were far ahead, running away from the field. When the morning came for Mr. S. to examine the results, he was flabbergasted by the great distance that separated you from the others. He walked back from the pegboard to the front of the class, looked you in the eye (you were fairly close to him, sitting in the second row of desks), and, with a hostile, belligerent expression on his face, accused you of cheating. It wasn't possible for anyone to read so many books, he said, it defied all logic, all sense, and you were an idiot if you thought you could get away with a stunt like that. It was an insult to his intelligence, an insult to the hard work of the other students, and in all his years of teaching you were the most brazen liar who had ever set foot in his classroom. His words felt like bullets to you, he was machine-gunning you to death in front of the other children, publicly accusing you of being a fraud, a criminal, you had never been so brutally attacked by anyone, you who had been so conscientious, so hungry to prove that you were a good student, and even as you tried to answer his accusations, telling him that he was wrong, that you had read the books, had read every page of every book, the magnitude of his anger was too much for you, and suddenly you began to cry. The bell rang, sparing you from further humiliation, but as the other students filed out of the classroom, Mr. S. told you to stay, he wanted to talk to you, and a moment later you were standing face to face with him beside his desk, hiccupping forth an avalanche of tears, insisting through broken, throttled breaths that you had been telling the truth, that you weren't a cheat or a liar, and if he wanted to see the list of books you had read, you would give it to him the next morning, your innocence would be proved, and bit by bit Mr. S. began to back down, slowly understanding that perhaps he had been wrong. He took his handkerchief out of his pocket and handed it to you. As you brought it to your face to blow your nose and wipe away your tears, you breathed in the smell of that freshly laundered handkerchief, and even though the fabric was clean, there was something sour and sickening about that smell, the smell of failure, the smell of something that had been used once too often, and every time you think about what happened to you that morning more than half a century ago, you are holding that handkerchief again and pressing it into your face. You were twelve years old. It was the last time you broke down and cried in front of an adult.

ACKNOWLEDGMENTS

The work in this collection originally appeared in the following publications and books:

"Portrait of an Invisible Man" and "The Book of Memory": *The Invention of Solitude*. New York, Sun Books; 1982. Reprinted by Penguin USA; 1988.

"The Red Notebook" (*Granta*, 1993), "Why Write?" (*The New Yorker*, 1995), "Accident Report" (*Conjunctions*, 2000), and "It Don't Mean a Thing" (*Granta*, 2000): *The Red Notebook: True Stories*, New York, New Directions; 2002.

Hand to Mouth. New York, Henry Holt; 1997.

Winter Journal. New York, Henry Holt; 2012.

Report from the Interior. New York, Henry Holt; 2013.

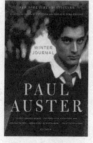